ESSAYS ON THE SEMITIC BACKGROUND OF THE NEW TESTAMENT

BY THE SAME AUTHOR

An Introductory Bibliography for the Study of Scripture (co-authored with G. Glanzman, S.J.; Woodstock Papers 5; Westminster: Newman, 1960)

Die Wahrheit der Evangelien (Stuttgarter Bibelstudien 1; Stuttgart: Katholisches Bibelwerk, 1965 [a brief form of this work appeared in *The Historical Truth of the Gospels* (Glen Rock, N.J.: Paulist Press, 1964)]

The Genesis Apocryphon of Qumran Cave I: A Commentary (Biblica et orientalia 18; Rome: Pontifical Biblical Institute, 1966); second, revised edition, 1971

Pauline Theology: A Brief Sketch (Englewood Cliffs, N.J.: Prentice-Hall, 1967)

The Aramaic Inscriptions of Sefîre (Biblica et orientalia 19; Rome: Pontifical Biblical Institute, 1967)

The Jerome Biblical Commentary (co-edited with R. E. Brown, S.S. and R. E. Murphy, O.Carm.; Englewood Cliffs, N.J.: Prentice-Hall, 1968; London: Geoffrey Chapman, 1968)

The Gospel According to Luke (Anchor Bible 28) [forthcoming]

Essays on the Semitic Background of the New Testament

Joseph A. Fitzmyer, S.J.

GEOFFREY CHAPMAN
LONDON 1971

Geoffrey Chapman Ltd
18 High Street, Wimbledon, London SW 19

Geoffrey Chapman (Ireland) Ltd
5–7 Main Street, Blackrock, County Dublin

This edition first published 1971

This book is set in 11/13 *pt Baskerville*
Printed in Great Britain by The Sidney Press Ltd, Bedford

CONTENTS

ABBREVIATIONS

PROTOCANONICAL AND DEUTEROCANONICAL BOOKS OF THE BIBLE

Old Testament

Gn Genesis
Ex Exodus
Lv Leviticus
Nm Numbers
Dt Deuteronomy
Jos Joshua
Jgs Judges
Ru Ruth
1 Sm 1 Samuel
2 Sm 2 Samuel
1 Kgs 1 Kings
2 Kgs 2 Kings
1 Chr 1 Chronicles
2 Chr 2 Chronicles
Ezr Ezra
Neh Nehemiah
Tb Tobit
Jdt Judith
Est Esther
Jb Job
Ps(s) Psalms
Prv Proverbs
Eccl Ecclesiastes (Qoheleth)
Ct Canticle of Canticles
Wis Wisdom
Sir Sirach (Ecclesiasticus)
Is Isaiah
Dt-Is Deutero-Isaiah
Jer Jeremiah
Lam Lamentations
Bar Baruch
Ez Ezekiel
Dn Daniel
Hos Hosea
Jl Joel
Am Amos
Ob Obadiah
Jon Jonah
Mi Micah
Na Nahum
Hab Habakkuk
Zeph Zephaniah
Hag Haggai
Zech Zechariah
Dt-Zech Deutero-Zechariah
Mal Malachi
1 Mc 1 Maccabees
2 Mc 2 Maccabees

New Testament

Mt Matthew
Mk Mark
Lk Luke
Jn John
Acts Acts of the Apostles
Rom Romans
1 Cor 1 Corinthians
2 Cor 2 Corinthians
Gal Galatians
Eph Ephesians

Phil	Philippians	Jas	James
Col	Colossians	1 Pt	1 Peter
1 Thes	1 Thessalonians	2 Pt	2 Peter
2 Thes	2 Thessalonians	1 Jn	1 John
1 Tm	1 Timothy	2 Jn	2 John
2 Tm	2 Timothy	3 Jn	3 John
Ti	Titus	Jude	Jude
Phlm	Philemon	Ap/Rev	Apocalypse/ Revelation
Heb	Hebrews		

APOCRYPHA OF THE OLD TESTAMENT

Apoc. Bar.	*Apocalypse of Baruch*
Apoc. Mos.	*Apocalypse of Moses*
Assump. Mos.	*Assumption of Moses*
Enoch	*I Enoch*
4 Ezr	*Apocalypse of Ezra* (=chapters 3–14 of *2 Esdras*)
Jub	*Book of Jubilees*
Pss Sol.	*Psalms of Solomon*
T. Asher, *T. Levi*, etc.	*Testament of Asher*, *Testament of Levi*, etc.

CD	Cairo (Genizah text of the) Damascus (Document)
DJD	Discoveries in the Judaean Desert (of Jordan) [Oxford: Clarendon]
Hev	Nahal Hever (Naḥal Ḥeber) caves
Mur	Wadi Murabba'ât caves
p	Pesher (Qumran commentary on OT books)
Q	Qumran (caves)
1Q, 2Q, 3Q, etc.	Numbered caves of Qumran, yielding written material; followed by standard abbrevi-

	ations of biblical and apocryphal books (e.g., 4QEx^{a}) or by numbers officially assigned to texts in the volumes of the series DJD (e.g., 1Q*19*, 4Q*175*)
1QapGn	Cave 1, Genesis Apocryphon
1QH	*Hôdāyôt*, Thanksgiving Psalms
1QM	*Milḥāmāh*, War Scroll *or* Rule of the War
1QpHab	Pesher on Habakkuk
1QpMic	Pesher on Micah (=1Q*14*)
1QpPs	Pesher on the Psalms (=1Q*16*)
1QpZeph	Pesher on Zephaniah (=1Q*15*)
1QS	*Serek ha-Yaḥad*, Rule of the Community *or* Manual of Discipline
1QSa	Appendix A (Rule of the Congregation) to 1QS (=1Q*28a*)
1QSb	Appendix B (Blessings) to 1QS (=1Q*28b*)
4QAhA	Cave 4, Aaron text, copy A (to be published by J. Starcky)
4QarP	Aramaic papyrus fragment (to be published by J. Starcky)
4QCatena^{a}	Catena of OT Passages, copy a (=4Q*177*)
4QD^{b}	Damascus Document, copy b (to be published by J. T. Milik)
4QFlor	Florilegium *or* Eschatological Midrashim (=4Q*174*)
4QHen^{a}	Enoch, copy a (to be published by J. T. Milik)
4QHen astr^{b}	Enoch, astronomical section, copy b (to be published by J. T. Milik)
4QḥʻA^{c}	*Ḥ^{a}zût ʻAmram*, Vision of ʻAmram, copy c (to be published by J. Starcky)
4QM^{a}	*Milḥāmāh*, Rule of the War, copy a [*ZAW* 69 (1957) 131–51]

4QpHos^{a,b}	Pesher on Hosea, copies a, b (=4Q*166–167*)
4QpIs^{a-e}	Pesher on Isaiah, copies a–e (4Q*161–165*)
4QpNah	Pesher on Nahum (=4Q*169*)
4QpPs 37	Pesher on Ps 37 (now part of 4QpPss^{a} [=4Q*177*])
4QpPss^{a}	Pesher on Psalms, copy a (=4Q*177*)
4QPatrBless	Patriarchal Blessings [*JBL* 75 (1965) 174–87]
4QS	*Serek ha-Yaḥad*, Rule of the Community *or* Manual of Discipline
4QTest	Testimonia (=4Q*175*)
11QMelch	Cave 11, Melchizedek fragments [*Oudtestamentische Studiën* 14 (1965) 354–73]
11QPs^{a}	Psalms Scroll, copy a (=DJD 4)
11QPs^{a} DavComp	Davidic Composition, a prose insert in 11QPs^{a}

PUBLICATIONS AND INSTITUTIONS

AASOR	*Annual of the American Schools of Oriental Research*
AB	Anchor Bible (Garden City)
AcOr	*Acta orientalia*
AER	*American Ecclesiastical Review*
AG	W. F. Arndt and F. W. Gingrich, *A Greek-English Lexicon of the New Testament* (Chicago, 1957)
AJSL	*American Journal of Semitic Languages and Literatures*
AJT	*American Journal of Theology*
ALBO	Analecta lovaniensia biblica et orientalia (Louvain)
Albright, *AP*	W. F. Albright, *The Archaeology of Palestine* (Harmondsworth, 1960)
AnalGreg	Analecta gregoriana (Rome)
ANEP	J. B. Pritchard, ed., *The Ancient Near East in Pictures* (Princeton, 1955)

ANET	J. B. Pritchard, ed., *Ancient Near Eastern Texts* (rev. ed.; Princeton, 1955)
AP	A. E. Cowley, *Aramaic Papyri of the Fifth Century B.C.* (Oxford, 1923)
APOT	R. H. Charles, *Apocrypha and Pseudepigrapha of the Old Testament* (2 vols; Oxford, 1913)
ARM	A. Parrot and G. Dossin, ed., *Archives royales de Mari* (Paris, 1950–)
ATD	Das Alte Testament deutsch (Göttingen)
ATR	*Anglican Theological Review*
BA	*Biblical Archaeologist*
BANE	G. E. Wright, ed., *The Bible and the Ancient Near East* (Fest. W. F. Albright; New York, 1961)
BASOR	*Bulletin of the American Schools of Oriental Research*
BCCT	J. L. McKenzie, ed., *The Bible in Current Catholic Thought* (New York, 1962)
BC	F. J. Foakes Jackson and K. Lake, ed., *Beginnings of Christianity* (5 vols; London, 1920–33)
BeO	*Bibbia e oriente*
BFTh	*Beiträge zur Förderung christlicher Theologie*
Bib	*Biblica*
BIES	*Bulletin of the Israel Exploration Society*
BIFAO	*Bulletin de l'institut français d'archéologie orientale*
BJRL	*Bulletin of the John Rylands Library*
BKAT	Biblischer Kommentar: Altes Testament (Neukirchen)
BMAP	E. G. Kraeling, *Brooklyn Museum Aramaic Papyri* (New Haven, 1953)
BO	*Bibliotheca orientalis*
BT	*The Bible Today*
BTS	*La Bible et terre sainte*
BZ	*Biblische Zeitschrift*
BZAW	Beihefte zur *ZAW* (Berlin)
BZNW	Beihefte zur *ZNW* (Berlin)

CBQ	*Catholic Biblical Quarterly*
CC	*La civiltà cattolica*
ChQR	*Church Quarterly Review*
CIG	*Corpus inscriptionum graecarum* (Berlin, 1828–)
CIL	*Corpus inscriptionum latinarum* (Berlin, 1862–)
CIS	*Corpus inscriptionum semiticarum* (Paris, 1881–)
CJT	*Canadian Journal of Theology*
ConNeot	*Coniectanea Neotestamentica*
CRAIBL	*Comptes rendus de l'Académie des Inscriptions et Belles-Lettres*
CSCO	Corpus scriptorum christianorum orientalium (Louvain)
CSEL	Corpus scriptorum ecclesiasticorum latinorum (Vienna)
DACL	*Dictionnaire d'archéologie chrétienne et de liturgie* (15 vols; Paris, 1924–53)
DJD	Discoveries in the Judaean Desert of Jordan (Oxford, 1955–)
DTC	*Dictionnaire de théologie catholique* (16 vols; Paris, 1903–65)
EBib	Etudes bibliques (Paris)
EstBíb	*Estudios bíblicos*
EstEc	*Estudios eclesiasticos*
ET	*Evangelische Theologie*
ExpT	*Expository Times*
FRLANT	Forschungen zur Religion und Literatur des Alten und Neuen Testaments (Göttingen)
GCS	Griechische christliche Schriftsteller (Berlin)
GJV	E. Schürer, *Geschichte des jüdischen Volkes im Zeitalter Jesu Christi* (3 vols; Leipzig, 1901–11)
HeythJ	*Heythrop Journal*
HJ	*Hibbert Journal*
HNT	Handbuch zum Neuen Testament (Tübingen)
HTR	*Harvard Theological Review*
HUCA	*Hebrew Union College Annual*

ICC	International Critical Commentary
IEJ	*Israel Exploration Journal*
Int	*Interpretation*
IER	*Irish Ecclesiastical Record*
ITQ	*Irish Theological Quarterly*
JA	*Journal asiatique*
JAOS	*Journal of the American Oriental Society*
JBL	*Journal of Biblical Literature*
JBR	*Journal of Bible and Religion*
JEA	*Journal of Egyptian Archaeology*
JEOL	*Jaarbericht . . . ex oriente lux*
JJS	*Journal of Jewish Studies*
JNES	*Journal of Near Eastern Studies*
JPOS	*Journal of the Palestine Oriental Society* (Jerusalem, 1921–37)
JQR	*Jewish Quarterly Review*
JRel	*Journal of Religion*
JSS	*Journal of Semitic Studies*
JTS	*Journal of Theological Studies*
Jud	*Judaica*
KB	L. Koehler and W. Baumgartner, *Lexicon in veteris testamenti libros* (Leiden, 1953)
Mansi	G. D. Mansi, *Sacrorum conciliorum nova et amplissima collectio* (31 vols: Florence, 1758–98)
Mus	*Muséon*
MTZ	*Münchener theologische Zeitschrift*
NKZ	*Neue kirkliche Zeitschrift*
NT	*Novum Testamentum*
NTA	*New Testament Abstracts*
NTD	Das Neue Testament deutsch (Göttingen)
NTS	*New Testament Studies*
NTSup	Novum Testamentum Supplements (Leiden)
OTS	*Oudtestamentische Studiën*
PAM	Palestine Archaeological Museum
PEFQS	*Palestine Exploration Fund Quarterly Statement*

PEQ	*Palestine Exploration Quarterly*
PG	J. Migne, *Patrologia graeca* (Paris)
PJB	*Palästina-Jahrbuch*
PL	J. Migne, *Patrologia latina* (Paris)
PSB	L. Pirot, *La sainte Bible*, rev. by A. Clamer (12 vols; Paris, 1935–)
PW	Pauly-Wissowa, *Realencyclopädie der classischen Altertumswissenschaft* (Stuttgart, 1893–)
QDAP	*Quarterly of the Department of Antiquities in Palestine*
RB	*Revue biblique*
RBibIt	*Rivista biblica italiana*
RechBib	Recherches bibliques (Bruges)
REG	*Revue des études grecques*
RevBén	Revue bénédictine
*RGG*³	K. Galling, ed., *Die Religion in Geschichte und Gegenwart* (3rd ed.; 7 vols; Tübingen, 1957–65)
RHPR	*Revue d'histoire et de philosophie religieuses*
RHR	*Revue de l'histoire des religions*
RQ	*Revue de Qumran*
RScRel	*Revue des sciences religieuses*
RSR	*Recherches de science religieuse*
RTP	*Revue de théologie et de philosophie*
SBT	Studies in Biblical Theology (London and Naperville, Ill.)
SBU	*Symbolae biblicae upsalienses*
ScEccl	*Sciences ecclésiastiques* (now called *Science et esprit*)
SE	F. L. Cross, ed., *Studia evangelica* (*SE* 1=TU 73 [Berlin, 1959]; *SE* 2=TU 87 [Berlin, 1964]; *SE* 3=TU 88 [Berlin, 1964])
SEA	*Svensk exegetisk årsbok*
SMR	*Studia montis regii*
SNTS	Society for New Testament Studies
SPB	Studia postbiblica (Leiden)
ST	*Studia theologica*

Str-B	H. L. Strack and P. Billerbeck, *Kommentar zum Neuen Testament* (6 vols; Munich, 1922–61)
StCath	*Studia catholica*
SZ	*Stimmen der Zeit*
TDNT	G. Kittel, ed., *Theological Dictionary of the New Testament* (Grand Rapids, 1964–). English version of *TWNT*
TGl	*Theologie und Glaube*
ThStKr	*Theologische Studien und Kritiken* (Hamburg; now Berlin)
TLZ	*Theologische Literaturzeitung*
TQ	*Theologische Quartalschrift*
TRu	*Theologische Rundschau*
TS	*Theological Studies*
TU	Texte und Untersuchungen (Berlin)
TWNT	G. Kittel, ed., *Theologische Wörterbuch zum Neuen Testament* (8 vols; Stuttgart, 1933–). German original of *TDNT*
TZ	*Theologische Zeitschrift*
VC	*Vigiliae christianae*
VD	*Verbum domini*
VDBS	F. Vigouroux, *Dictionnaire de la Bible, Supplément* (7 vols; Paris, 1928–)
VDI	*Vestnik drevnei istorii*
VerbC	*Verbum caro*
VT	*Vetus Testamentum*
VTSup	Vetus Testamentum Supplements (Leiden)
WO	*Die Welt des Orients*
ZAW	*Zeitschrift für die alttestamentliche Wissenschaft*
ZDPV	*Zeitschrift des deutschen Palästina-Vereins*
ZKG	*Zeitschrift für Kirchengeschichte*
ZKT	*Zeitschrift für katholische Theologie*
ZNW	*Zeitschrift für die neutestamentliche Wissenschaft*

Ant.	Josephus, *Antiquities of the Jews*
CCD	Confraternity of Christian Doctrine translation of the Bible
JW	Josephus, *Jewish War*
LXX	Septuagint (Greek translation of the OT)
MT	Masoretic Text
NEB	*The New English Bible*
Vg	Vulgate

FOREWORD

The essays which are collected in this volume were written over a period of fourteen years and represent reflections on a variety of New Testament problems which have been illustrated by data from the Semitic world of the eastern Mediterranean. The unity of such a collection is obviously not organic or closely-knit. This is admitted at the outset. But this disadvantage is somewhat offset by the convenience of having a number of essays on this aspect of New Testament studies brought together between the covers of one volume.

Essays on the Semitic background of the New Testament will always have a certain importance, even though they will not appeal to everyone, and even though one detects a tendency to disregard such discussions in favour of other aspects of New Testament study. These essays will say little to those whose main concern in New Testament study is philosophical or hermeneutical. At present, New Testament studies are highly marked by an introspective or hermeneutical thrust, even though not everyone would be inclined to concentrate on it. No one, however, who undertakes the study of the New Testament today can help but be caught up in this syndrome from time to time. But there is, fortunately, an area of New Testament studies that enables one to push forward a little from this point of view. Many have been the discoveries in recent years in the Hellenistic and Semitic worlds of the eastern Mediterranean that bear on some aspect or other of the New Testament. The data of such discoveries have to be assessed, interpreted, and judged for their relevance to the interpretation of the New Testament. Eventually, such data too will be caught up in the reflective, hermeneutical process. However, before that, they have to be understood more or less in and for themselves. It is hoped that this collection of essays will make more convenient to students of the New Testament the discussion of some of the problems raised by such discoveries in the Semitic area.

Some of the essays in this volume seek to interpret the relevance of the Qumran texts and fragments to the interpretation of certain New Testament passages. Others seek to do the same with various Aramaic texts that have come to light in the past decade and a half. The thread that links together the vast majority of the essays is a connection between New Testament passages and the Dead Sea Scrolls or contemporary Aramaic studies. One essay may seem out of place. It is the discussion of the *logoi* of Jesus that are preserved in the Oxyrhynchus Gospel fragments and the related Coptic Gospel according to Thomas. But anyone who is aware of some of the recent discussions about the Syrian origin of this Gospel, whether in its earlier Greek form or the later Coptic version, will realize that its inclusion in this collection of essays is not out of place.

In assembling these essays for republication, I have been able to make a number of minor changes in wording, add a few references to the notes about material published on the same topics since my original articles, and occasionally change a paragraph or two in the interest of clarity or clarification. This constitutes at most a minor revision of the essays that are now brought together. None of the basic theses of these essays has been altered.

Grateful acknowledgement is hereby expressed to the editors of the following periodicals who granted permission for the reprinting of the essays that originally appeared as articles in their publications: *The Catholic Biblical Quarterly*, *Concilium*, *Harvard Theological Review* (copyrighted by the President and Fellows of Harvard College), *Journal of Biblical Literature*, *New Testament Studies*, and *Theological Studies*. My gratitude is also due to Herder and Herder of New York for permission to reprint the essay, 'The Bar Cochba Period', from *The Bible in Current Catholic Thought* (Fest. M. J. Gruenthaner; New York, 1962), and to SPCK for permission to reprint the essay, 'Jewish

Christianity in Acts in Light of the Dead Sea Scrolls', from *Studies in Luke-Acts* (Fest. P. Schubert; ed. L. E. Keck and J. L. Martyn; London, 1966).

Lastly, it is my pleasant task to express my appreciation to the staff of Geoffrey Chapman Ltd and Brenda Hall for their collaboration in the production of this collection of essays.

Joseph A. Fitzmyer, S.J.

I

THE USE OF THE OLD TESTAMENT

1

THE USE OF EXPLICIT OLD TESTAMENT QUOTATIONS IN QUMRAN LITERATURE AND IN THE NEW TESTAMENT*

The problem of the use of the Old Testament in the New Testament is a vast one, complicated by side-issues of textual variants and involved in the kindred problem of the relation or harmony of the two Testaments. It is also a problem which has been well worked over by many scholars. Books have been written on the subject, comparing the text of the Old Testament quotations with the existing Greek and Hebrew recensions or comparing the exegetical principles and methods of the New Testament writers with those of the rabbis.[1] In particular, Paul's use of the Old Testament has been the special object of such study. It would seem useless, then, to take up again such a well-worked subject, were it not for the new light which has been shed on the problem by the discovery of the Qumran scrolls. The Jewish roots of the New Testament have always made it *a priori* likely that its use of the Old Testament would resemble that of contemporary Judaism to some extent. Indeed, resemblances with the rabbinical writings have long since been established. Yet one of the main difficulties in this comparative

* Originally published in *NTS* 7 (1960–61) 297–333.

[1] A convenient sketch of previous work, together with references to the pertinent literature, can be found in E.E. Ellis, *Paul's Use of the Old Testament* (Edinburgh, 1957) 1–5. See also J. Bonsirven, *Exégèse rabbinique et exégèse paulinienne* (Bibliothèque de théologie historique; Paris, 1939) 264–5.

study has always been the extent to which one can trust the contemporaneity of the so-called early material incorporated in these writings.[2] Now, however, we have in the Qumran scrolls Jewish writings which antedate for the most part the composition of the New Testament books—or at the latest are in part contemporary with them. Moreover, in many of these scrolls, which are admittedly sectarian writings and perhaps not characteristic of all contemporary Jewish thought, we find the Old Testament used in a manner and with a frequency which rivals that of the New Testament. It is certainly to our advantage, then, to examine this use of the Old Testament in the Qumran literature, in order to see what can be learned from it for the study of the related New Testament problem. For in both cases we are dealing with documents stemming from a group in which a theology built on the Old Testament motivated its way of life. Indeed, it would be difficult to find a more ideal set of documents to illustrate the New Testament use of the Old Testament than the Qumran scrolls, in which we see how contemporary Jews made use of their Scriptures.

Some of the methods of Qumran exegesis have already been studied;[3] a thorough, systematic investigation of all the evidence

[2] See E. E. Ellis, *op. cit.*, 42, 83.

[3] See W. H. Brownlee, 'Biblical Interpretation among the Sectaries of the DSS', *BA* XIV (1951) 54–76; F. F. Bruce, *Biblical Exegesis in the Qumran Texts* (Grand Rapids: Michigan, 1959); M. H. Gottstein, 'Bible Quotations in the Sectarian Dead Sea Scrolls', *VT* III (1953) 79–82; K. Elliger, *Studien zum Habakuk-Kommentar vom Toten Meer* (Beiträge zur historischen Theologie 15; Tübingen, 1953) 118–64; E. Osswald, 'Zur Hermeneutik des Habakuk-Kommentars', *ZAW* LXVIII (1956) 243–56; J. van der Ploeg, 'Bijbeltekst en theologie in de teksten van Qumrân', *Vox theologica* XXVII (1956–57) 33–45; B. J. Roberts, 'The Dead Sea Scrolls and the O.T. Scriptures', *BJRL* XXXVI (1953–54) 75–96; 'Some Observations on the Damascus Documents and the Dead Sea Scrolls', *ibid.*, XXXIV (1951–52) 366–87; J. A. Sanders, 'Habakkuk in Qumran, Paul and the Old Testament', *JRel* XXXVIII (1959) 232–44; G. Vermès, 'Le "Commentaire d'Habacuc" et le Nouveau Testament', *Cahiers Sioniens* V (1951) 337–49; P. Wernberg-Møller, 'Some Reflexions on the Biblical Materials in the Manual of Discipline', *ST* IX (1955) 40–66; C. Roth, 'The Subject Matter of Qumran

is still needed. The present study is limited to one aspect of Qumran exegesis and its bearing on the New Testament. It is hoped that it will be a useful contribution to the whole.

In both the Qumran literature and the New Testament we frequently find what has been called *le style anthologique*, the working of Old Testament expressions and phrases into the very fabric of the composition, in a manner which resembles a *cento*. It is well known that a book like the Apocalypse, which does not contain a single explicit quotation from the Old Testament, abounds none the less in Old Testament allusions. The same is true of the Qumran War Scroll, as clearly appears from the studies of J. Carmignac.[4] Such a *style anthologique* involves an implicit exegesis and is usually due to thorough acquaintance with and a reverent meditation upon the Old Testament. However, in this discussion I am not concerned with this *use* of the Old Testament by way of allusion or verbal echoes or reminiscences, even though it is an important aspect of the whole problem.

Attention will be centred rather on the *explicit quotations* of the Old Testament, such as are found in both the New Testament and in Qumran literature. In doing so, I am also leaving out of consideration the *pesharim* and 4QTestimonia. In an effort to delimit the problem I have deliberately excluded the *pesher*,[5] for it is a unique type of *midrash* having no exact counterpart in the

---

Exegesis', *VT* X (1960) 51–65; J. C. Trever, 'The Qumran Covenanters and Their Use of Scripture', *Personalist* XXXIX (1958) 128–38; G. Vermès, 'A propos des commentaires bibliques découverts à Qumrân', *RHPR* XXXIII (1955) 95–102; M. Black, 'Theological Conceptions in the Dead Sea Scrolls', *SEA* XVIII–XIX (1953–54) 72–97.

[4] 'Les citations de l'Ancien Testament dans "La guerre des fils de lumière contre les fils de ténèbres"', *RB* LXIII (1956) 234–60, 373–90.

[5] I have thus excluded the 1QpHab (M. Burrows, ed., *The Dead Sea Scrolls of St Mark's Monastery*, vol 1 [New Haven, 1950] pl. 55–61), 1QpNah (D. Barthélemy and J. T. Milik, *Qumran Cave I* [DJD 1; Oxford, 1955] 77–80); 1QpPs 57; 1QpPs 58 (*ibid.*, 81–2); 1QpZeph (*ibid.*, 80); 4QpNah (J. M. Allegro, 'Further Light on the History of the Qumran Sect', *JBL* LXXV [1956] 89–93); 4QpPs 37 (*ibid.*, 94–5 and *PEQ* LXXXVI [1954]

New Testament. There is no book or part of a book in the latter which is, strictly speaking, a *pesher*.[6] I am likewise omitting 4QTestimonia since I treat it below.[7]

There is, however, in the Qumran literature a body of isolated explicit quotations of the Old Testament, which are introduced by special formulae and are cited to bolster up or illustrate an argument, to serve as a *point de départ* in a discussion or to act as a sort of proof-text. This conscious and deliberate quotation of the Old Testament in the Qumran literature provides the most apt frame of reference in our comparative study. Hence, though it may appear arbitrary at first to exclude from our consideration the Qumran *pesher*—which is the biblical commentary *par excellence* in the sect—the reason for this exclusion becomes clear upon reflection. The isolated explicit quotations are closer in their use to those found in the New Testament and furnish the more valid type of Old Testament exegesis with which to compare those of the New. To be sure, the exegetical principles underlying the *pesher* and the isolated quotations are often the same, and there will be occasion to point this out; in this way the evidence of the *pesharim* will be used indirectly.

Fortunately, a good group of passages in the Qumran literature can be found, containing explicit quotations. Three of these passages occur in the *Manual of Discipline* (1QS), thirty in the

---

69–75; 4QpHos[a] (*JBL ibid.*, 93); 4QpHos[b] (J. M. Allegro, 'A Recently Discovered Fragment of a Commentary on Hosea from Qumran's Fourth Cave', *JBL* LXXVIII [1959] 142–7); 4QpGn 49 (*JBL* LXXV [1956] 174–6); 4QpIs[a] (*ibid.*, 177–82); 4QpIs[b] ('More Isaiah Commentaries from Qumran's Fourth Cave', *JBL* LXXVII [1958] 215–18); 4QpIs[c] (*ibid.*, 218–20); 4QpIs[d] (*ibid.*, 220–1).

[6] This has been recognized, among others, by W. Baumgartner, *TRu* XIX (1951) 117; F. F. Bruce, *Biblical Exegesis in the Qumran Texts*, 71–2; *NTS* II (1955–56) 181. See further A. G. Wright, 'The Literary Genre Midrash (Part 2)', *CBQ* XXVIII (1966) 417–57, esp. 418–22. Cf. B. Lindars, *New Testament Apologetic* (London: SCM, 1961); N. Perrin, 'Mark xiv. 62: The End Product of a Christian Pesher Tradition', *NTS* XII (1965–66) 150–5.

[7] See pp. 59–89.

Damascus Document (CD), five in the *War Scroll* (1QM), and four in the text labelled provisionally 4Q*Florilegium*.[8] In all, forty-two passages involving forty-four certain explicit Old Testament quotations and two probable ones occur in the published Qumran literature. This is a manageable group with which one can work.

In this treatment of the explicit quotations I shall first of all discuss briefly the introductory formulae and then the classes into which the quotations fall. In doing so, I shall be exposing the exegetical principles and methods at work in the two groups of quotations. I shall concentrate mainly on the new Qumran material, but also show how it illustrates the New Testament usage.

I. THE INTRODUCTORY FORMULAE

The fundamental attitude of both the Qumran sect and the early Christian Church toward the Old Testament is manifested in the introductory formulae used by their writers. While these formulae were often stereotyped in both literatures, they nevertheless indicate the conscious and deliberate appeal made by these writers to the Old Testament as the 'Scriptures'. The motivation and religious presuppositions of the two groups, which were founded on the Old Testament, are often best re-

[8] 4Q Florilegium was published at first only in part; see J. M. Allegro, 'Further Messianic References in Qumran Literature', *JBL* LXXV (1956) 176–7 [= Document II]; 'Fragments of a Qumran Scroll of Eschatological *Midrāšîm*', *JBL* LXXVII (1958) 350–4. See now 4Q*174* (DJD 5, 53–7). That this text is actually 'a more complex type of *pesher*—one that employs additional biblical material [that is, isolated explicit quotations] to expound the biblical passage under consideration', has been shown by one of my students, W. R. Lane, 'A New Commentary Structure in 4Q Florilegium', *JBL* LXXVIII (1959) 343–6. See also the improvements in the understanding of the text suggested by Y. Yadin, 'A Midrash on 2 Sam vii and Ps i–ii (4Q Florilegium)', *IEJ* IX (1959) 95–8. A few further examples of explicit quotations are to be found in the more recently published 11QMelchizedek (see pp. 245–68 below).

vealed by the formulae used to introduce the quotation itself. Quotations so introduced obviously differ from mere allusions, in which it is often difficult to decide to what extent or degree the use of an Old Testament expression was intended by the writer to carry the impression that a reference to it was actually being made. Modern writers are wont to use a phrase or expression from older classical sources, but it is not always with the same degree of deliberate reference. There is no doubt of the reference to the Old Testament, however, when the quotation is explicitly introduced by a formula. I shall list the introductory formulae used in the Qumran literature and indicate those which have counterparts in the New Testament. Certain features will emerge from the classification of them. A purely mechanical division of them is best made according to the verb used: (A) 'to write', (B) 'to say', (C) other formulae.[9]

(A) *Written:* Though we never find in the Qumran literature any expression which corresponds to the noun *hē graphē* (or *hai graphai*) as a designation for the Old Testament, such as we find in the New Testament, there are eight formulae which employ the verb *ktb* of the Old Testament. This, in itself, is not surprising for the same usage is found in the later books of the Old Testament and manifests only the common Jewish regard for their normative Scriptures.

(*a*) *ky' kn ktwb* (1QS 5:15; CD 11:18; 2Q*25* 1:3), 'for it is written', which seems to be the Hebrew equivalent of the New Testament formula, *houtōs gar gegraptai* (Mt 2:5; see also 1 Cor 15:45).

(*b*) *k'šr ktwb* (1QS 8:14; 5:17; CD 7:19; 4QFlor 1:12; 4QpIs[c] 4–7 ii 18; 4QCatena[a] 10–11:1; 4Q*178* 3:2; this is probably the full form of the abbreviation *kk* found in CD 19:1), 'as it was written'. This formula is, of course, found in the Old Testament (1 Kgs 21:11; Dn 9:13, though the more usual form is *kktwb*). Compare the variant, *w'šr ktwb* (4QpIs[e] 1–2:2). A

[9] A sketchy comparison of some of these formulae can be found in E. E. Ellis, *op. cit.*, 48–9; R. H. Charles, *APOT* II, 789.

variety of New Testament formulae corresponds to this one:

kathōs gegraptai (also found in the LXX: 2 Kgs 14:6; Dn 9:13 [Theodotion]): Lk 2:23; Acts 15:15; Rom 1:17; 2:24; 3:10; 4:17; 8:36; 9:33; 11:26; 15:3, 9, 21; 1 Cor 1:31; 2:9; 2 Cor 9:9; 13:15.

kata to gegrammenon (plural is used in Dn 9:13 [LXX]: 2 Cor 4:13.

kathōs estin gegrammenon: Jn 6:31; 12:14.

kathaper gegraptai: Rom 3:4; 9:13; 10:15; 11:8.

hōs gegraptai (used in *2 Esdras* 20:35): Lk 3:4 [see below under (*e*)]; Mk 7:6.

hōsper gegraptai: 1 Cor 10:7.

(*c*) *k'šr ktwb bspr* [*mwšh*] (4QFlor 1:2; cf. 4QpIs[c] 1:4), 'as it was written in the book of Moses'. A fuller form is found in *k'šr ktwb 'lyw bšyry dwyd 'šr 'mr*, 'as it was written concerning him in the hymns of David, who said . . .' (11QMelch 9–10; cf. also 11QMelch 24). Compare the New Testament expression: *kathōs gegraptai en biblō tōn prophētōn* (Acts 7:42; see also Mk 1:2; Lk 2:23; Acts 13:33; 1 Cor 9:9; 14:21); also *estin gegrammenon en tois prophētais* (Jn 6:45).

(*d*) *ky ktwb* (CD 11:20), 'for it was written', the Hebrew equivalent of the New Testament *gegraptai gar* (Mt 4:6, 10; 26:31; Lk 4:10; Acts 1:20; 23:5; Rom 12:19; 14:11; 1 Cor 1:19; 3:19; Gal 3:10; 4:27 [in Gal 4:22 it occurs without an explicit quotation!]). Possibly we should also compare *dioti gegraptai* (1 Pt 1:16) and *hoti gegraptai* (Mk 14:27; Gal 3:13).

(*e*) *'šr ktwb bspr yš'yh hnby' l'ḥryt hymym* (4QFlor 1:15), 'as it was written in the book of Isaiah the prophet for the end of days'. See also 4QFlor 1-3 ii 3 (*bspr dny'l*); 4QCatena[a] 7:3; 4QCatena[b] 1:4. Compare: *hōs gegraptai en biblō logōn Ēsaïou tou prophētou* (Lk 3:4).

(*f*) *whmh 'šr ktwb 'lyhmh bspr yḥzq'l hnby' 'šr* . . . (4QFlor 1:16), 'These are the ones about whom it was written in the book of Ezekiel the prophet, who . . .'. See CD 1:13; 4QCatena[a] 1–4:7;

5–6:11. Compare: *houtos estin peri hou gegraptai* (Mt 11:10; Lk 7:27).

(*g*) *w'yn ktwb ky 'm* ... (CD 9:5), 'And is it not written that ...?' Compare: *ouk estin gegrammenon en tō nomō hymōn hoti* ... (Jn 10:34, quoting Ps 82:6 as the 'Law') or *ou gegraptai hoti* ... (Mk 11:17).

(*h*) *w'l hnśy' ktwb* (CD 5:1), 'and concerning the prince it was written'. The strict formula here is probably only *ktwb*, and thus corresponds to the use in the New Testament of *gegraptai* alone (Mt 4:4; 21:13; Lk 4:4, 8; 19:46). Cf. 4Q*180* 5–6:2, 5.

(B) *Said:* The Old Testament was not only looked upon as the *written* tradition of Israel both by the Qumran sect and the New Testament writers, but it was also the collection of what had once been 'said'. Just as we find in the New Testament formulae a frequent use of the verb *legein*, so too in the Qumran literature there is a correspondingly frequent use of the verbs *'mr* (16 times), *dbr* (3 times), *hgyd* (3 times). The verb 'say' is thus used more frequently than the verb 'write', as is true of the Mishnaic formulae in contrast to those in Paul's letters, where forms of the verb 'write' are more numerous.[10]

(*a*) *k'šr 'mr* (CD 7:8 [=19:5], 14, 16; 20:16; [13:23], 'as it said', or possibly sometimes 'as he said'; it is often not possible to determine who or what the subject is in these formulae. A similar formula is *k'šr dbr* (CD 19:15). With these should be compared the New Testament expressions *kathōs eirēken* (Heb 4:3), *kata to eirēmenon* (Lk 2:24; Rom 4:18), *kathōs eipen hē graphē* (Jn 7:38); *kathōs legei* (Heb 3:7). See below, p.255.

(*b*) *'šr 'mr* (CD 4:20), 'as it (or he) said'. This formula also occurs in a fuller form, listed below under C (*d*).

(*c*) *w'šr 'mr* (CD 9:2; 16:6), 'and as for what it (or he) said'.

[10] See B. M. Metzger, 'The Formulas Introducing Quotations of Scripture in the N.T. and the Mishnah', *JBL* LXX (1951) 305, and cf. the slightly revised form of this article in Metzger's *Historical and Literary Studies: Pagan, Jewish, and Christian* (NTTS 8; Leiden: Brill, 1968) 52–63; E. E. Ellis, *op. cit.*, 48–9.

This formula is frequently found in the *pesharim* (1QpHab 6:2; 7:3; 9:2–3; 10:1–2; 12:6; 4QFlor 1:7; 4QpIs[a] D 5; 4QpIs[a] 1:3 [4–5]; 4Q*161* fr. 8–10:6; 4Q*183* 1 ii. 9; 11QMelch [2], [3], [11]). But in the latter case its use is different from that in CD, for a formal commentary is being written in the *pesharim*, and this formula is used to reintroduce a portion of a verse already fully quoted in order to comment upon it.[11] In CD there is no such reintroduction, and the formula acts almost as any other one.

In some cases, however, it is clear that God is the subject of the verb of saying.

(*d*) *'šr 'mr 'l* (*'lyhm*) (CD 6:13; 8:9), 'as for what (or: about whom) God said'. Similarly, . . . *k'šr hgdth lnw m'z l'mwr* (1QM 11:5–6), 'as you spoke to us of old saying . . .', . . .*'l 'šr 'mr lw* (CD 9:7), 'Who said to him . . .'. ⟨*'mr*⟩ *lhm bqdš* (CD 3:7), 'He said to them in Qadesh'. New Testament counterparts of these expressions can be found in the following: *elalēsen de houtōs ho theos* (Acts 7:6); *kathōs eipen ho theos hoti* (2 Cor 6:16); *ho gar theos eipen* (Mt 15:4); *ho theos eipen* (Acts 7:7; see also 7:3). In both bodies of literature we have the same underlying idea of the Old Testament Scriptures as the 'Word of God'.[12] At the same time we find formulae which express the instrumentality of the Old Testament writer: *'šr 'mr byd yḥzq'l* (CD 19:11–12); *k'šr dbr 'l byd yš'yh hnby' bn 'mwṣ l'mwr* (CD 4:13–14); *w'šr d*[*brt*]*h byd mwšh l'mwr* (1QM 10:6). The same instrumentality is sometimes noted in the New Testament in such phrases as *elalēsen ho theos dia stomatos tōn hagiōn ap' aiōnos autou prophētōn* (Acts 3:21), or *hōs kai en tō Hōsēe legei* (Rom 9:25).[13]

(*e*) *'šr 'mr yš'yh* (CD 6:7–8), 'as Isaiah said'. Note that the subject of the verb of saying is sometimes the human author of

[11] See M. Burrows, 'The Meaning of *'šr 'mr* in DSH', *VT* II (1952) 255–60. K. Elliger, *op. cit.*, 123–5, calls this expression in the *pesharim* a 'Wiederaufnahmeformel'.

[12] For the same underlying presupposition in the Mishnaic use of the Old Testament, see B. M. Metzger, *op. cit.*, 306.

[13] See also CD 19:7, quoted below in C(*b*.)

the Old Testament composition. Further: *w'šr 'mr mwšh (lyśr'l)* (CD8:14; 19:26–27); *wmwšh 'mr* (CD 5:8); *w'šr hgyd (mwšh) lnw* (1QM 10:1). This type of formula has its counterpart also in the New Testament: *prōtos Mōÿsēs legei* (Rom 10:19; see also Heb 12:21); *Dauid gar legei eis auton* (Acts 2:25; see also 2:34; Rom 11:9); *pros de ton Israēl legei (Ēsaïas)* (Rom 10:22); see further Rom 9:27; 10:16, 20; 15:12; Jn 1:23.[14] Cf. 11QMelch 15: [']*šr 'mr [l'ḥryt hymym byd yš']yh hnby' 'šr 'm[r]*, 'who said concerning the end of days through Isaiah the prophet, who said'.

(*f*) *ky hw' 'šr 'mr* (CD 10:16; 16:15), 'for that is what it (or: he) said'. Cf. 11QMelch 14. This formula has a perfect counterpart in the New Testament expression *houtos gar estin ho rhētheis dia Ēsaïou tou prophētou legontos* (Mt 3:3); *touto estin to eirēmenon dia tou prophētou Iōēl* (Acts 2:16). See also Mt 11:10; Lk 7:27.[15] It should not be confused with a somewhat similar expression, *houtos estin ho Mōÿsēs ho eipas tois huiois Israēl* (Acts 7:37).

(C) *Other formulae*. There are a number of formulae which use neither 'writing' nor 'saying'. In some of these we again find God the subject of the verb.

(*a*) *k'šr hqym 'l lhm byd yḥzq'l hnby' l'mwr* (CD 3:21), As 'God confirmed (it) for them through Ezekiel the prophet, saying . . .'. *wm'z hšm['th mw]'d gbwrt ydkh bktyym l'mwr* (1QM 11:11), 'And of old you caused us to hear the appointed time of the power of your hand against the Kittim, saying . . .'; *wylmdnw m'z ldwrwtynw l'mwr* (1QM 10:2), 'And he taught us of old for our generations, saying . . .'.

14 For the Mishnaic idea of instrumentality see B. M. Metzger, *op. cit.*, 306.

15 This formula also occurs in the *pesharim* (see 1QpHab 3:2, 13–14; 5:6). Once again there is a slight difference in the usage; in CD it introduces an Old Testament quotation supporting the injunction which precedes, whereas in 1QpHab it repeats a portion of a longer text which has already been given and partly expounded. See M. Burrows, *op. cit.*, 257. K. Elliger, *op. cit.*, 124, calls this a 'Rückverweisungsformel'. It should be noted, moreover, that the New Testament counterpart is used in the same way as the formula in CD and not as that in the *pesher*.

(*b*) The famous formulae of fulfilment or realization which are frequently found in the New Testament have practically speaking no equivalent in the Qumran literature. This may strike us as strange, since the expression has its roots in the Old Testament itself (1 Kgs 2:27; 2 Chr 36:21) and the Qumran sect did look upon certain events in their history as 'fulfilling', as it were, the utterances of the prophets. While there are no formulae which employ the verb *ml'*, there are two examples of a formula which comes close to the idea, but even these differ from the New Testament formulae in referring to a future event.

bbw' hdbr 'šr ktwb bdbry yš'yh bn 'mwṣ hnby' 'šr 'mr . . . (CD 7: 10–11), 'when the word will come true which is written in the words of the prophet Isaiah, son of Amoz, who said . . .' (Rabin).

bbw' hdbr 'šr ktwb byd zkryh hnby' . . . (CD 19:7), 'when the word will come true which was written by Zechariah the prophet . . .'. Yet even this type of expression finds a very close parallel in the New Testament, without, however, containing the verb *plēroun*. In 1 Cor 15:54 we read: *tote genēsetai ho logos gegrammenos*, 'Then will come true the word which is written . . .'. One other formula should be mentioned here, which does refer to the past, but again lacks the idea of fulfilment. It is *hy' h't 'šr hyh ktwb 'lyh* (CD 1:13), 'this is the time about which it was written'. But this formula in many respects is closer to the *houtos estin* type quoted above.

Probably the real reason for the lack of 'fulfilment' formulae in the Qumran literature is that they are a peculiarly New Testament type. More fundamental still is the difference of outlook which characterizes the two groups. The Qumran theology is still dominated by a forward look, an expectation of what is to come about in the *eschaton*, whereas the Christian theology is more characterized by a backward glance, seeing the culmination of all that preceded in the advent of Christ. As F. F. Bruce expresses it, 'The New Testament interpretation of the Old

Testament is not only eschatological but Christological'.[16] This difference is probably brought out most significantly in the use and non-use of the 'fulfilment' formulae when Scripture is quoted.[17]

(*c*) Just as we find a few explicit quotations of the Old Testament in the New, which are directly intended to be such, but which lack an introductory formula (see Mt 7:23; Lk 8:16; Mk 10:6–8; Rom 10:18; 2 Cor 10:17 [contrast 1 Cor 1:31]; 13:1; Eph 5:31; Gal 3:11 [contrast Rom 1:17]; Heb 10:37–38), so too we find the same phenomenon in CD 6:3, quoting Nm 21:18. These should not be confused with mere allusions, for they are obviously intended to be quotations. Perhaps we should refer to them as 'virtual citations'.[18]

(*d*) The converse of this phenomenon is also found both in the New Testament and in the Qumran literature, that is, the use of the well-known introductory formulae to cite a passage which is not found in the Old Testament (or at least which is not found in any of its known texts or versions). Mt 2:23, 'in fulfilment of the saying of the prophets, "He shall be called a Nazarene"', is a prime example of this phenomenon; see further 1 Cor 2:9; Eph 5:14; Jas 4:5; 2 Pt 2:22; possibly also 1 Tm 5:18. This same phenomenon appears in the CD 9:8–9, *'šr 'mr l' twšyʿk ydk lk*, 'As for that which it said, "Your own hand shall not avenge you"'. Likewise CD 16:10, *'šr 'mr [l]'yšh lhny' 't šbwʿth*, 'As for that which it said, "It is for her husband to annul her oath"'. Again CD 4:15, *'šr 'mr ʿlyhm lwy bn yʿqb*, 'concerning which Levi, the son of Jacob spoke'; it is just possibly a reference to a Testament of Levi, though the

[16] *Biblical Exegesis in the Qumran Texts*, 68. The same idea has been stressed by K. Stendahl, 'The Scrolls, and the New Testament: an Introduction and a Perspective', *The Scrolls and the New Testament* (New York, 1957) 17. See further C. F. D. Moule, 'Fulfilment Words in the New Testament: Use and Abuse', *NTS XIV* (1967–68) 293–320.

[17] The same absence of these formulae has been noted in the Mishnah by B. M. Metzger, *op. cit.*, 306–7.

[18] J. Bonsirven (*op. cit.*, 27–8) mentions the occurrence of the same feature in the Tannaitic literature.

text quoted is not found in the Greek *Testaments of the Twelve Patriarchs*.[19] Such a feature, found both in the New Testament and in the Qumran literature, would hardly warrant the conclusion that other works were regarded as 'canonical' than those which subsequently came to be regarded as such in the various canonical lists; it is much more likely that the introductory formulae were at times used loosely also of other literature which served some didactic or ethical purpose.

One last remark concerning the introductory formulae is in order. Many of the features which I have pointed out as emerging from a study of these formulae, for instance, the idea of the Old Testament as the word of God, the instrumentality of the human author, the absence of fulfilment formulae in Qumran literature, are also found in the formulae used to introduce the Old Testament in the Mishnah. Some years ago B. M. Metzger made a comparative study of the formulae in the Mishnah and the New Testament. Many of the points which I have noted can be paralleled in his article. However, the significant difference is the great diversity in the actual formulae. 'By far the majority of quotations in the Mishnah are introduced by the verb *'mr*.'[20] The forms most frequently attested are the participle *'wmr* or the Niphal perfect *n'mr* or *šn'mr* (with some other variations). But there is not one formula involving this verb in his list which corresponds to anything in the list constructed from the Qumran texts. The Mishnah also employs the root *ktb* in both nominal and verbal forms. Yet once again not one of the examples given parallels any of the usages from the Qumran literature. There are, of course, a few formulae found in the New Testament which have closer parallels with the Mishnaic material (such as the use of *hē graphē* for *hktwb*; or *hy'k 'th qwr'* for *pōs anaginōskeis* [Lk 10:26]). But such a comparison as I have made shows that the Hebrew equivalents of

[19] See the notes on these passages in C. Rabin, *The Zadokite Documents: I. The Admonition; II. The Laws* (2nd ed.; Oxford, 1958).

[20] *Op. cit.*, 298. See also J. Bonsirven, *op. cit.*, 29–32.

the New Testament introductory formulae are far more numerous in the Qumran literature than in the Mishnah. Consequently, the comparative study of the Qumran and the New Testament introductory formulae would tend to indicate a closer connection of the New Testament writings with the contemporary Qumran material than with the later Mishnaic.

II. THE CLASSES OF OLD TESTAMENT QUOTATIONS

The next step in this study of the Old Testament quotations used in both literatures is to examine the way in which the writers made use of the quotation. I have tried to determine the extent to which the Qumran author respects the meaning and original sense of the passage which he quotes. It is obviously of importance to know whether the Old Testament text which is quoted is understood according to its original context, or is adapted to a new situation, or is entirely twisted to the purpose of the one quoting. In sifting the forty-two passages, I have found that they fall into four categories. They are the following: (A) the Literal or Historical class, in which the Old Testament is actually quoted in the same sense in which it was intended by the original writers; (B) the class of Modernization, in which the Old Testament text, which originally had a reference to some event in the contemporary scene at the time it was written, nevertheless was vague enough to be applied to some new event in the history of the Qumran sect; (C) the class of Accommodation, in which the Old Testament text was obviously wrested from its original context, modified or deliberately changed by the new writer in order to adapt it to a new situation or purpose; (D) the Eschatological class, in which the Old Testament quotation expressed a promise or threat about something to be accomplished in the *eschaton* and which the Qumran writer cited as something still to be accomplished in the new *eschaton* of which he wrote. In classifying this material I have tried to let the texts speak for themselves, without trying to impose on them any preconceived ideas. I readily admit that in a few instances it is difficult to decide whether a particular text should be in one class or another, since the borderline especially between class B (Modernization) and class C (Accommodation) is at times debatable.

Having discovered these four classes of Old Testament quotations in Qumran literature, I tried to see to what extent they were also verifiable of the New Testament. All four classes can be illustrated by New Testament passages as well. I do not want to imply that these four classes exhaust the grouping of the New Testament quotations. It would lead us too far astray to try to analyse all the New Testament examples in the same way as those of the Qumran literature. This must be left to someone else. However, I have made enough of a check to know that all of the four classes found in the Qumran material can be paralleled as well in the New Testament. There is, moreover, a small group of Old Testament texts which have been used by both the Qumran writers and the authors of the New Testament books. By comparing the way in which the same quotation is treated in both literatures, one can discern still more clearly the similarities and differences which appear in the methods of quotation. Thirty-two of the quotations found in the Qumran texts are not found in the New Testament; in three cases, however, the *Damascus Document* explicitly quotes an Old Testament passage to which a New Testament writer merely alludes (CD 4:12–18, quoting Is 24:17—see Lk 21:35; CD 6:3–11, quoting Is 54:16—see Rom 9:22; CD 19:11–12, quoting Ez 9:4—see Rev 9:4). But five Old Testament quotations are explicitly quoted by both the New Testament and the Qumran literature.[21]

(A) *The Literal or Historical Class*

The first category of Old Testament citations is that in which the Qumran author quotes the Old Testament in the same sense

[21] In one case (Lv 19:18) CD 9:2 quotes the first part of the verse, while the New Testament (Mt 5:43; 19:19; 22:39; Mk 12:31; Lk 10:27; Rom 13:9; Gal 5:14; Jas 2:8) quotes the second half.

in which it was used in the original writing. As will be seen, almost all of the seven examples which are found in this category cite precepts which the Qumran sect still regards as valid. It is not surprising, then, that the same sense of the Old Testament passage would be preserved in such quotations. This use of the Old Testament is found in the following instances:

(1) *k'šr 'mr byn 'yš l'štw wbyn 'b lbnw* (CD 7:8–9, quoting Nm 30:17), 'As it said, "Between a man and his wife and between a father and his son"'. *Context:* An instruction is being given concerning the observance of the Law and in particular the rule of binding oaths formulated in Nm 30. The rules there stated are still in force, apparently in the same sense in which they were originally intended, as far as the sect of Qumran is concerned. The text of CD reads *wbyn 'b lbnw*, whereas the Masoretic text has *lbtw*, which is obviously correct, since there is no mention of a son's vow in Nm 30, nor does the context of CD demand it. Hence, the reading *lbnw* should be regarded as a curious mistake which has crept into the text of CD.[22]

(2) *w'šr 'mr l' tqwm wl' ttwr 't bny 'mk* (CD 9:2, quoting Lv 19:18). 'And as for what it said, "You shall not take vengeance nor bear a grudge against the sons of your own people"'. *Context:* Among the Laws in the second part of the *Damascus Document* the injunction against vengeance and bearing a grudge from the Holiness Code is cited as still having validity in the community. CD further specifies by concrete examples who such a person would be. There is no perceptible change in the meaning of the text which is cited.

(3) *w'yn ktwb ky 'm nwqm hw' lṣryw wnwṭr hw' l'wybyw* (CD 9:5, quoting Na 1:2), 'Is it not rather written that "He is the one who takes vengeance on his enemies and he bears a grudge against his adversaries"?' *Context:* In support of the prohibition of seeking revenge, which was discussed in (2) above, the *Damascus Document* now cites a verse from the writings of the

[22] See C. Rabin, *op. cit.*, 28.

prophets to confirm the injunction derived from the Law.[23] Nahum was describing God's vengeance and insisted that it was reserved to God and did not belong to man. The words of the prophet are now cited in the same sense.

(4) *l' hqym 't mṣwt 'l 'šr 'mr lw hwkḥ twkyḥ 't r'yk wl' tś' 'lyw ḥṭ'* (CD 9:7–8, quoting Lv 19:17), 'He has not carried out the command of God who said to him, "You must indeed reprove your neighbour and not bear sin because of him"'. *Context:* This passage is related to the two foregoing ones in which a prohibition of revenge is formulated. Again a precept of the Holiness Code in Leviticus is quoted, and is intended in the same sense as the original.[24]

(5) *ky hw' 'šr 'mr šmwr 't ywm hšbt lqdšw* (CD 10:16–17, quoting Dt 5:12), 'For that is what it said, "Be careful to keep the Sabbath day holy"'. *Context:* The regulations for the observance of the Sabbath in the community of Qumran are begun with the prescription that no one is to work on the sixth day from the setting of the sun, for that is what is meant by the precept. CD here quotes the Deuteronomic decalogue in the same sense in which it was originally intended, but adds the further prescription about the determination of the time, 'when the sun's full disc is distant from the gate'.

(6) *w'šr 'mr mwṣ' śptyk tšmwr lhqym* (CD 16:6–7, quoting Dt 23:24), 'And as for what it said, "A spoken promise you must be careful to observe"'. *Context:* This quotation is found in a passage of CD dealing with oaths. Whoever binds himself by an oath to return to the Law of Moses must do so, and the Qumran interpreter adds, 'even under pain of death'. The Deuteronomic precept, obviously still valid for the Qumran

[23] This combining of texts from the Torah and the prophets is well known in the combined quotations in Paul and rabbinical literature; see below, pp. 71–2; E. E. Ellis, *op. cit.*, 49–51. In this passage quoted from Nahum it should be noted that the well-known reverence for the Tetragrammaton, attested elsewhere in Qumran literature, is evidenced here again, for the author has written *hw'* instead of *Yhwh*, found in MT.

[24] CD has a slight variant in reading *r'yk* instead of MT's *'mytk*.

community, is applied here to the case of conversion to the Law.

(7) Possibly we should also list here CD 3:7, quoting Dt 9:23; some hesitation arises because the text of CD appears to be corrupt, and it is difficult to say for sure that an explicit quotation was here intended. It reads ⟨*’mr*⟩ *lhm bqdš ‘lw wršw ’t* ⟨*h’rṣ wybḥrw brṣwn*⟩ *rwḥm wl’ šm‘w lqwl ‘śyhm*, ‘⟨He said⟩ to them in Qadesh, “Go up and inherit the ⟨land”; but they chose the desire⟩ of their spirit(s) and did not heed the voice of their Maker’.[25] *Context:* A historical survey of the fidelity of the Patriarchs to the commandments of God and of the infidelity of the sons of Jacob who walked in the stubbornness of their hearts, doing as they pleased, is being given in the *Damascus Document.* As a part of the narrative Dt 9:23 is quoted, obviously in its historical sense.

These are the seven cases which have been found to preserve the literal or historical sense of the Old Testament passage, as they were quoted by the Qumran authors. Similar texts can be found in the New Testament. I shall cite but a few examples. Jn 6:31 quotes Ps 78:24 in a sentence which relates the event of the feeding of the forefathers in the desert with manna. ‘Our forefathers in the desert had manna to eat: as the Scripture says, “He gave them bread out of heaven to eat!”’ The words of the Psalm are quoted in the same sense which they have in the Old Testament. Again in Jn 10:34 Jesus says, ‘Is it not declared in your Law, “I said, ‘You are gods!’” ?’,[26] when he wants to show that he is not guilty of blasphemy in saying that he is God’s Son. It is a mere quotation of the words of the Psalm without any change in meaning. Several clear examples of this usage are also found in Stephen’s speech in Acts where he is

[25] See C. Rabin, *op. cit.*, 10.

[26] The Fourth Gospel is here quoting Ps 82:6, where *’lhym* has been interpreted by some scholars to mean ‘judges’. However, from the fact that it is parallel to *bny ‘lywn*, a good case can be made out for the meaning ‘gods’. On this text, see below, pp. 261–2; cf. J. A. Emerton, ‘Melchizedek and the Gods: Fresh Evidence for the Jewish Background of John X. 34–36’, *JTS XVII* (1966) 399–401.

giving a résumé of Israel's history. 'And he [God] said to him [Abraham], "Leave your country and your relatives and come to the country that I will show you"' (Acts 7:3, quoting Gn 12:1). Or again, 'This is what God said, "His descendants will be strangers, living in a foreign land, and they will be enslaved and misused for four hundred years, and I will sentence the nation that has enslaved them, and afterward they will leave that country and worship me on this spot"' (Acts 7:6–7, quoting Gn 15:13–14). The foregoing New Testament examples are mainly historical and resemble that last quotation (see (7) above) cited from CD.[27] There are, however, also examples in the New Testament in which precepts are quoted from the Old Testament as still valid in the same manner as the Qumran quotations. When Jesus quotes Scripture to Satan in the Temptation scenes, he is made to use it in the same sense (see Mt 4:4; Lk 4:4, quoting Dt 8:3; Mt 4:6; Lk 4:10, quoting Ps 91:11; Mt 4:7; Lk 4:12, quoting Dt 6:16; Mt 4:10; Lk 4:8, quoting Dt 6:13). There is here merely a reaffirmation of what was written earlier. Likewise in the Sermon on the Mount Jesus cites a number of Old Testament precepts, implicitly affirming their validity and sometimes specifying them still further in a way which resembles the Qumran specification (see Mt 5:21, 27, 31, 33, 38, 43).[28]

There are, then, clear examples in both bodies of literature of Old Testament quotations used in the literal or historical sense. In this respect we see the same type of use of the Old Testament in the New Testament and in the Qumran literature.

(B) *The Class of Modernized Texts*

In the second class there is a group of quotations in which the words of the Old Testament refer to a specific event in their

[27] See further Acts 7:37, 49–50; Rom 4:3, 18; 9:15–16; 11:3–4; 1 Cor 10:7; Heb 6:13–14; 9:20.

[28] Further examples of precepts quoted in the New Testament are Mt 15:4; 22:24, 37; Mk 7:10; 12:19, 29; Lk 2:24; 10:27; Rom 7:7; 13:9; Gal 5:14; Jas 2:11.

original context, but which are nevertheless vague enough in themselves to be used by the Qumran author of some new event on the contemporary scene. In other words, the same *general* sense of the Old Testament text is preserved, but it is applied to a new subject. Usually it is the new situation which determines the use of the old Testament text; a situation is found in the Old Testament which is analogous to the new one and the two are linked together by the common element in such wise that the old one sheds light and meaning on the new and invests it with a deeper significance. In some quarters the name *typological* is applied to such use of the Old Testament.[29] However, I have preferred to avoid this name because it is not always univocally used. In this class of quotations one normally finds the Old Testament text quoted in the same way it is found in the original context, without modification or deliberate changing of it. A new reference or a new dimension, however, is given to it in the way it is quoted.

The principle at work in such application of an Old Testament text to a new subject or situation is abundantly attested also in the *pesharim*, and in this regard we find an identical use of the Old Testament both in the commentaries of Qumran and in the isolated explicit quotations. Two passages of the *pesher* on Habakkuk explain the principle which underlies this common type of exegesis of the Old Testament.

God told Habakkuk to write the things which were to come upon the last generation, but the consummation of the period he did not make known to him. And as for what it says, 'That he may run who reads it', this means the Righteous Teacher, to whom God made known all the mysteries of the words of his servants the prophets (1Q Hab 7:1–5).

The second passage reads:

This means that the last period extends over and above all that the prophets said, for the mysteries of God are marvellous (1QpHab 7:7–8).

In these two comments we find the recognition of a revelation

[29] Cf. E. E. Ellis, *op. cit.*, 126.

made to the prophet Habakkuk for the last generation, but also of the fact that the words in Habakkuk's oracle transcend the immediate reference of his own day and in the light of the charismatic interpretation of the Righteous Teacher they are now referred to a situation in the time of the Qumran sect.[30] An analogous notion is found in the New Testament, in Rom 15:4, 'For everything that was written in earlier times was written for our instruction, so that by being steadfast and through the encouragement the Scriptures give, we might hold our hope fast'. Or again, 'These things happened to them as a warning to others, but they were written down to instruct us, in whose days the ages have reached their climax' (1 Cor 10:11; cf. Rom 4:23–24). In both groups we find the conviction that they were living in the 'end of days' and that the Old Testament writings have a special pertinence in their time.

There are eleven Qumran passages in which cases of the modernization of an Old Testament passage are found.

(8) *hy' hʿt 'šr hyh ktwb ʿlyh kprh swryrh kn srr yśr'l* (CD 1:13–14, quoting Hos 4:16), 'This is the time about which it was written, "Like a wild heifer, so Israel is wild"'.[31] *Context:* The *Damascus Document* is describing the faithless backsliders of the last generation, obviously of its own time, and it applies to them the description of Israel's apostasy taken from the oracle of Hosea. This is a clear case of an Old Testament text being cited in the same general sense in which it was originally uttered, but merely applied to a new situation. The situation of which the Qumran author writes is thus invested with a new meaning by being associated with the apostate Israel of Hosea's day.

(9) *wbkl hšnym h'lh yhyh blyʿl mšwlḥ byśr'l k'šr dbr 'l byd yšʿyh hnby' bn 'mwṣ l'mr pḥd wpḥt wpḥ ʿlyk ywšb h'rṣ* (CD 4:12–18, quoting Is 24:17), 'And during all those years Belial will be let

[30] See also 1QpHab 2:8–10. F. F. Bruce, *op. cit.*, 7–17, has well analysed this exegetical principle.

[31] M. H. Gottstein (*VT* III [1953] 82) has pointed out that the text of CD, reading *kn*, agrees rather with the Targum and the Peshitta than with MT.

loose against Israel, as God spoke through Isaiah the prophet, the son of Amoz, saying, "Terror and pit and snare are upon you, O inhabitant of the earth"'. *Context:* The *Damascus Document* envisages the years before the consummation of the end-time as a period when Belial is let loose upon the earth with three nets to ensnare the house of Israel; they are allegorized as harlotry, wealth and bringing unclean offerings to the sanctuary. The Old Testament text which is cited is taken from Isaiah's vision of the cataclysm in which the world is to be involved on the day of Judgment (Is 24:1–27:13). The words cited, however, are vague enough to be applied by the writer to the evils of his own time. The only real connection between the Isaian text and the interpretation (which is here called *pšrw*) is the mention of three things: 'Terror, pit and snare'; they become the three nets, and so the evil times in which the sect finds itself living take on the character of the Isaian day of judgment.[32]

(10) *wkl 'šr hwb'w bbryt lblty bw' 'l hmqdš lh'yr mzbḥw ḥnm wyhyw msgyry hdlt 'šr 'mr 'l my bkm ysgwr dltw wl' t'yrw mzbḥy ḥnm 'm l' yšmrw l'śwt kprwš htwrh lqṣ hrš'* (CD 6:11–14, quoting Mal 1:10), 'And all who have been brought into the covenant, (agreeing) not to come to the sanctuary to kindle a fire on his altar in vain, shall become those who have closed the portal, as God said, "Who among you will close its portal and not kindle a fire on my altar in vain?"—unless (it be those who) take care to act according to the explanation of the law for the period of wickedness'.[33] *Context:* This passage refers most likely to the community's abstention from participation in the sacrifices of the Jerusalem temple.[34] Those who entered the covenant

[32] See F. F. Bruce, *op. cit.*, 28; B. J. Roberts, *BJRL* XXXIV (1951–52) 371.

[33] There are two variants in the text of Malachi cited in CD: it omits *gm* after *my*, which is found in MT (see also *dioti kai en hymin* of LXX) and it reads *dltw* instead of MT's *dltym*. If the reading in CD should rather be *dlty*, 'my portals' (confusion of *waw* for *yodh* by the medieval scribe), we would have a better parallel with 'my altar' in the second member.

[34] See pp. 466–7 below.

of the community were regarded as fulfilling the task indicated in the words of Malachi: Yahweh's yearning for someone to close the doors of the temple and to prevent polluted sacrifices from being offered to him. The community by its covenant 'has closed the doors' in withdrawing to the desert to study the Law. The text of Malachi is thus modernized in being applied to the sect's withdrawal from the temple.

(11) *spry htwrh hm swkt k'šr 'mr whqymwty hmlk 't swkt dwd hnplt* (CD 7:15–16, quoting Am 9:11), 'The books of the Law are the hut of the king, as it said, "And I shall raise up the fallen hut of David"'.[35] *Context:* This passage forms part of a larger interpretation given to another passage from Am 5:26–27, where we find the word *skwt*, 'Sakkuth', an astral deity worshipped in Israel in the days of Amos. For that idolatry they were exiled 'beyond Damascus'. In this reference to Damascus the sect of Qumran saw some reference to its own history. But just as the MT wrongly vocalized the operative words here as 'Sikkuth', so too the Qumran commentator misunderstood *skwt*. The translation of *skwt mlkkm* (Am 5:26) in the Greek version as *tēn skēnēn tou Moloch* probably gives us the interpretation of this difficult verse which was current when the *Damascus Document* was composed, for it enables us to see how *skwt* could be related to *swkt dwyd* of Am 9:11. God's promise to raise up the fallen hut of David is seen to be verified in the sect's renewed reverence for the Law. The 'hut of David' is allegorized as the books of the Law and the text of Amos is thereby modernized. The promise of ultimate restoration of Israel which is to follow upon the destruction foreseen by the prophet belongs to what is regarded today as an appendix to Amos' prophecy.

(12) *whkwkb hw' dwrš htwrh hb' dmśq k'šr ktwb drk kwkb my'qb wqm šbṭ myśr'l hšbṭ hw' nśy' kl h'dh wb'mdw wqrqr 't kl bny št* (CD 7:18–21, quoting Nm 24:17), 'And the star is the Interpreter of

[35] MT has the imperfect *'qym*, whereas CD has read the perfect with *waw*-conversive. The latter is also found in the other passage in the Qumran literature which quotes this text from Amos (4QFlor 1-3 ii 11-13): see (40) on p. 50 below.

the Law, who came to Damascus, as it was written, "A star comes forth[36] from Jacob and a sceptre rises from Israel". The sceptre is the prince of the whole congregation, and at his rising "he shatters all the sons of Seth".' *Context:* The history of the sect is being interpreted in terms of Old Testament passages. Two personages in the sect are identified as the star and the sceptre mentioned in the oracle of Balaam, which was often regarded as the promise of a messianic figure. The Qumran writer saw the promise fulfilled in two important figures in his community. In the interpretation and application of this verse to the new situation we find the same technique here which is abundantly attested in the *pesher* on Habakkuk, namely, the use of the third personal pronoun as the copula in a phrase of identification.[37] Moreover, one should note the 'atomization' of the text, which is characteristic of the interpretation found in the *pesharim*, for what may have been intended as the promise of *a* messianic figure in the oracle of Balaam has become here the promise of two figures, the star and the sceptre. This oracle of Balaam was obviously a favourite Old Testament text in the Qumran community, for it occurs at least twice elsewhere: 4QTest 9–13[38] and 1QM 11:5–7 (see (30) below). For all this

[36] The perfect of the verbs is used here and it is difficult to say just what nuance of the perfect the sect saw in them. In view of the fact that this oracle is also quoted in 4QTestimonia 9–13 along with other texts which promise the *future* coming of expected figures, it is quite likely that the perfect should be regarded as the so-called prophetic perfect. It should also be noted that one of the members of the verse is omitted ('and he shatters the temples of Moab').

[37] The same device is also found in the New Testament; see, for example, 1 Cor 10:4; 2 Cor 3:17; Gal 3:16. Cf. 1QpHab 12:3, 4, 7, 9; 4QpPs 37 1:5; 2:12; 4QpIs^b 2:10(?).

[38] In 4QTestimonia the interpretation of this verse is contested. The first paragraph (quoting Dt 5:28–29 and 18:18–19 [or better, Ex 20:21; see below, pp. 82–3]) refers to the coming of a prophet like Moses, the second paragraph (quoting Nm 24:15–17) to the coming Davidic Messiah and another figure, probably a priestly 'Interpreter of the Law', and the third paragraph (quoting Dt 33:8–11) to the coming priestly Messiah. In *T. Levi* 18:3 the oracle of Balaam is applied to the Aaronitic Messiah.

text may have meant to early Christianity (see Justin, *Dial.* 106, 3), it is not cited in the New Testament.

(13) *wypr'w byd rmh llkt bdrk rš'ym 'šr 'mr 'l 'lyhm ḥmt tnynym yynm wr'š ptnym 'kzr htnynym hm mlky h'mym* [*wyy*]*nm hw' drkyhm wr'š hptnym hw' r'š mlky ywn hb' l'śwt bhm nqmh* (CD 8:9–12, quoting Dt 32:33), 'And they rebelled high-handedly by walking in the way of the wicked; about them God said, "Their wine is the venom of dragons, the pitiless poison of cobras". The dragons are the kings of the nations; and their wine is their ways and the poison of cobras is the chief of the kings of Greece, who has come to wreak vengeance on them.' *Context:* The text describes the community's enemies from whom it has separated itself, for these preferred to follow the stubbornness of their hearts and to walk rebelliously in the way of the wicked. The enemies are described by the use of a part of the Song of Moses, in which Israel's enemies are depicted and compared to Yahweh and his people. The text is thus modernized by being applied to a new enemy of Israel. Once again there are atomized comments on certain words of the verse of Deuteronomy, and there is a play on the words *r'š* meaning 'head, chief' and *r'š* meaning 'poison'. Both of these features are found in the exegesis of 1QpHab.

(14) *w'šr 'mr mšh l' bṣdqtk wbyšr lbbk 'th b' lršt 't hgwym h'lh ky m'hbtw 't 'bwtk wmšmrw 't hšbw'h wkn hmšpṭ lšby yśr'l* (CD 8:14–16, quoting Dt 9:5), 'And as for what Moses said, "It is not because of your righteousness nor because of the uprightness of your heart that you are entering to inherit (the land of) these nations, but rather because he loved your fathers and he has kept the oath". So is the case with those who return in Israel ....'[39] *Context:* This passage stresses the idea that those who have joined the community, having turned from the impiety of Israel and forsaken the way of the people, are not to think that they have done this by any merit of their own; it is rather due

[39] The first part of this quotation agrees with MT; the last part, however, is dependent on Dt 7:8, but is not introduced as an explicit quotation.

to God’s love of their forefathers and the oath which he swore to them. The words of Moses which are quoted are taken from his second discourse, addressed to Israel when it was about to cross the Jordan. Though the two situations are not parallel, there is a common element which permits the words of Moses to be applied to the new situation. (See the use of the same text in CD 19:26.)

(15) *kk šwmr hbryt whḥsd l’hb⟨yw⟩ wlšmrw mṣwty⟨w⟩ l’lp dwr* (CD 19:1, quoting Dt 7:9), ‘As it was written, “(He) keeps the covenant and mercy for ⟨those⟩ who love ⟨him⟩ and for those who keep ⟨his⟩ commandments for a thousand generations”’.[40] *Context:* The passage announces that all those who enter the new covenant and perfect themselves in the observance of the ordinances of the community will find that God is faithful to the covenant and to them for a thousand generations. Once again a part of Moses’ second discourse is cited in which the election of Israel and Yahweh’s divine favour toward it are made known. The *Damascus Document* modernizes the text in applying it to the new situation of the community.

(16) *hw’h hbyt ’šr [yʿśh] l[k b’]ḥryt hymym k’šr ktwb bspr [mwšh mqdš ’dwny k]wnnw ydykh Yhwh ymlwk ʿwlm wʿd hw’h hbyt ’šr lw’ ybw’ šmh* (4QFlor 1:2–3, quoting Ex 15:17b–18), ‘That is the house which [He will make for] you [in the] end of days, as it was written in the book of [Moses, “A sanctuary, O Lord,] your hands have [e]rected, Yahweh will reign for ever and ever”. That is the house to which there will not come [. . . .’[41] *Context:* This Old Testament quotation is used within what appears to be the commentary of a *pesher* or *midrash* on 2 Sm 7:10 ff.[42] After the verse from 2 Samuel has been quoted, the

[40] The text of CD is obviously corrupt here, reading *l’hb* and *mṣwtyy*, neither of which makes any sense. I have accordingly corrected them to agree with MT.

[41] The restoration of the lacunae follows that of Y. Yadin, *IEJ* IX (1959) 95–8. The latter part of the comment contains an allusion to Dt 23:3–4 and Ez 44:9.

[42] See above, p. 7, n. 8.

commentary begins and brings in as part of its comment a verse from the national anthem of ancient Israel (sometimes called the Song of Miriam). In the Exodus context Yahweh has brought his people into his inheritance where he will reign forever. 4QFlor now quotes this verse, applying it to the Qumran community, which is the new Israel, the new 'house'. The modernization of the verse of Exodus is presented as intended by God for 'the end of days'. The Qumran sect thought that it was living already in that period; but if that existence should rather be regarded as something still in the future, then possibly this example belongs to the class of eschatological quotations in class D.

(17) *pšr hdb[r 'šr] srw mdrk [hʿm] 'šr ktwb bspr yšʿyh hnby' l'ḥryt hymym wyhy kḥzqt [hyd wysyrny mlkt bdrk] hʿm hzh* (4QFlor 1:14–16, quoting Is 8:11), 'The interpretation of the passage (is about those) who turned away from the path of the people, (about) whom it was written in the Book of Isaiah the prophet for the end of days, And it was "while he grasped me by [the hand that he turned me aside from the path] of this people"'.[43] *Context:* This is the beginning of the commentary on Ps 1:1, 'Happy is the man who walks not in the counsel of the wicked'. As part of the commentary, Is 8:11 is quoted, a verse from the 'Book of Emmanuel', oracles which pertain to the Syro-Ephraimite war and the first Assyrian invasion. According to Isaiah, Yahweh is with his people to turn them aside from the path of the terrifying invaders. 4QFlor quotes the text, which is vague enough to be modernized and applied to the situation in the 'end of days'.

(18) *whmh 'šr ktwb ʿlyhmh bspr yḥzq'l hnby' 'šr lw[' yṭm'w ʿwd bg]lwlyhmh hmh bny ṣdwq w['n]šy ʿṣ[t]w rw[* . . . (4QFlor 1:16–17, quoting Ez 37:23), 'And they are the ones about whom it was written in the book of Ezekiel the prophet, who "will no [longer

[43] The reconstruction offered here is that of Y. Yadin (*op. cit.*, 96), which is based on MT. It should be noted, however, that the text of 4QFlor, in so far as it is preserved, agrees rather with 1QIs^a, which differs from MT somewhat, *kḥzqt yd ysyrny*.

defile themselves with] their [i]dols". They are the sons of Zadok and the men of His council. . . .'[44] *Context:* The continuation of the commentary on Ps 1:1 identifies those who turned aside from the way of the people, the 'happy ones' of Ps 1:1, as the sons of Zadok, the members of the community. They are the ones about whom Ezekiel wrote. The words of the prophet were part of a promise to unite Israel and Judah again in one kingdom in the days when they will not defile themselves with idols and abominable practices. They are here referred to a new situation which is found in the Qumran community.

There are, then, eleven instances in which the Old Testament texts have been quoted and related by Qumran authors to contemporary events or the situation in which they lived. In most cases the situation itself already existed and it was enhanced with special meaning because of a similarity or an analogy which they saw between it and some Old Testament situation. There is little doubt that they believed that their own history was guided by the hand of God and that these similarities or analogies were somehow intended by him.[45]

The New Testament too has similar groups of texts in which one finds the Old Testament modernized. No less than the

[44] We are again following the reconstruction of the text suggested by Y. Yadin, *ibid.* He has more correctly identified the text of Ezekiel as 37:23 than Allegro, who proposed 44:10.

[45] Modernization of the prophet's text is very frequent in 1QpHab, as might be expected (see 1:5, 6, 7, 8, 9, 10*c–d*, 11, 13*c–d*, 14–15, 16*a–b*, 17; 2:2*d*, 5–6, 8*a*, 12–13, 15, 16, 17). Cf. E. Osswald, *op. cit.*, 247 ff.—I am touching here on an acute modern hermeneutical problem. As far as I am concerned, the interpretation of any Old Testament text should be one that a Jew and a Christian could work out and agree on, from the standpoint of philology, exegesis, and Old Testament biblical theology. I see no reason why a Jewish synthesis of Old Testament theology would be *radically* different from a Christian synthesis. To admit this is not to deny the 'harmony of the Testaments', nor to abandon one's Christian heritage. Nor is it said merely to be irenic. The Christian interpretation of the Old Testament must begin with that which a Jewish interpreter, writing with the empathy of his own heritage and a recognition of the value of modern historical, critical interpretation of the Bible, would set forth. The difference between the Jewish and the Christian interpretation of the Old Testament lies not in the primary literal sense of

Qumran authors, the New Testament writers considered their history to be guided by the hand of God. But for the New Testament authors his word spoken through the prophets and writers of the Old Testament had already seen fulfilment in the new events and situations of the early Christian history. Due to the predominantly backward glance of the New Testament writers, which we have already noted, the number of such modernized texts in the New Testament is considerably greater. While some commentators prefer to regard the fulfilment quotations in the New Testament as literal realizations of prophecy, I believe that most of them belong more properly in this group of modernized texts. For the words cited usually have a specific reference in their Old Testament context. The new reference which they acquire in the New Testament is due to the application of those words to a new situation by the New Testament writer—a God-directed situation, whose meaning for the Christian community is enhanced by the significance of the previous divine intervention. I am not trying to deny that the New Testament writer regarded the new event as a fulfilment of what was uttered of old; he explicitly says so. But what does he mean by it? Cognizance must be taken of the fact that

---

the Old Testament text (arrived at with the same philological, historical, and literary critical means), but in the plus value that the Old Testament takes on when it becomes part of the Christian Bible. One may call this a fuller dimension that the Hebrew Scriptures have because of their relation to the book of the Christian community. This fuller sense is one which a Christian interpreter would not expect a Jewish reader to accept. But it is at the same time one which the Jewish reader, with his keen sense of God's providence, must also learn to live with. If twentieth-century Christians have not worked out for themselves a 'theology of Israel' (how it is that God in his providence has permitted the Jewish people to survive and maintain its corporate religious identity, despite the fact that Christianity's first theologian characterized them as 'a disobedient and contrary people' [RSV, Rom 10:21, adapting Is 65:2]), similarly Jews of the twentieth century have scarcely reckoned sufficiently with the historical dimension of their existence in a culture which has developed largely in a belief that Yahweh, the God of Israel, intervened again in man's history in the person, life, and career of Jesus of Nazareth. This cultural problem underlies the hermeneutical problem briefly sketched above.

the Old Testament passage which he quotes usually has a more immediate, literal reference which cannot be simply ignored.

For instance, when Matthew (4:15–16) cites the words of Isaiah (8:23–9:1): 'Zebulon's land, and Naphtali's land, along the road to the sea, across the Jordan, Galilee of the heathen! The people that were living in darkness have seen a great light, and on those who were living in the land of the shadow of death a light has dawned', he introduces them thus: 'And he left Nazareth and went and settled in Capernaum, by the sea, in the district of Zebulon and Naphtali, in fulfilment of what was said by the prophet Isaiah. . . .' The words quoted from the prophet belong to the Emmanuel oracle and in their original context refer to the liberation to come after the Assyrian conquest. But the great light of which the prophet spoke could also carry a further meaning, which it acquires in the use of it by Matthew, who applies it to the Galilean ministry of Christ.[46]

When Luke (4:16–21) records the episode of Christ's reading from the scroll of Isaiah in the synagogue of Nazareth, he quotes Is 61:1–2. Jesus' commentary on it begins: 'This passage of Scripture has been fulfilled here in your hearing today!' New meaning is given to those words of Isaiah by the event taking place—a new meaning which has little to do with the original context in which the words are understood either of the Servant of Yahweh or of Deutero-Isaiah himself. But they are expressed in a general enough way so that they could be used of the New Testament situation.

Similarly, when Paul writes, 'As God's fellow-worker, I appeal to you, too, not to accept the favour of God and then waste it. For he says, "I have listened to you at a welcome time, and helped you on a day of deliverance!" Now the welcome time has come' (2 Cor 6:1–2, quoting Is 49:8). Paul here quotes the words of Deutero-Isaiah, which refer immediately to the return from exile, but which are general enough to be applied to his

[46] Further examples in Matthew: 8:17; 11:10; 13:35; 15:8; 21:42.

own preaching and apostolic activity among the Corinthians. Further examples of this use of the Old Testament texts in the New Testament could easily be cited; those already mentioned suffice to show the existence of them.[47]

(C) *Accommodated Texts*

Akin to the second class of Old Testament quotations is another group, which has in common with the foregoing the application of the text to a new situation or subject. However, it differs in this that the Old Testament text in this case is usually wrested from its original context or modified somehow to suit the new situation. I have included here the instances in which the Old Testament text appears somewhat confused when compared with the existing Hebrew and Greek recensions, although it is admittedly not easy to determine in each case whether mere textual corruption has occurred or a different recension was used.

Twelve passages are found in the Qumran literature in which accommodations of the Old Testament texts have been made.

(19) *ky' yrḥq mmnw bkwl dbr ky' kn ktwb mkwl dbr šqr trḥq* (1QS 5:15, quoting Ex 23:7), 'But he shall keep far away from him in everything, for so it was written, "From everything deceitful you must withdraw"'. *Context:* The community's rule-book prescribes that the member must avoid all contact with the impure, wicked outsider. As support for this prescription, it cites Ex 13:7, a text which actually has to do with law-suits and social conduct: 'You must not pervert the justice due to your poor in his case. Avoid false charges; do not have innocent and guiltless persons put to death, nor acquit the wicked.' The phrase, 'avoid false charges', contains in Hebrew the word *dbr*, which also has the generic meaning of 'thing', and so the *Manual*

[47] See further Lk 22:37; Jn 12:38; 13:18; 19:24; Acts 3:25; 13:33–34; Rom 9:29; 10:15–16; 15:21; 2 Cor 6:2; Heb 1:5, 8–9, 10–12, 13; 3:7–11; 4:3, 7; 5:6; 8:8–12; 10:16–18.

of Discipline was able to quote the phrase without any regard to its original judicial context and apply it to the question of contact with wicked outsiders. The possibility of so using the text was probably also due to the fact that the Hebrew text cited contains the indefinite pronoun *kwl* (thus agreeing with the Septuagint's *apo pantos rhēmatos adikou* rather than with MT which omits it).[48] We have, then, in this instance a clear case of the accommodation of the Old Testament verse to a new situation, in which the original context is wholly disregarded.

(20) *k'šr ktwb ḥdlw lkm mn h'dm 'šr nšmh b'pw ky' bmh nḥšb hw'h ky' kwl 'šr lw' nḥšbw bbrytw lhbdyl 'wtm w't kwl 'šr lhm* (1QS 5:17–18, quoting Is 2:22), 'As it was written, "Desist from the man whose breath is in his nostrils, for by what can he be reckoned?" For all who are not reckoned in his covenant, they and all they have are to be excluded.' *Context:* This text continues the prohibition of contact with the wicked outsider begun in the previous passage. Here the *Manual of Discipline* quotes a text of Isaiah, actually a gloss, in which the writer counsels the people to cease trusting in the proud man, 'Cease trusting a man in whose nostrils is breath, for of what account is he?' The Qumran author twists the sense of the verb *nḥšb* to carry the meaning of 'being reckoned in the covenant' of the community, and so uses it to support the prohibition of contact with wicked outsiders. The warning of Isaiah has been turned into a sort of precept about an entirely different matter.

(21) *llkt lmdbr lpnwt šm 't drk hw'h' k'šr ktwb bmdbr pnw drk .... yšrw b'rbh mslh l'lwhynw hw'h mdrš htwrh ['šr] ṣwh byd mwšh l'śwt kkwl hnglh 't b't wk'šr glw hnby'ym brwḥ qwdšw* (1QS 8:13–16, quoting Is 40:3), '. . . to go into the desert to prepare there the way of Him, as it was written, "In the desert make ready the way of. . . ., make straight in the wilderness a highway for our God". This is the study of the Law which he commanded through Moses to be done according to all that was revealed from time to time and according to what the prophets revealed

[48] As was pointed out by M. H. Gottstein, *op. cit.*, 79.

through his holy spirit.'[49] *Context:* The *Manual of Discipline* is expressing the desert mystique of the community, which withdrew from the abodes of the men of deceit to go into the wilderness to relive there the experience of their forefathers in the desert. The motivation for this withdrawal is derived from Is 40:3, which is actually part of the Book of the Consolation of Israel. There, according to some interpreters, it is Yahweh who calls to his prophet, but more likely it is the voice of a herald which cries. Yahweh is going to put himself at the head of his people and lead them to freedom from exile across the desert, as he had done at the Exodus from Egypt into the Promised Land. But the Qumran author interprets the verse in a very specific way, disregarding the historical context; the preparation of the way of the Lord in the desert motivated the community's retreat into the wilderness of Qumran to live lives in perfect conformity with the Law and the utterances of the prophets, the study of which was their main occupation. This is an accommodated use of the Isaian verse. The same text is used in the New Testament about John the Baptist by all four evangelists (Mt 3:3; Mk 1:3; Lk 3:4–6; Jn 1:23), in a form which is closer to the Septuagint than to the Hebrew. Here we find an almost identical use of the text, for the apparent reason in citing it is to explain John's presence in the desert of Judah, where he is preaching and baptizing. Admittedly, the abrupt beginning of the Gospel of Mark makes it almost impossible to discern the motive in the use of the Isaian text, but in Matthew and Luke the connection between John and the *phōnē boōntos* is made explicit, 'It was he who was spoken of by the prophet Isaiah, when he said . . .'. The linking of *en tē erēmō* with *phōnē boōntos*, as in the Septuagint, is part of the reason why the verse could be applied to John in the desert. Hence, in both the Qumran and the New Testament contexts the sense of the original has been dis-

[49] Except for the four dots instead of the Tetragrammaton the quotation agrees with the text of the Masoretes. 1QIs[a], however, reads *wyšrw* instead of *yšrw*.

regarded, in that there is no longer a reference to Yahweh at the head of his people returning from exile, and the text is used to explain the presence of the community and of John in the desert.[50]

(22) *wkl kbwd ʾdm lhm hwʾ kʾšr hqym ʾl lhm byd yḥzqʾl hnbyʾ lʾmr hkhnym whlwym wbny ṣdwq ʾšr šmrw ʾt mšmrt mqdšy btʿwt bny yśrʾl mʿly hm ygyšw ly ḥlb wdm* (CD 3:20–4:2, quoting Ez 44:15), 'And all the glory of Adam is theirs, as God swore to them through Ezekiel the prophet, saying, "The priests and the levites and the sons of Zadoq who have kept charge of my sanctuary when the children of Israel went astray from me, they shall bring me fat and blood"'. *Context:* In this passage the *Damascus Document* is explaining that when God pardoned the impiety of Israel and made his covenant with it—that is, established the Zadoqite community at Qumran—he destined it for eternal life and all the glory of Adam. This community was made up of priests, levites and the sons of Zadoq, whose lot it would be to minister to Yahweh in the end of days. As part of this explanation the text of Ezekiel is cited in which the promise is made that Yahweh will be served by 'the levitical priests, sons of Zadoq'. However, in quoting this text of Ezekiel, the *Damascus Document* inserts the conjunction 'and' twice, so that the phrase becomes 'the priests and the levites and the sons of Zadoq', probably with the intention of including in such an expression all the members of the community. There is here an accommodation of the text of Ezekiel, which consists in a deliberate manipulation of the text in order to suit the purpose of the passage in which it is quoted.[51]

(23) Perhaps one of the most striking cases of accommodation which occurs in the Qumran literature is found in the following passage, in which four Old Testament passages are used. It also has a striking parallel in the New Testament. *bwny*

[50] Cf. C. F. D. Moule, *NTS* XIV (1967–68) 294, n. 1, for a rather different interpretation of this use of Isaiah.

[51] See the similar interpretation of F. F. Bruce, *op. cit.*, 31.

hḥwṣ 'šr hlkw 'ḥry ṣw hṣw hw' mṭyp 'šr 'mr hṭp yṭypwn hm nytpśym bštym bznwt lqḥt šty nšym bḥyyhm wyswd hbry'h zkr wnqbh br' 'wtm wb'y htbh šnym šnym b'w 'l htbh w'l hnśy' ktwb l' yrbh lw nšym wdwyd l' qr' bspr htwrh hḥtwm (CD 4:19–5:2, quoting Mi 2:6; Gn 1:27; 7:9; Dt 17:17), 'The builders of the wall—who have walked after Zaw (Zaw is a preacher, as it said, "They must indeed preach")—are those caught in two ways: in harlotry, by marrying two women in their lifetime, whereas the principle of creation is: "Male and female he created them", and "those who entered the ark went into the ark by twos"; and concerning the prince it was written, "Let him not multiply wives unto himself". But David had not read the sealed book of the Law....'

Context: The meaning of the first part of this passage is not clear. The passage itself forms part of the explanation of the three nets of Belial, which was cited earlier (see (9) above), but just who the 'builders of the wall' are is obscure. They are said to have walked after a mysterious *Zaw*, a 'preacher'. He is described in terms of a verse of Micah (2:6). In its original context this verse describes the people's protests against the prophet's threats, which they believe are contrary to the traditional faith in the alliance with Yahweh: *'l-tṭpw yṭypwn l'-yṭpw l'lh*, '"Do not keep on harping", they harp; "One should not be harping upon such things"'. Explicitly introduced as a quotation in CD, this becomes *hṭp yṭypwn*, 'They must indeed preach'. If the text is sound, then we have a deliberate manipulation of the prophet's words, first of all by the omission of the negative, and secondly by the complete disregard of the context. But the accommodation of the sense of a text is still more evident in the next two verses from Genesis which are cited to support the prohibition of polygamy (which is the net of 'fornication' let loose by Belial). One does not have here the characteristic introductory formulae, but the intention to quote Scripture is evident from the use of the texts which are cited as the 'principle of creation'. As proof against polygamy CD quotes the description of the creation of man in the image of God from Gn 1:27 (in which passage there is really no reference to monogamous marriage) and the story of the entrance of the animals into Noah's ark *in pairs* from Gn 7:9. This is rounded off by an Old Testament text which forbids the prince a multiplicity of wives, a text which has some pertinence in the context in which it is used. Now there is the almost identical use of the first text from Genesis (1:27) in the New Testament, in this case joined to Gn 2:24 ('That is why a man leaves his father and mother, and clings to his wife, so that they form one flesh'), as the scriptural support for the prohibition of divorce. Indeed, in Mk 10:6 the quotation is introduced by the words, 'From the beginning of creation', which certainly resembles the 'principle of creation' phrase of the *Damascus Document*.[52] In both cases, then, there is a description of man in the image of God ('male and female he created them') cited in support of a notion which actually goes beyond the immediate intention of the verse in Genesis.

(24) *wlwqḥym 'yš 't bt 'ḥyhw w't bt 'ḥwtw wmšh 'mr 'l 'ḥwt 'mk l' tqrb š'r 'mk hy'* (CD 5:7–9, quoting Lv 18:13), 'And they marry each man the daughter of his brother and the daughter of his sister, whereas Moses said, "You shall not approach your mother's sister, she is your mother's kin"'.[53] *Context:* This passage describes the second of the two ways the 'builders of the wall' are caught in the net of harlotry, namely, by marriage between an uncle and his niece. But to prevent such marriages the author of CD invokes a text of Leviticus which actually forbids the marriage of a man with his *aunt*. The marriage of a man with his niece is not explicitly forbidden in the Leviticus passage on forbidden degrees of kinship (18:6 ff.), but the Qumran author extends the legislation by analogy, which we must recognize as a sort of accommodation of the text cited.[54]

[52] Cf. Mt 19:4. See the similar explanation of F. F. Bruce, *op. cit.*, 29. Cf. D. Daube, *The New Testament and Rabbinic Judaism* (Jordan Lectures in Comparative Religion II; London, 1956) 71–85.

[53] The text in CD agrees neither with MT (*'rwt 'ḥwt-'mk l' tglh ky-š'r 'mk hw'*) nor with LXX. Possibly CD has preserved a different Hebrew recension here.

[54] Cf. F. F. Bruce, *op. cit.*, 28 for a similar explanation.

(25) *wyšmy'm wyḥpwrw 't hb'r b'r ḥprwh śrym krwh ndyby h'm bmḥwqq hb'r hy' htwrh wḥwpryh hm šby yśr'l hywṣ'ym m'rṣ yhwdh wygwrw b'rṣ dmśq 'šr qr' 'l 't kwlm śrym ky dršwhw wl' hwšbh p'rtm bpy 'ḥd whmḥwqq hw' dwrš htwrh 'šr 'mr yš'yh mwṣy' kly lm'śyhw wndyby h'm hm hb'ym lkrwt 't hb'r bmḥwqqwt 'šr ḥqq hmḥwqq lhthlk bmh bkl qṣ hršy' wzwltm l' yśygw 'd 'md ywrh hṣdq b'ḥryt hymym* (CD 6:3–11, quoting Nm 21:18 and Is 54:16), 'And he caused them to listen, and they dug the well, "a well which princes dug, which the nobles of the people sunk with a tool". The well is the Law and those who dug it are the converts of Israel, who went out of the land of Judah and sojourned in the land of Damascus, all of whom God called princes, for they sought him and their glory was not withdrawn (?) on the lips of anyone. And the tool is the Interpreter of the Law, as Isaiah said, "Who bringeth forth a tool for his work". And the nobles of the people are those who have come to dig the well with the tools which the lawgiver set up, to walk according to them in the whole period of wickedness and without which they will not succeed, until there rises one who teaches righteousness in the end of days.' *Context:* In this passage God, remembering the covenant which he had made with the forefathers of Israel, raised up men of understanding from both Aaron and Israel, who dug the well of the Torah. CD applies to the Torah Israel's Song of the Well, found in Nm 21:18, where it refers to a well in the desert provided by Yahweh for his thirsty people. A completely allegorical meaning is given to the well in the CD context, without any reference to the original context of the song.[55] The second text which is quoted comes from Is 54:16, which is part of Deutero-Isaiah's description of the future glory of Jerusalem. Yahweh, consoling Israel in her tribulation from

[55] The meaning of 'staff' which is usually employed for *mḥwqq* in this passage can hardly be correct. Aside from the fact that the digging of a well with a staff is rather peculiar, the rapprochement of the two texts (Nm 21: 18 and Is 54:16) here suggests that the author of CD understood *mḥwqq* in the same sense as *kly*, hence our translation 'tool'. In MT *bmš'ntm* may well be a gloss; cf. LXX. It is difficult to say what the connecting link between

outside enemies, makes it known that it is he who has made the smith who produces the tool or weapon suited to its work; hence he shall not permit any weapon forged against Israel to succeed. CD quotes this verse completely out of its context, relating to it the 'tool' of the former quotation from Numbers, for the word *mḥwqq* can have two meanings, 'a tool', as in Nm 21:18, and 'a lawmaker', as in Gn 49:10, which obviously led to its allegorization as the 'Interpreter of the Law'. So he becomes the tool brought forth by Yahweh and suited for *his* work, for a task ordained by Yahweh. The verse of Isaiah thus quoted is used with complete disregard of its original context.

(26) *k'šr 'mr whglyty 't skwt mlkkm w't kywn ṣlmykm m'hly dmśq* (CD 7:14–15, quoting Am 5:26–27), 'As it said, "I shall exile Sikkuth your king and Kiyyun your images from the tents of Damascus"'. *Context:* This is one of four quotations in a passage to which I have referred earlier. In it we are told that when the two houses of Israel, Ephraim and Judah, separated, those who were turned back were put to the sword, but those who remained firm escaped to the land of the north, as it said. . . . CD looks upon a certain event in the history of the community as fulfilling this utterance of Amos. The text of Amos is somewhat different. First of all, it seems evident from what I have said earlier (see (11) above) that the author of CD did not understand what Sakkuth and Kewan were, i.e., astral deities worshipped by idolatrous Israelites. Secondly, the text of Amos has been somewhat telescoped. His words were: 'But you have carried around Sakkuth, your king, and Kewan, your images, the star of your god, which you have made for yourselves, so I will carry you into exile beyond Damascus.' This form of the text, taken from the Masoretic Bible, actually fits the context in

---

the well and the Torah was in the passage. According to W. H. Brownlee (*BA* XIV [1951] 56), the link was the Hebrew radicals *b'r* which could be vocalized as *be'ēr*, 'a well', or as *bē'ēr*, 'he explained', as in Dt 1:5. He also saw a connection between *krwt*, 'to dig', and *krt*, 'to cut; form (a covenant)'. F. F. Bruce (*op. cit.*, 31), on the other hand, saw a connection in the 'obvious appropriateness of pure water as a figure of sound doctrine'.

CD better than the form cited there. For the commentary continues to speak about the 'star', explained in terms of Nm 24:17 (see (12) above), but the 'star' does not appear in the form of the Amos text cited in CD. This may be due, of course, to some corruption in the transmission of the text of CD. At any rate, as B. J. Roberts has already pointed out:

> The source is Am 5:26 f., but the context of the original is wholly disregarded, and terms of offensive associations are correlated to personalities with the highest possible prestige. Thus Torah is represented by Sikkuth, a pagan astral deity-king, and—even if this happened through ignorance and the connection with the festival *par excellence* of all Jews was made by false etymology and a change of vocalization—there is still greater incongruity in the subsequent correlation of obnoxious idols with the spurned prophets and their ignored oracles, and again, of an astral deity with the Messianic 'Star of Jacob'. . . . The significance in each instance lies in the 'key-words': they are symbols of historical events, but these are only intimated as fulfilments of the uttered oracle, and do not of themselves offer the means of reconstructing a historical account. Such a reconstruction is rendered still more difficult by the obvious dissociation of the interpretation from the context of the original oracle.[56]

If the text is sound, the use made of the Old Testament quotation can only be classed as one of accommodation. One finds a rather different use of this passage in Acts 7:42–43, where Stephen uses it in his historical résumé of Israel's infidelity, citing it as an example of what happened to Israel because of her idolatry. He thus uses the text in a way which is far more faithful to the original context than does the author of CD.

(27) *'l y'l 'yš lmzbḥ bšbt ky 'm 'wlt hšbt ky kn ktwb mlbd šbtwtykm* (CD 11:17–18, quoting Lv 23:38), 'Let no one offer (anything) on the altar on the Sabbath except the burnt-offering of the Sabbath, for thus it was written, "apart from your Sabbath-offerings"'. *Context:* As part of the regulations made to enforce the Old Testament law of observance of the Sabbath, CD proscribes the offering of anything except the Sabbath holocaust.

[56] *BJRL* XXXIV (1951–52) 373.

However, in its use of Lv 23:38 it completely disregards the sense of the original. The words quoted occur at the end of a list of festivals and their sacrifices; it is stated that the latter are to take place each on its proper day in addition to the Sabbaths of the Lord, the gifts, votive-offerings and voluntary offerings. The words are quoted in CD, however, with a different sense given to *mlbd*, which no longer means 'besides, in addition to', but 'except'. The words are thus wrested from their original context and used to serve the purpose of the author of the *Damascus Document.*

(28) *ky ktwb zbḥ ršʿym twʿbh wtplt ṣdqm kmnḥt rṣwn* (CD 11: 20–21, quoting Prv 15:8), 'For it was written, "The sacrifice of the wicked is an abomination but the prayer of the righteous is like a delightful offering"'.[57] The *Damascus Document* here forbids the sending of an offering to the sanctuary through the intermediary of a man afflicted with any uncleanness, thus empowering him to convey uncleanness to the altar. In support of this prohibition Prv 15:8 is cited, but with a change in the meaning of the text. For in its original context it is a proverb referring to moral wickedness in contrast to righteousness; here, however, the question of moral evil is disregarded and the verse is cited to forbid the use of an unclean man as the bearer of a gift to the altar.

(29) *['l] yqdš 'yš 't m'kl p[yhw l']l ky hw' 'šr 'mr 'yš 't rʿyhw yṣ[w]dw ḥrm* (CD 16:14–15, quoting Mi 7:2), 'Let no one declare holy to God the food of his mouth, for that is what it said, 'Each traps his neighbour with a vow"'. *Context:* This is a prohibition of the dedication of any food to God so that it might not be used to help one's neighbour. In support of this prohibition, Mi 7:2 is cited, again with complete disregard of the sense of the original context. Micah is describing the moral collapse of Israel: 'The godly has perished from the land, and there is none righteous among men. They all lie in wait for

[57] This agrees with neither MT nor LXX completely; possibly a different recension of the verse is here preserved.

blood; each hunts his brother with a net.' The last part of this verse contains the Hebrew word *ḥrm*, which in Micah means a 'snare, trap', but in CD has been understood in the sense of 'something consecrated, dedicated, removed from profane use'. This play on the word is responsible for the accommodation of the text.

(30) *wlw' kwḥnw wʿṣwm ydynw ʿśh ḥyl ky' bkwḥkh wbʿwz ḥylkh hgdwl k'[šr] hgdth lnw m'z l'mwr drk kwkb myʿqwb qm šbṭ myśr'l wmḥṣ p'ty mw'b w*qrqr kwl bny šyt wyrd myʿqwb wh'byd śryd [m]ʿyr whyh 'wyb yršh wyśr'l ʿśh ḥyl* (1QM 11:5–7, quoting Nm 24:17–19), 'Nor has our strength or the might of our hands done valiantly, but it is by your strength and the power of your great might, as you declared to us of old, saying, "A star comes forth out of Jacob, a sceptre rises from Israel; and it crushes the foreheads of Moab and breaks down all the sons of Seth; and it goes down from Jacob to destroy the remnant of the city and the enemy is dispossessed and Israel acts valiantly"'.[58] *Context:* This is part of the discourse of the High Priest before the eschatological battle, when he encourages the troops to fight valiantly. However, they are to remember that any success will not be due to them but to the promise of victory which he finds in the oracle of Balaam. The promise of messianic figures, which is the normal understanding of the verse,[59] is here completely set aside in the new context of encouragement.

The twelve passages from Qumran literature, which have been examined, contain sixteen Old Testament quotations, all of which manifest a loose application of the Old Testament verse to a new situation with either a manipulation of the text itself or a complete disregard for the original context. The accommodation was often made by the adoption of another meaning which the same Hebrew radicals could support, by giving the words an allegorical meaning, by atomizing the sense

[58] See above, p. 26. This text is also cited in (12). For a discussion of the form of the text used here and a comparison with MT and versions, see J. Carmignac, *RB* LXIII (1956) 238.

[59] See pp. 82–4 below.

of the Old Testament expression or by omitting words (for example, negatives).[60]

It has long been recognized that there are Old Testament quotations in the New Testament, which appear to be based on the literal sense of the original text, but which give it an extension of meaning that it did not have in its original context. Such quotations are not always introduced in the New Testament as a sort of proof, but often merely as an illustration—a distinction which we should also admit in certain cases in the Qumran literature. A clear case of the accommodation of a text in the New Testament is furnished by Mt 12:32, where Jesus, speaking to the Sadducees about the resurrection of the dead, is presented as asking them, 'Did you never read what was said to you by God, "I am the God of Abraham, the God of Isaac, and the God of Jacob"? He is not the God of dead men but of living!' To confute the Sadducees, Christ quoted Ex 3:6 (or 15, 16). But in this passage there is certainly no reference at all to the resurrection of the dead; and L. Venard remarks, 'L'idée de la survivance des patriarches . . . dépasse le sens primitif direct de ce passage'.[61] In fact, it is the same type of disregard for the original context which we found so frequently in the Qumran passages listed above.

Paul, writing frequently in the rhetorical style of a preacher, often fails to take into consideration the original context of the Old Testament and twists the quotation which he uses to his own purpose. For instance, in Rom 2:23–24 he says to the Jew, 'Will you boast of the law and yet dishonour God by breaking it? For, as the Scripture says, "The very name of God is abused among the heathen because of you"' (Is 52:5). Paul is here quoting the fuller text of the Septuagint; but in any case the meaning of the original is that at the time of the Babylonian captivity God's name was despised among the Gentiles because

[60] Similar devices have been found also in the *pesher* on Habakkuk; see the list in W. H. Brownlee, *BA* XIV (1951) 60–2.

[61] 'Citations de l'Ancien Testament dans le Nouveau Testament', *VDBS* II, 43.

fortune had turned against the Israelites, and it looked as though Israel's God was impotent to help or rescue them and thus on their account God's name was continually blasphemed. In Paul's context, however, the name of Yahweh is an object of blasphemy among the Gentiles who see that the Jews boast of the Law but do not observe it and hence spurn the will of God. This is obviously a free adaptation of the text of Isaiah, which goes beyond the original sense of it. Paul likewise indulges in a play on words in order to bring in an Old Testament text, when he applies Dt 21:23 to the crucified Christ. 'Christ ransomed us from the Law's curse by taking our curse upon himself (for the Scripture says, "Cursed be anyone who is hung on a tree") in order that the blessing given to Abraham might through Jesus Christ reach the heathen.' The only connection here between the verse of Deuteronomy and the Pauline use of it is the double pun of the Law's curse and the word 'cursed' and the crucifixion of Christ and 'hung on a tree'. The orator Paul is the one who makes the connection by putting them together. Again in Eph 4:8 he atomizes the sense of the text in quoting Ps 68:19, 'So it says, "When he went up on high, he led a host of captives, and gave gifts to mankind". What does "he went up" mean, except that he had first gone down to the under parts of the earth? It is he who went down who has also gone up above all the heavens, to fill the universe.' Here Paul completely disregards the original context of the Psalm in order to retain only the words 'he went up' and 'he gave'.

Further examples could easily be cited to illustrate many of the same devices which are found in the Qumran literature. These can be found in the lists which L. Venard and J. Bonsirven have supplied.[62]

[62] *Ibid.*; J. Bonsirven, *op. cit.*, 320 ff. See especially J. Schmid, 'Die alttestamentlichen Zitate bei Paulus und die Theorie vom sensus plenior', *BZ* III (1959) 161–73, where the instances from Paul's letters which are discussed give numerous examples of this use of Scripture.

(D) *The Eschatological Class of Texts*

The last group of Old Testament quotations may be called eschatological, for they usually express in the Old Testament context a promise or threat about something still to be accomplished in the *eschaton*, which the Qumran writer cites as something still to be accomplished in the new *eschaton* of which he writes. In some ways this group of quotations occupies a middle ground, as it were, between the first group and the other two, for in many cases the Old Testament text is quoted in the sense originally intended, but it is also extended to a new situation which is expected.

There are ten passages in the Qumran literature of this sort. (31) *bbw' hdbr 'šr ktwb bdbry yšʿyh bn 'mwṣ hnby' 'šr 'mr ybw' ʿlyk wʿl ʿmk wʿl byt 'byk ymym 'šr b'w mywm swr 'prym mʿl yhwdh* (CD 7:10–12, quoting Is 7:17), 'When the utterance will come true which was written in the words of Isaiah the son of Amoz, the prophet, who said, "There will come[63] upon you and upon your people and upon your father's house days such as have ⟨not⟩ come to pass since the day when Ephraim parted from Judah"'. *Context:* The *Damascus Document* here describes what will happen at the time of God's visitation: He will requite those who despise his commandments and ordinances and the words of Isaiah will be fulfilled at that time. These words are part of the Emmanuel Oracle in the book of Isaiah; the prophet's threat of a coming visitation by God is reaffirmed by the Qumran

[63] CD reads *ybw'* whereas MT and 1QIs^a have *yby' Yhwh*. B. J. Roberts (*BJRL* XXXIV [1951–52] 372) ascribes the change to the unwillingness of the author to attribute these events to God. This is possible, but it is more likely that the medieval copyist confused a *waw* and a *yodh*. The general reluctance of the Qumran scribes to write the tetragrammaton would account for its omission here; in such case *yby'* would be preferable. If we should not restore the negative according to MT, then the translation would run, 'He will bring upon you and upon your people and upon your father's house days such as have come to pass since the day when Ephraim parted from Judah'. However, I prefer to restore it with C. Rabin (*op. cit.*, 28).

author as something to come true in the *eschaton* awaited by them.[64]

(32) *bbw' hdbr 'šr ktwb byd zkryh hnby' ḥrb ʿwry ʿl rwʿy wʿl gbr ʿmyty n'm 'l hk 't hrʿh wtpwṣynh hṣ'n whšybwty ydy ʿl hṣwʿrym whšwmrym 'wtw hm ʿnyy hṣ'n* (CD 19:7–9, quoting Zech 13:7), 'When the utterance will come true which was written by Zechariah the prophet, "Rise, O sword, against my shepherd and against the man, my companion. The oracle of God: Strike the shepherd and you will disperse the flock; and I shall turn my hand against the little ones." Now these who give heed to him are the poor of the flock.' *Context:* This passage occurs in MS. B of the *Damascus Document* and should parallel the previous quotation; however, the text is quite different, even though the context is roughly the same. When God visits the land, those who reject his commandments and statutes will receive the recompense of their wicked deeds and the utterance of Zechariah will come to pass. Just what the context in Zechariah is has been a matter of dispute among scholars, since many believe that it is misplaced. In the words themselves there is clearly a threat uttered; this is repeated by the Qumran author as something to take place at the awaited visitation of God upon the enemies of the sect. 'The poor of the flock' which is to be dispersed is the Qumran community. In a similar manner this text has been used in the New Testament; in Mk 14:27 it refers to the disciples who deserted Jesus as his passion approached. In both cases the text was used of a coming trial.

(33) *k'šr hyh bqṣ pqdt hr'šwn 'šr 'mr byd yḥzq'l lhtwt htyw ʿl mṣḥwt n'nḥym wn'nqym* (CD 19:11–12, quoting Ez 9:4), 'As it was in the time of the first visitation, as he said through Ezekiel, "to set a mark upon the foreheads of those who sigh and groan"'.[65] *Context:* At the time of God's visitation the 'poor of

[64] There is a play on words in the sentence. In Is 7:17 we find the words *mywm swr 'prym mʿl yhwdh*. The word *swr* is first explained by *bhprd*, 'when the two houses separated', and then by *śr*, 'Ephraim became ruler over Israel'. See the note in C. Rabin, *op. cit.*, 28.

[65] The ending of this quotation is somewhat telescoped in CD.

the flock' will be dispersed, but will escape, whereas the others will be handed over to the sword. The sparing of the poor of the flock is likened to what happened at God's first visitation, when those who sighed and groaned at the abominations wrought in the city were signed with a mark and spared from destruction by the sword. This same thing is to take place again in the *eschaton* awaited by the community, to which Ezekiel's words are now applied. Cf. Ap 7:3; 9:4; 14:1.

(34) *hw' hywm 'šr ypqd 'l k'šr dbr hyw śry yhwdh kmśygy gbwl 'lyhm 'špk km[ym] 'brh* (CD 19:15–16, quoting Hos 5:10), 'That is the day on which God will visit, as it said, "The princes of Judah have become like those who remove the boundary-stones; upon them I shall pour out wrath like [wa]ter"'. (Cf. CD 8:2–3.) *Context:* When God comes in his day of visitation, extinction is threatened for all who will not hold fast to the ordinances. In support of this, CD quotes a part of Hosea's description of the guilt of Judah and Israel and the punishment which awaits them from God's wrath. It is now applied to those who in the community's estimation do not observe his ordinances.

(35) *wbqṣ hhw' yḥrh 'p 'l byśr'l k'šr 'mr 'yn mlk w'yn śr w'yn šwpṭ w['y]n mwkyḥ bṣdq* (CD 20:15–17, quoting Hos 3:4), 'And in that time the anger of God will be kindled against Israel, as it said, "There is no king and there is no prince and there is no judge and there is none to reprove in righteousness"'.[66] *Context:* This passage is part of a description of the time which lasted from the 'gathering in' of the Teacher until the annihilation of all the men of war who returned with the 'Man of the Lie', forty years during which God's anger will be enkindled against Israel, with no one to direct men in the way of righteousness. CD compares the situation to that which would exist later in Israel in the days described by the Old Testament writer.

(36) *w'šr hgyd lnw ky' 'th bqrbnw 'l gdwl wnwr' lšwl 't kwl*

[66] The ending of this quotation in CD is different from that of MT. See the note in C. Rabin, *op. cit.*, 40.

'wybynw lp[*nyn*]*w* (1QM 10:1–2, quoting Dt 7:21–22), 'And as (Moses) declared to us that "You are in our midst, a great and awesome God, to despoil all our enemies before us"'. *Context:* This is part of the discourse of the High Priest to be used before the eschatological battle; he quotes the significant words of Moses' second discourse in which he explained to the Israelites the strength and power which Yahweh would give them against their enemies. The *War Scroll* now applies them to the combatants of the coming eschatological war.[67]

(37) *wylmdnw m'z ldwrwtynw l'mwr bqrbkm lmlḥmh w'md hkwhn wdbr 'l h'm l'mwr šm'h yśr'l 'tmh qrbym hywm lmlḥmh 'l 'wybykmh 'l tyr'w w'l yrk lbbkmh w'l tḥ*[*pzw w'*]*l t'rwṣw mpnyhm ky' 'lwhykm hwlk 'mkm lhlḥm lkm 'm 'wybykm lhwšy' 'tkmh w*[*š*]*wṭrynw ydbrw lkwl 'twdy hmlḥmh* (1QM 10:2–5, quoting Dt 20:2–5), 'And he taught us of old for our generations saying, "When you approach the battle, the priest shall stand and address the people saying, 'Hear, O Israel, you are approaching the battle today with your enemies; fear not, let not your heart waver, do not tremble nor stand in dread of them, for your God walks with you to do battle for you against your enemies, to save you'. And our officers shall speak to all those prepared for the battle."' *Context:* This is a continuation of the High Priest's exhortation before the eschatological battle. With a few slight inversions the exhortation which Moses addressed to the Israelites is applied to the new situation which will arise in the end of days. The same quotation is used again in 1QM 15:8–9 in a similar way, but without being introduced as an explicit quotation.

(38) *w'šr d*[*brt*]*h byd mwšh l'mwr ky' tbw' mlḥmh b'rṣkmh 'l hṣr hṣwrr 'tkmh whry'wt*[*mh*] *bḥṣwṣrwt wnzkrtmh lpny 'lwhykm wnwš'tm m'wybykm* (1QM 10:6–8, quoting Nm 10:9), 'And as you s[pok]e through Moses, saying, "When war comes in your land, against an enemy who oppresses you you

[67] This text is also listed by J. Carmignac (*RB* LXIII [1956] 235) as one of the explicit quotations, even though he admits that 'pour intégrer ce texte dans sa propre phrase il le retouche assez profondément'.

shall sound a war-blast on the trumpets and you will be remembered before your God and saved from your enemies"' *Context:* This is still another part of the High Priest's exhortation addressed to the warriors who are to engage in the eschatological battle. Here he cites the words of Moses who ordered the making of two silver trumpets and gave instructions for their use. In case of an invasion they were to be blown and Yahweh would deliver Israel. These words of Moses are now recalled and applied to the coming war in which evil will be wiped out in the end of days.

(39) *wm'z hšm[ʿth mw]ʿd gbwrt ydkh bktyym l'mwr wnpl 'šwr bḥrb lw' 'yš wḥrb lw' 'dm tw'klnw* (1QM 11:11—12, quoting Is 31:8), 'Of old you made [known the sea]son of the power of your hand against the Kittim, saying, "And Assyria shall fall by the sword, not of man, and a sword, not of man, shall devour him"'. *Context:* Another part of the High Priest's exhortation cites the promise uttered by Isaiah, that Assyria would fall by Yahweh's might, which he would manifest on behalf of his chosen ones. Assyria here is modernized to refer to the Kittim of Assyria (see 1QM 1:2), the enemy of the new Israel, whose definitive destruction was awaited by the community in God's good time.[68]

(40) *hw'h ṣmḥ dwyd hʿwmd ʿm dwrš htwrh 'šr* [***] *bṣywn b'ḥryt hymym k'šr ktwb whqymwty 't swkt dwyd hnwplt hy'h swkt dwyd hnwpl[t ']šr yʿmwd lhwšyʿ 't yśr'l* (4QFlor 1–3 ii 11–13, quoting Am 9:11), 'He is the scion of David who rises with the Interpreter of the Law, who [***] in Zion in the end of days, as it was written, "And I shall raise up the fallen hut of David". It is the fallen hut of David which will stand up to save Israel.' *Context:* This passage is part of the *pesher* on the dynastic oracle of 2 Sm 7:11 ff. The 'seed' to be raised up by God in the future is identified as the 'scion of David' and in him the promise of

[68] 'Nous avons ici un bel exemple d'exégèse "extensive", qui dépasse le sens littéral, la ruine d'Assour, pour appliquer ce texte à la ruine définitive de tous les ennemis du peuple juif' (J. Carmignac, *RB* LXIII [1956] 239).

the ultimate restoration of Israel is to be accomplished, by applying to him the words of the oracle of Amos. The Qumran author related the two texts as an expression of his messianic hope, that Yahweh will yet save Israel by raising up the fallen hut of David in the end of days. Both of the Old Testament texts involved here are actually given an eschatological twist. This text of Amos is unique in that it occurs twice in the Qumran literature (see (11) above) and also in the New Testament (Acts 15:16). There is, however, no similarity in the use of this text in the three places. In the *Damascus Document* it occurs in a passage which is not too clear and in which the books of the Law are said to be the 'hut of the king', and this hut is related to the 'fallen hut of David'. In 4QFlor the scion of David is associated with the Interpreter of the Law, but he is to bring about the salvation of Israel. In the New Testament James uses the text in his speech to the assembly in Jerusalem; without any reference to a scion of David he asserts the fulfilment of the verse in the conversion of the Gentiles to the Gospel, 'Symeon has told how God first showed an interest in taking from among the heathen a people to bear his name. And this agrees with the predictions of the prophets which say . . .' (Acts 15:14–15). He has thus extended the sense of the text far beyond its original intention in seeing in the conversion of the Gentiles the fulfilment of the promise to 'possess the remnant of Edom and all the nations over whom my name is called'.

As the texts are used in the Qumran literature, all ten in this class apply Old Testament verses to some eschatological event, either the battle in which the community is to take part, or the day of Yahweh's visitation. The *eschaton* which was often envisaged in the Old Testament text itself has now found a new emphasis in being identified with the *eschaton* of the community.

There are a few examples of the 'eschatological' use of the Old Testament in the New Testament. The number of quotations, however, in this class from the New Testament is considerably less than in the other groups, and the Qumran quotations are proportionally more numerous. This is probably due again to the fact that Christian writers were more often looking back at the central event in which salvation had been accomplished rather than forward to a deliverance by Yahweh, which seems to characterize the Qumran literature.

In Rom 11:26–27 Paul quotes Is 59:20–21 and 27:9 in support of his contention that only partial insensibility has come upon Israel, to last until all the heathen have come in, and then all Israel will be saved, 'just as the Scripture says, "The deliverer will come from Zion, he will drive all ungodliness away from Jacob and this will be my agreement with them, when I take away their sins"'. Paul is looking forward to a point in the Christian *eschaton*, wherein he believes the words of Isaiah will finally find fulfilment. Similarly, in Mt 7:23 Jesus, discussing the division of men which his coming was to effect, announced that not everyone who said to him 'Lord, Lord', would enter the kingdom of heaven, but only those who did the will of his Father. 'Many will say to me *on that day*, "Lord! Lord". Was it not in your name that we prophesied, and by your name that we drove out demons, and by your name that we did many mighty acts? Then I will say to them plainly, "I never knew you! Depart from me, you who do wrong!"' In the last sentence Jesus is quoting Ps 6:9 (without an introductory formula), 'Depart from me all evildoers'. The day to which he refers is the day of eschatological judgment. We likewise find this use of the Old Testament in paraenetic passages. 'Do not take your revenge, dear friends, but leave room for God's anger, for the Scripture says, "Vengeance belongs to me; I will pay them back, says the Lord"'. Here (Rom 12:19) Paul is citing Dt 32:35, referring the words to a future punishment by God of those who seek vengeance. See further Heb 10:30, 37–38; 1 Cor 15:54–55.[69]

[69] Earlier in my discussion I mentioned forty-two passages in the Qumran

CONCLUSION

The foregoing analysis of the isolated explicit quotations of the Old Testament which occur in various Qumran writings reveals four generic uses of those quotations, literal or historical, modernized, accommodated, eschatological. These uses can likewise be illustrated from the many Old Testament quotations which exist in the New Testament.[70] Moreover, the introductory formulae which are found in the Qumran texts appear to be without parallel in the Mishnah, despite the common use of the verbs 'to say' and 'to write', while a great number of the Qumran expressions prove to be the exact Semitic equivalents of the New Testament formulae. There is, further, a variety of minor exegetical devices common to the Qumran texts and the New Testament (which are not without parallels, however, in the rabbinical writings). The conclusion drawn from these details is that the exegetical practice of the New Testament writers is quite similar to that of their Jewish contemporaries, which is best illustrated by the Qumran literature.

We may characterize both the Qumran and the New Testament use of the Old Testament *in general* as a literal exegesis, when this is defined in opposition to the allegorical exegesis of Philo and the Alexandrian school of later times. There are, it is true, some allegorical interpretations in both, but these are not

---

literature which contain Old Testament quotations, but have presented an analysis of only forty of them. In two cases introductory formulae are used, but the quotation introduced is not from the Old Testament, or at least cannot be found in any of the known texts or versions. They are CD 9:8–9 and 16:10.

[70] I have re-examined all the New Testament quotations in the light of the four categories which emerged from my analysis of the Qumran passages. Many of them fall easily into the same categories, as I have tried to indicate above. However, I do not want to give the impression that these four categories exhaust the uses of the Old Testament in the New; there is always the danger in such a comparative study of creating a Procrustean bed. Further analysis of the New Testament passages along lines which I have suggested here may necessitate more categories than the four which emerge from the Qumran material.

characteristic. Nor is it a *strictly literal* exegesis which respects the original meaning and context of the words quoted; however, examples of this do occur occasionally. Normally, it is an exegesis based on the words quoted, even though the relevance of them to their historical setting means very little to the Qumran or New Testament writers. This is often due to the fact that both the Qumran sect and the early Christians believed that they were living in some sense 'in the end of days'. This notion, however, did not have a univocal meaning for the two groups. At Qumran many of the Old Testament texts were applied to events in the recent history of the sect; in this respect there is some similarity to the backward glance of the New Testament writers. But the messianic hope at Qumran shifted the emphasis much more to a *coming fulfilment* of the Old Testament scriptures. Again, common to both was the implicit desire to enhance some recent event in their histories or some idea or person with an Old Testament association, as a result of a certain analogy which they saw between the event and some event in Israel's history.

In the isolated explicit quotations many of the exegetical devices are found to be at work which have been found also in the *pesharim* (for example, the actualization of the text, the atomistic interpretation of it, the use of textual variants, a play on words, a deliberate manipulation of the text to suit the new context better). These devices were not, therefore, exclusive to the *pesher*, which was essentially a sort of midrashic running commentary on a continuous text of a prophet or some other Old Testament writing. The data which we have collected above confirm the criticism which B. Gärtner wrote[71] of K. Stendahl's thesis about the 'formula quotations' in Matthew, which the latter labelled as *pesher*-type quotations.[72] Aside from the diffi-

[71] 'The Habakkuk Commentary (DSH) and the Gospel of Matthew', *ST* VIII (1954) 1–24.

[72] *The School of St Matthew and Its Use of the Old Testament* (Uppsala, 1954; reprinted, Philadelphia, 1968) 200 ff.

culties which that thesis encounters on the textual basis, it is evident that many of the devices which are found in the *pesharim* are not exclusive to them. Moreover, the 'formula quotations' in Matthew are all of the so-called 'fulfilment' type. As I have pointed out earlier, this type of introductory formula is singularly absent from the Qumran texts.[73] So I question the advisability of continuing to speak of *pesher*-type quotations or a *pesher*-type interpretation, unless this is defined more accurately and restricted to definite cases.

There is no evidence at Qumran of a systematic, uniform exegesis of the Old Testament. The same text was not always given the same interpretation (see the variants in CD 7 and 19 and compare the use of Nm 24:17 and Am 9:11 in different contexts). Nor does any pattern appear in the Old Testament quotations in the Qumran texts such as that which C. H. Dodd has detected in the New Testament.[74]

A. von Harnack once maintained that Paul was the originator of typological exegesis. E. E. Ellis[75] has shown, however, that such typological interpretation of the Old Testament existed in pre-Pauline strata of the New Testament. But many of the examples cited in classes B and C above will show that this type of interpretation was also pre-Christian, being practised by contemporary Jews as well, even though we do not find in the Qumran material any Semitic equivalent of the Pauline *typos* or *typikōs*.

The similarities in the exegetical practices of the two groups do not affect anything more than the periphery of their theologies. Both depend on the Old Testament, but both have certain presuppositions in the light of which they read the Old Testament. It is these presuppositions which distinguish the two groups despite the similarities in their exegetical procedures.

[73] In this I disagree with B. Gärtner's remarks (*op. cit.*, 14) about the similarity of these 'fulfilment' quotations to certain Qumran formulae.

[74] *According to the Scriptures: the Sub-Structure of New Testament Theology* (London, 1953).

[75] *Op. cit.*, 129 and 90 ff.

The foregoing study has a certain pertinence also for the question of the *sensus plenior* of Scripture. This is not the place for an extended discussion of this pertinence, but it should be noted at least. Many passages in the Old Testament are claimed to have such a sense because of the subsequent use of them in the New Testament. The interpretation in the latter is often said to be *homogeneous* with the literal sense of the Old Testament. However, J. Schmid has recently shown that this theory does not adequately explain the Pauline use of the Scriptures, since many of his examples can hardly be said to be homogeneous.[76] The evidence which I have amassed in my analysis reveals that many of the Qumran cases of modernized or accommodated interpretations might just as easily be called the *sensus plenior* of the Old Testament passages, because they are derived by the same exegetical methods and devices. Some of them at least are no less homogeneous than those in the New Testament. In both cases there is a similar use of the Old Testament. As a result, one would be is forced to admit that the New Testament interpretations are instances of the *sensus plenior* of the Old Testament and the Qumran interpretations are not, simply because the former are found in inspired texts.[77] Certainly, the extension of the meaning of an Old Testament

[76] *Op. cit.*, 173.

[77] R. E. Brown ('The Sensus Plenior in the Last Ten Years', *CBQ* 25 [1963] 265–85) criticized this position, saying that my view 'is perhaps handicapped by Benoit's theory that SP [= *sensus plenior*] may be uncovered only by the NT'. I would not ascribe it to Benoit's restrictive theory, since I do admit that *genuine* dogmatic tradition or development (in conciliar or papal definitions) can also be a source of learning the *sensus plenior* of an Old Testament passage, and even of a New Testament text. The *dogma* of the Trinity is a good example of the latter. But I cannot understand how Brown can say that 'Qumrân by its relation to Judaism is *part of a stream of divine revelation* [my italics] and so the Qumran exegetes could come to recognize a SP of the OT' (p. 272, n. 55). To accord Qumran literature such a quality is to equate it with the Old Testament, the New Testament, and genuine Christian tradition. As far as I am concerned, the *sensus plenior* of an Old Testament text could be given in a later Old Testament book, or in the New Testament, or in *genuine* Christian dogmatic tradition (such as that mentioned

passage in the New could be the result also of a rhetorical device. The mere occurrence of an Old Testament quotation in the New does not give the Old Testament passage a *sensus plenior*, in particular when the extended sense is a sheer accommodation. I would admit the *sensus plenior* only when some basic homogeneity is detected between the Old Testament meaning and the sense the text acquires by its use in the New Testament. This is demanded by the idea of the unity or harmony of the inspired Testaments. But inspiration does not exclude the possibility of New Testament writers accommodating an Old Testament text, even arbitrarily suiting it to their heterogeneous purpose. Because this does happen at times (e.g. 1 Cor 9:9), a real hermeneutical problem arises.

Finally, to forestall a possible objection, one should remember that the New Testament writers and even the Qumran authors did not read their Scriptures as a modern biblical scholar does. My entire discussion above might imply that I think they did. To modern critical scholarship their way of reading the Old Testament often appears quite arbitrary in that it disregards the sense and context of the original. Yet if we are ever going to discover the sense in which such writers used their Scriptures and the presuppositions which they brought to the reading of them, their quotations of the Old Testament must be analysed somewhat along the lines which I have attempted, that is, of a comparison of the text and context in which they occur with the text and context of the original. The introductory formulae used by the Qumran and New Testament writers reveal a profound reverence for the Old Testament as the word of God; they obviously believed, moreover, that their interpretative use of it was legitimate for the

---

above). The common element here is Spirit-guided inspiration or assistance (*assistentia* in the technical theological sense). I cannot ascribe either of these to Qumran literature, any more than I can to other intertestamental literature or rabbinic writings. It should be obvious that this is a hermeneutical problem that is tied to the Catholic idea of biblical inspiration.

religious purpose of their compositions. Nowhere do they make the claim that they are quoting it according to what we call its strict literal sense; that they do on occasion appears from class A above. But generally their use of the Old Testament was a free, sometimes figurative, extension or accommodation of the words to support a position already taken.[78]

[78] See further S. L. Edgar, 'Respect for Context in Quotations from the Old Testament', *NTS* IX (1962–63) 55–62; J. J. O'Rourke, 'The Fulfilment Texts in Matthew', *CBQ* XXIV (1962) 394–403; 'Explicit Old Testament Citations in "the Gospels"', *SMR* VII (1964) 37–64.

2

'4QTESTIMONIA' AND THE NEW TESTAMENT*

A Hebrew text, discovered in Qumran Cave 4, was published by J. M. Allegro, who gave it the provisional title of '4QTestimonia'.[1] Its contents are described as 'a group of *testimonia* of the type long ago proposed by Burkitt, Rendel Harris and others to have existed in the early Church'.[2] *Testimonia* is the current name for systematic collections of Old Testament passages, often of messianic import, which are thought to have been used by early Christians. This name is derived from a work of Cyprian, *Ad Quirinum*, whose subtitle is *Testimoniorum libri tres*.[3] Cyprian's work, at least in its first two books,[4] is a collection of Old Testament passages, compiled with an apologetic purpose *adversus Iudaeos*. Similar collections were made by other patristic writers as well. But the existence of such collections of *testimonia* in the primitive Church and the relation of them to the formation of the New Testament have often been denied and affirmed during the past sixty years. To some scholars it seems that such collections, which they also call 'florilegia',

* Originally published in *TS* 18 (1957) 513–37.

[1] J. M. Allegro, 'Further Messianic References in Qumran Literature', *JBL* 75 (1956) 182–7, Document IV. See now the definitive edition of this text, 4Q*175*, in J. M. Allegro, *Qumrân Cave 4: I* (*4Q158–4Q186*) (DJD 5; Oxford: Clarendon, 1968) 57–60.

[2] *JBL* 75 (1956) 186. J. T. Milik, DJD 1, 121, has also referred to this text as *testimonia;* see also *RB* 60 (1953) 290.

[3] Edited by G. Hartel, CSEL 3/1 (1868) 33–184.

[4] The third book is generally regarded as a later edition; cf. J. Quasten, *Patrology* 2 (Utrecht and Antwerp, 1953) 363.

'anthologies', or 'a catena of fulfilments of prophecy', must be the basis of some of the Old Testament quotations in the New Testament. Others have denied the existence of such *testimonia.* Consequently, if the provisional title, '4QTestimonia', given to the new Qumran text proves to be correct, then Allegro is right in saying that 'this document will certainly revive interest in the question' of the *testimonia.*[5]

The present article, at any rate, will bear out Allegro's prediction of interest. I propose to give a brief survey of the problem of the *testimonia* in the study of the New Testament and then try to situate the new document in the context of that problem. Our discussion will treat: (1) the hypothesis of the *testimonia* collections, (2) the reaction to the hypothesis, (3) extant *testimonia,* and (4) the significance of '4QTestimonia'.

THE HYPOTHESIS OF THE TESTIMONIA COLLECTIONS

While the majority of the OT quotations in the NT agree substantially with the text of the Septuagint (LXX), as we know it today, there is a good number of quotations that are closer to the Masoretic Hebrew text (MT). Some, however, diverge considerably from both. The Epistle to the Hebrews, for instance, is a striking example of dependence on the LXX, while a certain group of quotations in the Gospel according to Matthew has always been considered outstanding for its departure from this text. The picture presented by the OT quotations in the NT is a complicated one and has evoked study from the early centuries of the Church's existence on. The facile solution, often employed to explain the discrepancies between the quotations and the known Greek or Hebrew texts of the OT, is that of the 'quotation from memory'. Even St Jerome took refuge in this solution: 'In omnibus paene testimoniis quae de Vetere Testamento sumuntur istiusmodi esse errorem, ut aut ordo mutetur aut verba, et interdum sensus quoque ipse diversus sit vel Apostolis vel Evangelistis non ex libro carpentibus

[5] Allegro, *art. cit.*, 186, n. 107.

testimonia, sed memoria credentibus, quae nonnumquam fallitur.'[6] It would be foolish to deny that the NT writers, especially Paul in his letters, quoted the OT at times from memory. But to use this solution everywhere would be a gross oversimplification.

Recourse to the hypothesis of previously compiled collections of OT passages, especially to those which might have depended on different recensions of the OT books, has often been had by scholars in recent times to explain some of the problems that arise from the use of the OT by Paul and Matthew. It is thought that these collections of *testimonia* were composed for various purposes, devotional, liturgical, or apologetic. Providing handy summaries of the main OT passages for the busy missionary or apostolic teacher, they would have dispensed him from consulting the OT itself or from carrying it around with him. To use a phrase of Rendel Harris, they would have been 'a controversialists' *vade mecum*'.[7] It has even been suggested that Paul refers to such collections, when he instructs Timothy to bring along with him 'the cloak that I left with Carpus at Troas, and the books, especially the parchments (*tas membranas*)' (2 Tm 4: 13).

The use of such collections of *testimonia* was postulated to explain four problems of OT citations in the NT: (*a*) the attribution of citations to wrong OT authors; (*b*) the 'formula quotations'[8] found in Matthew; (*c*) the divergence of the OT

[6] *Comm. in Michaeam* 2, 5 (*PL* 25, 1255 [ed. 1865]). For ancient discussions of the use of the OT in the NT, see H. Vollmer, *Die alttestamentlichen Citate bei Paulus, textkritisch und biblisch-theologisch gewürdigt nebst einem Anhang über das Verhältnis des Apostels zu Philo* (Freiburg and Leipzig, 1895) 1–6.

[7] Rendel Harris, *Testimonies* 1 (Cambridge, 1916) 55.

[8] This term has been used by Sherman Johnson, 'The Biblical Quotations in Matthew', *HTR* 36 (1943) 135, and adopted by K. Stendahl, *The School of St Matthew and Its Use of the Old Testament* (Uppsala, 1954; reprinted Philadelphia: Fortress, 1968) 45, as the translation of the German 'Reflexionszitate'. Such quotations are introduced by the evangelist himself into his account of an event, which he regards as the fulfilment of a saying of the OT. The German term is actually a better expression than the current English phrase, as it reveals the nature of the quotation.

citations from the LXX and their closer agreement with the Hebrew; (*d*) the composite quotations.

Citations Attributed to Wrong Authors

The chief cases of such ascription are Mk 1:2–3 and Mt 27:9–10.[9] In Mk 1:2–3 we read: 'As is written in the prophet Isaiah: "Here I send my messenger on before you; he will prepare your way. Hark! Someone is shouting in the desert: Get the Lord's way ready, make his paths straight."'[10] Although the second citation in verse 3 is taken from Is 40:3, the first is drawn from Mal 3:1, or possibly from Ex 23:20. Yet both are introduced by the phrase, 'As is written in the prophet Isaiah'. Rendel Harris suggested that this ascription in the earliest of our Synoptic Gospels was due to 'some collection of Testimonies'.[11] If we imagine a collection of prophetic texts strung together, some with and some without their sources indicated, the solution suggested by Harris would not be impossible.[12] Krister Stendahl has pointed out that a stronger argument for such an interpretation is that both the Malachi and Isaiah texts contain the phrase *pinnāh derek*, 'to prepare the way', an expression which occurs only here and in two closely related Isaiah passages, 57:14 and 62:10.[13] Possibly a collection of texts existed that dealt

[9] A third case might be added, Mt 13:35, if the reading in Sinaiticus is adopted, where *Ēsaiou* is added after *dia* in the phrase *dia tou prophētou legontos*. But Isaiah is not quoted; the text comes rather from Ps 78:2. If the name of Isaiah is omitted with most of the other MSS., the sense of the word *prophētou* can be explained with K. Stendahl (*op. cit.*, 117–18) by showing that the quotation comes from a psalm of Asaph, whom early Jewish tradition regarded as a prophet (1 Chr 25:2).

[10] Translations of the NT are taken from E. J. Goodspeed, *The Complete Bible: An American Translation* (Chicago, 1951).

[11] Rendel Harris, *op. cit.*, 49; see also 21–22.

[12] V. Taylor in his commentary, *The Gospel according to St Mark* (London, 1953) 153, admits that 'Mark may have inadvertently introduced it from a collection of Messianic proof-texts', while observing that there are good reasons for the view of Holtzmann, Lagrange, and Rawlinson that the Malachi-Exodus text might be a 'copyist's gloss'.

[13] Stendahl, *op. cit.*, 51.

with 'preparing the way' and in the course of time it was thought that all the passages were from Isaiah.[14]

In Mt 27:9–10 Jeremiah is said to have written, 'They took the thirty silver pieces, the price of the one whose price had been fixed, on whom some of the Israelites had set a price, and gave them for the Potter's Field as the Lord directed me.' But this saying is partly a quotation and partly a paraphrase of Zech 11:13 with a possible allusion to Jer 18:1 (LXX) and Ex 9:12. Once again Rendel Harris suggests that 'Matthew has been using a *Book of Testimonies*, in which the history and tragic end of Judas was explained as a fulfilment of ancient prophecy, and that the mistake . . . either existed in the *Book of Testimonies*, or was accidentally made by the evangelist in using such a book.'[15]

The 'Formula Quotations'

In the Gospel according to Matthew there are ten citations from the OT which form a special group within that Gospel. They occur in various places throughout the work: four in the infancy stories, five in the ministry narratives, and one in the account of the passion.

	Group A		*Group B*
1:22–23	(Is 7:14)	4:15–16	(Is 8:23; 9:1)
2:15	(Hos 11:1)	8:17	(Is 53:4)
2:17–18	(Jer 31:15)	12:17–21	(Is 42:1–4)
2:23	(Is 11:1)	13:35	(Ps 78:2)
27:9	(Zech 11:12–13)	21:4–5	(Zech 9:9; Is 62:11)

The citations of Group A are found in passages that are peculiar to Matthew; those of Group B occur in passages that have Synoptic parallels, but which Matthew has modified to suit the incorporation of the quotation (contrast the Marcan parallels). Now several points are to be noted in connection with these passages of Matthew. First of all, they have a special introductory formula, either *hina* (*hopōs*) *plērōthē to rēthen* or *tote*

[14] See N. J. Hommes, *Het Testimoniaboek* (Amsterdam, 1935) 174 ff., who maintains that such a group of texts did exist under the heading of Isaiah in pre-Christian times.

[15] Rendel Harris, *op. cit.*, 56.

eplērōthē to rēthen tou prophētou legontos, not found with the other OT citations in the first Gospel.[16] Secondly, this type of citation is found in the Synoptic tradition only in Matthew;[17] it is a *Reflexionszitat*, added by the writer and not attributed to another person. Thirdly, the language of these citations is generally judged to be different from the other citations of the OT in Matthew and from those in Mark and Luke. They manifest a much greater similarity to the Hebrew text of the OT than the others, which are more faithful to the LXX.[18] Such peculiarities of this group of citations demand an explanation and that has often been found in the theory of the *testimonia*.[19] It is thought that Matthew drew upon a collection of such texts, since their use admirably suited the purpose he had in writing his Gospel.

Citations that Diverge from the Text of the LXX

This feature of some of the OT citations has already been mentioned, especially in the case of the formula quotations. Such a deviation from the LXX text, however, is found in a number of instances outside of Matthew. According to E. F. Kautzsch,[20] who made a thorough study of the eighty-four Pauline citations and compared them with the LXX (Alexandrinus), thirty-four of them agree with the LXX, while thirty-six depart from it 'leviter'. There are ten passages where the citations 'longius recedunt' from the LXX, 'ita tamen ut dissensus . . . ad liberam allegandi rationem referendus videatur'. In two passages (Rom 12:19; 1 Cor 14:21) the 'quotation' is judged to be quite free,

[16] Chiefly for this reason we have not included in this group the quotation of Mi 5:2, which occurs in Mt 2:6. However, a case might be made out for its inclusion in Group A. Stendahl treats it in his discussion of the formula quotations; cf. *op. cit.*, 99–101.

[17] The quotation of Zech 9:9, employed in Mt 21:5, is also found in Jn 12:15, but this is outside the Synoptic tradition.

[18] See Johnson, *art. cit.*, 152.

[19] See T. Stephenson, 'The Old Testament Quotations Peculiar to Matthew', *JTS* 20 (1918–19) 227–9; L. Vaganay, *Le problème synoptique* (Paris, 1954) 237–40.

[20] E. F. Kautzsch, *De Veteris Testamenti locis a Paulo apostolo allegatis* (Leipzig, 1869) 109.

but is still capable of being recognized as a quotation. Finally, in two other passages Paul cites Job clearly according to the Hebrew text.[21] Kautzsch suggests that Paul only knew Job in the Hebrew and had no acquaintance with the Greek translation of that book. But these differences that exist between the various classes of citations are significant enough to make Vollmer have recourse to 'Citatenkomposition'[22] as well as to different Greek versions (Aquila or Theodotion or Symmachus) to explain the variants. It should be noted, however, that deviation from the text of the LXX, taken by itself, is rarely considered sufficient evidence to postulate the previous existence of a quotation in a collection of *testimonia*. But it is often a confirmation of one of the other reasons for such a postulate.

The Composite Quotations

Perhaps the chief reason for postulating the existence of collections of *testimonia* in the early Church is the phenomenon of composite quotations found in various NT books. We met an example of such a quotation in discussing the text of Malachi that is attributed to Isaiah in Mk 1:2. The term, composite quotation, designates the stringing together of two or more OT quotations which are given more or less completely. It is to be distinguished from a conflated quotation, such as Mt 22:24: 'Master, Moses said, "If a man dies without children, his brother shall marry his widow and raise up a family for him."' Here we have parts of Gn 38:8 and Dt 25:5 fused together. Moreover, a composite quotation is different from allusions to the OT which are strung together. The Apocalypse is generally said to contain not a single OT quotation, yet is replete with OT allusions. The clearest examples of composite quotations are the citations that are strung together without intervening comments or identification of their author(s). Such citations are rare in the Gospels; the following is usually given as an example:

[21] See Stendahl, *op. cit.*, 159, for slightly different figures, but substantial agreement.

[22] Vollmer, *op. cit.*, 48.

'*My house shall be called a house of prayer*, but you make it *a robbers' den*' (Mt 21:13). The italicized words come from Is 56:7 and Jer 7:11; in both cases the text is quite similar to the LXX. See further examples in Mk 10:6–8 (Gn 1:27; 2:24); Mt 19:18–19 (Ex 20:12–16 or Dt 5:16–20 and Lv 19:18).

It is in the Pauline letters that we find the best examples of composite quotations. We shall give but two examples. In the first instance the 'catchword-bond' that unites them is 'heathen' or 'nation'. In the second the unifying element is rather the description of the man who is not upright, with the enumeration of different parts of the body as a secondary element.[23]

Rom 15:9–12
As the Scripture says,
'I will give thanks to you for this among the heathen,
And sing in honour of your name.' (Ps 17/18:50; cf. 2 Sm 22:50)
And again,
'Rejoice, you heathen, with his people.' (Dt 32:43 LXX)
And again,
'Praise the Lord, all you heathen, (Ps 116/17:1)
And let all nations sing his praises.'
Again Isaiah says,
'The descendant of Jesse will come, (Is 11:1, 10)
The one who is to rise to rule the heathen;
The heathen will set their hopes on him.'

Rom 3:10–18
As the Scripture says,
'There is not a single man who is upright, (Ps 13/14:1–3)
No one understands, no one searches for God.
All have turned away, they are one and all worthless;
No one does right, not a single one.'
'Their throats are like open graves, (Ps 5:10)
They use their tongues to deceive.'
'The venom of asps is behind their lips.' (Ps 139/40:4)
'And their mouths are full of bitter curses.' (Ps 9B/10:7)

[23] See J. Huby, *Saint Paul, Epître aux Romains* (11th ed.; Paris, 1940) 145, n. 1.

'Their feet are swift when it comes to shedding blood, (Is 59:7–8; cf. Prv 1:16)
Ruin and wretchedness mark their paths,
They do not know the way of peace.'
'There is no reverence for God before their eyes.'[24] (Ps 35/36:2)

Further examples may be found in Rom 9:25–29 (Hos 2:25,1; Is 10:22–23; 1:9); 10:15–21 (Is 52:7; 53:1; Ps 18/19:5; Dt 32:21; Is 65:1–2); 11:8–10 (Dt 29:3 [cf. Is 29:10]; Ps 68/69: 23–24); 11:26 (Is 59:20; 27:9); 11:34–35 (Is 40:13; Jb 41:3); 2 Cor 6:16–18 (Lv 26:12 [cf. Ez 37:27]; Jer 51:45; Is 52:11; Ez 20:34; 2 Sm 7:14).[25]

Composite quotations are also found in the early patristic writers (e.g., Clement of Rome, Barnabas, Justin Martyr) and they obviously served as a basis for the later extended collections of *testimonia* by Tertullian, Cyprian, and Pseudo-Gregory of Nyssa. After studying the composite quotations in the NT and the early Fathers, E. Hatch postulated the existence of collections of such texts. This was the beginning of the *testimonia* hypothesis in 1889, although Hatch did not use this name for

[24] M. Dibelius, 'Zur Formgeschichte des Neuen Testaments ausserhalb der Evangelien', *TRu*, N. F. 3 (1931) 228, finds it hard to believe that Paul himself sought out all these passages from the OT for the purpose of incorporating them in the Epistle to the Romans. He, too, thinks in terms of a pre-existing list of passages that Paul simply made use of here.

[25] It may be debated whether the following passages are really composite quotations, because of the intervening comments: Rom 9:12–13 (Gn 25: 23; Mal 1:2–3); 9:33 (Is 28:16; 8:14); 10:6–8 (Dt 30:12; Ps 106/7:26); 10:11–13 (Is 28:16; Jl 2:32); 12:19–20 (Dt 32:35; Prv 25:21–22); Gal 4: 27–30 (Is 54:1; Gn 21:10–12); 1 Cor 3:19–20 (Jb 5:13; Ps 93/94:11); 2 Cor 9:9–10 (Ps 111/12:9; Is 55:10; Hos 10:12). Composite citations are also found in Heb 1:5 (Ps 2:7; 2 Sm 7:14); 1:7–13 (Dt 32:42 LXX and 4Q Deut; Ps 103/4:4; 44/45:7–8; 101/2:26–28; 109/10:1); 2:12–13 (Ps 21/22: 23; Is 8:17–18); 5:5–6 (Ps 2:7; 109/10:4); 1 Pt 2:6–10 (Is 28:16; Ps 117/18:22; Is 8:14; 43:20–21; Ex 19:6 [cf. 23:22]; Hos 1:6, 9).—L. Cerfaux proposes the extended use of a florilegium in 1 Corinthians; see 'Vestiges d'un florilège dans 1 Cor. 1,18–3,24?', *Revue d'histoire ecclésiastique* 27 (1931) 521–34; *Recueil Cerfaux* 2 (Gembloux, 1954) 319–32.

it.[26] A thorough study of the Pauline composite citations was undertaken by Hans Vollmer, who published his results in 1895.[27] He believed that some combinations of texts were due merely to the juxtaposition of certain key-words ('zufällige Berührung eines Stichwortes').[28] Such a case is found in Rom 11:26, where the *kai hautē* of Is 59:21 brings to mind the *kai touto* of 27:9; such a similarity would be sufficient reason to join these two verses. Likewise in Rom 10:6–8 the *anabēsetai* of Dt 30:12 provides the link with *katabēsetai* of Ps 107:26. But he also found other cases of combined citations that reveal a deliberate process of compilation ('eine planmässige Zusammenstellung').[29] The latter citations reveal a tendency in Paul to cite passages

[26] E. Hatch, *Essays in Biblical Greek* (Oxford, 1889) 203: 'It would be improbable, even if there were no positive evidence on the point, that the Greek-speaking Jews, who were themselves cultured, and who lived in great centres of culture, should not have had a literature of their own. It is no less improbable that such a literature should have consisted only of the Apocalyptic books, and the scanty fragments of other books, which have come down to us. It may naturally be supposed that a race which laid stress on moral progress, whose religious services had variable elements of both prayer and praise, and which was carrying on an active propaganda, would have, among other books, manuals of morals, of devotion, and of controversy. It may also be supposed, if we take into consideration the contemporary habit of making collections of *excerpta*, and the special authority which the Jews attached to their sacred books, that some of these manuals would consist of extracts from the Old Testament. The existence of composite quotations in the New Testament, and in some of the early Fathers suggests the hypothesis that we have in them relics of such manuals.' —Prior to Hatch's study, C. Weizsäcker thought that Paul had composed for himself a sort of 'creed' in the form of citations from the OT which he used in his teaching. He compared the quotations in Rom 1–4 with those in Galatians and showed how they could be separated from their context to give this impression. Similarly the citations in Rom 9–11. 'Dieser Schriftbeweis ist nun ohne Zweifel nicht erst bei Abfassung der Briefe so aufgestellt, sondern der Apostel hat ihn sich überhaupt zurecht gemacht, und nur in diesen Briefen bei gegebenen Anlass verwendet' (*Das apostolische Zeitalter der christlichen Kirche* [Freiburg, 1886] 113–14; 3rd ed. [1902] 110–11).

[27] Vollmer, *op. cit.* (see n. 6 above).

[28] *Ibid.*, 36.

[29] *Ibid.*, 37.

from the three parts of the OT: the Law, the Prophets, and the Writings (or at least from two of them). See the examples cited above from Rom 11:8–10 and 15:9–12.[30]

Whereas E. Hatch had postulated a collection of Greek testimonies, compiled by Hellenistic Jews, Vollmer preferred to think that the compilations had already existed in Hebrew, in which such passages were assembled for dogmatic purposes from the Law, the Prophets, and the Writings. This, he thought, could be established by such a passage as 2 Cor 9:10, where the word 'rain' is the unitive element of the last three quotations (Is 55:10; Dt 28:11–12; Hos 10:12) that are fused together—even though this word does not appear in the parts quoted by Paul. Such a compilation of texts would have been impossible in Greek, since the unitive element is lacking in the third text according to the LXX. Hence, the 'rain' texts must have been collected in Hebrew, and probably in pre-Christian times.[31]

Whenever the *testimonia* hypothesis is discussed, the names of Burkitt and Rendel Harris always come to the fore. Though the idea did not originate with Burkitt, it seems that he was the first to use the name, *testimonia*, to designate the systematic collection of such OT texts.[32] Harris gathered evidence to support the hypothesis both from the NT and from the early Fathers.[33]

[30] This manner of quoting the OT had been pointed out long ago by Surhenus: '*spr hmšyh* sive *biblos katallagēs*, in quo secundum veterum theologorum Hebraeorum formulas allegandi et modos interpretandi conciliantur loca ex Vetere in Novo Testamento allegata' ([Amsterdam, 1713] Book 2, Thesis 11, p. 49). He showed that Paul was following good rabbinical practice in citing the OT in this fashion.

[31] Vollmer, *op. cit.*, 41–2. But the case is weakened by the fact that the words for 'rain' are not the same in all the passages; moreover, in the third instance the verb *ywrh* is used in a figurative sense (and contains a play on its meaning). For further criticism of this example, see O. Michel, *Paulus und seine Bibel* (Gütersloh, 1929) 42–3; Hommes, *op. cit.*, 349.

[32] F. C. Burkitt, *The Gospel History and Its Transmission* (Edinburgh, 1907) 126.

[33] Rendel Harris, *Testimonies*, 2 vols (Cambridge, 1916, 1920). Stendahl, *op. cit.*, 207, has pointed out that most of the patristic material to which

However, Harris went beyond Burkitt in maintaining that the passages all belonged to one Testimony Book. Nor was he content to regard the collections as *testimonia pro Iudaeis*, as E. Hatch had done, but considered them as Christian compilations (therefore, in Greek), *testimonia adversus Iudaeos*. 'If such collections of Testimonies on behalf of the Jews existed in early times, before the diffusion of Christianity, then there must have been, *a fortiori*, similar collections produced in later times, when the Christian religion was being actively pushed by the Church in the Synagogue.'[34] His contention is supported by the existence of such collections *adversus Iudaeos* in the writings of Cyprian, Tertullian, and Pseudo-Gregory of Nyssa.

But Harris went still further with his theory. The various composite quotations and those that are attributed to wrong authors not only belonged to an original Testimony Book, but they were actually part of 'the missing *Dominical Oracles* written by Matthew and commented on by Papias'.[35] Matthew, a member of the apostolic company, who is credited with the composition of *ta kyriaka logia*, is now claimed as the author of the *testimonia*. The five books of Papias' commentary could conceivably refer to this Testimony Book, divided into five parts, just as the first Gospel is. In this way Harris thought that he had found an answer to the oft-repeated question, 'What were the logia on which Papias commented?'

THE REACTION TO THE HYPOTHESIS

It is not surprising that the theory of the *testimonia* in the extreme form presented by Rendel Harris was not accepted by most scholars. While the evidence he had collected might support the contention that collections of *testimonia* did exist in the

---

Harris refers was previously collected by A. von Ungern-Sternberg, *Der traditionelle alttestamentliche Schriftbeweis 'De Christo' und 'De Evangelio' in der alten Kirche bis zur Zeit Eusebs von Caesarea* (Halle a. S., 1913).

[34] Rendel Harris, *op. cit.*, 1, 2.

[35] *Ibid.*, 109, 116–17.

early Church and possibly even prior to NT writings, there is certainly no evidence that they formed one book, nor that they had anything to do with the Logia of Papias' statement about Matthew.[36] Consequently, the extreme form of the hypothesis has been generally abandoned, but many scholars admit that *testimonia* collections must have preceded various sections of the NT.[37]

There have been a few scholars, however, in recent times who have questioned both the existence of *testimonia* and the extent to which they were used in the early Church. So far we have seen that the existence of *testimonia* collections was a mere postulate; they are a convenient way of explaining certain puzzling features in the NT. But possibly these features can be explained in another way.

It has often been pointed out that Paul had rabbinical tradition to give him the model for his composite quotations from the Law, the Prophets, and the Writings. This method of 'stringing together' texts like pearls on a thread was known to the rabbinical schools; he who strung the texts together was called *ḥārōzā'* (from *ḥrz*, 'to pierce', 'to bore through' in order

[36] For criticism of Harris' work see A. L. Williams, *Adversus Judaeos* (Cambridge, 1935) 6–10; Hommes, *op. cit.*, 251. ('Papias is de *Deus ex machina* in zijn systeem'); L. Cerfaux, 'Un chapitre du Livre des "Testimonia" (Pap. Ryl. Gr. 460)', in *Recueil Cerfaux* 2, 226, note; Stendahl, *op. cit.*, 209 ff.; P. Feine and J. Behm, *Einleitung in das Neue Testament* (10th ed.; Heidelberg, 1954) 24; J. A. Findlay, 'The First Gospel and the Book of Testimonies', in *Amicitiae corolla: Essays Presented to J. R. Harris*, ed. H. G. Wood (London, 1933) 57–71; Ch. Guignebert, in RHR 81 (1920) 58–69.

[37] See, for instance, W. Sanday and A. C. Headlam, *Commentary on the Epistle to the Romans* (*International Critical Commentary*; Edinburgh, 1908) 264, 282; J. Moffatt, *An Introduction to the Literature of the New Testament* (Edinburgh, 1920) 23–5; M. Simon, *Verus Israel: Etude sur les relations entre chrétiens et juifs dans l'empire romain* (*135–425*) (*Bibliothèque des Ecoles Françaises d'Athènes et de Rome* 166; Paris, 1948) 186; Vaganay, *op. cit.*, 237–40; H. Lietzmann, *An die Galater* (HNT 10; 2nd ed.; Tübingen, 1923) 33; D. Plooij, 'Studies in the Testimony Book', *Verhandelingen der Koninklijke Akademie van Wetenschappen te Amsterdam* (Literature Section, New Series, Part 32, No. 2; 1932) 5–27.

to put on a string). Such a stringing together of texts was especially common at the beginning of synagogal homilies.[38] Since the Torah was the definitive deposit of God's revelation to Israel, there was no idea of a progressive revelation. Moses had revealed all and no prophet could ever add to the Torah. The Law was only to be explained, and the Prophets and Writings quoted in conjunction with a passage from the Law were intended only to show how Scripture repeated what was already in the Torah. Given such an interpretative method of quoting Scripture in rabbinical circles, Paul's composite quotations might be judged merely to be an imitation of this method. If that is so, then one of the main reasons for postulating the existence of the *testimonia* disappears.

O. Michel, in his painstaking study of the OT in the Pauline letters, uses this argument and goes even further in denying the existence of *testimonia* collections, mainly because 'es fehlt jede Spur spätjüdischer Florilegien. Das bleibt zu beachten.'[39] He remarks:

There are no traces of pre-Christian *florilegia*, neither of the late Hellenistic Jewish type (Hatch), nor of the late rabbinical sort (Vollmer). Moreover, the hypothesis of R. Harris, that there were early Christian *florilegia*, which would have been composed prior to the writings of the NT, cannot be regarded as probable. Collections of that sort occur first in an early Christian setting; they can be proved to exist with Melito of Sardis and Cyprian. Probably their origin can be traced to an even earlier time; the Epistle of Barnabas perhaps supposes them. But the impression we get is that the Gentile Christian Church compiled these *florilegia* for missionary and polemical purposes.[40]

Others have not been so radical in their denial as Michel. Their criticism of the hypothesis affects rather the way in which the *testimonia* are said to have been used or the extent to which

[38] See A. F. Puukko, 'Paulus und das Judentum', *Studia orientalia* 2 (1928) 62; Michel, *op. cit.* (n. 31 above) 12–13, 83; Hommes, *op. cit.*, 324–54. Cf. n. 30 above.

[39] Michel, *op. cit.*, 43.

[40] *Ibid.*, 52.

they were employed. For example, C. H. Dodd is of the opinion that the theory as proposed by Harris 'outruns the evidence, which is not sufficient to prove so formidable a literary enterprise at so early a date'.[41] Dodd has studied fifteen of the OT passages that occur in the NT, which are cited by two or more writers in prima facie independence of one another (Ps 2:7; 8:4–6; 110:1; 118:22–23; Is 6:9–10; 53:1; 40:3–5; 28:16; Gn 12:3; Jer 31:31–34; Jl 2:28–32; Zech 9:9; Hab 2:3–4; Is 61:1–2; Dt 18:15, 19). An examination of the contexts of these passages shows that they served as units of reference usually wider than the brief form of the words actually quoted. For the context, and not merely the individual verse of the OT that is quoted, has often influenced the vocabulary and the idea of the passage of the NT into which it is incorporated. The fifteen passages and their contexts should be reckoned as wholes or units of reference in the OT for some of the essential articles of the primitive kerygma.[42] Hence it seems that large sections of the OT, especially of Isaiah, Jeremiah, and the Psalms, were

[41] C. H. Dodd, *According to the Scriptures: the Sub-Structure of New Testament Theology* (London, 1952) 26.

[42] Dodd divides the OT citations into four groups to illustrate these themes (see pp. 107–8):

	Primary Sources	Supplementary Sources
Apocalyptic-eschatological Scriptures	Jl 2–3; Zech 9–14; Dn 7	Mal 3:1–6; Dn 12
Scriptures of the New Israel	Hos; Is 6:1–9:7; 11:1–10; 28:16; 40:1–11; Jer 31:10–34	Is 29:9–14; Jer 7:1–15; Heb 1–2
Scriptures of the Servant of the Lord and the Righteous Sufferer	Is 42:1–44:5; 49:1–13; 50:4–11; 52:13–53:12; 61; Ps 69; 22; 31; 38; 88; 34; 118; 41; 42–43; 80	Is 58:6–10
Unclassified Scriptures	Ps 8; 110; 2; Gn 12:3; 22:18; Dt 18:15–19	Ps 132; 16; 2 Sm 7:13–14; Is 55:3; Am 9:11–12

selected as the result of a convention among early Christian evangelists and teachers to support their kerygmatic activities. These sections reveal, then, their method of biblical study. Consequently, particular verses quoted from such OT passages should be regarded 'rather as pointers to the whole context than as constituting testimonies in and for themselves. At the same time detached sentences from other parts of the Old Testament could be adduced to illustrate or elucidate the meaning of the main section under consideration.'[43] The quotations from the OT, then, are not to be accounted for by the postulate of a primitive anthology or isolated proof-texts. 'The composition of "testimony books" was the result, not the presupposition, of the work of early Christian biblical scholars.'[44]

K. Stendahl is in agreement with this last statement of Dodd. His book, *The School of St Matthew and Its Use of the Old Testament*,[45] presents a thorough study of the quotations of the first Gospel. Along with many others, he distinguishes two sorts of quotations in Matthew. He calls one group a 'liturgical' type, because the text of these quotations agrees closely with that of the LXX, the version of the OT which was standard for the liturgy. The other group is a *pesher* type of quotation, which manifests a dependence on a Greek text of the OT, but which also 'presupposes an advanced study of the Scriptures and familiarity with the Hebrew text and with the traditions of interpretation known to us from the Versions'.[46] The latter type is distinguished by the introductory formulas of express fulfilment—the 'formula quotations'. They are called a *pesher* type, because they are considered to be the result of a targumizing procedure, resembling the interpretation of Habakkuk that is found in the Qumran *pesher* on Habakkuk (1QpHab). 'All of Matthew's formula quotations give evidence of features of text

[43] *Ibid.*, 126.

[44] *Loc. cit.*

[45] See n. 8 above.

[46] Stendahl, *op. cit.*, 203.

interpretation of an actualizing nature, often closely associated with the context in the gospel.'[47] Stendahl believes that the Habakkuk text found in 1QpHab never existed as a 'text' outside the commentary. The eschatological conviction of the Qumran sect explains the remarkable freedom they exercised with regard to the text. As the significance of Habakkuk's words became gradually more and more understood through the coming and the instruction of the Teacher of Righteousness, the prophet's message could be made more lucid. Hence the scholarly study, in which the sect engaged,[48] would make it possible, in the light of this greater comprehension of Habakkuk's message, to choose or reject among the various traditions of interpretation they were acquainted with. This study resulted in the adoption of variant readings, or perhaps even in a deliberate change of the text, to suit their theological ideas. Hence the text in the *pesher* would not really represent the text found in a copy of Habakkuk used by them, for instance, for liturgical purposes. Stendahl believes that a similar interpretative or targumizing process was at work on the OT text that is found in the formula quotations of Matthew. The special formulas of introduction would correspond to the Qumran *pesher* formula, *pšrw 'l. . .* . Consequently, the fact that the text of these quotations differs from the LXX in contrast to the 'liturgical' type of citation is to be explained more by this interpretative process than by appeal to citations from the Hebrew or to derivation from a list of *testimonia*.

Moreover, Stendahl finds that the formula quotations of Matthew show a greater similarity to the LXX than is often claimed—a fact which makes it necessary to correct the prevailing view that they are dependent on the MT. He believes that the formula quotations originated in Greek, the language of the Matthaean Church; he denies, therefore, that the first Gospel

[47] *Ibid.*, 200–1.

[48] For the Qumran sect's study of the Scriptures see 1QS 6:6–7 and the activity of the *dôrēš hattôrāh* in CD 8:6 ff.; 9:8; 4QFlor 2 (Allegro, *art. cit.*, 176).

ever existed as a consistent Aramaic unity. The first Gospel is for him a handbook for teaching, preaching, and church government, into which the formula quotations have been worked, side by side with the other type of quotation. They are the specific product of the School of St Matthew.

In the last chapter of his book Stendahl asks the question, 'Did Matthew make use of Testimonies?' He thinks that a Book of Testimonies might explain (1) the composite quotations, (2) the ascription to wrong authors, and (3) the readings which differ from the editions known to us—especially if these differences remain constant in the testimony tradition. He admits, moreover, that the *testimonia* might fit well into the picture of early Christian preaching. But there are simpler alternatives than the testimony hypothesis to explain the composite quotations. The *midrashim* provide us with an example of a storehouse of quotations brought together by means of association; rabbinical methods account for most of the features Harris wanted to explain by his Book of Testimonies. 'This is not to say that the primitive church did not know and use testimonies, oral or even written, but so far as Matthew is concerned, these testimonies are not responsible for the form of the quotations, least of all for that of the formula quotations.'[49] Thus Stendahl's position comes close to that of Dodd.

ARE THERE ANY EXTANT LISTS OF TESTIMONIA?

When we ask this question, we mean aside from the evidence in the patristic writers such as Cyprian and Pseudo-Gregory of Nyssa. There are two texts that have been considered as *testimonia* that we must now consider. The first is a Greek text published by C. H. Roberts in 1936, bearing the identification P. Ryl. Gk. 460.[50] It is a fragmentary papyrus, which had been

[49] Stendahl, *op. cit.*, 217.

[50] C. H. Roberts, *Two Biblical Papyri in the John Rylands Library, Manchester* (Manchester, 1936) 47–62. 'It is not to be expected that the text of such a manuscript would be of any importance for textual criticism; neither its omissions . . . or additions . . . are of any significance, although a tendency to disagree with Vaticanus (B) may be noticed' (p. 56).

acquired by the John Rylands Library, Manchester, in 1917; its provenance was probably the Fayyûm and it is dated in the fourth century A.D. This fragment of two columns belongs to two other scraps of an Oslo papyrus codex published by G. Rudberg in 1923.[51] When put together, the three pieces contain the following verses of the OT in Greek:

Folio i recto	Is 42:3–4
	66:18–19
Folio i verso	Is 52:15
	53:1–3
Folio ii verso	Is 53:6–7; 11–12
Folio ii recto	An unidentified verse
	Gn 26:13–14
	2 Chr 1:12
	Dt 29:8, 11

Roberts published together with the photograph of the Rylands papyrus the text of both the Rylands and the Oslo fragments. The latter were described by their first editor 'as a *Textbuch für kultische Zweck* [sic], the property of some poor Christian community in Egypt, and the editors of the Oslo papyri write that "Isaiah combined with Genesis suggests that the book was meant for liturgical use"'.[52] But since the verses from Isaiah include parts of the famous Servant passages from chapters 52–3, while all the other extracts in this papyrus, if not 'messianic' in character, can be related to the history of Christ or of Christianity, Roberts suggested that we have a part of a Book of Testimonies in these fragments.

But because the passages from Isaiah found in this text are not among those that appear in Harris' *Testimonies* and because there is no trace of introductory formulas, Roberts did not think that he had found a 'fragment of *the* Testimony Book desider-

[51] G. Rudberg, *Septuaginta-Fragmente unter den Papyri Osloenses* (*Proceedings of the Scientific Society of Kristiania* 1923/2; Kristiania, 1923); later republished by S. Eitrem and L. Amundsen, *Papyri Osloenses* 2 (1931) 10 f.

[52] Roberts, *op. cit.*, 49–50.

ated by Dr Harris'.[53] Rather, it was probably a collection of 'prophetic' passages of the OT, composed for a devotional purpose in the fourth century, when the need for polemics against the Jews would be less than in the second.

While one cannot say with certainty that this papyrus fragment belongs to a list of *testimonia*, it is most probable that it does. I have found no reviewer of Roberts' publication who questions his identification of this text.[54] If one rejects this identification, one may well ask for an alternative satisfactory explanation. The fact that the fragments date from the fourth century A.D. does not exclude the previous existence of such a list, of which this might be a copy.[55] Whether one wishes to ascribe to this collection of texts a merely devotional scope, as does Roberts, or a polemical (anti-Jewish) purpose, as does L. Cerfaux,[56] the fact is that this papyrus bears witness to the existence of such lists at a fairly early date. It lends some sup-

[53] *Ibid.*, 53.

[54] See H. I. Bell, in *JEA* 23 (1937) 138: 'Mr Roberts is almost certainly right in describing it as a portion of a book of "Testimonies". . . . Every one of the extracts contained in them can, without too much forcing, be made to serve as a "testimony".' L. Cerfaux, in *Revue d'histoire ecclésiastique* 33 (1937) 71: 'Il est clair maintenant que nous avons affaire à des *Testimonia*.' E. C. Colwell, in *JRel* 18 (1938) 462: 'The most important of the editor's conclusions is that this papyrus in its disagreements with the testimonies of Cyprian and Gregory of Nyssa shows that there were various testimony books in use in the early Christian centuries.' J. Finegan, *Light from the Ancient Past* (Princeton, 1946) 324. Only H. G. Opitz, in *ZKG* 56 (1937) 436, expressed himself with a bit of caution.

[55] See L. Cerfaux, *Recueil Cerfaux* 2, 225, note 31: 'Notre collection est assez artificielle et tardive. Le texte a été revisé à la bonne tradition des LXX: les variantes ne sont guère que celles des grands onciaux. Néanmoins, il subsiste des indices que l'auteur a travaillé sur des florilèges antérieurs.'

[56] In *Revue d'histoire ecclésiastique* 33 (1937) 71–2: 'M. Roberts estime que son florilège est simplement messianique et qu'il a été formé par un motif de piété. Il paraît cependant assez proche de deux chapitres des *Testimonia* de Cyprien pour que nous lui soupçonnions une parenté plus marquée avec la littérature antijuive. On peut le comparer en effet avec *Test.*, I, 21: *Quod gentes magis in Christum crediturae essent* et avec *Test.*, II, 13: *Quod humilis in primo adventu suo* (*Christus*) *veniret*. Il est construit comme *Test.*, II, 13, com-

port to the hypothesis of the *testimonia*, which cannot be lightly dismissed.

Strangely enough, C. H. Dodd, who devoted a whole book to the OT passages cited in the NT and who more or less rejects the idea of collections of *testimonia* prior to the NT, does not mention this papyrus. Perhaps he does not consider it of any value for the early period. In itself it is not proof for the period in which the NT was formed. Consequently, O. Michel's view would still seem to be valid.

It is at this point that we return to the Qumran fragments published by Allegro. '4QTestimonia' is a fragment that is apparently almost complete in itself, lacking only the lower right-hand corner. 'It is clearly not part of a scroll, for there is none of the close stitching at the left-hand side one associates with a scroll page.'[57] It consists of a single page measuring about 23 cm. high and 14 cm. wide. Its text is a compilation of the following biblical passages: Dt 5:28–29;18: 18–19; Nm 24:15–17; Dt33: 8–11; and finally a section which 'has no apparent messianic import and is not entirely scriptural'.[58] J. Strugnell, one of the international group of scholars working in Jerusalem on the publication of the Cave 4 documents, has discovered this same passage among other 4Q fragments, to which he has given the provisional title of 4Q Psalms of Joshua. The fragments seem to be part of an apocryphal work used by the Qumran sect and hitherto unknown.

The following is a translation of 4QTestimonia:

And .... [=Yahweh] spoke to Moses, saying,

---

mençant par trois longues citations d'Isaïe (la première et la troisième communes avec ce chapitre) et continuant par une seconde série de citations scripturaires. Avec *Test.*, I, 21 il a en commun le deuxième texte d'Isaïe et le début du troisième. La deuxième série de citations du pap., ayant son point de départ en Gen., est très proche de la série correspondante de *Test.*, I, 21; on se base de part et d'autre sur un même principe en recourant aux bénédictions et promesses de l'Ancien Testament.'

[57] Allegro, *art. cit.*, 182.

[58] *Ibid.*, 186.

Dt 5:28 'You (or I) have heard the sound of the words of this people who have spoken to you. They have spoken well everything that they have said. (29) If only this were their determination: to fear me and to keep all my commandments throughout all the days that it might go well with them and with their children forever.'

Dt 18:18 'A prophet like you I shall raise up for them from the midst of their brothers, and I shall put my words in his mouth, and he will tell them all that I command him. (19) Whoever does not listen to my words which the prophet will speak in my name, I shall seek a reckoning from him.'

Nm 24:15 And he uttered his message and said, 'Oracle of Balaam, son of Beor, and oracle of the man whose eye is clear; (16) oracle of one who hears the sayings of El, and who knows the knowledge of Elyon; who sees the vision of Shaddai, (who) falls, yet with opened eye. (17) I see him, but not now; I watch him, but not near. A star shall march forth from Jacob, and a sceptre shall rise from Israel; it shall crush the heads of Moab and destroy all the children of Sheth.'

Dt 33:8 And of Levi he said, 'Give to Levi your Thummim, and your Urim to your loyal bondsman, whom you tested at Massah, and with whom you strove at the waters of Meribah; (9) who said to his father and to his mother, I do (not) know you; and whose brother(s) he did not acknowledge and whose sons he did not recognize. For he kept your word and guarded your covenant; (10) he shall make your judgments clear to Jacob, your Torah to Israel. He (or they) shall set incense before you, and a whole burnt offering on your altar. (11) Bless his might, ... [= O Yahweh], and accept the work of his hands. Smite the loins of his adversaries and those who hate him, that they may never rise (again).'[59]

4QPs Jos At the time when Joshua finished praising and uttering his hymns of thanksgiving, he said, 'Cursed be the

[59] I call attention to the reading, *bl yqwmw*, instead of the MT *mn yqwmwn* in v. 11. At the time of the composition of this list the archaic *mn* (= *man*, the interrogative pronoun) was probably no longer understood and

> man who rebuilds this city; with his firstborn may he lay its foundation, and with his lastborn may he set up its gates' (Jos 6:26). Now behold, an accursed man, one belonging to Belial, arises, to be a fowl[er's sn]are to his people and a destruction to all his neighbours. He arose [and made his sons] rulers so that the two of them became vessels of violence. They returned and built (i.e., built again) [this city and es]tablished for it a wall and towers, to provide a refuge for wickedness [. . .] in Israel and a horrible thing in Ephraim, and in Judah [. . . and they] caused pollution in the land, and great contempt among the sons of [Jacob. They shed bl]ood like water on the rampart of the daughter of Zion and within the boundary of Jerusalem.[60]

The 4QTestimonia resemble the Roberts Papyrus in that they are strung together without introductory formulae and intervening comments on the text. In the same article Allegro also published part of another fragment from Qumran Cave 4, which he entitled provisionally '4QFlorilegium'.[61] Only four of the nineteen lines it was said to contain were published in that article. Further fragments of the same text were subsequently published, and the title of this article referred to a 'scroll of eschatological midrāšîm'.[62] Now that the full text of this

---

so was changed to *bl*, just as the archaic *yqwmwn* was changed to *yqwmw*. A less likely possibility, however, is that this fragment preserves for us a reading that is older than that of the MT. For *mn* as *man*, see F. M. Cross and D. N. Freedman, 'The Blessing of Moses', *JBL* 67 (1948) 204; W. F. Albright, 'The Old Testament and Canaanite Language', *CBQ* 7 (1945) 23–4; *id.*, 'A Catalogue of Early Hebrew Lyric Poems', *HUCA* 23/1 (1950–51) 29.

[60] For other translations and further studies of 4QTestimonia, see my bibliography in *CBQ* 30 (1969) 68–70.

[61] Allegro, *art. cit.*, 176–7, Document II.

[62] Allegro, 'Further Light on the History of the Qumran Sect', *JBL* 75 (1956) 95, had previously revealed that 4QFlorilegium also contains a 'comment on Ps 2:1–2'; 'all that remains of the *pešer* itself, apart from the introduction, is: ". . . the chosen ones of Israel in the last days, that is, the time of trial which is com[ing]."' The other fragments were published in 'Fragments of a Qumran Scroll of Eschatological Midrāšîm', *JBL* 77 (1958) 350–4. References to further studies of this text can be found in my bibliography in *CBQ* 30 (1969) 67–8.

Qumran document (4Q*174*) is available,[63] it is apparent how ineptly the original title was chosen. Certainly Allegro's second title, 'eschatological midrash', is better suited to the nature of the text, mainly because of the interwoven commentary on the texts cited (2 Sm 7:10–14 [=1 Chr 17:9–13]; Ex 15:17–18; Am 9:11; Ps 1:1; Is 8:11; Ez 37:23; Ps 2:1). However, in the definitive edition of the text in DJD Allegro continues to label it 'Florilegium', implying that it is somehow related to the anthological literature to which the Testimonia belong. This general relationship can be admitted, but even though 4QFlorilegium is important as a genre that illustrates NT usage of OT citations with interwoven commentary, nevertheless it is not a *testimonia* list as such.

THE SIGNIFICANCE OF THE 4QTESTIMONIA

The first question that must be answered with regard to the 4QTestimonia text is, 'Is it really a collection of *testimonia*?' If a doubt arises about Allegro's identification, it is because of the last section, a *pesher* on Jos 6:26 quoted from the 4Q Psalms of Joshua. Until we see the other fragments of this work, we cannot be sure about its character. Allegro admits that the part here quoted has no messianic import. There is, of course, no reason why all the texts must have it, for we are not sure of the reason why they were so compiled. Hence, the presence of such a text in the list does not prevent it from being a collection of *testimonia*. Yet its presence is peculiar, even though we do admit that its incorporation in such a list can be compared to the NT use of extracanonical works like Enoch (see Jude 14).[64]

Moreover, the first section quoted in this text comes from Dt 5:28–29, which de facto has no more messianic import than the

[63] See 4Q*174* in DJD 5, 53–7.

[64] N. Wieder, 'Notes on the New Documents from the Fourth Cave of Qumran', *JJS* 7 (1956) 75–6, thinks that rabbinical haggadah may help solve the riddle of the relationship between the first three *testimonia* and the final section. The rabbis regarded the story of Hiel (1 Kgs 16:34), to which the last passage refers, as testimony to the truth of the biblical prophecies of Joshua.

4Q Psalms of Joshua. But it is closely joined to Dt 18:18–19 in the first paragraph (note the paragraph dividers on the plate published by Allegro). Mgr P. W. Skehan is quoted as saying that 'the combination of Dt 18:18–19 with Dt 5:28–29 is already found in the Samaritan Pentateuch at Ex 20:21'.[65] This fact likewise explains the first few words of the fragment, *wydbr* : : : : *'l mwšh l'mwr*, 'And (Yahweh) spoke to Moses saying'. They differ from the introductory formula of Dt 5:28, *wy'mr yhwh 'ly*, which Allegro thinks has been changed 'for the purpose of the Testimonia selection'.[66] As a matter of fact, the introductory phrase found in 4QTestimonia is identical with that used in the Samaritan Hebrew Pentateuch at Ex 20:21b; it reads *wydbr yhwh 'l mšh l'mr*.[67] That there is some connection here between this text and the Samaritan Pentateuch is obvious, even though we have not yet discovered just what it is. At any rate, the close joining of the two passages of Deuteronomy in one paragraph shows that they were regarded as a unit, which ends with the promise of a prophet to come.

The promise of a prophet, a successor to Moses, in the first paragraph, followed by the Oracle of Balaam in the second, and the Blessing of Moses (Jacob) accorded to Levi in the third, presents a sequence that can only be described as a collection of *testimonia* used in Qumran theological circles. Nm 24:17 must have enjoyed a certain favour in these circles, for it is quoted once in the War Scroll (1QM 11:6) and once in the Damascus Document (CD 7:18–20).[68] If, then, the identification of this text as a list of *testimonia* compiled in view of Qumran theology is rejected, we have a right to ask for a better explanation of the text.

[65] See R. E. Brown, "The Messianism of Qumrân', *CBQ* 19 (1957) 82. See further P. W. Skehan, *CBQ* 19 (1957), 435–40.

[66] Allegro, *art. cit.* (n. 1 above) 182, note 48.

[67] A. von Gall, *Der hebräische Pentateuch der Samaritaner* (Giessen, 1918) 159. Cf. H. Petermann, *Pentateuchus Samaritanus*, fasc. 2: Exodus (Berlin, 1882) 189: *wmll yhwh 'm mšh lmymr*.

[68] See J. Carmignac, 'Les citations de l'Ancien Testament dans "La guerre des fils de lumière contre les fils de ténèbres"', *RB* 63 (1956) 237–9.

To regard this sequence of texts from the OT as *testimonia* does not ipso facto mean that it is a messianic *testimonia* list, even in the loose sense. It is well known that 1QS 9:11 refers to the 'coming of a prophet and the Messiahs of Aaron and Israel'. The prophet that is meant here is almost certainly the Prophet-like-Moses; the Messiah of Aaron is an expected anointed high-priestly figure; the Messiah of Israel is an expected anointed king, the ideal Davidic heir. To a number of scholars the first three paragraphs of 4QTestimonia refer to Qumran messianic belief: Dt 5:28–29 and 18:18–19 would allude to the Prophet-like-Moses who is awaited; Nm 24:15–17 to the Messiah of Israel; and Dt 33:8–11, the blessing of Levi, to the Messiah of Aaron. This is the view of A. Dupont-Sommer, G. Vermes, T. H. Gaster, and many others.[69] The fact that the two passages derived from Dt 5 and 18 were undoubtedly derived from the Samaritan text tradition, which quotes them together at Ex 20:21b, does not really militate against the reference of these passages to the Qumran belief in the coming prophet. The real difficulty in the list is the reference of Nm 24:15–17 to the kingly Messiah, since the same passage is referred to in CD 7:18–20 and interpreted of *two* figures, not one: the Star is understood to be the Interpreter of the Law (probably a priestly figure), and the Sceptre is the Prince of all the congregation (probably the Davidic Messiah). This means that the first three paragraphs of 4QTestimonia cannot be taken as exact allusions to the three expected figures of 1QS 9:11. It is more complicated than that. But in any case, one cannot deny the *testimonia*-character of the text.

Accepting, then, the identification of this text as most likely a

[69] See, e.g., A. Dupont-Sommer, *Ecrits esséniens découverts près de la Mer Morte* (Paris: Payot, 1959) 328–33; G. Vermes, *The Dead Sea Scrolls in English* (Pelican; Harmondsworth and Baltimore: Penguin, 1965) 247–9; T. H. Gaster, *The Scriptures of the Dead Sea Sect* (London: Secker and Warburg, 1957) 353–9 (who notes on p. 327 that 'the same passages of Scripture are used by the Samaritans as the stock *testimonia* to the coming of the Taheb, or future "Restorer"'[?]).

collection of *testimonia*, one asks what light it sheds on the problem of *testimonia* in NT study. The particular sequence of texts found in 4QTestimonia and in the Roberts Papyrus does not agree with any of the NT or patristic composite citations. In fact, one of the striking features about the whole problem of the *testimonia* is that there are very few composite citations that are repeated in the various NT or patristic writers. Even the sequence of Is 28:16, Ps 117/18:22, Is 8:14 (found in Mt 21:42, Rom 9:33, 1 Pt 2:6–8, and *Ep. Barn.* 6, 2, 4) appears with such differences and omissions that it would be hard to establish that they all came from one collection.[70] Such a fact should not be lost sight of.

On the other hand, we do have in 4QTestimonia a collection of OT passages strung together in a way that resembles the composite citations of the NT. If we are right in thinking that 4QFlorilegium is related to the *testimonia*, then we have a concrete example of how *testimonia* were worked into the text of a sectarian writing. This use of OT citations will illustrate the Pauline usage of OT quotations with intervening comments.[71] If the hypothesis of *testimonia* lists had been excogitated to explain the existence of the Roberts Papyrus and the 4QTestimonia, we might have reason to suspect it. But most of the discussion antedates the publication of these documents, which, in turn, confirm the existence of such collections. One can now point to 4QTestimonia to answer Michel's objection, 'Es fehlt jede Spur spätjüdischer Florilegien'. For this text from the fourth cave at Qumran bears witness to the existence of such a literary procedure in late Judaism. Moreover, both Dodd and Stendahl will have to alter their views slightly. While the collections of *testimonia* that are found in patristic writers might be regarded as the result of early Christian catechetical and mis-

[70] Harris, *op. cit.*, 1, 26–32, makes much of this example. Dodd, *op. cit.*, 26, comments: 'Indeed striking, but it is almost the only one of its kind.' Stendahl, *op. cit.*, 212, thinks that it is rather 'a *verbum Christi*', which served as the 'nucleus for the later formation of the testimony'.

[71] See the texts listed in n. 25 above.

sionary activity, 4QTestimonia shows that the stringing together of OT texts from various books was a pre-Christian literary procedure, which may well have been imitated in the early stage of the formation of the NT. It resembles so strongly the composite citations of the NT writers that it is difficult not to admit that *testimonia* influenced certain parts of the NT.

Even if we have not uncovered in these texts any exact parallel for the sequences of OT passages cited in the NT, it is not without significance that the extant *testimonia*, especially those of Qumran, contain passages which are quoted in the NT —outside of composite quotations. Dt 18:18–19 is used in Acts 3:23; 7:37; 2 Sm 7:11–14 in 2 Cor 6:18; Jn 7:42; Heb 1:5 (in a composite quotation); Am 9:11 in Acts 15:16. Like the early Christian Church, the sect of Qumran had favourite texts of the OT. From what we have already learned about Qumran theology, it is not surprising that many of these texts are the same as those in the NT. Given the use of similar texts and given a similar way of handling OT texts, we must conclude that the 4QTestimonia document is an important discovery for the understanding of the formation of the NT.

Stendahl's study of the quotations in Matthew is a careful comparison of the passages cited with the various Greek and Hebrew texts and versions of the OT. He has convincingly shown that the formula quotations in Mt depend much more on the LXX than was previously thought.[72] On the other hand,

[72] An extensive criticism of Stendahl's book can be found in B. Gärtner, 'The Habakkuk Commentary (DSH) and the Gospel of Matthew', *ST* 8 (1954) 1–24. He questions Stendahl's interpretation of the double readings in the Habakkuk *pesher*, which led him to maintain that the OT text found in 1QpHab was not known outside this commentary. Utilizing a fragment of a Greek translation of Habakkuk, found in the Judean desert and published by D. Barthélemy, 'Redécouverte d'un chaînon manquant de l'histoire de la Septante', *RB* 60 (1953) 18–29, Gärtner has convincingly shown that 'in three passages where DSH [= 1QpHab] offers a reading differing significantly from the MT, the Greek version agrees with DSH.... Similarly on a number of other points it seems to me that the Greek version gives evidence that the sect had its own peculiar tradition of the text of the Minor Prophets' (p. 5).

recently published preliminary reports about the Qumran biblical texts indicate that we shall have to revise some of the notions commonly held about the relation of the LXX to the MT. Fragments from Cave 4 have revealed a Hebrew text of various biblical books that support the readings of the LXX against those of the MT.[73] The text tradition of the LXX must be taken seriously and the differences between it and the MT can no longer be written off merely as 'free' translations or as mistranslations. Theological opinions of the translators influenced their work at times, as is well known, but outside of such areas where this is obvious or proven, the LXX should be regarded as a witness of a different Hebrew recension, when it does not agree completely with the MT. The discrepancy in readings, however, between the LXX and the MT varies in value according to the OT book under discussion.[74]

The Qumran discoveries have brought to light Hebrew recensions, differing from the MT, which were in use in Palestine in the last centuries B.C. and in the first A.D. It is possible that such recensions influenced also the NT.[75] If readings from

---

Consequently, 'one may ask whether the sect in general had knowledge of what we call the MT to the Minor Prophets' (p. 6). If this is so, then there is no basis for Stendahl's contention that the sect deliberately altered the text according to its theological interpretations. Gärtner also criticizes Stendahl's use of the term *pesher* to designate the type of quotation that would have been produced by the school of St Matthew. He shows that the manner of citation in Matthew is quite different from that of the *pesher* on Habakkuk. See the comments of K. Stendahl in the reprint of his book (cf. n. 8 above) pp. i–xiv.

[73] See F. M. Cross, Jr, 'A New Qumrân Biblical Fragment Related to the Original Hebrew Underlying the Septuagint', *BASOR* 132 (1953) 15–26; Moshe Greenberg, 'Stabilization of the Text of the Hebrew Bible, Reviewed in the Light of the Biblical Materials from the Judean Desert', *JAOS* 76 (1956) 157–67. Cf. F. M. Cross, Jr., *IEJ* 16 (1966) 81-95.

[74] See F. M. Cross, Jr, 'The Scrolls and the Old Testament', *Christian Century*, Aug. 10, 1955, 920–1; P. Katz, 'Septuagintal Studies in the Mid-Century', *The Background of the New Testament and Its Eschatology: Studies in Honour of C. H. Dodd* (Cambridge, 1956) 200–8.

[75] A text of Exodus from Qumran Cave 4 (4QEx[a]) reads *ḥmš wšbʿym npš wymt*, thus confirming the LXX version of Ex 1:5, which has *pente kai*

the OT were taken from Hebrew texts of this sort—often betraying a 'Septuagintal tendency'—and were incorporated into lists of *testimonia*, this could explain the different textual tradition that sometimes appears in the quotations in the NT. As for the formula quotations, which as a group are closer to the Hebrew than to the LXX, when compared with the 'liturgical' type of quotations, it may be that the 'Septuagintal tendency' that Stendahl has found in them is due to dependence on a Hebrew text with such a tendency, such as we know existed in Palestine at the beginning of our era. It should be noted that Allegro has emphasized the 'Septuagintal tendency of the text tradition used by the compiler of 4Q[Testimonia]'.[76] But the further publication of the 4Q biblical fragments must be awaited before this aspect of the problem can be pursued.

In conclusion, the text of 4QTestimonia furnishes pre-Christian evidence of a literary process that led to the use of composite quotations in the NT and thus supports the hypothesis of *testimonia*. The discovery of this text thus confirms the opinion of Vollmer that Hebrew collections of OT passages did exist among the Jews before the time of Christ. This discovery, however, does not invalidate the views of C. H. Dodd about the

---

hebdomēkonta eteleutēsan, whereas the MT mentions only 'seventy' persons. Acts 7:14, however, mentions 'seventy-five'; see *RB* 63 (1956) 56. Heb 1:6 quotes Dt 32:43, agreeing with the LXX against the MT; a text from 4Q now confirms the reading in the LXX and Hebrews: *whšthww lw kl 'lhym*; see P. W. Skehan, *BASOR* 136 (1954) 12–15. Allegro, *art. cit.* (supra n. 1) 176, n. 25, seems to think that Am 9:11, which is quoted in 4QFlorilegium and in CD 7:16, is 'in the form offered by . . . Acts 15:16, against MT and LXX'. The MT has *'qym*; 4QFlorilegium and the Damascus Document have *whqymwty*, a waw-conversive perfect instead of the imperfect. This is supposed to reflect a text tradition preserved in Acts by *kai anoikodomēsō*; see C. Rabin, *The Zadokite Documents* (Oxford, 1954) 29, whom Allegro quotes. This interpretation is certainly possible, but there is just a chance that too much is being derived from the form of the waw-conversive perfect. Actually the LXX reads *anastēsō*, a form that is certainly closer in meaning to *qwm*, used by both the MT and the 4QFlorilegium, than is the *anoikodomēsō* of Acts.

[76] Allegro, *art. cit.* (supra n. 1) 186, n. 107. In Dt 18:19 the word *hnby*,

use of OT contexts among early Christian writers and teachers. But it is not possible to regard the use of *testimonia* as the final term of such a development, as Dodd has suggested. Nor does it rule out the activity of a 'School of St Matthew', as postulated by K. Stendahl, but the activity of that school will have to be explained otherwise. While I would not go so far as to say with Allegro that 'this *testimonia* document from Qumran is one of the most important of the works found',[77] it is true that it throws new light on an old problem.[78]

'the prophet', is found in the 4Q text, in the LXX, and in the citation used in Acts 3:23, but it is missing in the MT. In Dt 33:8 the LXX and 4Q Testimonia read, 'Give to Levi', which is not found in the MT.

[77] J. M. Allegro, *The Dead Sea Scrolls* (Harmondsworth, 1956) 139.

[78] See further P. Prigent, 'Les récits évangéliques de la Passion et l'utilisation des "Testimonia"', *RHR* 161 (1962) 130–2; J.-P. Audet, 'L'hypothèse des Testimonia: Remarques autour d'un livre récent', *RB* 70 (1963) 381–405; P. Prigent, *Les Testimonia dans le christianisme primitif: L'épître de Barnabé I–XVI et ses sources* (EBib; Paris: Gabalda, 1961); R. A. Kraft, Review of P. Prigent, *JTS* n.s. 13 (1962) 401–8; 'Barnabas' Isaiah Text and the "Testimony Book" Hypothesis', *JBL* 79 (1960) 336–50; E. D. Freed, *Old Testament Quotations in the Gospel of John* (NTSup 11; Leiden: Brill, 1965) 44–5; M. Treves, 'On the Meaning of the Qumran Testimonia', *RQ* 2 (1960) 569–71.

II

THE SEMITIC BACKGROUND OF VARIOUS GOSPEL PASSAGES

3

THE ARAMAIC QORBĀN INSCRIPTION FROM JEBEL ḪALLET EṬ-ṬÛRI AND MK 7:11/MT 15:5*

When Jesus was arguing with the Pharisees, he reproached them with nullifying what God had commanded in order to observe their own traditions. As an example he cited the commandments, 'Honour your father and your mother', and 'Whoever abuses his father or mother must be put to death'. In contrast, the Pharisees and scribes were teaching, 'If a man says to his father or mother, "Anything of mine that might have been of use to you is Korban" (that is, a gift), they let him off from doing anything more for his father or mother' (Mk 7:9–13 = Mt 15:3–6). Mark has preserved the Aramaic word in his account, *korban, ho estin dōron, ho ean ex emou ōphelēthēs* (7:11), which he also translated for his Gentile readers, whereas Matthew has simply *dōron ho ean ex emou ōphelēthēs* (15:5). Commentators have been accustomed to explain the word *korban* in Mark by appealing to the Mishnah and to statements in Josephus.

A recently discovered tomb in the area south-east of Jerusalem has yielded an inscribed ossuary-lid that sheds new light on this verse in Mark. The tomb was found at Jebel Ḫallet eṭ-Ṭûri, a spot south of Bîr-'Ayyûb in the extension of the Cedron Valley just before it becomes the Wâdi en-Nâr. It is a Jewish tomb dating from the beginning of the Christian era. The inscription has been published with a photo and facsimile by Fr

* Originally published in *JBL* 78 (1959) 60–5.

Jozef T. Milik in an article entitled 'Trois tombeaux juifs récemment découverts au Sud-Est de Jérusalem'.[1]

According to Milik's description, the inscription consists of two lines scratched with a fairly broad-pointed nail (about 0.2 cm. wide). The characters are firmly made but not deeply incised, with the exception of a few at the beginning. The length of the first line of the inscription is 54 cm. and of the second 38 cm. The letters have an average height of 2.5 cm. It is written on a lid 64.5 cm. long, 19.5 cm. wide and about 3 cm. thick.

The inscription reads as follows (Milik's translation):[2]

kl dy 'nš mthnh bḥlth dh *qrbn 'lh mn dbgwh*	Quiconque réutilisera à son profit cet ossuaire-ci, malédiction (*litt.* offrande) de Dieu de la part de celui qui est dedans!

Milik comments, 'La lecture matérielle et la traduction sont certaines.' Since he was kind enough to show me the ossuary-lid while I was in Jerusalem, I was able to check his reading and

[1] *Studii Biblici Franciscani Liber Annuus* 7 (1956–57) 232–9. The text and Milik's translation can also be found in *RB* 65 (1958) 409.

[2] The script of the inscription is described as close to the Herodian type (related to the Uzziah inscription and 1QIs[b], 1QM, 1QH, 1QapGn), introduced into public use *c.* 30 B.C. Milik dates the inscription on paleographical evidence to the end of the first century B.C. He also calls attention to a few of the grammatical peculiarities of the text: 1) the emphatic state of *hlth* written with *he* instead of *aleph*, a phenomenon which he finds paralleled in the Elephantine papyri, twice in the *Genesis Apocryphon* (see E. Y. Kutscher, 'The Language of the Genesis Apocryphon, a Preliminary Study', *Scripta Hierosolymitana* 4 [1957] 26), and in two unpublished texts from Qumran Cave 4 (very frequently in 4QHen[a] [from the second century B.C.] and by way of exception in 4QHen astr[b] [end of the second-beginning of the first century B.C.]; 2) both *dy* and *d* occurring as the relative pronoun; this feature too is found in 1QapGn (see Kutscher, p. 6 [six instances of *d* against 60–70 of *dy*]; 3) *dh* as the demonstrative adjective feminine instead of *d'*; the latter alone is found in Qumran Aramaic with one doubtful exception (see *RB* 63 [1956] 413); 4) *ḥlth*, 'box, ossuary', is also found in the Phoenician Ešmun'azor inscription (*CIS* 3: 3, 5, 7, 10, 21) and in *Midraš Tanna'im* (ed. D. Z. Hoffmann, 175 f.).

agree that it is certain. It was only subsequently that I developed some doubts about the translation.

To justify his translation, Milik explains that the beginning of the inscription, *kl dy 'nš mthnh*, is syntactically impossible. He supposes that the scribe began with *kl dy*, originally intending to continue with a finite verb (e.g., *ythnh*). This supposition is based on traces of a letter within the *aleph* of *'nš* which Milik considers may well be a *yodh*. The scribe is thought to have corrected himself, recalling a more general formula requiring a participle and *kl 'nš*. Consequently, the first line would more properly be transcribed thus: *kl* {*dy*} *'nš mthnh bḥlth dh*. But such an explanation and his translation do violence to the text, which can be understood more simply on closer examination.

First of all, there is no doubt that there are extra traces within the *aleph*; but they are not of the form of a *yodh* at all. They seem to be nothing more than attempts to write *aleph* correctly and are of the same type as the extra traces within the *lamedh* of *kl*.

Secondly, the elimination of *dy* must be regarded as gratuitous. It is rather to be construed as a compound relative pronoun,[3] having a function both in the main clause and in the subordinate clause. In the main clause *kl dy* obviously acts as the subject of the nominal sentence whose predicate is *qrbn*. In the subordinate clause *dy* serves as the complement (or possibly as the internal object) of *mthnh*. The subject of this participle is the indefinite *'nš*.

Thirdly, Milik's translation disregards or misinterprets the preposition *b* before *ḥlth dh*. Part of this difficulty lies in the sense he gives to the participle, 'réutilisera à son profit'. The root of the verb is *hny*, known in Jewish Aramaic, Syriac, and Modern

[3] This analysis of *dy* as a compound relative is based on the usual interpretation to *kl* as a construct state in this *kl dy* expression. See P. Leander, 'Laut- und Formenlehre des Ägyptisch-Aramäischen', *Göteborgs Högskolas Årsskrift* 34 (1928) #18j; J. A. Fitzmyer, 'The syntax of *kl, kl'* in the Aramaic Texts from Egypt and in Biblical Aramaic', *Bib* 38 (1957) 175–6. If one prefers to regard *kl* as the absolute and *dy* as a simple relative, then *dy* alone is the subject of the nominal sentence.

Hebrew and meaning, 'to be pleasing, profitable'. Brockelmann relates it to Arabic *hani'a*, Sabaean *hn'm*, 'lucrum'.[4] In the Ithpeel it means 'to enjoy, to derive profit from, to profit from'. The Ithpeel is found elsewhere with the preposition *b*,[5] which at first sight might seem to confirm Milik's translation of the first line. However, it should be noted that we here find a direct object *dy*, which prevents us from regarding the construction as *hny b*. Hence we must restore to *beth* its basic prepositional force.

Fourthly, the translation of *qrbn* as 'malédiction' is highly questionable. What reason is there for supposing that *qrbn* is used here like the *qwnm* of later rabbinical writings? Moreover, such a translation leaves the syntax of the sentence completely unexplained; the only way it could possibly be saved would be to emend the beginning of the first line thus: *⟨l⟩kl {dy} 'nš mthnh. . . .*

Consequently, the inscription should rather be translated as follows:

> 'All that a man may find-to-his-profit in this ossuary
> (is) an offering to God from him who is within it.'[6]

This translation is confirmed by the Peshitta version of Mt 15:5, which uses precisely the same verb in connection with *qrbn*. It reads as follows:[7] *qurbān(y) meddem d^{e}teth^{e}nē' men(y)*. It is

[4] *Lexicon Syriacum* (Halle/S., 1928) 178.

[5] J. Levy (*Chaldäisches Wörterbuch über die Targumin* [Leipzig, 1881] lists an example from Ez 16:31 which illustrates this usage: 'Eine Buhlerin *dmthny' b'gr'* die sich Nutzen (od. Vergnügen) verschafft durch den Buhlerlohn oder für Buhlen.'

[6] For similar uses of *kl dy* see Dn 2:38; 6:8; Ezr 7:21, 23, 26; Cowley, *AP* 15:19, 24, 27; 40:3; 49:4; Kraeling, *BMAP* 2:8, 10; 7:22, 31, 35; 1QapGn 22:30. For the indefinite use of *'nš* see *AP* 28:8, 10; *BMAP* 8:5, 8; 1QapGn 21:13. For further uses of the emphatic in *he* see *AP* 14:5 (*'lhth*); 14:4, 6, 9; 6:6 (*mwm'h*); *Aḥiqar* 204 (*'rdh*); *BMAP* 12:9 (*byth* [but not 3:4, where *byth* is followed by *zy* and a proper name; *pace* Kraeling, it is to be interpreted as a prospective suffix followed by *zy* and a proper name similar to *'nny zy 'ḥwhy*, *AP* 30:18–19; 31:18; cf. *byth zy 'sḥwr*, *AP* 15:30]); 1QapGn 22:2 (*'nh*); 7:1 (*'r'ḥ*); 19:18 (*ḥlmh*); 17:16 (*ktrh?*). For further uses of *daleth* see 1QapGn 2:25; 20:10, 27; 21:29; 22:21, 22 (*bis*). The form *bgwh* is also found in Zakir b. 3; Ezr 5:7; 6:2.

[7] P. E. Pusey, G. H. Gwilliam, *Tetraeuangelium sanctum, simplex Syrorum versio* (Oxford, 1901) 94.

to be noted that the syntax of this verse closely parallels the main part of the ossuary inscription. Instead of *kl dy* we have *meddem de*; instead of the generic *'nš mthnh* we have the finite verb with a personal (2 sg.) subject; instead of *bḥlth dh* we have *men(y)*, though the preposition is admittedly different. In both cases the predicate of the sentence is *qrbn*. Whereas the Syriac has *qurbān(y)* 'my offering', the ossuary-lid has preserved a fuller and more formal expression *qrbn 'lh mn dbgwh*. In other words, the use of *qrbn* in the ossuary inscription is identical with that preserved in the Greek of Mark: *korban ho ean ex emou ōphelēthēs*. We have to do with a dedicatory formula in common use among the Jews of the last few centuries B.C. and well into Christian times. Probably it is a vestigial survival of much older mortuary offerings. Whether we classify this formula with other *ndrym*, as does the Mishnah, or speak of it as a *horkos*, as does Josephus, makes little difference as long as we recognize its basic character as an expression that *puts a ban* on something, reserving it for sacred use and withdrawing it from the profane.

Milik has pointed out the pertinence of this inscription to the NT passages in Matthew and Mark. He does not stress, however, the similarity of the two expressions, as his interest lies rather in the evolution of various *qrbn* expressions with their successive changes, which he believes are due to 'scrupule religieux'.[8] According to him the ossuary-lid already manifests the fashion of the first century B.C. in substituting *'lh* for the tetragrammaton of the expression *qrbn Yhwh* found in Nm 9:13; 31:50.[9] Later in the first century A.D. *qrbn* is used alone (as we find it in Mt 15:5 and Mk 7:11). Still later in the second century A.D. we find the palliative *qwnm* being used instead of *qrbn*, 'à cause de sa signification sacrale'.

We should, however, beware of stressing such an evolution merely on the basis of these texts. There is no doubt about the

[8] *Op. cit.*, 238.
[9] To these references of Milik add Nm 9:7.

OT roots of the expression. But in addition to *qrbn Yhwh* from Numbers, we also find another expression in Lv 23:14, *'d hby'km 't qrbn 'lhykm*. This is admittedly not the stereotyped formula *qrbn 'lh* of the ossuary lid, but then neither is *qrbn Yhwh* of Nm 9:7, 13; 31:50. It shows, however, that the combination *qrbn 'lh* did exist earlier. Furthermore, the testimony of Josephus indicates that *qrbn 'lh* was also in use as late as the first century A.D. and that *qrbn* alone was known as an oath-formula in the late fourth century B.C.

All who consecrate themselves in fulfilment of a vow—Nazirites as they are called, people who grow long hair and abstain from wine—these too, when they dedicate their hair and offer it in sacrifice assign their shorn locks to the priests. Again, those who describe themselves as 'Corban' to God—meaning what the Greeks would call 'a gift'—when desirous to be relieved of this obligation must pay down to the priests a fixed sum.[10]

And again,

This [acquaintance of various cities in ancient times with the Jewish nation] is apparent from a passage in the works of Theophrastus[11] on *Laws*, where he says that the laws of the Tyrians prohibit the use of foreign oaths, in enumerating which he includes among others the oath called 'Corban'. Now this oath will be found in no other nation except the Jews and, translated from the Hebrew, one may interpret it as meaning God's gift.[12]

Such evidence seems to preclude any attempt to show that a development in the use of this dedicatory formula existed at an early period. It is more likely that a variety of formulae existed side by side, some expanded and formal like the ossuary in-

[10] *Ant.* 4, 72–3. Important words in Greek are: *kai hoi korban hautous onomasantes tō theō, dōron de touto sēmainei kata Hellēnōn glōttan.* Translation of H. St J. Thackeray, *Josephus* (Loeb Classical Library IV; London, 1930) 511. *tō theō* must be taken with *korban* and therefore reflects *qrbn 'lh*. Cf. H. Grégoire, 'La première mention de *Korbân* ou *Korbanâs* dans l'épigraphie grecque', *Bulletin de l'académie royale de Belgique*, Classe des lettres, 1953, 657–63; H. Hommel, 'Das Wort korban und seine Verwandten', *Philologus* 98 (1954) 132–49.

[11] The pupil of Aristotle, who lived *c.* 372–288 B.C.

[12] *Against Apion* 1, 166–7. *dēloi d', hōs an eipoi tis, ek tēs Hebraiōn methermēneuomenos dialektou dōron theou.* Thackeray's translation, LCL I, 229–31.

scription, others abbreviated like the NT expression or that indicated by Josephus. A similar variety of formulae that existed in the later period, when there admittedly was a semantic development, confirms this—in general at least.

For I do admit that the expressions found in the Mishnah reveal a later stage of development in the use of the *qrbn* formula. There is some indication that the nominal sentence formula (such as we have in Mark/Matthew and in the ossuary inscription) was still in use. In Nedarim 1:4 we find the expression *qrbn š'wkl lk*, 'What I eat of thine be . . . "a Korban"'.[13] But the development is seen, first of all, in the substitution of *qwnm*, *qwns*, *qwnḥ* for *qrbn* (Nedarim 1:2). Secondly, there is an obvious development in the meaning of the word in some of the rabbinical formulae; it no longer means merely 'an offering to God', pronounced over some object to remove it from profane use, but acquires the force of an asseverative and even an imprecatory interjection. It is frequently followed by a *š*-clause (a remnant of the old formula) and a conditional clause: *qwnm š'th nhnh ly 'm 'yn 'th b' wnwtn lbny kwr 'ḥd šl ḥytyn wšty ḥbywt šl yyn*, '*Konam* be the benefit thou hast from me if thou come not and give my son a *kor* of wheat and two jars of wine!' (Nedarim 8:7).[14] Or *qwnm šdy š'yny ḥwrš bh l'wlm* (said of a cow, which a neighbour refuses to lend), '*Konam!* if I ever again plough my field with it' (Nedarim 4:6). In my opinion, this usage is definitely a development beyond that which is found in the NT or ossuary expression—at least we have no evidence of this usage at an earlier period.

[13] Translation of H. Danby, *The Mishnah* (London, 1933) 265.

[14] *Ibid.*, 275. It does not seem to be correct to say with Rengstorf (Kittel *TDNT* 3, 865) that 'the sentence [in Mt/Mk] . . . has its literal and real counterpart in the rabbinical expression *qwnm š'th nhnyth ly*', because this is a quotation of only half of the pertinent saying. Aside from this point Rengstorf's treatment of *korban* is very well done. See also Str-B I, 711–17. It is rather characteristic of commentators on Mk 7:11 that they cite only *half* of these rabbinical statements; see e.g., E. Klostermann, *Das Markusevangelium* (HNT III; 4. Aufl.; Tübingen, 1950) 69; V. Taylor, *The Gospel according to St Mark* (London: Macmillan, 1953) 342; M.-J. Lagrange, *Evangile selon Saint Marc* (EBib; Paris, 1929) 185.

Now it is precisely this imprecatory usage that Milik has imposed upon *qrbn* in the translation he has given of the inscription. But since the syntax of the latter reveals the same construction as that found in the NT, I prefer to give it the simple meaning of 'an offering to God' rather than 'a curse of God'. We should not lose sight of the fact that the ossuary inscription has preserved for us the formula complete in itself; it is thus of far greater importance for the interpretation of Mark 7:11 than the somewhat cryptic formulae that we find in the casuistic passages of Nedarim. In it we have a concrete example of how the formula was used. The new inscription does not alter the sense of the word in Matthew or Mark but provides a perfect contemporary parallel.[15]

[15] See further Z. W. Falk, 'Notes and Observations on Talmudic Vows', *HTR* 59 (1966) 309–12; J. Bligh, 'Korban!', *HeythJ* 5 (1964) 192–3; S. Zeitlin, 'Korban', *JQR* 53 (1962) 160–3; 'Korban: A Gift', *JQR* 59 (1968) 135–5. To be noted is the discovery of a stone jar, inscribed with the word *qrbn* and two birds (turtle-doves?), recently found in the excavation of Jerusalem by B. Mazar south of the temple area (see 'The Excavations in the Old City of Jerusalem', *Eretz-Israel* 9*: W. F. Albright Volume* [Jerusalem: Israel Exploration Society, 1969] 168–70 [+pl. 45, #5]. The word designates the vessel as a 'gift', probably for the service of the temple. Since it is an isolated word, it does not add much to the meaning of *qorbān* found in the ossuary inscription. It undoubtedly illustrates the Mishnah, *Maaser Sheni* 4:10. See also G. W. Buchanan, 'Some Vow and Oath Formulas in the New Testament', *HTR* 58 (1965) 319–26. He discusses the *qorbān* formula, but with no reference to this Aramaic inscription. It is mentioned, however, in the inconsequential article of J. D. M. Derrett, '*Korban, ho estin dōron*', *NTS* 16 (1969–70) 364–8. Derrett suggests that the word be vocalized 'properly *ḳārebān*'. But this is impossible!

4

'PEACE UPON EARTH AMONG MEN OF HIS GOOD WILL' (LK 2:14)*

It was Dr Claus-Hunno Hunzinger who first pointed out the pertinence of a Qumran expression to the understanding of the Lucan Christmas greeting: *kai epi gēs eirēnē en anthrōpois eudokias* (2:14).[1] He found the phrase *b^e^nê r^e^ṣônô*, 'sons of his good pleasure', in one of the Qumran Thanksgiving Hymns (1QH 4:32–33). Though it had previously been pointed out, perhaps best by J. Jeremias,[2] that *eudokias* must refer to God and not to man, there was no direct parallel for the expression 'men of God's good pleasure'. Now at last there was found in the Qumran texts a contemporary expression that provided the missing Hebrew equivalent.

Fr Ernst Vogt, S.J., wrote a résumé of Hunzinger's article[3] and stressed especially that *eudokia* and *rāṣôn* express God's will in electing and predestining man rather than his pleasure in man's goodness. The phrase 'sons of his good pleasure' indicates

* Originally published in *TS* 19 (1958) 225–7.

[1] 'Neues Licht auf Lc 2:14 *anthrōpoi eudokias*', *ZNW* 44 (1952–53) 85–90.

[2] '*Anthrōpoi eudokias* (Lc 2:14)', *ZNW* 28 (1929) 13–20.

[3] '"Pax hominibus bonae voluntatis" Lc 2:14', *Bib* 34 (1953) 427–9. An English translation of this article, with some revisions, appears in K. Stendahl (ed.), *The Scrolls and the New Testament* (New York, 1957) 114–17. The author here points out that the phrase occurs again in 1QH 11:9. See also C. H. Hunzinger, 'Ein weiterer Beleg zu Lc 2:14 *anthrōpoi eudokias*', *ZNW* 49 (1958) 129–30. If Allegro's restoration is acceptable, another occurrence of the phrase would be found in 4QpPs^a^ 1–2 ii 24–25 (DJD 5, 44): [*pišrô 'al 'anšê*] *r^e^ṣôn*[*ô*].

in Qumran literature those who are the object of divine predilection. Moreover, since 'men' and 'sons' are frequently interchanged in kindred Qumran expressions, *b^e^nê r^e^ṣônô* can easily be the Hebrew equivalent of *anthrōpois eudokias*.

The Qumran expression contains a pronominal suffix which makes it clear that the good will refers to God. But the Greek of Luke's verse merely has *eudokias* without a possessive—a fact which has led to the frequently used but erroneous interpretation 'men of good will' (i.e., who have good will). Both Hunzinger and Vogt have pointed out that *eudokia* without *autou* could pass as the Greek equivalent of *r^e^ṣônô*. In Sir 15:15 and 39:18, *r^e^ṣônô* is translated merely by *eudokia*.[4]

However, I wish to call attention here to the reading which is found in the Coptic (Sahidic) version. There we read: *awō tirēnē hiǧ^e^m pkah h^e^n ^e^nrōme ^e^mpefwōš*, 'And peace upon the earth among men of his will'.[5] The *apparatus criticus* in modern New Testaments and the commentators often cite the Sahidic version in support of the genitive *eudokias*, the reading of the better manuscripts, against the nominative *eudokia*.[6] But they fail to indicate that the Sahidic also includes the personal pronominal prefix, *pef-*. This prefix corresponds, then, to the Hebrew pronominal suffix found on *r^e^ṣônô* in the Qumran expression. Such a detail of the Coptic translation should not be lost sight of, as it gives us valuable testimony that *eudokias* was understood in the past as 'of *his* good will'. It thus confirms the interpretation based on the Qumran expression: 'Peace upon earth among men of his good will'.

The expression *b^e^nê r^e^ṣônô*, being Hebrew, fits in well with the hypothesis, often used today, that the source of Luke's first two chapters was originally a Hebrew composition.[7] Recently, how-

[4] See N. Walker, 'The Renderings of *Rāṣôn*', JBL 81 (1962) 182–4.

[5] *The Coptic Version of the New Testament in the Southern Dialect, Otherwise Called Sahidic and Theban* (Oxford, 1911) 30–2.

[6] See, e.g., A. Merk, *Novum Testamentum graece et latine* (7th ed.; Rome 1951) 195; K. Aland *et al.*, *The Greek New Testament* (United Bible Societies, 1966) 207.

[7] See P. Winter, 'Some Observations on the Language in the Birth and

ever, the Aramaic equivalent of the Lucan phrase has turned up in a Qumran text being prepared for publication by M. l'Abbé J. Starcky. The latter, with whom I have had occasion to go over the text for the Cave 4 concordance, has graciously permitted me to cite the relevant passage here. The fragmentary manuscript in which the phrase occurs has been tentatively labelled *ḥᵃzût 'Amram* ᶜ, and assigned the siglum 4Q ḥ'Aᶜ; it tells of the vision enjoyed by Amram, the father of Aaron, Moses, and Miriam. The pertinent text is found in fragment 9, line 18. Unfortunately, only the beginning of the lines has been preserved in this fragment; what is left seems to be the end of the work. Though Aaron is not named, it seems that he is the subject.

18 *šby'y b'nwš r'wt[h wy]qrh wyt'm[r*
19 *ytbḥr lkhn 'lmyn* (vacat)

'he will be seventh among men of [his] good will [and ho]nour and it (he?) will be said . . .
he will be chosen as a priest forever.'

The phrase which interests us is *b'nwš r'wt[h]*, 'among men of [his] good will'. The text is unfortunately damaged and the pronominal suffix lost; but it can be supplied on the basis of the one found on the parallel, coordinated noun, *[wy]qrh*. The suffix refers most likely to God, as it does in the Hebrew counterpart, *bᵉnê rᵉṣônô*. The most interesting detail in the phrase is the noun *'nwš*, 'men', for it is the exact equivalent of the Lucan[8] expression, *anthrōpois eudokias*. Since *rᵉ'û* is the normal Aramaic cognate for the Hebrew *rāṣôn*, we now have both an Aramaic and a Hebrew equivalent for Luke's expression.[9] The occur-

---

Infancy Stories of the Third Gospel', *NTS* 1 (1954–55) 111–21; see also the literature cited there.

[8] Actually *'nwš* is a singular noun, but its collective force is quite frequently found, as here.

[9] This is not the first instance in which a NT expression, previously identified in Qumran Hebrew, has turned up in Aramaic dress as well. In the *Genesis Apocryphon*, published by N. Avigad and Y. Yadin (Jerusalem,

rence of the same phrase in both languages indicates its common and frequent usage and confirms the interpretation that Dr Hunzinger first suggested.[10]

1956), a few words can be read on the left-hand side of column 1, lines 1–4 (see the photo of column 2). The editors say that these words 'are as yet unclear' (p. 16). But in line 2 one can clearly read *'p rz ršʿ' dy*. The words *rz ršʿ'* are the Aramaic equivalent of the Hebrew *rzy pšʿ* (1Q27 1:2; 1QH 5:36; 1QH fr 50:5) and of the Greek *mystērion tēs anomias*, 'the mystery of iniquity' (2 Thes 2:7).

[10] See further R. Deichgräber, 'Lc 2:14: *anthrōpoi eudokias*', *ZNW* 51 (1960) 132 [The phrase is also found in the Samaritan Marqa's commentary on the Pentateuch.]; E. F. F. Bishop, 'Men of God's Good Pleasure', *ATR* 48 (1966) 63–9; F. Vattioni, 'Pax hominibus bonae voluntatis', *RBibIt* 7 (1959) 369–70; H. Rusche, '"Et in terra pax hominibus bonae voluntatis"', *Bibel und Leben* 2 (1961) 229–34.

5
THE NAME SIMON*

Speculation about the 'change' in the name of the apostle Peter (cf. Mt 16:18; Jn 1:42) will undoubtedly always be in order. In this respect the recent article of Cecil Roth of Oxford[1] raises an interesting point. He suggests that the apostle's name Peter prevailed in time over Simon because of a current tendency of contemporary Judaism to avoid the use of the name *Simōn* in Greek or *Šim'ôn* in Hebrew. The latter name was 'commonly or even methodically modified or eliminated, for some reason or the other, among the Jews at the beginning of the Christian era. One finds it difficult to avoid the conclusion that the modification of the name of the Apostle by the elimination of "Simon" was connected with this and due to the same cause, whatever that may have been.'[2] Roth offers parallels of persons whose name was Simon, but who were known more usually by a patronymic or a nickname (ben Sira, ben Zoma, ben Azzai, ben Nanos, bar Cochba), and suggests that it was a peculiarly 'patriotic' name, borne by great national and revolutionary leaders such as Simon Maccabee, Simon the High Priest (Sir 50:1–2), Simeon ben Šeṭaḥ (politician-Rabbi of the second century B.C.), Simon the rebel (Josephus, *JW* 2, 4, 2, #57; *Ant.* 17, 10, 6, #273), Simon the son of the founder of the Zealots, Judah the Galilean (Josephus, *Ant.* 20, 5, 2, #102), Simon bar Giora (leader in the First Revolt), Simon bar Cochba (leader

* Originally published in *HTR* 56 (1963) 1–5.

[1] 'Simon-Peter', *HTR* 54 (1961) 91–7.

[2] *Ibid.*, 94.

of the Second Revolt).[3] Roth raises the question: Was the name Simon forbidden by the Romans because of hyper-patriotic associations, or was it possibly regarded as too sacred for normal use by nationalistic Jews? Could possibly a 'proto-Midrashic interpretation' of the Blessing of Jacob in Gn 49:5–7, a 'comminatory' verse, have resulted in an inhibition to use the name, so that the person who bore it came to be referred to only by a patronymic periphrasis ('the son of so-and-so') or a nickname (such as Kaipha=Peter)? His conclusion: 'It seems certain that in the first century and perhaps for some time afterwards the use of the name Simon was deliberately avoided by Jews, whether from symbolic or patriotic or superstitious reasons, or even out of sheer nervousness.'[4]

Such a thesis, however, for all its interesting speculative and suggestive character, has to face a certain *factual* aspect of the problem of the 'change' of the name of the apostle from Simon to Peter. It is an aspect that Roth has for some reason or other been silent about; it certainly will not hurt to recall it here. For it so happens that *Simōn* or *Šmʿwn* is the most frequently attested name for Jews[5] of the period which Roth discusses. Admittedly, we do not have the complete onomasticon of the Jews even of Palestine for the first century B.C. or for the first two centuries A.D. But any number of names of Jews of this period are known to us, and the most significant feature is that the name 'Simon' is one which occurs most frequently in precisely this period, viz. of Roman domination.

Some years ago G. Hölscher pointed out that the name was not in great use among the Jews of an earlier period.[6] The old

[3] See below pp. 305—54.

[4] *Ibid.*, 96–7.

[5] Included are the names of those who were so named as Jews, even though they may have subsequently been converted to Christianity.

[6] 'Zur jüdischen Namenkunde', *Vom Alten Testament: Karl Marti zum siebzigsten Geburtstage gewidmet* (BZAW XLI, Giessen, 1925) 148–57. See also M. Noth, *Die israelitischen Personennamen im Rahmen der gemeinsemitischen Namengebung* (Stuttgart, 1928) 60.

tribal name given to individuals turns up in more or less common usage in the fifth century B.C., being attested in the Aramaic texts from Elephantine, among the Jewish names recorded in the Murašu texts from Nippur, and in the Old Testament (Ezr 10:31). In Hellenistic times *Šmʿwn* became still more common, because it was assimilated to the Greek name *Simōn*.

The names *Šmʿwn* (regarded as the equivalent of the Greek name *Simōn*), *Yhwdh* and *Ywsp* become ever more numerous, and in the time of the Roman Empire these three names belong to the most frequently used Jewish names. Besides them there occur quite often from the Augustan period on the name *Lwy*, and more rarely those of *Bnymyn* and *R'wbn.* Only in Talmudic times are still others of these tribal names attested as the names of individuals.[7]

Further on he adds:

When one surveys the Hebrew masculine names which were in use from early Roman times until about A.D. 200 among the Jews of Palestine, the name *Šmʿwn* (*Simōn*) is by far the most popular.[8]

Hölscher did not document the remarks which he published, and in the absence of the full onomasticon of the Jews of the period we can only appeal to the *known* lists of Jewish names. The most recent treatment of the name *Šmʿwn* has been presented by J. T. Milik in connection with his study of the proper names found on the ossuaries discovered in the tombs of the property of the Franciscan Friars on the slope of the Mount of Olives, called Dominus Flevit. Though he wrote in complete independence of Hölscher, it is interesting to note that his findings confirm those of the latter.

This biblical name (the patriarch, Ezr 10:31 = 1 Esdras 9:32; Sir 51:30) is one of the most frequently used among the Jews, and remained popular in the Greco-Roman period due to its phonetic identity [*sic*] with the Greek name *Simōn* which was equally current among the Greeks. Josephus knows 29 persons with this name, which is always written *Simōn*, except for *Symeōn* the patriarch and the ancestor of Matthatiah; Niese, *Index*, p. 564. In the Jewish community of Egypt *Simōn* (never *Sym(e)ōn* before the Byzantine period) takes second place only after Sabbathai, being attested some thirty times; Tcherikover, pp. 28 and 232–3. To these should be added the three

[7] *Op. cit.*, 150–1.

[8] *Op. cit.*, 155.

'sages' of the *Letter of Aristeas* (#47, 48, 49). In the New Testament (Bauer, 1367) there are nine examples[9] and thirty-two on the ossuaries: Bene Ḥazir, line 1; Frey #1254, 1317, 1318, 1173 (*Simōnos*, Lydda), 1182 (read *Šm*'[*wn*], Gezer), Bethphage col. 1, line 10; Frey #1350, 1351 and 1352, 1354, 1355 (*Simōnos*, twice), 1194 (er-Ram), 1191 (Michmas), 1292–1297–1299, 1298, 1411, 1384, 1246; *Kedem* II, pp. 24–5, n. 5; p. 31, n. 29; *AJA* 1947, pp. 351 ff., n. 1 and 2; *LA* VII, pp. 232 ff., n. 3 (twice), 4, 6, 10, 12; *PAM* 36. 911 (published by Sukenik in the *Kraus-Festschrift*) and unpublished: *PAM* 32.314 (Ḥizmeh), 42.125 (*Simōnos*) and finally three others described in the archives of the PAM of which two are mentioned below under no. 9.[10]

This gives some indication of the places where the occurrences of the name Simon can be found. Later on Milik gives a table in which he compares the number of occurrences of various Jewish names found in Egypt, Josephus, the Palestinian ossuaries, the New Testament and the new texts from Murabba'ât.[11] A glance at this table reveals that *Simon* or *Symeon* heads the list as the most frequently attested among the following not unusual names of the period in question: Joseph, Salome, Judah, Mary, John, Eleazar, Jesus, Martha, Matthias, Sapphira, Jonathe, Zachary, Azariah, Jairus, Menahem. In each group of texts listed the name most frequently attested is Simon (in some form or other).[12] Finally, Milik notes: 'The frequency of proper names on the ossuaries is, then, practically identical

[9] As a matter of fact, there are nine instances in the New Testament spelled *Simōn*; see W. F. Arndt and F. W. Gingrich, *A Greek-English Lexicon of the New Testament and Other Early Christian Literature* (Chicago, 1957) 758. But to these should be added two instances of *Symeōn* (Lk 2:25, 34 and Acts 13:1, the former referring to the devout old man of Jerusalem, the latter to Simeon Niger, who is perhaps also the Simeon of Acts 15:14. See S. Giet, 'L'assemblée apostolique et le décret de Jérusalem. Qui était Siméon?', *RSR* 39 [1951] 203–20).

[10] B. Bagatti and J. T. Milik, *Gli scavi del 'Dominus Flevit'* (Monte Oliveto—Gerusalemme): Part I, La necropoli del periodo romano (Pubblicazioni dello Studium Biblicum Franciscanum XIII; Jerusalem, 1958) 76–7.

[11] *Ibid.*, 108.

[12] A slight qualification should be made here because in the column in which the instances from Murabba'ât are recorded, the total is given for Simon as '*ca* 14 + 7', i.e. 14 occurrences in Hebrew or Aramaic texts and 7

with that of the New Testament—which is natural because the majority of the graffiti date from the first half of the first century A.D.'[13]

To the foregoing evidence must likewise be added the occurrences of the name in the texts from the cave in the Wâdi Ḫabra (=Naḥal Ḥever), which likewise come from the time of the Second Revolt; so far we have learned the names of two of Bar Cochba's officers: Masabbalah bar Simon (*Mśblh br Šmʿwn*) and Simon bar Judah (*Šmʿwn br Yhwdh*).[14]

In all of the texts from Murabbaʿât or Wâdi Ḫabra it is, moreover, significant that Bar Cochba, who is frequently mentioned, is never referred to merely by his patronymic, ben/bar Kosibah, but always either as *Šmʿwn* or *Šmʿwn bn/br Ksbh* or *Šmʿwn nsyʾ Yśrʾl*.[15]

In view of such evidence it is difficult to agree with Roth's

---

occurrences in Greek texts. While the total is greater for Simon than for any other name, the name Joseph appears more frequently in the Greek texts, 9 times. A further slight modification is in order, for in checking the Hebrew and Aramaic texts of Murabbaʿât I have found 17 instances of persons with the name *Šmʿwn*, apart from the frequent mention of *Šmʿwn bn Kwsbh*, Bar Cochba himself. See P. Benoit, J. T. Milik and R. de Vaux, *Les Grottes de Murabbaʿât* (DJD 2; Oxford, 1961): 9 i 1 (*Šmʿwn br sk.* [ ]); 28 i–ii 9 (*Šmʿwn br Pnḥs*); 29:10 (*Šmʿwn br Šby* and *Šmʿwn br Zkryh*); 29 verso 4 (*Šmʿwn br Šby br H*[ ]—possibly the same person as the first one mentioned in 29:10); 30:9 (*Šmʿwn br Symy*): 31 i 4 (*Šm*[*ʿwn*]); 31 iv 2 ([*Š*]*mʿwn*); 33:2 (*Šmʿwn br Ḥnyn*); 39 iii 1 (*Šmʿwn br M.*[ ]); 41 i–iv 4 (*Šm*[*ʿw*]*n br* [*?*]); 41 i–iv 7 (*Šmʿwn*); 48:1 ([*Šmʿ*]*wn* [*bn?*]); 48:2 (*Šmʿ*[*wn*]); 73:3 ([*Š*]*mʿwn br YŠ*[ ]); 74:1 (*Šmʿwn*); 29 verso 6 (*Šmʿwn bn* . . [ ]).

[13] *Gli scavi* . . ., 108.

[14] See Y. Yadin, 'Expedition D', *IEJ* II (1961) 36–52, especially 44–5. Cf. 'New Discoveries in the Judean Desert', *BA* 24 (1961) 48.

[15] Even granting that the tradition preserved by Origen and a number of New Testament MSS. is worthless, that Barabbas' name was really Jesus Barabbas (i.e. *Yšwʿ br ʾbʾ*), is it not somewhat gratuitous to suggest that the first name of the brigand was really Simon? The question of the use of patronymics alone as the identification of Jews is a complicated one and has an old tradition behind it (Barrakkab, Barhadad, Bartholomew, Barsabba [Murabbaʿât 25 i 4]; cf. Acts 1:23; 15:22). See A. Alt, 'Menschen ohne Namen', *ArOr* 18 (1950) 9–24; reprinted in *Kleine Schriften zur Geschichte des Volkes Israel* (München, 1959) 3, 198–213.

conclusion that 'in the first century and perhaps for some time afterwards the use of the name Simon was deliberately avoided by Jews'. It seems rather that since Simon or Simeon was such a commonly used name, the patronymics or nicknames were frequently used as a means of distinguishing those who bore the name of the tribal patriarch of old. Even though we do not have a complete listing of all the names of Jewish males in the Roman period, the evidence which has come to light in the various areas seems all to point in the direction of the great frequency of the name Simon.

The names found on the Palestinian ossuaries and in the texts from Murabba'ât and the Wâdi Ḫabra are obviously not those of 'personalities' or 'well-known persons', aside possibly from the officers of Bar Cochba. The fact that ordinary people used the name Simon in this period argues against its prohibition or the avoidance of it out of any superstitious or patriotic motive. By the same token it seems idle to try to explain the 'change' of the name of the apostle from Simon to Peter as a reflection of this supposedly current tendency.[16]

A FURTHER DISCUSSION*

In his article on the name Simon (*HTR* 56 [1963] 1–5) Father Joseph A. Fitzmyer, S.J., assembles a number of instances to show that this 'is the most frequently used name for Jews of the period . . . of Roman domination'. From this he deduces that my suggestion (*HTR* 54 [1961] 91–7) that its use was deliberately avoided for some reason by Jews at this time (this perhaps explaining the change of the name of the Apostle Simon to Peter) can have no basis.

On the contrary, I am inclined to think that his investigation strongly supports my view; he seems to have misunderstood me, unless the inadequacies of language led me to express myself

[16] See further B. Lifshitz, 'Notes d'épigraphie grecque', *RB* 76 (1969) 92–8, especially 94 (#5, *Simōnos Barsemia*); T. Nöldeke, *Zeitschrift für Assyriologie* 20 (1907) 134.

* Originally published in *HTR* 57 (1964) 60–1.

awkwardly. For what I proposed was not that the name Simon (Simeon) was not applied at this period—i.e., was not given by Jewish parents to their children—but that, when given, there was a tendency for it not to be used, the patronymic, 'the son of . . .' being normally substituted.

Clearly in an official act, or on a tombstone, this would not have been the case. The number of funerary inscriptions recording persons officially named Simon is irrelevant, so long as we do not know how they were actually called at home and in the market-place. The recently discovered documents from the Engedi neighbourhood confirm what we already knew, that the leader of the Second Revolt was Simon; but from the literary sources already available it is certain that colloquially he was known as Bar Kosiba (or Bar Kochba). Similarly, we have positive evidence Simon Bar Giora, the leader of the last desperate resistance in Jerusalem in the siege of 69/70, was normally referred to as Bar Giora, and Rabbi Simeon ben Zoma a generation later as Ben Zoma, and so on. As I say in my article: when in this period a man was generally called by a patronymic of this type, and his *Eigenname* is known, that name in a majority of cases was Simon. The fact that it was so popular, as Father Fitzmyer has shown, may perhaps confirm my suggestion that it had patriotic associations, this being the reason for its avoidance in actual usage.

Cecil Roth

Dr Roth's note makes his position clearer. I shall leave to others the judgment whether I misunderstood what was originally written.

But the problem still remains. How do we know that 'there was a tendency for it (the name Simon) not to be used'? Granted, 'we do not know how they were actually called at home and in the market-place'. So we can only depend on the evidence available, not only in the usual literary sources, but in other material as well, which I tried to present. The name

Simon was omitted in several cases, as Dr Roth pointed out (*HTR* 54 [1961] 91–3). But does such an omission really support his contention of a 'tendency' to avoid the name in actual usage (possibly because it had patriotic associations)? Was the name really 'consistently eliminated' (p. 92)? Indeed, it is not the only name omitted in the list he cites (see his footnote 9). Perhaps the reason why it is the most frequently omitted name there is rather the fact that it was the name most frequently given and used. The use of the patronymic in place of it served as a means of distinguishing the many who bore the name, as has been already suggested (*HTR* 56 [1963] 5; see above, p. 110).

But if the evidence for the 'tendency' is slight, that for the application of it to the problem of Simon-Peter is even more so. Every instance cited by Dr Roth (pp. 91–3) shows that when Simon was omitted, a patronymic was used. If the Apostle Simon were called only Bar Jonah later on in his career, then there might be some parallelism. But after trying to build a case on the evidence of patronymics, how can one suddenly introduce 'or a nickname (such as "Kaipha" = Peter would have been)' (p. 96)?

I suspect that our disagreement is basically one of methodology and that neither of us has the same estimate of the sources used by the other.

6

THE SON OF DAVID TRADITION AND MT 22:41–46 AND PARALLELS*

Any discussion of the development of Tradition in its relation to Scripture should cope with examples of this relation in Scripture itself. The problem of Scripture and Tradition in the Christian Church developed in its own way once the canon of the New Testament was fixed. But there is a relationship between those realities which is manifest in the New Testament itself, particularly as Old Testament traditions are taken up and adapted to the formation of later Scriptures. Even if such New Testament examples are not in every respect comparable to instances of the later development of Christian doctrine, nevertheless they have facets which merit a renewed consideration for the light they shed on the contemporary problem.

One passage which lends itself readily to such a consideration is the debate about the Messiah as the son of David in Mt 22:41–46 and its parallels (Mk 12:35–37a; Lk 20:41–44). The figure of the Davidic Messiah expected in Judaism about the time of Christ was the product of a long tradition. However complicated its previous history was, it receives in the Synoptics a significant interpretation. We turn then to this episode as an example of an evolving tradition rooted in the Old Testament motif of the son of David.

* Originally published in *Concilium* (British Edition) 10/2 (1966) 40–6.

Mt 22:41–46	Mk 12:35–37a	Lk 20:41–44
[41]Now when the Pharisees were gathered together, Jesus asked them a question, [42]saying,	[35]And as Jesus taught in the temple, he said,	[41]But he said to them,
'What do you think of the Messiah? Whose son is he?' They said to him, 'The son of David.'	'How can the scribes say that the Messiah is the son of David?	'How can they say that the Messiah is the son of David?
[43]He said to them, 'How is it then that David, inspired by the Spirit, calls him Lord, saying,	[36]David himself, inspired by the Holy Spirit, declared,	[42]For David himself says in the book of Psalms,
[44]The Lord said to my Lord, Sit at my right hand, till I put your enemies under your feet?	The Lord said to my Lord, Sit at my right hand, till I put your enemies under your feet.	The Lord said to my Lord, Sit at my right hand, [43]till I make your enemies a stool for your feet.
[45]If David thus calls him Lord, how is he his son?' [46]And no one was able to answer him a word, nor from that day did any one dare to ask him any more questions.	[37]David himself calls him Lord; so how is he his son?'	[44]David thus calls him Lord; so how is he his son?'

This pericope forms part of the Synoptic account of the last days of Jesus in Jerusalem. In its earliest form (Mk 12) the passage records a Dominical saying, 'As Jesus taught in the temple, he said. . . .' In Mark there is scarcely any evidence of debate; and the setting is hardly different in Luke. But in Mt 22 the Gospel tradition has clothed the saying with controversy so that it rather resembles an apophthegm.[1] In any setting the substance of the saying is the same: Jesus questions the contemporary tradition about the Messiah as the Son of David, implying that the Davidic Messiah must be understood in some other way. Among others, R. Bultmann believes that the early Church, not Jesus himself, has made this identification of Jesus and the Son of David.[2] But V. Taylor has effectively shown that this saying cannot be wholly due to a community-formula-

[1] R. Bultmann, *The History of the Synoptic Tradition* (New York, 1963) 51, 137, 405 (*Die Geschichte der synoptischen Tradition* [4th ed.: Göttingen: Vandenhoeck and Ruprecht, 1958] 54, 145; Ergänzungsheft [3rd ed.] 22).

[2] R. Bultmann, *Theology of the New Testament* (London, 1956) I, 28. Similarly E. Klostermann, *Das Markusevangelium* (HNT 3; Tübingen, 1950) 129. B. H. Branscomb, *The Gospel of Mark* (Moffatt New Testament Commentary; London, 1937) 222–5.

tion, since the allusive character of the saying, half-concealing and half-revealing the 'messianic secret', is difficult to explain as the doctrinal belief of a community. It stands in contrast to the tone and frankness of such passages as Acts 2:34–36; 5:31; 10:42–43; Rom 1:2–4; etc.[3]

Before asking in what sense the saying is to be understood, we must review the prior tradition about David.

THE DAVIDIC TRADITION IN THE OLD TESTAMENT

Within the Old Testament itself the Davidic tradition apparently grew up independently of Israel's ancient *credo* derived from the early period of its salvation history. Only with the passage of time were the two traditions fused, in fact about the time of the exile and in such writers as Ezekiel, Second Isaiah, Haggai, Zechariah, and Nehemiah. Yahweh's intervention on behalf of David was at that time seen to be a continuation of the salvific deeds recalled in Israel's ancient *credo*.

The earliest tradition about David is embedded in the work of the Deuteronomist and concerns David's role in the story of the Ark of the Covenant (1 Sm 4:1–7, 11; 2 Sm 6:1–15, 17–20a), his accession to the throne (1 Sm 16:1–2; 2 Sm 5:25; 6:16, 20b–23; 9:1–13), his dynasty (2 Sm 7:1–29; 11:2–20, 26; 1 Kgs 1:1–2, 46), and his last words (2 Sm 23:1–7). At this stage David is depicted as the zealous worshipper of Yahweh (2 Sm 6:6–9), 'chosen' by him to rule over all Israel in place of Saul (2 Sm 6:21), and favoured by his word (1 Sm 25:31; 2 Sm 3:9–10; 5:2). David is the obedient servant whose respect for Yahweh is shown in his slaying of the Amalekite who raised his hand against Saul, Yahweh's Anointed. Yet Yahweh has not favoured David for himself alone; David is to rule over Israel and his kingly role affects all Israel. Yahweh's choice of David

[3] *The Gospel According to St Mark* (London, 1953) 493. See also R. P. Gagg, 'Jesus und die Davidssohnfrage: Zur Exegese von Markus 12. 35–37', *TZ* 7 (1951) 18–30; O. Cullmann, *The Christology of the New Testament* (2nd ed.; London, 1963) 132.

is, therefore, an event of corporate salvific significance for the history of Israel.[4]

Two passages in particular stress this aspect of David's role: the Oracle of Nathan (2 Sm 7:14–17) and the 'Last Words of David' (2 Sm 23:1–17). Nathan makes it clear that Yahweh's favour is not limited to David himself: 'When your days are fulfilled and you lie down with your fathers, I will raise up after you your offspring who shall come forth from your body; and I will establish its kingdom. He shall build a house for my name and I will establish his royal throne forever. I will be his father and he shall be my son' (2 Sm 7:12–14). And the significance of this oracle is seen in David's 'last words' in which the psalmist of Israel is hailed as 'the anointed of the God of Jacob' (2 Sm 23:1). David is explicitly called *māšîaḥ*, an anointed agent of Yahweh. The oracle is a 'covenant' made by Yahweh with the Davidic dynasty: 'For Yahweh has made with me an everlasting covenant' (23:5). The Davidic tradition is now framed in convenantal terms and rivals, as it were, the ancient covenant of Sinai. It thus gives Israel's traditions a new centre of gravity.

This basic tradition about David underwent development in the Royal Psalms, in the Prophets, and in post-exilic writings. In the psalms which mention David (Pss 18, 72, 89, 132, 144) his title of 'Anointed' is explicitly repeated (Ps 18:51; 89:39, 52 [cf. v. 20]; 132:10, 17). Ps 132:2 ascribes to him a more prominent role in the building of the temple; he is said to have made a *vow* to build it. Yahweh's promise in the oracle of Nathan becomes a divine *oath* (Ps 132:11; 89:4, 36–37, 50). But above all these Psalms stress the enduring and unshakable character of the Davidic dynasty (Ps 18:51; 89:5, 30, 37; 132:10–12). It will last for ever, and the very cultic hymns of the Psalter attest to its continuance. Ps 2, a royal psalm which does not mention David, promises universal dominion to a Davidic king. The king is Yahweh's 'Anointed', indeed his very son, 'You

[4] See S. Mowinckel, *He That Cometh* (Oxford, 1956). S. Amsler, *David, roi messie* (Cahiers theologiques 49; Neuchâtel, 1963). R. A. Carlson, *David, the Chosen King* (Stockholm, 1964).

are my son, today I have begotten you' (2:7). Another royal psalm, probably composed for the enthronement of some Davidic king, depicts him as one invited by Yahweh to sit at his right hand and to share his exalted, heavenly glory: 'The Lord says to my lord, "Sit at my right hand, till I make your enemies your footstool"' (Ps 110:1). Thus an intimate relationship between Yahweh and the anointed Davidic heir is established.

The continuance of the Davidic dynasty is assured at the time of the Syro-Ephraimite war, as Isaiah announces to Ahaz in a moment of impending doom the birth of a royal heir; 'a child' is to be born who will be a 'wonderful Counsellor, mighty God, everlasting Father, prince of peace', and will sit 'upon the throne of David' (Is 9:6–7). He will be 'a shoot from the stump of Jesse' (11:1). To Hezekiah the prophet eventually announces Yahweh's further message, 'I will defend this city to save it, for my own sake and for the sake of my servant David' (37:35).

As Jeremiah confronted the last of the Davidic kings before Nebuchadnezzar's invasion, he called Israel to a renewed fidelity to its ancient *credo*. But he juxtaposed to this appeal allusions to the Davidic tradition. He announced that the Davidic king Jehoiakim would 'have none (i.e., no heir) to sit upon the throne of David' (Jer 36:30); and yet the same prophet uttered the promise of a 'new covenant' and proclaimed that Israel would 'serve Yahweh their God and David their king, whom I will raise up for them' (30:9).

In Jeremiah's words there is a significant development, for 'David' is now regarded as a future occupant of the throne to be raised up by Yahweh. The ideal king will be a 'David'. 'Days are coming, says the Lord, when I will raise up for David a Righteous Branch; he shall reign as king and deal wisely and shall execute justice and righteousness in the land' (Jer 23:5). Salvation, justice, and righteousness are the qualities linked with the reign of the new son of David. Ezekiel's message is similarly reassuring in the wake of the destruction of Jerusalem:

'They shall be my people and I will be their God; my servant David shall be king over them and they shall all have one shepherd' (Ez 37:23–24).

Significant in this prophetic development of a future sense of 'David' is the complete absence of the title *māšîᵃḥ*. The word occurs but twice in the Prophets: once applied to Cyrus (Is 45:1), and once to the king or the nation (Hab 3:13). The prophets echo indeed the oracle of Nathan in some sense. But even though David was clearly hailed earlier as Yahweh's 'Anointed', they significantly do not speak of the 'coming of a Messiah'. They only announce the hope of a restored kingdom of David, because Yahweh has promised it.

In post-exilic times the Davidic tradition develops still further. A king no longer rules in Jerusalem, for foreign domination prevents this. Yet the Davidic lineage continues in Zerubbabel, the governor of Judah, who has been 'chosen' by Yahweh (Hag 2:23; see Zech 6:12–14). The significant post-exilic development of the Davidic tradition is seen in the Chronicler's work. Here the portrait of David is not only idealized, but the account of his reign is schematized. Though 1 Chr opens with genealogies beginning with Adam, the real history of Israel starts with the death of Saul and the accession of David (1 Chr 10). The Chronicler aims to depict what the ideal kingdom of Israel under God should be like and idyllically describes the reigns of David and Solomon, not as they were, but as they should have been. David is idealized and becomes the real founder of the temple and its cult. The perpetuity of David's reign is stressed (1 Chr 28:4).

In this connection the Chronicler's modifications of the Oracle of Nathan are significant:

2 Sm 7:12, 16	1 Chr 7:11, 14
I will raise up after you your offspring who shall come forth from your body. . . . Your house and your kingdom shall be made sure before me forever; your throne shall be established forever.	I will raise up after you your offspring, who shall be one of your own sons. . . . I will confirm him in my house and in my kingdom forever, and his throne shall be established forever.

Whereas in 2 Sm 'your offspring' (*zarʿᵃkā*) was used in a collective sense, the Chronicler employs it of a particular descendant in the Davidic line (*ʾ*^a^*šer yihyeh mibbānêkā*, lit., 'who shall be from among your sons'). Again, 'I will confirm *him* in *my* house and in *my* kingdom forever', a significant change from the original oracle. The shift makes it clear that a Davidic king to come will be Yahweh's representative in the restored Israelite theocracy. But once again we note the absence of the title *māšîaḥ* for the Davidic king. If David himself is so named in 2 Chr 6:42, this refers to the historic David, not to the ideal, expected Davidic ruler; but the word 'anointed' may here even refer to Solomon.

Finally, only in the second century B.C. apocalypse of Daniel is there explicit mention of an expected 'anointed prince' in Jerusalem: '. . . from the going forth of the word to restore and build Jerusalem to (the coming of) an Anointed One, a Prince, there shall be seven weeks' (Dn 9:25, *ʿad māšîaḥ nāgîd*). Who is this anointed prince or 'Messiah'? A Son of David? Probably. Yet this occurrence of the word in Daniel is part of a larger, complex picture of messianic expectations which emerge in the second century B.C.

THE DAVIDIC MESSIAH IN LATER JUDAISM

That Dn 9:25–26 fed the Jewish hopes of a restored kingdom of God under the leadership of an ideal king, even called 'the Messiah', can be seen in the literature of Qumran. 1QS 9:11 clearly alludes to Dn 9:25, 'until the coming of a Prophet and the Messiahs of Aaron and Israel'.[5] Both the Danielic text and the Qumran literature reflect this stage in the development of Jewish beliefs when it is legitimate to speak of the coming of 'a (*or* the) Messiah', or even of 'the Messiahs'. Granted that one should beware of reading into these terms all the connotations of New Testament Christology, it would be hypercritical to insist at this stage that one should simply speak of 'Anointed Ones'.[6] For it is precisely these texts which show that a genuine

[5] For a bibliography on Qumran Messianism, see my article below, p. 130, n. 7.

[6] Cf. J. Carmignac, *Les textes de Qumran* (Paris, 1963) II, 13; L. Silber-

Old Testament theme of an anointed agent of Yahweh had developed into the expectation of a Messiah—and, in the specific case in which we are interested, of a Davidic Messiah. (The expected Prophet and the priestly Messiah, or Messiah of Aaron, do not concern us here.)

In the Qumran literature the Davidic Messiah is called the 'Messiah of Israel' (1QSa 2:14, 20; cf. 1QS 9:11; CD 20:1). In 4QPatrBles 2:4 (a sort of commentary on Gn 49:10) we read of the coming of 'the Messiah of Righteousness, the shoot of David' (*'d bw' mšyḥ hṣdq ṣmḥ dwyd*), for to him and to his seed has been given the royal mandate over his people for everlasting generations.[7] Important too is the interpretation of the Oracle of Nathan in 4QFlor 1:11–13.[8] Having quoted 2 Sm 7:11–14 in abbreviated form, the author comments, 'This is the Shoot of David who is to arise with the Interpreter of the Law who [will arise] in Zi[on in the l]ast days; as it is written, *And I will raise up the booth of David that is fallen.* That is the booth of David which is fall[en and after]wards he will arise to save Israel.' A salvific mission is thus clearly associated with the Davidic Messiah. One could also cite 4QpIs[a] 8–10:11–17, which relates Is 11:1 to the 'Shoot of David', and 4QTest 9–13, which applies part of the oracle of Balaam (Nm 24:15–17) to the Davidic Messiah.[9] See also *Enoch* 48:10; 52:4. Qumran literature thus attests the full flowering of an Old Testament tradition about David. The title *māšîaḥ* is given to an ideal son of David, expected in the 'end of days'. Elements of that belief sown like seeds in the Old Testament gradually grew and matured into an extra-biblical tradition intimately associated with the biblical books. So far no text has turned up in the

---

man, 'The Two Messiahs of the Manual of Discipline', *VT* 5 (1955) 77–82; M. Smith, 'What is Implied by the Variety of Messianic Figures?', *JBL* 78 (1959) 66–72.

[7] See J. M. Allegro, *JBL* 75 (1956) 174–5.

[8] See *JBL* 77 (1958) 353; cf. 4Q*174* 1–2 i 11–13 (DJD 5, 53).

[9] See *JBL* 75 (1956) 180–1, 183–4; Cf. DJD 5, 13–14, 58, and see my comments above, p. 84.

Qumran caves giving this future Davidic Messiah the title 'Son of God', although it is possible that one text speaks of God 'begetting the Messiah' (1QSa 2:11–12).[10] Again, no text yet applies to him the words of Ps 2:7 or the words of Ps 110.

Outside of Qumran but still in pre-Christian times the expectation of a son of David as a Messiah is also attested in the (probably Pharisaic) *Psalms of Solomon*: 'Raise up, O Lord, unto them their king, the son of David . . . that he may reign over Israel thy servant. . . . There shall be no unrighteousness in their midst in his days, for all shall be holy and their king the Anointed of the Lord' (17:23, 36; see 18:6, 8).[11] This expectation is echoed in the later rabbinical tradition. Though we can never be sure how early the elements of this rabbinical tradition are, it is at least a legitimate continuation of an understanding of the Davidic tradition well attested among the Jews of Palestine in pre-Christian times.[12]

[10] See D. Barthélemy and J. T. Milik, *Qumran Cave I* (DJD 1) 110, 117. On the problem of the reading see my remarks on p. 153 below. Though no published text from the Qumran caves uses the title 'Son of God' for the Messiah, there are reports that the title does occur in unpublished Qumran Cave 4 material. A. J. B. Higgins (*CJT* 6 [1960] 202, n. 12) writes, 'Prof. D. N. Freedman, however, in a private communication from Jerusalem, kindly informs me that the (Davidic) Messiah is called the Son of God in unpublished Qumran material.' Again, A. D. Nock (*Gnomon* 33 [1961] 584) speaks of unpublished Qumran evidence for 'the use of royal ideology, stating the Messiah's relation to God in terms of sonship'. These rumours refer to an Aramaic text acquired by the Palestine Archaeological Museum in July 1958, which is apparently part of J. T. Milik's Pseudo-Daniel fragments. Aramaic phrases for 'the son of God' and 'the son of the Most High' (cf. Lk 1:32, 35) are found in it (see *TS* 25 [1964] 429). But we shall have to await Milik's publication of *Qumran Cave IV* in the DJD series to get the text and to assess it. It is not yet clear that the title is given to a messianic figure.

[11] In this text we meet for the first time the title, Son of David, used in connection with the expectations of Palestinian Jews. See further E. Lohse, 'Der König aus Davids Geschlecht: Bemerkungen zur messianischen Erwartung der Synagoge', *Abraham unser Vater: Juden und Christen im Gespräch über die Bibel: Festschrift für Otto Michel* (Leiden, 1963) 337–45.

[12] In this regard one could cite the Targum on the Prophets, to Is 11:1; Midrash Ps 18, #36; Ps 21, #1. See further Str-B 4, 452–65.

THE SON OF DAVID QUESTION IN THE SYNOPTICS

Against the background of such a tradition and its development the words of Jesus in Mt 22:41–46 must now be judged. In conversation with the Pharisees Jesus raises a question about the Davidic origin of the Messiah.[13] Having posed it, he raises the problem of Ps 110: How could David, the reputed and inspired author of that Psalm, be the father of the messianic king whom he calls 'lord'? 'The Lord (*Yahweh, Kyrios*) said to my lord (*la'ᵃdōnî, tō kyriō mou* [=the anointed king]), "Sit at my right hand. . . ."'

The explanation of this saying of Jesus is not easy and has taken various forms in the history of its exegesis. We single out three general interpretations. (1) J. Klausner and others have thought that Jesus' argumentation implies that he is calling in question the Davidic origin of the Messiah. 'Jesus had already declared himself Messiah. But the Messiah was to be the *son of David*, whereas Jesus was a Galilean and the son of Joseph the carpenter! How could he be the Messiah? To evade this serious difficulty Jesus must find a passage of Scripture according to which the Messiah need not necessarily be the Son of David; and like an expert Pharisee he finds it.'[14] (2) Many ancient and modern commentators have understood his question to imply that the Messiah is something more than a mere son of David, having a more exalted, transcendent origin than David, seeing that the latter calls him 'lord'. Jesus would insinuate thereby a secret about himself, but no further specification is made in the text.[15] (3) J. Schniewind and others press beyond the second interpretation in specifying that Jesus is in fact referring to the vision of the 'Son of Man' in Dn 7:13. Jesus is indeed the son of

[13] One might be tempted to think that the question arose out of the Essene belief in two Messiahs, one of Aaron, the other of Israel. There is, however, no evidence that such a background to the question was involved here. The problem is wholly concerned with the Davidic Messiah.

[14] *Jesus of Nazareth: His Life, Times and Teaching* (New York, 1926) 320. See also C. G. Montefiore, *The Synoptic Gospels* (London, 1909) I, 290–2.

[15] E.g. V. Taylor, *op. cit.*, 492; A. H. McNeile, *The Gospel According to St Matthew* (London, 1915) 328.

David, but he is more; he is the Son of Man in a unique sense.[16]

Regarding these interpretations several points should be noted. The first explanation is generally abandoned because it is inexplicable how Jesus would have intended to attack a well-founded belief in the Davidic origin of the Messiah (see above for the Old Testament texts). The New Testament gives no evidence of such an intention; indeed, such a denial of the Scriptures would have given his opponents ground for the charge against him (cf. Jn 8:5). Again, it is really farfetched to maintain that Jesus did not know that he was of Davidic lineage.[17] An early level of New Testament tradition attests it (Rom 1:3), and ostensibly without any apologetic intent. It is also echoed in later levels (Mk 10:47–48; Mt 1:1; Lk 3:31; 2 Tm 2:8). Would not Jesus' denial of the Davidic origin of the Messiah have left some other trace in view of the New Testament stress on his role as one who fulfilled the Old Testament?

The real choice lies today between the second and the third explanations. Here I think a distinction must be made. For it is not unlikely that the evangelists, especially Matthew with his secondary additions to the episode, was implying something like the third explanation in recording it.[18] But the question is legitimately asked whether Jesus himself in the original *Sitz im Leben* of the incident implied all that the early Church understood by it in the light of its Easter and Pentecostal faith.

It is not impossible that the Synoptic accounts of this episode represent only a torso of the full account. Since the rest of the dialogue resembles similar altercations with Pharisees (cf. Mk 2:9, 17–19; 3:4), it may be that it was they who asked the first

[16] *Das Evangelium nach Markus* (10th ed.; Göttingen, 1963) 164–5. Cf. P. Bonnard, *L'évangile selon saint Matthieu* (Commentaire du Nouveau Testament; Neuchâtel, 1963) 330–1.

[17] See W. Michaelis, 'Die Davidssohnschaft Jesu als historisches und kerygmatisches Problem', *Der historische Jesus und der kerygmatische Christus* (ed. H. Ristow and K. Matthaie; 2nd edition; Berlin, 1961) 317–30, especially 321–4.

[18] *Ibid.*, 318–19; cf. B.M.F. van Iersel, *'Der Sohn' in den synoptischen Jesusworten* (NTSup 3; Leiden, 1964) 171–3.

question, something like, 'You too teach, don't you, that the Messiah is David's son?' And rather than answer it with 'yes' or 'no', Jesus posed a counter-question (cf. Mt 22:17). Jesus' answer then would have had the form of a scribal debate, aimed more at meeting the Pharisees on the level of haggadic scriptural interpretation than of suggesting that he was personally of some other than Davidic origin.[19] The question is one of emphasis, for the latter aspect cannot be fully excluded.

The background of such debate has been plausibly suggested by D. Daube, who has noted in Mt 22 four types of exegetical questions often grouped also in rabbinical tradition.[20] There is the Pharisees' question about tribute to Caesar (15–22), the Sadducees' question about levirate marriage and the resurrection (23–33), the Pharisees' question about the great commandment of the Law (34–40), and finally the Pharisees' question about the Messiah, son of David (41–46). These questions correspond respectively to the rabbinical grouping of four questions concerning *hokmāh* ('wisdom', i.e., halakic interpretation of legal texts), *bōrût* ('vulgarity', i.e., questions designed to ridicule a belief), *derek 'ereṣ* ('the way of the land', i.e., the principle of moral conduct), and *haggādāh* ('legend', i.e., the interpretation of biblical passages with apparent contradictions). In this case, Jesus would be propounding a *haggādāh* question arising from the contradiction of the Messiah as David's son and David's lord. It implies that both ideas are correct: the Messiah is David's son (in his earthly appearance), but also David's Lord.[21] We cannot be certain about this because the passage is so cryptic. It is not impossible that he also implied in his answer[22]

[19] Cf. R. P. Gagg, *op. cit.*, 24–9. I would not necessarily agree with all the individual details of this article.

[20] *The New Testament and Rabbinic Judaism* (London, 1956) 158–63. In quoting Daube, I do not mean to imply that he equates this four-question structure with Jesus' ministry itself; it may be due to the evangelists, as he suggests.

[21] See J. Jeremias, *Jesus' Promise to the Nations* (SBT 24; London, 1958) 53.

[22] See O. Cullman, *op. cit.*, 132–3.

that the Messiah was therefore less involved politically than the common belief depicted him to be.

At any rate, a more developed stage of the Son of David tradition developed with the writing of the Synoptic Gospels. As the evangelists incorporated this episode into their Gospels, it was almost certainly with a view to exploiting the nuances of the title *kyrios* and applying to Jesus the Messiah the words of Ps 110:1. By that time *kyrios*, used of Jesus, carried with it the clear suggestion that he was somehow on a par with Yahweh of the Old Testament. The use, moreover, of Ps 110:1 elsewhere in the New Testament clearly emphasizes Jesus' exaltation to Lordship and heavenly glory (see Mk 16:19; 1 Cor 15:25; Eph 1:20; Col 3:1; Heb 8:1; 10:12, 13; 12:2), and at times stands in contrast to his Davidic relationship (Acts 2:29–35; 13:23–39; Heb 1:3–13).[23]

In this regard three things should be noted: (1) It is highly questionable that the Davidic Messiah was given the title of Son of Man in pre-Christian times.[24] It is unlikely therefore that Jesus himself was referring to a well-known identification of the Messiah in his cryptic question. (2) The disciples, as depicted in the earliest Gospel strata, apparently did not make this equation during the earthly ministry of Jesus.[25] (3) Even though Ps 110 has no clear reference to the Son of Man or, most likely, even to the ideal and expected Davidic Messiah, these links are plausibly traced to Jesus himself. The allusion to Ps 110 in the trial scene (Mt 26:64 par.) suggests this and undoubtedly should be regarded as the springboard for the further development of the Son of David tradition in the Synoptics.[26] The term of this development, climaxing in Jesus' glorious exaltation and divine sonship, receives explicit formulation in *Ep. Barnabae* 12, 10,

[23] See E. Lövestamm, 'Die Davidssohnfrage', *SEA* 27 (1962) 72–82.

[24] See H. H. Rowley, 'The Suffering Servant and the Davidic Messiah', *The Servant of the Lord and other Essays on the Old Testament* (3rd ed.; Oxford, 1965) 82–4.

[25] *Ibid.*, 84

[26] See, however, N. Perrin, 'Mark XIV. 62: The End Product of a Christian Pesher Tradition', *NTS* 12 (1965–66) 150–5.

when Ps 110:1 is quoted in support of the belief that Jesus was 'not the son of a man, but the son of God'.

Thus the Davidic Messiah is a prime example of a biblical motif which developed in a tradition, even extrabiblically attested, but which was never completely divorced from its biblical roots. It grew and evolved beyond the limits of the Old Testament assertions and received a strong further impetus in Jesus' debate with the Pharisees over the Davidic origin of the Messiah.[27]

[27] See further A. Suhl, 'Der Davidssohn in Matthäus-Evangelium', *ZNW* 59 (1968) 57–81; E. Lohse, '*Huios David*', *TWNT* 8, 482–92.

7

THE ARAMAIC 'ELECT OF GOD' TEXT FROM QUMRAN CAVE 4*

A fcw years ago there was on display in the U.S.A. a group of Dead Sea Scrolls, lent by the Department of Antiquities of the Hashemite Kingdom of Jordan to the Smithsonian Institution of Washington, D.C. Under the direction of Dr Gus Van Beek, the curator of the section for Old World Archaeology, the Smithsonian Institution handsomely mounted the fourteen texts and other materials from the excavated Qumran caves and the community centre of Khirbet Qumran. The exhibit was sent round the country for display in various museums.[1]

The most important text in the exhibit was undoubtedly the Psalms Scroll from Qumran Cave 11, published by Dr J. A. Sanders, of Union Theological Seminary.[2] However, another piece in the exhibit is of no little interest to students both of the New Testament and of Jewish Messianism in the last two cen-

* Originally published in *CBQ* 27 (1965) 348–72.

[1] Its itinerary: Washington, D.C. (Smithsonian Institution), Feb. 28–Mar. 21, 1965; Philadelphia, Pa. (University of Pennsylvania Museum), Apr. 3–25; Berkeley, Cal. (Lowie Museum, University), May 8–30; Los Angeles, Cal. (Claremont Graduate School), June 12–July 8; Omaha, Nebr. (Joslyn Art Museum), July 17–Aug. 8; Baltimore, Md. (Walters Art Gallery), Aug. 21–Sept. 19; Ottawa, Ont. (National Museum of Canada); London, Engl. (British Museum); Jordan.

[2] *Psalms Scroll of Qumran Cave 11* (DJD 4; Oxford: Clarendon Press, 1965). Other publications: J. A. Sanders, 'The Scroll of Psalms (11QPss) from Cave 11: A Preliminary Report', *BASOR* 165 (1962) 11–15; 'Ps 151 in 11QPss', *ZAW* 75 (1963) 73–86; 'Two Non-Canonical Psalms in 11QPs[a]', *ZAW* 76 (1964) 57–75. P. W. Skehan, 'The Apocryphal Psalm 151', *CBQ*

turies B.C. and the first century A.D., because it mentions an 'Elect of God'. It is to a reconsideration of this text that we turn our attention.

The text was published by M. l'abbé Jean Starcky in a collection of recondite essays commemorating the fiftieth anniversary of the school of Ancient Oriental Languages of the Institut Catholique de Paris. It was labelled by him as 'an Aramaic Messianic Text from Qumran Cave 4' and given the siglum 4QMess ar.[3] But the title is a 'come-on' which excites our curiosity, as did the titles of some earlier articles on Qumran texts. For the text is unfortunately very poorly preserved and has been deteriorating still more in the Palestine Archaeological Museum since its arrival there in 1952. One enigmatic phrase in it should have been reason enough for the early publication of the text, since it bears on the question of God's begetting of

25 (1963) 407–9; 'A Broken Acrostic and Psalm 9', *CBQ* 27 (1965) 1–5. W. H. Brownlee, 'The 11Q Counterpart to Ps 151, 1–5', *RQ* 4 (1963) 379–87. J. Carmignac, 'La forme poétique du Ps 151 de la grotte 11', *RQ* 4 (1963) 371–8. I. Rabinowitz, 'The Alleged Orphism of 11QPss 18.3–12', *ZAW* (1964) 193–200. A. Dupont-Sommer, 'Notes qoumraniennes', *Semitica* 15 (1965) 71–8. J. Strugnell, 'More Psalms of "David"', *CBQ* 27 (1965) 207–16. M. Delcor, 'Zum Psalter von Qumran', *BZ* 10 (1966) 15–29. J. A. Sanders, 'Variorum in the Psalms Scroll (11QPs[a])', *HTR* 59 (1966) 83–94. J. Strugnell, 'Notes on the Text and Transmission of the Apocryphal Psalms 151, 154 (=Syr. II) and 155 (=Syr. III)', *HTR* 59 (1966) 257–81. Y. Yadin, 'Another Fragment (E) of the Psalms Scroll from Qumran Cave 11 (11QPs[a])', *Textus* 5 (1966) 1–10. J. A. Sanders, *The Dead Sea Psalms Scroll* (Ithaca, N.Y.: Cornell Univ. Press, 1967). R. Polzin, 'Notes on the Dating of the Non-Massoretic Psalms of 11QPs[a]', *HTR* 60 (1967) 468–76. R. Meyer, 'Die Septuaginta-Fassung von Psalm 151:1–5 als Ergebnis einer dogmatischen Korrektur', *Das ferne und nahe Wort* (ed. F. Maass; *BZAW* 105; Berlin: Töpelmann, 1967) 164–72. A. Hurvitz, 'The Language and Date of Psalm 151 from Qumran', *Sepher Sukenik: Eretz Israel* 8 (Jerusalem: Israel Exploration Society, 1967) 82–7. M. Delcor, 'L'hymne à Sion du rouleau des Psaumes de la grotte 11 de Qumrân (11QPs[a])', *RQ* 6 (1967–68) 71–88. D. Lührmann, 'Ein Weisheitspsalm aus Qumran (11QPs[a] XVIII)', *ZAW* 80 (1968) 87–8.

[3] 'Un texte messianique araméen de la grotte 4 de Qumrân', *Ecole des langues orientales anciennes de l'Institut Catholque de Paris: Mémorial du cinquantenaire 1914–1964* (Travaux de l'Institut Catholique de Paris 10; Paris: Bloud et Gay, 1964) 51–66.

the Messiah.[4] Because this Aramaic text clearly bears the phrase *bḥyr 'lh'* in a context that has something to do with birth, one can understand how Starcky would be led to describe it as 'de caractère à la fois astrologique et messianique'.[5] But the question arises whether it really has anything to do with a Messiah or with an astrological horoscope.

Moreover, it will be recalled that *ho eklektos tou theou*, the exact Greek translation of the Aramaic *bḥyr 'lh'*, is applied to Jesus in some MSS. of Jn 1:34, 'I myself have seen it and have borne witness that this is God's Chosen One'. Though the best MSS. read *ho huios tou theou*, the reading *ho eklektos tou theou* has been preferred by the *NEB*, *La Bible de Jérusalem*, A. Loisy, A. von Harnack, R. Schnackenburg, and R. E. Brown.[6] A few verses later Jesus is given the title *Messias* by Andrew (1:41). The collocation of these titles, 'Elect of God' and 'Messiah', might suggest that the former was an exclusive title for the latter, and that therefore the mention of the Elect of God in this text refers to one of the Messiahs expected at Qumran. An inferior reading in Lk 23:35 has the phrase, 'the Messiah, the Elect of God' (Peshitta, Syr^{sin}, C*) instead of the more usual wording, 'God's Messiah, the Elect One'. However, it is so weakly attested that it scarcely merits the textual critic's attention.

I. QUMRAN MESSIANISM

But this text is important not only because it supplies an extra-biblical attestation of the individual use of the title 'Elect of

[4] See 1QSa 2:11–12 (DJD 1, 110), and further comments below (see p. 153).

[5] *Op. cit.*, 51.

[6] The reading *ho huios tou theou* is found in P^{66}, P^{75}, S^{c}, B, c, f, l, q, vg, whereas *ho eklektos tou theou* is read in Sinaiticus (prima manus), P^{5} (probably), a few MSS. of the *Vetus latina* (e, ff^{2}), the Curetonian and Sinaitic Syriac versions, and is supported by Ambrose. The modern editors who prefer to read *ho eklektos* do so in the conviction that it is more probable that this reading was changed to *ho huios* than vice versa. Moreover, *ho eklektos* is more in harmony with what seems to have been the early Gospel tradition about the heavenly voice at Jesus' baptism (cf. Mk 1:11; Mt 3:17, which echoes Is 42:1). Cf. Lk 23:35; 9:35.

God', thus illustrating Jn 1:34, but also because it has been related to the larger question of Qumran messianism. J. Starcky discussed the relevance of the text to this larger question in an important article published under the title, 'The Four Stages of Messianism at Qumran'.[7] It is well for us to give a brief summary of his position in this article first, because it will serve as a background to our discussion. This article is, indeed, a significant contribution to the study of Qumran messianism, even if some details in his reconstruction are open to question.

The four separate stages which Starcky distinguished in the messianism of Qumran correspond in general to those periods which have been distinguished by the archaeologists and palaeographers who have worked on the Qumran material. Starcky speaks of the Maccabean period (equalling the archaeological phase Ia), the Hasmonean period (equalling the archaeological phase Ibα), the period of Pompey and Caesar (equalling the archaeological phase Ibβ), and finally the Herodian period (equalling the archaeological phase II).

[7] 'Les quatres étapes du messianisme à Qumran', *RB* 70 (1963) 481–505. Beware of the résumé in *NTA* 8 (1963–64) 430 (#1185). Older discussions of Qumran messianism can be found in the following: G. R. Beasley Murray, 'The Two Messiahs in the Testaments of the Twelve Patriarchs', *JTS* 48 (1947) 1–12. M. Black, 'The Messiah of the Testament of Levi XVIII', *ExpT* 60 (1948–49) 321–2; 61 (1949–50) 157–8. R. E. Brown, 'The Messianism of Qumran', *CBQ* 19 (1957) 53–82; 'The Teacher of Righteousness and the Messiah(s)', *The Scrolls and Christianity* (ed. M. Black; SPCK Theological Collections 11; London, 1969) 37–44, 109–12. M. Burrows, 'The Messiahs of Aaron and Israel (DSD IX, 11)', *ATR* 34 (1952) 202–6; J. S. Croatto, 'De messianismo qumranico', *VD* 35 (1957) 279–86; 344–60. E. L. Ehrlich, 'Ein Beitrag zur Messiaslehre der Qumransekte', *ZAW* 58 (1956) 234–43. J. Gnilka, 'Die Erwartung des messianischen Hohenpriesters in den Schriften von Qumran und im Neuen Testament', *RQ* 2 (1959–60) 395–426. R. Gordis, 'The "Begotten" Messiah in the Qumran Scrolls', *VT* 7 (1957) 191–4. A. J. B. Higgins, 'The Priestly Messiah', *NTS* 13 (1966–67) 211–39. K. G. Kuhn, 'Die beiden Messias Aarons und Israels', *NTS* 1 (1954–55) 168–79; translated and adapted in K. Stendahl, *The Scrolls and the New Testament* (New York: Harper, 1957) 54–64; 'Die beiden Messias in den Qumrantexten und die Messiasvorstellung in der rabbinischen Literatur', *ZAW* 70 (1958) 200–8. W. S. LaSor, '"The Messiahs of Aaron and

Starcky discusses the various Qumran texts which come from these periods and traces the development of the messianic expectations of the Qumran sect through them.

In the Maccabean period the Righteous Teacher arose, and his reform-activity got under way in the time of Jonathan who became High Priest *c.* 152 B.C. Starcky follows J. T. Milik and G. Vermes in identifying the persecuting Wicked Priest of the *Pesharim* on *Habakkuk* and *Ps 37* with Jonathan. The Righteous Teacher, whose reform-activity began after the sect's first twenty years of amorphous existence, is regarded as the author of the *Thanksgiving Psalms* and of the *Manual of Discipline*. But the oldest copy of the latter, as yet unpublished, is 4QS^{e} which dates from the end of the second century B.C. This copy of the *Manual of Discipline* lacks the long paragraph which runs from 1QS 8:15b to 9:11 (from *l'śwt* to *wyśr'l*).[8] Hence the oldest copy of the *Manual of Discipline* never had the passage mentioning the advent of a Prophet and the Messiahs of Aaron and Israel—i.e., it lacked the crucial sentence, 'They shall swerve

Israel"', *VT* 6 (1956) 425–49; 'The Messianic Idea in Qumran', *Studies Presented to A. A. Neuman* (Leiden: Brill, 1962) 343–64. R. B. Laurin, 'The Problem of the Two Messiahs in the Qumran Scrolls', *RQ* 4 (1963) 39–52. J. Liver, 'The Doctrine of the Two Messiahs in Sectarian Literature in the Time of the Second Commonwealth', *HTR* 52 (1959) 149–85. K. Schubert, 'Der alttestamentliche Hintergrund der Vorstellung von den beiden Messiassen im Schrifttum von Chirbet Qumran', *Judaica* 12 (1956) 24–8; 'Die Messiaslehre in den Texten von Chirbet Qumran', *BZ* 1 (1957) 177–97; 'Zwei Messiasse aus dem Regelbuch von Chirbet Qumran', *Judaica* 11 (1955) 216–35. L. H. Silberman, 'The Two "Messiahs" of the Manual of Discipline', *VT* 5 (1955) 77–82. K. Smyth, 'The Dead Sea Scrolls and the Messiah', *Studies* 45 (1956) 1–14. L. Stefaniak, 'Messianische oder eschatologische Erwartungen in der Qumransekte?', *Festschrift J. Schmid* (Regensburg: Pustet, 1962) 294–302. N. Wieder, 'The Doctrine of the Two Messiahs among the Karaites', *JJS* 6 (1955) 14–25. A. S. van der Woude, *Die messianischen Vorstellungen der Gemeinde von Qumran* (Studia semitica neerlandica 3; Assen: van Gorcum, 1957); 'Le Maître de Justice et les deux messies de la communauté de Qumran', *La secte de Qumran et les origines chrétiennes* (RechBib 4; Bruges: Desclée de Brouwer, 1959) 121–34.

[8] See J. T. Milik, *RB* 67 (1960) 413: 'Dans S^{e}, sur la ligne correspondante, *byd Mšḥ* est suivi immédiatement par IX 12ss.'

from no counsel of the Law to walk in all the stubbornness of their hearts, but shall be guided by the primitive precepts by which the men of the community were first instructed, until there will come a prophet and the Messiahs of Aaron and Israel.' Furthermore, though in the *Thanksgiving Psalms* the term *nēṣer* occurs, 'a shoot, sprout' (1QH 6:15; 7:19; 8:6, 8, 10), it does not refer to the 'scion of David', but to the Qumran community, regarded as a 'plantation'. It alludes not to Is 11:1, but to Is 60:21. The Righteous Teacher has gathered up a shoot from the dried-up trunk of Israel and transplanted it to the desert to bring forth a plantation, the community of the true Israel. Again, the reference in 1QH 3:9–10 to the 'Wonderful Counsellor' of Is 9:5 refers not to an individual, but in some way to the Qumran community (to the *'ṣt hyḥd* of 1QS). The upshot of all this is that in the texts which come from the early period, when the Righteous Teacher was still active, we find no titles used of himself; there is no evidence that he considered himself a 'messiah', nor did he even await one. The Righteous Teacher was a leader in the line of the prophets like Moses or a reformer like Ezra, but not a Messiah, 'car il n'attendait pas de Messie' (p. 487). In other words, in the earliest Qumran texts one is hard put to discern any sort of messianic expectation.

This expectation, however, is detected in the second or Hasmonean period, when either toward the end of the reign of John Hyrcanus or the beginning of that of Alexander Jannaeus a new generation of Essenes emerges. This new generation was undoubtedly influenced by the entrance into the community of persecuted Pharisees. Toward the end of the second century B.C. a Pharisaic influence had previously been noted.[9] From this period come the copy of the *Manual of Discipline* from Cave 1 (1QS, dated palaeographically to the beginning of the first century B.C.), the appendices to it (1 QSa, 1QSb) and the *4QTestimonia*. Starcky attributes to the scribe who composed

[9] See J. T. Milik, *Ten Years of Discovery in the Wilderness of Judaea* (SBT 26; London: SCM, 1959) 87–93.

the *Testimonia* those additions which were made to the original text of the *Manual of Discipline.*

Now it is significant that in these texts of the second period we find the full-blown Messianic expectations which we have come to identify with the Essenes of Qumran: the advent of a Prophet and of the Messiahs of Aaron and Israel (cf. 1QS 9:11). *4QTestimonia* (in which OT texts are quoted in a *catena*: Dt 5:28–29 and 18:18–19; Nm 24:15–17; and Dt 33:8–11) refers to the prophet, a political Messiah, and a priestly Messiah.[10] In 1QSa 2:11–12, 14, 20 the Messiah of Israel and a Priest are mentioned, and in 1QSb there is a blessing for the High Priest (1:21–3:21) which precedes that of the Prince of the Congregation (5:20–29). Under Pharisaic influence the early views of the priestly nucleus of the community were modified and the expectation of a Messiah grew. To this same period Starcky relates the basic form of the *Testaments of the Twelve Patriarchs* with its frequent mention of the Messiahs of Levi (priestly) and of Judah (Davidic). In fact, he thinks that both *Jubilees* and the *Testaments of the Twelve Patriarchs* (in its original form composed by a Pharisaic author) prepared the way for the author of 1QSa to add the paragraph in 1QS 8:15–9:11. Starcky further relates to this period a text as yet unpublished: 4QAhA, which he claims has to do with 'a suffering Messiah in a perspective opened by the Servant Songs' (p. 492). He claims that this text depicts the Messiah of Aaron as the Servant of Yahweh.

From the Pompeian period (63–37 B.C.) Starcky maintains that we have the messianic references found in the *Damascus Document.* This text alludes to Pompey in mentioning 'the head of the kings of Yawan who comes to wreak his vengeance on them' (CD 8:11–12=19:24–25). But in the oldest copy of the *Damascus Document* which is the unpublished 4QD^{b} dated palaeographically to 75–50 B.C., there is reference to a flight of the Essenes to Damascus camps. Also in this text we see the two Messiahs become *one*: 'the Messiah of Aaron and Israel' (CD

[10] On this text and its messianic references, see my remarks above, pp. 83–4.

19:10–11; 20:1; 12:23; 14:19). In the passage of 4QD[b] which corresponds to CD 14:19 the singular of 'Messiah' is found (*'d 'mwd mšyḥ 'hrwn wyśr'l*), which shows that it is not due to a medieval copyist, as was at times suspected. This Messiah arises from both Aaron and Israel, which would mean that at least his father would be an Aaronid, and his expiation for the iniquity of the community would imply a *priestly* role. Yet he will also be the Messiah of Israel, a royal Messiah; he is now regarded as the 'Prince of the *Whole* Congregation' (CD 7:20). The two Messiahs merge into a priestly figure.

But the 'Interpreter of the Law' (CD 7:18) is identified by Starcky with the eschatological Prophet (1QS 9:11), who is now none other than the Righteous Teacher, believed to return at the end of time with the Messiah of Aaron and Israel: '. . . to walk according to them in the whole period of wickedness and without them they shall achieve nothing, until he comes who shall teach uprightness at the end of days' (*'d 'md ywrh hṣdq b'ḥryt hymym*, CD 6:10–11). Starcky finds a further reference to this eschatological Prophet in a tiny unpublished papyrus fragment (4QarP), one line of which begins *lkn 'šlḥ l'lyh qd*[*m*], 'I shall send you Elijah befo[re] . . .', an obvious allusion to Mal 3:23. The preceding line of this fragment reads *tmyny lbḥyr wh'* [ ], 'the eighth as an Elect One; and behold [ ]'. Starcky sees in this 'eighth' a reference to David, who was the eighth son of Jesse and chosen as king (1 Sm 16:10–13). And so for this period Starcky concludes, 'After the taking of Jerusalem in 63, the Essenes awaited only one Messiah and his precursor' (p. 498). To this same period Starcky would also relate the *Psalms of Solomon*, which mention the 'Anointed of the Lord' (17:23–24, 36; 18:6, 8).

Finally, in the fourth or Herodian period (roughly from 4 B.C. to A.D. 68), when the Essenes returned to the mother-house at Qumran to rebuild it after the earthquake of 31 B.C., there developed among them an anti-Roman or Zealot tendency. To this period belongs the *Rule of the War* in which the primary role is played by the High Priest. The 'Prince of the Whole Congregation' is mentioned only in the inscription to be put on his shield (5:1). It was a troubled period, marked by the oppression of Roman procurators; and then it was that older documents, the *Manual of Discipline*, the *Thanksgiving Psalms*, and the *Damascus Document*, were recopied. In the *Rule of the War* there is once again the duality of Messiahs, *byd mšyḥykh ḥwzy t'wdwt*, 'through your Messiahs, the seers of things ordained' (1QM 11:7–8). This, however, seems to be an archaic survival or at most a parallel development to what otherwise appears at this time. In this period too belongs the mention of the 'Messiah of Uprightness, the scion of David' (4QPatrBles 1:3–4), of the 'Scion of David who will rise with the Interpreter of the Law' (4QFlor 1:11), and of the 'scion of David, who will arise in the end of days' (4QpIs[a] D 1). To this same period Starcky would assign the Parables of the book of *Enoch*, which conflate the titles 'Son of Man', 'the Elect One', 'the Anointed', and the 'Just One', applying them all to one person. Starcky attributes this section of *Enoch* to non-Essene Ḥasidim of the pre-Christian period. Finally, to this Herodian period Starcky also assigns the recently published text which mentions explicitly 'the Elect of God'.

Starcky concludes: 'The evolution which we believe we have detected among the Essenes agrees with what we know of the history of the sect and of Judaism in the last two centuries B.C.: an eclipse of messianism in the Hellenistic era; its re-awakening in the time of the Hasmonean kings, with a duplication in terms of a temporal and sacerdotal Messiah; then the absorption of the messianic prerogatives by the future High Priest at the beginning of the Roman period; and finally the renewal of the traditional conception of the Son of David at the very moment when Jesus was going to realize this expectation' (p. 504).

Starcky's reconstruction of the messianism of Qumran has much to commend it. It has been recognized for some time now that some Qumran texts mention no Messiah, some mention a Messiah from Aaron and Israel, and some mention Messiahs from Aaron and Israel. The only way in which this fluctuation of material can be coped with is to line up the Qumran texts in as definite a chronological order as possible. This Starcky has done. He has coped with the fact that a number of these texts have undergone subsequent reduction and editing, and has tried to evaluate the different forms of the texts. (By way of a momentary digression, we might point out the pertinence of such a mode of ancient composition that is well attested in the Qumran literature to the problem of how three different Synoptic accounts of the same Gospel tradition could come into being. Ancient authors did expand existing compositions by adding further material.)

Our criticism of Starcky's reconstruction concerns a number of minor points. First of all, in both of his articles he fails to treat distinctly titles which may represent different trends and beliefs in Judaism. When he finds, for instance, the title 'Elect of God', he immediately concludes that it refers to the Messiah and then cites Is 42:1 (a passage from the Servant Songs).[11] In this he betrays his Christian outlook, and is not disciplined enough in his interpretation of pre-Christian Jewish material. It is not *per se* evident that the title 'Elect of God' was messianic in Qumran circles. It is true that the titles 'Son of Man', 'Elect One' (but not 'the Elect of God'), 'Anointed' and 'Just One' are conflated and applied indiscriminately to one figure in the Parables of *Enoch*. But the date of this section in *Enoch* is quite disputed, and should it be due to a Jew or a Jewish Christian in the first or second century A.D., as Milik would have it,[12] then the first attestation of the conflated titles applied

[11] See J. Starcky, 'Un texte messianique . . .', p. 59: '. . . il s'agit de l'élu de Dieu, c'est-à-dire du Messie (*Is.*, 42:1 et 61, 1).'

[12] Cf. J. T. Milik, *Ten Years*, 33. For a fuller discussion of the problem see P. Grelot, 'Le Messie dans les apocryphes de l'Ancien Testament: Etat de la question', *La venue du Messie: Messianisme et eschatologie* (RechBib 6; Bruges: Desclée de Brouwer, 1962) 19–50, esp. 42–50.

to one person would be in the NT itself.[13] But the 'Elect of God' is a distinct title attested in the NT (Jn 1:34) and in Qumran writings (1QpHab 10:13 and 4QMess ar), which is not found otherwise in the OT nor in Intertestamental Literature, even though it may have its roots in the OT and a congener in 'the Elect One' of *Enoch*.

In a similar way, Starcky's remarks about the cryptic fragment (4QarP) which mentions the sending of Elijah before . . . (?) are tantalizing. If what he says is true, then this tiny fragment preserves the earlier hint of a late Jewish belief in Elijah as the precursor of the Messiah. Starcky identifies him with the 'eschatological Prophet' and in the same context speaks of the Essenes of the Pompeian period expecting 'un seul Messie et son précurseur' (p. 498). But is it really so? Form-critical studies on the Baptist accounts in the Synoptics have shown that John the Baptist expected Jesus to be Elijah and that it was Jesus himself who corrected this notion and taught the people that John was Elijah redivivus (Mt 11:3–14). Then because John was the precursor of Jesus, who was the Messiah, the belief apparently grew that Elijah was the precursor of the Messiah—but it grew up in Christian circles and cannot be traced certainly to any writer earlier than Justin Martyr.[14] Whatever the significance of this tiny papyrus scrap is, it should be thoroughly assessed and not too quickly related to the idea of a 'precursor' of the Messiah.[15]

Secondly, the title 'Messiah' must be used with care, as a number of writers have stressed since the discovery of the Dead Sea Scrolls, and not immediately be associated with Jesus of Nazareth, as Starcky is inclined to do (p. 504). It is a specific

[13] See my comments below, pp. 138, 252-4.

[14] See J. A. T. Robinson, 'Elijah, John and Jesus: An Essay in Detection', *NTS* 4 (1957–58) 263–81; reprinted in *Twelve New Testament Studies* (SBT 34; London: SCM, 1962) 28–52, esp. 37. Cf. J. Jeremias, 'Êl(e)ias', *TDNT* 2, 928–44. A. J. B. Higgins, 'Jewish Messianic Belief in Justin Martyr's *Dialogue with Trypho*', *NT* 9 (1967) 298–305.

[15] Concerning the 'eighth' mentioned in this fragment, see footnote 31 (below, p. 159).

term which has well-known OT roots. Used of prophets (possibly Ps 105:15; 1 Chr 16:22; Is 61:1), priests (Lv 4:3, 5, 16; Ex 29:7, 29; 30:30; Nm 35:25), and kings (1 Kgs 1:34; 1 Sm 24:7, 11; 26:9, 11; 2 Sm 23:1), it designated in common an anointed agent, sent by God to overcome opposition to him and eventually to secure his reign among men. Only in two places in the OT do we read of promises to raise up an Anointed One or a Priest with him for this purpose (1 Sm 2:35; Dn 9:25–26). And yet this sort of text fed the messianic expectations of some Jews in late Judaism, so that the Messiah came to be related with the 'end of days'. The Qumran texts in some cases openly allude to Dn 9:25 (*'d mšyḥ ngyd*); cf. 1QS 9:11. In my opinion, both the text in Daniel and the Qumran texts manifest a stage in the development of Jewish beliefs when it is thoroughly legitimate to speak of the coming of 'a/the Messiah' or even of 'the Messiahs'. Granted that one should not read into these terms all the connotations of NT Christology, and an effort should be made not to conflate the title 'Messiah' with other so-called messianic titles, nevertheless it is a hypercritical tendency that leads some to say that we should speak of 'Anointed Ones', or of 'Consacrés', or even of messiahs (with a small *m*) in the Qumran texts.[16] For it is precisely these texts which show that the genuine OT theme of an Anointed One had definitely developed into the expectation of a Messiah (or Messiahs). One should not water down the Qumran expressions lest their import in recording phrases which reflect genuine messianic hopes among Jews of the NT period be obscured. After all, the texts do use the word *māšîᵃḥ* as a substantive, and not just as an adjective, and in an individual, not a collective sense.

Thirdly, and more importantly, as R. E. Brown has pointed out,[17] Starcky has dated the *Damascus Document* too late in

[16] See, for instance, J. Carmignac, *Les textes de Qumran* (Paris: Letouzey et Ané) 2 (1963) 13; L. H. Silberman, 'The Two "Messiahs" of the Manual of Discipline', *VT* 5 (1955) 77–82; M. Smith, 'What is Implied by the Variety of Messianic Figures?', *JBL* 78 (1959) 66–72.

[17] 'J. Starcky's Theory of Qumran Messianic Development', *CBQ* 28 (1966) 51–7.

ascribing it to the third or Pompeian period. Milik dates his oldest copy of it (4QD[b]) to 75–50 B.C., and this is scarcely the original autograph. Again, Starcky has misinterpreted the phrase, 'the head of the kings of Yawan' (CD 8:11) as a reference to Pompey, whereas the Romans are usually referred to in Qumran literature as the Kittim. 'Yawan' means Greece, and the phrase almost certainly refers to the Seleucid kings and Alexander. Furthermore, the reference to 'forty years' in CD 20:13–15 argues for a date for CD shortly prior to 100 B.C. This would put the composition of CD in the second or Hasmonean period. If so, it would come from roughly the same period as 1QS. This text clearly speaks of two Messiahs (1QS 9:11). As far as Brown is concerned, the messianic texts in CD do not unequivocally speak of only one Messiah. Grammatically, 'a Messiah of Aaron and Israel' (CD 12:23–13:1; 14:19; 19:10–11) and 'a Messiah from Aaron and from Israel' (CD 20:1) could mean a Messiah from Aaron and a Messiah from Israel. This is supported by the interpretation given to Nm 24:17 in CD 7:18–20, which calls for two figures: the Star as the Interpreter of the Law, and the Sceptre as the Prince of the whole Congregation. Starcky understood the former to be the eschatological Prophet (of 1QS 9:11), but Brown more rightly identifies him as a priestly figure (cf. *T. Levi* 18:3). The other figure is the Davidic Messiah. This is confirmed by 4QFlor 1–3 i 11 (DJD 5, 54). Consequently, Brown insists that 'from the Hasmonean period on there was at Qumran an expectation of two Messiahs, a special king and a special priest, anointed (and hence messiahs) as kings and priests would be. . . . But we do not think there is sufficient evidence that during one period, the Pompeian period, this expectation was narrowed down to one figure who would be both prince and priest' (pp. 56–7). Brown prefers to speak of a revival of hope in the Davidic Messiah in the Herodian period, and agrees with Starcky that belief in him became stronger in this period because of the Roman occupation. It is a question of emphasis.

Lastly, we come to Starcky's interpretation of the 'Elect of God' text itself.

II. THE TEXT OF 4Q MESS AR

The reader is referred to Starcky's publication for the physical description and the dimensions of the text. Starcky relates the script of the roughly ten fragments which make up the text to F. M. Cross' class of the 'round semiformal' type of Herodian script,[18] which would yield a rough dating of 30 B.C. to A.D. 20. But he even entertains the possibility of extending it to the First Revolt (A.D. 70) and actually prefers a date in the first century A.D. J. Carmignac, who has also studied this new Aramaic text, points out that it was most likely copied by the same scribe who copied the Hebrew texts of the Pesher on Ps 37, the Pesher on Isaiah a, and the Pesher on Hosea b (now relabelled 4QpHos[a] —see 4Q*166* in DJD 5, 31–2).[19]

My transcription of the text follows in the main that of Starcky's publication. I have checked his transcription against the photo accompanying his article and the clearer ones which accompany the original text in the Smithsonian exhibit (PAM 43,590 and 43,591). Any variant readings of my own will be noted in the commentary. In Starcky's article a note at the bottom of the photo labelled 'Fragment i, I' indicates that a small fragment on the lower left does not really belong to the text. It does not appear in the photo on the left, where the two otherwise overlap.

One might also question whether the fragment which bears

[18] 'The Development of the Jewish Scripts', *BANE* 138, 173–4.

[19] See 'Les horoscopes de Qumran', *RQ* 18 (1965) 199–217, esp. 207–10. Confusion is the only word for the way in which J. M. Allegro has published at different times various parts of the same text. E.g., 4QpPs37 col. i (last 11 lines) and col ii were published in 'A Newly Discovered Fragment of a Commentary on Psalm XXXVII from Qumrân', *PEQ* 86 (1954) 69–75. Then fragments of col. iii appeared in 'Further Light on the History of the Qumran Sect', *JBL* 75 (1956) 94 (+pl. 3), together with further lines of col. i (*ibid.*, 9, pl. 4). Then in his book, *The People of the Dead Sea Scrolls* (Garden City, N.Y., 1958) pl. 48, he presents a photo of col. i–ii which is almost unreadable. Cf. H. Stegemann, *RQ* 14 (1964) 235–70.

the end of ll. 1–2 in Col. II is correctly placed. The last words make little sense as they now stand, and though the space between the lines agrees with that to which it is attached, the ‘join’ is not a perfect one. Though I was able to get very close to the plate containing the text both in Washington and in Philadelphia, I did not arrive at any certain judgment about this problem. Though we must reckon with the possibility that the edge of the fragment has deteriorated a bit or shrunk, yet the judgment will rest with those who can examine the ‘join’ again at first hand. Having raised the question of the correctness of this ‘join’, I shall otherwise go along with Starcky’s restoration.[20]

Col. I

1. *dy yd’ trtyn ’*[ ] *kmh* [ ]*w šwmh šb*[*q*] *mn* [ ]
2. *ś‘rh*[*w*]*ṭlwpḥyn ‘l* [ ]
3. *wšwmn zw‘yrn ‘l yrkth* [*btr trt*]*yn šnyn dn mn dn yd‘* . . *lyh*
4. *b‘lymwth lhwh klhwn* [*k’n*]*wš dy l’ yd‘ md‘*[*m ‘d*] *‘dn dy*
5. [*y*]*nd‘ tltt spry’* [ ]
6. [*b’*]*dyn y‘rm wyd‘ św*[*kl’*]*šn ḥzwn lm’th lh ‘l ’rkwbt*[*h*]
7. *wb’bwhy wb’*[*b*]*htwhy* . . [ ]*ḥyn wzqynh ‘mh lh*[*ww*]*n mlkh w‘rmwm*[*h*]
8. [*w*]*yd‘ rzy ’nš’ wḥwkmth lkwl ‘mmy’ thk wyd‘ rzy kwl ḥyy’*
9. [*wk*]*wl ḥšbwnyhwn ‘lwhy yswpw wmsrt kwl ḥyy’ śgy’ thw’*
10. [*ḥ*]*šbwnwhy bdy bḥyr ’lh’ hw’ mwldh wrwḥ nšmwhy*
11. [*ḥ*]*šbwnwhy lhwwn l‘lmyn* [ ]
12. [ ]*’ dy l*[ ] . . [ ]*lyn*
13. [ ]*t ḥšb*[*wn*
14. [ ]*b*
15. [ ]*why*
16. [ ].
17. [ ].*š*

[20] Many of the letters of this fragmentary text are restored; the reader should consult Starcky’s edition, where some are marked with a dot (indicating a probable reading) and others with a small circle (indicating a possible reading).

Col. II

1. .[ ] *dy m*[ ] *npl lqdmyn bny šḥwh* [
2. [ ]. .*t' b'yš ṭlwpḥ' l*. .[
3. [ ]. . . .[
4. [ ]*m'th*[
5. [ ]*bś*[*r'*
6. *mw*[ ]*h* [
7. *wrwḥ nš*[*mwhy* *ḥšbwnwhy lhwwn*]
8. *l'lmyn* [
9. . . . .[
10.
11.
12. *wmdynn* . .[
13. *wyḥrbwn t*.[ ].*m*[ ] *wbmln ytbyn dy l*.[
14. *myn yswpwn t*.[ ]*mn* [ ]*bbn yḥrbn kwl 'ln yhk*[*wn*]
15. *yt*.[
16. [ ]. .[ ]. *wkl*[*h*]*n ytbnwn k'yryn 'wbdh*
17. *ḥlp qlh* [ ]*yswdh 'lwhy ysdwn ḥṭ'h wḥwbth*
18. [ ]. .[ ]*ḥdwh*[*y*]. *qdyš w'yry*[*n*]*m'mr*
19. [*'*]*mrw 'lwhy* [ ]
20. [ ]. . .[ ].*b my*[ ]*pwn*
21. [ ].*zh*

There is one further fragment (no. 3) on which Starcky reads .]*mglyn*[.

III. TRANSLATION[21]

Col. I: [1]two . . . of the hand. [ ] [ ] it lef[t] a mark from [like] [2]barley [and] lentils on [ ][3] and tiny marks on his thigh [. After tw]o years he knows this from that. . . . [4]In his youth he will become like [like a ma]n who does not know anyth[ing, until] the time when [5]he shall become skilled in the three books. [6][Th]en he will become wise and will be endowed with disc[retion] . . . visions to

[21] Restorations are indicated by square brackets [ ]; parentheses ( ) indicate words added for the sake of a smoother translation.

come to him upon [his] knees. [7]And with his father and with his forefa[th]ers . . . [ ] life and old age; (and) with him there will be counsel and prudence [8][and] he will know the secrets of man. And his wisdom will go forth to all the peoples, and he will know the secrets of all living things. [9][Al]l their calculations against him will come to naught, although the opposition of all living beings will be great.[10] [But] his [cal]culations [will succeed] because he is the Elect of God. His birth and the (very) spirit of his breath [11][ ] his [cal]culations will exist forever. [ ] [12][ ] [13][ ] calcu[lation]

Col. II: [1][ ] which. [ ] fell to the east. Children of perdition(?) [ ] [2][ ] . . . (was) evil. The lentil(?) . . . [ ] [3][ ] [4][ ] to come [ ] [5][ ] fle[sh] [6][ ] [7]and the spirit of [his] breath [his calculations will exist] [8]forever [ ] [9][ ][10–11][ ] [12]and cities . . . [ ] [13]and they will lay waste . . . [ ] . . . [ ] and with dwelling which . . . [ ] [14]waters will cease . . . [ ] from [ ] . . . will devastate (the) gates(?). All these will co[me] [15][ ] [16][ ]. and all of [th]em [and] upon it they will base its foundation. Its sin and its guilt [18][ ] . . . [in] hi[s] breast [ ]. a Holy One and Watcher[s] a saying [19][ ]. they have [sp]oken against him.

[20][ ] [21][ ]

IV. COMMENTARY

The preserved text introduces us to a description of a new-born child, as it were, *in medias res*. In the lines best preserved a description is given of the qualities of this child: of his health and his growth, of his intelligence and his wisdom, of his long life and his old age. His favoured position and the success of his plans seem to be ascribed to the fact that he is an 'Elect of God'. Since the first lines of what is called Col. I are not really the beginning of the text, it is impossible to say for certain to whom all this is ascribed. But it is to be noted that there is no mention in the text of an Anointed One, a Messiah; nor is it even certain that the phrase 'Elect of God' is to be understood in a messianic sense.

Col. I

The first three lines of Col. I seem to describe certain physical characteristics of the child.

1. *dy yd' trtyn:* 'Two ? of the hand.' In the context *trtyn* could refer to the fem. pl. *śwmn*, 'marks', a word now lost, but which would have been at the end of the preceding column. Starcky reads *dy yd' trtyn '*[*w*]*kmh*, 'de la main (au nombre de) deux; *noire* (est une marque et . . .]'. The text is so broken, however, that the last word, while not impossible, is highly questionable. The letters *kmh* could be the interrogative 'how' (cf. 1QapGn 20:2).

śwmh šb[*q*] *mn* [ ]*:* 'It left a mark from [ ].' The only word which is certain here is *śwmh*, 'a mark'. Quite unlikely is the form suggested by Starcky for the end of this line, *šm*[*q*]*mq*, 'red, reddish'. With what would it agree? The syntax of *šmqmq š'rth* is almost impossible, unless one supposes that the latter word is masc. despite its fem. form. J. Carmignac (*op. cit.*, 210) has also questioned whether the traces of the letters correspond to *šmqmq*; he prefers to read (*w*)*śwmqyn ś'ry'*, ('et) roux (seront) les cheveux'. This makes more sense, but no justification is given for the form *śwmqyn*; the adjective is normally written either *śamôq* or *śimmûq*: cf. 1QapGn 21:17 (*ym' śmwq'*, 'the Red Sea'), 18 bis. Cf. G. Dalman, *Aramäisch-Neuhebräisches Handwörlerbuch* (Göttingen: E. Pfeiffer, 1938) 293. There is the further problem of the reading of *ś'yr'*; see below. The reading *šb*[*q*] *mn* does not help much in the context, but at least it deserves some consideration. If it has any point, then Carmignac's suggested comparison of the child with David, as the 'rejeton de David', has little basis. The word *śwm'* also occurs as *swm'* in later Aramaic, whereas in Hebrew the form is *šwmh*. It is difficult to be certain therefore of the exact form of the initial sibilant.

2. *ś'rh* [*w*]*ṭlwpḥyn*: 'Barley and lentils.' Just what such a phrase is doing in a description of the bodily features of a new-born babe is a good question. Starcky read the beginning of this line thus: *š'rt*[*h w*]*ṭlwpḥyn* '*l* [. . . .], taking *š'rt*[*h*] with the end of the preceding line. Aside from the fact that *ś'r*', 'hair', is normally masc. in Aramaic (cf. 1QapGn 20:3), the collocation of the consonants *ś'r* (whatever the ending is!) with *ṭlwpḥyn* would seem more naturally to suggest 'barley'. Hence we take *ś'rh* as fem. sg. absol. in a collective sense. For the collocation *ṭlpḥn* with *ś'rn*, see *AP* 2: 4, 5; 3: 5, 6. Most likely the mention of 'barley and lentils' here is part of a comparison; the marks on the body of the infant resemble barley and lentils. The reference is probably to moles; this meaning is attested for *šwmh* in rabbinical literature.

3. *wšwmn zw'yrn 'l yrkth*: 'And tiny marks on his thigh.' The form *zw'yrn* is fem. pl. absol. of the *qutail* (diminutive) type, 'very little'.

[*btr trt*]*yn šnyn dn mn dn yd'* . . .: 'After two years he knows this from that.' The restoration of the lacuna is conjectural, being suggested only by the context of growth. It is complicated by the reading of the last word. At the end of the line Starcky read *wd'h tlyh*, and he understood *šnyn* earlier in the line to mean 'teeth'. He translated the line thus, '[bien rang]ées sont les dents les unes par rapport aux autres, et (sa) science sera élevée'. Whatever one thinks of *šnyn* as 'teeth' (a possibility scarcely to be excluded), the translation of *wd'h tlyh* is impossible. Starcky had to insert *sa* ('his') in parentheses.

J. Carmignac (*op. cit.*, 211) correctly realized that the first of these two words should be read as *yd'*; but his reading *yd'* [*hp*]*lyh* is likewise improbable. He translates the phrase: 'il saura parler distinctement'. He adds the justification that 'after having spoken of teeth, it is normal enough for one to think of mentioning the distinctness of diction'. Carmignac explains *hplyh* as the causative of *ply*, 'parler distinctement'. This meaning is attested for Hebrew, but we fail to find this causative usage in Aramaic. There is the further problem of the causative in *h*- in Qumran Aramaic, which is otherwise unattested. Moreover, the use of the infinitive as a complement without *l* should be justified from more contemporary texts than the Palestinian Talmud.

The phrase seems to indicate a growth in the child's knowledge, in particular his power to distinguish and discern. If it refers to this, perhaps the length of time of 'two years' will be questioned, as such a length might imply something other than the infant's great powers of intellect, which the context would seem to suggest. But the fragmentary context hinders further conjecture.

4. *bʿlymwth lhwh* . . .: 'In his youth he will become. . . .' As the third word Starcky read *kltyš*, 'like (something) sharpened', and referred it to the child's acuity of intellect. *lṭyš* would then be pass. ptc. of *lṭš*, 'polish, sharpen'. J. Carmignac questions this reading and prefers *klyyš*, 'like a lion'. But is such an orthography (a doubled y) ever found in Qumran Aramaic? Hebrew knows the form *layiš*, 'lion'. When the word turns up in Late Aramaic (especially in the Targums; cf. Ez 19:2), it becomes *lêtā* (with *t*, not *š*); cf. Arabic *laythu*^{n}. Once again, this undermines Carmignac's speculation which compares the new-born child with a lion, as in Gn 49:9. The allusion to 1 Sm 17:34–36 is too far-fetched to be treated seriously.

[*k'n*]*wš dy l' ydʿ mdʿ*[*m ʿd*]*ʿdn dy* [*y*]*ndʿ tltt spry'*: 'Like a man who does not know anything, until the time when he shall become skilled in the Three Books.' The source of the child's extraordinary knowledge and wisdom is thus indicated. There is no problem with the reading of [*k'n*]*wš dy l' ydʿ*. Starcky preferred to read *mdʿ*[*n*], a Palmyrene form which means the same as *mdʿ*[*m*], because he thinks that the space is too small for *m*. Cf. *CIS* 2.3912, i, 5 and 3959 for the form. Our reading of the end of line 4 is based on a phrase in the Aramaic description of the

New Jerusalem published by M. Baillet; see 2Q*24* 4:19 (*'d 'dn dy*, followed by a verb). J. Carmignac was independently tempted to read this, but believes that the PAM 43,591 photograph reveals the last letter to be *zayin*, not *yodh*. I am not as confident about this as he is, and prefer to read *dy*. At the end of line 4 Starcky read *md'[n] mn 'dn rz [m]nd' tltt spry'*, translating, 'rien du temps du secret de la science des trois livres'. J. Carmignac, however, prefers to read *dy l' yd' md' '[d] 'dn rz [m]nd'* . . ., translating, 'qui n'a pas la connaissance, j[usqu'] au temps du secret de [la con]naissance des trois livres'. Theoretically, either of these restorations and interpretations is possible, but the piling up of so many construct states is improbable. Nor is it likely that both *md'* and *mnd'* would be used within the same phrase. In my interpretation [illegible]rst *yd'* is participial and the form *ynd'* is imperfect (cf. Dn 2:9, 30; 4:14; 1QapGn 2:20).

Starcky understood the reference to the Three Books as an allusion to the mystery involved in the manifestation of the Elect of God. He accordingly suggested that the books were of eschatological, and perhaps even of astrological, character. He rightly rejected the identification of them with the three parts of the OT, the *Tôrah*, *Nᵉbî'îm*, and *Kᵉtûbîm* (see Sirach, Prologue 1). J. Carmignac, however, believes that the *spr hhgy* (=*sēper ha-hᵒgî*, 'the book of Meditation') is one of them (see 1QSa 1:7; CD 10:6; 13:2), and asks whether the *Manual of Discipline* and the *Damascus Document* might not constitute the other two. This would be a plausible suggestion, if we were sure that this text were actually a sectarian document, i.e., one composed in the interests of the theology of the Qumran sect. But since Essene tenets are notoriously absent from certain Qumran texts and these could be of extraneous authorship, one always remains uncertain in this matter. For instance very little Essene theology is found in the *Genesis Apocryphon*.

The Three Books are probably apocalyptic, and not specific, real books; rather they allude to such writings as the 'books of the living' (*Enoch* 47:3), the book of man's deeds (Ps 56:9; Dn

7:10; *Enoch* 90:17) and the 'heavenly tablets' (*Jubilees* 30:22; *Enoch* 81:1–2) to which the Intertestamental Literature often makes reference. See R. H. Charles, *APOT* 2,216. Note too that the phrase *yd' spr* is found in Is 29:11–12 in a context dealing with heavenly revelation contained in a sealed scroll. In any case, the Three Books (specific since *spry'* is emphatic) are at least holy and heavenly (see *Enoch* 103:2; 108:3–7). These are the source of the newborn child's knowledge, wisdom, and acquaintance with the secrets of men and of all living things.

6. *[b']dyn y'rm wyd' św[kl']*: 'Then he will become wise and will be endowed with discretion.' Though *w'dyn* is found in Ezr 5:5, the more normal compound form of *'dyn* at this period is *b'dyn* (see Dn 2:14, 35, 46; etc.; 1QapGn 1:3, 13, 19; 20:21; 22:2, 18). Carmignac restores *[w]b'dyn*, but gives no parallels for it. Our restoration *yd' św[kl']*, lit., 'he will know discretion', is based on 2 Chr 2:11 (*yôdēa' śēkel ûbînāh*). Since the full writing of a short *u* in a closed syllable is well attested in Qumran texts, whereas it is apparently avoided for a short *i*, the form *śuklā* is preferred to the other possibility, *śiklā*. The phrase expresses the child's growth in wisdom and spiritual qualities. Cf. Lk 2:47, 52; Prv 8:12.

[ ]*šn ḥzwn*: Or perhaps *ḥzyn*. In the first case the word would be 'visions' (fem. pl. absol. of *ḥzwh*); in the second, the masc. pl. ptc. 'seeing'. But how does either fit in with the following words?

lm'th lh 'l 'rkwbt[h]: 'To come to him upon his knees.' The only problem in this phrase is to decide whether *lh* should be understood as a sort of ethical dative, or as a directional dative, indicating the term of the coming. Starcky understood it as ethical, 'pour aller sur ses genoux'. Cf. 1QapGn 20:2, 6, 34; 21:6 (?), 8, 17, 19. J. Carmignac, however, translates 'verront [=(seront) voyantes] venir à lui sur les genoux', taking *lh* as directional (cf. Dn 3:2). He gives no justification for the reading *'rkwbh*, nor any indication of his understanding of the last word in the line. Does the phrase denote reverence or adoration?

7. *wb'bwhy wb'[b]htwhy:* 'And with his father and with his forefathers'; or 'among' (them). The first part of this line suggests that the child will enjoy an abundant life and an old age similar to that of his forebears. Our reading follows that of Starcky, which is better than that suggested by Carmignac: *wb'byy' wb*[ ]*htwhy*, 'pendant la croissance, pendant ses [ ]'. He compares the beginning of line 4 with the beginning of this line, believing that he can discern an enumeration of four stages of life after youth: 'Et pendant la croissance et pendant ses [ ] et (pendant) [ ] et (pendant la) vieillesse'. But the lacunae and the words added in parentheses reveal the improbability of this reading. It might be more plausible, if one could read 'pendant *sa* croissance', (parallel with *b'lymwth*); but this would force us back to Starcky's reading, which Carmignac rejects. For the form *'bhtwhy* Starcky refers to G. Dalman, *Grammatik*, 198, 1. 24.

[ ] *ḥyn wzqynh:* 'Life and old age.' Perhaps the lacuna should be filled with some word denoting length of life, *'rykyn* or *'rk* (cst. st.); cf. *CIS* 1.135 (*'rk ḥym*). The form *zqynh* does not seem to be attested elsewhere. Following *ḥyn* (an absol.), it is probably an absol. sg. fem., meaning 'old age'. In form it is a *qatîl-at* type, resembling *'ᵃbîdah*, 'work'. See H. Bauer and P. Leander, *Grammatik des Biblisch-Aramäischen* (Halle/S.: M. Niemeyer, 1927) #51j″. One would have expected *dqynh* in this phase of Aramaic, but the form of this root with the archaic *z* persists even later.

'mh lh[*ww*]*n mlk' w'rmwm*[*h*]*:* 'With him there will be counsel and prudence', i.e., *milkāh wa'armûmāh.* The form of the last word is otherwise unattested, but is seemingly related to later *'armûmît*, as Starcky suggested. J. Carmignac (*op. cit.*, 214) believes that the description of the child's spiritual qualities is inspired by Is 11:2. There is not, however, a single quality in Is 11:2 which is mentioned here in an Aramaic equivalent. Though the later Targum Ps-Jonathan does use the word *mylk* for Hebrew *'ēṣāh*, 'counsel', there is no certain indication that

the author is suggesting that the new-born child is the scion of David.

8. [*w*]*yd*ʿ *rzy* ʾ*nš*ʾ: 'And he will know the secrets of man.' If Starcky's reading of the first word is correct, it must be the impf. Peal of *yd*ʿ in its assimilated form (*yidda*ʿ). With it one should compare the restored form in line 5. The phrase seems to be parallel to the end of this line, *wyd*ʿ *rzy kwl ḥyy*ʾ. It is not easy to determine the meaning of the 'secrets of man'. The phrase could be contrasted with the 'secrets of God' (1QpHab 7:8; 1QS 3:23; 1QM 3:9). Possibly one should relate to it the expression in *Enoch* 38:3, 'the secrets of the righteous'; see also 58:5. Recall 1QH 1:29, where *rzyhm* seem to refer to the secret thoughts of man. Cf. 1 Cor 2:11; Rev 2:23. Such knowledge of the secrets of man is due to the new-born child's wisdom, of which there is mention in the next part of the line.

wḥwkmth lkwl ʿ*mmy*ʾ *thk*: 'And his wisdom will go (forth) to all the peoples.' The phrase immediately makes one think of the wisdom of Solomon, to which both Starcky and Carmignac refer (see 1 Kgs 10:2; 5:9–14). Starcky wonders whether there is not also a reference to the Servant of Yahweh who is made a 'light to the nations' (Is 42:1–6; 49:6). In my opinion there is not the slightest trace of this motif here. Starcky continues, 'Quoi qu'il en soit, Salomon est le type du roi-messie (1 Chr., 17, 10–14).' Is he? Cf. E. Lohse, '*Solomōn*', *TWNT* 7, 459–65. We cannot deny that the description of this child—whoever he be—echoes the OT story of Solomon. But this does not immediately suggest the child's messianic character.

*wyd*ʿ *rzy kwl ḥyy*ʾ: 'And he will know the secrets of all living things' (or 'beings'). This may again reflect the OT account of Solomon's knowledge of trees, beasts, birds, reptiles, and fish (1 Kgs 5:13 [Engl. 4:33]). Cf. Wis 7:20.

9. [*wk*]*wl ḥšbwnyhwn* ʿ*lwhy yswpw*: 'All their calculations against him will come to naught' or 'all their plots against him will cease.' Starcky reads *yswpw*[*n*]; but although the photos reveal a tear in the skin, there is no certainty that the form was

yswpwn. It is apparently the short impf. *yswpw*. The form which Starcky read is the more normal form, but *yswpw* must remain in this case a sort of *lectio difficilior*. In any case, the latter form, read also by Carmignac, is not to be regarded as a Hebraism. If the context were better preserved, perhaps we would understand the precise modal usage of the short impf. At any rate, one should note within two lines the use of *rāz* and *ḥešbôn* and recall a similar collocation of these words in 1QH 1:29. Though the word *ḥšbwn* had originally a mathematical or commercial connotation ('reckoning, calculation'), in this context it apparently refers to plots or machinations. Is it a reference to astronomical calculations? Starcky thinks so. Cf. Dn 4:30 for the idiom *swp ʿl*.

wmsrt kwl ḥyy' śgy' thw': 'Although (lit., "and") the opposition of all living beings will be great.' This phrase explains the 'calculations' of the preceding. The problematic word is *msrt*, which Starcky translates 'et *la corruption* de tous les vivants deviendra grande', deriving *msrt* from *sry*, 'be corrupt'. This would refer to the growing corruption of mankind, an apocalyptic theme. Starcky prefers this meaning to another which he had proposed in *RB* 70 (1963) 502, 'le châtiment', from *ysr*. There is another possibility, a form derived from *srr*, 'be rebellious'. In form it could be like *m*^e^*gillat* from *gll*. The form *śgy'* is fem. sg. absol., with a final *aleph* instead of *he*.

bdy bḥyr 'lh' hw': 'Because he is the Elect of God.' This is the reason for the success of the new-born child's future plans. Starcky writes, 'il s'agit de l'élu de Dieu, c'est-à-dire du Messie (Is., 42, 1 et 61, 1)'. But this identification is not at all certain. True, the word *b*^e^*ḥîrî*, 'my Elect One, my Chosen One', does occur in Is 42:1; yet it is used of the Servant of Yahweh, who is not without further ado a Messiah. In Is 61:1 an anointed messenger is mentioned, but he is not called an 'Elect of God'.

The title 'Elect of God' is not an OT phrase. The closest one comes to it is *b*^e^*ḥîr YHWH* which stands in apposition to *b*^e^*gibʿat Šā'ûl* in 2 Sm 21:6. But the translation of this phrase is not without its problems, because the text seems to be corrupt. As it stands, it would mean, 'on the hill of Saul, the chosen one of Yahweh'. But modern editors emend the text, appealing to the LXX, 'on Gibeon, the mountain of Yahweh'.[22] The OT *roots* of the title 'Elect of God' are probably to be found rather in the pronominal usage of the singular *bḥyr*, used of Moses (Ps 106:23; *Môšeh bᵉḥîrî*), of David (Ps 89:4: *kāratti bᵉrît libᵉḥîrî, nišbaʿtî lᵉDāwîd ʿabdî*), and of the Servant of Yahweh (Is 42:1: *hen ʿabdî ʾetmok-bô, bᵉḥîrî rāṣᵉtāh napšî*); and in a collective sense also of Israel (Is 43:20; 45:4).[23]

Outside of this Aramaic text the title occurs once in the plural in a Qumran Hebrew text (1QpHab 10:13: *ʾšr gdpw wyḥrpw bḥyry ʾl*, 'who insulted and outraged the Elect of God'). There it is applied to the Qumran community as such.[24]

The title, however, is not found elsewhere in Intertestamental Literature. In the book of *Enoch* a character is referred to as the 'Elect One' in the Parables (section II, cc. 37–71; e.g. 40:5; 45:3–4; 49:2, 4; 51:3, 5; 52:6, 9; 61:5, 8, 10; 62:1). From *Enoch* 45:3, 4; 55:4 it is clear that this term has developed from a passage like Is 42:1, for we read of 'my Elect One'. From such passages as *Enoch* 48:10; 52:4; 62:1, 5, it is apparent that the title 'the Elect One' was used interchangeably with 'Son of Man' and 'his Anointed'. These passages suggest that 'the Elect One' was a title given to someone regarded as a Messiah. R. H. Charles is certainly of this opinion.[25] But there is a problem connected with these references to which I have already

[22] The LXX actually reads *kai exēliasōmen autous tō kyriō en Gabaōn Saoul ekletous kyriou*, 'and we shall hang them up to the Lord in Gibeon of Saul (as) chosen ones of the Lord'. The LXX takes *eklektous* with *autous*, revealing an underlying *bḥyry Yhwh*, which may be due to a dittography. As the MT stands, *bḥyr Yhwh* must refer to Saul.

[23] The plural usage can also be found: Ps 65:9, 15, 22; Ps 105:6, 43; 106:5; 1 Chr 16:13; Sir 46:1. These refer either to Israel or to Yahweh's faithful ones in Israel.

[24] Cf. 1QpHab 9:12, where *bḥyrw* is used of the Righteous Teacher; and 5:4 where *bḥyrw* = *bḥyryw*.

[25] See *APOT* 2, 184–5.

alluded: the fact that the 'Elect One' is found only in that part of *Enoch* which is as yet unattested at Qumran. Indeed, J. T. Milik is of the opinion that section II, 'The Parables' (or 'Similitudes'), is 'probably to be considered the work of a Jew or a Jewish Christian of the first or second century A.D., who re-utilized the various early Enoch writings to gain acceptance for his own work and gave the whole composition its present form'.[26] But in any case the formula is not quite the same as that found in this Aramaic text, and we should therefore not conclude too hastily to the messianic character of the latter.

mwldh wrwḥ nšmwhy [ ]: 'His birth and the (very) spirit of his breath. . . .' Supply something like 'are blessed' or 'are from God'. The latter suggestion is not impossible in the light of 1Q*28a*2:11 (*'m ywlyd* [*'l*]*'*[*t*] *hmšyḥ*, 'if [or 'when'] God begets the Messiah'),[27] for it is clear that the idea of the divine begetting of an Anointed One is not an impossible notion for an Essene in the 1st century A.D. The phrase *rwḥ nšmwhy* creates little difficulty; its redundancy is derived from OT parallels

[26] *Ten Years of Discovery in the Wilderness of Judaea* (SBT 26; London: SCM, 1959) 33. See further J. Albertson, 'An Application of Mathematical Probability to Manuscript Discoveries', *JBL* 78 (1959) 133–41; H. E. Robbins, 'Comments on a Paper by James Albertson', *JBL* 78 (1959) 347–50; P. Grelot, *op. cit.*, 42–50.

[27] This is the reading of D. Barthélemy in DJD 1,110. Since the text is not perfectly preserved, there was some hesitation at first about the reading of *ywlyd*. In fact, Barthélemy translated it as if it were *ywlyk* (following a suggestion of J. T. Milik). However, further investigation of the skin of the text convinced others that *ywlyd* is the correct reading. Cf. F. M. Cross, Jr., *The Ancient Library of Qumran* (Anchor A 272; Garden City: Doubleday, 1961) 88, n. 67 (which now differs from his main text on p. 67); J. M. Allegro, *JBL* 75 (1956) 177, n. 28; J. Starcky, *op. cit.*, 61, n. 1. See further M. Smith, '"God's Begetting the Messiah" in 1QSa', *NTS* 5 (1958–59) 218–24; R. Gordis, 'The "Begotten Messiah" in the Qumran Scrolls', *VT* 7 (1957) 191–4. O. Michel and O. Betz, 'Von Gott gezeugt', *Judentum, Urchristentum, Kirche: Festschrift für Joachim Jeremias* (BZNW 26; Berlin: Töpelmann, 1960) 3–23; 'Nocheinmal: "Von Gott gezeugt"', *NTS* 9 (1962–63) 129–30; E. Lohse, '*Huios*', *TWNT* 8, 361–3. Cf. the confident remarks of T. H. Gaster, *The Scriptures of the Dead Sea Sect* (London: Secker and Warburg, 1957) 39, n. 13.

such as Gn 7:22 (*nišmat rûᵃḥ ḥayyîm*) and Jb 34:14, where the breath of man is regarded as derived from God. Cf. Is 11:4 (*rûᵃḥ śᵉpātāyw*); 1Q28b 5:24. On the absence of *waw* before *mwldh*, cf. 1QapGn 20:3, 4, 5.

The crucial word in this broken phrase is *mwldh*. At first sight one would be tempted to read the line thus: *bdy bḥyr 'lh' hw' mwldh*, 'because the Elect of God is his begotten one'. The word *mwldh* would then be the pass. ptc. Aphel of *yld*. But even though *mwld* is found in Mishnaic Hebrew in the sense of 'issue, descendant' (= *môlēd*; cf. M. Jastrow, *Dictionary*, 742), apparently also in 1Q27 1 i 5 (*mwldy 'wlh*, 'descendants of iniquity'), and looks like the masc. form of the OT *môledet* (Lv 18:9; Gn 48:6), it is unattested in Aramaic. We know of no instances of the pass. ptc. Aphel in Qumran Aramaic. Again, the suffix on *mwldh*, referring to God, would be strange. J. Carmignac (*op. cit.*, 215) also wants to exclude this meaning, because it seems to contradict the context, presenting as begotten of God a person who is '[like a ma]n who does not know anything'.

At any rate, it seems preferable with Starcky, Dupont-Sommer (*RB* 71 [1964] 298–9) and Carmignac to take *mwldh* as meaning 'his birth'. It is a *maqtal* form of the root *yld*, and the noun in this sense is well attested both in Hebrew (cf. 1QH 3:11; 12:8; 4Qastr 2:8 [*JJS* 9 (1964) 291–4]) and in Aramaic. Carmignac, however, reads *bdy bḥyr 'lh' hw' mwldh*, translating, 'parceque sa naissance est choisie de Dieu'. He begins a new sentence with what follows, 'le vent de son souffle . . .'. He rejects Starcky's interpretation, which we follow, because *mwld*, 'birth' (even in the astrological sense of 'thème de géniture') can scarcely be coordinated with 'the spirit of his breath' to form together the subject of the following sentence. Moreover he thinks that although *bḥyr* is used as a noun in Hebrew and can be applied to an individual (4QpIs^{d} 1:3, *'dt bḥyrw*; 1QpHab 9:12; 4QpPs37 1:5; 2:5) or to the collectivity of the Qumran community (*passim*), and even to celestial beings (1QM 12:5), it is and remains a ptc. in Aramaic. He appeals to 1QapGn 22:6 (*gbryn bḥyryn lqrb*, 'men chosen [i.e. suited] for war'). It is certainly used there in its participial sense. But one cannot escape the fact that the normal understanding of *bḥyr 'lh*' is 'Elect of God', a construct chain which means indeed 'chosen by God'. Cf. the OT phrase *bᵉrûk Yhwh* (Gn 24:31; 26:29). Given the immediately preceding context which refers to a person, the most natural explanation is to regard this title as applied to the person. After all, the expression does occur elsewhere in Qumran literature, even though in Hebrew and used in the plural of members of the Qumran community (see 1QpHab 10:13 [*bḥyry 'l*]).[28]

There is the further question whether *mwldh* is used in an astrological sense. Granted that the Hebrew counterpart *hmwld* does occur in 4Qastr in a sense that may be such, it is still not certain that this meaning is intended *here*.[29] It seems rather that the author is giving reasons why the 'plans' of the new-born child will prosper (?); among them is the fact that he is the 'Elect of God' and his birth and the (very) spirit of his breath are under divine influence. The fact that both coordinated nouns (*mwldh wrwḥ nšmwhy*) end in pronominal suffixes suggests that they *are* to be taken together.

11. *[ḥ]šbwnwhy lhwwn lʿlmyn:* 'His calculations will exist forever.' Or it is possible that some predicate adjective preceded this phrase. On *lʿlmyn*, see below 2:8 and 1Q*23* 20:3; also Dn 2:4; 3:9; 5:10; 6:7, 22, 27.

[28] See the text of 4QarP above (p. 134), where *lbḥyr* is hardly used in a participial sense. Perhaps the expression *bḥyry šmym*, applied to celestial beings in 1QM 12:5, should also be considered, for the last word (*šmym*) may simply be a surrogate for 'God'. The plural use of *bḥyr 'l* supplies the Palestinian Semitic background for the NT phrase *eklektoi* (*tou*) *theou* which is used of Christians in Rom 8:33; Col 3:12; Ti 1:1. This plural, however, has little to do with the specific use of *bḥyr 'lh* for an individual—which is our real problem in this Aramaic text.

[29] See J. M. Allegro, 'An Astrological Cryptic Document from Qumran', *JSS* 9 (1964) 291–4.

Col. II

1. *npl lqdmyn:* 'Fell to the east.' Starcky translates this phrase thus: 'tomba aux temps anciens', and alludes to the fall of the angels (Gn 6:1–4). The broken context makes it almost impossible to be sure; but the absol. state would seem to call for 'east' rather than 'former times'.

bny šḥwh: 'Children of perdition', lit., 'of (the) pit'. We are not sure that the fragment bearing these words is rightly placed. The phrase makes no sense here. Starcky compares the Hebrew *bny hšḥt* (CD 6:15; 13:14) and *'nšy hšḥt* or *šḥt* (1QS 9:16, 22). Aramaic *šaḥwâ* is apparently the equivalent of Hebrew *šaḥat*.

7. *wrwḥ nš[mwhy]:* The traces of the letters here suit the phrase which is found in 1:10. Starcky, however, reads *wrwḥ bśr*['], 'et l'esprit de la chair', comparing 1QH 13:13; 17:25.

8. *l'lmyn:* Starcky excludes this reading, which alone is acceptable in my opinion. He reads *l'lywn*, but senses the difficulty, noting that it occurs only with *'l* preceding it (1QapGn 12:17; 20:12, 16; 21:2, 20; 22:15, 116bis.-21). See above 1:11.

13. *wyḥrbwn:* 'And they will lay waste', apparently 3 pl. masc. impf. Aphel of *ḥrb*. Starcky translates 'et seront détruits'.

wbmln ytbyn: Starcky reads *wbmln ytbn*, and translates only: 'et par des paroles . . .'. The phrase is too damaged for any plausible interpretation.

14. *myn yswpwn:* 'Waters will cease', i.e., 3 pl. masc. impf. Peal of *swp* (cf. 1:9). Starcky, however, translates, 'les eaux augmenteront', regarding the root as *ysp*, and comparing *yswpwn* with *ykwlwn* of 1QapGn 20:19. He appeals to the explanation of E. Y. Kutscher (*Scripta hierosolymitana* 4 [1958] 13). The latter regards *ykwlwn* as 'entirely "un-Aramaic" (=*yklwn*). It looks like a Hebrew pausal verb form.' *yswpwn*, however, may only represent the full writing of an otherwise reduced vowel (=*yikk*^{u}*lûn*); cf. 1QS 1:16 *y'bwrw*, 4:4 *y'rwkw*, 5:17 *yṣqwdw*; see J. T. Milik, *RB* 67 (1960) 41. In my opinion *yswpwn* is the ordinary form of the impf. of *swp*. Cf. Ap 21:1;

4Ezr 6:24; *Assump. Mos.* 10:6; *Pss Sol.* 17:21; *T.Levi* 4:1. The cessation of flood-waters is an apocalyptic motif.

bbn yḥrbwn: This reading is far from certain; Starcky read *bmn* instead of our *bbn*.

16. *wkl*[*h*]*n ytbnwn kʿyryn:* 'And all of them will be as intelligent as Watchers.' Starcky links the last word in the line with this phrase, translating, 'et tous ceux-là comprendront, comme les Veilleurs, son oeuvre'. He thus makes *ʿwbdh* the direct object of the reflexive *ytbnwn*, which, while not impossible, may not be necessary. For 'the Watchers', cf. 2:18; Dn 4:10, 14, 20; 1QapGn 2:1, 16; CD 2:18; *Jub* 4:15; *T. Reuben* 5:6–7; *T. Naphtali* 3:5; *Enoch* 12:2–3; 20:1; 39:12–13. They represent a class of angelic beings, sometimes identified with archangels, sometimes with the fallen angels. See R. H. Charles, *The Book of Enoch or 1 Enoch* (Oxford: Clarendon, 1912) 6.

ʿwbdh ḥlp qlh: 'His deed instead of his voice. . . .' Perhaps this refers to the exemplary conduct of the new-born child. His action is to be contrasted with his words.

17. *yswdh ʿlwhy ysdwn:* 'And upon it they will base its foundation.' Starcky read *yswrh ʿlwhy ysrwn*, 'ils lui infligeront son châtiment'; but J. Carmignac has also independently recognized that *yswdh* must be read here (*op. cit.*, 216).

18. *qdyš wʿyryn*: 'A Holy One and Watchers.' See above 2:16. Note the compound occurrence also in Dn 4:10, 14, 20.

V. CONCLUDING GENERAL REMARKS

The text which J. Starcky has published certainly presents a fragmentary portion of a prediction or pronouncement about a new-born child. Comparing it with other horoscopic material still to be published, Starcky calls this text 'astrologique'. However, we find in it no reference to stars or to signs of the Zodiac which might suggest its horoscopic nature. That it has parallels in Graeco-Roman physiognomic literature is likely, and perhaps this would be a truer designation of its literary form. For the text describes the temperament and character of the child from its outward appearance. The text is of interest in that its predictions of the qualities of the child provide an extra-biblical parallel for the utterances of the old man Simeon in the Lucan Infancy Narrative, 'This child is marked for the rise and the fall of many in Israel, to be a symbol that men will reject, and thus the thoughts of many minds will be laid bare' (2:34–35).

But we find even greater difficulty in Starcky's designation of this text as messianic. Granted that the idea of God's begetting the Messiah is not impossible for the Qumran community (see 1QSa 2:11–12), nevertheless one must ask whether the title, 'Elect of God', immediately refers to a Messiah. Starcky thinks so. But since this title is never found in the OT, and one can only appeal to the pronominal expression, 'my Chosen One', one must face the fact that the latter is used not only of David (Ps 89:4), of the Servant of Yahweh (Is 42:1), but even of Moses (Ps 106:23). In the NT it is applied to Jesus (Jn 1:34), who happens to be the 'Messiah'. But this represents the usual NT piling up of titles with which we are all familiar.

Given such hesitation about the messianic character of this fragmentary text, I would like to make a different proposal. In the Intertestamental Literature there is a certain fascination with the birth of Noah. His birth is quasi-miraculous, his radiance fills the whole house with light like the sun; he stands in the hands of the midwife, and speaks with the Lord of uprightness. The fascination with his birth is in part due to the late Jewish speculation about the so-called 'Fallen Angels' of Gn 6:1–4, for the Noah story begins in Genesis immediately after this enigmatic passage. Elaborate descriptions of the character of Noah were composed. We should recall the 'Noah Apocalypse' in *Enoch* 106–8, *Jub* 4–10; the fragmentary text in the *Genesis Apocryphon*, col. 2; 1Q*19* fr. 3; and Josephus, *Antiquities* 1, 3, 1–9, #72–108. Another text from Cave 4, as yet unpublished, also deals with the wondrous birth of Noah, and even gives the baby's weight.[30]

Given such material, the question arises whether we are not really dealing with another text belonging to the Noah literature of late Judaism. There is certainly no phrase in the two fragmentary columns which cannot be understood of Noah. Wis 10:4 implies that Noah was saved from the deluge because of his wisdom: 'When the earth was deluged because of him, Wisdom again saved the upright man, steering him with a cheap piece of wood.' Noah's wisdom would be hailed in col. 1, line 8 of this Aramaic text. Nowhere else, however, in this Intertestamental Literature is Noah referred to as the 'Elect of God'. The closest one comes to any title of this sort is found in Josephus, who, speaking in general of the patriarchs and their long lives, gives as the reason for it: 'in the first place, they were beloved of God (*theophileis*)' (*Ant.* 1, 3, 9, #106). If Josephus could say of Noah that he was *theophilēs*, then the author of this Aramaic text could conceivably call him the 'Elect of God'. Much of the vocabulary of this text can also be found in *Enoch* 106–8, 'secrets', 'books', 'sin', 'destruction', 'waters', etc. The mention of the child who would enjoy long life and old age after the fashion of his father (Lamech, who lived 777 years according to Gn 5:31 [MT]) and his forefathers takes on meaning, if it refers to Noah. Cf. Josephus, *Ant* 1, 3, 7, #98, *gēras kai biou mēkos homoion tois tachion eperchomenōn.* Again, the mention of the 'Holy One and Watchers' (2:18, 16) recalls the occurrences of these figures in col. 2 of the *Genesis Apocryphon* which deals with the birth of Noah. They are otherwise unknown in any passage of Intertestamental Literature dealing with a Messiah.[31]

The upshot of all this is to question Starcky's identification of this text as messianic, and to suggest that its pertinence to other

[30] See J. T. Milik, *Ten Years*, 35.

[31] Is it not possible too that the 'eighth' who is an 'Elect', according to the papyrus fragment 4QarP, is a reference to Noah? See 2 Pt 2:5, 'except for Noah, the preacher of uprightness, the eighth'.

literature concerned with the birth of Noah be given some consideration. If it is not messianic, then it can scarcely be used to fill out the picture of Qumran messianic expectations in the Herodian period.[32]

[32] See also I. D. Amusin, '"Izvrannik Voga" b Kumranskich tekstach', *VDI* 1 (92, 1966) 73–9.

8

THE STORY OF THE DISHONEST MANAGER (LK 16:1–13)*

There are few passages in the Synoptic Gospels more puzzling than the well-known story about the Dishonest Manager (or Unjust Steward). Summer after summer Christians used to hear it read as the climactic Scripture message in the liturgy of the eighth Sunday after Pentecost (Lk 16:1–9), and usually came away wondering what it was all about. Commentators have often discussed its meaning, and what some have proposed has not always been enlightening. Preachers have isolated sentences of it for sermons on extraneous topics, often without attempting to analyse the story itself. Over thirty years ago the noted French exegete, Père M.-J. Lagrange, O.P., wrote of it: 'I admit that it is not easy to preach on this subject, because many people imagine that only an edifying story can be told in church.' Whether a clear and definitive explanation of this story will ever be arrived at is hard to say. But there is a growing consensus of opinion about various features of it which will always have to be respected. It is my purpose to try to distil this consensus from some recent studies of the story, and to support an interpretation which, I believe, sheds most light on this puzzling episode.

An initial difficulty—which must be recognized—was caused by the liturgical isolation of this story from its Gospel context. Such a difficulty is associated with many of the Gospel episodes taken over into the liturgy, where they acquire a certain setting

* Originally published in *TS* 25 (1964) 23–42.

not native to them. The proper understanding of the story will only be had when it is considered in its own Gospel setting. Secondly, an added difficulty is often encountered with Gospel passages used in the liturgy, because past practice has often been cavalier in abridging episodes and suppressing important verses. A classic example of this was found in the no longer used Last Gospel of the Roman Mass, where only the first fourteen verses of the prologue of John's Gospel were read and the important ending in vv. 15–18 was omitted. Liturgical usage also abridged the story of the Dishonest Manager, using only vv. 1–9, although the account itself is actually four verses longer. But since the Lucan story is made up of a parable and a multiple conclusion, the result of the abridgment was the adoption of only the parable and *a part* of the conclusion. The relation of the conclusion to the parable itself created a major difficulty in the understanding of the Lucan story as a whole. The liturgical abridgment eliminated some of this difficulty, but enough of the Lucan conclusion remained to complicate the task of anyone who would preach a homily on the story.

THE GENERAL LUCAN CONTEXT

The story of the Dishonest Manager forms part of the Lucan narrative of Jesus' journey to Jerusalem (9:51–19:27). It is found in the specifically Lucan 'travel account', that extended insertion of additional material (Lk 9:51–18:14) which the Evangelist had made into what he had otherwise taken over from Mark. This artificial, literary report of what Jesus said and did on his way to Jerusalem from Galilee comes from two different sources of Gospel traditions: Q (the source for those episodes common to him and to Matthew) and a private source (peculiar to Luke alone).[1] The story of the Dishonest Manager

[1] This analysis of the story of the Dishonest Manager is based on a modified form of the Two-Source theory of the Synoptic problem, similar to that proposed by J. Levie, J. Schmid, A. Wikenhauser, etc. For further details concerning it, the Q-material common to Mt and Lk, the latter's 'travel account', the literary tendencies of the individual Evangelists, see A.

belongs to the latter, being found only in Luke. It is an isolated account of a parable uttered by Jesus which Luke has made part of his 'travel account'.

In the immediate context of chapter 16 there are two stories about riches, separated by sayings of Jesus derived from various contexts. Vv. 1–13 relate the story of the Dishonest Manager, told to the disciples; vv. 19–31 tell the story of Dives[2] and Lazarus. Both of these stories are parables about riches, a subject of no little importance in the third Gospel.[3] But the two stories are separated by isolated logia (or sayings) on Pharisaic hypocrisy (16:14–15), on John the Baptist (16:16), on the Law (16:17), and on divorce (16:18).[4] A similar combination of two

---

Wikenhauser, *New Testament Introduction* (New York, 1958) 209–53; A. Robert and A. Feuillet, *Introduction à la Bible* 2 (Paris, 1959) 233–95; A. H. McNeile, *An Introduction to the Study of the New Testament* (2nd ed.; Oxford, 1953) 59–91; P. Feine–J. Behm, *Einleitung in das Neue Testament* (12th ed., by W. G. Kümmel; Heidelberg, 1963) 11–44.

[2] Since the recent publication of the oldest Greek text (P^{75}) of Luke's Gospel in *Papyrus XIV–XV: Evangiles de Luc et Jean: Tome I, XIV: Luc chap.* 3–24*; Tome II, XV: Jean chap.* 1–15 (ed. V. Martin and R. Kasser; Cologny-Genève, 1961), should we continue to call the rich man by the usual Latin appellative, Dives? His name appears in this 2nd–3rd century Greek text as *Neuēs*. This puzzling name seems to be a scribal abbreviation of *Nineuēs*, the rich man's name recorded in the ancient Coptic (Sahidic) translations of Lk, i.e., 'Nineveh'. See my article, 'Papyrus Bodmer XIV: Some Features of Our Oldest Text of Luke', *CBQ* 24 (1962) 170–9; cf. H. Cadbury, 'A Proper Name for Dives', *JBL* 81 (1962) 399–402.

[3] See X. Léon-Dufour, in Robert-Feuillet, *op. cit.*, 251; J. Dupont, *Les béatitudes* (Bruges, 1958) 52, 212–17, 320–5.

[4] Though the story of the Dishonest Manager is addressed to the disciples, the following saying is uttered in the hearing of the Pharisees; they have listened to 'all this' (*tauta panta*). The latter expression might seem at first to refer to the preceding story (16:1–13); and as used by the Evangelist in his account, it does. But one must not insist on such connections between episodes when it is a question of their setting in the life of Jesus itself. For this reason the attempt of R. Pautrel to interpret the parable together with vv. 14–15 is misleading and has found little support; see '"Aeterna tabernacula" (Luc, XVI, 9)', *RSR* 30 (1940) 307–27.—Moreover, vv. 16–18 represent the combination of three isolated sayings. The first of them (16:16) is a key verse in Luke's theology, expressing the significance of John the Baptist (see H. Conzelmann, *The Theology of St Luke* [tr. G. Buswell; New York, 1961] 22 ff.; W. Wink, *John the Baptist in the Gospel Tradition* [SNTS

parables separated by independent sayings is found in Lk 12:13–37 (the parable of the Rich Fool, 12:13–21; logia, 12:22–34; the parable on watchfulness, 12:35–37). There is another connection between the two parables in chapter 16 and chapter 12. The parable of the Rich Fool teaches the folly of the pursuit of riches and of the belief that one is secure in the possession of wealth. The story of the Dishonest Manager admonishes Christians about the prudent use of riches (the parable) and the danger of slavish servitude to them (the conclusion). The first of the immediately following independent logia (16:14–15) characterizes the money-loving (*philargyroi*) Pharisees as men enmeshed in such servitude and unable to judge by any other standard than that which is an abomination in the sight of God. And shortly thereafter the story of Dives and Lazarus follows. There is, further, an extrinsic connection of this teaching on riches in chapter 16 with the foregoing parable of the Prodigal Son (15:11–32), which deals with the improper use of wealth. In its Lucan context, therefore, the story of the Dishonest Manager forms part of a group of instructions on the use of wealth.

THE GOSPEL STORY ITSELF

1 Jesus said to the disciples: 'There was a certain rich man who had a manager, and he heard complaints that this man was squandering his property. 2 So he called him and said: "What's this I hear about you? Prepare for me an account of your management; you can't be manager around here any longer." 3 Then the manager said to himself: "What am I going to do? My master is taking my job as manager away from me. I am not strong enough to dig; I'm ashamed to beg.—4 Ah, I know what I'll do, so that when I lose this job, I'll be welcome in people's homes." 5 He summoned his master's debtors one by one. He said to the first of them: "How much do you owe my master?" "One hundred jugs of olive oil," was the answer. 6 He said to the man: "Here, take your note; sit down and,

Monographs 7; Cambridge, 1968] 51-7). It really has, however, nothing to do with vv. 14–15 or vv. 17, 18. All three verses (16–18) have counterparts, if not strict parallels, in Mt in different contexts (Mt 11:12–13; 5:18; 5:32).

hurry, write one for fifty." 7 Then he said to another debtor: "How much do you owe?" He answered: "A hundred bushels of wheat." Again he said: "Here, take your note and write one for eighty." 8a And the master approved of that dishonest manager because he had acted prudently.'

8b For the children of this world are more prudent in dealing with their own generation than the children of light are. 9 I tell you, make friends with the wealth of dishonesty, so that when it gives out,[5] you will be welcomed into everlasting tents.

10 The man who is trustworthy in little things is also trustworthy in what is big; and the man who is dishonest in little things is also dishonest in what is big. 11 If, then, you are not trustworthy when handling the wealth of dishonesty who will trust you with the wealth that is real? 12 And if you are not trustworthy when handling what belongs to another, who will give you what is your own?[6]

13 No servant can serve two masters; either he will hate the one and love the other, or he will be devoted to the one and despise the other. You cannot serve both God and wealth.

THE LUCAN CONCLUSION TO THE PARABLE

In analysing the story of the Dishonest Manager, the reader must learn to look at it as a parable to which several concluding verses of diverse origin have been added by the Evangelist. This analysis represents the consensus of opinion among Protestant and Catholic scholars who have studied the story on Form Critical methods. Though it is a matter of debate among them just where the parable ends, no one denies the obvious conflated nature of the story as a whole and the traces of the compilatory process that produced it.

Where does the parable end? According to R. Bultmann, W. Grundmann, J. Jeremias, A. R. C. Leaney, H. Preisker, W.

[5] The preferred reading of the Hesychian recension is *eklipē* (3 sg.), 'it gives out', referring to *mamōnas*. The inferior reading of the Koine tradition is *eklipēte* (2 pl.), 'you give out' (=die), and is the source of the Latin *cum defeceritis*.

[6] 'Your own' (*hymeteron*) is the reading of Sinaiticus, P^{75}, Alexandrinus, Codex Bezae, Koridethi, the Latin and Syriac versions; it is preferred by Aland, Merk and Bover. But Nestle and Kilpatrick read 'our own' (*hēmeteron*), the *lectio difficilior*, which is however less well attested (Vaticanus, Origen).

Michaelis, etc., it consists only of vv. 1–7. In v. 8 *ho kyrios* ('the master') is interpreted as Jesus and vv. 8–13 are further commentary put on his lips. Others would include v. 8 in the parable (so D. Buzy, J. M. Creed, A. Descamps, J. Dupont, A. Loisy, L. Marchal, T. W. Manson, K. H. Rengstorf, J. Schmid, etc.). In this interpretation *ho kyrios* is usually said to be the master of the parable itself (and different explanations are proposed). Still other commentators would include even v. 9 in the parable (so D. R. Fletcher, P. Gaechter, J. Knabenbauer, M.-J. Lagrange, W. Manson, A. Rücker, and most of the older Catholic commentators—many of the latter did so because they felt bound by the liturgical form of the story and were generally reluctant to adopt Form Critical methods of analysis). This last view has so many problems connected with it that it is generally abandoned today.

In my opinion 16:1–8a constitute the parable proper, and vv. 8b–13 represent the added Lucan multiple conclusion. In including the first part of v. 8 in the parable, we are following the view of B. Weiss, F. Tillmann, B. T. D. Smith, W. O. E. Oesterley, L. M. Friedel, J. Volckaert, P. Samain, etc. The main reason for doing so is that without v. 8a the parable has no real ending. From the beginning the reaction of the master to the manager's conduct is expected; it is finally given in v. 8a: 'and the master approved of that dishonest manager because he had acted prudently.'[7] In this view *ho kyrios* is the same as the master in vv. 3, 5.[8] It also is the most natural reading of the first

[7] This division has been well worked out by F. Tillmann, 'Zum Gleichnis vom ungerechten Verwalter. Lk 16, 1–9', *BZ* 9 (1911) 171–84, esp. 177 ff.

[8] J. Jeremias (*The Parables of Jesus* [tr. S. H. Hooke; London, 1958] 33) argues that the absolute use of *ho kyrios* refers in some instances in Luke's Gospel to God, but in all others (18 times in all) to Jesus. Consequently, Jeremias along with many others (J. M. Creed, E. Klostermann, W. Grundmann, K. H. Rengstorf, J. Schmid, etc.) understand 'the master' in v. 8a as Jesus. In this they appeal to the sense of v. 8b, which almost certainly reflects a statement of Jesus and seems out of place in the mouth of the master of the parable. These writers also appeal to Lk 18:6, where an observation of *ho kyrios* is recorded, who cannot be anyone else but Jesus. And in 18:8

part of the verse. To interpret 'the master' as a reference to Jesus is unexpected, and it is really read back into the first part of the verse only by reflection on its second part and the change of subject in v. 9. The change of subject, however, in v. 9 seems precisely to lend support to the view that 'the master' in v. 8a refers to the one in the parable. It is clear that the 'I' of v. 9 ('I tell you') can refer only to Jesus. So the first part of v. 8 is still part of the parable.

Moreover, v. 8b is not part of the original parable at all. J. Jeremias has pointed out how out of place it is on the lips of the master of the parable.[9] It actually reads like a generalizing commentary on the parable: 'the children of this world are more prudent in dealing with their own generation than the children of light are.' While the Palestinian origin of this part of the verse finds support in interesting Essene parallels,[10] the

---

there follows a similar introduction of a saying by *legō hymin* (see 16:9).—However, the situation in chap. 16 is not the same as that in chap. 18. There is an earlier mention of *kyrios* in 16:3, 5, whereas there is nothing similar in Lk 18. Moreover, in Lk 12:42, although the first instance of the absolute use of *ho kyrios* refers to Jesus, the second one is generic and does not refer to him at all, as is commonly recognized by commentators. The attempt to distinguish two different meanings for 'the master' in 16:8a is artificial. A. Descamps ('La composition littéraire de Luc XVI 9–13', *NovT* 1 [1956] 47–53) would have us believe that in Luke's source *ho kyrios* referred to Jesus, but in Luke's Gospel he has been identified with the master of the parable. No reasons, however, have been proposed for this distinction. For a more recent attempt to explain *ho kyrios* as referring to Jesus, see I. H. Marshall, 'Luke xvi. 8—Who Commended the Unjust Steward?' *JTS* 19 (1968) 617–19; H. Drexler, 'Miszellen: zu Lukas 16:1–7', *ZNW* 58 (1967) 286–8. (On p. 288, n. 8, the author calls my attempt to interpret the manager's action after he has been reported to the master in a more favourable light than it is usually understood 'aussichtslos'. But he does not bother to justify this estimate of it.)

[9] *The Parables of Jesus*, 33.

[10] 'The children of this world' (*hoi huioi tou aiōnos toutou*) may be a reflection of the Qumran expression *kl bny tbl* (CD 20:34). More pertinent is the expression 'children of light' (*tous huious tou phōtos*), which was found only in Jn 12:36; 1 Thes 5:5; Eph 5:8 until the Qumran scrolls were discovered. It is now seen to be a favourite Essene designation for their community of the New Covenant. See 1QS 1:9; 2:16; 3:13, 24, 25; 1QM 1:1, 3, 9, 11, 13.

saying preserved here represents an independent logion of Jesus which has been joined to the parable (either by Luke or his source). For it follows strangely on v. 8a, and indeed on the whole preceding parable.

When the Lucan conclusion to the parable is studied, the traces of its compilation in the Greek text are not hard to find. Let us work backwards, beginning with v. 13. First of all, though Lk 16:1–12 is without any real Synoptic parallel, 16:13 is paralleled in Mt 6:24, where the context is that of the Sermon on the Mount and entirely unrelated to such a parable as this one. This verse alone, then, in the whole story of the Dishonest Manager is derived from the Q-material, and has been added to the otherwise peculiarly Lucan material.[11] Secondly, vv. 10–12 form a unit describing the trustworthy (*pistos*) servant and comparing him with one who is not. The adjective *pistos* is the catchword bond linking the three verses.[12] The subject of these

---

The peculiar dualistic character of the expression is well known. It is not found either in the OT or in rabbinical literature. While the contrast of light and darkness is almost a natural figure for good and evil, and is found in the OT, the division of all humanity into two groups so designated is unknown outside of the Qumran literature and the NT. This is one of the reasons for maintaining that the expression is not just part of the general Palestinian intellectual climate of the first century A.D. See H. Braun, 'Qumran und das Neue Testament', *TRu* 28 (1962) 186–7; P. Benoit, 'Qumrân et le Nouveau Testament', *NTS* 7 (1960–61) 276–96, esp. 289–90.

[11] Note too the change of vocabulary. The parable itself concerns a 'manager' (*oikonomos*), but the conclusion mentions a 'servant' (*oiketēs*). This points to a different original context for 16:13, preserved neither in Lk nor in Mt. It is not at all certain that Lk has borrowed the saying from the Matthean tradition, as A. Descamps (*op. cit.*, p. 52) would have it. Another indication of its isolated character is given by the fact that it is used in the Coptic *Gospel according to Thomas* (ed. A. Guillaumont, H.-Ch. Puech, G. Quispel, W. Till, Y. 'Abd-al-Masiḥ; New York, 1959) Log. 47: 'Jesus said: It is impossible for a man to mount two horses and to stretch two bows, and it is impossible for a servant to serve two masters, otherwise he will honour the one and offend the other.'—Cf. J. Dupont, *Les béatitudes*, 107–13.

[12] The adjective *pistos* echoes the fuller expression in Lk 12:42, *ho pistos oikonomos ho phronimos*, 'the faithful, prudent manager'. It is in such an expression that one finds the link between the two characteristics of the ser-

verses is responsibility in handling wealth (or lack of it). It has only an extrinsic connection with the parable of the Dishonest Manager, the point of which is rather another characteristic of that man. This unit of three verses, then, records an instruction on responsibility, which is really extraneous to the parable, but which draws out of it some further implications. When the verses are scrutinized more closely, v. 10 is seen to be a development of Lk 19:17, or at least a reflection of it. This verse occurs in the parable of the Minas: 'Congratulations! You are a good slave! Because you were trustworthy in a small matter, you shall have authority over ten cities.'[13] The verse is more at home in that parable. Lk 16:10 reflects, therefore, a genuine tradition, but it has been attached to a different story of a manager; here it has become the basis of a developed unit of three verses.[14] Thirdly, the joining of the vv. 10–13 to v. 9 is due to another catchword bond, *mamōnas* ('wealth').[15] Three sayings,

---

vants in the parable (prudence) and the conclusion (trustworthiness). Cf. 1 Cor 4:2.

[13] Lk 19:17 is actually Q-material, having a parallel in Mt 20:21, 23. This fact may point to a different original context.

[14] Bp A. Descamps, the rector of the Catholic University of Louvain, has suggested (*op. cit.*, pp. 49–52) that vv. 9–12 are a secondary Lucan construction. V. 9 would have been composed by Luke with vocabulary drawn from the parable proper (16:1–8) and from the isolated saying of 16:13; v. 10 would have been composed on the basis of Lk 12:42 and 19:11–27; and so on. While such an analysis is not absolutely incorrect, it encounters several telling difficulties, not the least being that vv. 10–12 seem to have been composed in Aramaic because of the play on *mamōnas* and *pistos* (see note 15 below). In this respect the critique of J. Dupont (*Les béatitudes*, pp. 109–10) is to be noted. None of the reasons brought forth by Descamps are sufficient to exclude the less radical possibility that vv. 10–12 represent genuine sayings of Jesus derived from another context.

[15] *Mamōnas* is the Greek form of the Hebrew *māmôn* or Aramaic *māmônā*. Though unknown in OT Hebrew, the word has turned up in the Qumran literature (1QS 6:2; 1Q*27* 1 ii 5; CD 14:20 [in the last two instances it occurs only in very fragmentary contexts]). There is, however, another Qumran expression, which does not use *māmôn*, but *hôn ḥāmās*, 'the wealth of violence' (1QS 10:19), which is close in sense to the Lucan 'wealth of dishonesty' (16:9).—The etymology of *māmôn* is uncertain, but it is commonly

dealing with mammon (16:9, 11, 13) and the responsibility or slavish involvement that it entails, are joined together as a multiple conclusion to the parable.[16] (The connection of v. 8a with 8b has always been problematic, and has been discussed above.)

For these reasons—all of which match the general patterns of the recording of Jesus' parables in the Synoptic tradition[17]—the unity of the story of the Dishonest Manager should not be stressed.

THE MEANING OF THE PARABLE ITSELF

As A. Descamps notes, there is nothing against the attribution of the parable to Jesus himself.[18] Like many of the other parables used in the Gospels, its historical basis in the life of Jesus himself offers no difficulty. One may wonder why it should be called a parable, since it lacks the usual introduction which states the comparison. But this is not the only parable of this sort; at the end of the chapter the story of Dives and Lazarus is similar, but

---

explained as derived from the root *'mn* ('to be firm'; causative: 'to trust in, believe'). *Māmôn* (<*ma'môn*) would, therefore, designate that in which one puts one's trust. If this is correct—and vv. 10–12 seem to suggest that it is—the play on the words *mamōnas* and *pistos* is obvious. See F. Hauck, '*Mamōnas*', *TDNT* 4, 389–90; J. Dupont, *Les béatitudes*, 109–10; A. M. Honeyman, 'The Etymology of Mammon', *Archivum linguisticum* 4/1 (Glasgow, 1952) 60–5.—Commentators have often related Luke's phrase to the rabbinical expression *māmôn dišqar*, 'wealth of deceit'. But this expression has a far more pejorative sense than Luke's, suggesting ill-gotten gains or wealth that has been amassed at the expense of justice. In Luke's usage, however, the word designates the tendency that wealth has to make men dishonest. Distracting men from the service and devotion of God, it enslaves them in a pursuit of itself and ends in making them dishonest.

[16] The reasons given by A. Descamps (*op. cit.*, 49–50) for the Lucan construction of 16:9 are not impossible; they are better than his analysis of vv. 10–12.

[17] See J. Jeremias, *The Parables of Jesus*, 20–88; C. H. Dodd, *The Parables of the Kingdom* (rev. ed.; New York, 1961) 1–20; R. E. Brown, *The Parables of the Gospels* (Paulist Press Doctrinal Pamphlet; New York, 1963).

[18] *Op. cit.*, 48.

only in the Codex Bezae is the latter explicitly called a parable (*eipen de kai heteran parabolēn*, 'and he proposed another parable').

In trying to determine the main message of the parable (16:1–8a), certain crucial questions have to be answered. Four of them may be singled out: (1) In what way was the manager dishonest? (2) What was the Palestinian economic situation behind the parable? (3) Why does the master praise the manager's actions? (4) What is the point of the comparison in the parable?

(1) In what way was the manager dishonest? This may seem like a simple question, but in many ways it is fundamental to the understanding of the whole parable (and the subsequent conclusion). From the outset of the parable the manager is accused[19] of having squandered his master's property. We are not told in what way he did this, and it is really immaterial. The manager neither subsequently denies the accusation, nor tries to defend himself, nor even attempts to beg off (as the slave does in Mt 18:26). So a reason is already found in the accusation why he could be called 'the dishonest manager' (*ton oikonomon tēs adikias*, 16:8).

But is not this last description of him due rather to his conduct subsequent to the accusation and the master's decision to call for an inventory? After all, this description does not occur until v. 8a, and might seem to suggest this. The answer to this question depends on whether the manager's subsequent conduct was wrong or not. A very common interpretation of the parable so understands it: he summoned the debtors and suggested to them to falsify their receipts or notes. This was a further dishonest act. Such an interpretation, however, has always encountered the difficulty of explaining how the master (either the master of the parable or Jesus) could commend such

[19] The verb *dieblēthē* could mean 'was calumniated, was accused falsely' (as in *4 Mc* 4:1; Josephus, *Ant.* 7, 11, 3 §267) of having squandered the property. But this meaning does not suit the context. The manager does not try to defend himself, and his subsequent conduct would be illogical if he had not been guilty.

a corrupt manager and hold him up for instruction and example to Christians. In this interpretation, according to which the subsequent conduct of the manager is also flagrantly dishonest (though the text does not say so), the description of him in v. 8a is then said to be merited on two counts: (1) for squandering his master's property; (2) for involvement in graft.

In such an interpretation of the parable, commentators customarily point out that the master commends the manager for his 'prudence', not for his dishonesty. This 'prudence' is then explained as astuteness or cleverness in dealing with his fellow men. So it is not the manager's corruption which is made the object of the application, but only general prudence (if the parable is understood as ending with v. 7) or prudence in the use of money (if v. 8 or v. 9 is included). Or, as J. Jeremias, who limits the parable to vv. 1–7, explains it, the parable describes a criminal threatened with exposure who adopts unscrupulous but resolute measures to ensure his future security. The clever, resolute behaviour of the man threatened with catastrophe becomes an example for Jesus' listeners. Christians too must be aware that they face the crisis of the *eschaton*.[20]

Yet all of this interpretation *presupposes* that the manager's subsequent conduct was dishonest and corrupt. But there is not a detail in the parable text itself which imposes such an interpretation or clearly intimates that the manager was further involved in crooked knavery. It is, to say the least, strange that the only reaction of the master to the subsequent actions of his manager is one of praise for his prudence.[21] Again, there is an

[20] *The Parables of Jesus*, 34.

[21] H. Preisker ('Lukas 16, 1–7', *TLZ* 74 [1949] 85–92) believes that the sense of the adverb *phronimōs* (16:8a) is different from that found elsewhere in the Synoptics (except Mt 14:16b). Elsewhere the adjective *phronimos* describes the person who has grasped the eschatological condition of man (Mt 7:24; 24:45; 25:2, 4, 8, 9; Lk 12:42). But J. Jeremias (*The Parables of Jesus*, 34) has more correctly noted that the adverb is used precisely in this eschatological sense in the parable. The manager stands for the Christian confronted with the crisis that the kingdom brings in the lives of men. In

interesting parallel in the parable of the Dishonest Judge (Lk 18:2–8), who 'neither feared God nor respected men'. The judge in this parable merits a description very similar to that of the dishonest manager, *ho kritēs tēs adikias* ('the dishonest judge', 18:6). This description, moreover, is given to him only at the end of the parable, even though from the outset of it he is said to be unscrupulous—again we are not told precisely in what way. He finally yields to the pestering widow to be rid of her; but no further dishonest conduct is ascribed to him. In fact, the parable was told to teach Christians to 'pray always and not give up' (18:1, probably a secondary application). The similarity with the parable of the Dishonest Manager is striking. Nothing in the latter, subsequent to the reproach of the master, is clearly branded as knavery.

(2) What is the Palestinian economic situation reflected in the parable? According to the usual interpretations, the manager who handled the estate of the rich man had charge not only of his household but also of his financial affairs. In various transactions conducted by him (renting of farms to tenants, loans against a harvest, etc.) the neighbours contracted debts with the master of the estate. The manager kept the accounts of such transactions, and the master who lived perhaps in another part of the country presumably checked up on the manager from time to time. Otherwise he was trusted. He was empowered to handle debts and see to their reduction. In the parable the manager's squandering of the property had been reported and an account was demanded. Realizing that his situation was desperate, he summoned the debtors and in a last act of knavery had them change the amounts on the receipts in order to ingratiate himself with them against the time when his job would be taken away from him. This was a form of graft. One

---

the Lucan conclusion of v. 8b (of distinct origin) the comparative *phronimōteroi* has a little broader meaning because of the reference to the dealings with one's own generation. But even so, the implied contrast is still between those dealings and the reaction to the kingdom.

must presume that this was eventually brought to the master's attention. His only recorded reaction is one of admiration and praise for the manager's astuteness.

However, if there is nothing in the text that clearly labels the manager's subsequent conduct as dishonest, then possibly some other economic situation is reflected in the parable. Another situation has, in fact, been suggested by a number of writers in this century, though it has not been widely adopted. M. D. Gibson was apparently the first to propose it in 1903 on the basis of modern Near Eastern customs.[22] Her suggestion was subsequently supported by others.[23] But none of these writers was able to adduce much evidence for it from antiquity, their parallels being drawn from modern Near and Far Eastern practices. However, a recent writer has amassed an impressive array of data from rabbinical writings and Jewish law to suggest that the practice was known in antiquity too. He is J. Duncan M. Derrett, a reader in Oriental Laws in the University of London.[24]

[22] 'On the Parable of the Unjust Steward', *ExpT* 14 (1902–3) 334.

[23] W. D. Miller, 'The Unjust Steward', *ExpT* 15 (1903–4) 332–4; E. Hampden-Cook, 'The Unjust Steward', *ibid.* 16 (1904–5) 44; P. Gaechter, 'The Parable of the Dishonest Steward after Oriental Conceptions', *CBQ* 12 (1950) 121–31; C. B. Firth, 'The Parable of the Unrighteous Steward (Luke xvi. 1–9)', *ExpT* 63 (1951–52) 93–5; J. Volckaert, 'The Parable of the Clever Steward', *Clergy Monthly* 17 (1953) 332–41; G. Gander, 'Le procédé de l'économe infidèle décrit Luc 16:5–7, est-il répréhensible ou louable?' *VerbC* 7 (1953) 128–41. See also G. Chastand, *Etudes sociales sur les paraboles évangéliques* (Toulouse, 1925) 68–75.—Though the same basic interpretation is common to all these writers, there are variations in details.

[24] 'Fresh Light on St Luke xvi. I. The Parable of the Unjust Steward', *NTS* 7 (1960–61) 198–219; 'II. Dives and Lazarus and the Preceding Sayings', *ibid.*, 364–80. Derrett's competence in the field of Oriental law may be presumed; his explanation of the legal and economic background of the parable seems well enough supported. However, his flight from conclusions generally admitted today about the composition of the Gospels and the recording of Jesus' parables is another matter; few will follow him in his views on this subject. The same can be said of the general explanation which he proposes for the parable. I have tried to sift from his discussion what seems valid for the understanding of the story as a whole.

Derrett explains the parable as reflecting the Palestinian laws and customs of agency and usury. A duly appointed manager acted as the agent for his master and was legally empowered to act in his name. His job was fiduciary. But 'there was no agency for wrongdoing'. A criminal act on the part of the manager did not necessarily involve the master; and if the latter ordered a criminal act, which the manager carried out, the manager had to bear the responsibility for it and could not take refuge in superior authority. The agent could involve the master in transactions with third parties (e.g., tenant farmers, borrowers, etc.). But custom permitted him to make a profit for himself, which may not have been precisely authorized by the master. Though he was not remunerated by his master, he was normally compensated for his expenses. In many cases he was a household slave, a *ben bayit* ('a son of the house', one born in the familia). Incompetence, misuse of discretion, negligence, and downright swindling were grounds for reprehension by the master and even for the unilateral dismissal of the agent. But he could not be sued in court as a debtor. The agent, however, could release debts owed to his master, and the latter was expected to ratify and abide by such acts.

In the parable the manager was such an agent. Reported as dishonest in his management of the property, he was upbraided by the master and was going to be dismissed. The master demanded that he draw up an inventory of the estate and an account of his handling of it, so that it could be made over to another manager. His social equals, other managers, would not welcome him, once dismissed; and since he could not face the prospect of hard labour or begging, the crisis forced him to build up good will with the general public (the debtors included). In his management of the estate, he had indulged in the commonly practised usury of the time. He lent his master's goods or land to fellow Jews at an interest apparently customary to the practice of his day, even though unauthorized to do so by his master. This was his profit. Such a practice, however, was a violation of the Torah and especially of the Pharisaic, rabbinical interpretation of it (see Dt 15:7–8; 23:20–21; Ex 22:24; Lv 25:36–37). However, as far as the courts were concerned, there were ways of getting around the law. Rabbinical casuistry discussed the legality of contracts for loans and the way in which they were recorded. For instance, if a receipt or note read, 'I will pay Reuben 1 denarius on the 1st of Nisan; and if I do not, then I will pay $\frac{1}{4}$ denarius annually in addition', this was declared to be usury, and the sum could be recovered in the courts by the debtor. However, if the receipt merely said, 'I owe Reuben 10 kor of wheat', this was declared not to be usury in the strict sense (and hence not recoverable), even though the borrower had not actually received the equivalent of 10 kor of wheat. He may have received only 5 or 8, but was constrained by the prevailing customs to write a larger sum on the note, and the difference represented the commission for the agent.[25]

When the parable is read in the light of such an economic background, it is understood in a quite different way. The manager, in the interests of ingratiating himself with others than his master, now that his job is virtually lost, has summoned the debtors and ordered them to write new notes or bonds which represent the real amounts owed to the master.[26] He returns the old ones, gets new ones, and prepares his ac-

[25] While the rabbinical writings know of this custom of usury and discuss various aspects of it, the question inevitably arises about the antiquity of this material. Does it really reflect a situation in Palestine in the time of Christ? There are certain indications that it does. Josephus, for instance, records that when Herod Agrippa I was almost bankrupt (*c.* A.D. 33–34), he borrowed money through an agent Marsyas from a Near Eastern banker, who forced Marsyas to sign a bond for 20,000 Attic drachmae, though he received 2500 drachmae less (*Ant.* 18, 6, 3, §157). Perhaps one could also appeal to the Murabba'ât texts (18 r 4 [DJD 2, 101]; 114 [DJD 2, 240–1]).

[26] Note that Luke's text does not speak of falsifying the text or even of changing it. Nor do we find the technical expression for cancelling a debt, used in the Pap. Flor. I. 61, 65 [A.D. 85]: *ekeleuse to cheirographon chiasthēnai*, 'he ordered the receipt crossed out' (i.e., marked with a *chi*). All that Luke's text says is that the debtor is to write fifty or eighty, presumably a new *cheirographon* (although the newness of it is not essential to this interpretation).

count for the master. The manager has, therefore, merely foregone his own profit or commission on the transactions. In this case his subsequent conduct is hardly dishonest, since he is renouncing what in fact was usury.

(3) Why does the master approve of the manager's actions? The master may well have been ignorant of the precise usurious nature of the original transactions; but it is to be presumed that he was aware of the custom of managers. Since 'there was no agency for wrongdoing', and usury was a violation of the Mosaic legislation, the master could hardly have authorized it. There was the duty of releasing the debts of distressed fellow Jews. While the master might have tried to claim the usurious gains from the debtors, since the receipts were written to include them, there was nothing to prevent him from releasing them from what they did not really owe him in terms of the main transaction. If, therefore, his manager reduced the debts by eliminating the usurious gain without the knowledge of the master, he would have been expected to approve and ratify such an act subsequently. This was apparently what he did in effect, when 'he approved of the dishonest manager'. The master was not cheated of anything that was really his. He commends the prudence of the manager in foregoing his profits to win favour with the debtors and others in view of the impending dismissal. While the verb *epēnesen* directly expresses praise for the manager's prudence, it may also reflect the official act of approval or ratification of the reduction of the debts and the elimination of the usury.

(4) What is the point of comparison in the parable? The conclusion in v. 8a states the important element of the parable: 'The master approved of that dishonest manager because he had acted prudently.' His prudence in the face of the crisis that was before him is commended; it is not just prudence in general, but rather his prudent use of material wealth with respect to it. He used his wealth (the profits that were coming to him) to ensure his future in view of the crisis. In this interpretation the

full eschatological nuance of the adverb *phronimōs* is thus brought out, for the Christian situation is one dominated by a need for decisive action. The dishonest manager has become the model for Christians, who are expected to grasp the dramatic situation of the kingdom and the crisis that it brings into the lives of men. It is a situation which calls for a prudent use of one's material wealth. In this there is a connection between this parable and those of the Rich Fool and Dives and Lazarus.

Is there even a slight allegorization of the parable? Modern students of the parables, who have followed A. Jülicher, A. T. Cadoux, C. H. Dodd, and J. Jeremias, tend to restrict the meaning of the Gospel parables to *one* point. Such a position was a reaction against the hyperallegorization of the parables practised in the interpretation of them for centuries. More recent writers, however, have questioned—and rightly so—the 'strait jacket' exegesis of the parables which has since developed.[27] In some cases there may have been at least a second point of comparison, or even more. Can or should this be admitted for the parable of the Dishonest Manager?

A. Descamps speaks of the slight allegorization of the images in the parable. 'Jesus could scarcely utter this parable without making perceptible a slight allegorical nuance in the images—such as that of the master demanding an account from his manager (God calling man to judgment), of the haste with which the manager sets to work (the urgency of the present situation for the disciple). . . .'[28] Such a restricted use of allegory can be admitted, but any further allegorization of it would have to be carefully scrutinized and would have to remain within known Gospel modes of thought and expression. Above all, the tendency to anachronism would be inadmissible.

[27] See P. Benoit, *RB* 55 (1948) 598; R. E. Brown, 'Parable and Allegory Reconsidered', *NovT* 5 (1962) 36–45 (reprinted in *New Testament Essays* [Milwaukee, 1965; London 1966] 254–64); and more recently D. O. Via, Jr., *The Parables: Their Literary and Existential Dimension* (Philadelphia, 1967) 13-17, 155-62.

[28] *Op. cit.*, 48–9.

THE MEANING OF THE LUCAN MULTIPLE CONCLUSION TO THE PARABLE

The Lucan conclusion, which begins with v. 8b and ends with v. 13, should be understood as three further lessons which are drawn from the parable. In a sense, they are inspired allegorizations of the parable, exploiting its various aspects. However, since the material is more than likely derived from other contexts, as already pointed out, the conclusion is much rather the result of conflation than mere allegorization. C. H. Dodd is undoubtedly right when he looks on these verses as 'notes for three separate sermons on the parable as text'.[29] In other words, Luke records three different ways in which the early Church moralized the parable. The first sermon is outlined in vv. 8b–9, where a further eschatological lesson on prudence is drawn from the parable. In the parable itself the dishonest manager by his prudence was the model for Christians facing the crisis which the coming of the kingdom has brought into their lives. The first conclusion rather equates the manager with the children of this world. Both of them are more prudent than the children of light; i.e., the manager and the children of this world manifest a prudence in their dealings with one another which is greater than that manifested by the children of light.[30] The second sermon is found in vv. 10–12, drawing a lesson of responsible management of what is entrusted to one. The eschatological nuance disappears in this application; the emphasis is shifted rather to day-by-day responsibility and fidelity. There are three points: the contrast of responsibility in the little and big things of life; the contrast of responsibility in handling the wealth of dishonesty[31] and real wealth; the

[29] *Parables of the Kingdom*, 17.

[30] Some might prefer to distinguish v. 8b and v. 9 into two distinct applications. This is possible, since v. 8b and v. 9 are distinct in origin. However, they do have a common eschatological reference and both seem to concentrate on the need of prudent, decisive action in 'the children of light'.

[31] See note 15 above (pp. 169-70).

contrast of responsibility in handling the goods of another and one's own. Finally, the last sermon, which really has nothing to to with the parable, sums up a general attitude toward wealth (or mammon). If a man allows himself to get involved in the pursuit of it and reduces himself thereby to a slavish servitude, he cannot serve God. Mammon becomes almost a god itself.

When the story of the Dishonest Manager is analysed along lines such as these, it is seen to have a certain intelligibility. The analysis is complicated, because of the conflation present in the story. But this interpretation has the advantage of reckoning with the separate elements of it and of interpreting them in their own right. At the same time, there is seen to be a unity in it all, which was what the inspired Evangelist was striving for in uniting the disparate elements in his 'travel account'. When the story is analysed in this fasion, there is no need to invoke irony as the key to the interpretation of the passage. This has often been suggested[32] but has never been very convincing.

HOMILETIC CONSIDERATIONS

The preacher who would present the Gospel of the Dishonest Manager would do well in his homily to recall the general Lucan context of the passage (that this is but one of the Lucan stories inculcating a Christian attitude towards riches). Secondly, he would do well to explain to the congregation the distinction between the parable itself (16:1–8a) and the multiple conclusion (16:8b–13), with its further lessons which the inspired Evangelist draws from the parable. Thirdly, a brief exposé of the Palestinian economic situation

[32] See J. F. McFadyen, 'The Parable of the Unjust Steward', *ExpT* 37 (1925–26) 535–9; R. Pautrel, '"Aeterna tabernacula" (Luc, XVI, 9)', *RSR* 30 (1940) 307–27; J. A. A. Davidson, 'A "Conjecture" about the Parable of the Unjust Steward (Luke xvi, 1–9)', *ExpT* 66 (1954–55) 31; H. Clavier, 'L'ironie dans l'enseignement de Jésus', *NovT* 1 (1956) 3–20, esp. 16–17; G. Paul, 'The Unjust Steward and the Interpretation of Lk 16, 9', *Theology* 61 (1958) 189–93; D. R. Fletcher, 'The Riddle of the Unjust Steward: Is Irony the Key?', *JBL* 82 (1963) 15–30.

reflected in the parable would clear up most of the obscure phrases in the story. This would enable the preacher to drive home the main point of the parable (as explained above). Finally, a brief explanation of any of the added applications would be in order. It should be obvious that a homily based on this Gospel pericope is going to be mainly informative and expository; the moralizing tendency of the preacher would have to be curtailed in this case.

To bring this long discussion to a close, we can recapitulate the essentials by presenting the Gospel text in the following form.

The Parable Proper

1 *Jesus said to the disciples: 'There was a certain rich man* (the owner of an estate) *who had a manager* (a servant empowered to handle the household and financial affairs of the estate; he could contract loans in the name of the master, had to keep the accounts, and could even liquidate debts), *and he heard complaints* (literally, "he [the manager] was accused", but we are not told by whom; it need not have been by the debtors) *that this man was squandering his property* (through negligence, swindling, incompetent use of discretion, etc.). 2 *So he called him and said: "What's this I hear about you? Prepare for me an account of your management* (i.e., give me an inventory and prepare an account of the debtors and what they owe me; the purpose of this account is to prepare for the transfer of management to a new man); *you can't be manager around here any longer* (the master has decided to dismiss the servant)." 3 *Then the manager said to himself* (soliloquy): "*What am I going to do? My master is taking my job as manager away from me. I am not strong enough to dig* (as a servant trained to a 'white-collar' job, he knows that he cannot endure the life of a labourer accustomed to hard, physical labour); *I'm ashamed to beg.*—4 *Ah, I know what I'll do, so that when I lose this job, I'll be welcome in people's homes*' (literally, 'I have known [an aorist expressing decision] what I shall do, that when I am removed from management they will receive me into their houses.' The third plural verb is indefinite, since no persons have yet been mentioned to whom it might refer. It is a Semitic way of paraphrasing the passive.—His decision is to take means to secure his future.). 5 *He summoned his master's debtors one by one* (i.e., those with whom he had transacted various "deals"). *He said to the first of them: "How much do you owe my master?"* (It should

not be presumed that he does not know how much was owed. His question is part of the dramatic presentation of the story.) "*One hundred jugs of olive oil*" (literally, 'one hundred baths of olive oil'. Since the Hebrew measure 'bath' equals between eight and nine gallons, this really represents an amount closer to a thousand gallons), *was the answer.* 6 *He said to the man: "Here, take your note* (literally, 'receive your written statement', the IOU or *cheirographon* ['bond'] originally written by the debtor expressing what he owed to the master), *sit down, and, hurry, write* (one for) *fifty* (i.e., write a new IOU for the real amount of the debt owed to the master, now minus the interest originally demanded by the manager. Fifty baths of oil are the manager's commission. The exorbitant rate [100%] should not be pressed too literally, for high figures are characteristic of Jesus' parables.[33] The rate is exorbitant to drive home the real point in the parable; no one is expected to take the figures seriously.). 7 *Then he said to another debtor: "How much do you owe?" He answered: "A hundred bushels of wheat"* (literally, 'a hundred kor of wheat', which is a considerable sum, since the Hebrew kor equals roughly ten to twelve bushels in our metric system. Again, a more realistic modern equivalent would be a thousand bushels of wheat, cut down to eight hundred.). *Again he said: 'Here, take your note and write* (one for) *eighty* (The manager gives up his claim to twenty-five per cent commission). 8 *And the master approved of that dishonest manager* (Since the dishonesty is to be understood as the squandering of the master's estate, reported in v. 2, this description of the manager is not to be regarded as derived from his conduct subsequent to the master's calling him to task. The master's approval or praise commends the manager for having made prudent use of the resources that were his in the situation. There is also the nuance that he gave his approval to the reduction of the debts.), *because he had acted prudently* (i.e., he had sized up the urgency of the situation, and in this he becomes the model for Christians, who should face up to their eschatological situation).

The Lucan Conclusion

8b *For* (The Greek conjunction *hoti* ['because'] introduces a further lesson drawn from the parable; it is a redactional suture joining to the parable itself a Lucan reflection, based on the words of Jesus.) *the children of this world* (See note 10. The children of this world are contrasted with the children of light [=Christian disciples]. The manager is now equated with them. Their shrewdness in their

[33] See J. Jeremias, *The Parables of Jesus*, 22.

dealings with one another becomes an example of the shrewdness which should characterize the Christian disciples in their endeavours to enter the kingdom.) *are more prudent* (The nuance of prudence in the face of the eschatological situation is not completely lost here, for this is the frame of reference for the Christians' activity. But they are compared to the children of this world in their dealings with their own generation. In this conclusion, therefore, the word *phronimos* takes on a further nuance.) *in dealing with their own generation than the children of light are.* 9 *I* (Jesus, the Master) *tell you, make friends with the wealth of dishonesty* (i.e., use prudently the wealth that you have to insure your status when the eschaton arrives. It does not mean that Christians are to make use of ill-gotten gain; the expression is pejorative and expresses only the tendency of wealth as such. It tends to lead man to dishonesty.), *so that when it gives out* (i.e., when the crisis has come), *you will be welcomed into everlasting tents* (i.e., probably into heaven. The expression 'everlasting tents' is not found in the OT, nor in rabbinical writings, but appears first outside of Luke in 2 Esdras 2:11 [3rd c. A.D.].[34] The saying seems to be inculcating a prudent use of wealth in view of one's future—eschatological—status. The expressions seem to be modelled on v. 4 of the parable.). 10 *The man who is trustworthy in little things is also trustworthy in what is big* (Note that this second application has switched from the eschatological situation of the manager and his prudence in face of the crisis to the day-by-day fidelity in responsible positions. This and the next two verses comment not on the subsequent conduct of the manager, for which he was praised as prudent, but rather on the idea of what was expected of him by his own master, when he first gave him the job.). 11 *If, then, you are not trustworthy when handling the wealth of dishonesty, who will trust you with the wealth that is real* (The contrast is between that which is material wealth and that which is spiritual.)? 12 *And if you are not trustworthy when handling what belongs to another, who will give you what is your own* (Material wealth is treated as something that does not belong to man; his real wealth is something that is truly part of himself. If he is not trustworthy in handling the former, how can he trust himself in the disposition of the latter?)?

13 *No servant* (the Greek word here is *oiketēs*, a more general expression than *oikonomos*, 'manager') *can serve two masters; either he will hate the one and love the other, or he will be devoted to the one and despise the*

[34] For an entirely different interpretation of this phrase, see R. Pautrel, *op. cit.*, 319 ff.

other (The third application made on the parable. It is only loosely connected with it, and really is linked more closely to the preceding vv. 10–12. Devotion to wealth is not compatible with devotion to God; that is why wealth is called the mammon of dishonesty [16:9].). *You cannot serve both God and wealth.*

At the beginning of this article I mentioned a growing consensus of exegetical opinion about this Gospel story. I hope that I have made it clear that this is a consensus about the composite nature of it. Unfortunately, the same consensus is not found about the interpretation of it. The understanding of the parable which I have presented, however, has the advantage of giving an intelligible and coherent meaning to the whole. It is not, moreover, without some foundation.

In the new arrangement of Scripture readings for a three-year liturgical cycle of Sundays, it was wise to adopt the whole story of the Dishonest Manager (16:1–13) and not just the old liturgical form of it. In no case should it have been simply omitted—just because it is difficult to explain or preach about. With the adoption of the full text, the multiple Lucan conclusion is in the liturgy with its perennially valid message for the edification and instruction of God's People in this twentieth century.[35]

[35] The new Gospel for the 25th Sunday of the Year, year C, is Lk 16:1–13; the shorter form is Lk 16:10–13. The Gospel for Friday of the 31st week, years 1 and 2, is Lk 16:1–8.

III

PAULINE PASSAGES

9

A FEATURE OF QUMRAN ANGELOLOGY AND THE ANGELS OF 1 COR 11:10*

The Qumran texts have brought to light a feature of Jewish thought about angels which helps us to interpret the meaning of the phrase *dia tous angelous*, 'on account of the angels', in 1 Cor 11:10. This phrase has been the subject of many interpretations from the time of Tertullian on. The evidence from Qumran, however, does not just add another interpretation to the many that have already been given; rather it adds a detail to one interpretation already rather common, thus supporting it and rendering the other interpretations less probable. It is my purpose in this study to indicate the bearing of the new evidence from Qumran on this Pauline expression.

In 1 Cor 11:3–16, Paul is dealing with an abusive practice that had arisen in the Church of Corinth. It had been reported to him that women were praying and 'prophesying' in the liturgical gatherings with heads uncovered. It has been asserted that Greek women were accustomed to wear a veil on the streets and often even at home, if they were married, but usually removed it in religious assemblies.[1] This custom is supposed to have been imitated by the Christian women of Corinth in their

* Originally published in *NTS* 4 (1957–58) 48–58. The postscript of 1966 was originally prepared for the reprint of this article in *Paul and Qumran* (ed. J. Murphy-O'Connor; London: Chapman, 1968) 31–47.

[1] E. B. Allo, *Saint Paul, Première Épître aux Corinthiens*, Paris (1956) 258; see also 263. The chief source of evidence for Greek women taking part in a religious ceremony with uncovered head is the Andania Mysteries in-

religious assemblies. Though it is not certain just how the abuse arose, we are certain from the way Paul speaks about it that he looked upon it as such, especially because it was contrary to the custom of other Christian communities. In this regard the Church of Corinth was not in conformity with the *paradosis*, 'tradition', which Paul had passed on to them (v. 2).[2] So he writes to correct the abuse.

Four reasons may be distinguished in the course of Paul's remarks why a woman should veil her head in assemblies of public prayer. (1) Theologically, the order of creation found in the Genesis story shows that woman is subordinated to man; she is destined to be his companion, helper and mother.[3] Hence she should manifest that subordination by wearing a veil. (2) Philosophically (or sociologically), natural decency would seem to demand it. (3) As a matter of ecclesiastical discipline, the 'churches of God' recognize no other practice in worship. (4) 'On account of the angels' (v. 10). The last reason causes a

---

scription. See W. Dittenberger, *Sylloge Inscriptionum Graecarum* (Leipzig) vol. II (1917) no. 736, 4. Also important is the *Lycosurae lex sacra* (*ibid.* III [1920] no. 999). For the bearing of these inscriptions (and others) on 1 Cor 11:10, see S. Lösch, 'Christliche Frauen in Corinth (1 Kor 11, 2–16). Ein neuer Lösungsversuch', *TQ* 127 (1947) 230–51. Though many details about the wearing of the veil in antiquity, both by Jewish and Greek women, have been preserved for us, none of them bears directly on the problem of the Church in Corinth. We do not know the exact nature nor the origin of the abuse that Paul was trying to handle. Was it a reaction against a custom that he was trying to introduce? G. Delling, *Paulus' Stellung zur Frau und Ehe* (Stuttgart, 1931) 98, seems to think so; likewise A. Schlatter, *Die korinthische Theologie* (Beiträge zur Förderung christlicher Theologie 18/2; Gütersloh, 1914) 23, 54. On the use of the veil in antiquity see R. de Vaux, 'Sur le voile des femmes dans l'Orient ancien', *RB* 44 (1936) 397–412; A. Jeremias, *Der Schleier von Sumer bis heute* (Der Alte Orient 31/1–2; Leipzig, 1931).

[2] S. Lösch (*op. cit.*, 225–30) rightly rejects the idea that there was a movement in Corinth in favour of the emancipation of women, which Paul was trying to combat.

[3] Paul is obviously speaking in vv. 3–9 of the order of creation; cf. 1 Tm 2:13. Further on, however, in v. 11 he introduces another point of view, namely, *en kyriō* 'in the Lord'. Under this aspect Paul says, in Gal. 3:28, *ouk eni arsen kai thēlu*, 'there is neither male nor female'.

difficulty, because it is abruptly added to a verse which is the conclusion of the theological reason set forth in vv. 3–9. As several commentators have remarked, it is a surprise to find it there.[4] Moreover, it is added without any explanation, and all the attempts that have been made to integrate it with the preceding argument have not succeeded. Hence it is best to regard it as a subsidiary reason stated succinctly.

Because the context of this verse will be necessary for the interpretation, I shall give the translation of the entire passage. Goodspeed's translation,[5] which is being used, is a good example of the way modern translators have wrestled with v. 10.

I appreciate your always remembering me, and your standing by the things I passed on to you, just as you received them. But I want you to understand that Christ is the head of every man, while a woman's head is her husband, and Christ's head is God. Any man who offers prayer or explains the will of God with anything on his head disgraces his head, and any woman who offers prayer or explains the will of God bareheaded disgraces her head, for it is just as though she had her head shaved. For if a woman will not wear a veil, let her cut off her hair too. But if it is a disgrace for a woman to have her hair cut off or her head shaved, let her wear a veil. For a man ought not to wear anything on his head, for he is the image of God and reflects his glory; while woman is the reflection of man's glory. For man was not made from woman, but woman from man, and man was not created for woman, but woman was for man. That is why she ought to wear upon her head something to symbolize her subjection, on account of the angels, if nobody else. But in union with the Lord, woman is not independent of man nor man of woman. For just as woman was made from man, man is born of woman, and it all really comes from God. Judge for yourselves. Is it proper for a woman to offer prayer to God with nothing on her head? Does not nature itself teach you that for a man to wear his hair long is degrading, but a woman's long hair is her pride? For her hair is given

[4] So P. Bachmann, *Der erste Brief des Paulus an die Korinther* (4. Aufl.; Leipzig, 1936) 356; J. Sickenberger, *Die Briefe des hl. Paulus an die Korinther und Römer* (Bonner Bibel 6; Bonn, 1932) 51; J. Héring, *La première épitre de Saint Paul aux Corinthiens* (Neuchâtel, 1949) 94.

[5] In J. M. P. Smith (ed.), *The Complete Bible, an American Translation* (Chicago, 1951) New Testament section, 162.

her as a covering. But if anyone is disposed to be contentious about it, I for my part recognize no other practice in worship than this, and neither do the churches of God.

The Greek text of v. 10 reads as follows: *dia touto opheilei hē gynē exousian echein epi tēs kephalēs dia tous angelous.*

The words *dia touto*, 'that is why', indicate the conclusion to the preceding theological argument. Because of them the unexpected addition of *dia tous angelous*, 'on account of the angels', has made some commentators think that this phrase was a gloss.[6] But Robertson and Plummer have pointed out that it cannot be dismissed so lightly: 'Marcion had the words, and the evidence for them is overwhelming. An interpolator would have made his meaning clearer.'[7] Nor is it possible to admit any of the many purely conjectural and often far-fetched emendations, such as *dia to euangelion*, 'on account of the gospel'; *dia tas agelas*, 'on account of the crowds'; *dia tous agelaious*, 'on account of the men who crowded in'; *dia tous andras*, 'on account of the vulgar' or 'gazing men'; *dia tous engelastas*, 'on account of the mockers'; *dia tous ochlous*, 'on account of the mobs'; *dia tēs angelias*, 'throughout [the whole of] her [divine] message'.[8] Consequently, one must try to understand the words as they stand.

V. 10 contains another difficult expression that has tormented interpreters and no satisfying solution has really been found for it—the word *exousian*. Since this is actually the keyword in the verse, I shall indicate briefly the main attempts to interpret it, as its meaning affects the phrase *dia tous angelous*. Four interpretations are currently proposed and unfortunately no new light from Qumran has been shed on this problem.

In itself *exousia* means 'power, authority, right to do some-

[6] C. Holsten, *Das Evangelium des Paulus* (Berlin, 1880) 472–4, eliminates the whole verse. J. M. S. Baljon, *Novum Testamentum Graece* (Groningen, 1898) 525; A. Jirku, 'Die "Macht" auf dem Haupte (1 Kor 11:10)', *NKZ* 32 (1921) 711, consider *dia tous angelous* a gloss.

[7] *First Epistle of St Paul to the Corinthians* (ICC; Edinburgh, 1911) 233.

[8] See R. Perdelwitz, 'Die *Exousia* auf dem Haupt der Frau', *ThStKr* 86 (1913) 611–13; A. P. Stanley, *Epistles of St Paul to the Corinthians* (3rd ed.; London, 1865) 186.

thing; ability; dominion'.[9] But what is its meaning when Paul says, 'That is why the woman should have *exousian* upon her head'?

(1) Most commentators understand *exousia* today in a figurative sense as a *symbol of the power* to which the woman is subjected (by metonymy). Theophylact expressed it thus: *to tou exousiazesthai symbolon*, 'the symbol of being dominated'.[10] It must be admitted that this sense of the word fits the context well, but the chief difficulty with this interpretation is a philological one, since it attributes to *exousia* a passive sense, which is otherwise unknown. Apropos of this interpretation W. M. Ramsay has remarked: '. . . a preposterous idea which a Greek scholar would laugh at anywhere except in the New Testament, where (as they seem to think) Greek words may mean anything that commentators choose'.[11] *Exousia* should indicate a power that the woman possesses or exercises (cf. Rev 11:6; 14:8; 20:6), not one to which she is subjected or subordinated.[12] One may

[9] See W. Bauer, *Griechisch-Deutsches Wörterbuch zu den Schriften des Neuen Testaments* (4. Aufl.; Berlin, 1952) 502; Liddell-Scott-Jones, *A Greek-English Lexicon* (9th ed.; Oxford, 1925–40) vol. I, 599; C. Spicq, 'Encore la "Puissance sur la tête" (1 Cor 11:10)', *RB* 68 (1939) 557–62. Fr Spicq has studied the uses of *exousia* especially in Ben Sira and the Greek papyri and has shown that the word was used specifically of the authority of a husband over his wife or of a father over his children.

[10] *Expos. in Ep. I ad Cor.* (*PG* 124, 697C); the symbolical meaning has been proposed by Theodoret (*PG* 82, 312D); Chrysostom (*PG* 61, 218); A. Lemonnyer, *Épîtres de saint Paul, première partie* (Paris, 1908) 145; R. Cornely, *Commentarius in S. Pauli apostoli epistolas, II: Prior epistola ad Corinthios* (Paris, 1909) 319; P. Bachmann, *op. cit.*, 356; Str-B 3, 436; J. Huby, *Saint Paul, Première épître aux Corinthens* (Paris, 1946) 248–9; C. Spicq, *op. cit.*, 558; J. Kürzinger, *Die Briefe des Apostels Paulus, die Briefe an die Korinther und Galater* (Würzburg, 1954) 28; *et al.*

[11] *The Cities of St Paul. Their Influence on his Life and Thought* (London, 1907) 203.

[12] This is the weak point, in my opinion, in Spicq's study of *exousia* (see above in n. 9). Granted that metonymy is a legitimate way to interpret the word, and granted that *exousia* does mean in the papyri and Ben Sira the authority of the husband over his wife or of the father over his children, the fact remains that *echein exousian* in the New Testament is used in an *active* sense of a power which one exercises. Even in the examples from the papyri

rightly ask why St Paul says 'power' (or 'authority'), if he really means 'subjection'. Then, too, the shift from an abstract idea like power to the specific meaning of an article of feminine attire is not an easy one to explain, even by metonymy.[13] Wendland asks what evidence there is for the veil as a sign of subordination to a man.[14] Consequently, if this interpretation of *exousia* is to be retained, one must say that Paul has created the figurative meaning to suit his context.

(2) Because of this philological difficulty, some commentators have preferred to interpret *exousia* rather as a symbol of the power, the honour and the dignity of the woman. 'The woman who has a veil on her head wears authority on her head: that is what the Greek text says.'[15] The woman who veils her head exercises control over it and does not expose it to indignity; if she unveils it, everyone has control over it and she loses her dignity.[16] Such an interpretation has the advantage of giving to *exousia* an active meaning, but it seriously forces the context, since Paul is not speaking of the dignity of woman nor of her dignified actions. The context treats rather of woman's subordination to man according to the Genesis account of creation.[17]

---

which Spicq cites the word *exousian* seems to me to have this meaning; thus *didonai exousian* means to transfer the authority to another so that he can exercise it.

[13] Allo (*op. cit.*, 266–7) cites the use of a similar expression in Diodorus Siculus (1, 47, 5), who reports that the statue of an ancient Egyptian goddess bears *treis basileias epi tēs kephalēs*, that is, three diadems, signs of a triple royalty. But there is an important difference to be noted: 'here it is question of the power of its wearer and not of the power of someone else' (J. Héring, *op. cit.*, 95); see also J. Weiss, *Der erste Korintherbrief* (Göttingen, 1910) 274.

[14] *Die Briefe an die Korinther* (Das Neue Testament Deutsch 7; Göttingen, 1954) 83.

[15] W. M. Ramsay, *op. cit.*, 203. E. B. Allo, *op. cit.*, 267, combines this interpretation with the first one: Paul is stressing not only the subordination of the woman, but also strives to bring out her dignity. See Delling, *op. cit.*, 99, n. 4.

[16] Robertson and Plummer, *op. cit.*, 232.

[17] J. Huby, *op. cit.*, 248.

(3) A fairly common interpretation of *exousia* today explains the word in the sense of a *magical power* that the veiled woman possesses to ward off the attacks of evil spirits. Since woman is the secondary product of creation, she requires this additional force 'as the weaker sex' against the fallen angels.[18] She needs this magic force, which is the veil, especially in times of prayer and ecstasy, when the angels draw near, for her natural frailty is not sufficient to protect her. The advantage of this interpretation is that it preserves the active meaning of *exousia* and provides a closer connection with what precedes for the phrase *dia tous angelous*. But the major difficulty with this opinion is the lack of evidence showing that a woman's veil was ever thought of as having such a function in antiquity. J. Héring believes that M. Dibelius proved this very point. Yet H. Lietzmann, whose commentary made this interpretation popular, admits the difficulty: 'Freilich ist bisher die Vorstellung von einer apotropäischen Wirkung des Schleiers nicht nachgewiesen.'[19]

(4) In 1920 G. Kittel proposed a new interpretation of *exousia* which has been adopted in some quarters. He pointed out that an Aramaic word, *šlṭwnyh*, meaning a 'veil' or an 'ornament of the head', occurs in the Jerusalem Talmud.[20] It is given there as the equivalent of the Hebrew *šbys* of Is 3:18. Now the root of this word is *šlṭ*, and is identical with the com-

[18] Thus O. Everling, *Die paulinische Angelologie und Dämonologie* (Göttingen, 1888) 37; M. Dibelius, *Die Geisterwelt im Glauben des Paulus* (Göttingen, 1909) 13–23; J. Weiss, *op. cit.*, 274; J. Lietzmann, *An die Korinther I–II* (4. Aufl.; Tübingen, 1949) 55; R. Reitzenstein, *Poimandres* (Leipzig, 1904) 230, n. 1; J. Héring, *op. cit.*, 90, 94–5; E. Fehrle, *Die kultische Keuschheit im Altertum* (Religionsgeschichtliche Versuche und Vorarbeiten 6; Giessen, 1910) 39; *et al.*

[19] *Op. cit.*, 55. W. G. Kümmel's added note on p. 184 is scarcely pertinent.

[20] *Sabbath* 6: 8b, commenting on Is 3:18: *hšbysym: šlṭwnyh kmh d't 'mr šbys šl sbkh.* 'Was die *šebisim* anlangt, so sind damit gemeint die *šalṭonayya*, wie du sagst: der *šabis* des Kopfnetzes.' ('Die "Macht" auf dem Haupt (1 Kor 11:10)', *Rabbinica* (Arbeiten zur Vorgeschichte des Christentums 1/3; Leipzig, 1920) 20. Though this opinion is usually ascribed to G. Kittel, he was actually anticipated by J. Herklotz, 'Zu 1 Kor 11:10', *BZ* 10 (1912) 154. See Levy, *Wörterbuch über die Talmudim und Midraschim*, IV, 562a.

mon Aramaic verb meaning 'to have power, dominion over'. Hence, either by a mistranslation or by a popular etymology, the Greek *exousia* was taken as the equivalent of the Aramaic *šlṭwnyh*. The proponents of this explanation of *exousia* point out that an ancient variant reading in 1 Cor 11:10 is *kalymma*, 'a veil',[21] found in Irenaeus (*PG* 7, 524B), which is supported by *velamen* of Jerome (*PL* 25, 439A) and a codex of the Vulgate. Origen (*PG* 13, 119B) combined the two readings, *velamen et potestatem*. Though we cannot rule out the possibility that the reading *kalymma* or *velamen* is an interpretation of the text or an attempt to eliminate a difficulty of the original text,[22] nevertheless it does show that the word was understood in antiquity in the sense of 'a veil'. This interpretation has been adopted by W. Foerster and M. Ginsburger and seems to underlie the translation given in RSV.[23] The main difficulty with this meaning of *exousia* is that the Greeks of Corinth would never have understood what Paul meant by it.[24] I must admit that this is a real difficulty, but the presupposition on the part of those who propose it usually is that the Church of Corinth was wholly, or almost wholly, Greek. It is, however, beyond doubt that there were *Jewish* elements in the Corinthian community who would have understood the word *exousia* in the sense of *šlṭwnyh*.[25] Consequently, until a better suggestion is made for the sense of *exousia* I prefer to go along with Kittel.

Having given a survey of the main interpretations of *exousia*

[21] Treated as a variant by Nestle, Merk. But is it certain that the text of Irenaeus offers nothing more than a paraphrase of our verse?

[22] See J. Héring, *op. cit.*, 95.

[23] Foerster proposes it only as a conjecture in *TDNT* 2, 574. Ginsburger's discussion ('La "gloire" et l'"autorité" de la femme dans 1 Cor 11:1–10', *RHPR* 12 [1932] 248) was apparently written independently of Kittel's study. G. Delling (*op. cit.*, 105, n. 68) regards this interpretation as 'die annehmbarste Lösung'.

[24] Thus Str-B 3, 437; Allo, *op. cit.*, 264.

[25] According to Acts 18:1–5 Paul on his first arrival in Corinth was given hospitality by 'a Jew named Aquila, a native of Pontus, who had recently come from Italy with his wife Priscilla. . . . Every Sabbath he would preach

we can turn to the phrase *dia tous angelous*. The figurative meanings that have been given to the phrase can be dismissed immediately, as it is obvious that they are 'last-resort' solutions. For instance, Ephraem thought that *angelous* meant *sacerdotes*,[26] while Ambroisiaster commented: *angelos episcopos dicit, sicut in Apocalypsi Ioannis.*[27] But though the word *angelos* is found in the New Testament in the sense of a human messenger (Lk 7:24; 9:52; Jas 2:25), it is never used thus by Paul.

Likewise to be rejected is the interpretation, 'in imitation of the angels', or 'because the angels do so'. Support for this opinion has been sought in Is 6:2, where the angels covered their faces and loins with their wings in the presence of the Lord. So a woman in prayer should cover her head. Just as the angels, who are subordinate to God, veil themselves in his presence, so should woman 'as a subordinate being'[28] follow their example. But one may ask, with J. Huby, why this imitation of the attitude of the angels during divine worship should be prescribed for women only.[29] Moreover, what evidence is there for understanding *dia* in this sense?

---

in the synagogue, and try to convince both Jews and Greeks.' When he turned in anger from the Jews to preach to the heathen, 'he moved to the house of a worshipper of God named Titus Justus, which was next door to the synagogue. But Crispus, the leader of the synagogue, believed in the Lord and so did all his household. . . .' See Allo, *op. cit.*, 12–13; J. Holzner, *Paulus* (Freiburg im B., 1937) 206.

[26] *Commentarii in Epistulas D. Pauli, nunc primum ex Armenio in Latinum sermonem translati* (Venice, 1893) 70. This was likewise the opinion of Pelagius (*PL* 30, 781B) and of Primasius of Hadrumetum (*PL* 118, 532D).

[27] *PL* 17, 253. Similarly D. Bornhäuser, '"Um der Engel willen", 1 Kor 11:10', *NKZ* 41 (1930) 475–88; P. Rose, 'Power on the Head', *ExpT* 23 (1911–12) 183–4.

[28] W. Meyer, *I. Korinther 11–16 Leib Christi* (Zurich, 1945) 26. Similarly K. Roesch, '"Um der Engel willen" (1 Kor 11:10)', *TGl* 24 (1932) 363–5; Robertson and Plummer, *op. cit.*, 233–4 (as a suggestion 'worth considering'); J. Mezzacasa, 'Propter angelos (1 Cor 11:10)', *VD* 11 (1931) 29–42; S. Lösch (*op. cit.*, 255, n. 80) labels K. Roesch's *exposé* as 'die einzig richtige, von den Kirchenvätern übereinstimmend vertretene Deutung'.

[29] *Op. cit.*, 251.

In mentioning above the third interpretation of *exousia* I indicated a meaning of *angelous* that is fairly common among that group of commentators, namely, *fallen angels*. As far as I know, Tertullian was the first to suggest this meaning for *angelous* in this passage. In *De virginibus velandis* 7, he says, *propter angelos, scilicet quos legimus a deo et caelo excidisse ob concupiscentiam feminarum.*[30] Tertullian's suggestion has been illustrated by reference to Gn 6:2, 'the sons of the gods (*b^e^nê 'elôhîm*) noticed that the daughters of men were attractive; so they married those whom they liked best'. Lietzmann adds that this passage in Genesis often excited the fantasy of later Jewish writers, for whom bad angels preying on weak, defenceless women were a literary commonplace.[31] He refers, in particular, to the *Testament of Reuben* 5, where women are warned *hina mē kosmōntai tas kephalas kai tas opseis autōn* because the women before the Flood bewitched the angels in that way.[32] But J. Héring thinks that, since it is not certain that the Corinthians were *au courant* with such Jewish beliefs, it is preferable to suppose with M. Dibelius an allusion to Hellenistic ideas, according to which a woman in a state of ecstasy (as in sleep) was by her weakness particularly exposed to the attacks of certain spirits.[33] Hence *exousia* gives her a magic protection against such attacks.

Against this opinion one may point out that the *weakness* of woman is a notion that the interpreters have introduced. Paul speaks of woman's subordination to man; he says nothing of her weakness. Hence a woman's need of an added protection intro-

[30] *PL* 2, 947A; cf. *Contra Marcionem* 5, 8 (CSEL 47, 597); *De cultu feminarum* 2, 10 (CSEL 70, 88).

[31] *Op. cit.*, 55. He refers to W. Bousset, *Die Religion des Judentums im neutestamentlichen Zeitalter* (Berlin, 1906) 382. See also L. Jung, *Fallen Angels in Jewish, Christian and Mohammedan Literature* (Philadelphia, 1926) 97 ff.; W. Weber, 'Die paulinische Vorschrift über die Kopfbedeckung der Christen', *Zeitschrift für wissenschaftliche Theologie* 46 (1903) 487–99. See n. 18 above for others who hold this opinion.

[32] Compare *Enoch* 6 (Charles, *APOT* 2, 191); 19:1 (2,200); *Jub* 4:22 (2, 19); *Apoc. Bar.* 56:12 (2,513); *Tb* 6:14; 8:3.

[33] *Op. cit.*, 94; cf. M. Dibelius, *Die Geisterwelt*, 18 ff.

duces into the context a consideration that is quite foreign to Paul's argumentation. But the most decisive reason against this interpretation is that *angeloi*, used with the article, never designates bad or fallen angels in the Pauline writings.[34] Moreover, sensuality is never attributed to any of the good angels in any of the Christian or Jewish writings of the period.[35] One of the other problems that is met in interpreting this verse is visualizing just what kind of veil Paul has in mind. It is far from certain that he means a veil that covers the face after the fashion of the oriental women in modern times (at least until fairly recently); he speaks of a covering for the head. If it is merely a head-covering, is that sufficient protection against the fallen angels? Consequently, I believe that this opinion must be abandoned, especially since the new evidence from Qumran rules it out.

The most common opinion has always regarded *angelous* as meaning good angels. Theodoret specified this view, by understanding the word of guardian angels.[36] J. Moffatt expands this notion: 'Paul has in mind the midrash on Gn 1:26 f., which made good angels not only mediators of the Law (Gal 3:19), but guardians of the created order. Indeed, according to one ancient midrash, reflected in Philo, when God said, "Let us make man", he was addressing the angels.'[37] Consequently, a woman should wear a veil on her head out of respect for the angels who are guardians of the order of creation (to which Paul alludes in vv. 8–9).

But Moffatt adds another function of the angels, which some commentators either give as the only one, or join, as he does, to

[34] Compare 1 Cor 13:1; Mt 13:49; 25:31; Lk 16:22; Heb 1:4, 5. See Bachmann, *op. cit.*, 357; and p. 203 below.

[35] See Allo, *op. cit.*, 266. J. Héring (*op. cit.*, 95) thinks that he can weaken this point made by Allo by pointing out that the angels of Gn 6 were also good, 'before permitting themselves to be seduced'. This is hardly *ad rem.*

[36] *PG* 82, 312D-313A. So too E. Zolli, *Christus* (Rome, 1946) 88; Str-B 3, 437; Kittel, *op. cit.*, 26, regards the angels rather as guardians of the woman's chastity.

[37] *The First Epistle of Paul to the Corinthians* (London, 1947) 152. See also L. Brun, '"Um der Engel willen" 1 Kor 11:10', *ZNW* 14 (1913) 298–308.

their task as guardians of the created order. This second function is their assistance at gatherings of public worship.[38] I would separate this function from the former for two reasons. First, it is supported elsewhere in the Old and New Testament. In Ps 137 (138):1 we read *enantion angelōn psalō soi* (LXX). In Rev 8:3 an angel is the mediator of the prayers of the saints.[39] Secondly, two passages in the Qumran literature so far published mention the presence of angels in sacred gatherings.

In column 7 of the *War Scroll* the physical requirement of those who would take part in God's war, an eschatological war, are set forth.

No one who is lame or blind or crippled or who has a permanent blemish in his flesh, nor any person afflicted with a disease in his flesh—none of these shall go with them to war. All of them are to be men who volunteer for battle, perfect both in spirit and in body and prepared for the day of vengeance. Nor shall any man go down with them who is not yet cleansed from his bodily discharge on the day of battle, for holy angels accompany their armies (1QM 7:4–6).[40]

The Hebrew of the last clause reads as follows: *ky' ml'ky qwdš ʿm ṣb'wtm yḥd.* The same reason is given in the so-called Rule of the Congregation for the exclusion of similar cases of physical unfitness from assemblies of the 'congregation'.

Nor shall anyone who is afflicted by any form of human uncleanness whatsoever be admitted into the assembly of God (*bqhl 'lh*); nor shall anyone who becomes afflicted in this way be allowed to retain his place in the midst of the congregation. No one who is afflicted with a bodily defect or injured in feet or hands, or who is lame or blind or deaf or dumb, or who has a visible blemish in his body, or who is an old man, tottering and unable to stand firm in the midst of the congregation of the men of renown, for holy angels are (present) in their [congre]gation. If anyone of these persons has something to say

[38] See G. Kurze, *Der Engels- und Teufelsglaube des Apostels Paulus* (Freiburg im B., 1915) 12.

[39] See further Tb 12:12; 1 Cor 4:9; Eph 3:10; 1 Tm 5:21; Heb 1:14 for functions of the angels that are similar.

[40] *'Ôṣar hammegillôt haggenûzôt* (Jerusalem, 1954) Milḥemet . . . lûaḥ 22.

to the holy council, let an oral deposition be taken from him; but let him not enter, for he is contaminated (1QSa 2:3–11).[41]

The Hebrew for the clause we are interested in is *ky' ml'ky qwdš* [*b'd*]*tm*.

In these two passages every sort of bodily defect, affliction or discharge was considered a thing unworthy of the sight of the angels, who were believed to be present at the gathering of the army for the eschatological war and at the meeting of the congregation or the assembly of God. The volunteer for the holy war had to be perfect not only in spirit but also in body. One gathers from the expression *lr'wt 'ynym* (1QSa 2:7) that bodily defects offend the sight of the angels who are present.

It is interesting to note in this connection that similar bodily defects excluded descendants of Aaron from service in the temple, according to Lv 21:17–23.

'Say to Aaron, "None of your descendants, from generation to generation, who has a defect, may draw near to offer his God's food; for no one who has a defect may come near, no one who is blind, or lame, or has any perforations, or has a limb too long; no one who has a fractured foot, or a fractured hand, or is a hunchback, or has a cataract, or a defect of eyesight, or scurvy, or scabs, or crushed testicles—no one of the descendants of Aaron, the priest, who has a defect, may come near to offer the Lord's sacrifices; since he has a defect, he may not come near to offer his God's food. He may eat his God's food, some of the most sacred as well as the sacred; only he must not approach the veil nor come near the altar, because he has a defect in him, lest he profane my sanctuaries." '

There is no mention of angels in this passage of Leviticus, but it is clear that a bodily defect was considered in ancient Judaism as a source of irreverence toward that which was *qōdeš*, even independently of any moral culpability. In the two passages from the Qumran literature the angels are specified as *ml'ky qwdš*, and the exclusion of bodily defects from their sight is put on the same basis of reverence. From this notion one may interpret the meaning of *dia tous angelous* in 1 Cor.

[41] D. Barthélemy, J. T. Milik, *Qumrân Cave I*, DJD 1, 110.

The context shows that it is a question of a sacred assembly, for men and women are praying and 'prophesying'.[42] In v. 16 Paul refers to the 'custom' which is current in the 'Church of God' (the resemblance of this last expression to *qhl 'lh* in 1QSa 2:4 should be noted).[43] In such an assembly, Paul says, the woman is to wear upon her head a veil *dia tous angelous*. We are invited by the evidence from Qumran to understand that the unveiled head of a woman is like a bodily defect which should be excluded from such an assembly, 'because holy angels are present in their congregation'.

Furthermore, the Pauline context supports such an interpretation. 'Any woman who prays or "prophesies" with uncovered head disgraces her head, for it is just as though she had her head shaved. For if a woman will not wear a veil, let her cut off her hair too. But if it is a disgrace for a woman to have her hair cut off or her head shaved, let her wear a veil' (v. 6). 'Does not nature itself teach you that . . . a woman's long hair is her pride? For her hair is given her as a covering' (vv. 14–15). In Paul's view there is no difference between the unveiled head of a woman and the shaven head of a woman; and the latter is an unnatural condition. This is not much different from saying that the unveiled head of a woman is like a bodily defect. Hence *dia tous angelous* should be understood in the sense of 'out of reverence for the angels', who are present in such sacred gatherings and who should not look on such a condition.

Though this evidence from Qumran has not solved the problem of *exousia*, it has, I believe, made the interpretation of *dia tous angelous* as 'fallen angels' far less plausible, and consequently the interpretation of *exousia* as a magical power loses much of its force.

One last remark. It may be asked whether it is valid to cite evidence from the Qumran texts to interpret a passage in the

[42] This is the common interpretation of the situation in this passage; see Allo's remarks (*op. cit.*, 257) against Bachmann's understanding of the context.

[43] On *qhl* and *ekklēsia* see Kittel's *TDNT* 3, 524–6.

epistles to the Corinthians. These letters have always been looked upon as the special preserve of those who would point out 'Hellenisms' in Paul's thought or language. Influence from the Greek world on the Apostle's writings cannot be denied, given his background as a Jew of the Diaspora and his vocation as the missionary to the Gentiles. It is to be expected that the Epistles to the Corinthians will continue to be better understood as our knowledge of their Hellenistic background increases. But Paul was a Jew and his chief education was rabbinical, based on a thorough study of the Old Testament and saturated with the ideas of contemporaneous Judaism. Hence it is not surprising that some of the background should appear even in the most Greek of his letters.[44]

No one knows *how* the theological ideas of the Qumran sect influenced Paul. That they *did* so is beyond doubt. J. Coppens, in an early article on the relation of the Qumran scrolls to the New Testament, stated that the influence of the sect was more apparent in the later writings of Paul than in the 'great epistles'.[45] As the Qumran texts continue to be published, one sees this influence appearing abundantly throughout Paul's letters. Consequently, if my suggestion that *dia tous angelous* of 1 Cor 11:10 is to be explained in terms of Qumran angelology were an isolated case of such influence in the Epistles to the Corinthians, I might suspect its validity. But a glance at the list of rapprochements between Qumran and the New Testament writings recently published by R. E. Murphy[46] will show that it is not alone. And that list is far from complete, as its author admits. Consequently, one should not be surprised to find a

[44] In the same vein writes S. Lyonnet ('L'étude du milieu littéraire et l'exégèse du Nouveau Testament', *Bib* 37 [1956] 1–3), apropos of the results of J. Dupont's researches into Pauline gnosis.

[45] 'Les documents du Désert de Juda et les origines du Christianisme', *ALBO* ser. 2, no. 41 (1953) 26.

[46] 'The Dead Sea Scrolls and New Testament Comparisons', *CBQ* 18 (1956) 263–72.

detail of Qumran angelology shedding light on a passage of the Pauline Letters which is otherwise heavily 'Hellenistic'.

Postscript (1957)

After my arrival in Jerusalem I found that there were two other passages in the Qumran Cave 4 material that supported the interpretation set forth in this article. One is in an unpublished fragment of the Damascus Document (provisional abbreviation 4QD[b]). A translation of it appears in J. T. Milik, *Ten Years of Discovery in the Wilderness of Judea*, London, 1959, 114: 'Fools, madmen (*mšwgʿ*), simpletons and imbeciles (*mšwgh*), the blind, the maimed (*ḥgr*), the lame, the deaf, and minors, none of these may enter the midst of the community, for the holy angels [are in the midst of it].' The second passage was pointed out to me by Dr Claus-Hunno Hunzinger, who has found it in a Cave 4 fragment of the *Milḥamah*, which he is preparing for publication (4QM[a]). Enough of the context has been preserved to show that bodily defects were to be excluded from the presence of the angels. In the immediately preceding lacuna reference was most probably made to a nocturnal pollution. The text reads: *[ly]lh hh'wh l[w' yṣ]' 'tmh l[mlḥ]mh ky' ml'ky qwdš bmʿrkwtmh* ('for the holy angels are among their battle-lines'). In all of these passages the force of *ky'* should not be overlooked; it gives the reason for the exclusion of the defects in the camps, the battle-lines and the assemblies. It parallels the Pauline use of *dia*.

Postscript (1966)

The interpretation of 1 Cor 11:10 which I have proposed in the above article finds support in the independent study of H. J. Cadbury, 'A Qumran Parallel to Paul', *HTR* 51 (1958) 1–2. It has been favourably adopted by K. H. Schelkle, *Die Gemeinde von Qumran und die Kirche des Neuen Testaments* (Patmos: Düsseldorf, 1960) 82.

Criticism of my interpretation can be found in J. Héring, *The*

First Epistle of Saint Paul to the Corinthians (tr. A. W. Heathcote and P. J. Allcock; London: Epworth, 1962) 108; H. Braun, 'Qumran und das Neue Testament: Ein Bericht über 10 Jahre Forschung (1950–59)', *TRu* 29/3 (1963) 213–14; J. C. Hurd, Jr., *The Origin of 1 Corinthians* (New York: Seabury, 1965) 184, n. 4.

Both Braun and Hurd have noted my omission of a reference to Col 2:18 in the discussion of the Pauline use of *hoi angeloi*. It should certainly have been included in footnote 34. But I am not sure that they are right in saying that the omitted reference militates against my thesis at that point. Is it certain that the angels mentioned in Col 2:18 are 'fallen' or 'bad' angels? It seems to me that the argument in Colossians (whether this is genuinely Pauline or not) does not depend on whether the angels are good or bad. The 'worship of angels' (Col 2:18) is apparently to be understood in terms of the other references to spirits in that letter, i.e. to those beings, good or bad, whom certain Christians in the Colossian church were venerating and whose cult was jeopardizing the cosmic role of Christ. The author's opposition to this cult is just as intelligible if the angels be good or bad.

Braun further criticizes the interpretation of both Cadbury and myself, maintaining that its main point is forced, viz. that the uncovered or shorn head of a woman is comparable to a bodily defect. I probably would never have made such a comparison personally, nor have I found any ancient data to support it. But it should not be overlooked that it is Paul who (at least implicitly) suggests this comparison. He equates the unveiled head of a woman with the shaven or shorn head (1 Cor 11:5–6); again it is Paul who regards such a condition as disgraceful (*aischron*). Is his attitude toward the uncovered head of the woman so radically different from that of the Qumran author who would exclude bodily defects from the sight of the angels?

Lastly, Braun asserts that 'the magically protective effect of a headcovering *is* attested in b. Shabbat 156b' (p. 214 [his italics]). He refers to W. G. Kümmel's revision of Lietzmann's commentary on 1 Cor (HNT 9 [1949] 184). When, however, one checks this reference, one sees how far-fetched the parallel is, as far as the Pauline passage is concerned. I shall quote Kümmel's note in Braun's own language: 'In einer späten talmudischen Erzählung (*Schabbat* 156b, s. W. Foerster, *ZNW* 30 (1931) 185 f.) wird ein Rabbi zum Dieb, als ihm das Kopftuch vom Haupt gleitet: da ist das Kopftuch deutlich ein magischer Schutz gegen den "bösen Trieb" (die Stelle kann unmöglich auf die Kopfbedeckung als "Unterordnung unter Gott" gedeutet werden, so W. Foerster, *TWNT*, vol. II, p.571, Anm. 72). Damit ist, wenn nicht die apotropäische, so doch die magisch beschützende Wirkung einer Kopfbedeckung deutlich belegt.'—But is the head-covering which protected the rabbi against his 'evil impulse' to steal really a parallel to Paul's 'veil' on a woman's head in a sacred assembly? Is the 'evil impulse' (*yṣryh*) comparable to a bad angel? Finally, is this 'late Talmudic narrative' of the Babylonian tractate *Shabbat* (156b; ed. Goldschmidt, I. 717) a tale that might have been known to Paul? After all, it is told of R. Naḥman bar Isaac who belonged to the fourth generation of Babylonian Amoraim and died *c.* A.D. 356 (see H. L. Strack, *Introduction to the Talmud and Midrash* [Philadelphia: Jewish Publication Society of America, 1931] 130). In short, none of the above mentioned points of criticism seems to be serious enough to invalidate the interpretation.

Hurd speaks of the Qumran parallels as being 'rather distant'. I am fully aware of this difficulty and know no more to say about it than what has already been said on pp. 200–2 above. But until a better solution to this *crux interpretum* comes along, the Qumran parallel seems to shed most light on the problem. For a recent discussion of the passage which makes no reference to Qumran or my interpretation, see M. D. Hooker, 'Authority on Her Head: An Examination of 1 Cor 11:10', *NTS* 10 (1964) 410–16.

10

QUMRAN AND THE INTERPOLATED PARAGRAPH IN 2 COR 6:14–7:1*

That there are contacts between the literature of the Qumran Essene sect and the Pauline corpus is no longer a question of doubt. One may discuss, of course, whether the contacts are direct or indirect, but the general fact is admitted today.[1] There is one passage, however, in the Pauline corpus which has not received the detailed attention it deserves in view of the large number of contacts which it contains and the bearing which they have on its nature. This is the puzzling passage in the Second Epistle to the Corinthians 6:14–7:1.

The problem presented by this passage is perhaps best summed up by a quotation from a commentary written in 1915, well before the discovery of the Qumran texts. At that time A. Plummer wrote, 'This strongly worded admonition to make no compromise with heathenism comes in so abruptly here that a

* Originally published in *CBQ* 23 (1961) 271–80.

[1] To admit this is not to subscribe to a form of pan-Qumranism. The word 'contact', however, is deliberately chosen here, and not 'parallel'. Parallels in literature are legion, and there is undoubtedly truth in the remarks of S. Sandmel, 'Parallelomania', *JBL* 81 (1962) 1–13. Again, one often sees quoted E. R. Goodenough's famous dictum about literary parallels: a parallel by definition consists of straight lines in the same plane which never meet, however far produced in any direction. But the definition is derived from mathematics and applied to literature. To repeat the dictum as if it closes the discussion or absolves one from investigating the literary relationship of authors is only a form of obscurantism—something little better than parallelomania or pan-Qumranism. Moreover, it enables one to avoid asking the question when a *literary* parallel might cease to be such and actually prove to be a 'contact'.

number of critics suppose that it is a fragment of another letter and some maintain that the fragment is not by St Paul.'[2] Three main reasons are given for this critical view. First, the paragraph radically interrupts the chain of thought between 6:13 and 7:2. In the preceding context (6:1–13) Paul is making an eloquent plea for his reconciliation with the Corinthian community, appealing to his own past experience and his efforts expended on their behalf. In the immediately preceding verses (11–13) he pleads, 'I have kept nothing back from you, men of Corinth; I have opened my heart to you (*hē kardia hēmōn peplatyntai*). It is not that I am cramping you, it is your own affections. To pay me back, I tell you, my children, you must open your hearts too (*platynthēte kai hymeis*).' Then comes the puzzling paragraph about avoiding relations with unbelievers (6:14–7:1). Finally, Paul resumes his pleas for open-hearted reconciliation in 7:2 with *chōrēsate hēmas*, 'Make room for me in your hearts. I have not wronged or harmed or got the better of anybody.' And the plea continues for two more verses. The second reason is that the passage has a self-contained, independent character, forming a unit intelligible in itself, like a short homily. It is devoid of any concrete details which would suggest that it was dealing with a specifically Corinthian problem. Thirdly, it has been denied Pauline authorship, because six of the key-words in the passage are not found elsewhere in the New Testament, and some of them are *hapax legomena* in the whole Greek Bible. These are *heterozygeō*, *metochē*, *symphōnēsis*, *synkatathesis*, *Beliar*, *molysmos*.[3] These three reasons, together with

[2] *A Critical and Exegetical Commentary on the Second Epistle of St Paul to the Corinthians* (New York: Scribner, 1915) 204. The critics are divided: (a) some regard the passage as a non-Pauline interpolation; (b) others think that it is Pauline, but belongs to some lost letter of the Apostle (perhaps that referred to in 1 Cor 5:9); (c) still others maintain that it is Pauline, but is merely misplaced within 2 Cor, e.g., that it should follow 2 Cor 6:2. A good summary of critical opinion on this question can be found in E.-B. Allo, *Saint Paul: Seconde Épître aux Corinthiens* (EBib; Paris: Gabalda, 1937) 189–93.

[3] Some critics add to this list the rare words *emperipatēsō* and *eisdexomai*,

a few subsidiary considerations, have been well presented in a careful scrutiny of the usual attempts to defend the authenticity of the passage[4] and its nexus in the letter by the Dutch Catholic scholar W. Grossouw.[5] Without appealing to the Qumran contacts, he concluded to the non-Pauline character of the passage.

It was apparently K. G. Kuhn who first noted the relationship between this paragraph and the Qumran writings and pointed out in a footnote that this passage, more than any other text in Paul's letters, contains 'des affinités de terminologie frappantes avec les textes des Esséniens'.[6] He concluded that 'Paul is perhaps citing here precisely an Essene text.' However, the evidence of these Qumran contacts has not been examined in detail. This I propose to do and to attempt to come to some conclusion about the bearing of them on the nature of this passage in 2 Cor.

First of all, I cite the passage (2 Cor 6:14–7:1) for the convenience of the reader.

Do not be misyoked with unbelievers. What partnership can uprightness have with iniquity? Or what fellowship can light have with darkness? What harmony can there be between Christ and Beliar? Or what part can a believer have with an unbeliever? What agree-

---

which never appear otherwise in the New Testament, and *pantokratōr* which otherwise occurs only in the Apocalypse. But these three words are found here in citations from the Old Testament and may not be used with the same validity as criteria.

[4] Attempts to explain the nexus between the preceding context and the paragraph either by internal analysis of them or by an appeal to Pauline anacolutha (which are claimed to be more numerous in 2 Cor than in other Pauline letters) have been more marked by rhetoric than success. See A. Plummer, *op. cit.*, 205; E.-B. Allo, *op. cit.*, 185–6; C. Spicq, *Épîtres aux Corinthiens* (La Sainte Bible [de Pirot-Clamer] 11/2; Paris: Letouzey et Ané, 1948) 348; A. Menzies, *The Second Epistle of the Apostle Paul to the Corinthians* (London: Macmillan, 1912) 50. (The latter is a good example of the forced attempt to explain the nexus by an analysis of the preceding context and the passage itself.)

[5] 'Over de echtheid van 2 Cor 6:14–7:1', *StudCath* 26 (1951) 203–6.

[6] *RB* 61 (1954) 203, n. 1; see also *ET* 11 (1951) 74; F.-M. Braun, 'L'arrière-fond judaïque du quatrième évangile et la communauté de l'Alliance', *RB* 62 (1955) 33–4.

ment has the temple of God with idols? For we are the temple of the living God; as God has said,

'I shall dwell among them and move about among them,
and I shall be their God and they will be my people.'
(Lv 26:12; Ez 37:27)

Therefore, 'come forth from them, (Is 52:11)
and separate from them, says the Lord,
and touch nothing that is unclean';
then 'I shall welcome you.' (Ez 20:34)
And 'I shall become a father to you, (2 Sm 7:14)
and you will be my sons and daughters,
says the Lord Almighty.'

Since we have such promises, dear friends, let us purify ourselves from all that can taint body and spirit, and let us perfect our holiness in the fear of God.

The elements in this passage which suggest Qumran contacts or the reworking of Qumran ideas are the following: (*a*) the triple dualism of uprightness and iniquity, light and darkness, Christ and Beliar (together with the underlying notion of the 'lot'); (*b*) the opposition to idols; (*c*) the concept of the temple of God; (*d*) the separation from impurity; (*e*) the concatenation of Old Testament texts. Each of these elements is known to have a significant Qumran background which is the basis of our discussion.

(*a*) *The triple dualism.* The purpose of the contrast brought out by the triple dualistic expressions is to divide mankind into two classes, those who follow Christ and those who do not. A similar division of mankind, by now well known, is expressed in many ways in the Qumran literature, but most significantly by the expressions 'sons of light' and 'sons of darkness'. Though the expression 'sons of light' does not occur here, Paul does employ the Greek equivalent of it elsewhere.[7] But the contrast of

[7] The expression 'sons of darkness' does not appear in the New Testament, but 'sons of light' occurs in 1 Thes 5:5 and Eph 5:8 (and outside the Pauline corpus in Jn 12:36 and Lk 16:8). Moreover, the fuller context of 1 Thes 5:4–8 and Eph 5:8–13 exploits the contrast of light and darkness in ways reminiscent of several Qumran passages. See also Rom 13:12–13.

light and darkness in *tís koinōnia phōti pros skotos*[8] in a context of mixing believers with unbelievers is merely another way of saying 'sons of light' and 'sons of darkness'. Pertinent to our discussion here is the well-known passage of the *Manual of Discipline*, 'to love all the sons of light, each according to his lot in God's counsel, and to hate all the sons of darkness, each according to his guilt in God's vengeance' (1QS 1:9–11). Again, 'may he be cut out of the midst of the sons of light because he swerved from following God for the sake of his idols and of that which casts him into iniquity' (1QS 2:16–17).[9] See further 1QS 3:3, 13, 19–20, 24–25; 1QM 1:1, 3, 9, 11, 13; 13: 5–6, 9, 15–16; 1QH 12:6; 4QFlor 1:9. While the opposition of light and darkness is not only a natural one, and one found as a symbolic representation of the forces of good and evil in many literatures, among which we may mention the Old Testament itself (Is 45:7; Mi 7:8; Jb 29:3), it is to be noted that the figure is found neither in the Old Testament nor in Rabbinical literature as a means of expressing two great classes of mankind.[10] In this Corinthian passage mankind is divided according to light and darkness just like the 'sons of light' and the 'sons of darkness' in the Qumran literature.

Several nouns occur in this passage as expressions for the general idea of association with one or other of these classes of mankind: *metochē*, *koinōnia*, *symphōnēsis*, *meris*. It is especially the last one which indirectly suggests that the Qumran notion of

[8] The expression *koinōnia pros* is peculiar; it is found also in Sir 13:2 where it can be explained as reflecting the Hebrew original *ytḥbr 'l* (the preposition *'el*). H. Windisch (*Der zweite Korintherbrief* [Meyer-Kommentar 6; 9th ed.; Göttingen: Vandenhoeck und Ruprecht, 1924]) also suggests a Semitism as the reason for it. If it really is such, then this point of syntax would be an additional support to our thesis.

[9] Note also the proximity of two other ideas in this text which are found in the Corinthian passage under discussion, 'idols' and 'iniquity'.

[10] G. Graystone ('The Dead Sea Scrolls and the New Testament', *ITQ* 23 [1956] 33; *The Dead Sea Scrolls and the Originality of Christ* [New York: Sheed and Ward, 1956] 71–2) tried to minimize the importance of the Qumran phrase 'sons of light' by maintaining that even if it did not occur

'lot' likewise underlies this passage. This will be clarified by referring to a passage in Col 1:12, another Pauline verse which has likewise been shown to have been influenced by Qumran ideas: *eis tēn merida tou klērou tōn hagiōn en tō phōti*, 'to share the lot of the saints in light'. Here we find the noun *meris* explicitly associated with *klēros* in a context of light, and perhaps because of this association K. G. Kuhn was inclined to equate *meris* in 2 Cor 6:15 with the Hebrew word used at Qumran for 'lot', viz. *gôrāl*.[11] However, it is significant that *meris* in the Septuagint never translates *gôrāl*, whereas *klēros* quite frequently does.[12] However, even in the Septuagint these words are related, as passages like Dt 10:9; Jer 13:25 and Wis 2:9 show. When we recall that the members of the Essene community regarded themselves not only as the 'sons of light', but also as the 'lot of light' (*gôral 'ôr*; see 1QM 13:9, 5–6; CD 13:12;[13] 4QIs[d] 13:12) and the 'lot of God' (*gôral 'El*; see 1QS 2:2; 1QM 1:5, 15; 13:5; 15:1; 17:7), it is difficult to escape the

---

in the Old Testament, it is almost a natural Hebraism, using the frequent 'sons of. . . .'. A natural Hebrew idiom, indeed, but the significant fact remains that the expression had not been found outside of the New Testament before the discovery of the Qumran Scrolls. It is, moreover, paralleled only there. See further my remarks above, pp. 167-8, n. 10.

[11] *RB* 61 (1954) 203, n. 2.

[12] Cf. E. Hatch and H. A. Redpath, *A Concordance to the Septuagint and the Other Greek Versions of the Old Testament (Including the Apocryphal Books)* (Graz: Akademische Druck- und Verlagsanstalt, 1954) 2, 911 (*meris*), 770 (*klēros*). O. Procksch has maintained that *klēros* is the usual rendering of the Hebrew *naḥ*^a^*lāh*, 'inheritance', in the Old Testament (see the article '*klēros*' in Kittel, *TWNT* 1, 108). As a matter of fact, it occurs 48 times as the equivalent of *naḥ*^a^*lāh* over against 62 times as the translation of *gôrāl*. The Pauline usage may well reflect the meaning 'inheritance' at times, but when the Colossian passage is compared with such a Qumran passage as 1QS 11:7–8, 'To those whom God has chosen . . ., he has given a share in the lot of the saints (*wynḥylm bgwrl qdwšym*)', the later Qumran nuance of *gôrāl* as 'lot' or 'party' seems to be more appropriate in the Colossian passage.

[13] In the light of the other passages where this expression occurs it seems preferable to read *h*'[*wr*] here instead of C. Rabin's *h*'[*mt*]; see *The Zadokite Documents* (Oxford: Clarendon, 1954) 67.

conclusion that this notion underlies the division of mankind described in this passage in Corinthians.

The dominantly ethical character of the cosmic dualism of Qumran[14] is manifest in the contrast of uprightness and iniquity which is often associated with that of light and darkness. This we find also in the 2 Cor passage, where the two pairs are juxtaposed. It is interesting to compare with this the following Qumran texts: 'All iniquity and [wick]edness you will destroy forever and your uprightness will be manifested to the sight of all whom you have made' (1QH 14:16). Again, 'Then iniquity shall depart before uprightness, as darkness departs before the light' (1Q27 1 i 5–6). Here the two pairs are linked. See further CD 20:20–21.

The last couple in the Pauline text is Christ and Beliar. Christ, of course, does not appear in the Qumran texts, and his appearance in the 2 Cor passage is clear proof of the Christian *reworking* of the Qumran material. But Belial frequently is opposed to God as the leader of the hostile lot.[15] At the end of the eschatological war described in the *War Scroll* the priests, levites and all the elders of the community 'shall bless in their places the God of Israel and all his faithful works and the indignation which he has directed against Belial and all the spirits of his lot. And they shall answer and say, "Blessed be the God of Israel . . ., but cursed be Belial with his hostile purpose . . .!"' (1QM 13:1–4). Here we find Belial set over against the God of Israel, just as he is pitted against Christ in the Corinthian text. Belial, as a demon or personified force, occurs further in 1QS 1:18, 24; 2:19, 5 ('all the men of Belial's lot'); 10:21 (?); 1QM 1:1, 5, 13; 4:2; 11:8; 13:[2], 4, 11; 14:9; 15:3; 18:1, 3; 1QH 6:21;

[14] See G. Mensching, 'Dualismus. I. Religionsgeschichtlich', *RGG*[3] 2 (1958) 272–4; G. Gloege, 'Dualismus. II. Theologisch', *ibid.*, 274–6.

[15] Beliar, the New Testament form of the name, is merely the result of a late dissimilation of the liquid consonants and is actually identical with the name Belial. The name can now be safely interpreted as the name of a demon opposed to God on the basis of the Qumran parallels and the suggestion of some commentators that it refers to Anti-Christ (e.g., H. Lietz-

1Q40 9:3 (?); 4QFlor 1:8 bis, 9; 2:2; 4QTest 23 (?); 4QM[a] 6.[16] The Hebrew word *b^elîya'al* occurs in the Old Testament as a common noun, meaning 'worthlessness, evil, perversion', as it does often also in the Qumran *Hôdāyôt.* There is, further, the expression, *'yš bly'l* or *bny bly'l*, 'an evil man', 'evil men'. This is undoubtedly the root of the Qumran expression, but Belial as the proper name of a demon is otherwise unknown in the Old Testament.[17] Before the discovery of the Qumran texts this usage was known only in this unique New Testament passage and in several Jewish intertestamental compositions, such as *Jubilees* (1:20; 15:33 [?]), the *Testaments of the Twelve Patriarchs* (Reuben 4:11; 6:3 [?]; Simeon 5:3 [explicit contrast of God and Beliar]; Levi 19:1 [where light and darkness are coupled with the Lord and Beliar]; Dn 1:7 [?]; 4:7; 5:1; Naphtali 2: 6; 3:1), the *Ascension of Isaiah* (3:11) and the *Damascus Document* (4:13, 15; 5:18; 8:2; 12:2 [?]; 19:14). But several of these works were favourites with the Essenes of Qumran, often copied by them, if not actually composed by them.[18] It is,

---

mann, *An die Korinther, I–II* [Handbuch zum Neuen Testament 9; 4th ed.; Tübingen: Mohr, 1949] 129) can be dismissed. See further W. Foerster, '*Beliar*', *TDNT* 1,607.

[16] Cf. H. W. Huppenbauer, 'Belial in den Qumrantexten', *TZ* 15 (1959) 81–9.

[17] C. Spicq (*op. cit.*, 348) considers it possible that this meaning may occur in 2 Sm 22:5 and Ps 18:5, 'comme Dieu de la mort et du monde souterrain'. Similarly W. Foerster, *op. cit.* This is, however, most unlikely since the word *bly'l* in each case stands in parallelism with *mawet* ('death') and *še'ôl* ('Hades'), which supports the abstract meaning given by the dictionaries, 'rivers of destruction'. However, cf. P. Joüon, '*b^elîya'al* Bélial', *Bib* 5 (1924) 178–83.

[18] Five fragmentary MSS. of *Jubilees* have come to light in Qumran Cave IV alone. The same cave has yielded an Aramaic text of the *Testament of Levi* and a Hebrew text of the *Testament of Naphtali*. Even though the latter two are not exactly the same as the Greek version known to us in the *Testaments of the Twelve Patriarchs*, they probably served as the sources of the latter (see J. T. Milik, *Ten Years of Discovery in the Wilderness of Judaea* [SBT 26; London: SCM, 1959] 34–5). Moreover, the *Damascus Document* has turned up in eight fragmentary copies from Cave 4 and one from Cave 6 (see *RB* 63 [1956] 55, 60–1, 407, n. 1; 62 [1955] 398–406).

therefore, significant that the unique occurrence of Beliar in the New Testament should be in this otherwise puzzling paragraph which manifests so many contacts with the Qumran literature. Considering the triple contrast of light and darkness, uprightness and iniquity, Christ and Beliar, it is difficult to deny the reworking of Qumran expressions and ideas.[19]

(*b*) *Opposition to idols.* Following the triple dualistic contrast is the question, 'What agreement has the temple of God with idols?' This question reflects the same attitude found in the Qumran text already cited, 'May he be cut off from the midst of the sons of light because he has swerved from following God for the sake of his idols and of that which casts him into iniquity' (1QS 2:16–17). We do not find here the explicit contrast of idols with the temple of God in the Qumran text, but both elements are frequent in this literature, opposition to idols and the temple of God. This suggests a common conceptual background; see further 1QS 2:11, 17; 4:5; 1QH 4:19; CD 20:9; *T. Reuben* 4:6.

(*c*) *The temple of God.* The contrast of idols with the temple of God leads to the assertion, 'For we are the temple of the living God.' This assertion introduces an idea into the sixth

[19] Another possible contact which may strengthen the evidence thus far adduced is found in the use of *heterozygeō*. This verb obviously reflects the prohibition of Dt 22:10, forbidding a man to plough with an ox and an ass yoked together (see also Lv 19:19). The commentators usually refer to these passages to illustrate the incongruity of the association stressed here. It is, moreover, an Old Testament figure to speak of yoking in the sense of believing a teaching, following a doctrine (see Ps 106:28; Nm 25:3). Hence, the basic idea used here is an Old Testament derivative. But it should be noted that the same nuance occurs also in the Qumran *Hôdāyôt*. If it is correct that the person speaking in the first singular is the Righteous Teacher, the founder of the Qumran movement, as many maintain, then he refers to his followers as 'all those who are yoked to my counsel' (*kwl nṣmdy swdy*, 1QH 5:24), and as 'those who are yoked to my testimony' (*nṣmdy t'wdty*, 1QH 6:19). This is obviously a use of 'yoking' in the sense of following a doctrine.

chapter of 2 Cor which is otherwise quite foreign to it. The 'we' must be understood of the believers, the followers of Christ, the men of his lot. As a community they constitute the temple of God. The same theme can be found also in genuine Pauline passages like 1 Cor 3:16–17 and Eph 2:21–22.[20] But the idea of the community as the 'holy of holies' is a notion cherished by the Qumran Essenes. 'At that time the men of the community shall be set apart as a sanctuary for Aaron (*byt qwdš l'hrwn*), being united as the Holy of Holies, and those who walk in perfection as a house of community for Israel (*wbyt yḥd lyśr'l*, 1QS 9:5–7).[21] Again, 'when all these things shall come to pass in Israel, the council of the community shall be established in truth as an eternal planting, a sanctuary (*byt qwdš*) for Israel and a foundation of the Holy of Holies (*wswd qwdš qwdšym*) for Aaron' (1QS 8:4–6; see further 5:6; 8:8–9; 11:8 [*wswd mbnyt qwdš*]; 4QFlor 1:6 [*lbnwt lw' mqdš 'dm lhywt mqṭyrym bw' lw' lpnyw m'śy twrh*]).

[20] The whole context here forbids us to think of the 'temple of God' in terms of the individual Christian, like the figure employed in 1 Cor 6:19 (*pace* H. Lietzmann, *op. cit.*, 129). K. G. Kuhn (*RB* 61 [1954] 203, n. 2) has indicated that the theme of the human body as the temple of God has parallels rather in the Hellenistic world, especially in Philo, whereas the theme of the community-temple has previously lacked parallels in the literature prior to or contemporary with the New Testament. See the bibliographical references cited by him; but also K. Prümm, *Diakonia Pneumatos, der zweite Korintherbrief als Zugang zur apostolischen Botschaft, Auslegung und Theologie* (Rome: Herder) II/1 (1960) 361–4; G. W. MacRae, 'Building the House of the Lord', *AER* 140 (1959) 361–76; J. Pfammatter, *Die Kirche als Bau* (AnalGreg 110; Rome: Gregorian University, 1960). B. Gärtner, *The Temple and the Community in Qumran and the New Testament: A Comparative Study in the Temple Symbolism of the Qumran Texts and the New Testament* (SNTS Monograph Series, 1; Cambridge: University Press, 1965).

[21] 'Holy of Holies' is an expression used for objects consecrated to Yahweh, especially to his service in the temple of Jerusalem or in the desert Tent. For a discussion of its various uses, see S. R. Driver, *The Book of Daniel* (Cambridge Bible for Schools and Colleges; Cambridge: University Press, 1901) 137. When all the evidence is reviewed, it is seen to be an expression reserved either for the temple or some part of it, and often for the inner-

(*d*) *Separation from all impurity.* It would be surprising in a text which already reveals so many contacts with the Qumran literature, if we did not find some reference to its ideas on purity and defilement. Avoidance of ritual defilement was a major preoccupation of the Essenes and affected many aspects of their way of life. They were expected to 'make a distinction between the clean and the unclean' (CD 6:17), 'not to let their property be mixed with the property of men of deceit who have not purified their conduct by separating from iniquity and by walking with perfect conduct' (1QS 9:8–9). Again, 'let him not come to the water to share in the purification of holy men—for they will not be cleansed, unless they have turned from their wickedness—for he is impure among all those who transgress his word' (1QS 5:13–14). The abhorrence of all unclean idols (*glwly ndh*, 1QS 4:5) was prescribed. Moreover, the regulations for ritual purity among the Essenes were numerous (see 1QS 4:10; CD 7:3; 9:21; 10:10 ff.; 11:19 ff.; 12:19; 1QM 13:5). In the light of such prescriptions the counsel in 2 Cor, to 'cleanse ourselves from everything that can taint body and spirit' in an effort toward perfect holiness, takes on new meaning. It resembles strongly the general Qumran proscription of all contact with outsiders.

(*e*) *Concatenation of Old Testament texts.* The last point of contact to be noted in this passage is the series of Old Testament quotations strung together in the manner of *Testimonia.* We have, first of all, a conflated quotation of Lv 26:12 and Ez 37:27, then an inverted quotation of Is 52:11, followed by part of Ez 20:34 and finally 2 Sm 7:14. The unifying thread running through all the citations is the theme of God's chosen people, 'God's lot', to use the Qumran expression. Collections of Old Testament texts grouped about a certain theme occur elsewhere in Paul's letters and the question has often been

---

most sanctuary. It is therefore a most apt expression for the idea of an object (or a community) withdrawn from profane use and dedicated to God.

raised whether Paul constructed them himself or made use of already existing *testimonia*. The main argument for denying that Paul made use of previously existing *testimonia* has been that there was no evidence for the existence of such lists prior to the patristic writers. But we now have a *testimonia* document from Qumran Cave 4, which groups various texts from the Old Testament.[22] I have discussed the pertinence of this document for the New Testament elsewhere in detail.[23] We need note here only that the early appearance of such a literary form at Qumran does not prove that Paul used already existing *testimonia*; but the likelihood is increased now that a pre-Christian example of it has turned up. Once again the discovery of such a form precisely at Qumran yields another point of contact between it and the 2 Cor passage.[24] Finally, it should be noted that the introductory formula, *kathōs eipen ho theos hoti . . .*, which occurs only here in the New Testament, has its Qumran counterpart in CD 6:13; 8:9 (*'šr 'mr 'l*),[25] but is found neither in the Old Testament nor the Mishnah.

Having examined the five points of contact between this passage and the Qumran literature, we may conclude. Not all the points in this comparison are of equal importance or value, but the cumulative effect of so many of them within such a short passage is the telling factor. We are faced with a paragraph in

[22] See J. M. Allegro, 'Further Messianic References in Qumrân Literature', *JBL* 75 (1956) 182–7, Document IV.

[23] '"4QTestimonia" and the New Testament', pp.59–89 above.

[24] One of the Old Testament passages cited here, 2 Sm 7:14, is used in a Qumran text which at first sight seemed to be related to the *testimonia* form, a text provisionally labelled '4QFlorilegium'. However, further investigation of the text has shown that 'florilegium' is a misnomer for the *genre* employed there, for it is actually 'a more complex type of *pesher*—one that employs additional biblical material [i.e., isolated explicit quotations from other Old Testament books] to expound the biblical passage under consideration' (W. R. Lane, 'A New Commentary Structure in 4Q Florilegium', *JBL* 78 [1959] 343–6). See further pp. 7, 81–2 above.

[25] See my article, 'The Use of Explicit Old Testament Quotations in Qumran Literature and in the New Testament', pp. 3–58 above.

which Qumran ideas and expressions have been reworked in a Christian cast of thought. Some of the contacts can be shown to exist also in genuinely Pauline passages, e.g., the temple of God, the idea of the 'lot', the *testimonia*-form. But when the total Qumran influence is considered along with the other reasons (the interrupted sequence of the surrounding context, the self-contained unit and the strange vocabulary), the evidence seems to total up to the admission of a Christian reworking of an Essene paragraph which has been introduced into the Pauline letter. The problem of how it got there remains unsolved, for 'there is no evidence in MS., or version, or quotation, that any copy of the Epistle ever lacked this passage'.[26] At any rate, this solution seems preferable to those which are content with merely writing the passage off as a digression or just another case of Pauline anacoluthon due to his practice of dictation. It certainly is not a case of anacoluthon, for the grammar is intact. To label the passage as a digression or as a Pauline 'quotation' of an Essene paragraph (as did K. G. Kuhn) is no solution, for the problem still remains, why did he digress *here* with a heavily Qumran passage? Hence, I believe that it is preferable to regard the passage as a non-Pauline interpolation.[27]

[26] A. Plummer, *op. cit.*, 205

[27] See further J. Gnilka, '2 Cor 6:14–7:1 in the Light of the Qumran Texts and the Testaments of the Twelve Patriarchs', *Paul and Qumran: Studies in New Testament Exegesis* (ed. J. Murphy-O'Connor; London: Chapman, 1968) 48–68.

IV
THE EPISTLE TO THE HEBREWS

11

'NOW THIS MELCHIZEDEK . . .' (HEB 7:1)*

To show the superiority of Christ's priesthood over that of Aaron and the levites, the author of the epistle to the Hebrews introduces a comparison between Jesus and Melchizedek. The comparison is briefly stated in Heb 5:6–10 for the first time, but at the end of the following hortatory section the author returns to the Melchizedek theme and affirms that Christian hope is like an anchor firmly rooted in the heavenly sanctuary where Christ has gone on ahead of us, 'forever a high priest according to the order of Melchizedek' (6:20). There follows in chapter 7 an extended discussion of Christ and Melchizedek, which C. Spicq has called the 'culminating point of the epistle's argument'.[1] Whether this view of chapter 7 is correct or not, much has been written on Melchizedek and his relation to Heb. It is our purpose here to sift from the recent studies those elements which seem pertinent to his appearance in Heb and relate to them some new data bearing on the Melchizedek tradition which have come to light in the Qumran literature and in the newly discovered Vatican codex of the Palestinian Targum Neofiti I.

Before turning to the new data, I must stress with several modern writers[2] that the detailed comparison of Christ and

* Originally published in *CBQ* 25 (1963) 305–21.

[1] *L'épître aux Hébreux* (EBib; 3d ed., Paris) 2,203.

[2] See R. Bloch, 'Midrash', *VDBS* 5, 1279; H. Rusche, 'Die Gestalt des Melchisedek', *MTZ* 6 (1955) 230–52. This is certainly a more valid analysis

Melchizedek in Heb 7 is an excellent example of a midrash on Gn 14:18–20. Introducing his implicit quotation of Gn by *houtos gar ho Melchisedek*, the author of Heb first gives a brief résumé in vv. 1–2 and afterwards takes up various elements of it for comment. Thus in this section of Heb are verified the five characteristics of midrash, pointed out by R. Bloch,[3] viz., its *point de départ* in an OT passage (Gn 14:18–20 implicitly quoted), its homiletic character (here for apologetic purposes), its attentive analysis of the text (the interpretation of the names and explanation of the blessing and tithes), its adaptation of the OT text to a present situation (the priesthood of Christ), and its haggadic character (an elaborative exposé in which the interest is centred on the biblical account rather than on the historical figure as such). Even in its outward form this section bears resemblance to a classic midrash in *Genesis Rabbah* 43:6.[4] Moreover, the manner in which Heb introduces into the midrash on Gn 14 phrases from Ps 110 (see Heb 7:11, 15, 17, 21, 28) is strikingly similar to the technique of the so-called 4QFlorilegium,[5] a Qumran text which bears the name *midrāš* as part of an opening formula.[6] The latter text is really a commentary on 2 Sm 7:10–14, followed by one on Ps 1:1 and Ps 2:1; but into the commentary on these passages other OT passages have been introduced (Ex 15:17–18 and Am 9:11 into the part on 2 Sm; Is 8:11 and Ez 37:23 into that on Ps

---

of Heb 7 than Spicq's view that the entire chapter 7 is nothing more than an exegesis of Ps 110:4 (*op. cit.*, 205).

[3] *Op. cit.*, 1265–7.

[4] See H. Freedman, *Genesis* (Midrash Rabbah 1; London, 1951) I, 355 ff. A. G. Wright, 'The Literary Genre Midrash (Part Two)', *CBQ* 28(1966) 437, classes this passage among 'small midrashic units' in the New Testament, which are built on implicit citations of the Old Testament.

[5] See J. M. Allegro, 'Fragments of a Qumran Scroll of Eschatological *Midrāšîm*', *JBL* 77 (1958) 350–4. Cf. my comments on this text above, pp. 7, 81–2.

[6] *Ibid.*, 353 (I, 14). Cf. W. R. Lane, 'A New Commentary Structure in 4Q Florilegium', *JBL* 78 (1959) 343–6; Y. Yadin, 'A Midrash on 2 Sam. vii and Ps. i–ii (4Q Florilegium)', *IEJ* 9 (1959) 95–8.

1:1). The only difference is that the OT texts are here introduced by explicit formulae, whereas they are not in Heb.[7] But the midrashic technique is basically the same. Further, Helga Rusche has recently shown that the treatment of Melchizedek in Heb is not characterized by the extreme allegorical speculations found in Philo, Josephus, several Gnostic writers and the Rabbis.[8] The theological conception used is related much more to controllable Jewish apocalyptic writers with their expectations of a messianic priesthood rooted in Gn 14. Since the two intertestamental writings in which she finds the relevant material are *Jubilees* and the *Testaments of the Twelve Patriarchs*—texts with known connections with the Qumran literature—another point of comparative interest is thus established between Qumran and Heb.[9]

Ps 110:4

Before we take up the use of Gn 14 in Heb, a few preliminary remarks are in order about the author's use of Ps 110. Heb first cites it in 1:13 and uses it again in 5:5–10, to set up the comparison of Jesus and Aaron. The role of high priest was not usurped in either case, but bestowed by divine appointment. This idea forms part of the development of Heb at this point, where Jesus is shown to have all the qualities of the 'perfected' (or 'qualified') high priest. In proof, the author cites Ps 2:7, 'You are my son; this day I have begotten you', and joins to it Ps 110:4, 'The Lord has sworn and will not go back on his

[7] See my essay, 'The Use of Explicit Old Testament Quotations in Qumran Literature and in the New Testament', pp. 3–58 above.

[8] *Op. cit.*, 238–44.

[9] Y. Yadin, 'The Dead Sea Scrolls and the Epistle to the Hebrews', *Aspects of the Dead Sea Scrolls* (Scripta hierosolymitana 4; Jerusalem, 1958) 36–55; C. Spicq, 'L'épître aux Hébreux, Apollos, Jean-Baptiste, les Hellénistes et Qumran', *RQ* 1 (1958–59) 365–90; H. Kosmala, *Hebräer—Essener—Christen. Studien zur Vorgeschichte der frühchristlichen Verkündigung* (SPB 1; Leiden, 1959). F. F. Bruce, '"To the Hebrews" or "To the Essenes"?', *NTS* 9 (1962–63) 217–32; J. Coppens, 'Les affinités qumrâniennes de l'Epître aux Hébreux', *NRT* 84 (1962) 128–41, 257–82 (=ALBO 4/1).

word: "You are a priest forever according to the order of Melchizedek".' As Dom J. Dupont, and more recently a young Swedish scholar, E. Lövestam, have pointed out,[10] all the clear instances of the use of Ps 2:7 in the NT relate it to the Resurrection. As of the time of his resurrection Christ became a 'son of God' in a special sense (in the understanding of the early kerygma reflected here)—God's son endowed with universal and everlasting *royal dominion* (cf. Rom 1:4).[11] To this notion derived from Ps 2:7, Heb now links another from Ps 110:4: God's appointment of the risen royal Son as the possessor of the eternal *priesthood* of Melchizedek.

Though the messianic character of Ps 110 is debated among OT commentators,[12] there is rather general agreement that it is at least a royal psalm, one in which some Davidic king is addressed as the hero[13] and associated with the past as the successor of Melchizedek. Like Ps 2, it echoes the dynastic covenant established in the oracle of Nathan (2 Sm 7:8–16). But the psalmist thinks of the reigning Israelite king, 'not . . . as a simple historical figure, but as a religious figure who incorporates in himself the kingdom of Israel and its hope for a future in which the kingship of Yahweh will become universally effective. In this sense the Ps is messianic since it repeats the

[10] J. Dupont, 'Filius meus es tu', *RSR* 35 (1948) 522–43; E. Lövestam, *Son and Saviour: a Study of Acts 13,32–37* (*ConNeot* 18; Lund, 1961) 15–37; E. Käsemann, *Das wandernde Gottesvolk* (FRLANT 37, Göttingen, 1939) 58–9; R. H. Fuller, *The Mission and Achievement of Jesus* (SBT 12; London, 1954) 87.

[11] See E. Lövestam, *op. cit.*, 37.

[12] See the summary by J. L. McKenzie, 'Royal Messianism', *CBQ* 19 (1957) 25–52, esp. 34–6 (reprinted in *Myths and Realities* [Milwaukee-London, 1963] 203–31).

[13] The opinion of H. H. Rowley, 'Melchizedek and Zadok (Gen 14 and Ps 110)', *Festschrift für Alfred Bertholet* (Tübingen, 1950) 461–72, according to which David addresses Zadok in v. 4, does not seem to have convinced many; see V. Hamp, 'Melchisedech als Typus', *Pro Mundi Vita: Festschrift zum eucharistischen Weltkongress 1960* (München, 1960) 16–17; J. W. Bowker, 'Psalm CX', *VT* 17 (1967) 31–41; H. H. Rowley, 'Melchizedek and David', *VT* 17 (1967) 485.

messianic outlook of the dynasty of David.'[14] It has been maintained that v. 4, in which the Israelite monarch is presented as a king-priest, is a gloss, because it is unique in the OT. However, the excision of it has to be based on something more than a hunch, and the otherwise early date of the Ps points to its composition in the time of David or Solomon,[15] when the connection of the Davidic dynasty with the city of Melchizedek was still fresh and when many of the inhabitants were not Israelites. Ps 110:4 thus presents the king as the heir of Melchizedek, succeeding him as a priest forever.[16]

In Heb 5 the author applies this verse of Ps 110 to Jesus, undoubtedly understanding it as messianic (although he does not expressly state this link).[17] Having first introduced Ps 2:7 to establish the risen Jesus as the possessor of *regal* inheritance, he adds Ps 110:4 to present this Kingly Son of God as one appointed also to an *eternal priesthood.*

Whatever the puzzling Hebrew phrase *'al dibrātî Malkî-ṣedeq* means, no one has ever suggested that it be understood in terms of hereditary succession. Hence the priesthood of the king is due to something else. The commonly accepted interpretation of the form *'al dibrātî* is that it is an alternative, per-

[14] J. L. McKenzie, *op. cit.*, 35–6. H.-J. Kraus, *Psalmen* (BKAT 15/10; Neukirchen, 1959) 763–4; V. Hamp, *op. cit.*, 18.

[15] Since Gunkel the early date of the Ps in the time of David or Solomon has been widely admitted; see H.-J. Kraus, *op. cit.*, 755; E. R. Hardy, 'The Date of Psalm 110', *JBL* 64 (1945) 385–90; H. G. Jefferson, 'Is Ps 110 Canaanite?', *JBL* 73 (1954) 152–6; H. Schmid, 'Jahwe und die Kulttraditionen von Jerusalem', *ZAW* 67 (1955) 175, n. 42. See further W. E. Brooks, 'The Perpetuity of Christ's Sacrifice in the Epistle to the Hebrews', *JBL* 89 (1970) 205–14.

[16] A. Caquot, 'Remarques sur Psaume CX', *Semitica* 6 (1956) 33–52, rightly stresses the emphasis in the Psalm on the eternal aspect; cf. R. Tournay, 'Le Psaume CX', *RB* 67 (1960) 5–41, esp. 19, n. 2.

[17] It is apparently part of the author's own theology to apply Ps 110:4 to Christ as the messianic priest. No rabbi is attested as having applied Ps 110:4 to the Messiah before the second half of the 3d cent. A.D. See C. Spicq, *op. cit.*, 204, n. 4.

haps older, form of the construct *ʿal dibrat.*[18] Elsewhere in the OT this phrase means 'for the sake of' (Eccl 3:18; 8:2; 7:14). This causal meaning, however, though defended here by a few scholars,[19] scarcely suits the context of the Ps, and has been avoided both by ancient versions and many modern commentators in favour of a modal sense.[20] The LXX rendered it *kata tēn taxin Melchisedek*, and was followed by Heb 5:6; 6:20; 7:11, 17 and the Vg, *secundum ordinem Melchisedech*. But the Greek word *taxis* is of little help, for neither its basic meaning, 'arrangement, fixed order, succession', nor its Hellenistic meaning, 'office, post' of a priest, nor even the meaning 'character, quality' (apparently used in 2 Mc 9:18), has won any general adherence of scholarly opinion. And yet, there is little doubt of its meaning in Heb, for in 7:15—a verse often strangely omitted in many discussions of the meaning of the Greek or Hebrew phrase—it has been paraphrased by the author, *kata tēn homoiotēta Melchisedek*, 'according to the likeness of Melchizedek'.[21] Does the Peshitta reflect this in Ps 110:4 or preserve its own ancient interpretation: *badmûteh deMelkîzedeq*, 'in the

[18] P. Joüon (*Grammaire de l'hébreu biblique* [2d ed.; Rome, 1947] #93i-m) and G. Beer-R. Meyer (*Hebräische Grammatik* [Sammlung Göschen Berlin, I, 1952] #45d) explain the final *yodh* as *ḥireq compaginis*; but Gesenius-Kautzsch-Cowley (Hebrew Grammar [Oxford, 1946] #90k-1), H. Bauer-P. Leander (*Historische Grammatik der hebräischen Sprache des Alten Testaments* [Halle a. S., 1918] #65j–k) more correctly explain it as an obsolete case-ending. Cf. H.-J. Kraus, *op. cit.*, 753.—Despite a superficial resemblance to (and perhaps a common origin with) the Aramaic *ʿl dbr* (Cowley, *AP* 6,6 [in a context of swearing]; *BMAP* 4,13) and *ʿl dbrt dy* (Dn 2:30; 4:14), the phrase in the Ps seems to be different.

[19] Cf. among others Koehler-Baumgartner, *Lexicon in Veteris Testamenti libros* (Leiden; 1958) 202; V. Hamp, *op. cit.*, 18; J. M. P. Smith (*American Translation* [Chicago, 1951] 561): 'A Melchizedek, because of me.' See also B. D. Eerdmans, *The Hebrew Book of Psalms* (Leiden, 1947) 499: 'For the sake of Melchizedek' (explained as 'for the memory of').—Still less convincing are the attempts of A. Caquot (*op. cit.*, 44), 'Tu es prêtre pour toujours. (Il l'a juré) à propos de Melchisedeq'; and of R. Tournay (*op. cit.*, 19, n. 2), 'sur ma parole (jurée)'.

[20] H.-J. Kraus, *op. cit.*, 752; CCD 3,287; Gesenius-Buhl, 155.

[21] It has been noted independently by R. Tournay, *op. cit.*, 19, n. 2.

likeness of Melchizedek'? Heb 7:15 is so obviously an allusion to Ps 110:4 that Nestle prints it in boldface except for *homoiotēta*. It is this notion of 'likeness' which is exploited in the midrashic commentary, even though the text of Heb may not really solve the problem of *'al dibrātî* or *kata tēn taxin*. In reality, *kata tēn homoiotēta* may be no more than a paraphrase of the preposition *kata* alone.

GN 14:18-20

We turn now to the midrash of Heb 7. But it will be well to juxtapose first of all the pertinent verses of Gn as they appear in the MT, the *Genesis Apocryphon*[22] and the *Targum Neofiti I*.[23] Various features of these comparative texts will enter into our discussion of the development in Heb.

MT	*1QapGn*	*Neofiti I*
[17]The king of Sodom went out to meet him, after his return from killing Chedorlaomer and the kings who were with him,	[12]The king of Sodom heard that Abram had brought back all the captives [13]and all the booty, and he went up to meet him. He came to Salem, that is Jerusalem, and Abram was	The king of Sodom went out to meet him after he returned from killing Chedorloamer and the kings who were with him in the plain of Phordesaya,[24] that is the King's Plain. . . .[25] And
to the Valley of Shaveh, that is the King's Valley.	camped in the Valley of [14]Shaveh (that is, the King's Valley, in the	the upright king, the king of Jerusalem, that is the great Shem,

[22] N. Avigad and Y. Yadin, *A Genesis Apocryphon: A Scroll from the Wilderness of Judaea* (Jerusalem, 1956). See also my *The Genesis Apocryphon of Qumran Cave I: A Commentary* (Biblica et Orientalia, 18; Rome: Pontifical Biblical Institute, 1966: 2nd revised edition, 1971).

[23] See A. Díez Macho, 'Una copia de todo el Targum jerosolimitano en la Vaticana', *EstBib* 16 (1956) 446–7; 'Una copia completa del Targum palestinense al Pentateuco en la Biblioteca Vaticana', *Sefarad* 17 (1957) 119–21; P. Boccaccio, 'Integer textus Targum hierosolymitani primum inventus in codice Vaticano', *Bib* 38 (1957) 237–9.—The text given here is taken from a microfilm supplied by the Vatican Library. The text is now available with a Spanish, French, and English translation in A. Díez Macho, *Neophyti I: Targum palestinense . . . Tomo 1: Genesis* (Madrid: Consejo superior de investigaciones científicas, 1969).

[24] See J. T. Milik, '"Saint-Thomas de Phordêsa"', *Bib* 42 (1961) 77–84.

[25] In the text of *Neofiti I* the beginning of each verse is indicated by two or three words of the Hebrew, set off in quotation marks and followed by *sōph pāsûq*. Thereafter follows the Aramaic version of the complete verse. See next note. Dots in the translation represent the omission of the Hebrew words.

[18]And Melchizedek, the king of Salem, brought out bread and wine;

and he was a priest of the Most High God; and he blessed him, saying, [19]'Blessed be Abram by the Most High God, the creator of the heavens and the earth!

[20]And blessed be the Most High God, who has delivered your enemies into your hand!' And he gave him a tenth of everything.

[21]And the king of Sodom said to Abram,

'Give me the men, but the goods take for yourself.'

[22]But Abram said to the king of Sodom, 'I raise my hand to Yahweh, the Most High God, the creator of the heavens and the earth, [23]that I shall not take so much as a thread or a sandal-strap from anything that is yours, lest you say, [24]"I have enriched Abram".'

(Gn 14:17–24)

Valley of Beth Kerem). And Melchizedek, the king of Salem, brought out [15]food and drink for Abram and all the men who were with him. And he was a priest of the Most High God. And he blessed [16]Abram and said, 'Blessed be Abram by the Most High God, lord of the heavens and the earth! And blessed be the Most High God, [17]who has delivered your enemies into your hand!' And he gave him a tenth of all the flocks of the king of Elam and his confederates. [18]Then the king of Sodom drew near and said to Abram, 'My lord Abram, [19]give me the men that are mine from the captives who are with you, whom you have rescued from the king of Elam, and [20]all the flocks (are) left for you.' Then Abram said to the king of Sodom, 'I raise [21]my hand this day to the Most High God, the lord of the heavens and the earth, [22]that I shall not take so much as a thread or a sandal-strap from anything that is yours, lest you say, 'From my flocks comes all the wealth of [23]Abram. . . ."'

(22:12–23)

brought out bread and wine; and he was a priest serving in the great priesthood before the Most High God. . . . And he blessed him saying, 'Blessed is Abram before the Most High God, who by his word created the heavens and the earth. . . . And blessed is the Most High God (who) has broken your enemies before you.' And he gave him a tenth of everything. . . .

And the king of Sodom said to Abram, 'Give me the men, but the money take for yourself.'

. . . And Abram said to the king of Sodom, 'Behold, I raise my hand in oath before Yahweh, the Most High God, who by his word created the heavens and the earth . . . that I shall not take so much as a thread or a shoe-lace from all that is yours, lest you become proud and say, "I have enriched Abram".'[26]

(fol. 23 v., ll. 14 ff.)

[26] *Neofiti I*, f. 23v., line 14 ff.: "*wyṣ' mlk*": *wnpq mlk' dsdwn* {*lq*} *lqdmwtyh* ***mn*** *btr dy ḥzr mn dqṭl yt kdr l'm(r) wyt mlkyy'; dhwn 'myh bmyšr prdsy' hy' mšrh dmlk'*: "*wmlky ṣdq mlk šlm*": *wmlk' ṣdq mlk' dyrwšlm hw' šm rwbh*—f. 24r, l. 1 ff.: *'pq lḥm wḥmr whw' hwh khn mšmš bkhnt(t) rbth qdm 'lh' 'l'h*: "*wybrkhw wy'mr*": *wbryk ytyh w'mr bryk hw' 'brm qdm 'lh' 'yl'h dbmymryh qnh šmy' w'r'*: "*brwk 'l 'lywn*": *wbryk hw' 'lh' 'ly' dy tbr b'ly dbbk qdmk wyhb lh ḥd mn 'šrh mn klh*: "*wy'mr mlk sdwm*": *w'mr mlk' dsd(m) l'brm hb ly npšt' wmmwnh sb lk*: "*wy'mr 'brm*": *w'mr 'brm lmlk' dsdm h' zqp{y} ydy bšbw'h qdm yyyy 'lh' 'ly' dbmmryh qnh šmy' w'r'*: "*'m mḥwṭ*": *'m mn ḥwṭ rṣw'h dmsn 'n 'sb mn kl mh dy lk dl' tyhwwy mtg'y wtymr 'n' 'tryt yt 'brm.*

THE NAME MELCHIZEDEK

'First of all, his name is interpreted as the king of uprightness' (Heb 7:2). The author's minute, attentive, midrashic analysis of the OT text centres first on the name of Melchizedek, in a way which was apparently traditional among the Jews of his time. But in fact this analysis contributes little to the development of the argument in Heb. In the light of the modern study of Northwest Semitic personal names, *Malkî-ṣedeq* must have meant originally either '(the god) Ṣedeq is my king', or 'My king is upright'. The first element *malkî-* (with *yodh*) was suffixal, meaning 'my king', like *Malkî-'ēl* ('El is my king' [Gn 46:17]), *Malkî-yāh* or *Malkî-yāhû* ('Yahweh is my king' [Ezr 10:31; Jer 38:6]), and a host of names with similar suffixal elements like *'ābî* ('my father'), *'āḥî* ('my brother'), *'ēlî* ('my god'), *'ammî* ('my kinsman'), *zimrî* ('my protection'), etc.[27] As for the second element *ṣdq*, it was most likely the name of a god,

[27] Compare *'Abî-'ēl* (1 Sm 9:1),*'Abî-yāh* (1 Sm 8:2), *'Abî-yāhû* (2 Chr 13: 20), *Abi-dDagan* (*ARM* 2,83.21), *Abi-milki* (*EA* 148,2), *Ilima-abi* (*BASOR* 95 [1944] 22), *Ili-milku* (*EA* 151,45), *'Ēlî-melek* (Ru 1:2), *'Ēlî-'ēl* (1 Chr 11:46), *'Elî-yāh* (2 Kgs 1:3), *Ili-Eraḫ* (*ARM* 1,63.6), *Aḫi-milku* (KB 2,148), *'Aḥî-melek* (1 Sm 21:2), *'Ammî-'ēl* (Nm 13:12), *'Ammî-šadday* (Nm 1:12), *Zimrî-dDagan* (*ARM* 1,85.11). See C.-F. Jean, 'Les noms propres de personnes dans les lettres de Mari', *Studia Mariana* (Leiden, 1950) 63–98.—M. Noth (*Die israelitischen Personennamen im Rahmen der gemeinsemitischen Namengebung* [Stuttgart, 1928] 24–5) rejects the explanation that the *yodh* is a suffix, as maintained by Delitzsch, Bauer-Leander, T. Bauer, *et al.*, and sees in it 'nur einen Rest alter Kasusendungen'. In the light of the foregoing material this is most unlikely. All the examples which he offers can be explained otherwise quite easily. Moreover, he is responsible for another analysis of *Malkîṣedeq* often quoted today (p. 161, n. 4), '(the god) Milk is upright'. This is due to his desire to interpret all instances of *mlk* in Canaanite names as a theophoric element. But just as he was forced to admit *ṣdq* as a divine name (in South Arabic *ṣdqḏkr*, *ṣdqyd'*, *ṣdqyp'*; cf. also Chagar Bazar *Ṣidqi-epuḫ*, Mari *Ṣidqu-la-nasi*, Ugaritic *Ṣdq'il*) as well as an epithet, 'upright' (in names like *ṣdqyh*, *yhwṣdq*; cf. Aleppo seal, *Aḫi-ṣaduq*), so too *mlk* in personal names can be either a theophoric element or a simple epithet (as in the examples cited above). Cf. also *Malkî-ram* (1 Chr 3:18), *Malkî-šûa'* (1 Sm 14:49). See W. F. Albright, *JBL* 69 (1950) 389; *AASOR* 6 (1926) 63; contrast W. W. Baudissin, *Kyrios* (Giessen, 1929) 3, 44–51 (*Malkî-ṣedeq* = '(mein) Malk ist gerecht' [?]).

Ṣedeq, a form of the name which Philo Byblius gives in a Phoenician pantheon as *Sydyk*[28] and which Damascius writes as *Sadykos*.[29] However, it is not possible to exclude the meaning of *ṣdq* as an adjective, 'upright'.[30] At any rate, *Malkî-ṣedeq* is related to the name of the Jerusalem king in the time of Joshua, *'Adōnî-ṣedeq* ('Ṣedeq is my lord', or possibly 'My lord is upright' [Jos 10:1, 3]), and to the Amorite name of the Babylonian king, *Ammi-ṣaduqa* (16th cent. B.C.).

Neither of these possible meanings of the name of Melchizedek was preserved, however, in first-century Jewish tradition. Both Philo and Josephus record the popular etymology of their day, *basileus dikaios*.[31] This is reflected in later Targums,[32]

[28] Eusebius, *Praep. evang.* 1, 10, 13–14, 25; GCS 43/1, 46, 48 (ed. K. Mras, 1954): MS. variants: *Sydek* and *Sedek*. See further R. A. Rosenberg, 'The God Ṣedeq', *HUCA* 36 (1965) 161–77; M. C. Astour, 'Some New Divine Names from Ugarit', *JAOS* 86 (1966) 277–84, especially 282–3.

[29] Photius, *Bibl.*, cod. 242, p. 573 H (cited by W. W. Baudissin, *op. cit.*, 3, 411–12).—This form of the name is close to that in *Ammi-ṣaduqa*, *Aḫi-ṣaduq* and the OT name, *Ṣadoq* (which should probably be *Ṣaddûq* [2 Sm 8:17]).

[30] Cf. *Yehôṣādāq* (Hag 1:1), *Yôṣādāq* (Ezr 3:2); perhaps the *a–u* vowels are indicative of an adjectival form in *Ammi-ṣaduqa* and *Aḫi-ṣaduq*. Cf. the Phoenician inscription of Yeḥawmilk: *k mlk ṣdq h'*, 'for he is a loyal king' (line 9).

[31] Josephus, *Ant.* 1, 10, 2, #180; *JW* 6, 10, 1, #438; Philo, *De legum allegoria* 3, 79.

[32] *Neofiti I:* 'And the upright king, the king of Jerusalem, the great Shem, brought out' *(wmlk' ṣdq mlk' dyrwšlm hw' šm rwbh 'pq); Fragmententargum:* 'And Melchizedek, the king of Jerusalem, that is the great Shem' *(wmlky ṣdq mlk' dyrwšlm dhw' šm rb'); Ps.-Jonathan:* 'And the upright king, that is Shem, the son of Noah, the king of Jerusalem, went out . . .' *(wmlk' ṣdyq' hw' šm br nḥ mlk' dyrwšlym npq); Onqelos:* 'And Melchizedek, the king of Jerusalem, brought out . . .' *(wmlky ṣdq mlk' dyrwšlm 'pyq)*.—By equating Melchizedek with Shem, the rabbinical tradition thus incorporated him into the Israelite nation and provided him with a genealogy; see Gn 10:1; 11:10–26. C. Spicq (*op. cit.*, 205) further points out that the haggadah identified Melchizedek with Shem, the eldest son of Noah, because from Adam to Levi the cult was supposed to have been cared for by the first-born. See also H. W. Hertzberg, 'Die Melkiṣedeq-Traditionen', *JPOS* 8 (1928) 170; J. J. Petuchowski, 'The Controversial Figure of Melchizedek', *HUCA* 28 (1957) 127–36.—The meaning 'upright king' is used by H. E. del

and underlies the phrase used in Heb itself, *basileus dikaiosynēs*, 'king of uprightness'. Some authors[33] try to defend the translation in Heb as the original one (invoking *ḥireq compaginis*), but unconvincingly. It is to be noted that in the *Genesis Apocryphon* the name is still written as one word, and may reflect a period before the popular etymology set in with the consequent tendency to write the name as two words *Malkî-ṣedeq*. The form preserved in *Neofiti I* is problematical and probably reflects an even later stage of the popular etymology; *mlk' ṣdq* may be a mistake for *mlky ṣdq*, but it may also be an attempt to write *mlk' ṣdyq'* of the tradition in Pseudo-Jonathan. At any rate, there can be no doubt that the explanation of the name used in Heb is one which was in accord with the current popular etymology and in the long run better suited to the purpose of the author of Heb.

THE KING OF 'SALEM'

The analysis of the text of Gn is continued, 'He is also the king of Salem, that is the king of peace' (7:2), according to the usual translation. *Basileus salēm* is once again the use of a contemporary, popular etymology known to us from Philo, *basilea tēs eirēnēs*.[34] However, in this case the meaning is interesting, because the sense of the Hebrew text of Gn itself is not without its problems. Is the expression *melek šālēm* topographical or not? This question has not always been answered in the affirmative. Most recently W. F. Albright has explained the verse with the aid of an haplography which results in an interesting interpretation. He would read, *ū-Malkî-ṣédeq mélek šelôm⟨ōh⟩ hôṣî' léḥem wa-yáyin*, 'And Melchizedek, a king allied to him, brought

---

Medico ('Melchisedech', *ZAW* 69 [1957] 160–70) to eliminate the proper name (Melchizedek) from the text of both Gn and Ps 110, since 'upright king' and 'peaceful king' are epithets of the king of Sodom mentioned in the previous verse of Gn. The explanation is more ingenious than convincing.

[33] C. Spicq, *op. cit.*, 182 ('roi de justice'); similarly P. Joüon, *Grammaire*, #93m; Gesenius-Kautzsch-Cowley, *Hebrew Grammar*, #90*l* ('king of righteousness') ; *et al.*

[34] *De legum allegoria* 3,79.

out bread and wine.'[35] The word *šlm* is explained by him as produced by 'the simplest possible haplography', due to the following *hôṣî'*; he compares such expressions as *'îš šelômî* (Ps 41:10), *'anšê šelômekā* parallel to *'anšê berîtekā* (Ob 7), etc. The phrase, *melek šelôm⟨ōh⟩*, would then mean 'a king of his alliance' (his 'peace', literally). Along with H. Gunkel and others Albright believes that Gn 14:18–20 had originally nothing to say about Jerusalem—the identification of Salem with it would seem to be a later tradition, reflected in Ps 76:2 ('In Salem is his abode, his dwelling is in Zion'). When it arose is not certain at all, but it was current in the first century A.D., as is evident not only from Josephus, who stated, 'Solyma was in fact the place afterwards called Hierosolyma',[36] but also from the *Genesis Apocryphon* (22:13): Abram 'came to Salem, that is Jerusalem'.[37] The *Targum Neofiti I* agrees with the previously known Targums in reading *mlk' dyrwšlm*, 'king of Jerusalem'. Now given such a long-standing interpretation of *šlm* of Gn 14 as Jerusalem, it is noteworthy that Heb merely transcribes *šālēm* into Greek as *salēm* and interprets it like Philo as *basileus eirēnēs*. Whether Albright's interpretation, eliminating the topographical name, will rally scholarly opinion to it or not, it at least provides an understandable background for the interpretation common to both Philo and Heb. It is also to be noted that the Alexandrian background of Philo and Heb may well account for the interpretation common to them over against that found in Josephus, the *Genesis Apocryphon* and the Targums, which may reflect rather a Palestinian interpretation of *mlk šlm*.

However, in the long run it must be admitted that the ex-

[35] 'Abram the Hebrew: A New Archaeological Interpretation', *BASOR* 163 (1961) 52.

[36] *Ant.* 1,10,2, # 180 (*tēn mentoi Solyma hysteron ekalesan Hierosolyma*); *JW* 6,10,1, # 438.

[37] See *CBQ* 22 (1960) 281; cf. P. Winter, 'Note on Salem-Jerusalem', *NT* 2 (1957) 151-2. This identification gives the lie to the statements of H. E. del Medico (*op. cit.*, 163), who neglects the Jewish tradition on Ps

planation of the names of Melchizedek and of Salem does not really advance the main argument of the midrash. But just as in the later midrashim, even the minor elements of the OT text are exploited to suggest that Christ, the new high priest, *kata tēn taxin Melchizedek*, brings the messianic blessings of uprightness and peace. This seems to be the reason for the adoption of the current popular etymologies. Through Christ come the messianic blessings of 'uprightness' (see Is 9:5–6; 32:1; Jer 23:5–6; Dn 9:24; Mal 3:20 ; Acts 3:14; 1 Cor 4:30) and of 'peace' (Is 9:5; 32:17; Zech 9:9–10; Eph 2:14). As king and priest forever he establishes the new order of hope (Heb 6:15–20), and in him the fruits of the traditional priestly blessing (Nm 6:23–26) take on a new nuance.

MELCHIZEDEK'S LACK OF GENEALOGY

The first of the three main points of the Melchizedek theme used in the midrash of Heb to show the superiority of Jesus' priesthood over that of Aaron is the lack of genealogy: like Melchizedek Jesus too is *agenealogētos*. What ultimately underlies the lack of Melchizedek's genealogy in Gn is that he appears in the original story—in the source which has found its way into Gn 14—as a Canaanite priest-king. His name is of traceable Canaanite origin; if Albright's interpretation of Gn 14:18 be correct, he would be a vassal Canaanite king bound by treaty to Abram; otherwise he would be the king of a Canaanite town of Salem. He is further described as a priest of El 'Elyon (*wᵉhû' kôhēn lᵉ'ēl 'elyôn*). As this phrase stands in the MT (and in the final redaction of Gn), it certainly refers to the service of Yahweh. Indeed, a few verses later (14:22) Abram swears with uplifted hand by 'Yahweh El 'Elyon'. But it has long been suspected that *Yhwh* in 14:22 is a later gloss, since it does not appear in the LXX nor in the Peshitta, and is now found to be lacking in the Aramaic translation of this verse in the *Genesis*

76:2 and rejects Josephus' statements as interpolations of a later date, because 'the identification of Salem with Jerusalem was not followed in the first centuries of our era'.

Apocryphon (22:21).[38] If this be so, then Melchizedek's service of El 'Elyon in 14:18 likewise suggests his Canaanite background. For El is the name of a well-known henotheistic Canaanite deity of the second millennium B.C. Despite the fact the *El* and *'Elyān* later appear on an 8th century Aramaic inscription from Sefire, apparently as the names of a pair of Canaanite gods (Sf I A 11),[39] *'elyôn* eventually became an epithet of the supreme God, the creator of the heavens and the earth, the lord of the gods and the universe. God Most High eventually revealed himself and his personal name, Yahweh, to the patriarchs of his chosen people Israel.[40] But as in the case of other OT passages which reflect a strong Canaanite background (Nm 24:16; Is 14:14; cf. Dn 3:26), it is not unlikely that El 'Elyon in Gn 14:18 was understood as not yet identified as Yahweh; rather it is the name of the Canaanite deity whom the king Melchizedek served as priest.

This question is involved in that of the character of vv. 18–20 in Gn 14. They interrupt the story of the meeting of Abram with the king of Sodom, and though it is now generally recognized that there is no solid reason to reject them as a 'later addition',[41] nevertheless they probably are part of an independent poetic saga, as old as the rest of Gn 14, but incorporated in the story of Abram's meeting with Sodom's king. It

[38] See *CBQ* 22 (1960) 291. O. Eissfeldt, 'El and Yahweh', *JSS* 1 (1956) 29, n. 1, remarks: 'That *yhwh* . . . is secondary may be taken as certain.'

[39] See A. Dupont-Sommer and J. Starcky, 'Les inscriptions araméennes de Sfiré (Stèles I et II)', *Mémoires présentés à l'Académie des Inscriptions et Belles-Lettres* 15 (1958) 193–351, esp. 17, 34; cf. J. A. Fitzmyer, *The Aramaic Inscriptions of Sefîre* (Biblica et orientalia 19; Rome: Pontifical Biblical Institute, 1967) 37–8.

[40] On the relation of El and 'Elyon consult the excellent survey of the question by R. Lack, 'Les origines de *'Elyon*, le Très-Haut, dans la tradition cultuelle d'Israël', *CBQ* 24 (1962) 44–64.

[41] See F. M. Th. Böhl, 'Die Könige von Genesis 14', *ZAW* 36 (1916) 72–3; H. Gunkel, *Genesis* (HKAT 1/1; Göttingen, 1922) 284–5; B. Vawter, *A Path Through Genesis* (New York, 1956) 132; J. Chaine, *Le livre de la Genèse* (Lectio divina 3; Paris, 1949) 202–3.—The recent attempt of G. R. Castellino, 'Il sacrificio di Melchisedec', *Eucaristia* (ed. A. Piolanti; Rome, 1957)

has been proposed that the hero of these verses (or of the whole saga) was Melchizedek, and that it was a *hieros logos* of the Jerusalem sanctuary with the aetiological purpose of showing Abram paying tithes to the Jerusalem priest-king.[42] It is rather more likely that the saga told of the co-operation of Melchizedek, an allied king, who went forth to refresh Abram and his troops, to bless him and give 'him a tithe of everything' (i.e., pay him tribute). Such a hypothesis accounts at least for the choppy character of the three verses and their relation to the whole.

With the insertion of the Melchizedek verses in Gn 14 and the identification of El 'Elyon as Yahweh, Melchizedek was adopted into Israelite tradition. By the time of the establishment of the Maccabean royal priesthood Melchizedek's designation becomes the official title of the Hasmonean dynasty.[43] Josephus, who calls Melchizedek *Chananaiōn dynastēs* ('a lord of the Canaanites'), mentions that he was the first to officiate as the priest of God,[44] and according to Philo God made him 'both king of peace, for that is the meaning of "Salem", and his own priest (*hierea heautou*)'.[45] This Jewish adoption of Melchizedek underlies the treatment of him in Heb, for the author knows that Melchizedek does not share a common ancestry with Abram (7:6).

But the rootless character of the vv. 18–20, to which we have referred, is precisely what provides the author of Heb with a starting-point for his comparison. In good rabbinical fashion

---

12, to defend the unity of Gn 14 amounts to no more than an assertion that it is unified.

[42] See W. F. Albright, *AASOR* 6 (1926) 63; H. W. Hertzberg, *op. cit.*, 169–79; H. Haag, *Bibellexikon* (Zürich, 1951) 1101–2.

[43] See 1 Mc 14:41; cf. Josephus, *Ant.* 16, 6, 2, #162; *Assumptio Mos.* 6:1; *Jub* 32:1; *T. Levi* 8:14–15.

[44] *JW* 6, 10, 1, #438; *Ant.* 1, 10, 2, #181.

[45] *De legum allegoria* 3, 79. See note 32 above for the rabbinical mode of adoption.

the argument is based on the very silence of the OT account; the principle is, as Strack-Billerbeck pointed out long ago, 'quod non in thora, non in mundo'.[46] More recently V. Hamp has labelled it *typologia e silentio*.[47] Because these verses are an insertion in the Abram story, there is no mention of Melchizedek's origins or destiny. The omission of such details led to the formulation of the legend (in a four-lined poetic composition) that he was

> *apatōr, amētōr, agenealogētos,*
> *mēte archēn hēmerōn mēte zōēs telos echōn,*
> *aphōmoiōmenos de tō huiō tou theou,*
> *menei hiereus eis to diēnekes.*[48]

It is an elaboration of the very silence of Gn.

But the point of the comparison is that Melchizedek, who appears in the OT with the title *kôhēn*, 'priest', lacks the all-important priestly genealogy. This situation undoubtedly caused speculation in Jewish circles, because the legitimacy of the priestly family depended on its genealogy,[49] on its ability to trace its descent from Levi via Aaron and Zadok. Aaron was the first high priest appointed by Moses at God's command (Ez 28:1 ff.; Lv 8:2 ff.), and was the model of all Jewish priests of the levitical line. But Aaron's ancestry is given in the OT; he

[46] Str-B 3, 694.

[47] *Op. cit.*, 9.

[48] The possibility that Heb 7:3 depends on an older tradition about Melchizedek is not unlikely. However, that it actually goes back to the middle of the second millennium B. C. and is reflected in the Amarna letters of Abdu-Heba of Urusalim (*EA* 287, 25; 'Behold this land of Jerusalem: (It was) not my father (and) not my mother (who gave (it) to me, (but) the arm of the mighty king (which) gave (it) to me' [*ANET* 488]) is rather unlikely.—One may wonder, however, whether the last two lines would antedate Christian times; or, if so, whether 'son of God' in such a case would mean anything more than 'angel', as in Gn 6:2.

[49] See Ez 40:46; 43:19; 44:15; Ezr 2:61–63; Neh 7:63–65; Philo, *Spec. leg.* 1,110 (cf. Lv 21:7–14); Josephus, *Contra Ap.* 1–7, #31–6; *Ant.* 11, 3, 10, #71; Mishnah, *Middoth* 5, 4; *Kiddushin* 4, 4; Tosephta, *Sanhedrin* 7, 1. Cf. M. D. Johnson, *The Purpose of the Biblical Genealogies* (SNTS Monograph 8; Cambridge: University Press, 1969) 79–80.

was descended from Levi, the son of Jacob the patriarch, via Kohath and Amram (Ex 6:16–19). His birth is mentioned explicitly in Ex 6:20 and his death in Nm 20:24–28. Hence he was scarcely *apatōr*, *amētōr*, *agenealogētos*; nor could he be said to be without an end to his life. Nothing similar is stated, however, of Melchizedek, the priest of God Most High. And yet in him the author of Heb finds the *type* of Jesus, the 'perfected' Son. The word *typos* is not used, but rather an equivalent expression, by which Jesus is not compared to Melchizedek, but Melchizedek to the 'Son of God' (*aphōmoiōmenos de tō huiō tou theou*)—a form of comparison which resembles the Pauline typology of Adam and Christ in Rom 5:14. In this regard, O. Michel has noted that Melchizedek 'has no independent meaning for salvation, but is only a pointer referring to the Son set up by God himself'.[50]

At this point the midrash introduces an element from Ps 110 to complete the comparison, and to emphasize the superiority of Christ. Nothing in Gn indicates that Melchizedek will 'remain a priest forever'. This element is derived from the divine promise made under oath to the Israelite king that he will be a priest *leʿôlām*. This was, if you will, a midrashic element already introduced into Ps 110. Now with the aid of Ps 110:4 Heb emphasizes that Jesus knows 'no end to his days', but only a 'life that cannot end' (7:15) and a priesthood that is 'untransferable' (7:24).[51] Thus it is that Melchizedek who has not received his priesthood *via generationis carnalis* nor transmitted it to others by the same means—because the Gn story knows no genealogy of him—is the type of Jesus the Son and high priest forever. Precisely in that respect in which his priesthood is farthest removed from the Aaronitic type, viz. the lack of hereditary human descent or genealogy, either antecedent or subsequent, is Melchizedek the prefigured Jesus.[52] We may

[50] *TDNT* 4, 570.

[51] The meaning of *aparabatos* is problematical; see AG 80.—C. Spicq (*op. cit.*, 197) defends the sense used here on the basis of both etymology and context.

[52] Melchizedek is used as the type of Jesus because he is 'a priest forever',

wonder at this point whether the author of Heb ever knew the Lucan and Matthaean genealogies of Jesus. But he does know that 'our Lord sprang from the tribe of Judah' (7:14) according to the flesh—and that is why he hastens to answer this objection with the comment, 'with reference to which (tribe) Moses said nothing at all about priests'. But the similarity with Melchizedek is found precisely in this, that he possesses 'a life which cannot end' (*zōē akatalytos*). Thus has the author of Heb established his basic comparison of Jesus with Melchizedek.

THE TITHES

Two further elements in the Gn story are now pursued, to illustrate the superiority of Christ's priesthood over that of Aaron. The first is tithes. Gn 14:20 relates that after Melchizedek blessed Abram, 'he paid him a tithe of everything'. Who paid whom? The text puzzled Jerome who saw that either interpretation was possible.

(Melchisedech) decimas praedae atque uictoriae acceperit ab eo (Abraham) siue—quoniam habetur ambiguum—ipse dederit ei decimas substantiae suae et auitam largitatem ostenderit in nepotem.[53] utrumque enim intellegi potest et iuxta hebraicum et iuxta septuaginta interpretes, quod et ipse acceperit decimas spoliarum et Abrahae dederit decimas substantiae suae.[54]

Modern commentators also raise the question,[55] for no subject

---

according to Ps 110:4. It should be recalled here, however, that in the fragment of Qumran Cave 4, to which I referred above on p. 103, the Aramaic phrase is found, *ytbḥr lkhn ʿlmyn*, 'he will be chosen as a priest forever' (literally, as a priest of [the] ages). It is part of a text that Starcky labels provisionally 'the Vision of Amram' (4QḥʿA^c 9:19). If it refers to Aaron, as Starcky thinks, then the permanence of his priesthood, which would be of interest to the Essene community, would be stressed. This perdurance of the Aaronid priesthood would then conflict with the argument of the author of Hebrews. Unfortunately, we shall have to await the full publication of this fragmentary text in order to be more definite about the meaning of the phrase and the person to whom it refers.

[53] Jerome followed the rabbinical identification of Melchizedek with Shem; see note 32 above and *Ep.* 73 (*Ad Evangelum*) #5 (CSEL 55, 18–19).

[54] *Ep.* 73, # 6 (CSEL 55, 20).

[55] See F. M. Th. Böhl, *op. cit.*, 72–3, whom we are following in part here.

is expressed in the MT or LXX and the subject of the preceding verb is not Abram but Melchizedek. Once again, the answer is probably to be sought in the fact that vv. 18–20 are an insertion, and that it was originally Melchizedek who as a vassal, an 'allied king', paid tithes to Abram. However, in Heb 7:2 there is no doubt about the subject of the sentence, because in his summary of Gn the author has inserted the name *Abraam*.[56] This is the contemporary understanding of the Gn text, as can be seen from the *Genesis Apocryphon* (22:17: 'And he gave him a tithe of all the goods of the king of Elam and his companions'—which can only refer to Abram), and from Josephus ('Abram then offered him the tithe of the spoil, and he accepted the gift').[57] From this contemporary interpretation of the Gn text Heb draws the conclusion of the superiority of Melchizedek's priesthood over that of Levi: Levi the otherwise privileged collector of tithes according to Mosaic legislation (Dt 10:8–9; 12:2) actually paid tithes to Melchizedek through Abram, 'for Levi was still in the loins of his father Abraham, when Melchizedek met the latter' (7:10). Though descended from the same patriarch Abraham, the levitical priests were permitted even as mortal men to tithe their own brothers. But the patriarch himself paid tithes not to a kinsman, but to a

---

Also G. Wuttke, *Melchisedech der Priesterkönig von Salem; eine Studie zur Geschichte der Exegese* (BZNW 5; Giessen, 1927) 20–1; H. Haag, *Bibellexikon*, 1101–2 ('Ob Abraham dem M. "den Zehnten von allem" gab oder umgekehrt, ist umstritten. Im heutigen Zusammenhang hat Abraham kaum etwas zu verzehnten, weil er ausdrücklich auf die Kriegsbeute verzichtet [14,23]'). See further R. H. Smith, 'Abram and Melchizedek', *ZAW* 77 (1965) 129-53.

[56] The boldface printing of *Abraam* (Heb 7:2) as part of the OT quotation in E. Nestle, *Novum Testamentum graece*, ed. 24 (1960), in the British and Foreign Bible Society's text, *Hē Kainē Diathēkē*, ed. 2 (1958), and in K. Aland *et al.*, *The Greek New Testament* (United Bible Societies, 1966) 758, is misleading at this point. Cf. A. Merk, *Novum Testamentum graece et latine* (9th ed.; Rome, 1964) 720.

[57] *Ant.* 1, 10, 2, #181.—The defective text of *Jub* 13, 25–6 has at least enough preserved to show that it too understood Gn 14:18–19 in the same way; see R. H. Charles, *APOT* 2, 33.

foreign king, who was a priest without ancestry, 'of whom it is testified that he lives' (7:9). This shows 'how great' Melchizedek was.

MELCHIZEDEK'S BLESSING

Lastly, Jesus' superiority over the Aaronitic line is shown by the fact that in Gn Melchizedek, the priest of El 'Elyon, blessed Abram. 'As is quite obvious, it is the inferior who is blessed by the superior' (Heb 7:7). Heb makes use of another current interpretation of Gn, when it links the phrase, 'And he was a priest of the Most High God', with the following verse, 'And he blessed him, saying. . . .' To the author of Heb the priestly act was the *blessing*;[58] no mention is made of the bringing out of bread and wine, much less of any sacrifice. An analogous understanding of Gn is seen in the *Genesis Apocryphon*, where the Aramaic version of Gn reads: 'And Melchizedek, the king of Salem, brought out food and drink for Abram and for all the men who were with him; and he was the priest of the Most High God, and he blessed Abram, saying . . .' (22:14–15). The addition to the text, 'for Abram and for all the men who were with him', as well as the translation of the Hebrew *leḥem wa-yayin* ('bread and wine') by the Aramaic *mēʾkal ū-mištêh* ('food and drink'),[59] show that the following phrase, 'and he was the priest of the Most High God', was scarcely intended as ex-

[58] See A. Vaccari, '"Melchisedec, rex Salem, proferens panem et vinum" (Gen. 14:18)', *VD* 18 (1938) 210–11; V. Hamp, *op. cit.*, 12–13.—Some authors have tried to maintain that though the utterance of a blessing in the OT is not exclusive to priests (see Gn 48:9; 49:28; Ru 2:4; Ps 128:5–6), it is normally uttered by them (Dt 10:8; 18:5; 21:5 [H. Gunkel, *op. cit.*, 286: 'Segnen ist Priesterrecht']). This argument lacks its force, however, precisely because it is not an exclusive prerogative.—The article of J. E. Coleran, 'The Sacrifice of Melchisedech', *TS* 1 (1940) 27–36, shows that no argument can be built up one way or the other from the use of the Hebrew expression *wᵉhûʾ*, for in Gn itself it is found several times to refer both to what follows and to what precedes (more frequently, however, to what precedes).

[59] In contrast to the later Targums, which translate it *lḥm wḥmr* (Neofiti I and Ps.-Jonathan), *lḥym wḥmr* (Onqelos), *mzwn wḥmr* (Fragmententargum).

planatory of what preceded. Josephus' understanding of the Gn text is no different.[60]

Thus, when the author of Heb set out to show the superiority of Jesus' priesthood over that of Aaron, he illustrated it from three elements in Gn alone: the lack of genealogy, the reception of tithes, and the blessing bestowed. It has often been noted that the author of Heb seems to be unaware of any sacrificial character of the Gn phrase, 'brought out bread and wine'.[61] In a composition that is otherwise so closely bound up with the notion of sacrifice, it is difficult to understand how he would have omitted it, if it were so understood in his day. It is significant that neither Josephus nor the *Genesis Apocryphon* so understands it. But it is well known that some of the Fathers understood these words in Gn in terms of the sacrifice of Melchizedek.[62] Their exegesis of the text, however, manifests the same midrashic, haggadic development as that of the author of Heb; it lacks only the charism of inspiration. However, it should be admitted with V. Hamp that even if the verb *hôṣî'* ('brought

[60] *Ant.* 1, 10, 2, #181: 'Melchizedek hospitably entertained Abraham's army, providing abundantly for all their needs, and in the course of the feast he began to extol Abraham and to bless God for having delivered his enemies into his hand.'

[61] Admittedly in this part of Heb the author is stressing the eternal character and superiority of Christ's priesthood and is not yet concerned (as in ch. 8–10) with his priestly *activity*. But he does draw two arguments from *actions* of Melchizedek (blessing and reception of tithes) to serve his purpose; if there were any special 'sacrificial' connotation to the bringing out of bread and wine, would he not have used this too?—Catholic exegetes admit frankly today that the verb *hôṣî'* is in no way sacrificial. See V. Hamp, *op. cit.*, 12; H. Rusche, *op. cit.*, 232; J. Chaine, *op. cit.*, 207, n. 89. Nor is there in the text any indication that the sacred author considered the bringing out of bread and wine to be 'un'azione sacra', nor that they were to be consumed 'in un'atmosfera religioso-sacrale di sacrificio'—*pace* G. R. Castellino, *op. cit.*, 16.

[62] But as P. Samain has pointed out, 'la tradition patristique n'établit pas qu'il y eut oblation' ('Melchisédech a-t-il offert un sacrifice, figure de l'Eucharistie?', *RevDTour* 1 [1946] 38–41). The usual patristic fluctuation of interpretation is noted in this question too. Tertullian (*Adv. Iud.* 3; CSEL 70, 258) makes no mention of sacrifice; nor do J. Firmicus Maternus (*De*

forth') can in no wise be forced into a sacrificial expression, nevertheless the bringing out of 'bread and wine' by the priest Melchizedek does prefigure the loving care of the high priest Christ who provides food to still the spiritual hunger of his chosen warriors in their earthly campaign. In this sense Gn 14: 18 can be said to prefigure the Eucharist.[63]

There can be little doubt that the 'rootless character' of vv. 18–20 in Gn 14 is responsible for the legends which grew up about Melchizedek. We noted that this started in the OT itself (in Ps 110); it is continued in the *Genesis Apocryphon*, Philo, Josephus and the Targums (which all manifest the Jewish adoption of him). Heb and later patristic writings carry on the adoption, until he becomes in the canon of the Mass of the Roman rite *summus sacerdos tuus Melchisedech*.[64] And the adoption

---

errore prof. rel. 18, 3; ed. K. Ziegler [1953] 62); Ambrosiaster (*Lib. quaest. vet. et novi test.* 109, 18; CSEL 50, 266); Justin (*Dial. c. Tryph.* 33; *PG* 6,545); Theophilus of Antioch (*Ad Autolycum* 2, 31; *PG* 6, 1104). Among these Ambrosiaster mentions the bread and wine as a type of the Eucharistic food offered to Christians by Christ; similarly Clement of Alexandria (*Strom.* 4, 161, 31; GCS 15,319), Epiphanius (*Pan.* 55, 6, 3–4; GCS 31, 331), Chrysostom (*In. Gen. hom.* 35, 5; *PG* 53, 328; *In Ps* 109, 8; *PG* 55, 276), Jerome (*Tract. in libr. Ps.* 109, 4; *CC* 78, 225). The sacrificial note was introduced especially in the West by Cyprian (*Ep.* 63, 4; CSEL 3/2, 703–4) and repeated by many thereafter. It is significant to note in Jerome's case that whereas he often speaks of the sacrificial aspect of Melchizedek's offering (*Comm. in ev. Matt.* 4, 26; *PL* 26, 202–3; *Hebr. quaest. in Gen.* 14, 18; *CC* 72, 19; *Ep.* 73, 3; *CSEL* 55, 16), nevertheless when he explains 'ipsa hebraica verba' (*Ep.* 73, 5), he makes no mention of sacrifice and even goes so far as to say, 'nec esse mirum, si Melchisedech uictori Abraham obuiam processerit et in refectionem tam ipsius quam propugnatorum eius panem uinumque protulerit et benedixerit ei' (*Ep.* 73, 6).—See G. Bardy, 'Melchisédech dans la tradition patristique', *RB* 35 (1926) 496–509; 36 (1927) 25–45; G. Wuttke, *op. cit.*, 43–59; H. Rusche, *op. cit.*, 246–50; R. Galdos, 'Melquisedec en la patrística', *EstEc* 19 (1945) 221–46; P. F. Cremin, 'According to the Order of Melchisedech: the Patristic Interpretation and its Value', *IER* 54 (1929) 385–91.

[63] *Op. cit.*, 14–15—The Council of Trent did not define that Melchizedek offered a sacrifice; see P. Samain, *op. cit.*, 41.

[64] See R. Le Déaut, 'Le titre de *Summus Sacerdos* donné à Melchisédech est-il d'origine juive?', *RSR* 50 (1962) 222–9.

of Melchizedek is not at an end, for in his little book on the *Holy Pagans of the Old Testament* J. Daniélou makes him out to be 'the High Priest of the cosmic religion'.[65]

[65] Tr. F. Faber; Baltimore, 1957, 104.

12

FURTHER LIGHT ON MELCHIZEDEK FROM QUMRAN CAVE 11*

A. S. van der Woude published a group of thirteen small fragments discovered in 1956 in Qumran Cave 11.[1] The title of his article attracts attention immediately, 'Melchizedek as a Heavenly Redemption-Figure in the Newly Discovered Eschatological Midrashim from Qumran Cave 11'.[1] Unfortunately, the state of preservation of these fragments is such that their interpretation will remain problematical; but they do contain a number of interesting phrases revealing new facets of the Melchizedek legend in Palestinian Judaism of the first century A.D., and these will affect in turn our understanding of the OT figure and the interpretation of certain NT passages.

The thirteen fragments furnish the better part of one column of the scroll or text to which they originally belonged; there are also a few isolated words at the beginning of the lines of a second column, but the context is broken and the rest of the lines lost so that they are of little interest to us here. We reproduce the text of Col. I, as it has been published by van der Woude. His reading of the text is in general accurate; occasionally there is room for a slightly different interpretation. He dates the text to the Herodian period, according to the cate-

* Originally published in *JBL* 86 (1967) 25–41.

[1] 'Melchisedek als himmlische Erlösergestalt in den neugefundenen eschatologischen Midraschim aus Qumran Höhle XI', *OTS* 14 (1965) 354–73.

gories established by F. M. Cross, Jr., and prefers a date in 'the first half of the first Christian century'.[2]

11QMelch offers another fragmentary example of a composition which comments on isolated OT texts taken from their original context and strung together with some theological intention. The editor of this text has compared it with that published by J. M. Allegro and often referred to as 4QFlorilegium.[3] In 11QMelch the sectarian comments on the OT passages are introduced by the word *pšr* (lines 4, 12, 17),[4] but they are really quite similar to those introduced by *mdrš* in 4QFlorilegium.[5] In the latter text the biblical verses quoted are drawn from 2 Sm 7:10b–11a; Ex 15:17–18; 2 Sm 7:11b–12; Am 9:11; Ps 1:1; Is 8:11; Ez 37:23; Ps 2:1.[6] We have a similar line-up of OT quotations in the text now under discussion: Lv 25:13; Dt 15:2; Is 61:1; Lv 25:10; Pss 82:1; 7:8—9; 82:2; Is 52:7; Lv 25:9. Although *pšr* has come to mean in modern parlance a special Essene type of commentary on a continuous text of some prophet or psalm, it is apparent that the word must have been used among the Essenes themselves

[2] *Ibid.*, 357.

[3] 'Fragments of a Qumran Scroll of Eschatological *Midrāšîm*', *JBL* 77 (1958) 350–4; see also 'Further Messianic References in Qumran Literature', *ibid.*, 75 (1956) 174–87, esp. 176–7.

[4] For discussions of the meaning of *pšr* and *mdrš*, see J. van der Ploeg, 'Le rouleau d'Habacuc de la grotte de 'Ain Fešḫa', *BO* 8 (1951) 2; 'Les manuscrits du Désert de Juda: Livres récents', *ibid.*, 16 (1959) 163; K. Stendahl, *The School of St Matthew and Its use of the Old Testament*, 200 ff.; J. A. Fitzmyer, 'The Use of Explicit Old Testament Quotations in Qumran Literature and in the New Testament', pp. 3–58 above, esp. p. 55; A. G. Wright, *CBQ* 28 (1966) 116–18, 418–22.

[5] See 11QMelch 14. For other Qumran texts of midrashic character see the remarks of J. T. Milik in 'Le travail d'édition des fragments manuscrits de Qumrân', *RB* 73 (1956) 61. Cf. also W. R. Lane, 'A New Commentary Structure in 4QFlorilegium', *JBL* 78 (1959) 343–6; Y. Yadin, 'A Midrash on 2 Sam VII and Ps I–II (4QFlorilegium)', *IEJ* 9 (1959) 95–8.

[6] In 4QFlor the main comments are made on 2 Sm 7 and on Pss 1–2; the others are introduced to illustrate the development of the midrashic comments. The correlation of Ps 2 and 2 Sm 7 in the one text is noteworthy, but unfortunately the text is very fragmentary and it only excites our curiosity.

as almost synonymous with *mdrš*. Perhaps we should regard the *pšr* as a special Essene type of *mdrš*. At any rate, van der Woude is correct in identifying 11QMelch as another example of an 'eschatological midrash' already found in the Qumran documents. As in the case of 4QFlor, an interpretation of the OT verses is given *l'ḥryt hymym*, 'for the end of days' (see lines 4, [15]; cf. line 20); compare 4QFlor 1:2, 12, 15, 19. Also to be noted is the similarity of phraseology in the comments of 4QFlor and 11QMelch; although different OT texts are commented upon, yet the mode of commenting is very similar. Several phrases recur: 'Belial', 'those who turn away from walking in the way of the people', etc.

THE TEXT[7]

1. [ ].........*yk* .....[
2. [ ]..[*w'*]*šr 'mr bšnt hyw*[*bl hzw't tšwbw 'yš 'l 'ḥwztw*
3. [*w'šr 'mr šmw*]*ṭ kwl bʿl mšh yd 'šr yšh* [*brʿhw lw' ygwś 't rʿhw w't 'ḥyw ky' qr'*] *šmṭh*
4. [*l'l pšrw l'ḥ*]*ryt hymym ʿl hšbwyym 'šr* [ ]*'sr*
5. ....*mh* ....*y h*.... *wmnḥlt mlky ṣdq k*[ ].....*hmh b*...[*mlky ṣ*]*dq 'šr*
6. *yšybmh 'lyhmh wqr' lhmh drr lʿzwb l*[*h*]*mh* [*wlkpr*] *ʿl ʿwwnwtyhmh w*....... [ ] .. [ ]*dbr hzh*
7. *bšnt hywbl h'ḥ*[*r*]*wn 'm*[*r*] *š*[ ]. *bly*[ ] *wy*[*wm* (?) *hkpw*]*rym h*[*w'*]*h* [ ] ..... [*yw*]*bl h*[ʿ]*śyry*
8. *lkpr bw ʿl kwl bny* [*'wr w*]*'nš*[*y g*]*wrl ml*[*ky*] *ṣdq*[ ]*m ʿly*[*hm*]*h ht*[ ] *lg*[ ]*wtmh ky'*
9. *hw'h ḥqq šnt hrṣwn lmlky ṣ*[*dq*]*l* .. [ ] *wqdwšy 'l lmm*[*š*]*lt mšpṭ k'šr ktwb*
10. *ʿlyw bšyry dwyd 'šr 'mr 'lwhym* [*n*]*ṣb bʿ*[*dt 'l*] *bqwrb 'lwhym yšpwṭ wʿlyw 'm*[*r* ʿ]*lyh*
11. *lmrwm šwbh 'l ydyn ʿmym w'šr '*[*mr ʿd mty t*]*špwṭw ʿwwl wpny ršʿ*[*y*]*m tś*[*'w s*]*lh*

[7] The reader is referred to the *editio princeps* for indications of the certainty or probability of the reading of various letters.

12. *pšrw ʿl blyʿl wʿl rw[ḥ]y gwrlw ʾš[r]..m bsp[ ] .. wqyʾl* . [
13. *wmlky ṣdq yqwm nq[m]t mš[p]ṭy ʾ[l myd b]lyʿl wmyd kwl [rwḥy gwrl]w*
14. *wbʿzrw kwl ʾly [ʿwlmym h]wʾh ʾ[šr ʾmr k]wl bny ḥ[y]l whp*[ ]
15. *hzwʾt hwʾh ywm h[hrgh ʾ]šr ʾmr [lʾḥryt hymym byd yšʿ]yh hnbyʾ ʾšr ʾm[r mh] nʾww*
16. *ʿl hrym rgl[y] mbś[r m]šmyʿ šlwm mb[śr ṭwb mšmyʿ yšwʿ]h ʾwmr lṣywn [mlk] ʾlwhyk*
17. *pšrw hhr[ym]tbyʾw[ty]hmh ʾ*[*]tp*[*]lkwl* . [
18. *whmbśr hw[ʾh m]šwḥ hrw[ḥ] ʾšr ʾmr dn[yʾl mbśr]*
19. *ṭwb mšmy[ʿ yšwʿh] hwʾh hk[tw]b ʿlyw ʾšr [ʾmr*
20. *lnḥ[m ?]*.....[*]l [y]śkylmh bkwl qṣy ḥ[rwn*
21. [*]ʾmt l* .[ ]...[
22. [ ]...[
23. [ ]*.h srh mblyʿl wt*. [ ]..[
24. [*]bmšpṭ[y] ʾl kʾšr ktwb ʿlyw [ʾwmr lṣy]wn mlk ʾlwhyk [ṣy]wn h[yʾh*
25. [ ]... *mqym[y] hbryt hsrym mlkt [bd]rk hʿm wʾl[w]hyk hwʾh*[
26. [ ]..........*d blyʿl wʾšr ʾmr whʿbrtmh šwp[r trwʿh] bḥ[wdš] h[šbyʿy*

Written vertically in the right-hand margin, beginning about line 11: *bmwšh kyʾ*

TRANSLATION[8]

1. [ ]........... your .....[ ]
2. [ ].. [and wh]at he said, '*In this year of ju*[*bilee each of you will return to his possession*'] (Lv 25:13)
3. [and what he said,] '*Let every creditor* [*re*]*mit the due that he claims* [*from his neighbour; let him*

[8] Italics in the translation indicate the parts of OT verses which are quoted in the Hebrew text of the Qumran document.

not dun his neighbour or his brother for there is proclaimed] a remission (Dt 15:2)

4. [of God.' Its meaning for the en]d of days concerns *those taken captive* whom [he] imprisoned (Is 61:1)

5. ... MH .... Y H .... and from the heritage of Melchizedek K[ ] ...... their BW .. [Melchized]ek who

6. will restore them to them, and he will *proclaim release* to them, to set them (?) free [and to atone] for their iniquities and .... [ ] .. [ ] this word. (Lv 25:10)

7. In the year of the la[st] jubilee he sai[d] S[ ]. BLY. [ ] and [tha]t is the d[ay of Atone]ment [ ] ..... the [t]enth [ju]bilee

8. to atone in it for all sons of [light and] men [of the l]ot of Mel[chi]zedek [ ]M upon [th]em HT [ ] LG [ ] WTMH for

9. he has decreed a year of good favour for Melchize[dek] L .. [ ] and the holy ones of God for a re[ig]n of judgment. As it is written

10. about it in the songs of David, who said, '*'Elohim has [ta]ken his stand in the as[sembly of 'El], in the midst of gods ['lwhym) he gives judgment*'. And about it he sa[id, '*A-] bove it* (Ps 82:1) (Ps 7:8–9)

11. *take your throne in the heights; let God ('l) judge* (the) *peoples.*' And he s[aid, '*How long*] *shall you judge unjustly and li[ft up] the face of* (the) *wic[ke]d'?* [Se]lah. (Ps 82:2)

12. Its interpretation concerns Belial and concerns the spir[it]s of his lot whi[ch] .. M

in the boo[k of] .. WQY'L .. [ ]
13. And Melchizedek shall exact the ven[ge]ance of the jud[g]ments of God ('[*l*]) [from the hand of Be]lial and from the hand(s) of all [the spirits of] his [lot].
14. And all the [eternal] gods (*'ly*) are for his help. [T]his is wh[at he said, A]ll the sons of mi[gh]t (?) and the P[ ]
15. this. This is the day of the [(about) wh]ich he said [for the end of days through Isai]ah the prophet who sai[d, *'How*] *beautiful* (Is 52:7)
16. *upon the mountains are the feet* [*of*] *the heral*[*d proclaiming peace; the herald of good, proclaiming salvat*]*ion,* (and) *saying to Zion, "Your God* [*is king*]*."'*
17. Its interpretation: The mounta[ins] their pro[du]ce ' [ ] TP [ ] for all. [ ]
18. and the herald i[s the on[e an]ointed with the Spir[it] (about) whom Dan[iel] spoke, [the herald of]
19. good, proclaimin[g salvation.] This is what is wr[itt]en about him, what [he said
20. to conso[le?] .. .. [ ] L [will in]struct them about all the periods of wra[th]
21. [ ] truth for. [ ]
22. [ ]
23. [ ]. H she turned from Belial and she .[ ]
24. [ ] with the judgment[s of] God (*'l*), as it is written concerning him, [*'Saying to Zi*]*on, "Your 'Elohim is king."'* (Now) Zi]on i[s
25. [ ] . . . the establisher[s of] the covenant

are those who turn away from walking [in
the p[ath of the people. And (as for) your
'Elohim (*'l*[*w*]*hyk*), he (is) [ ]

26. [ ] . . . . L . . . . . D Belial, and what
he said, *'And you shall sound the horn* [*loud*] *in* (Lv 25:9)
the [*seventh*] *mo*[*nth*]

COMMENTARY

The thread which apparently runs through the whole text and ties together its various elements is Lv 25. Parts of three verses of that chapter are quoted: v. 9 in line 26, v. 10 in line 6, and v. 13 in line 2. The fragmentary text begins *in medias res* with a reference to a jubilee year; it is part of a quotation of Lv 25:13, the first part of the thread running through the text. Into this context of a jubilee year and the regulations prescribed for it in Lv 25 the figure of Melchizedek is introduced. He is apparently being given a special role in the execution of divine judgment which is related to a jubilee year. In the course of the midrashic development the year of jubilee mentioned first in line 2 becomes 'the last jubilee' (line 7) or 'the tenth jubilee' (line 7, at the end). In other words, it seems to refer to the end of the 490 years, or 'the seventy weeks of years' of Dn 9:24–27. It is called the year of 'release' (*šmṭh*) proclaimed for the Lord (lines 3–4) and of 'liberation' (*drr*), such as was announced to the captives of Is 61:1. It is a year which involves atonement for iniquity, and the Day of Atonement is somehow related to it; unfortunately, line 7, where the latter seems to be mentioned, is very fragmentary. It is impossible to specify the relation further.

The characteristics of this year of 'release' and 'liberation' are 'peace, welfare (literally, good), and salvation' (see lines 16, 19). These are ensured because of a judgment in which a figure is involved who is either Melchizedek himself, or someone who enjoys 'the heritage of Melchizedek' (lines 5–6). Even though Melchizedek's name must be partly restored in lines 5, 8, and 9, it is nevertheless read with certainty in line 13. So there is little doubt that he is somewhow connected with the year of jubilee with which the text deals. Not only is 'a year of good favour' (*šᵉnat rāṣôn*, cf. Is 61:2) decreed by God in his regard, but Pss 82 and 7 are quoted in reference to him (lines 10–11). These quotations imply that he is somehow God's agent for the execution of divine judgment on man in this year of jubilee. Depending on how strictly and literally these OT quotations are to be applied to him, Melchizedek seems to enjoy a status among or even above such heavenly beings as 'the holy ones of God' (*qᵉdōšê 'El*). The application of Ps 82:1 to him in line 10 is problematical; van der Woude is of the opinion that *'lwhym* in line 10 refers directly to Melchizedek, who thereby is made to take his stand in the assembly of *'El* and in the midst of *'lwhym* he gives judgment.[9] When Ps 7:8–9 is applied to him, it emerges that Melchizedek is somehow exalted even above the *ʿᵃdat 'El*; and when Ps 82:2 is referred to Belial and the spirits of his lot (line 12), we learn that Melchizedek will exact the vengeance of divine judgment from them, being aided in this by 'all the [eternal] *'ēlîm*', i.e., by the angelic spirits of heaven.

The day of judgment to be executed by Melchizedek (or whoever shares his heritage) is apparently further identified with the salvation proclaimed by the herald of Is 52:7 (see lines 15–16). It is not surprising that the year of jubilee, the 'year of good favour', the 'releases', and the 'liberation' are somehow identified in this text with 'salvation', even the salvation of Is 52:7. But what is striking is that the *mᵉbaśśer*, or 'herald', of the Isaian text is said to be 'anointed with the Spirit'. In line 18 van der Woude restored the article before [*m*]*šyḥ*, thus identifying the 'herald' explicitly with 'the Messiah'. His reading was subsequently challenged by Y. Yadin (see commentary below), who proposed the reading *mšwḥ hrw*[*ḥ*], 'anointed with the Spirit'. This, of course, eliminates the reference to a single Messiah (cf. 4QPatrBless 3). But Yadin's reading is, nevertheless, interesting in that it makes of the

[9] *Op. cit.*, 364.

herald of Is 52:7 a messianic figure, i.e., one anointed. This reading is probably a further allusion to Is 61:1, a passage to which we have already referred in the general comments above (p. 246). The connection of these Isaian passages with Dn 9 receives a further support, if my restoration of the end of line 18 is correct, 'and the herald is the one anointed with the Spirit (about) whom Daniel said . . .'. I proposed to read *Danîyel* and referred it to the *māšîaḥ nāgîd* of Dn 9:25. This identification of the herald with the Anointed One of Dn 9, though not certain, is in reality not so striking as the mention of the *m^ebaśśer* or 'herald of good tidings', as someone anointed, or as a messianic figure. It is known that the 'herald' of Is 52:7 became a figure expected in the beliefs of Palestinian Judaism. He was in fact identified with the Anointed King or King Messiah by R. Jose the Galilean (*c.* A.D. 110), according to *Derekh 'Ereṣ Zuṭa.*[10]

What is to be noted above all in this text, therefore, are the associations which are made with Melchizedek. He is associated with the deliverance of divine judgment, with a day of atonement, with a year of jubilee, and with a role that exalts him high above the assembly of heavenly beings. Such associations make the comparison in Hebrews between Jesus the high priest and Melchizedek all the more intelligible. The tradition is not the same; but what we have in 11QMelch at least furnishes a new light on the comparison. It reveals an almost contemporary Jewish understanding of Melchizedek, which is not without its pertinence for the midrash on him which is incorporated into Heb 7.[11] Whether Melchizedek is the same as the 'herald'

[10] See also *Pesiqta* 51a, 20. Cf. G. Friedrich, *euangelizomai*, *TDNT* 2, 716–17; Str-B 3, 9–10.

[11] For a fuller discussion of this subject, see my article, '"Now this Melchizedek . . ." (Heb 7:1)', pp. 221–43 above. J. F. X. Sheehan, 'Melchisedech in Christian Consciousness', *ScEccl* 18 (1966) 127–38, takes me to task for my interpretation of the Melchizedek midrash in Heb 7. He attempts to set forth 'the cumulative thrust of the dogmatic, patristic, and even linguistic evidence in favour of the "classical" or "traditional" notions of the role of the bread and the wine in the Melchisedech episode' (p. 128). By so doing, he hopes to show that Melchizedek is still 'among the most

in this text is difficult to say because of the fragmentary state of the document. If he were, then the identification of these various titles with him would be still more interesting, in that they would illustrate in a Jewish text the conflation of expected figures similar to that found in the NT when the many titles, derived from independent OT themes, are applied to Jesus.[12] The fragmentary state of the text, however, prevents us from saying whether this midrash has any connection with either Gn 14:18–20 or Ps 110, the two places in the OT where Melchizedek is explicitly mentioned. What is preserved is a midrashic development which is independent of the classic OT loci. And this is, in my opinion, the reason for saying that the tradition found here is not the same as that in Hebrews, even though it does shed some light on the more general development. J. A. Sanders has suggested to me that possibly the thought-development of Ps 110 underlies the midrash in this text. Possibly there is an echo of Ps 110:6 in line 11, but then this is a quotation of Ps 7:8–9 (the verb *yādîn* occurs in both places). But beyond this extremely superficial echo the influence of Ps 110 on what is preserved of the midrash in this fragmentary text is almost nil.

Did the author of this text consider Melchizedek to be the

---

beloved of the Old Testament pre-figures of the Eucharistic sacrifice' (p. 127). I am particularly unimpressed by what he calls the 'linguistic' evidence; the use of the copula *w*-, followed by a pronoun, can indeed have subordinate meaning (e.g., 'since'), but does it always have it? This explanation is not acceptable in Gn 14:18 without further ado. Nor has he asked himself whether what he calls 'the cumulative thrust of the dogmatic' and 'patristic . . . evidence' is not really an accommodation of the OT text by a later tradition. For an independent confirmation of my views on the subject, one can consult I. Hunt, 'Recent Melkizedek Study', *BCCT* 21–33. See also F. Moriarty, 'Abel, Melchizedek, Abraham', *The Way* 5 (1965) 95–104, esp. 102.

[12] There is a similar conflation of the Son of Man, Messiah, and Elect One in *Enoch* (e.g., see chapters 48–52). But it is not easy to show the conflation of other titles and the application of them to one person in earlier or contemporary Jewish writings. This, then, is an important aspect of 11QMelch.

archangel Michael? Van der Woude inclines to think that he did, because Melchizedek is called *'lwhym* and is exalted above the heavenly court in lines 10–11. He mentions that Jewish tradition regarded Melchizedek as 'high priest' and that Michael is called the heavenly high priest in the Babylonian Talmud (*Ḥagigah* 12b). The medieval writing *Yalkut ḥadaš* (fol. 115, col. 3, n. 19) makes the identification explicit: *myk'l nqr' mlky ṣdq . . . kwhn 'l 'lywn šhw khn šl m'lh.* This identification is, then, clear in later Jewish tradition; but is it in the mind of the author of this text? Is it an early tradition which he might be reflecting? It is impossible to answer these questions in my opinion. If the interpretation of van der Woude be correct, then this is the earliest attestation of this identification. But it is complicated by the fact that the author of the text seems to refer to Melchizedek as *'Elôhîm* (see lines 10 and possibly 25). This is the suggestion of van der Woude himself and it seems correct. See below for the details. This is the basis for his opinion too that Melchizedek is presented in this text as a heavenly redemption-figure.

The following remarks on various phrases will help to give a more detailed interpretation of the text in support of the general commentary supplied above.

2. *[w']šr 'mr:* 'And what he said', i.e. God. This formula commonly introduces an OT quotation, not only in this text (see lines [3], 10, 11, [14], 15 *bis*, 18, 19, 26), but also in other Qumran literature (cf. my article, 'The Use of Explicit Old Testament Quotations in Qumran literature and in the New Testament', pp. 3–58 above). Van der Woude (*op. cit.*, 360–1) has shown that in the Qumran texts there is really no parallel to the NT and rabbinical instances in which the subject of *'mr* could be understood as 'Scripture' or 'a Scripture passage'. In Qumran literature the sense is rather that of a personal subject, either expressed (Levi, CD 4:15; Moses, CD 8:14; 19:26; Isaiah, CD 6:8; Jeremiah, CD 8:20; or God, either with or

without an intermediary, CD 6:13; 8:9; 19:22: 9:7; 4QFlor 1:7; CD 3:19–20; 19:11; 4:14) or understood, as in this case. Van der Woude translates the expression, however, in the present, 'und das, was Er sagt'. The form *'mr* could indeed be the participle, *'ômēr*; and given the fluctuation in the NT between *legei* and *eipen* (see Heb 1:5–13; cf. G. Kittel, *TDNT* 4, 105–6), one might be inclined to say that either participle or perfect were possible. Indeed, both are used in rabbinical writings. However, the perfect is to be preferred in my opinion because of the tendency to *plena scriptio* in the Qumran writings; we would expect *'wmr* here, if the author meant the participle.

bšnt hyw[bl hzw't]: 'In this year of jubilee.' The OT text quoted is probably Lv 25:13, since Lv 25 is further quoted in lines 6 and 26. Theoretically, Lv 27:24 is also possible. The references to *ywbl*, *šmṭh*, and *drwr* in the context of the returning exiles of the Babylonian captivity are better understood in the quotation of Lv 25. This year of jubilee is further identified in line 9 as a year of good favour (*šnt hrṣwn*) decreed by God for Melchizedek and 'the year of the last jubilee' (*šnt hywbl h'ḥrwn*) in line 7, 'the tenth jubilee'. It is not easy to determine the sense in which Lv 25:13 is used here because of the fragmentary state of the text. Van der Woude may be right in thinking of an eschatological possession of the holy land by the returning captives. At least this would be the sense of line 4. Cf. 1QM 2:6 (*bmw'd šnt hšmṭh*), 2:8 (*wbšny hšmṭym*).

3. *[šmw]ṭ kwl b'l mšh yd:* 'Let every creditor remit.' The author of the text now associates Dt 15:2 with the year of jubilee. The text agrees with the MT except for *yd*, which is read instead of the latter's *ydw*. Dt 15:2 is immediately concerned with the Sabbatical year, but van der Woude has pointed out the relation of the two verses to each other which is suggested by the LXX, in which *bšnt hywbl* of Lv 25:13 is rendered by *en tō etei tēs apheseōs* and the same word *aphesis* is used in Dt 15:2 for *wzh dbr hšmṭh*. The use of *aphesis* for both *ywbl* and *šmṭh* forms the link between the two.

4. [*l'l*]*:* 'Of God', or more literally, 'for God'. The MT has at this point *lYhwh*, but given the Qumran reluctance to write the tetragrammaton (see my *The Genesis Apocryphon of Qumran Cave I: A Commentary* [Rome, 1966] 159), van der Woude's restoration is most plausible. Compare the same substitution of *'l* for *Yhwh* in the quotation of Ps 7:9 in line 11 below. It is interesting to note that Dt 15:2 is also used in 1Q*22* ('Dires de Moïse') 3:4–6, where it is joined to phrases taken from Lv 25. At the end, instead of *lYhwh*, we find the restoration *l*[']*l*[*why 'lwhyk*]*m*, an extended paraphrase demanded by the space. In this text God is called *'l*, and apparently not *'lwhym*; see below on line 10.

[*pšrw l'ḥ*]*ryt hymym:* 'Its meaning for the end of days', i.e., its eschatological meaning. The form *pšrw* is also found in lines 12, 17. But the restoration follows the phrase found in 4QpIs[b] 2:1; 4QpIs[c] 10 (*JBL* 77 [1958] 215, 219); 1QpHab 2:5 (with deleted *aleph*).

'l hšbwyym 'šr: 'Concerns those taken captive whom. . . .' The immediate allusion here is undoubtedly to Is 61:1 (*lqr' lšbwym drwr*), the text to which further reference is made in the following lines. For the *plena scriptio*, see 1QIs[a] 49:26. A return to the holy land formed part of the salvific hope of contemporary Judaism; and van der Woude is more inclined to apply the words here to all the diaspora rather than to the Qumran community. Once again it is the fragmentary state of the text which hinders any certain judgment, but there must be some reference to the Qumran community in these words, given their esoteric way of interpreting Scripture in terms of their own community. The use of the preposition *'l* here sheds light on the Greek *eis* used in Eph 5:32. The Isaian passage is quoted in Lk 4:18–19.

5. *wmnḥlt mlky ṣdq:* 'And from the heritage of Melchizedek.' Unfortunately, the fragmentary state of the text once again hinders any real comprehension of this phrase. Van der Woude appeals to Dt 32:8 apropos of the noun *nḥlt*, 'when the Most High gave to the nations their inheritance'. But this seems

scarcely *ad rem* to me. Rather, *nḥlt* more likely refers to the priestly 'inheritance' of the levites, *kî kehunnat Yahweh naḥalātô* (Jos 18:7). We should recall that Melchizedek is called *kôhēn* in Gn 14:18 (see my remarks on pp. 233–8 above). It may be that the priests of the Qumran community are thus envisaged; and perhaps an ideal one, possessing the 'heritage of Melchizedek' and thus possessing no land of his own, is here regarded as the person to proclaim the year of jubilee and release to the 'captives', to those who are to return to their own possessions.

The end of this line presents a problem, because it is impossible to say whether the name *mlky ṣ]dq* is the *nomen rectum* of a construct chain whose *nomen regens* would be the antecedent of the relative pronoun or is itself the antecedent. The latter seems more plausible in the entire context of the document, but then one may ask who it is that enjoys the 'heritage of Melchizedek'. Note the writing of the name in two words; contrast 1QapGn 22:14. See further pp. 229-31 above.

6. *yšybmh 'lyhmh:* 'Will restore them to them.' The prepositional phrase must refer to the captives mentioned in line 4. But who is the subject and what is the direct object? In the opinion of van der Woude the rest of the line alludes to Is 61:1 and so the subject should likely be the Anointed One of line 18. This may be a little far-fetched, in that the Anointed One is not yet named.

wqr' lhmh drr: 'And he will proclaim release to them.' This phrase could be an allusion to Is 61:1 (so van der Woude) or to Jer 34:8 (which is closer in verbal form; cf. 34:15, 17), or to Lv 25:10 (*ûqerā'tem derôr*). The occurrence of *derôr* in both Lv 25 and Is 61 is undoubtedly the reason for relating the texts in this midrash. Cf. Lk 4:18, where Jesus appears as the anointed instrument of Yahweh, performing that which the expected figure in this text is to perform.

l'zwb l[h]mh: 'To set them free.' This is the restoration suggested by van der Woude, who also mentions another possibility, *l'zwr*, 'to help'. Is *lhmh* to be taken as the direct object here? D. R. Hillers has pointed out to me two possible parallels of this phrase: CD 5:6 (*wy'zbm lw 'l*) and Sir 3:13 (*'zwb lw*). Possibly, then, we should rather translate the phrase, 'to show forebearance to them'.

[*wlkpr*] *'l 'wwnwtyhmh:* 'To atone for their iniquities.' For the idiom, see line 8 and CD 4:9–10 (where God is the subject); 1QS 11:14 (with *b'd* instead of *'l*); 1QS 3:6 (*ykwprw kwl 'wwnwtw*); see also 1Q22 3:7, where the phrase is also partially restored. Underlying the words is undoubtedly the biblical expression found in Dn 9:24 (*l^ekappēr 'āwōn*), a passage which has otherwise influenced this midrash.

[ ]*dbr hzh:* 'This word', before which we should probably restore the article *h*-. But cf. Dt 15:2 (*wzh dbr hšmṭh*).

7. *bšnt hywbl h'ḥ*[*r*]*wn:* 'In the year of the last jubilee', i.e., the end of the 490 years, or the tenth jubilee (according to the end of this line).

bly[ ]: Van der Woude rules out the possibility of reading here *'blym*, 'mourners' (Is 61:2). One might also think of Belial, but how would it fit into the context?

wy[*wm hkpw*]*rym h*[*w'*]*h:* 'That is the Day of Atonement.' Van der Woude does not translate this phrase, nor does he try to explain it. Recall also the mention of 'the Day of Atonement' in 1Q*34bis* 2+1:6 (see Milik's note in DJD 1, 153), and in 1QpHab 11:7. Perhaps my suggestion is completely out of place here, and is too much influenced by the Epistle to the Hebrews in which both Melchizedek and the Day of Atonement play a significant role. The restoration, indeed, is not certain, but is possible and does not lack some plausibility, given the mention of the Day of Atonement in Lv 25:9. See also line 26 below, and compare the related text of 1Q22 3:9–12.

[*hyw*]*bl h*[*'*]*śyry:* 'The tenth jubilee.' This phrase is most likely an explanation of the 'last jubilee' mentioned at the beginning of this line. It seems to be an obvious reference to Dn 9:24–27, which alludes to Jer 25:11 and 29:10. Cf. 2 Chr 36:20–21. The plausibility of this interpretation is enhanced by *T.*

Levi 17:2 ff.: 'In each jubilee there shall be a priesthood. In the first jubilee the first who is anointed to the priesthood shall be great and shall speak to God as to a father. . . .' But in the succeeding six jubilees the priesthood deteriorates and becomes progressively corrupt. Finally, after the seventh jubilee, 'then shall the Lord raise up a new priest' (18:2). This reference to the *Testament of Levi* supplies some background which makes the 'tenth jubilee' a little more intelligible in terms of Melchizedek's priestly role. And yet, it must be emphasized that Melchizedek does not appear in *T. Levi* 17–18, where this development is found. Be this as it may, it is important not to stress this too much nor to judge the situation too much from the standpoint of the author of the Epistle to the Hebrews, where Melchizedek is set in contrast to the levitical priesthood.

8. *lkpr bw ʿl kwl bny* [*ʾwr*]*:* 'To atone in it for all (the) sons of light.' The prepositional phrase *bw* ('in it') refers to the tenth jubilee, which seems to be the time of salvation and atonement, or possibly to the Day of Atonement during it. Parallel expressions can be found in 1QS 5:6 (*lkpr lkwl hmtndbym*); 1QM 2:5 (*lkpr bʿd kwl ʿdtw*); cf. *Jub* 34:18; 1Q*22* 3:9–12.

[*w*]*ʾnš*[*y g*]*wrl ml*[*ky*] *ṣdq:* 'And men of the lot of Melchizedek.' This phrase seems to be the counterpart of Belial and 'the spirits of his lot' (line 12). If the reading *ml*[*ky*] *ṣdq* is correct here, then it is quite interesting, because it would be a parallel to *ʾnšy gwrl ʾl* (1QS 2:2; 1QM 13:5; 17:7), in which Melchizedek's name is substituted for that of God. However, van der Woude indicates that the reading is not entirely certain, even though he prefers it to the other possibility *ʾl* [*h*]*ṣdq*, a phrase which is not without some parallelism in 1QM 18:8; 1QH fr 7:8.

9. *hwʾh ḥqq šnt hrṣwn lmlky ṣ*[*dq w*]*l* . . .: 'He has decreed a year of good favour for Melchizedek and for. . . .' The first word *hwʾh* may be simply a pronoun, being used as an emphatic expression of the subject, but it may also be a surrogate for Yahweh (as in 1QS 8:13). The verb *ḥqq* probably refers to the

divine determination of historical periods (compare 1QpHab 7:13; 1QS 10:1). The phrase *šnt hrṣwn*, lit. 'the year of good favour', meaning a year in which God manifests his good will and predilection toward men. It is an echo of Is 61:2 (*liqrō' šᵉnat rāṣôn laYhwh*); cf. 1QH 15:15 (*mwʿd rṣwn*) and Lk 4:18.

wqdwšy 'l: 'The holy ones of God', i.e., the angels; cf. CD 20:8 (*kl wqdšy ʿlywn*). Reference seems to be made to these beings in the verses of the Psalms which are quoted in the following lines; cf. C. H. W. Brekelmans, *OTS* 14 (1965) 305–29.

lmmšlt mšpṭ: 'For a reign of judgment.' This is apparently the purpose of Melchizedek's exaltation and of the divine decree concerning him; it is the opposite of *mmšlt ʿwlh* (1QS 4:19).

k'šr ktwb ʿlyw: 'As it is written about it', or possibly 'about him'. In the first instance the preposition *ʿlyw* would refer to the judgment; in the second, to Melchizedek. Van der Woude prefers the latter, but P. W. Skehan has suggested to me the former possibility. The introductory formula has not previously been found as such in Qumran literature; it resembles a number of others, however. See pp. 8–10 above. The closest parallel seems to be CD 1:13 (*hy' hʿt 'šr hyh ktwb ʿlyh. . .*).

10. *bšyry dwyd*: 'In the songs of David.' Note that the psalm is referred to here as *šîr*, and not as *tᵉhillāh*; for the distinction see 11QPsᵃ DavComp 4–5, 9 (DJD 4, 92); cf. 2 Sm 22:1 (=Ps 18:1).

'lwhym [n]ṣb bʿ[dt 'l], bqwrb 'lwhym yšpwṭ: These words are taken from Ps 82:1, which the RSV translates as follows: 'God has taken his place in the divine council. In the midst of the gods he holds judgment.' However, in the context of this Qumran document one has to modify the translation slightly, because the author obviously understands *bʿdt 'l* as 'in the assembly of 'El (*or* God)', whereas the word *'lwhym* must refer to others than God. For this reason I have translated it, ''Elohim has taken his stand in the assembly of El, in the midst of gods he gives judgment.' The word *'Elohim* in the first instance ap-

parently refers to Melchizedek, who is to execute divine judgment in the year of good favour decreed for him. 'The midst of the gods' must then designate an angelic court, above which Melchizedek is exalted. This is the same interpretation as that of van der Woude, who thinks that Melchizedek is presented here as an exalted heavenly being, presiding over the angels who are his helpers and in whose midst he delivers judgment. For the form *qwrb* instead of *qereb*, a not infrequent *qutl* type found in the Qumran texts, see the remarks of M. H. Goshen-Gottstein, 'Linguistic Structure and Tradition in the Qumran Documents', *Scripta hierosolymitana* 4 (1958) 101–37, esp. 126–7.

w'lyw 'mr. 'And about it he (i.e., God) said.' A second quotation from the Psalms is thus introduced and applied to the judgment to be given by Melchizedek.

11. [']*lyh lmrwm šwbh, 'l ydyn 'mym*: 'Take your throne above it in the heights; let God ('El) judge (the) peoples.' Ps 7:8–9 is quoted in the same form as the MT, except that *'l* is substituted for *Yhwh*; see note on line 4 above. *'lyh* in Ps 7 refers to *'dt l'mym*, 'an assembly of peoples', but in this midrash it refers rather to the *'dt 'l* of Ps 82:1, the only feminine expression in the context. The phrase *lmrwm* refers to the heights of heaven, where 'El dwells, and is another indication of the exaltation of Melchizedek. The problematic word in this verse is *šwbh*, which has the same consonantal spelling as the MT. At first sight, it would seem to be a form of *šwb*, 'return' and possibly the author of the midrash so understood it. However, it makes little sense in the context, and possibly we should rather read *šybh* and understand it as a form of *yšb*, 'sit'. This certainly yields a far better sense; see H.-J. Kraus, *Psalmen* (BKAT XV/1; Neukirchen, 1960) 1, 54; M. J. Dahood, *Psalms I* (AB) 44.

w'šr '[*mr*]: See note on line 2.

['*d mty t*]*špwṭw 'wwl wpny rš'*[*y*]*m tś*['*w*]: 'How long shall you judge unjustly and lift up the face of (the) wicked?' This is a quotation from Ps 82:2; its form corresponds to the MT save for the *plena scriptio* of *tšpwṭw* and *'wwl*. Its collocation with the other two psalm verses just quoted might suggest that it refers to Melchizedek, as they do; but it would then imply that he is being rebuked by the words of the psalm which preserves a divine rebuke of unjust judges. This would be a little strange in the context. However, the explanation which is given immediately after the quotation shows that the words are not addressed to Melchizedek, but to Belial and the spirits of his lot, who are to be judged by Melchizedek.

[s]lh: 'Selah.' This word is found here, just as in the MT. It is also found in 11QPs[a] 25:12 (DJD 4, 46; =Ps 143:6). For a discussion of its meaning, see H.-J. Kraus, *Psalmen*, 1, xxv–xxvi.

bmwšh ky': 'In Moses, that . . .', i.e., in the Torah, or possibly in the Scriptures. These words are written vertically in the margin, beginning between lines 11 and 12. Perhaps they belong in line 10 after *w'lyw 'm[r]* and before the quotation of Ps 82:2. A. S. van der Woude thinks that these words belonged to a preceding column; they are, however, written very close to the beginning of this one. For a parallel to 'in Moses', see 2 Cor 3:15; cf. Jn 10:34 (where Ps 81:6 is quoted as 'the Law'); Jn 15:25 (Ps 24:19 so quoted).

12. *pšrw 'l bly'l w'l rw[ḥ]y gwrlw:* 'Its interpretation concerns Belial and concerns the spirits of his lot.' The words of Ps 82:2 are thus applied to Belial in a very vague way. Belial is well known in Qumran literature as the chief spirit of evil, 'the angel of hostility' (1QM 13:11), 'the prince of the dominion of evil' (1QM 17:5). Those identified as belonging to his lot are usually called *kwl 'nšy gwrlw* (1QM 4:2; cf. 1QS 2:4–5; CD 12:2). But in 1QM 13:2, 4, 11 we find *rwḥy gwrlw*, who are 'angels of destruction'. The same phrase is plausibly restored in line 13 below. Cf. 2 Cor 6:15; see pp. 209–13 above.

bsp[r] . . . wqy'l: Unintelligible.

13. *wmlky ṣdq yqwm nq[m]t mšpty ['l]:* 'And Melchizedek shall exact the vengeance of the judgments of God (*or* 'El).' Melchizedek now clearly appears in his role as an instrument of the execution of divine judgment. His role is described and related

to the *yôm nāqām lē'lôhênû* (Is 61:2), 'the day of vengeance for our God'. For 'the judgments of God', see line 24.

[myd b]lyʿl wmyd kwl [rwḥy gwrl]w: 'From the hand of Belial and from the hand(s) of all the spirits of his lot.' See note on line 12 above; cf. 1QS 4:18.

14. *wbʿzrw kwl 'ly [ʿwlmym]:* 'And all the eternal gods are for his help.' This is van der Woude's restoration. It is not, however, certain and presents a difficulty. He restores it on the basis of an expression which J. Strugnell says occurs in Qumran literature (see VTSup 7 [1959] 331). What is strange here is that the angels who are to be Melchizedek's helpers are called *'ly*, whereas in the rest of the text *'l* is used for God and *'lwhym* for angels (or Melchizedek). *bʿzrw:* b+infinitive construct with the suffix, 'for helping him'.

[h]w'h 'šr 'mr: 'This is what he said.' A similar expression is found in CD 10:16; 16:15; 1QpHab 3:2, 13–14; cf. p. 12 above.

[k]wl bny ḥ[y]l whp[ ]: 'All the sons of might (?) and the P[ ].' The expression *bny ḥyl* is found in the OT (2 Sm 2:7; 13:28; 17:10; etc.), and the introductory phrase which precedes should make this part of a quotation; but I have been unable to find any passage which is suited to this context.

15. *hw'h ywm h[hrgh]:* This is van der Woude's restoration, based on 1QH 15:17, where the word is also restored (cf. Jer 12:3). He translates it, 'das ist der Tag der Schlachtung', explaining it as the day of eschatological judgment. While not impossible, it does not seem to fit very well into the context which follows (with its quotation from Isaiah).

[']šr 'mr [l'ḥryt hymym byd yšʿ]yh hnby' 'šr 'm[r]: '(About) which he said for the end of days through Isaiah the prophet, who said. . . .' This full formula occurs here for the first time in Qumran texts; it should be compared with 4QFlor 1:15; CD 4:14; 19:10–11; 3:21.

[mh] n'ww ʿl hrym rgl[y] mbś[r] . . .: 'How beautiful upon the mountains are the feet of the herald', etc. The text is the same

as the MT of Is 52:7, except for the form *hrym* (without the article) and the *plena scriptio* of *'wmr*. Note, however, that *hhrym* occurs in line 17. There is, of course, the earlier passage of Na 2:1 which is echoed. 1QH 18:14 also alludes to Is 52:7.

16. *[m]šmy' šlwm:* 'Proclaiming peace.' Is this possibly the reason why this quotation of Is 52:7 is introduced into this midrash, because it contains a reference to *šlwm*, 'peace', and could be exploiting the pun on the 'king of Salem'? Cf. Heb 7:2; see pp. 231–3 above. It may be, though, that this observation is too much influenced by the Epistle to the Hebrews and the association did not really enter into the mind of the author of this text.

[mlk] 'lwhyk: 'Your God is king', or more literally, 'has reigned'.

17. *pšrw:* 'Its interpretation.' See note on line 4.

hhr[ym]: 'The mountains', here with the article. This suggests that the form in line 16 is a scribal error.

tby'w[ty]hmh: 'Their produce.' The third letter is clearly a *yodh* and not the expected *waw*.

18. *whmbśr hw]'h [m]šwḥ hrw[ḥ] 'šr 'mr dn[y'l] . . .:* 'And the herald is the one anointed with the Spirit (about) whom Daniel said. . . .' Van der Woude first read *whmbśr hw['h hmšyḥ hw'[h]*, 'and the herald is that Anointed One'. However, Y. Yadin ('A Note on Melchizedek and Qumran', *IEJ* 15 [1965] 152–4) called his reading of this line in question and proposed to read rather *[m]šwḥ hrw[ḥ]*, which is certainly better. It has been accepted by M. de Jonge and A. S. van der Woude in *NTS* 12 (1965–66) 301–2. This corrected reading makes an allusion to Is 61:1 rather clear. Given other references in this text to Dn 9:24–27, it is not impossible that the *dn*[ ] should be filled out as we have restored it here; it would thus contain a reference to the *māšîaḥ nāgîd* of Dn 9:25. In fact, even though van der Woude reads only a *daleth* before the lacuna, there is in my opinion also the trace of a *nun* after it. If this reading should prove acceptable, then one might have to reconsider van der

Woude's suggestion that the Anointed One mentioned here was more of a prophetic figure than a political ruler (p. 367). On the other hand, if Melchizedek himself is to be identified with the 'herald' who is also 'the Messiah', then one might hesitate. Melchizedek would be thought of more readily in terms of a priestly Messiah—he was in Gn 14 both priest and king.

What is above all striking here is the mention of the *m^e^baśśer* of Is 52:7 as one anointed. See the general remarks above, at the beginning of the commentary. Van der Woude restored the article before [*m*]*šyḥ*, but it is almost certainly not to be read thus. The singular reference to 'the Messiah' is thus eliminated. But one should note the joining of the allusion to Is 61:1 with that of Is 52:7—a significant joining of the two Isaian motifs that is paralleled in the New Testament.

19. *hw'h hk*[*tw*]*b ʿlyw 'šr* [*'mr*]*:* 'That is what is written about him, what he said. . . .' See note on line 9; cf. 4QFlor 1:16.

20. *lnḥm* . . . [*y*]*śkylmh bkwl qṣy ḥ*[*rwn*]*:* 'to console (?) . . . will instruct them about all the periods of wrath.' Cf. Is 61:2. *qṣy ḥrwn:* See 1QH fr. 1:5; 4QpHos[b] 1:12.

23. *srh mblyʿl wt.* [ ]*:* 'She turned from Belial and she . . . .' The feminine forms here probably refer to Zion.

24. *bmšpty 'l:* 'With the judgments of God (*or* El).' See line 13. *k'šr ktwb ʿlyw:* See note on line 9.

[*sy*]*wn h*[*y'h* . . .]*:* '(Now) Zion is. . . .' Perhaps some phrase like 'the abode of' should be restored in the lacuna, because Zion is actually being interpreted in terms of the upright ones in the community who have made the covenant with Yahweh.

25. *mqym*[*y*] *hbryt:* 'The establishers of the covenant.' The phrase *lhqm hbryt* can be found in different forms in 1QS 5:21; 8:10; 1QSb 5:23; 1QM 13:7; CD 3:13; 4:9. Cf. Gn 17:19. The phrase designates obviously members of the Qumran community.

hsrym mlkt [*bd*]*rk hʿm:* 'Those who turn away from walking in the path of the people.' The same phrase is found in 4QFlor 1:14 (see *JBL* 77 [1958] 353; but also Y. Yadin, *IEJ* [1959]

95); 1QSa 1:2–3; CD 8:16; 19:29. The phrase is derived from Is 8:11 (see LXX).

w'l[w]hyk hw'h [ ]: 'And (as for) your 'Elohim, he is. . . .' Van der Woude may well be right to suggest this phrase from Is 52 was explained in terms of Melchizedek; see line 10.

26. *bly'l:* See note on line 12 above.

w'šr 'mr: See note on line 2 above.

wh'brtmh šwp[r trw'h] bḥ[wdš] h[šby'y]: 'And you shall sound the horn loud in the seventh month. . . .' This is a quotation from Lv 25:9, in form identical with the MT, except for the 2nd pl. (*h'brtmh*) instead of the 2nd sg.; cf. LXX. Van der Woude thinks the quotation would refer to the sounding of the last trumpet on Judgment Day (cf. 1 Thes 4:16); but this seems a little far-fetched to me. Once again, it is the fragmentary state of the text which hinders any certain interpretation.

These remarks scarcely exhaust all the aspects of this interesting, though fragmentary, new text. Perhaps they will stimulate still further discussion of it. Even though it is not possible to say that the presentation of Melchizedek which is found in it directly influenced the midrash on him in Heb 7 (because the latter is developed almost exclusively in terms of the classic OT loci, Gn 14 and Ps 110), nevertheless its exaltation of Melchizedek and its view of him as a heavenly redemption-figure make it understandable how the author of the epistle to the Hebrews could argue for the superiority of Christ the high priest over the levitical priesthood by appeal to such a figure. The exalted status of Melchizedek which is presented in this text gives another aspect to the Christology of the epistle in which Jesus is depicted as a priest *kata tēn taxin Melchisedek.*[13]

[13] See further M. de Jonge and A. S. van der Woude, '11Q Melchizedek and the New Testament', *NTS* 12 (1965–66) 301–26; J. A. Emerton, 'Melchizedek and the Gods: Fresh evidence for the Jewish Background of John X. 34–6', *JTS* 17 (1966) 399–401; R. Meyer, 'Melchisedek von Jerusalem und Moresedek von Qumran', *VTSup* 15 (1966) 228–39; D. Flusser, 'Melchizedek and the Son of Man', *Christian News from Israel* 17 (1966) 228–39; M. P. Miller, 'The Function of Isa 61:1–2 in 11Q Melchizedek', *JBL* 88 (1969) 467–9.

V

EARLY CHRISTIANITY

13

JEWISH CHRISTIANITY IN ACTS IN THE LIGHT OF THE QUMRAN SCROLLS*

It is by now a well-worn platitude to say that the Qumran Scrolls have shed new light on Christian origins. Yet in a volume dealing with studies in Luke–Acts and dedicated to Prof. Paul Schubert, who has shown a long and sustained interest in such studies, there is room for a reassessment of the relationship between Qumran and the early church. The Qumran texts have brought to light many new details of Palestinian Judaism in the period in which Christianity emerged. They have been studied in detail by many scholars and from different points of view. It is not out of place, then, to review here the significance of these new finds for first-century Jewish Christianity as it is depicted in the Acts of the Apostles.

The Qumran literature comes from a group of Jews whose principal community centre existed on the northwest shore of the Dead Sea roughly between 150 B.C. and A.D. 70. These dates are supported by both archaeological and paleographical evidence.[1] The sect, whose beliefs and way of life are made known

* Originally published in *Studies in Luke-Acts: Essays Presented in Honor of Paul Schubert* (ed. L. E. Keck and J. L. Martyn; London: SPCK, 1966) 233–57.

[1] See R. de Vaux, *L'archéologie et les manuscrits de la Mer Morte* (Schweich Lectures, 1959; London, 1961). J. T. Milik, *Ten Years of Discovery in the Wilderness of Judaea* (SBT XXVI; Naperville, 1959) 133–6. F. M. Cross, Jr., *The Ancient Library of Qumran and Modern Biblical Studies* (Anchor, rev. ed.; Garden City, 1961) 117–27. N. Avigad, 'The Palaeography of the Dead Sea Scrolls and Related Documents', *Scripta hierosolymitana* IV (1958) 56–87.

to us in this literature, is revealed to be a community that is wholly Jewish, dedicated to the study and observance of the Torah, yet living a communal, religious, and ascetic mode of life for a considerable period before the emergence of Christianity. The data from these scrolls have made the majority of the scholars who have studied them identify the Qumran sect with the Essenes, even though some of the new material is not always perfectly reconcilable with what was previously known about the Essenes from the classical sources of Philo, Josephus, Pliny the Elder, Hippolytus, and Dio Chrysostom.[2] For my part, this identification is acceptable, and I shall not be concerned with any further attempt to establish it. I do admit, however, especially with J. T. Milik, traces of a Pharisaic influence on the group.[3] But there seems to be little reason to connect them in any way with the Sadducees,[4] the Zealots,[5] or the Ebionites.[6] It is also necessary to distinguish at times between the Essenes

[2] Philo, *Quod omnis probus liber sit* 72–91; *Apologia pro Iudaeis* 11, 1–18 (cf. Eusebius, *Praeparatio evangelica* 8, 11, 1–18); *De vita contemplativa* 1–90. Josephus, *Jewish War* 1, 3, #78–80; 2, 7, #111–13; 2, 8, #119–61; 2, 20, #566–8; *Antiquities* 13, 59, #171–2; 18, 1, 5, #18–22. C. Plinius Secundus (the Elder), *Naturalis historia* 5, 17, 4. Dio Chrysostom, 3, 1–4. Hippolytus, *Refutatio omnium haeresium* 9, 18–28. See A. Adam, *Antike Berichte über die Essener* (Kleine Texte 182; Berlin, 1961).

[3] *Ten Years*, 87–93. A. Dupont-Sommer (*The Essene Writings from Qumran* [tr. G. Vermes; Oxford, 1961] 145, 408) likewise admits such Pharisaic influence on the Qumran sect, although he rightly rejects the thesis of C. Rabin (*Qumran Studies* [Oxford, 1957]) that the sect was in fact Pharisaic.

[4] Despite the frequent use of the term 'sons of Zadok' to designate the members of the Qumran sect (1QS 5:2, 9; 1QSa 1:2, 24; 2:2; etc.). See R. North, 'The Qumran "Saducees"', *CBQ* XVII (1955) 44–68; J. Trinquet, *VT* I (1951) 287–92.

[5] Thus C. Roth, *The Historical Background of the Dead Sea Scrolls* (Oxford, 1958); 'New Light on the Dead Sea Scrolls', *Commentary* XXXVII/6 (June, 1964) 27–32.

[6] So J. L. Teicher in a series of articles in *JJS* II (1951) 67–99; III (1952) 53–5, 87–8, 111–18, 128–32, 139–50; IV (1953) 1–13, 49–58, 93–103, 139–53; V (1954) 38, 93–9; etc. Cf. M. A. Chevallier, *L'esprit et le messie dans le Bas-Judaïsme et le Nouveau Testament* (Paris, 1958) 136–43. This view is without foundation since it utterly neglects archaeological evidence and misinterprets most of the Qumran texts that it uses. See below, pp. 435–80; *TS* XX (1959) 451–5.

of Qumran—of the 'motherhouse', as it were—and those of the 'camps' in the land of Damascus. For in some details the Essene mode of life differed in these two situations.

The other term of our comparison is Jewish Christianity, precisely as it is presented in the Acts of the Apostles. The influence of the Essenes on the Christian church has been detected in other writings, and a consideration of these would give a more complete picture. But we are interested only in trying to assess the extent to which the picture of Jewish Christianity as it is painted in Acts has been illumined by what we know of the Qumran sect and its literature.

If a plausible case has been made for some contact between John the Baptist and the Qumran sect,[7] the extent to which similar contact can be shown between Jesus of Nazareth and this group is far less definable. With the data available at present it is almost impossible to determine it. But in any case it is widely admitted that some influence was exerted by the Qumran Essenes on the early church, at least as it is depicted in the writings of Paul, Matthew, and John.[8] One may debate whether this contact is direct or indirect, and whether it was exerted on the early Palestinian Church or only the New Testament authors. But the data in the Qumran texts provide at least an intelligible Palestinian matrix for many of the practices and tenets of the early church. Our discussion then is an attempt to assess the areas of influence and contact between the Essenes and the Jewish Christian church in Acts.

JEWISH CHRISTIANITY IN ACTS

Before attempting to compare the pertinent material, let us summarize briefly the picture of the Jewish Christian church in

[7] See J. A. T. Robinson, 'The Baptism of John and the Qumran Community', *HTR* L (1957) 175–91; reprinted: *Twelve New Testament Studies* (SBT XXXIV; Naperville, 1962) 11–27. W. H. Brownlee, 'John the Baptist in the Light of Ancient Scrolls', *Int* IX (1955) 71–90.

[8] See P. Benoit, 'Qumran and the New Testament', *Paul and Qumran* (ed. J. Murphy-O'Connor; London, 1968) 1–30.

Acts. When we open the book of Acts, we are immediately introduced to a group of disciples of Jesus of Nazareth who are at least vaguely aware of their identity as a group. They may be addressed simply as 'men of Galilee' (1:11), but they are also 'chosen apostles' (1:2). Scarcely any indication is given of their previous backgrounds, but they seem to have been part of the *'am hā-'āreṣ*. This is at least suggested by the conduct of Peter and John (8:14–25; 9:43; 11:2–3) who were not concerned with Pharisaic prescriptions and distinctions. Some of the eleven bear Greek names, and yet they are Palestinian Jews who have banded together, united by a belief in Jesus, 'a man certified by God with mighty works and wonders' (2:22), whom 'God raised' from the dead (2:32). These disciples are his 'witnesses' (1:8), and under the inspiration of God's Spirit they proclaim him and his message to 'all the house of Israel': God has made this Jesus 'both Lord and Messiah' (2:36). Such a christological belief sets them apart from the rest of the 'house of Israel' and makes them conscious of their Jewish *Christian* character.

But from the very beginning of the story in Acts this Christian group is marked as *Jewish* in its origins and background. Before the event of Pentecost they are depicted as men looking to this Lord and Messiah as the one who would 'restore the kingdom of Israel' (1:6). The 'men of Galilee' go up to the temple daily (2:46; 3:1, 11); they celebrate the festival of Weeks (2:1); they observe the Sabbath (1:12). One of their leaders, James, lends his support to the Jerusalem temple for a considerable time (21:8–26). The God whom they continue to worship is 'the God of Abraham, and of Isaac, and of Jacob, the God of our fathers' (3:13). In time 'a great number of the priests embraced the faith' (6:7), obviously a reference to members of Jewish priestly families. A nucleus of twelve—a number inspired by the twelve tribes of Israel—symbolizes the fact that the group is the New Israel.

These Jewish Christians carry their belief in Jesus of Nazareth as the Lord and Messiah from Jerusalem to Judea, Samaria, and Galilee (1:4, 8; 8:1; 9:31; cf. Lk 24:47). Gradually their numbers increase; the initial 120 members of the Pentecostal assembly in Jerusalem become three thousand (2:41), then five thousand (4:4). The number steadily grows (6:7), until a summary acknowledges, just before the message spreads to Gentile areas, that the 'church throughout all Judea, Galilee and Samaria enjoyed peace and was being built up' (9:31). During all this growth the Christian group is marked off from the Jewish people as such. 'None of the rest of the people dared to join them, but they held them in great esteem' (5:13). While one cannot apodictically exclude from the Palestinian church at this time converts from paganism, the picture in Acts 1–9 is certainly that of a predominantly Jewish Christian church.

Acts vaguely suggests that the Christian group looked on itself as the New Israel; this seems at least implied in the disciples' question about the restoration of the kingdom to Israel (1:6) and in the need felt to reconstitute the twelve (1:15–26). The corporate character of the Jewish Christians is formulated for the first time in the word *koinōnia* (2:42).[9] It is noteworthy that before the account mentions Saul and his career, there is scarcely any attempt to depict the community as *ekklēsia*. The sole exception to this is the summary statement at the end of the story of Ananias and Sapphira (5:11).[10] Once the career of Saul is begun, however, then the Christian community is referred to as *ekklēsia* (8:1, 3; 9:31; 11:22 ['the church in Jerusalem'], 26;

[9] The meaning of *koinōnia* in this text is debated. That it refers to the specific act of a contribution during a liturgical service is not very convincing but has been proposed by J. Jeremias (*Jesus als Weltvollender, BFTh* XXXIII 4 [Gütersloh, 1930] 78; cf. E. Haenchen, *Die Apostelgeschichte* [12th ed.; Göttingen, 1959] 153). The communal sharing of goods, property, and food was an important part of *koinōnia*, as 2:44–46 seems to make clear. But what the word immediately indicates is the corporate character of the Christian group, as it expressed itself in various ways (spiritual, material, and liturgical). See Ph.-H. Menoud, *La vie de l'Église naissante* (Cahiers théologiques XXXI; Neuchâtel, 1952) 22–34.

[10] The use of the word here reflects a later awareness on the part of the author, since it forms part of a 'summary'. See H. J. Cadbury, *BC* V, 402.

12:1, 5; 13:1; etc.). Moreover, in none of his statements in Acts about his early persecution of the young church does Paul speak of *ekklēsia*. The persecuted 'Jesus' is identified in 9:2–5 with 'some belonging to the Way'; in 22:4 he says, 'I persecuted this Way to the death'; and in 26:9, 15 'Jesus' is identified with 'many of the saints'. By the same token, it is only with the beginning of the story of Saul that we meet the expression, 'the Way' (9:2; cf. 19:9, 23; 22:4; 24:14, 22), as a designation of the Christian movement. Finally, we eventually see 'the Way' referred to as a 'sect' (*hairesis*, 24:14).[11] These details seem to indicate the rather nebulous awareness which the early Jewish Christian church had at first of its corporate character.

On the other hand, it is an awareness that grows as the account in Acts advances. Even though the account was written at a later date and from a standpoint which was considerably developed, nevertheless these expressions seem to reflect an early Jewish Christian community gradually becoming consciously structured in its corporate entity. The awareness of itself as *ekklēsia* comes with persecution and missionary effort, both of which are interrelated in the account in Acts.

Though indications are given of a small nucleus in the early community which has authority and shapes the group, nevertheless they are not such as to reveal the community as a well-defined organization. There are the 'chosen apostles' (1:2), the small band of the 'eleven' (1:26; 2:14) or the 'twelve' (6:2), which plays the important role of 'witnesses to his resurrection'. It is the 'teaching of the apostles' (2:42) which shapes the community. Singled out as exercising authority, however, are Peter (1:15; 2:14; 15:7) and James. The latter is recognized by

[11] Josephus never mentions the Christian movement as a *hairesis* among the Jews. But Acts three times (24:14; 24:5; 28:22) calls it such, using the very word that Josephus employs for the Pharisees, Sadducees, and Essenes (*Ant.* 13, 5, 9, #171; see also 20, 9, 1, #199; *Vita* 2, #10, 12; cf. Acts 15:5; 5:17; 26:5). This use of *hairesis* for Christianity records the impression that it made on contemporary Palestinian Jews. It was regarded as another 'sect' springing from the bosom of Judaism, espousing what was central to it (reverence of Yahweh, the Torah, and the temple).

Peter (12:17) and greeted officially by Paul (21:18); he also settles a disputed question for the local churches (15:13). But there is also mention of 'the apostles and the elders' (15:2, 4, 6, 22, 23; 16:4; cf. 21:18), whose advice and decision are sought. Eventually the community appoints seven 'assistants' to care for its dole.

The picture of the life of the early Jewish Christian community is painted in idyllic colours. It is a fervent community, practising a communal form of life; it is devoted 'to the teaching of the apostles, to a community-spirit, to the breaking of bread, and to prayers' (2:42). 'All who believed shared everything in common; they would sell their property and belongings and divide all according to each one's need' (2:44; cf. 2:46). 'One heart and soul animated the company of those who believed, and no one would say that he possessed anything of his own' (4:32).

The first suggestion of some diversity in the Palestinian church is met in 6:1, where the 'Hellenists' murmured against the 'Hebrews' because their widows were neglected in the daily distribution. *Hellēnistai* is the name for certain members of the Christian community. But 9:29 suggests that the name had already been in use among Palestinian Jews and was merely taken over by Christians to designate converts from such a distinctive group.[12] Its meaning among the Jews is a matter of debate. Since the time of John Chrysostom the 'Hellenists' have been understood as 'Greek-speaking Jews'.[13] Their presence in the Palestinian church would be understandable in the light of Acts 2:5, 9–10. They had come from the diaspora and had taken up residence in Jerusalem. This meaning, however,

[12] C. F. D. Moule, whose opinion I otherwise prefer (see 'Once More, Who Were the Hellenists?' *ExpT* LXX [1958–59] 100–2), considers the Hellenists of Acts 9:29 to be Christians. This is difficult to understand in the context. They are preferably to be regarded as Jews (so E. Haenchen, *Die Apostelgeschichte*, 280; M. Simon, *St Stephen and the Hellenists in the Primitive Church* [New York, 1958] 14–15).

[13] *Homily* 14 (in Acts 6:1); *PG* 60, 113; *Homily* 21 (in Acts 9:29); *PG* 60, 164.

has been questioned because Paul was such a diaspora Jew and calls himself *Hebraios* (Phil. 3:5; 2 Cor. 11:22); apparently he did not regard himself as a 'Hellenist'. Some years ago H. J. Cadbury argued that *Hellēnistēs* meant no more than *Hellēn* since it was a derivative of *hellēnizō*, which means 'to live as a Greek' not 'to speak Greek'. For him 'Hellenist' was a title for Gentile members of the Palestinian church.[14] His explanation, however, has not been widely accepted; many commentators still prefer Chrysostom's explanation, especially since the context of Acts 6 seems to demand that the 'Hellenists' were Jewish Christians of some sort. This is likewise the view of C. F. D. Moule, who recently made the attractive suggestion that *Hellēnistai* meant 'Jews who spoke *only* Greek', while *Hebraioi* means 'Jews who, while able to speak Greek, knew a Semitic language *also*'.[15] This explanation seems suitable. But it should also be recalled that such a linguistic difference would also bring with it a difference in outlook and attitude. More than likely the influence of Hellenism would be greater among the 'Hellenists' than among the 'Hebrews'. But in either case it is a question of degree, since this explanation allows the Hellenists to be Jews, as the context apparently demands.[16]

That the Hellenists were Jews of some sort is likewise recognized by O. Cullmann, who has tried to identify them in some vague way with the Qumran sectarians.[17] If this identification were correct, then the Hellenists would belong to the original Palestinian church from the beginning and would have had nothing to do with the diaspora. As Jews who differed from official Judaism and displayed more or less esoteric tendencies and an opposition to the Jerusalem temple, they would have

[14] *BC* V, 59–74; IV, 64.

[15] 'Once More, Who Were the Hellenists?', 100.

[16] Cf. M. Simon, *St Stephen*, 34–5. It is perhaps too strong a judgment to regard them as 'paganizing' Jews, as Simon suggests.

[17] 'The Significance of the Qumran Texts for Research into the Beginnings of Christianity', *JBL* LXXIV (1955) 213–26; reprinted: K. Stendahl (ed.), *The Scrolls and the New Testament* (New York, 1957) 18–32.

been called 'Hellenists' by the rest. From such a background would have come the 'Hellenist' converts of Acts 6:1, and with them Paul disputes in 9:29. But this specific identification of the Hellenists as Jews of Essene background (or of a kind of Judaism close to it) introduces an improbability into the discussion. It is difficult to see how such strict-living Essenes, rigorously observant of the Torah and cultivating a rather exclusive way of life, even hostile to the temporizing and levitically 'unclean' priesthood of Jerusalem, could give to others the impression that they were *hellēnizontes*, 'living like Greeks'. Not even their attitude toward the temple, supposing that it agreed with Stephen's, would imply their adoption of Hellenizing ways, which had become such an abomination to observant Jews since the time of Antiochus IV Epiphanes (cf. 2 Mc 4:13–17). And their connection with Pythagoreans is more alleged than substantiated. So we see no reason to identify the Hellenists of Acts specifically with converts from Essenism or a form of Judaism close to it.

At any rate, the distinction of Hellenists and Hebrews does not introduce into the Palestinian church a non-Jewish element. This does not mean, however, that there was not a variety of Jewish converts. For there were in the early Christian community converts from the priestly families (6:7) and 'believers who belonged to the party of the Pharisees' (15:5). The latter are depicted as Christians who insisted on the strict observance of the Mosaic law. And yet, they can hardly be identified simply with the 'Hebrews'. This latter group must have included also converts from the *'Am hā-'āreṣ*, from the Essenes and from the Samaritans, even though none of the last three groups are mentioned as such in Acts. Possibly some Essenes were included among the priests of 6:7, but one could never restrict this notice to them alone.

The persecution which raged against the early church in Palestine was an important factor in the spread of the gospel among the Gentiles. Yet when Saul made his way to Damascus, it was to the synagogues of that town that he was heading, presumably in pursuit of Jewish Christians (9:2). And even as the missionary effort among the Gentiles got under way, the church in Jerusalem remained notably Jewish. James, the 'brother of the Lord', became its leader; and though he is not called a bishop, his place of prominence there, his stability in one area, and his administrative decision for nearby local churches give him marks that resemble those of the residential bishop of later times. Be this as it may, his prominence reflects at least the predominance of Jewish Christians in the Palestinian church. Jewish practices were still admitted as part of the Christian way of life in Jerusalem as late as *c.* A.D. 58, when Paul after a long apostolate among the Gentiles went through the rite of the Nazirite at James' request (21:23–26).

These would seem to be the main features of the picture of the early Jewish Christian church which is painted in Acts. We want to see how our understanding of such a picture has been affected by the Qumran literature. This entails a consideration of the main points of contact detected between Acts and the Scrolls.[18]

But before we look at the details it would be well to recall that the comparison of the early Jewish Christian church with the Essene communities brings out fundamental differences far more than resemblances. These differences emerge when one considers the character and the goal of the two groups. Even if we admit the difference of Qumran Essenism from that of the 'camps' of Damascus, there is still a vast difference between the Essene movement and that of early Christianity. The difference is more manifest when the Jewish Christians are compared with

[18] Most of the data for this study were amassed when H. Braun's second article ('Qumran und das Neue Testament: Ein Bericht über 10 Jahre Forschung, 1950–59', *TRu* XXIX [1963] 142–76) arrived. My task has been considerably lightened by this invaluable survey. Since Braun's article takes up and discusses many of the small suggestions that have been made apropos of one verse or another, I shall not repeat them here. I concentrate on the major issues on which a judgment can be based.

the Qumran Essenes. The discipline there laid stress on celibacy, obligatory communal ownership of property, common meals, regulated prayer, study and esoteric interpretation of the Torah, probation for candidates, fines and a form of excommunication, and a structured organization in which monarchic and democratic elements were admitted. Such a strictly organized community the early Jewish Christian church never was. Nor did it have the exclusive character of the Essene movement; it did not retire to the desert or to the 'camps'. It adopted an attitude toward the law of Moses that would have been wholly inadmissible among the Essenes. It also had a backward look in that it regarded Jesus of Nazareth as the Messiah who had already come, whereas the Essene movement still shared the hope of the coming of, not *a* Messiah, but a prophet and two Messiahs.

And yet with such fundamental differences between the two groups there are a number of points of contact and influence which must be recognized. To such points we now turn our attention.

QUMRAN PARALLELS

1. Our discussion begins with those designations of the Essene and the Jewish Christian groups which are common to both Acts and the literature of the Scrolls.

The first designation is the absolute use of 'the Way' referring to the mode of life lived in these communities. *hē hodos* is found only in Acts (9:2; 19:9, 23; 22:4; 24:14, 22) among the New Testament writings; it succinctly describes the form of Christianity practised in Jerusalem and Palestine. E. Haenchen in his monumental commentary on Acts wrote, 'We do not know where the absolute use of *hodos* for Christianity comes from.'[19] He compares *tēn hodon tou kyriou* (18:25) and *tēn hodon tou theou* (18:26), but though these expressions fill out the meaning of 'the Way', they do not explain the origin of its absolute use.

[19] *Die Apostelgeschichte*, 268, n. 3. See also the comments of K. Lake and H. J. Cadbury, *BC* IV, 100; V, 391–2.

Acts 24:14 implies that 'the Way' was a term which the Christian community used of itself in contrast to the term *hairesis*, undoubtedly used of it by outsiders who associated it with other movements among the Jews. Haenchen rightly states that the rabbinical parallels listed in Strack-Billerbeck's *Kommentar* (2,690) are scarcely to the point.

However, the same absolute use of 'the Way' occurs in the Qumran writings to designate the mode of life of the Essenes.[20] The following passages best illustrate the use of it. 'Those who have chosen the Way' (1QS 9:17–18, *lbwḥry drk*); 'these are they who turn aside from the Way' (CD 1:13, *hm sry drk*; cf. CD 2:6; 1QS 10:21). 'These are the regulations of the Way for the master' (1QS 9:21, *'lh tkwny hdrk lmśkyl*). (See further 1QS 4:22; 8:10, 18, 21; 9:5, 9; 11:11; 1QM 14:7; 1QH 1:36; 1QSa 1:28.) At Qumran 'the Way' referred above all to a strict observance of the Mosaic law, especially as this was interpreted in the community. This is made clear in 1QS 8:12–15: 'When these become members of the Community in Israel according to these rules, they will separate from the gathering of the men of iniquity to go to the desert to prepare the Way of HIM, as it is written, "In the desert prepare the way of . . . ., make straight in the wilderness a highway for our God" (Is 40:3). This is the study of the Law [which] he ordered to be done through Moses' (cf. 1QS 9:19). The absolute use of 'the Way' among the Essenes may well go back to this passage in Isaiah. It should be noted too that there is a Qumran counterpart for the fuller expressions used in Acts; compare 'the way of the Lord' (18:25) and 'the way of God' (18:26) with *drk hw'h'* (1QS 8:13) and *drk 'l* (CD 20:18). While it might theoretically be possible that both groups (Christian and Essene) derived the

[20] For previous discussions see W. K. M. Grossouw, 'The Dead Sea Scrolls and the New Testament: A Preliminary Survey', *StCath* XXVII (1952) 1–8, esp. 5–6. F. Nötscher, *Gotteswege und Menschenwege in der Bibel und Qumran*, BBB XV (Bonn, 1958) 76–96, 100–1. V. McCasland, '"The Way"', *JBL* LXXVII (1958) 222–30.

use of 'the Way' from Is 40, nevertheless the close similarity of usage suggests in this case Essene influence.

There is, however, an important difference to be noted. Among the Essenes the expression 'the Way' has a dualistic connotation, for it is to be related to the doctrine of the Two Spirits (1QS 3:18 ff.), which are given to men and according to which all are to 'walk'. 'These are their ways in the world: To illumine the heart of man and to make plain before him all the ways of uprightness ⟨and⟩ truth' (1QS 4:2). The word *drk* is not used here absolutely; but it is impossible to divorce the absolute use of it entirely from reference to the 'ways' of these spirits. Such a dualistic connotation, however, is absent from Acts.

Another designation for the Qumran community with a possible bearing on the early Jewish Christian church in Acts is *yḥd*. According to Acts 2:42 the early Christians devoted themselves to *koinōnia*. This included the communal ownership of goods (4:32b–35; 6:1), the common 'breaking of bread' (2:42; 20:7), communal meals (2:46), and their contributions for the relief of the needy (11:29). But the word *koinōnia* probably denoted something more than such details: the communal spirit of co-operation and fellowship existing among the early Christians. Acts 4:32a is probably a description of it: 'The community of believers was of one heart and mind' (*kardia kai psychē mia*).

Even though the precise meaning of *koinōnia* is a matter of debate,[21] the term *yḥd* in Qumran literature sheds some light on it, in providing an intelligible Palestinian background for interpreting it. It is indeed impossible to establish any direct borrowing of the term. But to prescind for the moment from specific Qumran parallels for the elements of the life designated by *koinōnia*—parallels which are not perfect in all details—the sum total of them as expressed by *yḥd* should be included in any discussion of the meaning of *koinōnia*. For in the Qumran writings the word *yḥd* often designates the 'community' as such

[21] See note 9 above.

(1QS 1:1, 16; 5:1, 2, 16; 6:21; 7:20; etc. 1QSa 1:26, 27; 4QPatrBless 5; etc.). In this usage it certainly is more specific than *koinōnia.*[22] The latter may sum up the corporate spirit of the Christian group, but is not used as a name for it. But in the Qumran writings there is also a wider sense of *yḥd*. 'This is the rule for the men of the Community (*'nšy hyḥd*) who devote themselves to turning from all evil and to adhering to all that he has commanded according to his good pleasure: to separate from the congregation of the men of iniquity, to form a communal spirit with respect to the Law and to wealth' (*lhywt lyḥd*). In the first case *yḥd* seems to be the name for the group, 'community', whereas in the second instance it designates rather a common participation in the study and observance of the Torah and in the use of wealth. See also 1QS 6:7 ('The Many shall watch in common', *hrbym yšqwdn byḥd*).[23] Thus even though the word *yḥd* often is the designation for a far more structured community than *koinōnia* is, there is a nuance in the Qumran use of the word that sheds light on the Christian *koinōnia*.

2. The mention of *koinōnia* brings up the question of the community of goods in the early church and in the Essene sect. From Acts we learn of a communal ownership of property among the early Jewish Christians; see 2:44–45; 4:32–35. Selling what they owned, they contributed the proceeds to a common fund, administered at first by the apostles, but later by seven assistants. From it distribution was made, even daily (6:1), to all the faithful according to their needs. The main

[22] S. Talmon ('The Sectarian *yḥd*—A Biblical Noun', *VT* III [1953] 132–40) cites a few places in the Old Testament where *yḥd* may even have the meaning, 'congregation, community' (Dt 33:5; Ez 4:3; 1 Chr 12:18; Ps 2:2). Though the first instance is plausible, the others scarcely are.

[23] Recall that Philo (*Quod omnis probus liber sit*, 84 and 91) speaks of the Essene way of life as an 'indescribable communal life' (*tēn pantos logou kreittona koinōnian*), using of it the very word *koinōnia*. See also no. 85; *Apologia pro Iudaeis* 11, 10–13. Josephus, however, uses *to koinōnikon*, and this in a more restricted sense, as he refers it to the common sharing of possessions (*JW* 2. 8, 3, #122).

elements in this feature of common life were the surrender of private property, the deposit of it with the leaders of the community, punishment for deception, and a care of the needy from the common fund. When one reads Acts 2:44–45; 4:32–35, one gets the impression that the communal ownership was obligatory. However, 4:36–5:11 suggests that it was voluntary. 'Poverty . . . [as] a religious ideal' is the term that O. Cullmann uses to describe the situation.[24] This interpretation seems to be based on 4:32b: 'None of them ever claimed anything as his own.' The motivation for this communal ownership is never described as a fulfilment of the injunctions of Jesus recorded in Mk 10:21; Mt 19:21; Lk 18:22. It seems rather to be an ideal motivated by simplicity, detachment, and charitable sharing which springs from their corporate identity as the Jewish Christian community. As a mode of life common to all Christians it eventually disappears.

But an analogous situation was found among the Essenes of Qumran. They too seem to have practised a form of communal ownership of property though it is not in all respects identical to that of the early church. According to the *Manual of Discipline*, anyone who would enter the 'community' had to reckon with the surrender of his wealth. 'All those who dedicate themselves freely to his truth shall bring all their knowledge, their ability, and their wealth into God's Community in order to purify their knowledge in the truth of God's precepts and to determine exactly their abilities according to the perfection of his ways and their wealth according to his righteous counsel' (1QS 1:11–13; cf. CD 13:11). Explicit mention is made of the property of the whole assembly or of 'the Many' (*hwn hrbym*, 1QS 6:17). Before the probation is over, the candidate's belongings are not to be mingled with those of the community nor spent for common purposes.[25] The mingling of his property

[24] *The Scrolls and the New Testament*, 21.

[25] The meaning of *'rb* in the Qumran writings has been questioned. In my opinion, the word as used in 1QS 6:17, 22 describes the 'mingling' of the

with that of the community occurs only at the end of his second year of probation, when he becomes a full-fledged member (1QS 6:21–23). Deceit in the declaration or deposit of property results in exclusion from the 'Purity' (or sacred meal) of the community for one year, and a reduction of the food allowance by one quarter (1QS 6:24–25; cf. CD 14:20–21).[26] Fraud (or neglect) in the use of common property was punished with the obligation of restitution through one's labour and/or a fine (1QS 7:6). The emphasis on common ownership of property was such among the Essenes of Qumran that the group was characterized by its communal spirit with respect to the law and to wealth (*lhywt lyḥd btwrh wbhwn*, 1QS 5:2).[27]

But while entrance into the Qumran community was voluntary, the surrender of one's property and earnings (*'t hwnw w't ml'ktw*, 1QS 6:19) was not. The surrender was obligatory and detailed. In this the Qumran practice differs considerably from the early Christian communal ownership described in

individual's property with that of the group and does correspond to Josephus' expression (*anamemigmenōn*, *JW* 2, 8, 3, #122). The evidence of Josephus should not be written off too quickly in this regard; cf. C. Rabin, *Qumran Studies*, 22–36. His reasons are not very convincing. See also M. Black, *The Scrolls and Christian Origins* (New York, 1961) 32–9.

[26] The text of CD is at this point fragmentary. Since it also mentions a different fine ('six days'), we might ask whether this passage is really parallel to that in 1QS 6:24–25.

[27] See also CD 13:14; 14:12–16. The regulations regarding communal ownership were not the same in the 'camps' of Damascus as at Qumran itself. However, there has been a tendency to exaggerate the difference. Some of the passages which have been interpreted in terms of private ownership do not clearly state this. CD 14:12–16, for instance, does not necessarily mean that the wages are private. The *śkr* could well refer to the income of the 'work' of the members of the 'camp'; the income of two days would be put aside for the care of orphans, the poor, and the elderly. The passage seems to deal with the *community's* care of such persons, a corporate duty (*srk hrbym*). Likewise, in CD 13:14 the prohibition of trade or traffic with outsiders on an individual basis in any other manner than for cash is understandable in the context of communal ownership. If a member of the 'camps' sold to an outsider or worked for him, his recompense was to be cash, lest he bring into the community unclean produce or products. It does not necessarily mean that the cash was his own.

Acts 4:36–5:11, which is voluntary. If the passages in Acts 2:44–45; 4:32–35 are to be understood in a more obligatory sense, then they are closer to the Qumran practice. At any rate, there is in both groups a willingness to surrender property and earnings as a feature of common life. In the Essene community, however, this is but an element in a closely organized and structured community; since the early church is not depicted in Acts as so highly organized, the surrender of common property was of a looser sort.

As for the motivation of such a way of life, the Qumran literature itself is less explicit than the ancient sources about the Essenes. 1QS 9:22 expresses a certain contempt for riches and a salary: wealth and earnings are to be left to the men of perdition. But Josephus (*JW* 2, 8, 2, #122) explicitly calls the Essenes 'despisers of wealth' (*kataphronētai de ploutou*). And Philo too emphasizes their detachment.[28] In this respect we detect little difference between the Essenes and the early Jewish Christians.[29] Although the ultimate motivation for this poverty might be Old Testament passages such as Prv 30:8–9; 14:20–21; etc., nevertheless this does not account for the communal aspect of it practised in the two groups. The analogy existing between the early Jewish Christians and the Qumran community is such that one should reckon with an imitation of Qumran practices among the former, even if it is clear that modifications were introduced. In this respect we cannot agree with the radical rejection of any Qumran influence on the early Jewish Christians, such as has been proposed by H. H. Rowley, G. Graystone, and N. Adler.[30]

One last observation in this matter. Though there is provision

[28] *Quod omnis probus liber sit* 85–6; *Apologia pro Iudaeis* 11, 11.

[29] According to S. E. Johnson, 'The emphasis is upon communal life and not on poverty as such' (*The Scrolls and the New Testament*, 133).

[30] H. H. Rowley, *The Dead Sea Scrolls and the New Testament* (London, 1957) 13. G. Graystone, *The Dead Sea Scrolls and the Originality of Christ* (New York, 1955) 33–5. N. Adler, 'Die Bedeutung der Qumran-Texte für die neutestamentliche Wissenschaft', *MTZ* VI (1955) 286–301, esp. 299.

for the needy among the Jewish Christians of Acts (2:45; 4:34–35; 6:1), it is striking that the term *hoi ptōchoi* is never used there. Paul uses it in Rom 15:26; Gal 2:10, and one has been inclined to regard the term as a designation for the Jerusalem church. Indeed, it has often been suggested that it is the equivalent of *h'bywnym*. The latter, drawn from the Old Testament (Ex 23:11; Est 9:22; Ps 132:15), seems to have been a rare, non-technical designation for the Qumran sect in use among the Essenes themselves (see 1QpHab 12:3, 6, 10; 4QpPss^a 1–2 ii 9; 1, 3–4 iii 10 [*'dt h'bywnym*]; 1QM 11:9, 13; 13:14).[31]

3. Another area of contact between the early Jewish Christian church and the Essenes of Qumran which must be discussed is the organizational structure of the two groups. I have already tried to indicate the vagueness of detail that characterizes the description of the community of Christians in Acts. This vagueness must prevent us from being too absolute in any judgment about the similarity of it with the Qumran community, which was certainly much more structured than the Jewish Christian congregation.

Like the early Christians, the Essenes of Qumran considered themselves to be the Israel of the end of days. They patterned their way of life on the Israel of the desert wanderings. The original nucleus of the community seems to have been priestly, and this accounts for the title 'sons of Zadok' often applied to it. But apart from the priests there were also levites and laymen (1QS 2:19–21; cf. 1:18, 21; 2:1, 11). The latter were divided into tribes and groups called 'thousands, hundreds, fifties, and tens' (1QS 2:21; cf. 1QM 4:1–5, 16–17; 1QSa 1:14, 29–2:1; CD 13:1–2). This division is derived from Ex 18:21, 25 (cf.

[31] See L. E. Keck, 'The Poor among the Saints in the New Testament', *ZNW* LVI (1965) 100–29; 'The Poor among the Saints in Jewish Christianity and Qumran', *ZNW* LVII (1966) 54–78. My earlier remarks on this subject (*TS* XVI [1955] 344, n. 22) need some qualification (see below, pp. 438–41, 476–7). I would, however, still reject the suggestion that these 'poor' might be the Ebionites, or simply became the Ebionites later on.

Nm 31:48, 54); it probably designates various groups within the community with diverse status or functions. One may legitimately ask whether there were literally groups of 'thousands' at Qumran. The priestly element in the community was often called 'sons of Aaron', and the title probably included the levites too. But the non-priests were designated as 'Israel'. In the Damascene camps there were also proselytes (CD 14:3).

Both Aaron and Israel were accustomed to meet in a full assembly (*mwšb hrbym*) where they had fixed places and where they in common settled issues of a juridical and executive nature. Some writers have mentioned that there was also in the Qumran community a small 'council' (1QS 8:1, *'ṣt hyḥd*), entrusted with the study of legal matters.[32] The existence of a nucleus of fifteen members is certain, but just what its function was is not clear at all. This will be discussed further below. Finally, in addition to the full assembly authority was vested in various 'overseers' or 'superintendents'. At Qumran itself there was a '(lay)man appointed at the head of the Many' (*h'yš hpqyd brw'š hrbym*, 1QS 6:14) and a lay 'overseer of the Many' (*h'yš hmbqr 'l hrbym*, 1QS 6:11); the latter is probably the same as the 'overseer of the work of the Many' (*h'yš hmbqr 'l ml'kt hrbym*, 1QS 6:20). The first was apparently a sort of superior, and the second a sort of bursar. In the Essene 'camps' of Damascus there was a 'priest appointed over the Many' (*hkwhn 'šr ypqd ⟨br⟩'š hrbym*, CD 14:6–7; also mentioned in 4QD) and a lay 'overseer for all the camps' (*hmbqr 'šr lkl hmḥnwt*, CD 14:8–11), as well as a lay 'camp overseer' (*hmbqr lmḥnh*, CD 13:7–19). The latter was entrusted with teaching, reprehension, admission of candidates, and the administration of the property of the community in the camp (CD 13:7–19). He was assisted by a group of ten judges (CD 10:4–7). Even though it is not possi-

[32] E.g., J. T. Milik (*Ten Years*, 100); F. M. Cross, Jr. (*Ancient Library of Qumran*, 231); B. Reicke, 'The Constitution of the Primitive Church in the Light of Jewish Documents', *TZ* X (1954) 95–113, reprinted in *The Scrolls and the New Testament*, 151–2.

ble to give in full detail the functions of these different authorities, this brief sketch does make it plain that the Essene communities (either at Qumran or in the Damascene camps) had a structure that was much more organized than anything which emerges from the account in Acts about the early Jewish Christian church.

And yet there are certain elements in common which call for comment. First of all, the absolute use of *to plēthos* to designate the full congregation of the Jerusalem converts. It is commonplace to point out that there are two uses of *to plēthos* in Acts:[33] (a) 'crowd, large number of persons' (so 2:6; etc.); (b) 'the full assembly, congregation'. The latter meaning is found in Acts 6:5; cf. 6:2; 4:32. It refers to the full body of Jerusalem disciples. In a more restricted sense it is used in 15:12 of the body of the apostles and elders. Again, with the spread of Christianity it is applied to the community at Antioch (15:30).[34] Since both meanings are well attested in classical and Hellenistic Greek, it may seem that these have been simply used in the account of Acts. However, given the wide use of *rb*, *rwb* and *hrbym* in the Essene literature there is a likelihood that the designation of the Jewish Christian community as *to plēthos* was an imitation of current terminology. For in the Qumran writings the Essene assembly was often called *hrbym*, 'the Many'. Though pioneer translators sometimes sought to render it as 'the Great Ones', or 'the Masters', the commonly accepted explanation today refers it to the democratic assembly of the Essenes as they met in a session (*mwšb*) to decide common matters (see 1QS 6:1, 7–9, 11–18, 21, 25; 7:16; 8:19, 26; CD 13:7; 14:7, 12; 15:8). The Greek phrase, however, is hardly the literal translation of *hrbym*.[35] It may reflect the Hebrew *rb* or *rwb* (1QS 5:2, 9, 22;

[33] See K. Lake and H. J. Cadbury, *BC* IV, 47–8.

[34] In Acts 19:9 the meaning of *to plēthos* is disputed. E. Haenchen (*Die Apostelgeschichte*, 188, n. 1) maintains that it refers to the Jewish Christian community, while K. Lake and H. J. Cadbury (*BC* IV, 48) refer it to the 'congregation of the Jews'.

[35] *Pace* J. M. Allegro (*The Dead Sea Scrolls* [Pelican ed., Baltimore, 1957]

6:19). But it is to be noted that *rb* and *rwb* seem to designate rather the Essene assembly considered as distinct from the priests, whereas *hrbym* would include them.[36] For this distinction there is no equivalent in the early Christian church; it is a precision which has not been taken over. But this does not seem to invalidate the suggestion that the Essene use of *rb*, *rwb* and *hrbym* underlies in some way the early Christian use of *to plēthos* for the full congregation of disciples.

Secondly, several writers have discussed the possibility of Essene influence in the role of the twelve in the early Jewish Christian church. In Acts 'the twelve' are mentioned indeed, but rarely (explicitly only in 6:2; but cf. 1:15–26; 2:14). They have been compared to 1QS 8:1: 'In the council (?) of the Community [when there are? *or* there shall be?] twelve men and three priests, perfect in all that is revealed in the Law'. It has been suggested that the mention of 'twelve men' is 'an analogue to the college of the twelve apostles of Jesus', since it is 'not clear from the text whether the three priests are inside or outside the circle of twelve. Perhaps the inclusion of the three priests is to be preferred, because it enables one to see in the expression "priest" an especial mark of honour and to avoid the rather improbable result that the other twelve were laymen.'[37] But just why it is not clear that the twelve are distinct from the three is never explained; any normal reading of the line would suggest that the text mentions 15 persons. This number is confirmed, in fact, by a text from Cave 4 which is unfortunately as yet unpublished.[38] Consequently, there is little

---

144), *hrbym* would correspond more exactly to the Pauline use of *hoi polloi* (Rom 5:15, 19) or of *hoi pleiones* (2 Cor 2:6; cf. 1 Cor 9:19). Josephus uses *hoi pleistoi* (*Ant.* 18. 1, 5, #22) and *hoi pleiones* (*JW* 2, 8, 9, #146) of the Essene community as a whole.

[36] See H. Huppenbauer, '*rb, rwb, rbym* in der Sektenregel (1QS)', *TZ* XIII (1957) 136–7.

[37] See B. Reicke, 'The Constitution', *The Scrolls and the New Testament*, 151.

[38] See J. T. Milik, *VD* XXXV (1957) 73; *Ten Years*, 96; *RB* LXIV (1957) 589. See also A. Dupont-Sommer, *Essene Writings*, 90, n. 4. Curiously enough, Milik speaks later on (*Ten Years*, 143) of the early church and the Essenes

reason to think that the apostolic twelve in the early Christian church was modelled on the 'twelve men' mentioned in this one place in the *Manual of Discipline*. J. T. Milik and others have related the three priests mentioned there to the three priestly families descended from Levi through his sons Gershon, Kohath, and Merari (Gn 46:11).[39] In both Essene and Christian circles the number twelve is more plausibly explained as a derivative of the twelve tribes of Israel. The element that is common to the use of this number in both circles is its appearance in an eschatological context. Jesus' saying about the twelve thrones has to do with eschatological judgment (Mt 19:28; Lk 22:30), and the division of the Sons of Light in the eschatological war is according to twelve tribes (1QM 3:13–14; 5:1–2). The real problem in Acts—why the twelve disappear as an authoritative and administrative group within a relatively short time after the need was felt to reconstitute it by the election of Matthias—unfortunately receives no illumination from the Qumran material.

Thirdly, the organization of the Essene camps in the land of Damascus was somewhat different. Here a body of ten judges functions, 'four from the tribe of Levi and Aaron, and six from Israel' (CD 10:4). Again, they represent the priest and non-priest members, but the number twelve is not operative here. It is rather ten, the number otherwise used for small groups or 'cells' within the Essene community which gathered for various purposes (cf. 1QS 6:6; 1QSa 2:22; Josephus, *JW* 2. 8, 9, #146). But this does not seem to have any significance for the Jewish Christian church of Acts.[40]

---

as both holding the 'eschatological concept of the true Israel ruled by twelve leaders'.

[39] The connection between the 'three priests' and the 'pillars' of Gal 2:9 or the mention of Peter, James, and John (Mt 17:1) must be admitted to be extremely tenuous.

[40] Gathering in groups of ten was a principle also recognized in the Pharisaic-Rabbinical tradition; cf. Mishnah, *Megillah* 4:3. But it is debatable whether the idea of a group of ten, of whom one was a priest, had

Fourthly, another feature of organization that has often been discussed is the relation of the *episkopos* in the early church to the Essene *mbqr*. Since both words etymologically mean 'overseer', 'superintendent', the Essene institution has often been considered as a likely model for the early Christian episcopate.[41] As far as the early Jewish Christian church is concerned, the relation seems to be negligible, for the Greek word occurs in Acts only in 20:28, in Paul's discourse to the elders (*presbyteroi*, 20:17) of Ephesus summoned to Miletus. He bids them, 'Keep watch then over yourselves and over all the flock of which the holy Spirit has made you overseers' (*episkopous*). The assimilation of the 'overseer' to a shepherd is used in the instructions for the 'Camp Overseer' in CD 13:7–9: 'He shall bring back all those who have strayed, as a shepherd his flock' (cf. Ez 34: 12–16; Nm 27:16; 1 Pt 2:25; 5:2). This would seem to make plausible the suggestion that the *episkopos* was somehow an

---

anything to do with the 120 present in the first Jewish Christian assembly in Acts (1:15): 'ten members to each Apostle' (so J. T. Milik, *Ten Years*, 101; cf. *BC* IV, 12). The problem is that the apostles are not considered to be *hiereis* in Acts. See H. Braun, 'Qumran und das Neue Testament', 147.

[41] Josephus speaks of the Essene *epimelētai* (*JW* 2. 8, 6, # 134; 2. 8, 3, #123); this seems to be his equivalent for the Hebrew *mbqr* or *pqyd*. This Greek word is not used in the New Testament nor in the LXX. Although *episkopos* is used in extrabiblical Greek for a civic, financial, and religious 'overseer', it is also found in the LXX (Nm 4:16; 31:14; Jgs 9:28; 2 Kgs 11:15, 18; etc.). In most cases it translates some form of the root *pqd*, as does the verb *episkopein*. Only rarely does the latter translate the Hebrew *bqr* (Lv 13:36; 2 Esdras 4:15, 19; 5:17; 6:1; 7:14; Ps 26/27:4; Ez 34:11, 12). For further discussions of this problem see J. Jeremias, *Jerusalem zur Zeit Jesu* (Göttingen: 2nd ed.; 1958) II, 1, 132-3; K. G. Goetz, 'Ist der *mbqr* der Genizafragmente wirklich das Vorbild des christlichen Episkopats?', *ZNW* XXX (1931) 89–93; H. W. Beyer, *episkopos*, *TDNT* II, 614–16; B. Reicke, 'The Jewish "Damascus Documents" and the New Testament', *SBU* VI (1946) 16; W. Nauck, 'Probleme des frühchristlichen Amtsverständnisses (I Peter 5:2–3)', *ZNW* XLVIII (1957) 200–20; A. Adam, 'Die Entstehung des Bischofsamtes', *Wort und Dienst* NF V (1957) 103–13; W. Eiss, 'Das Amt des Gemeindeleiters bei den Essenern und der christlichen Episkopat', *WO* II (1959) 514–19; F. Nötscher, 'Vorchristliche Typen urchristlicher Ämter: Episkopos und Mebaqqer', *Die Kirche und ihre Ämter und Stände* (Festgabe J. Kardinal Frings; Köln, 1960) 315–38.

imitation of the Essene *mbqr*.[42] But the leaders of the Jewish Christian church in Palestine are never called *episkopoi* in Acts. And even if we find the apostles performing a role there that resembles a function of an Essene overseer as the Christians who have sold their property come and deposit the proceeds of it at the feet of the apostles (4:35, 37; 5:2; cf. CD 14:13 and possibly also 1QS 6:19–20), there is no trace of the use of such a title in the early Jewish Christian church. Nor does the passage in Acts 1:17–25 really contradict this impression. For although the word *episkopē* does occur in 1:20 in connection with the office that Matthias was elected to fill, it is actually part of an Old Testament quotation, Ps 109:8: *ten episkopēn autou labetō heteros*. In the context *episkopē* is related to both *apostolē* and *diakonia* (1:17, 25). Its sense is obviously generic, and it can in no way be used to show that the 'apostolate' was already an 'episcopate'. Even James who begins to rule the Jerusalem church in a manner that resembles the residential bishop of later date is never called *episkopos*. Indeed, his position of prominence seems to be due to the fact that he is 'a brother of the Lord'. In the New Testament the *episkopoi* emerge in churches of Hellenistic background (see Acts 20:28; Phil 1:1; 1 Tm 3:2; Ti 1:7), as groups of 'guardians' or 'overseers'. It is the Ephesian 'elders' who are called thus by Paul in Acts 20:28. They seem to have been set up by travelling apostles (like Paul) or by apostolic 'delegates' (like Timothy at Ephesus or Titus on Crete) to govern local churches, but it is only gradually that their monarchical function emerges. Granting then the common etymological meaning of *episkopos* and *mbqr*, and certain similar functions, it is nevertheless difficult to set up any direct connection between the Essene 'overseer' and the institution of the early Jewish Christian church in Palestine.[43]

[42] Cf. J. Dupont, *Le discours de Milet: Testament pastoral de saint Paul* (*Acts* 20:18–36) (Paris, 1962) 149, n. 1. This is not the place for a more detailed comparison, but CD 13:5–13 would lend itself to further discussion in this matter of the Christian 'overseer'.

[43] I do not exclude the possibility of Essene influence on the early

Fifthly, the early Christian church gave a special function to 'elders' in addition to the apostles. The *presbyteroi* occur in Acts 11:30; 15:2, 4, 6, 22, 23; 16:4; 21:18. These 'elders' were, however, a natural borrowing from the existing Jewish institution mentioned in Acts itself (4:5, 8, 23; 6:12; 23:14; 24:1; 25:15) and can in no way be traced to the Essene community specifically. The Essenes had such 'elders' too. In the ranks of the Qumran community the priests take precedence over the elders, as they meet in full assembly (1QS 6:8). They take their place along with the priests and the levites in pronouncing blessings and curses after the defeat of the enemy in the eschatological war (1QM 13:1). In general, respect for them is inculcated (CD 9:4). But there is nothing to indicate that the elders of the Christian community were in any way a derivative of the Essene institution. Both communities derived the institution rather from Old Testament tradition, as Acts 2:17 and *Damascus Document* 5:4 would suggest.

Finally, by way of contrast it is remarkable how frequently one reads of the role of the 'priests' and the 'Levites' in the Essene communities (e.g., 1QS 1:18, 21; 2:1, 11, 19; 1QM 7:15; 13:1; 15:4; CD 3:21; etc.) and how silent Acts is about such groups in the early Christian church. 'Priests' and 'levites' are mentioned in Acts only as indications of the former Jewish status of converts (6:7; 4:36). This remarkable difference between the two groups stems from their basic attitude toward the temple in Jerusalem. In both we find a kindred idea that the Jerusalem temple and its sacrificial cultus have been replaced by a community of the faithful.[44] But in the case of the Qumran Essenes this replacement was temporary; the Qumran com-

church in non-Palestinian areas. If, as seems likely, some Essene influence reached Damascus in the 'camps' and even further into the hinterlands of Asia Minor (see P. Benoit, *NTS* VII [1961] 287), then possibly the connection of the Essene *mbqr* with the Christian *episkopos* should be sought in such areas.

[44] See B. Gärtner, *The Temple and the Community in Qumran and the New Testament* (SNTS Monograph series, I; Cambridge, 1965) 99–101.

munity is the 'sanctuary for Aaron, . . . the Holy of Holies' (1QS 9:5–7; cf. 8:4–6; 5:6; 11:8; 4QFlor 1:6), but only because it has considered the Jerusalem temple defiled by the worldly, temporizing priests who serve it, and hence unfit for the sacrifice to God according to the prescriptions of Mosaic law.[45] Once God's victory is won, then the pure levitical service of God will be resumed. In the early church, however, the temple and its sacrifices soon cease to have significance for Christians. Even though we read of the apostles 'attending the temple together' (2:46) and 'going up to the temple at the hour of prayer, the ninth hour' (3:1), yet it is not long before the opposition to the temple develops. Stephen's speech reflects this and is the beginning of the development within the early Jerusalem community (cf. Acts 6:14) that culminates in the temple symbolism found in the writings of Paul, 1 Peter, and Hebrews. This temple symbolism is certainly similar to that of the Essene community, but there is a difference, too. This is found chiefly in the preservation within their community of the divisions of priests and levites who by their strict living were preparing themselves for the pure service of God in the ideal eschatological temple. As we have already remarked, there were undoubtedly some Essenes among the priests converted to Christianity (Acts 6:7), and they were most likely the bridge of contact between the two communities. However, it is important to note that they are never found continuing their function as priests even in some new way (such as blessing the bread and wine at the Christian communal meal instead of sacrificing, as did happen in the Essene community, 1QSa 2:18–19).

Such are the observations which seem pertinent to the discussion of influence of the Essene community on the structure and organization of the early Jewish Christian church.

4. When Matthias was elected to replace Judas in the num-

[45] See 1QpHab 9:4–7; 10:9–13; 11:4–12; 4QpIs[b] 2:7, 10; 4QpIs[c] 10–11; CD 11:17–20; 4QpNah.

ber of the twelve, it is noteworthy that the other eleven are not said to have laid hands on him or 'ordained' him, as is the case with the seven in Acts 6:6. Rather, once the requirements (2:21–22) are met, the commission is given to Matthias by the 'Lord' himself (2:24) through the casting of the lot. The use of this means of determining the will of God is known from the Old Testament: the lot determined priestly functions in the temple (1 Chr 24:5; 26:13–14; Neh 10:34; etc.) and service in the army (Jgs 20:9). It is also known to have been used in rabbinical circles. It is not surprising then that the lot was also in use in the Essene community, given its place in the general Jewish cultural heritage. But several expressions in the Matthias passage are better understood against the specific background of the Essene usage. In the Qumran community the lot was used in some way to determine the candidate's admission into the community and also his rank in it. Using an expression drawn from Nm 33:54 or Jos 16:1, the *Manual of Discipline* (6: 16) prescribes apropos of the candidate's admission that the lot be used: *k'šr yṣ' hgwrl 'l 'ṣt hrbym.* At subsequent periods in the candidate's probation further determination is made, and finally, 'if it be his lot to enter the Community then he shall be inscribed in the order of his rank among his brethren' (1QS 6:22, *'m yṣ' lw hgwrl lqrbw lyḥd yktwbhw bsrk tkwnw btwk 'ḥyw*). One's rank in the community was determined by lot, too: 'No man shall move down from his place nor move up from his allotted position' (1QS 2:23, *wlw' yrwm mmqwm gwrlw*). (See also 1QS 1:10; 9:7; CD 13:12; 20:4.) There are elements in this Essene practice which shed light on the details of the election of Matthias. For instance, Judas is said by his vocation as an apostle to 'have obtained the lot of this ministry' (Acts 1:17, *elachen ton klēron tēs diakonias tautēs*). Then, the Christian community prayed that God would indicate who was to take over *ton topon tēs diakonias tautēs* (1:25), an expression which finds its counterpart in *mqwm gwrlw* (1QS 2:23). Though these resemblances are *in se* superficial, taken in conjunction with the use of the lot to designate a man for a specific rank within the community, they do make the story of the election of Matthias a little more intelligible.[46] We would not be able to conclude, however, that the practice was due to imitation of an Essene custom.

5. The communal meal of the early Jewish Christian church (2:46) has often been compared to the religious common meal of the Essenes described in 1QS 6:4–5; 1QSa 2:11–22.[47] The brief notice of the Christian meal in Acts, however, contains so little detail that one cannot really make a valid comparison in this case. Previous discussions of the relationship of the Essene repast to the Christian Eucharist or the Last Supper have exploited the Gospel and Pauline material, as they must; but this is outside our perspective. Even though one were to admit that the Jerusalem church was the source of the tradition about the Last Supper in Matthew and Mark, there is little reason to bring it into this discussion. The only element which should be noted is that the account of the common meal in Acts is framed merely in terms of 'breaking bread', and there is no mention of 'wine', the other element in the Essene meal. Though one may be inclined to admit that the meal was eaten in anticipation of the messianic banquet in the Essene community (1QSa 2:14–20), this note is not found in the account in Acts.

6. The last topic to which we shall turn our attention is the interpretation of the Old Testament found in Acts and in the Essene literature. For despite the difference in the messianic views of the two communities, which we have already noted and which certainly coloured their interpretation of the Old Testa-

[46] Cf. W. Nauck, 'Probleme des frühchristlichen Amtsverständnisses', 209–14. E. Stauffer, 'Jüdisches Erbe im urchristlichen Kirchenrecht', *TLZ* LXXVII (1952) 203–4.

[47] E.g., F. M. Cross, Jr., *Ancient Library*, 235–7. M. Black, *The Scrolls and Christian Origins*, 102–15. K. G. Kuhn, 'The Lord's Supper and the Communal Meal at Qumran', *The Scrolls and the New Testament*, 65–93. J. van der Ploeg, 'The Meals of the Essenes', *JSS* II (1957) 163–75. E. F. Sutcliffe, 'Sacred Meals at Qumran?', *HeythJ* I (1960) 48–65. J. Gnilka, 'Das Gemeinschaftsmahl der Essener', *BZ* V (1961) 39–55.

ment, there is a remarkable similarity in other respects which shows the early Jewish Christian community to be very close to the Essenes. For the Christians of Acts the Messiah has come (2:36), but another definitive coming of his is still awaited (1:11; 3:21). This expectation manifests a similarity with the Essene expectation of a prophet and two Anointed Ones (1QS 9:11), who are in some way related to the day of God's visitation of his people (1QS 3:18). There is the common conviction that they are living in the 'end of days' (1QpHab 2:5; 9:6; 1QSa 1:1; 4QpIs^a A:8; 4QFlor 1:2, 12, 15, 19; CD 4:4; 6:11; etc.; cf. Acts 2:17: *en tais eschatais hēmerais*).[48] This conviction enables both groups to refer sayings of the Old Testament prophets and writings to events or tenets in their own history or beliefs. Especially pertinent is 1QpHab 7:1–5: 'God told Habakkuk to write the things which were to come upon the last generation, but the consummation of the period he did not make known to him. And as for what it says, "That he may run who reads it", this means the Righteous Teacher, to whom God made known all the mysteries of the words of his servants the prophets' (see also 1QpHab 7:7–8). This attitude underlies the constant actualization or modernization of the Old Testament texts being used either in the *peshārîm* or in isolated quotations in other writings. See CD 1:13 ('This is the time about which it was written', introducing Hos 4:16); 10:16; 16:15 ('For that is what it [*or:* he] said'); 1QM 10:1; 11:11. It is this same attitude that underlies the use of the Old Testament in Peter's speech on Pentecost, as the prophet Joel is quoted (cf. Acts 3:24).

The introductory formulas often reveal this attitude more than anything else. I have elsewhere[49] studied the similarity of these Essene formulas and their New Testament counterparts

[48] The phrase is derived from Is 2:2; cf. Mi 4:1; Dn 2:28. There is, however, a textual difficulty here: Vaticanus reads simply *meta tauta*; I have used what seems to be the better reading, based on Sinaiticus, Alexandrinus, and the Codex Bezae.

[49] 'The Use of Explicit Old Testament Quotations in Qumran Literature and in the New Testament', pp. 3–58 above, esp. pp. 7-16.

in detail. I shall give here only the list of those passages which occur in Acts and are pertinent to this discussion.

Acts		*Qumran Literature*
1:20	'for it is written'	CD 11:20
2:16	'this is what was said through the prophet Joel'	CD 10:16; 16:15
2:25	'for David says'	CD 6:7–8 (cf. 6:13)
2:34	'he says'	CD 4:20 (?)
3:21	'God spoke through the mouth of his holy prophets of old'	CD 4:13–14
3:25	'saying to Abraham'	?
4:11	'this is the . . .'	1QpHab 12:3; 4QpIs[b] 2:10
4:25	'spoke through the mouth of David his servant'	CD 4:13–14
7:6	'So God said'	CD 6:13; 8:9
7:7	'God said'	CD 6:13; 8:9
7:42	'As it is written in the book of the prophets'	4QFlor 1:2
7:48	'as the prophet says'	CD 6:7–8 (?)
13:33	'as it is written in the second psalm'	4QFlor 1:2; 11QMelch 9–10
13:33	'and in another place he says'	?
13:40	'Beware then lest what was said by the prophets come true [of you]'	?
15:15	'as it is written'	1QS 8:14; 5:17; CD 7:19; 4QFlor 1:2

28:25 'The holy Spirit has well said through Isaiah the prophet'	CD 4:13–14 ('God said . . .')

Two observations are pertinent. First, the Hebrew equivalents of the introductory formulas in the New Testament are found in greater abundance in the Qumran literature than in the early rabbinical compositions (such as the Mishnah).[50] Even if the formulas used show an affinity to those of the Essene writers, we cannot establish a definite borrowing of the Qumran literary practice by the early Christians. Secondly, it is not insignificant that the majority of explicit quotations introduced by such formulas in Acts are found in the early chapters which deal specifically with the early Jewish Christian church. A glance at the above list shows this. Several reasons, of course, can be suggested for the difference (e.g., that the latter part of Acts deals with Paul, his missions, his evangelization of the Greek world, etc.). But they should not be pressed to the extent of excluding all influence of Palestinian methods of Old Testament exegesis which the data would seem to suggest.

CONCLUSION

The features of Essene tenets and practices which we have surveyed have often shed important light on passages of Acts that describe the early Jewish Christian church. They at least provide concrete and tangible evidence for a Palestinian matrix of the early church as it is described in Acts. The evidence varies, since it is possible at times to think in terms of a direct contact or a direct imitation of Essene usage (as in the case of 'the Way'), while at other times the evidence is not so strong. Certainly, one cannot prove from such points of contact that the early Jewish Christian church developed out of an exclusively Essene framework. The most that one can say is that the early Jewish Christian church was not without some influence from the Essenes.

[50] See pp. 15–16 above.

It is not unlikely, as we have mentioned above, that among the 'great number of priests' (Acts 6:7) who were converted some were Essene and provided the source of Essene influence.

In my opinion, the influence of Qumran literature on Acts is not as marked as it is in other New Testament writings (e.g., John, Paul, Matthew, Hebrews). The parallels that do exist, striking though they may be, are not numerous. In an early article on the subject, S. E. Johnson wrote, 'It also appears that he [the author of Luke–Acts] is in closer touch with the Jewish sectarian background of Christianity than any other New Testament author.'[51] Now that much more of the Essene literature has been published and more of its contacts with the New Testament have been studied, we can see that this judgment would have to be modified, if Johnson meant by 'Jewish sectarian background' specifically the Essene background of the Qumran sect.

It has not been my express intention in this article to use Qumran material to support the historical character of Luke's account of the early Jewish Christian church in Acts. W. C. van Unnik has called Luke–Acts 'a storm centre in contemporary scholarship', and no little part of the reason why it has become such is precisely the need to distinguish the Lucan theologoumena in Acts from what might possibly be the historical data that it also contains. The effort to do this is not slight and it has created the storm. Perhaps a by-product of the above discussion of the light shed on the early Jewish Christian church by the discovery of the Qumran scrolls might be a contribution toward a better assessment of what is historical and what is Lucan theology. For it is obvious that Luke's picture of the early Jewish Christian community has been painted with a certain amount of hindsight, and there is need to read between the lines in seeking to understand it. However, since I am—for obvious reasons—not all that exercised over the so-called early

[51] 'The Dead Sea Manual of Discipline and the Jerusalem Church of Acts', *The Scrolls and the New Testament*, 129.

Catholicism of Luke, I may be permitted to cast some of his data in a different light. I admitted above (see p. 277) that the picture he has painted of the early Church was drawn at times in idyllic colours; but I sought to outline it with a minimum of Lucan theologoumena. Sometimes it is easy to spot the latter, especially when one can compare the Lucan presentation with other New Testament data (e.g., Pauline letters). But when such comparable material within the New Testament is lacking, the judgment about Luke's presentation of the early Church is reduced to speculation or subjective impressions, unless one has the advantage of outside controls, such as material from the Qumran scrolls. To use the latter is not easy. I have sought to make certain comparisons. Some of them bear on the problem of the historicity of the Lucan account; others shed light on Lucan theologoumena (e.g., Luke's use of the Old Testament and his introductory formulas). The material that is presented above must be assessed for what it is worth, and with reference to the double aspect of the problem.

14

THE BAR COCHBA PERIOD*

The number of historical documents pertaining to the second century A.D. in Palestine has always been small. It is consequently of interest to learn of new discoveries of original texts which come from that century and shed light on an otherwise obscure movement in the history of that part of the world. Though this movement has little direct bearing on Christianity, it is an important episode in the history of the Jewish people, for it is in effect the aftermath of the fateful destruction of Jerusalem by the Romans in A.D. 70 and the beginning of their long separation from the Holy City. That movement is the Second Jewish Revolt, which began under Bar Cochba in A.D. 132 and lasted until about 135, when the last remnants of the rebels were wiped out and the emperor Hadrian forbade the Jews to set foot in Jerusalem or even approach it within a certain radius.

In Josephus' writings we have a fairly lengthy and reasonably reliable account of the First Jewish Revolt, which began in A.D. 66 and ended with the destruction of the city of Jerusalem and of the temple of Yahweh in 70.[1] But the details of the Second Revolt under Bar Cochba, which apparently rivalled the first in scope and duration, have been only very briefly recorded by contemporary writers. Hence any new information, no matter how meagre, helps to fill out the picture.

* Originally published in *The Bible in Current Catholic Thought: Gruenthaner Memorial Volume* (ed. J. L. McKenzie; New York: Herder and Herder, 1962) 133–68.

[1] See *Jewish War* 2, 271 ff. to the end of Book 7; *Life* 17–410.

THE NEW FINDS

The new material has so far been published only in part and for some of it we must rely on preliminary reports. It comes from the caves in at least three different wâdies which empty into the west side of the Dead Sea. The first place which yielded written documents pertaining to the period of the Second Revolt was a pair of caves in the Wadi Murabba'ât, discovered sometime during 1951. Murabba'ât is part of the long wâdi which begins to the east of Bethlehem under the name Wâdi Ta-'âmireh and ends at the Dead Sea under the name Wâdi Darajeh. The site of the caves in this Jordanian torrent-bed is about a two-hour walk westward in from the Dead Sea, being situated some fifteen miles, as the crow flies, to the south-east of Jerusalem and some eleven miles south of Qumran Cave I. The caves open southward and are found about halfway up the north side of the gorge, which is some 600 ft deep.

News of the discovery of written material in the Murabba'ât caves arrived in Jerusalem in October 1951, and an archaeological expedition was mounted to explore and excavate four caves in that wâdi from 21 January to 21 March, 1952. Two of them were of little importance and yielded no written material; but the other two gave definite evidence of a prolonged occupation in the Roman period, in addition to artifacts of the Chalcolithic, Iron II and Arab periods.[2] From the Iron II period of occupation of one of the caves came the earliest Palestinian papyrus (*Mur* 17)[3] to be found to date, a palimpsest

[2] Details are derived from the full report and publication of the documents of the Murabba'ât caves, which are now available in P. Benoit, J. T. Milik and R. de Vaux, *Les Grottes de Murabba'ât* (Discoveries in the Judaean Desert 2; two parts, Texte, Planches; Oxford: Clarendon, 1961). Hereafter the siglum DJD will refer to this series. See further R. de Vaux, 'Les grottes de Murabba'ât et leurs documents', *RB* 60 (1953) 245–67; G. Lankester Harding, 'Khirbet Qumran and Wady Murabba'ât: Fresh Light on the Dead Sea Scrolls and New Manuscript Discoveries in Jordan', *PEQ* 84 (1952) 104–9 (+five plates); H. Seyrig and J. T. Milik, 'Trésor monétaire de Murabba'ât', *Revue numismatique*, sér. VI, vol. 1 (1958) 11–26.

[3] In accord with the system of abbreviation explained in *Qumrân Cave 1* (DJD 1; Oxford: Clarendon, 1955) 46–8, the siglum *Mur* (=Murabba'ât)

dating from the eighth century, which is bound to arouse palaeographic interest.[4] From the Roman period came documents written in Hebrew, Aramaic, and Greek, which gave evidence of a trilingualism in Palestine, which was already known in the time of Herod and is now confirmed anew.[5] Some of the documents of this Roman period belong to the first century B.C.; a few are dated in the first century A.D. (to the time just prior to the First Revolt—one even in the second year of Nero [*Mur* 18]).[6] But the most important ones are derived from the time of the Second Revolt or the decades immediately preceding it (in the latter case, though the documents were written earlier, they were probably carried to the caves by the refugees who fled there toward the end of the revolt). Later on, in 1955, six Bedouin shepherds found, in a hole not far from the Murabba'ât caves, an important fragmentary scroll of the OT Minor Prophets in Hebrew, which had been buried with a refugee who had fled to the wâdi during the revolt and died there.[7]

---

is used to indicate the texts of DJD 2. The system is also explained in *The Catholic Encyclopedia*, Supplement II, section 9, s.v. 'Dead Sea Scrolls', #VII (where M should be changed to Mur); and in *Evangelisches Kirchenlexikon* 3 (1958) 421.

[4] See F. M. Cross, Jr., *The Ancient Library of Qumran and Modern Biblical Studies* (Garden City, N.Y.: Doubleday, 1958) 14, n. 22.

[5] Cf. DJD 2, 69; M. Smith, 'Aramaic Studies and the Study of the New Testament', *JBR* 26 (1958) 304–13. It is not certain that Bar Cochba himself wrote in all three languages, but they were at least being used by those under him. See Y. Yadin, 'Expedition D.', *Yedîʿôt ha-ḥebrāh la-ḥaqîrat 'ereṣ yiśrā'ēl we-ʿattîqôtêhā* (=*BIES*) 25 (1961) 63; *IEJ* 11 (1961) 50. Among the Wâdi Ḫabra texts are three letters addressed to his officers, Yehonatan and Masabbalah, one in each language (Papyrus 3, 4, 12). Yadin thinks that the Aramaic of these texts is to be identified with the Aramaic of the Targum Onqelos; this identification, however, must await further study. See my article, 'The Languages of Palestine in the First Century A.D.', *CBQ* 32 (1970) 501-31.

[6] His name is spelled *nrwn qsr*, just as it has often been suggested apropos of Ap 13:18 (=666!). See D. R. Hillers, 'Revelation 13:18 and a Scroll from Murabba'at', *BASOR* 170 (1963) 65.

[7] See DJD 2, 8, 50, 181.

About the same time as the discovery and excavation of the Murabba'ât caves (1951–52) the Bedouins found further materials related to the Second Revolt in other caves whose location was for a long time kept secret. The reluctance of the finders to reveal the name of the area was suspected by the archaeologists and scholars in Jordan to have been related to the fact that the site was across the border in Israel. The texts found in this 'unknown site' were offered for sale in Jerusalem during July and August 1952.[8] They included Hebrew biblical fragments (Gn, Nm, Dt, Ps 7:14–31, 22), a complete phylactery, a fragmentary text of the OT Minor Prophets in Greek,[9] a letter written to Bar Cochba in Hebrew, two Aramaic contracts dated in the 'third year of the liberation of Israel, in the name of Simon ben Kosibah', two Greek and two Aramaic documents dated according to the system used in the Roman Province of Arabia (erected on the ruins of the Nabataean kingdom of Petra in A.D. 106), and finally some Nabataean papyri.[10] 'The group is to be dated toward the end of the first

[8] J. T. Milik, *Ten Years of Discovery in the Wilderness of Judaea* (SBT 26; London: SCM, 1959) 16.

[9] Partially published by D. Barthélemy, 'Redécouverte d'un chaînon manquant de l'histoire de la Septante', *RB* 60 (1953) 18–29; see further his *Les devanciers d'Aquila: Première publication intégrale du texte des fragments du Dodécaprophéton* (VTSup 10; Leiden: Brill, 1963). The parts preserved belong to Micah, Jonah, Nahum, Habakkuk, Zephaniah, Zechariah; they date from the end of the first century A.D. and are important evidence for the study of the Greek translation of the OT. See further E. Vogt, 'Fragmenta prophetarum minorum deserti Iuda', *Bib* 34 (1953) 423–6; P. Kahle, 'Die im August 1952 entdeckte Lederrolle mit dem griechischen Text der kleinen Propheten und das Problem der Septuaginta', *TLZ* 79 (1954) 81–94. Further fragments of the same text were subsequently published by B. Lifshitz, 'The Greek Documents from the Cave of Horror', *IEJ* 12 (1962) 201–14. They include fragments from Hosea, Amos, Joel, Jonah, Nahum, and Zechariah.

[10] One of the Nabataean papyri has been published by J. Starcky, 'Un contrat nabatéen sur papyrus', *RB* 61 (1954) 161–81; see further J. J. Rabinowitz, 'A Clue to the Nabatean Contract from the Dead Sea Region', *BASOR* 139 (1955) 11–14. J. T. Milik has also published a few of the documents from this site: 'Un contrat juif de l'an 134 après J.-C.', *RB* 61 (1954)

and the beginning of the second century A.D.; the *terminus ad quem* is the Second Jewish Revolt, for it was then that these documents were hidden in their caves.'[11] It is now known that the site of the discovery was a cave (or caves) in the Wâdi Seiyâl (or Naḥal Ṣe'ᵉlîm), which is in Israel between Masada and 'En-gedi. The site was explored between 24 January and 2 February 1960 by Israeli archaeologists, who found evidence of fairly recent Bedouin clandestine digging on the spot.[12] The archaeologists also found further material in the Wâdi Seiyâl caves: 'traces of Chalcolithic occupation at some sites and in many caves, two Iron Age and four Roman fortresses in the region, and a group of caves inhabited during the Bar-Kokhba revolt. The most important finds were an arsenal of arrows, including the iron arrow-heads as well as the shafts of wood and cane, coins from the time of Trajan until Severus Alexander, and some fragments of scrolls, including two parchments of a

---

182–90; 'Deux documents inédits du Désert de Juda', *Bib* 38 (1957) 245–68 (II. Acte de vente d'un terrain, 255–64; III. Acte de vente d'une maison, daté de 134 ap. J.-C., 264–8 [a restudy of the text published in *RB* 61 (1954) 182–90]). See further J. T. Milik, 'Note additionnelle sur le contrat juif de l'an 134 après J.-C.', *RB* 62 (1955) 253–4; J. J. Rabinowitz, 'Some Notes on an Aramaic Contract from the Dead Sea Region', *BASOR* 136 (1954) 15–16; S. Abramson and H. L. Ginsberg, 'On the Aramaic Deed of Sale of the Third Year of the Second Jewish Revolt', *BASOR* 136 (1954) 17–19.

[11] J. T. Milik, *Ten Years*, 16. For further details about the contents of this find see J. T. Milik, 'Le travail d'édition des manuscrits du Désert de Juda', VTSup 4 (1957) [Volume du Congrès; Strasbourg: 1956]) 17–26. See further *Bib* 34 (1953) 419.

[12] Y. Yadin, 'New Discoveries in the Judean Desert', *BA* 24 (1961) 34, has recently confirmed the location which was rumoured several years ago in Jerusalem: '. . . according to a reliable report that reached us several months ago, [the documents were] found by Bedouin in a cave of Nahal Tse'elim, north of Massada, i.e.—in Israel territory. . . . the team did indeed find traces of Bedouin search parties in some of the caves.' Likewise, 'Les repaires de Bar Kokhéba', *BTS* 33 (1960) 6. However, some of the texts mentioned above as coming from the 'unknown site' have been identified as coming from the so-called Cave of Horror in the Wâdi Ḫabra (e.g., the fragmentary text of the Minor Prophets in Greek, the siglum for which is 8HevXIIgr. See B. Lifshitz, *IEJ* 12 (1962) 201, n. 1. See further Y. Yadin, 'Expédition D—The Cave of the Letters', *IEJ* 12 (1962) 227–57, esp. 228–9.

phylactery containing parts of Exod. xiii, 1–16, and fragments of Hebrew, Aramaic and Greek papyri.'[13]

Further material pertaining to the Bar Cochba period has come from a third spot. In 1953 and again in April 1955 Y. Aharoni, an Israeli archaeologist, conducted some explorations in the Wâdi Ḫabra (or Naḥal Ḥever in Israel), some six kilometres, as the crow flies, slightly SW of 'En-gedi. Lacking proper equipment, he was not able to do a thorough job at that time, but he discovered that at least one cave was related to the Bar Cochba revolt. In its vicinity were found traces of two Roman camps, strategically built on the two sides of the steep cliffs forming the wâdi and so placed as to keep watch on the cave-mouth visible below them.[14] During a two-week campaign, from 23 March to 5 April 1960, a team of scholars of the Israel Exploration Society (J. Aviram, N. Avigad, Y. Aharoni, P. Bar-Adon and Y. Yadin) explored the desert area about 'En-gedi.[15] In the three-chambered Naḥal Ḥever cave they uncovered in the inmost chamber a burial niche containing a collection of baskets overflowing with skulls and also several layers of large mats covering human bones. A second spot in the cave yielded a basket of nineteen metal objects: twelve bronze jugs of varying sizes, three incense shovels, two large platters, a

[13] J. Aviram, 'Judean Desert', *IEJ* 10 (1960) 125. See also M. Cassuto Salzmann, 'Ricerche in Israele', *BeO* 3 (1961) 24; Y. Aharoni, 'Les nouvelles découvertes de la Mer Morte', *BTS* 29 (1960) 12–13; 'Expedition B', *BIES* 25 (1961) 19–33; *IEJ* 11 (1961) 11–24.—For the text of the phylactery see P. Wernberg-Møller, 'The Exodus Fragment from Massada', *VT* 10 (1960) 229–30; F. Vattioni, 'Ritrovati altri manoscritti sulla riva israeliana del Mar Morto', *RBibIt* 8 (1960) 71–2; 'Il frammento dell' Esodo scoperto a Massada', *ibid.*, 180.

[14] Y. Aharoni, 'Hever Valley (Wadi Habra)', *IEJ* 4 (1954) 126–7; 5 (1955) 272–3; also M. Cassuto Salzmann, *BeO* 3 (1961) 23–5.

[15] See J. Aviram, 'The Judean Desert Expeditions', *BIES* 25 (1961) 5–12; N. Avigad, 'Expedition A.', *ibid.*, 13–18; Y. Aharoni, 'Expedition B.', *ibid.*, 19–33; P. Bar-Adon, 'Expedition C.', *ibid.*, 34–48; Y. Yadin, 'Expedition D.', *ibid.*, 49–64; B. Lifshitz, 'The Greek Documents from Nahal Seelim and Nahal Mishmar', *ibid.*, 65–73. (All are in Modern Hebrew.) See *IEJ* 11 (1961) 3–62.

patera and a key. Most of the objects were clearly identified as Roman and cultic. At a third spot there was discovered a 4×5 cm. fragment of animal hide on which a few words of Ps 15 and the beginning of Ps 16 were written (dated by Y. Yadin to the second half of the first century A.D.). But the most important find in this cave came from still another spot; it was a goat-skin water-bottle stuffed with bundles of coloured raw wool, skeins of wool, beads, and a package which contained a batch of papyri bound together with four pieces of a wooden slat. 'After having been opened, the papyri were read by Yadin and found to contain fifteen letters from the leader of the Revolt, Bar-Kochba, written in Hebrew, Aramaic and Greek.'[16] According to another report four of the letters were written in Hebrew, two in Greek and the rest in Aramaic; they were letters written by Bar Cochba to officers stationed at the oasis of 'En-gedi.[17]

Finally, during the spring of 1961, when the Israeli archaeologists returned to the wâdi, a sensational discovery was made 'in the same cave where the "archives" of the second century Jewish leader Simon Bar-Kochba were found in April, 1960'.[18] The number of papyrus documents discovered there in 'a long, reed-like sheath' was first announced as seventy.[19] But subsequent reports have reduced the number to five documents found in a leather pouch and thirty-six in a water-skin; they too are letters of Bar-Cochba, deeds and contracts of the same

[16] J. Aviram, *IEJ* 10 (1960) 125–6; see further R. North, 'Report from Palestine', *CBQ* 22 (1960) 317.

[17] *BeO* 3 (1961) 25. Y. Yadin (*BA* 24 [1961] 48; *Bible et Terre Sainte* 34 [1961] 14) now specifies that one of the Greek letters 'is apparently not from Bar Kochba'. In fact, in his fuller report (*BIES* 25 [1961] 49–64) he lists eight papyrus letters as Aramaic (Pap. 1, 2, 4, 8, 10, 11, 14, 15), two as Greek (Pap. 3, 6), three as certainly Hebrew (Pap. 5, 7, 12) and two as probably Hebrew (Pap. 9, 13). B. Lifshitz subsequently published the two Greek letters in 'Papyrus grecs du désert de Juda', *Aegyptus* 42 (1962) 240–56 (+2 plates).

[18] Reuter's dispatch from Tel Aviv, dated 18 March; *Washington Post*, 19 March 1961, p. A3.

[19] *Ibid.*

period.[20] But most of this material is as yet unpublished and we are dependent so far only on preliminary reports.[21]

So much for the new finds which have provided the material which sheds new light on the Bar Cochba period. We turn now to an attempt to relate the new material, in so far as it is known, to what was previously known.

BAR COCHBA'S NAME

One of the most interesting features of the new data supplied by the texts found in the caves of the Wâdies Murabba'ât and Ḫabra is the spelling of the name of the leader of the Second Revolt. In English the most commonly used form is Bar Cochba (less frequently spelled Kochba, Kokhba or Cocheba). This name has clung to him in history mainly due to its use by ancient Christian authors who wrote it in Greek or Latin as *Chochebas* or *Chōchebas*.[22] Bar Cochba means 'the son of the star'. In the light of the new data this form is almost certainly to be regarded as a nickname, or at least as a name derived from a word-play on his real name. His full name is given as

[20] Y. Yadin, 'The Secret in the Cliffs: the Discovery of the Bar Kochba Letters', *Atlantic Monthly* 208/5 (Nov. 1961) 129–35. However, in a recent public lecture Yadin reported the number as 47 papyrus letters, contracts, deeds and 1 biblical fragment on skin. See further Y. Yadin, 'Expedition D—The Cave of the Letters', *IEJ* 12 (1962) 227–57, for a fuller description of the cave, its objects and documents (the archive of Babatha, Nabataean documents, Aramaic and Hebrew texts from the time of Bar Cochba).

[21] See Y. Yadin, 'The Nabatean Kingdom, Provincia Arabia, Petra and En-Geddi in the Documents from Naḥal Ḥever', *JEOL* 17 (1963) 227–41; H. J. Polotsky, 'The Greek Papyri from the Cave of the Letters', *IEJ* 12 (1962) 258–62; 'Three Greek Documents from the Family Archive of Babatha', *E. L. Sukenik Memorial Volume (1889–1953)* (Eretz-Israel 8; Jerusalem: Israel Exploration Society, 1967) 46–51 [in Hebrew; English summary, p. 69*].

[22] Justin Martyr wrote *Chochebas* (*Apol.* 1, 31; *PG* 6, 376); likewise Orosius (7, 31; CSEL 5, 468), Jerome's translation of Eusebius' *Chronicon* (283 F; GCS 47, 201). But Eusebius (*Eccl. Hist.* 4, 6, 2; 4, 8, 4; GCS 9, 306 and 316) has *Chōchebas*. This form of the name is also found in a few Rabbinical texts: *Seder 'Olam Rabbah* 30 (ed. R. Ratner, p. 146; one MS. has *br kkb'*); *Šilšelet haqqabbala* of R. Gedalya ben Yahya 40 (*br kwkb'*). See S. Yeivin, *Milḥemet bar Kôkbâ* (2nd ed.; Jerusalem: Mosad Bialik, 1953) 145, 233–4.

Simon ben/bar Kosibah in the new texts: *šmʿwn bn kwsbh* (*Mur* 43:1), *šmʿwn br kwsbh* (*Hev* 1, 3, 11) sometimes spelled *kwsbʾ* (*Mur* 24 B 3, C 3, 30, E 2, G 3, *Hev* 2, 12), *kwśbh* (*Hev* 14) or *kśbh* (*Hev* 8). The Greek form of the name occurs in *Hev* 6 as *Simōn Chōsiba*, giving us precious evidence of the pronunciation of the name.[23] His real name was, then, Simon the son of Kosibah—the latter is apparently the name of his father, and not of the locality from which he comes.[24]

However, in Rabbinical writings his name is often given as *bn* or *br kwzybʾ* (or *kwzbʾ*), 'the son of the lie',[25] a word-play involving the shift of the radicals *ksb* to *kzb*, the root meaning 'to

[23] See Y. Yadin, *BIES* 25 (1961) 54 ff.; *BA* 24 (1961) 48. The siglum *Hev* will hereafter refer to the texts of the Wâdi Ḫabra as they are cited in the *BIES* article of Yadin. An English translation of this article has appeared too: 'Expedition D', *IEJ* 11 (1961) 36–52. See further E. Y. Kutscher, 'The Languages of the Hebrew and Aramaic Letters of Bar Cochba and His Contemporaries', *Leshonenu* 25 (1961) 117–33; 26 (1962) 7–23. The Greek text of *Hev* 6 has been published by B. Lifshitz, *Aegyptus* 42 (1962) 248–52. It reads: '[A]nnanos to brother Jonathe, greetings! Since Simon (ben) Chosiba (*Simōn Chōsiba*) has again written to send [. . . for] the needs of our brothers [. . .], now sen[d] these things im[mediately i]n security. [Anna]nos. Farewell, brother!'

[24] It has been suggested that *bn* or *br kwzybʾ* in the Rabbinical writings may mean 'the man of Kozeba', a town or locality mentioned in 1 Chr 4:22 (*kôzēbāʾ*). But this suggestion can now be disregarded since the name is given in the new documents with a *samekh* or *śin* instead of a *zayin*. J. T. Milik (*RB* 60 [1953] 279–89) discussed the problem of the *bn X* names, whether they are always patronymics or could be designations of quality. However, in DJD 2, 126 he recognizes *bn kwsbh* as a patronymic, even though the etymology of *kwsbh* is quite obscure. This seems to be the better solution, until more evidence is forthcoming. Y. Yadin (*BIES* 25 [1961] 64) apparently also inclines toward the view that *bar Kôkᵉbā* and *bar Kôzibā* are nicknames. Cf. F. Nötscher, 'Bar Kochba, Ben Kosba: der Sternsohn, der Prächtige', *VT* 11 (1961) 449–51. For another discussion of the name, see now B. Lifshitz, *Aegyptus* 42 (1962) 240–56.

[25] Bab. Talmud, *Sanhedrin* XI, 1, 2; fol. 93b (ed. Goldschmidt, 7, 400); Jer. Talmud, *Taʿanith* 4, 68; *Echa Rabbah* 80, 2, 5 (ed. S. Buber, p. 158): 'Do not read *kôkāb*, 'star', but *kôzēb*, "liar".'—J. T. Milik (*RB* 60 [1953] 277–8: DJD 2, 126) suggests that of the two forms of the name attested in the Rabbinical writings, *kwzbʾ* and *kwzybʾ*, the defective form was the more original, since the dissyllabic form **Kosba* becomes **Kozba* ('*s* s'assimilant à la sonore suivante'). The form with *z* would be a phonetic shift introduced

lie'. Though the interpretation is questioned at times,[26] it still seems best to regard the Rabbinical *Kôzibā* form of his name as due either to the Rabbis who did not approve of his anti-Roman uprising or to those who later reflected ironically on its ill-fated outcome. To them he was the 'son of the lie'. The other form of the name, *Kôk^ebā*, is likewise due to a word-play attributed to his contemporary, the great Rabbi Aqiba, who did approve of his movement. In fact, he regarded him as a messiah, and applied to him the oracle of Balaam, 'A star shall advance from Jacob' (Nm 24:17).[27] The patronymic *bar Kôsibāh* was changed to the Aramaic *bar kôk^ebā*, 'the son of the

into the writing, especially by those who only heard the name and related it to an otherwise known root. However, the trisyllabic form of the name is preserved in Greek, *Chōsiba*. When this is considered together with the Rabbinical *plena scriptio*, *kwzyb'*, it appears that the more original form was *Kôsibah*. Hence, it is better to retain the suggestion that both *kwkb'* and *kwzb'* are the result of a play on the original name.

[26] E. Schürer (*Geschichte des jüdischen Volkes im Zeitalter Jesu Christi* [5th ed.; Leipzig: J. C. Hinrichs, 1920] 1, 683; [Engl. tr. of 2nd ed. by J. MacPherson; Edinburgh: T. and T. Clark, 1905: 1/2, 298]) maintains that it was 'not until a comparatively late period, and only by a few individual writers, in view of his miserable collapse, [that] it was taken to mean liar or deceiver'. Footnote 100 (Engl. 84): 'Since Barcosiba or Bencosiba is the prevailing form, even in the mouths of such as esteemed him highly, like Akiba, it cannot have had a disrespectful meaning.' It should be recalled, however, that Schürer's transliteration of the name with an *s* does not represent the real spelling of the name now known to us from the new finds, but is the frequently used German equivalent of Semitic *z* in the Rabbinical form of the name *kwzyb'*. What Schürer says might be accepted as correct, if we could be sure that R. Aqiba had not in fact used the correct form *kwsbh* (with a *samekh*), which was later normalized in the Rabbinical tradition to agree with the other form *kwzyb'*, precisely because of the ill-fated outcome of the revolt.

[27] Jer. Talmud, *Ta'anith* 4, 68d: 'R. Simon ben Yohai said, "R. Aqiba, my teacher, expounded the passage: 'There shall go forth a star (*kwkb*) out of Jacob' (Nm 24:17), as follows: 'There goes *kwzb'* out from Jacob.' When R. Aqiba saw Barcoziba, he said, 'This is the king Messiah.' Then R. Yoḥanan ben Torta said to him, 'Aqiba, the grass will grow out of your jaw-bone, and the Son of David will not yet have come.'"' Similarly the Midrash *Echa Rabbah* (2, 2, 4, ed. S. Buber, p. 101; tr. by J. Rabinowitz, in *Midrash Rabbah* [London: Soncino, 1951] 157).—Eusebius (*Eccl. Hist.* 4,

star', whence comes our English form Bar Cochba, the name which has persisted for him in our history books.

Coins minted during the first year of the Second Revolt bear the name with a title, 'Simon, Prince of Israel' (*šmʿwn nśyʾ yśrʾl*),[28] and the fuller form of the name and title is now attested in the new documents as 'Simon ben Kosibah, Prince of Israel' (*šmʿwn bn kwsbʾ nsyʾ yśrʾl* [*Mur* 24 B 2–3] or 'Simon bar Kosibah, the prince over Israel' (*šmʿwn br kwsbh hnsyʾ ʿl yśrʾl* [*Hev* 1]). The title, 'Prince of Israel', designates the supreme rank which Bar Cochba held during the period of his leadership of the revolt. There was, however, apparently also a priestly co-leader, for other coins of the same period mention Eleazar, the Priest (*ʾlʿzr hkwhn*).[29]

It is not unlikely that both the title, Prince of Israel, and the appellation, 'the son of the star', are due to the messianic character of the uprising. Thanks to the discovery of the Qumran texts, where we find a developed but complex messianic expectation formulated, it is easy for us to understand how Bar Cochba's movement could have been hailed as the event which was to free Jerusalem and redeem Israel. In the

---

6, 2; GCS 9, 306) is also aware that *Barchōchebas* is related to *kwkb*, 'star', when he says that he was 'a man who was murderous and a bandit, but relied on his name, as if dealing with slaves, and claimed to be a luminary who had come down to them from heaven and was magically enlightening those who were in misery'. This pejorative view of the leader of the Second Revolt agrees with that of other early Christian writers; see footnote 117.

[28] It is now universally admitted that these Simon coins date from the Bar Cochba period; see A. Reifenberg, *Ancient Jewish Coins* (2nd ed.; Jerusalem: Rubin Mass, 1947) 33–4, 64 (#190, 192, 193, 199); likewise DJD 2, 46. Some of the coins with the name *šmʿwn* bear a star, which may refer to Aqiba's appellation of the leader as a messiah (see A. Reifenberg, *op. cit.*, 60 [#164, 167]). Cf. C. Roth, 'Star and Anchor; Coin Symbolism and the End of Days', *ʾEreṣ Yiśrāʾēl* 6 (1960) 13*–15*.

[29] Perhaps this is R. Eleazar ben Azariah, the president of the Beth-Din in the place of Gamaliel II; see A. Reifenberg, *Ancient Jewish Coins*², 34 and 61 (#169, 170), 63 (#189, 189a), 64 (#196), 65 (#203); DJD 2, 47.—Y. Yadin (*BIES* 25 [1961] 59; *IEJ* 11 [1961] 46) mentions that *Hev* 11, a letter written by Simon bar Kosibah to two of his officers at 'En-gedi,

messianic expectations of the Qumran sect the Oracle of Balaam played an important role. It is used in the third paragraph of the *Testimonia* text from Cave 4, in 1QM 11:5–7, in CD 7:18–20. In the latter text it refers to the Davidic Messiah and to the Interpreter of the Law (probably a priestly figure), whereas its use in the *T. Levi* (18:3) is applied rather to the Aaronitic Messiah and in *T. Judah* 24:1 it is used of the Kingly Messiah.[30] Even granting that such messianic expectations might have been rather 'sectarian', and not necessarily characteristic of all contemporary Judaism, nevertheless they provide a background against which it is easy to understand how the uprising of the Jews in the second century after the horrible destruction of their 'holy city' and the temple of Yahweh in A.D. 70 could take on the colours and hues of a messianic movement. Simon ben Kosibah, as the leader of that Second Revolt, was the 'Messiah', the 'son of *the star*'. His revolt was dedicated to the 'Liberation of Jerusalem', and the 'Redemption of Israel', as the coins of his time attest.[31] We know nothing about his antecedents, and cannot even conjecture how he came to be the leader of the revolt. But at any rate he became for the Jews the 'Prince of Israel', the *nāśî'*, the name reminiscent of the OT eschatological leader of the people spoken of by the prophet Ezekiel, who was to be descended from David (see Ez 34:24; 37:25; 44:3).

---

contains a reference to a certain Baṭniyah bar Misah, who is called 'our master' (*rbnw*). It is not yet determined who he is, nor what relationship he had to the rebel leader. See further 'Les lettres de Bar Kokhéba', *BTS* 34 (1961) 15.

[30] See J. M. Allegro, 'Further Messianic References in Qumran Literature', *JBL* 75 (1956) 182–7, Document IV. Cf. ' "4QTestimonia" and the New Testament', pp. 58–89 above; 'The Use of Explicit Old Testament Quotations in Qumran Literature and in the New Testament', pp. 3–58 above. Likewise L. E. Toombs, 'Barcosiba and Qumran', *NTS* 4 (1957) 65–71.

[31] See A. Reifenberg, *Ancient Jewish Coins*², 60–6.

THE CAUSES OF THE SECOND REVOLT

The causes of the Second Jewish Revolt have always been a subject of great debate among the historians of second-century Palestine. How grateful we would be, then, if the new documents were to shed some light on this subject. However, the reports about the new discoveries and texts shed no new light on this area of our study and we are in no better position than previously. We present here a brief résumé only of what seems to be the state of the question regarding the sources today.

Ancient authorities assign various causes to the Second Revolt, most of which are not contradictory, but the problem is how to assess them. Modern historians do not always agree. E. Schürer has, however, effectively disposed of one claim that has often been put forward, that the revolt was due to the permission given by Hadrian to the Jews to rebuild the temple of Yahweh, but which was subsequently revoked by him.[32] There is really no foundation for the claim. The two reasons, however, which are seriously considered today as having played a major role in causing the Jews to revolt are those which come to us from Dio Cassius in his *Roman History* and from the *Life of Hadrian*, wrongly attributed to Aelius Spartianus.

The first reason which we shall discuss is that given by Dio Cassius, *viz.* that the Emperor Hadrian, who was visiting the Near East, attempted to rebuild the city of Jerusalem as an important centre of his empire and to erect on the site of the temple of Yahweh a shrine to the Roman god Jupiter Capitolinus. Dio Cassius' text follows:

At Jerusalem he [Hadrian] founded a city in place of the one which had been razed to the ground, naming it Aelia Capitolina, and on the site of the temple of the god he raised a new temple to Jupiter. This brought on a war of no slight importance nor of brief duration, for the Jews deemed it intolerable that foreign races should be settled in their city and foreign religious rites planted there. So long, indeed, as Hadrian was close by in Egypt and again in Syria, they remained

[32] *GJV* 1, 671, 3 (Engl. tr. 289–91); similarly H. Strathmann, 'Der Kampf um Beth-Ter', *PJB* 23 (1927) 103–5.

quiet, save in so far as they purposely made of poor quality such weapons as they were called upon to furnish, in order that theRomans might reject them and they themselves might thus have the use of them; but when he went farther away, they openly revolted.[33]

This reason, as given by Dio Cassius, seems to fill out with details what the biographer of Hadrian very succinctly said of him in the following words: 'sacra Romana diligentissime curavit, peregrina contempsit; pontificis maximi officium peregit'.[34] In other words, it was completely in character with Hadrian to attempt to rebuild Jerusalem after the fashion of Hellenistic cities and try to establish there the culture of the Greeks which he admired so much.

One of the problems connected with this cause for the Second Revolt is precisely the time when Hadrian began to build Aelia Capitolina. Dio Cassius' report seems to indicate that it was actually begun before the Revolt. Since this point enters into our later discussions of the dates of the revolt, it is important that we review here the reasons for thinking that Dio Cassius is correct.

The reign of Hadrian was marked by long journeys to the various parts of his empire. In the year A.D. 128 he undertook his second protracted visit to the Near East. While the data about his movements, his visits to various colonies, cities and countries, and his inspections of Roman legions and garrisons are relatively abundant, they are not sufficient to establish with certainty their detailed chronological order. But it seems that he was at Antioch in Syria in autumn A.D. 129, and from there made his way to Beirut in Phoenicia, via Palmyra and Damas-

[33] *Roman History* 69, 12, 1–2 (tr. by E. Cary, Loeb Classical Library, vol. 8, 449).

[34] *Vita Hadriani* 22, 10; in the *Scriptores historiae augustae* (tr. by D. Magie, Loeb Classical Library, vol. 1, 68–9). In connection with these testimonies it is customary for historians to discuss the *Epistle of Barnabas* (16, 4), but the value of this text, which is corrupt in a crucial spot, is quite debatable. See E. Schürer, *GJV* 1, 672 (Engl. tr. 290); H. Strathmann, *PJB* 23 (1927) 104; H. Bietenhard, 'Die Freiheitskriege der Juden unter den Kaisern Trajan und Hadrian und der messianische Tempelbau', *Jud* 4 (1948) 95–100.

cus. From Beirut he went to the province of Arabia, the former kingdom of the Nabataeans, and from Petra he came back to Jerash, where he apparently spent the winter of A.D. 129–30.[35] From Jerash he must have made his way to Judaea, for coins have been found commemorating his *parousia* or arrival there: *adventui Aug(usti) Iudaeae*.[36] He seems to have visited Eleutheropolis, Tiberias, Caesarea Maritima and Gaza.[37] In many of these places he was hailed as *restitutor*, *oikistēs*, *ktistēs*, *euergetēs*, which titles are generally attributed to his policy of setting the Roman garrisons to work in building Hellenistic-style cities in these areas.[38] While there is no direct evidence of Hadrian's visit to Jerusalem, it is quite likely that he visited the town, given its importance in the history of Palestine, its fairly recent destruction by Roman troops, and the fact that a garrison of the *Legio X Fretensis* was still stationed there. En route to Gaza and subsequently to Egypt, where he spent the winter of A.D. 130, he must have passed through Jerusalem. It is likely that he

[35] The inscription on the triumphal arch at Jerash, which was erected on the occasion of Hadrian's visit there, is dated to the fourteenth *tribunicia potestas* and the 192nd year of the era of Jerash (=the Pompeian era), i.e. 1 October 129–30. See W. F. Stinespring, 'The Inscription of the Triumphal Arch at Jerash', *BASOR* 56 (1934) 15–16; C. H. Kraeling (ed.), *Gerasa: City of the Decapolis* (New Haven: American Schools of Oriental Research, 1938) 401–2; C. C. McCown, 'New Historical Items from Jerash Inscriptions', *JPOS* 16 (1936) 69–78, esp. 75–6; M. I. Rostovtzeff, *CRAIBL* 1934, 267.—On the journeys of Hadrian in general see J. Dürr, *Die Reisen des Kaisars Hadrian* (Vienna: G. Gerold, 1881); B. W. Henderson, *The Life and Principate of the Emperor Hadrian A.D. 76–138* (London: Methuen, 1923) 128 ff.; B. d'Orgeval, *L'empereur Hadrien: oeuvre législative et administrative* (Paris: Ed. Domat Montchrestien, 1950) 25 ff.; W. F. Stinespring, 'Hadrian in Palestine, 129/130 A.D.', *JAOS* 59 (1939) 360–5.

[36] See H. Mattingly and E. A. Sydenham, *The Imperial Roman Coinage; Vol. II Vespasian to Hadrian* (London: Spink, 1926) 454 (#890–4); M. Bernhart, *Handbuch zur Münzkunde der römischen Kaiserzeit* (Halle a.d.S.: A. Riechmann, 1926), Textband, 103, n. 1; H. St J. Hart, 'Judaea and Rome: the Official Commentary', *JTS* n.s. 3 (1952) 172–98 (esp. pl. V, #1–4).

[37] See F.-M. Abel, *Histoire de la Palestine depuis la conquête d'Alexandre jusqu'à l'invasion arabe* (EBib; Paris: Gabalda) vol. 2 (1952) 74, 79 ff.

[38] See R. MacMullen, 'Roman Imperial Building in the Provinces', *Harvard Studies in Classical Philology* 64 (1959) 207–35.

ordered the rebuilding of the city as the *colonia Aelia Capitolina* at this time. At any rate, Hadrian was in Egypt by November A.D. 130, for he saluted the colossal statue of Memnon at Thebes on the 21st of that month.[39] Apparently he returned to Syria in the spring of A.D. 131 and then proceeded to visit the regions of Pontus and the Black Sea.[40] He passed the winter of 131–2 at Athens. The withdrawal to these more distant places is probably what Dio Cassius has in mind, when he refers to the outbreak of the Second Revolt.

A different reason, however, is given by the *Life of Hadrian* for the revolt, one which has nothing to do with the attempt to rebuild Jerusalem as a Hellenistic city. The biographer of Hadrian records it thus: 'moverunt ea tempestate et Iudaei bellum, quod vetabantur mutilare genitalia.'[41] The emperor Domitian had earlier forbidden castration. Dio Cassius records, 'He forbade that any person in the Roman Empire should thereafter be castrated.'[42] This prohibition was repeated by the Emperor Nerva.[43] But when Hadrian came along, he interpreted the prohibition in such wise that it included circumcision.[44] The rescript which he issued apropos of it probably does not date from the beginning of his reign; it belongs more likely to the period just before the Second Revolt, and for that reason it is given by the *Life* as a cause of the revolt.[45] Hadrian

[39] Cf. *CIG* 4737.

[40] See Arrian, *Periplus ponti Euxini* 1, 1 (ed. R. Hercher, 1885, p. 86).

[41] *Vita Hadriani* 14, 2.

[42] *Rom. Hist.* 67, 2, 3. See also Suetonius, *Domitian* 7, 1: 'Castrari mares vetuit'; Eusebius, *Chronicon* 272F (GCS 47, 190): 'Domitianus eunuchos fieri prohibuit'. H. Hitzig, 'Castratio', *PW* 3/2 (1889) 1772–3; B. d'Orgeval, *L'empereur Hadrien*, 324.

[43] Dio Cassius, *Rom Hist.* 68, 2, 4.

[44] See Ulpian, *Digesta* 48, 8, 4: 'Divus Hadrianus rescripsit: constitutum quidem est, ne spadones fierent, eos autem, qui hoc crimine arguerentur, Corneliae legis poena teneri. . . .' The *lex Cornelia de sicariis et veneficis* punished murder with death. This was applied to the physician who performed the castration; the eunuch was punished with exile and loss of property.

[45] This is accepted as a cause of the revolt by E. Schürer, *GJV*; M. Noth, *The History of Israel* (2nd English ed.; New York: Harper, 1960) 451–2;

made both castration and circumcision a crime punishable by death, by subsuming it under the existing *lex Cornelia de sicariis et veneficis*. Such a law naturally touched a major tenet of the religion of the Jews and it is not improbable that it contributed to their rebellion against Roman domination.

The widening of the prohibition of castration to include circumcision, however, was not specifically directed against the Jews. There is no evidence that Hadrian so intended it. On the contrary, when under Antoninus Pius permission was given to the Jews to circumcise their children again, the prohibition still was in effect for the non-Jewish peoples.[46] Consequently, it appears that the prohibition of circumcision was a general one, but affected an important Jewish religious rite—a rite for which the Jews were as prompt to rebel as for the building of a shrine of Jupiter on the site of Yahweh's temple in Jerusalem.

The prevailing opinion among modern historians of the period is to accept both the cause given by Dio Cassius and that supplied by the *Life of Hadrian*, since they are not conflicting reasons and both may have been the prime factors in the uprising. Whether there were other subordinate reasons we do not know for certain.[47]

H. Hitzig, 'Circumcisio', *PW* 3/2 (1899) 2570–1. But it is questioned by H. Bietenhard, *Jud* 4 (1948) 92–4.

[46] See Modestinus, *Digesta* 48, 8, 11: 'Circumcidere Iudaeis filios suos tantum rescripto divi Pii permittitur; in non eiusdem religionis qui hoc fecerit, castrantis poena irrogatur.' See E. Schürer, *GJV* 1, 677; E. M. Smallwood, 'The Legislation of Hadrian and Antoninus Pius against Circumcision', *Latomus* 18 (1959) 334–47.

[47] S. Perowne (*Hadrian* [London: Hodder and Stoughton, 1960] 149–50) summarizes thus the grievances which the Jews could have had against Hadrian by the year 130: 'First, he had declared himself the successor to Antiochus Epiphanes. He had finished Antiochus' own temple in Athens. Secondly, like Antiochus, he had adopted, or allowed others to adopt in addressing him, the style of god, of Zeus Olympios. Thirdly, he had permitted this style to appear on coins which circulated among Jewish communities. Fourthly, he had prohibited circumcision, which for the Jews was the very seal of their being and faith. Fifthly, he was on his way to patronize and caress the Greeks of Alexandria, who had shewn themselves the most

It should be noted, however, that Pausanias and Chrysostom were content to ascribe the Second Revolt merely to the general disobedience and the revolutionary tendency of the Jews, who were hankering after the restoration of their ancient political state.[48] But this is a description rather of the general background of the period under Roman domination, especially since the destruction of Jerusalem in A.D. 70. After Titus left the town in ruins and a garrison of the *Legio X Fretensis* was stationed there to maintain Roman military control, the lot of the Jews in the empire was not easy. Under Vespasian the procuratorial province of Judaea was administered as an imperial province with the official name *Iudaea*. It was not a part of the *provincia Syriae*, but depended directly on the emperor and thus had the appearance of independence, at least of the neighbouring Roman administration in Syria. *Iudaea* was governed by a *legatus* who resided at Caesarea Maritima. Roman colonists were settled in Flavia Neapolis (modern Nablus) and 800 veterans were given property in Emmaus. In Jerusalem itself some of the old inhabitants, both Jews and the Christians, who had returned from Pella, lived side by side with the Romans. In fact, in recent times it has become clear that more Jews actually lived in Jerusalem between the two revolts than we normally imagine, as ossuaries and other burials of the period attest. Vespasian had claimed the whole of the land of Judaea as his private property and tenant-farmers worked the land for him. The Jewish community, accustomed to pay a didrachm or half-shekel as a tax for the temple of Yahweh, now had to contribute the same to the *fiscus iudaicus* which eventually bene-

---

ardent enemies of the Jews. Sixthly, he had gone out of his way to honour the very man who had captured Jerusalem, almost two centuries before, and had violated the Holy of Holies [i.e., Pompey]. Seventhly, and finally, he had given orders for the obliteration of Jerusalem, for the construction on the site of a Roman colony, called by his own name, and containing, on the very site of the ancient Temple, a shrine where he himself should be venerated.'

[48] Pausanias, *Periegesis* 1, 5, 5; Chrysostom, *Adv. Judaeos* 5, 11; *PG* 48, 900.

fited the Roman temple of Jupiter Capitolinus. The temple cult was no more and with it passed away the influence of the Jerusalem Sanhedrin headed by the high priest. Religious emphasis among the Jews shifted to certain forms of synagogue worship and to the study of the Torah to ensure its careful observance (especially according to the traditions of the Pharisees and the Rabbis). The council of 72 Elders (or Rabbis) in Jamnia (Yabneh), under the leadership of R. Joḥanan ben Zakkai and later under R. Gamaliel II, took over the rule of the Jewish community in Palestine. It enjoyed a certain autonomy even though the land was still dominated by the Romans, who normally did not interfere with the workings of the council. It is often said to have fixed the calendar and the canon of the Scriptures[49] and functioned as a court of law. But both in Palestine and in the diaspora there was always the yearning for the 'restoration of Israel', a yearning fed by the recollection of what had taken place after the destruction of Jerusalem in 586 B.C. When Trajan (A.D. 98–117) was occupied with the threat of the Parthians, revolts of the Jews occurred in Cyrene, Egypt, Cyprus and in Mesopotamia (toward the end of his reign, *c.* 115–16).[50] These revolts were in part fired by the messianic expectations current among the Jews of the time. The general who finally put down the Mesopotamian revolt was the Romanized Moor, Lusius Quietus, who was subsequently rewarded with the governorship of Palestine.[51] We know little

[49] But cf. J. P. Lewis, 'What Do We Mean by Jabneh?', *JBR* 32 (1964) 125–32.

[50] See Dio Cassius, *Rom. Hist.* 68, 32, 1–3 (which ascribes much bloodshed and gruesome atrocities to the Jews in Cyrene, Egypt and Cyprus). Similarly Eusebius, *Eccl. Hist.* 4, 2, 1–5 (who mentions the revolts in Alexandria, the rest of Egypt, Cyrene and Mesopotamia in the 18th regnal year of Trajan). Cf. V. A. Tcherikover and A. Fuks, *Corpus papyrorum iudaicarum* (Cambridge, Mass: Harvard Univ. Press) vol. 1 (1957) 85–93; H. Bietenhard, *Jud* 4 (1948) 66–7.

[51] Dio Cassius, *Rom. Hist.* 68, 32, 5; Eusebius, *Chronicon* in Armenian translation by J. Karst, GCS 20, 219.—The *Seder 'Olam Rabbah* 30 (ed. B. Ratner, 146) speaks of a 'war of Quietus', but historians are reluctant to

about the conditions of Palestine between the two revolts, but the fact that Lusius Quietus was sent there as governor would indicate that elements of unrest were present there too. It is to this general background of unrest among the Jews, both in the diaspora and in the motherland, that the statements of Pausanias and Chrysostom are best related. Given such hopes of a liberating messiah to come and such hankering after the freedom of old, the two causes of the Second Revolt as stated by Dio Cassius and the *Life of Hadrian* become readily intelligible.

THE DATES OF THE REVOLT

The dates normally given for the Second Revolt are A.D. 132–5. The beginning of the revolt is usually reckoned according to the notice of Dio Cassius, that the Jews 'openly revolted', when Hadrian withdrew from their vicinity to more distant regions, as we have seen. These dates have been preferred by modern historians to those supplied by Epiphanius and the *Chronicon Paschale*. The former gives the forty-seventh year after the destruction of Jerusalem as the date of Hadrian's visit to Jerusalem and the building of Aelia Capitolina, which occasioned the revolt.[52] This, however, cannot be correct, for it would equal A.D. 117, the very year of Hadrian's accession to the imperial throne. The *Chronicon Paschale* also gives a misleading date, in associating the building of Aelia Capitolina with the third year of the 224th Olympiad, in the consulship of Aelius Hadrianus Augustus and Rusticius.[53] This would be the year A.D. 119. Although we cannot date precisely the year in which Hadrian began the

---

take this expression in a strict sense; moreover, the text may not be sound. See H. Bietenhard, *Jud* 4 (1948) 70–7.

[52] Epiphanius, *De mensuris et ponderibus* 14; *PG* 43, 259–61.

[53] *PG* 92, 613; ed. Dindorf, I, 474. For a modern, but isolated, attempt to defend these dates see W. D. Gray, 'The Founding of Aelia Capitolina and the Chronology of the Jewish War under Hadrian', *AJSL* 39 (1922–23) 248–56. See also M. Auerbach, *Zur politischen Geschichte der Juden unter Kaiser Hadrian* (Berlin, 1924) 325.

rebuilding of Jerusalem, it seems to have been before the Second Revolt, and most probably in the year A.D. 130. Dio Cassius' report implies that some time passed before the Jews openly rebelled. Hence the year is usually given as A.D. 132.

New light has been shed on the question by the dates given in one of the documents from a Murabba'ât cave. *Mur* 24 is an abstract of title-deeds written on a papyrus by a deputy of Bar Cochba, in whose name various farm-lands were rented out in return for crops to be paid into the 'treasury' of the Prince of Israel. It belongs to a *genre* called in Greek *diastrōma* and already known from the papyri found at Oxyrhynchus in Egypt.[54] In each case a record is made of the date, the competent authority, the names of the lessees, the fact of the rental, the duration of it, and the terms (stating the exact amount of wheat which is to be paid yearly to the 'treasury'); finally the signatures are appended. In *Mur* 24 there are eleven fragmentary texts of this sort, the wording of which offers at times slight variants. The item of interest to our discussion here is found in texts B and E of this document; it is the synchronism of dates which is given. We supply the text of one of the deeds in order to comment on it and explain the synchronism.[55]

Mur 24 *E* (*DJD* 2, 131)

[*b'śryn lš*]*bṭ šnt št*[*ym*] *lg'lt*[56]	[The 20th of She]bat, the 2nd year of the Redemption of

[54] Oxy P 274 (dated A.D. 89–97); see B. P. Grenfell and A. S. Hunt, *The Oxyrhynchus Papyri, Edited with Translations and Notes* (London: Egypt Exploration Fund, 1899) 2, 259–62.

[55] The lacunae in the text are restored with certainty due to the very similar wording of these parts in the other fragmentary texts, which fortunately do not have the lacunae always in the identical spot.

[56] *lg'lt yśr'l:* Milik rightly understands this expression as a synonym for *lḥrwt yrwšlm*, adducing as evidence the interchange of these expressions in different dates or years on coins (see A. Reifenberg, *Ancient Jewish Coins*², 60 [#163, *lg'lt yśr'l*, 170–2, 189–95]) and in the new documents (*Mur* 23 and 24). There is no reason to regard *lg'lt yśr'l* as the more messianic title given

[*y*]*śr'l 'l yd šm'wn bn k*[*ws*]*b' nsy'*	[I]srael by Simon ben K[osi]bah, the Prince of
[*yś*]*r'l bmḥnh šywšb bhrwdys*[57]	[Is]rael, in the camp which is situated at Herodium.
[*y*]*hwdh bn rb' 'mr lhll bn grys*[58]	[Ye]hudah ben Rabba' declared to Hillel ben Garis:
'ny mrṣwny [*ḥ*]*krt*[59] *hmk*[60] *hywm 't*	'I, of my own free will, have [ren]ted from you today
h'pr[61] *šhw' š ly bḥ*⟨*k*⟩*rty b'yr*	the farm-land, which is mine by my tenancy in 'Ir-

---

to the revolt and *lḥrwt yrwšlm* as the more political one, as suggested by B. Kanael, 'The Historical Background of the Coins "Year Four . . . of the Redemption of Zion"', *BASOR* 129 (1953) 20. For two hybrid coins in A. Reifenberg, *Ancient Jewish Coins*², #171–2, bear on the obverse *šnt 'ḥt lg'lt yśr* ('year one of the Redemption of Isr⟨ael⟩') and on the reverse *š b lḥr yśr'l* ('yr 2 of the Freed⟨om⟩ of Israel').

57 *bmḥnh šywšb bhrwdys:* Milik's translation links these words with the preceding *nsy' yśr'l*, 'Prince d'Israël en campagne, qui réside à Hérodium'. He interprets the expression to mean that Bar Cochba had his headquarters at Herodium. However, Y. Yadin ('Were the Headquarters of Bar Cochba at Herodium?', *Hā-'Āreṣ*, 10 March 1961, 10; see also *IEJ* 11 [1961] 51) has shown that the Hebrew need not mean that; the sense is rather that the contract was made in the camp at Herodium. This interpretation is confirmed by other documents found in the Wâdi Ḫabra cave in 1960, which make it unlikely that the headquarters of Bar Cochba were on Herodium. See further discussion below, pp. 335–7. Cf. *Mur* 18:2, where the place in which the text is written seems to be named; likewise *Mur* 19:1, 12; 115:2.

58 *hll bn grys:* The same individual is mentioned in other deeds (*Mur* 24 B 6, C 5, [F 4–5], [H 3], J 3), and is probably the administrator in charge of the lands in the village of 'Ir-Naḥaš, near Eleutheropolis, the modern Deir Naḫḫas, about a mile and a half ENE of Beit Jibrin.

59 *ḥkrt:* The verb *ḥkr* means to 'contract, farm', especially to 'give or take in rent on a fixed rental payable in kind' (Jastrow, 463). The details of the text bear out this meaning.

60 *hmk:* Defective spelling of the Mishnaic Hebrew *hymk* (*hêm^{e}kā*), an alternate form of *mmk*, 'from you'. See M. H. Segal, *A Grammar of Mishnaic Hebrew* (Oxford: Clarendon, 1958) 144.

61 *h'pr:* Normally this word means 'loose earth' (whence a number of

nḥš šḥkrt mšmʿwn nsyʾ yśrʾl	Naḥaš (and) which I have rented from Simon, the Prince of Israel.
t[62] *ʿpr hlz ḥkrty hmk mn hywm*	This land I have rented from you from today
ʿd swp ʿrb hšmṭh šhm šnym	until the end of the eve of Remission, which is (in) complete years,
šlmwt šny [m]ksh[63] *ḥmš t ḥkyr*	[fi]scal years, five. (This is) the rent
[šʾh]ʾ mwdd[64] *lk b[hr]wdys ḥnṭyn*	[which I sha]ll pay to you at [Her]odium: wheat
[ypwt wnqywt] šlw[št kwr]yn wltk	[of good quality and pure], thr[ee ko]rs and a letek,
[mʿsrt mʿsrt] t ʾlh	[tithed . . . having tithed] these
[šthʾ šwql ʿl gg hʾwṣr][65] *w[q]ym*	[which you will pay into the treasury]. (This document is) valid,

---

figurative meanings are derived); but here it equals 'a piece of farmland'.

[62] *t:* This form, which is found often in these documents (*Mur* 22 i 2; 24 A 8, B 18, C 16, D 11, E 8, 10, 13; 36 i–ii 3; 43 3, 5; 44 6, 7, 8, 9; 46 3, 5), is related by Milik to the Punic *t*, a form of the *signum accusativi* (See Z. Harris, *A Grammar of the Phoenician Language* [American Oriental Series 8; New Haven: American Oriental Society, 1936] 76; J. Friedrich, *Phönizisch-Punische Grammatik* [Analecta Orientalia 32; Rome: Pontifical Biblical Institute, 1951] #255).

[63] *šny mksh:* Lit. 'years of the toll', from the root *mks*, 'to pay a toll on' (Jastrow, 783). See now the important study of J. R. Donahue, 'Tax Collectors and Sinners', CBQ 33 (1971).

[64] *šhʾ mwdd:* The relative pronoun *š* precedes the 1st sg. impf. qal of *hyh* in an apocopated form; see M. H. Segal, *op. cit.*, 95. The 2 sg. is restored in 1:14. The rood *mdd*, 'to measure', is often used for measuring off a tithe; compare *šql* in 1:14.

[65] *ʿl gg hʾwṣr:* Lit. 'on the roof of the treasury'. Milik explains the expression by the shape of public granaries in the ancient East, especially in Egypt, which were great round silos with an opening on top through which the grain was poured. *ANEP* #90.

15 [*'ly l'mt kkh*[66]]	[therefore, against me].'
[*yhwdh bn rb' 'l npšh ktb*]	[Yehudah ben Rabba', for himself. There wrote (this)]
[*plwny bn 'lmwny mn m'mrh*[67]]	[at his dictation X ben Z].

There are several important items in this text which shed new light on the affairs of second-century Palestine. For the moment we are only interested in those which help to fix the date of the Second Revolt more precisely. These are, first of all, the date of the document itself, 'the 20th of Shebat, the 2nd year of the Redemption of Israel'; secondly, the reference to the 'end of the eve of Remission', and lastly the indication that the contract would last up to that time, a period of 'five complete years'. The 'remission' (*šᵉmiṭṭāh*) referred to is the observance of the regulation of Ex 23:10–11, according to which the land is to lie fallow every seventh year.[68] The contract is thus made to be valid up to the end of the sixth year of the current seven-year or Sabbatical cycle. Until that time there are five complete years, i.e. years when the rental on the harvest derived from the land must be paid. This means, therefore, that the 20th of Shebat of the second year of the Redemption of Israel falls in the second year of the Sabbatical cycle. Since Shebat corresponds roughly to January–February, the 20th of this month would equal the early part of February in our calendar.

Now Rabbinical tradition has recorded that the temple was destroyed by Titus during *môṣā'ê šᵉbî'ît*,[69] which means the year

[66] *l'mt kkh:* Lit. 'in accordance with thus'; ='*l kk* of the OT.

[67] *mn m'mrh:* 'At his dictation', the form of the suffix being an Aramaism, as in *npšh* (1:16). Milik understood this expression to refer to a command given by Bar Cochba to a deputy; but Y. Yadin (*IEJ* 12 [1962] 253–4), on the basis of similar texts in newer documents, has shown that the concluding formula records the name of the town clerk who acted as scribe.

[68] It may also refer to Dt 15:1 ff., which ordains that every seventh year a creditor's claims are to be remitted; *šmṭh,* the noun, is found explicitly in this connection. Cf. *Mur* 18:7.

[69] *Seder 'Olam Rabbah* 30 (ed. B. Ratner, 147); cf. Bab. Talmud, *'Arakhin*

after the Sabbath-year. Hence, the year itself was A.D. 68–9, beginning with the month of Tišri.[70] The subsequent Sabbath-years fell on 75–6, 82–3, 89–90, 96–7, 103–4, 110–11, 117–18, 124–5, 131–2.[71] The year 132–3 was, then, the first year of the new cycle and 133–4 its second year. Therefore, the document was written at the beginning of February of the year 134. This date is indicated as corresponding with the second year of the 'Redemption of Israel'. We have unfortunately no certitude as to what month was used as the beginning of the year in this reckoning. Milik has suggested Tišri.[72] In that case, there would

11b (ed. Soncino Press, 33, 65); *Ta'anith* 29a (ed. Goldschmidt, 3, 520). Milik (DJD 2, 125) says that Josephus mentions this year as a Sabbath year, but gives no references.

[70] Mishnah, *Roš haššanah* 1, 1; 'There are four "New Year" days: on the 1st of Nisan is the New Year for kings and feasts; on the 1st of Elul is the New Year for the Tithe of Cattle . . .; on the 1st of Tishri is the New Year for [the reckoning of] the years [of foreign kings], of the Years of Release and Jubilee years, for the planting [of trees] and for vegetables; and the 1st of Shebat is the New Year for [fruit-] trees . . .' (tr. H. Danby, *The Mishnah* [London: Oxford, 1954] 188). Josephus (*Ant.* 1, #81) also mentions an autumn New Year for 'selling, buying and other ordinary affairs' (i.e. the making and dating of contracts). Cf. J. Jeremias, *ZNW* 27 (1928) 98.

[71] Milik (DJD 2, 125) says: 'L'année sabbatique la plus proche de la fin de la Révolte, 135 ap J.-C. (date assurée par les sources romaines), est donc 130/1 et la deuxième année du cycle suivant correspond à 132/3.'–The same miscalculation has been noted by S. Zeitlin, 'The Fiction of the Bar Kokba Letters', *JQR* 51 (1960–61) 265–74, esp. 267. See also M. R. Lehmann, *RQ* 4 (1963–64) 56 for further arguments that corroborate my dating. Cf. also L. Kadman, *The Coins of Aelia Capitolina* (Corpus Nummorum Palaestinensium 1; Jerusalem: Universitas, 1956) 17, who shows that a Bar Cochba coin overstruck on a coin from Gaza with the double date of the third year of the visit of Hadrian and the 192nd year of the Era of Gaza (=A.D. 131–2) gives this year as the *terminus post quem* for the outbreak of the revolt. See further E. Koffmahn, 'Zur Datierung der aramäisch/hebräischen Verkunden von Murabba'at', *WZKM* 59-60 (1963-64) 119-36.

[72] Milik is, however, aware of a complication here, when he writes,' On se rappellera cependant que le Nouvel An d'automne ne valait que pour la datation des contrats. Il reste à étudier si cette ère telle qu'elle est attestée par les monnaies ne doit pas plutôt commencer au 1er Nisan, et s'il s'agit du 1er Nisan de 131 ou de 132' (DJD 2, 67); cf. *BTS* 33 (1960) 16. The year is

be a perfect agreement of the beginning of the Sabbatical cycle with that of the new era of the Redemption of Israel. In such a case, the revolt began on, or at least was officially reckoned from, 1 Tišri A.D. 132. This reckoning, however, does not agree with that proposed by Milik, viz. 1 Tišri A.D. 131, for he maintains that we must correct the normally accepted date. I have, however, used the same presuppositions as he has in my reckoning, and it seems to me that his calculation is off by one year. Reckoning the Sabbath-years from 68–9 one does not arrive at 130–1.

Rabbinical tradition has preserved the notice that Bar Cochba's revolt lasted for three and a half years (*mlkwt bn kwzyb' šlš šnym wmḥṣh*).[73] This has often been suspected, because the same tradition ascribes three and a half years to Vespasian's and Titus' siege of Jerusalem, and also because it is reminiscent of the apocalyptic passages in Dn 7:25 and 9:27, which are thought to have been operative in the creation of this tradition. However, one of the new texts from Murabba'ât is dated in the 'third year of the freedom of Jerusalem' (*Mur* 25 i 1) and two Aramaic contracts from the cave in the Wâdi Seiyâl are reported to be dated in the 'third year of the liberation of Israel' (see above). Finally, and best of all, there is *Mur* 30:8, which contains the date the '21st of Tišri of the fourth year of the Redemption of Israel'. This puts an end to a puzzling problem about the duration of the revolt as posed by the coins of the period. Coins had been found dated *šnt 'ḥt lg'lt yśr'l* ('the first year of the Redemption of Israel') or *š b lḥr yśr'l* ('the second year of the Freedom of Israel').[74] But none were dated after that

---

certainly A.D. 132, but no evidence so far has settled the month, Nisan or Tišri.

[73] *Seder 'Olam Rabbah* 30 (ed. B. Ratner, 146); cf. Jerome, *Comm. in Danielem* 9; *PL* 25, 577–8. The Midrash, *Echa Rabbah* 2, 2, 4 (ed. S. Buber, 101), attributes three and a half years to the siege of Beth-Ter alone; this is impossible.

[74] A. Reifenberg, *Ancient Jewish Coins*², #189, 197; see also p. 35.

year. Reifenberg's solution was to maintain that those which simply bore *lḥrwt yrwšlm* without a date were minted in the third year of the revolt, but after Jerusalem had again fallen into the hands of the Romans. It is now certain that the revolt lasted into the beginning of the fourth year at least, and so the Rabbinical tradition about three and a half years is not far off.

However, according to our calculation the 21st of Tišri of the fourth year of the Redemption of Israel would equal October A.D. 135 (according to Milik it is the year 134). Eusebius (*Eccl. Hist.* 4, 6, 3) mentions that the war 'reached its height in the eighteenth year of the reign of Hadrian in Beththera, which was a strong citadel not very far from Jerusalem; the siege lasted a long time before the rebels were driven to final destruction by famine and thirst'. The eighteenth regnal year of Hadrian is normally reckoned as 11 August 134–5.[75] If our reckoning of the beginning of the era of the 'Redemption of Israel' is correct, and *Mur* 30 is to be dated to the 21st of Tišri A.D. 135, then Eusebius' statement just quoted must be taken more seriously and exactly than it normally is. For it is usual to regard it as meaning that the revolt came to an end in Hadrian's eighteenth year.[76] However, what Eusebius actually says is that the war came to a head or a climax in Hadrian's eighteenth year (*akmasantos de tou polemou etous oktōkaidekatou tēs hēgemonias kata Bēththēra . . . tēs te exōthen poliorkias chroniou genomenēs*) and that the siege lasted a long time. The Armenian text of Eusebius' *Chronicon*, moreover, lists that the Jewish war came to an end in Hadrian's *nineteenth* year.[77]

Further corroboration of this is derived from another source. As a result of the final defeat of the Jewish rebels and the con-

[75] See *Vita Hadriani* 4, 7, where it is recorded that Hadrian's regnal year is to be reckoned from 11 August.

[76] So E. Schürer, *GJV* 1, 695 (Engl. tr. 310) and many others.

[77] Karst's German translation for the 19th year (GCS 20, 221): 'Der jüdische Krieg, der im Palästinerlande war, endigte, indem übel hergenommen die Juden kaum der Vernichtung entgingen.' Cf. H. Strathmann, *PJB* 23 (1927) 100, 111 n. 2.

clusion of the 'Jewish war' Hadrian was acclaimed *imperator* for the second time. For a long time the title *Imp. II* was not found with certainty in any inscription before A.D. 136. But it is now known that the second acclamation occurred toward the end of Hadrian's nineteenth *tribunicia potestas.*[78] The twentieth began on 10 December A.D. 135, and the earliest occurrence of *Imp. II* is thus dated before that, between April and December 135. But if the revolt had already begun its fourth year by the 21st of Tišri (=October) 135, it is hardly likely that Hadrian's troops had as yet put an end to it. So his second acclamation as *imperator* must have occurred between October and 10 December A.D. 135. This still leaves open the question whether the year is to be reckoned from 1 Nisan of 1 Tišri. But it confirms the data advanced above for the termination of the revolt in the year A.D. 135.

Rabbinical tradition has, however, recorded that Beth-Ter

[78] The evidence is complicated. Several inscriptions are known from the year A.D. 134–5 without any mention of Hadrian's second acclamation. The latest of these are *CIL* 3, #XXXV (dated 15 Sept. 134; cf. *CIL* 16, #79); *CIL* 16, #82 (dated 14 Apr. 135). Earlier ones of the same year are: *CIL* 3, #XXXIV; 6, #973; 9, #4359; 10, #7855. On the other hand, it is clearly found in several inscriptions dated to the *trib. pot.* XX (i.e. after 10 December 135): *CIL* 6, #976, 975; *Papyri Osloenses* (ed. S. Eitrem and L. Amundsen) 3, #78 (dated before 31 May 136); R. Cagnat, *Inscriptiones graecae ad res romanas pertinentes*, 3, #896; and probably also in *CIL* 14, #4235 (where [*trib. pot. X*]*X* is restored and the date is 14, 19, 24 or 29 Dec. 135). This would give a date between April and 10 December 135. However, the second acclamation occurs in an inscription which is dated in the *trib. pot. XVIII*, hence before 10 December 135. See *CIG* 12 *Suppl.* (1939), #239; W. Peek, *Archaiologikē Ephēmeris* 1931, 113, #9; C. Seltman, 'Appendix', *Hesperia* 17 (1958) 85; F. M. Heichelheim, 'New Light on the End of Bar Kokba's War', *JQR* 34 (1943–44) 61–3. It may also occur in an undated fragmentary inscription whose restoration is not certain (*CIL* 2, #478); see also *CIL* 6, #974. Since the date of the '21st of Tišri of the fourth year of the Redemption of Israel' is found in *Mur* 30:8, the interval in which the second acclamation took place thus becomes October to 10 December 135. However, it should be noted that there are a few inscriptions of the year 136 which do not mention *Imp. II* (*CIL* 14, #2088; 3, #749), and that S. Perowne (*Hadrian*, 165) reckons the fall of Beth-Ter in A.D. 136. Cf. B. W. Henderson, *Life and Principate*, 218, n. 4.

fell on the 9th of Ab (July). But this date probably represents a conflation of the celebration of three fast-days rather than the recollection of an actual historical date: one fast-day commemorated the three great Jewish defeats. As the Mishnah puts it, 'Five things befell our fathers on the 17th of Tammuz and five on the 9th of Ab. . . . On the 9th of Ab it was decreed against our fathers that they should not enter into the Land [of Israel; Nm 14:29 ff.], and the Temple was destroyed the first and the second time, and Beth-Tor [=Beth-Ter] was captured and the City was ploughed up.'[79]

THE PERIOD OF THE REVOLT ITSELF

The information about the course of the revolt is meagre indeed. From what there is it seems that Jerusalem was wrested once again from the control of the Romans. This is certainly implied in the coins which were minted with the inscription *lḥrwt yrwšlm*, 'Of the Liberation of Jerusalem'. It is not improbable that the cult of Yahweh on the site of the old temple was resumed, and that this was commemorated by the coins struck with the title *'l'zr hkwhn*, 'Eleazar, the Priest'. That an attempt was made by the Jews to rebuild the temple itself at this time would not surprise us, although there is no definite information regarding this point.[80]

[79] *Ta'anith* 4, 6 (tr. H. Danby, 200). Josephus (*JW* 6, #250) also knows of the tradition which assigns the double destruction of Jerusalem to the same day of the month: 'But now in the revolution of the years had arrived the fated day, the tenth of the month Lous, the day on which of old it had been burnt by the king of Babylon.' H. St J. Thackeray's comment: 'This is in accordance with Jer. lii. 12 f., where the burning of the temple by Nebuzaradan, captain of Nebuchadrezzar's guard, is stated to have occurred on the 10th day of the 5th month (Heb. Ab=Lous in the Syrian calendar). In 2 Kings xxv. 8, on the other hand, the day is given as the 7th of Ab; while, in Jewish tradition, the anniversary of the double burning has always been kept on the 9th Ab. A fictitious symmetry between corresponding events in the two sieges has probably been at work' (Loeb Classical Library, 3, 448–9).

[80] See S. Yeivin, *Milḥemet Bar Kôkbâ*, 78 f. Possibly the obscure reference in the *Epistle of Barnabas* (16, 1–7) should be considered in this connection; see note 34 above and H. Bietenhard, *Jud* 4 (1948) 95 ff.

Did Bar Cochba attempt to reinforce Jerusalem at this time? The archaeologists who have studied the problem of the 'Third Wall' of Jerusalem of which Josephus speaks (*JW* 5, #147) have not always been of one mind regarding it. The line of an ancient wall which has been traced roughly from the old Russian colony, past the front of the American Consulate, to the American School of Oriental Research, was regarded by E. Robinson and more recently by E. L. Sukenik and L. A. Mayer as the third north wall of the city of which Josephus speaks.[81] However, H. Vincent maintained still more recently that the Third Wall built in the time of Herod Agrippa I coincided roughly with the line of the present-day north wall of the Old City. Vincent's view has been supported by British excavations at the Damascus Gate.[82] For him the ancient wall which lies considerably to the north of it is nothing more than remnants of the rampart set up as an outer defence of the city under Bar Cochba. It is the 'wall of Bar Cochba'. But W. F. Albright is inclined to follow the view of Sukenik and Mayer. This is a knotty problem in which the experts do not agree themselves; it must await further excavation and investigation for a solution. But it deserves mention here for the possible connection it may have with the Second Revolt.

It is difficult to understand how Dio Cassius (*Rom. Hist.* 69, 13, 1) could write, 'At first the Romans took no account of

[81] *The Third Wall of Jerusalem: An Account of Excavations* (Jerusalem: Hebrew University Press, 1930). Albright, *AP* 158, favours this view. He reaffirms it in *BASOR* 183 (1966) 26, n. 21. Cf. W. Ross, 'The Four North Walls of Jerusalem', *PEQ* 1942, 69–81.

[82] H. Vincent and M.-A. Stève, *Jérusalem de l'Ancien Testament: Recherches d'archéologie et d'histoire* (Paris: Gabalda, 1954) vol. 1, 146–74. For more recent discussions of this problem, see K. M. Kenyon, 'Excavations in Jerusalem, 1965', *PEQ* 98 (1966) 73–88; *Jerusalem: Excavating 3000 Years of History* (New York: McGraw-Hill, 1967) 162 and plate 86; E. W. Hamrick, 'New Excavations at Sukenik's Third Wall', *BASOR* 183 (1966) 19–26; 'Further Notes on the "Third Wall"', *BASOR* 192 (1968) 21–5; R. P. S. Hubbard, 'The Topography of Ancient Jerusalem', *PEQ* 98 (1966) 130–54; M. Avi-Yonah, 'The Third and Second Walls of Jerusalem', *IEJ* 18 (1968) 98–125.

them [the Jewish insurgents]. Soon, however, all Judaea had been stirred up, and the Jews everywhere were showing signs of disturbance, were gathering together, and giving evidence of great hostility to the Romans, partly by secret and partly by overt acts.' This statement, however, is a brief summary of the whole revolt, and perhaps the liberation of Jerusalem itself was at first regarded as a minor, local skirmish by the Romans. Yet it was a local skirmish which apparently spread rapidly to all parts of Judaea.

Once Jerusalem had been liberated and Israel redeemed, the Prince of Israel had to organize the land for the continuation of the revolt. The administrative machinery and the division of the land into toparchies which had been set up by the Romans were apparently retained by Bar Cochba. He controlled the land of Judaea, especially the fertile Shephelah, and from the new documents we learn additional names of villages and districts under his control. In addition to Jerusalem, which name is probably to be read in *Mur* 29:9, 11; 30:8 (see DJD 2, 205), the following places came under his administration directly or indirectly: Herodium (*Mur* 24 B4, C4, E3, 14), Teqoa' (*Mur* 47: 6; *Hev* 1 and 14), 'En-gedi (*Mur* 46:4; *Hev* 12), Qiryat 'Arabayah (*Hev* 15), 'Ir-Naḥaš (*Mur* 24 B8, C7–8, E6–7), Beth Mašiko (*Mur* 42:1, 4), *M^{e}ṣad Ḥ^{a}sîdîn* (identified by Milik with Khirbet Qumran, *Mur* 45:6) and K^{e}par Biš, K^{e}par Šaḥalîm, K^{e}par Dikrîn (the three villages mentioned in Rabbinical writings as destroyed by the Romans [*Echa Rabbah* 53b; *Ta'anith* 4, 69a; *Gittin* 4, 6, 3]). Y. Yadin conjectures that Bar Cochba also controlled Masada at this time.[83] To this list must be added the place of his last stand, Beth-Ter (Eusebius, *Eccl. Hist.* 4, 6, 3).

Herodium is mentioned as the centre of a toparchy in *Mur* 115:2, 21, a Greek document of remarriage dated A.D. 124. In the time of Bar Cochba it probably continued to be the centre of the toparchy, for we learn that a camp was situated there

[83] *BIES* 25 (1961) 63. But cf. his book, *Masada: Herod's Fortress and the Zealots' Last Stand* (London: Weidenfeld and Nicolson, 1966) 207.

(*Mur* 24, E3). Indeed, Milik has suggested on the basis of the phrase, *šmʿwn bn kwsbʾ nsyʾ yśrʾl bmḥnh šywšb bhrwdys*, that Bar Cochba as the warlike Messiah had made his headquarters at Herodium, and that it was from there that he withdrew to Beth-Ter as the Romans closed in about him. As I indicated in note 57, the Hebrew need not be so interpreted. Moreover, new information from the Wâdi Ḫabra texts suggests that it is quite unlikely that his headquarters were there. In *Hev* 12, as Y. Yadin has pointed out,[84] Bar Cochba writes to two of his officers at ʿEn-gedi:

mšmʿwn br kwsbʾ lʾnšy ʿyngdy	From Simon bar Kosibaʾ to the men of ʿEn-gedi,
lmsblʾ [w]lyhw[n]tn b[r] bʿ̱yn šlwm bṭwb	to Masabbalaʾ [and] to Yehonatan ba[r] Baʿyan, greetings! In ease
ʾtn ywšbyn ʾklyn wš[w]tyn mn nksy byt	you are living, eating and dr[i]nking off the goods of the house
yśrʾl wlʾ dʾgyn lʾḥykn lkwl dbr	of Israel, and you care not a whit for your brothers. . . .

This rebuke is addressed to Masabbalah and Yehonatan at ʿEn-gedi. This fact must be coupled with a bit of information found in another papyrus, *Hev* 15, which reads as follows:

šmʿwn lyhwdh br mnšh lqryt ʿrbyh šlḥt lk try ḥmryn dy tšlḥ
ʿmhn (*tr!*) *gbryn lwt yhwntn br bʿyn wlwt msblh dy yʿmrn*
wyšlḥn lmḥnyh lwtk llbyn wʾtrgyn wʾt šlḥ ʾḥrnyn mlwtk
wymṭwn lk hdsyn wʿrbyn wtqn ythn wšlḥ ythn lmḥnyh
. . . . . *hwʾ šlm*

Simon to Yehudah bar Menasseh at Qiryat ʿArabayah. I have sent to you two asses, with which you will send

[84] *Hāʾāreṣ* (10 March 1961) 10; see also *BIES* 25 (1961) *passim*. See now E. M. Laperrousaz, 'L'Hérodium, quartier général de Bar Kokhba?', *Syria* 41 (1964) 347–58.

2. (two?) men to Yehonatan bar Ba'yan and to Masabbalah that they may gather and

3. send to the camp, toward you, palm-branches and citrons. And you send other men from your own quarters

4. and let them bring to you myrtle and willow twigs. Prepare them and send them to the camp.

5. . . . Farewell.

From this letter it is obvious that Bar Cochba is sending the two asses to 'Engedi via Qiryat 'Arabayah. There is no spot between Herodium and 'En-gedi which can be identified with this name. Yadin, following Mazar, had identified Qiryat 'Arabayah with *Birat 'Areva' d^{e}Bêt-leḥem*, mentioned in the Midrashim in connection with the birthplace of the Messiah, the modern village of 'Arṭas, near the pools of Solomon. If this identification is correct, the route which the asses are to take to go to 'En-gedi leads in the opposite direction. In another text (*Hev* 1) Bar Cochba orders the same Masabbalah and Yehonatan bar Ba'yah (*sic*) to punish the men of Teqoa' (*kwl gbr tqw'y*), who were spending time repairing their houses. Teqoa' apparently pertained to the jurisdiction of the officers stationed at 'En-gedi. Consequently, it would be strange, if Bar Cochba's own headquarters were at Herodium, that he would give such orders to the officers of 'En-gedi, given the relative proximity of Teqoa' to Herodium itself. It is better, then, to regard Herodium merely as one of the camps under Bar Cochba's control, the administrative centre of a toparchy as in the days of Roman domination. His headquarters are better sought either in Jerusalem or in Beth-Ter. Sending the letter to Yehudah bar Menasseh from one of these spots with the instruction that he should send men on to 'En-gedi is certainly more logical. The note was probably delivered to Yehonatan and Masabbalah, who kept it in their archives and carried it with the other missives of their chief to the cave in the Wâdi Ḫabra, when they fled there before the advancing Roman soldiers.

'En-gedi thus emerges as a source of supplies for the rebel chief. The oasis there was cut off from the rest of Judaea by the desert and was rich in produce. There was also a small port there for commercial traffic by boat on the Dead Sea. From the rebuke addressed by Bar Cochba to Yehonatan and Masabbalah it would appear that it was something of a sinecure for them, when their lot was compared to that of their 'brothers'.

Besides the military, priestly and intellectual leaders of the period of the Second Revolt, Simon ben Kosibah, Eleazar (ben Azariah?), and the Rabbi Aqiba, we now know of many other Jews who were engaged in the uprising, thanks to the new documents. Their names are preserved on the skin and papyrus documents which they carried with them to the caves of refuge. There is no need to retail them all here, but the more important ones are the names of the officers under Bar Cochba. In addition to Yehonatan bar Ba'yah (or Ba'yan) and Masabbalah bar Šim'ôn[85] there were Yešua' ben Galgulah, who is addressed as *rwš hmḥnyh* (*Mur* 42, 2), and, if Y. Yadin's conjecture is correct,[86] Šim'ôn bar Mattatyah, who is stationed at Masada. Just where Yešua' ben Galgulah had his camp is not certain. The administrators (*hprnsyn*) of the village of Beth-Mašiko address him as *rwš hmḥnyh*, when they write explaining the sale of a cow

[85] In a Greek letter (*Hev* 3) they are addressed as *Iōnathē kai Masabala.* Y. Yadin, *BIES* 25 (1961) 57, suggests the vocalization *Masabbalah* on the basis of Josephus (*JW* 5, #532), which has *masbalos* and *masambalos*. The text of *Hev* 3 has been published by B. Lifshitz, *Aegyptus* 42 (1962) 240–8. It was sent by a certain *Soumaios*, whom the editor takes to be Simon ben Kosibah himself, to *Iōnathē Baianou kai Masabala*. As in the Aramaic letter (*Hev* 15) quoted above, he instructs them to send *s*[*te*]*leou*[*s*] *kai kitria*, 'twigs(?) and citrons' for the 'Citron-celebration of the Jews' (⟨*e*⟩*is* [*k*]*itreiabolēn Ioudaiōn*), i.e., for Succoth or Tabernacles. The most interesting feature in it, however, if the *Soumaios* is really Bar Cochba, is his reason for writing in Greek: 'No[w] (this) has been written in Greek because the [de]sire has not be[en] found to w[ri]te in "Hebrew"' (*egraphē d*[*e*] *helēnisti dia t*[*o ho*]*rman mē eurēth*[*ē*]*nai hebraesti g*[*ra*]*psasthai*). Either Bar Cochba, the Jewish leader of the Second Revolt, or someone very close to him, prefers to communicate with his lieutenants in Greek rather than in 'Hebrew' (=Aramaic?)! See further my article in *CBQ* 32 (1970) 513–15.

[86] *BIES* 25 (1961) 63, apropos of a Wâdi Seiyâl text not yet published; see VTSup 4 (1957) 21.

by an inhabitant of their village to a certain Joseph ben Aristion (*Mur* 42), but no indication is given where that camp is situated. However, two other letters are addressed to him by Bar Cochba himself.

Mur 43

mšmʿwn bn kwsbh lyšʿ	From Simon ben Kosibah
bn glglh wlʾnšy hkrk[87]	to Yešuaʿ ben Galgulah and to the men of the fort,
šlwm mʿyd ʾny ʿly t šmym	greetings! I call the heavens to witness against me that
yps[*d*] *mn hgllʾym šhṣlkm*	(if) any of the Galileans who are with you is mistreated,
kl ʾdm šʾny ntn t kblym	I shall put irons
brglkm kmh šʿst[*y*]	on your feet, as I have done
lbn ʿplwl	to ben ʿAphlul.
[*š*]*mʿwn b*[*n kwsbh*] *ʿl* [*npšh*][88]	Simon b[en Kosibah], for [himself].

[87] The reading of this word is doubtful. Milik at first read *wlʾnšy ḥbrk*, 'aux hommes de ta compagnie' (*RB* 60 [1953] 277), a reading which was accepted by F. M. Cross, Jr., *RB* 63 (1956) 47: 'La première lettre du mot est sûrement ḥeth'. This reading was judged 'graphically impossible' by H. L. Ginsberg, *BASOR* 131 (1953) 25, who read instead *wlʾnšy hkrk*, 'and to the men of the fort'. Milik now reads (DJD 2, 160) the first letter as a *he* and the second as a *beth*, and understands the word as a name of a village mentioned by Jerome as *Caphar Barucha* and by Epiphanius as *Kapar Baricha*, situated about 3 mi. east of Hebron. According to this latest suggestion of Milik, *Yešuaʿ* would be the commander of a camp at *K^{e}par ha-Baruk*. But since the construction is peculiar (with an article and without *k^{e}par*), and the reading is not at all certain, it seems preferable not to introduce a proper name here. So we retain Ginsberg's suggestion, *hkrk*, 'the fort'.

[88] This restoration, if correct, would mean that Bar Cochba himself has written the letter, and it would be a precious autograph. The phrase *ʿl npšh* is certainly found elsewhere in the new texts (normally in contracts, *Mur* 18:9; 19:26; 21:21, 23; 24 C 19, D 20; 27:6; 28:11, 12; 29 verso 3 [where it is parallel to the Greek *cheiri heautou*]; 36:6; but also in a letter, *Mur* 42: 10). However, Y. Yadin, *BIES* 25 (1961) 58; *IEJ* 11 (1961) 45; *BTS* 43 (1961) 16, suggests that since at least one Bar Cochba letter (*Hev* 8) was signed *šmʿwn br yhwdh* (a secretary?), it might also be the case here. Possibly we should read the *ʿl* [*mʾmrh*], as in *Mur* 24 C 20 (where Milik has written

The second letter (*Mur* 44) reads as follows:[89]

mšm'wn lyšw' bn glgwlh [	From Simon to Yešua' ben Galgulah [the head of the camp]
šlwm štšlḥ tbw ḥmšt[	greetings! You should send and bring five [
kwryn ḥ[*ṭy*]*n* [ ].*š lbyty* [	kors of wheat [ ] . . . to my house [
'ṣlk bd't wttqn lhn [	near you with knowledge (?); and you should prepare for them [
mqwm pnwy yhw bw 'ṣlk [	a free (?) place. Let them be in it near you [observe]
t šbt ḥzw 'm yḥpṣw lbw [	the Sabbath. See (to it) that they be pleased at heart [
whtḥzq wḥzq t mqwm [	Take courage and fortify [that] place [
hw' šlwm wpqdty t my [	Farewell! And I have ordered the . . . [
šytn lk tḥṭyn šlh 'ḥr [	who will give you his wheat, other [
hšbt yṭlwn	the Sabbath they will take up

[*mn*] but admits in the note that '*l* is also possible).

[89] My translation is different from that of Milik, who believes that the text of this letter is intact. However, the grammatical difficulties which his translation encounters (e.g., the continual shift in person and number) make it unlikely that his interpretation is correct. There is not one line which joins necessarily with the beginning of the next, and the photo suggests that possibly we do not have the full width of the original papyrus letter. Hence I have tried to translate the lines only in the most obvious way and leave the rest blank except for line 1, where the restored title is derived from *Mur* 42:2. Milik's translation of *tšbt* (line 6) as 'pendant le sabbat' is almost certainly wrong; the sign of the accusative *t* suggests that some verb is missing in the preceding line.

In general, the new texts from the caves of Murabba'ât, Ḫabra, and Seiyâl reveal Bar Cochba as an administrator, giving orders to subordinates and settling problems which have arisen in the land under his control. Like the Roman Emperor before him, he is the proprietor of the land. Farms are rented out in his name and a yearly rent has to be paid in kind into his granaries.[90] This appears from the *diastrōmata* in *Mur* 24, where the land is rented from Simon the Prince of Israel (*mšm'wn nsy' yśr'l,* E 7). The deputy, Hillel ben Garis, acts as an administrator of the lands of *'Ir-Naḥaš* on his command ([*mn/'l*] *m'mrh,* C 20). The Wâdi Ḫabra texts are reported to contain similar details about the leasing of government-owned lands to a four-man syndicate which, in turn, subleased the plots among themselves. Amid the details which concern him Bar Cochba shows himself respecting the traditional Jewish feasts. In *Mur* 44 he is apparently ordering Yešua' ben Galgulah to provide hospitality for a caravan transporting grain over the Sabbath. He orders that Eleazar bar Ḥittah be sent to him 'immediately before the Sabbath' (*Hev* 8). He provides that the palm-branches and citrons be brought for the celebration of the feast of Succoth in one of the camps, and orders Yehuda bar Menasseh to make similar provision where he is (*Hev* 15). In other letters he orders the arrest of a certain Yešua' bar Tadmorayah (whose sword must be taken from him), confiscates wheat, seizes property, and even gives instructions about the harvesting of ripe and unripe grain. It is an abundance of such details which come to light in the new documents, which also reveal that the simple people in Palestine were leading fairly normal lives despite the revolt. They still exchanged property, married, and made their contracts of various sorts.

The list of the few names of villages which were controlled by Bar Cochba given above scarcely exhausts the places which

[90] See further S. Appelbaum, 'The Agrarian Question and the Revolt of Bar Kokhba', *E. L. Sukenik Memorial Volume* (Eretz-Israel 8; Jerusalem: Israel Exploration Society, 1967) 283–7 (in modern Hebrew with an English summary, p. 77*).

were under his authority. Dio Cassius (*Rom. Hist.* 69, 14, 1) mentions that the Romans finally captured 'fifty of their most important outposts and nine hundred and eighty-five of their most famous villages were razed to the ground'. Where Dio Cassius got such figures, we do not know, but they do give some indication of the extent of the control over the land which Bar Cochba must have had.

All of these details confirm the data given in Dio Cassius about the mode of warfare which was practised by the rebels. 'They did not dare try conclusions with the Romans in the open field, but they occupied the advantageous positions in the country and strengthened them with mines and walls, in order that they might have places of refuge whenever they should be hard pressed, and might meet together unobserved under ground.'[91] It was probably a guerrilla-type warfare, well organized on a village and toparchy basis, and resembling that of the Maccabees, especially in the early days of their struggle.

At first sight it might seem that the caves in the Wâdies Murabba'ât, Seiyâl and Ḫabra were actually the outposts (*phrouria*), of which Dio Cassius speaks (*Rom. Hist.* 69, 14, 1). The evidence found in them, however, indicates rather that they were used as places of refuge, like the *anaphygai* also mentioned by him (69, 12, 3). For it appears that Yešua' ben Galgulah fled from his camp to the cave in the Wâdi Murabba'ât, taking with him various household objects, family archives, the letters from his chief, Bar Cochba, and perhaps also his family.[92] Similarly, Yehonatan and Masabbalah fled from their camp at 'En-gedi to the cave in the Wâdi Ḫabra with a whole collection of letters from their chief.

Among the documents taken by the refugees to the caves were biblical scrolls and texts. From the Murabba'ât caves have come fragments of Gn, Ex, Nm (*Mur* 1), Dt (*Mur* 2), Is (*Mur* 3) and the large fragmentary scroll of the Minor Prophets (*Mur*

[91] *Rom. Hist.* 69, 12, 3.

[92] For the artifacts found in the Murabba'ât caves, see DJD 2, 29–48.

88). The latter was found in a hole near the caves, in which a refugee had been buried. Milik mentions that this is the oldest concrete example of a tomb-genizah, of which the Rabbinical writers speak.[93] The text of this scroll is fragmentary in many places, but a substantial portion of ten of the twelve books is preserved (Jl 2:20, 26–4:16; Am 1:5–2:1; 7:3–8:7; 8:11–9:15; Ob 1–21; Jon 1:1–4:11; Mi 1:1–7:20; Na 1:1–3:19; Hab 1:1–2:11; 2:18–3:19; Zeph 1:1; 1:11–3:6; 3:8–20; Hag 1:1–2:10; 2:12–23; Zech 1:1–4). Further, there is a phylactery (*Mur* 4), and possibly a Mezuzah (*Mur* 5). We have mentioned the biblical texts from the other areas earlier in our discussion. In all these biblical documents the remarkable aspect is the close agreement of their text with the *textus receptus* of later centuries. Milik lists for the text of the Minor Prophets (*Mur* 88) only 59 variants, the majority of which are simply cases of *scriptio plena* for *defectiva* or vice versa (about 30) and additions written above the line possibly by the copyist himself (about 8). Many of the others are quite insignificant (prepositional exchanges like *beth* for *kaph*, *'el* for *'al*, etc.).[94] When these texts are compared with the biblical texts from the Qumran caves, where a number of texts manifest different recensions, it looks very much as though we have in the Murabba'ât scrolls the stabilization of the text effected by the academy at Jamnia. Indeed, they apparently determined not only what books belonged to the Palestinian canon of the OT, but also what recension was to be copied in the future, with what spelling and in what script. The script of the Murabba'ât biblical texts bears a very strong resemblance to the script employed by the scribes in the medieval manuscripts. For this reason the biblical texts from the Bar Cochba period are important for the data which they supply for the study of the transmission of the OT.

In the new material which has been published so far there are

[93] DJD 2, 181; see Bab. Talmud, *Megillah*, fol. 26b.

[94] See DJD 2, 183–4, 205. Milik had previously pointed out that the only significant variant in the whole scroll was Hab 3:10: *zrmw mym 'bwt* (as in Ps 77:18) instead of the MT *zrm mym 'br* (VTSup 4 [1957] 20).

strikingly few references to the enemy Romans. The letter of the administrators of Bet-Mašiko to Yešua' ben Galgulah explains that they do not come up with Joseph ben Aristion, who has bought the cow, to give evidence of the purchase, because 'the Gentiles are drawing near to us' (*hgyym qrbym 'lnw*), *Mur* 42:5. Milik has reported that a short letter from the Wâdi Seiyâl addressed to Bar Cochba by Šim'ôn ben Mattatyah mentions *hg'ym* who have moved their camp (*qṣryhm*).[95] But the only explicit reference to the Romans found so far is in *Hev* 11, an Aramaic letter which mentions *rhwmyh* (i.e., *Rhômāyēh*).[96] Perhaps the texts found this year will supply further information about the Romans, who were systematically advancing through the country and wiping out the pockets of resistance, thus driving the refugees to the caves.

THE END OF THE REVOLT AND THE LAST STAND AT BETH-TER

Just where the emperor Hadrian was all during the Second Revolt is not clear. After leaving Palestine and Syria in A.D. 131, he went to Pontus and the Black Sea area and from there to Athens for the winter. On 5 May A.D. 134 he was once again in Rome.[97] By this time the revolt was well under way. He must have returned to Judaea afterwards, to judge by a remark of Dio Cassius about the outcome of the war, which I shall quote later.

The initial lack of concern on the part of the Romans about the Jewish uprising stemmed from the attitude of the Roman governor of Judaea, a certain Tineius Rufus (Eusebius, *Eccl. Hist.* 4, 6, 1). He undoubtedly underestimated the movement and soon it grew to proportions which were beyond his control. Dio Cassius (*Rom. Hist.* 69, 13, 1) mentions that 'all Judaea had been stirred up'. This is to be understood not in the restricted

[95] *Ibid.*, 21.

[96] *BIES* 25 (1961) 60; *IEJ* 11 (1961) 45. On p. 56 Yadin mentions that *hgw'yn* also occurs in one of his Hebrew documents.

[97] *CIG* 3, 5906, which is dated *pro g' Nōnōn Maiōn apo Rōmēs*; the year is given as *dēmarchikēs exousias to iē'*, *hypatos to g'*. See F.-M. Abel, *Histoire*, 2, 93.

sense of Judaea (as opposed to Samaria and Galilee), but in the sense of the Roman province, which included those areas as well. We have already seen the solicitude of Bar Cochba for the Galileans, who apparently had joined his ranks. Dio Cassius (*ibid.*) further adds that 'many outside nations, too, were joining them through eagerness for gain'. The result was that the rebels were getting the better of the Roman garrisons and aid had to be given to the governor. Leaving his own province in the charge of Caius Severus, the legate of the *Legio IV Scythica*, Publicius Marcellus, the governor of Syria, came to the aid of Tineius Rufus, as a Greek inscription attests,[98] probably with the *Legio III Gallica*. Eusebius (*Eccl. Hist.* 4, 6, 1) records that military aid was sent by the Emperor. E. Schürer[99] has made a catalogue of the Roman legions which took part in the Judaean war, using the various direct and indirect references to it found in inscriptions. The following groups of Roman soldiers were engaged at some time or other in putting down the rebellion: *Legio X Fretensis* and *Legio VI Ferrata* (both resident in Judaea),[100] *Legio III Cyrenaica* (brought in from the province of Arabia), *Legio III Gallica* (probably brought by the Governor of Syria), *Legio XXII Deiotariana* (brought in from Egypt), *cohors IV Lingonum*, *cohors I Thracum*; besides several detachments of *Legio I Italica*, *Legio V Macedonica*, *Legio X Gemina* and *Legio XI Claudia*.[101]

[98] *CIG* 3, 4033–4: *hēnika Poublikios Markellos dia tēn kinēsin tēn Ioudaikēn metebebēkei apo Syrias.*

[99] *GJV* 1, 687–9, n. 116 (Engl. tr. 303, n. 96). See further F.-M. Abel, *Histoire*, 2, 92.

[100] See B. Lifshitz, 'Sur la date du transfert de la legio VI Ferrata en Palestine', *Latomus* 19 (1960) 109–11. The transfer took place before the war began, possibly as early as A.D. 130.

[101] An epitaph of a Roman soldier, found at Beisân (ancient Scythopolis), shows clearly that the *Legio XI Claudia* was in Palestine at this time and engaged in operations in the north as well as at Beth-Ter. See M. Avi-Yonah, 'Greek and Latin Inscriptions from Jerusalem and Beisan', *QDAP* 8 (1939) 57–9. This inscription shows that in fact *Legio XI Claudia* was present during the Roman counter-offensive, and that the inscription at the spring in the village of Bittîr also dates from this period: CENTVR. VEXILL. LEG. V. MAC. ET. XI. CL (*CIL* 3/14, 155; cf. *ZDPV* 29 [1906]

Apparently the *classis syriaca* was also somehow involved in the war.

But this was not enough. Finally 'Hadrian sent against them his best generals. First of these was Julius Severus, who was dispatched from Britain, where he was governor,[102] against the Jews' (Dio Cassius, *Rom. Hist.* 69, 13, 2). Although Eusebius gives the impression that Tineius Rufus was always in charge of the operations against the Jewish rebels (*Eccl. Hist.* 4, 6, 1), it was actually Sextus Julius Severus who had the supreme command in the last period and who finally succeeded in putting an end to the rebellion.

Severus did not venture to attack his opponents in the open at any one point, in view of their numbers and their desperation; but by intercepting small groups, thanks to the number of his soldiers and his under-officers, and by depriving them of food and shutting them up, he was able, rather slowly, to be sure, but with comparatively little danger, to crush, exhaust and exterminate them. Very few of them in fact survived. Fifty of their most important outposts and nine hundred and eighty-five of their most famous villages were razed to the ground. Five hundred and eighty thousand men were slain in the various raids and battles, and the number of those that perished by famine, disease and fire was past finding out. Thus nearly the whole of Judaea was made desolate, a result of which the people had had forewarning before the war. For the tomb of Solomon, which the Jews regard as an object of veneration, fell to pieces of itself and collapsed, and many wolves and hyenas rushed howling into their cities' (Dio Cassius, *Rom. Hist.* 69, 13,3–14, 2 tr. E. Cary).

Not only the Roman sources mention the great number of Jews who perished in this war, but also the Rabbinical and

---

55, n. 1). See further J. Meyshan (Mestschanski), 'The Legion Which Reconquered Jerusalem in the War of Bar Kochba (A.D. 132–135)', *PEQ* 90 (1958) 19–25.

[102] This is confirmed by his *cursus honorum* given in a Latin inscription (*CIL* 3, 2830): *leg(ato) pr(o) pr(aetore) imp(eratoris) Traiani Hadriani Aug(usti) provinciae Daciae, co(n)s(uli) leg(ato) pr(o) pr(aetore) Moesiae inferioris, leg(ato) pr(o) pr(aetore) provinciae Britanniae, leg(ato) pr(o) pr(aetore) provinciae Iudeae, leg(ato) pr(o) pr(aetore) provinciae Suriae.*

Christian writings. The former abound in many legendary and imaginative details, but there can be little doubt about the correctness of the substantial account.[103] Eusebius reports (*Eccl. Hist.* 4, 6, 1): 'He [Rufus] destroyed in heaps thousands of men, women and children, and, under the law of war, enslaved their land.' The slow process of searching out the rebels, of starving them and of killing them off, recorded by Dio Cassius, is now confirmed by the discoveries in the caves of Murabba'ât, Seiyâl and Ḫabra, to which the Jews fled. The burial niche in the Wâdi Ḫabra cave, with its 'collection of baskets overflowing with skulls' and 'layer upon layer of large mats covering human bones',[104] gives eloquent testimony to the Roman mop-up operations. Whole families must have taken refuge in the caves at the advance of the Roman troops; there they died of hunger and thirst.[105] In the case of the Wâdi Ḫabra cave two Roman camps were built in a strategic position atop the cliffs of the gorge so as to keep watch on the opening of the cave, lest the refugees try to escape.[106]

To judge from the Rabbinical writings the greatest opposition to the Romans occurred in Judaea in the region called *har hammelek*, 'The Royal Mountain'.[107] The same sources relate that during the revolt R. Aqiba had preached that salvation

[103] Cf. E. Schürer, *GJV* 1, 694; Engl. tr. 311.

[104] *BA* 24 (1961) 39–40; cf. *IEJ* 4 (1954) 126–7; 5 (1955) 272–3.

[105] This is the conclusion too of the archaeologists who explored the various caves; see Y. Aharoni, *IEJ* 4 (1954) 127; 5 (1955) 272–3; Y. Yadin, *BIES* 25 (1961) 51; R. de Vaux, DJD 2, 48.

[106] 'These camps resemble those found around Masada. They are built with a wall of rough stones *ca.* 1 m. thick, except on the side which touches the cliff. The gates are protected by *claviculi* which, unlike those found in the camps around Masada, turn outwards. Inside the camps were traces of various square and round constructions. These camps seem to have had no other strategic or military purpose than to keep watch on the cave-mouths visible directly below them in the cliff side, at present very difficult of access' (*IEJ* 4 [1954] 126–7).

[107] See J. T. Milik (DJD 2, 126) for an attempt to identify the town and the region connected with this name in the Rabbinical literature. It is apparently the area about Eleutheropolis (Beth Gubrin).

would come to the Jews from Judah and Benjamin, while the other tribes would be the objects of divine rejection.[108] The great Rabbi's preaching fired them to an almost fanatical enthusiasm for wiping out the Romans. It will be remembered that Dio Cassius recorded the caution of the Roman general, Sextus Julius Severus, who was aware of the 'desperation' of the Jews (*Rom Hist.* 69, 13, 3). With craft they managed to annihilate a phalanx of the *Legio XXII Deiotariana.*[109] But in the end the *har hammelek* was devastated, Jerusalem fell to the Romans and the last stand was made at Beth-Ter.

Most of the sources are silent about the recapture of Jerusalem by the Romans, and consequently we do not know exactly when it occurred. Possibly it happened during the second year of the revolt or a little after it, and that is why no coins were issued in the third or the fourth year of the Liberation of Jerusalem. Neither Dio Cassius nor Eusebius mentions the Roman recapture of the town. However, a vague reference to it may be found in the contemporary writer, Appian, who lived both at Alexandria and at Rome in the time of Hadrian, and who wrote: 'Jerusalem, the greatest city, which Ptolemy I, king of Egypt, had destroyed [?], and when it was repopulated again Vespasian razed, and Hadrian again in my own day (did the same). . . .'[110] Was it at the fall of Jerusalem that Hadrian returned to the Near East? Both Appian and the Mishnah (*Ta'anith* 4, 6: the fall of Beth-Ter and the ploughing up of the

[108] See L. Ginzberg, *The Legends of the Jews* (Philadelphia: Jewish Publication Society of America, 1928) 6, 408.

[109] Julius Africanus ascribes it to the Pharisees who served the Romans poisoned wine. See A. von Harnack, 'Medizinisches aus der ältesten Kirchengeschichte', *TU* 8/4 (Leipzig: J. C. Hinrichs, 1892) 44; cf. J.-R. Viellefond, *Jules Africain: Fragments des Cestes* (Paris, 1932) 15.—Y. Yadin (*BA* 24 [1961] 42) suggests that the 19 metal vessels which were found in a basket in the Wâdi Ḫabra cave and which are clearly Roman objects were actually booty taken by Bar Cochba's fighters from the Romans and carried off with them to the refuge-cave. Cf. *BIES* 25 (1961) 52–3.

[110] *De bello syr.* 50 (=*Roman History* 11, 8, 50; ed. H. White, Loeb Classical Library, 2, 199).

City on the 9th of Ab) refer to a destruction of the city under Hadrian. This must refer to what had been built anew since the days of Titus and perhaps under Bar Cochba himself; but it was a destruction in view of the building of Aelia Capitolina.

According to Eusebius (*Eccl. Hist.* 4, 6, 3), the war reached its height at Beth-Ter, a strong citadel not very far from Jerusalem.[111] There the siege lasted a long time before the rebels were driven to final destruction by famine and thirst and 'the instigator of their madness paid the penalty he deserved'. Beth-Ter is identified today with *Khirbet el-Yehûd* ('the ruin of the Jews'), a site on a hill-top about 400 metres WNW of the modern village of *Bittîr*. It overlooks from the south the Wâdi el-Gharbi, through which the railroad makes its way from Jerusalem to Jaffa. The modern village of Bittîr has preserved the ancient name of the place where Bar Cochba made his last stand; it is situated some six and a half miles WSW of Jerusalem.

According to F.-M. Abel, the space within the roughly ellipse-shaped fortified enclosure, which crowns the summit of the hill and of which there are still some traces here and there, scarcely measures 300 × 150 metres.[112] Hadrian had apparently had a road built from Jerusalem to Eleutheropolis in A.D. 130, which made its way through the valley at the foot of the hill itself. The eighth milestone is found in the valley below the ruins and is dated to the year 130. In order to take the citadel, the Roman general had to lay siege to the area. Traces of the

[111] The spelling of the name of this place varies in the sources. The Greek MSS. of Eusebius have *Bēththēra*, *Biththēra*; Latin texts have *Bether* (Jerome, *In Zach.* 8, 9; *PL* 25, 1574), *Bethera*; Rabbinical sources also vary: *byttr*, *bytr*, *btr*. We have followed E. Schürer in regarding *byttr* as the most probably correct form. It is probably the same place as *Baithēr*, a town in Judah in the vicinity of Bethlehem, mentioned in Codex Alexandrinus at Jos 15:59. The word occurs in a phrase not found in the MT, and the Codex Vaticanus of the LXX reads *Thethēr*.—W. D. Carroll, 'Bittîr and its Archaeological Remains', *AASOR* 5 (1923–24) 78, tries unconvincingly to derive the form from *bêt-har* (*bêttar*), 'in view of the mountainous location of the place', and with reference to Ct 2:17.

[112] Abel, *Histoire*, 2, 94.

Roman *circumvallatio* are still visible today to the north and the west of the ruins. They permit one to reconstruct a wall of about 3800 metres, doubled in some places, and fitted with a watch-tower. The size of the *circumvallatio* and its position suggest a rather lengthy siege, thus confirming the suggestion made by Eusebius. Detachments of the *Legio V Macedonica* and the *Legio XI Claudia* left their names on the road to the spring; they seem to have been at least part of the Roman troops which were engaged in this final stage of the war.[113]

There is little information about the siege itself and the conquest of Beth-Ter in the sources. Of all the Rabbinical legends related to this struggle few are regarded as trustworthy by modern historians. E. Schürer and F.-M. Abel retain only one as having some credibility: that before Beth-Ter fell, Bar Cochba himself killed his uncle, the Rabbi Eleazar of Modin, a pious old man who apparently wanted to come to terms with the Romans.[114] There is no reason to doubt the substantial historicity of the accounts about the massacre of the Jews when the citadel was finally taken.

Dio Cassius (*Rom. Hist.* 69, 14, 3) records at the end of his account: 'Many Romans, moreover, perished in this war. Therefore Hadrian in writing to the senate did not employ the opening phrase commonly affected by the emperors, "If you and your children are in health, it is well; I and the legions are in health."' The losses on both sides were apparently heavy, and for that reason the Emperor despite the successful outcome of the war for Rome did not feel that he could send back the usual report to the senate in Rome. This notice found in Dio Cassius suggests, therefore, that in the final stages of the war

[113] On Beth-Ter see A. Alt, 'Die Ausflüge', *PJB* 23 (1927) 9–29 (12–15: 'Reste der römischen Zirkumvallation um Beth-Ter'); A. Schulten, 'Anhang: Beth-Ter', *ZDPV* 56 (1933) 180–4; W. D. Carroll, *AASOR* 5 (1924) 77–103; A. Dowling, 'Interesting Coins of Pella and Bittîr', *PEFQS* 38 (1907) 295–7; H. Strathmann, *PJB* 23 (1927) 114–18; E. Zickermann, 'Chirbet el-jehud (bettir)', *ZDPV* 29 (1906) 51–72.

[114] Jer. Talmud, *Ta'anith* 4, 68d–69a; Midrash, *Echa Rabbah* 2, 2, 4. Cf. *GJV* 1, 695 (Engl. tr. 311); Abel, *Histoire*, 2, 95.

Hadrian was once again in Judaea. At any rate, as a result of the victory over the Jews Hadrian was soon acclaimed *imperator* for the second time, and soon thereafter the title appears on his inscriptions. Within a short time he contracted an illness which was to prove fatal.

Sextus Julius Severus was rewarded by the Senate for his victory over the Jews,[115] and subsequently became the governor of the province of Syria. Apparently Tineius Rufus resumed the control of Judaea, for he is remembered in Jewish tradition as the tyrant and to him is attributed the death of the great Rabbi Aqiba.[116] Once Beth-Ter had fallen, many Jewish captives were sold into slavery by the Romans in markets set up at Mamre ('in tabernaculo Abrahae', Jerome, *In Zach.* 11, 4; *PL* 25, 1573; 'in mercato Terebinthi', Jerome, *In. Jer.* 6, 18, 6; CSEL 59, 390) and at Gaza (later called 'Hadrian's Market'); others were carried off to Egypt.

AELIA CAPITOLINA

The fate of the Jews was sealed. Not only were they defeated and massacred or enslaved, but an imperial edict added the crowning ignominy: they were forbidden access to their 'Holy City'—an edict which had its consequences until the Six-Day War in 1967. Eusebius in his *Ecclesiastical History* recorded:

> Hadrian then commanded that by a legal decree and ordinances the whole nation should be absolutely prevented from entering from thenceforth even the district around Jerusalem, so that not even from a distance could it see its ancestral home. Ariston of Pella tells the story. Thus when the city came to be bereft of the nation of the Jews, and its ancient inhabitants had completely perished, it was colonized by foreigners, and the Roman city which afterwards arose changed its name, and in honour of the reigning emperor Aelius Hadrian was called Aelia. The church, too, in it was composed of

[115] *CIL* 3, 2830: 'Huic [senatus, a]uctore [imp(eratore) Tra]iano Hadriano Aug(usto) ornamenta triumphalia decrevit ob res in [Ju]dea prospere gestas. [d(ecurionum)] d(ecreto).'

[116] Cf. P. Benoit, 'Rabbi Aqiba ben Joseph sage et héros du Judaïsme', *RB* 54 (1947) 54–89, esp. 87–9.

Gentiles, and after the Jewish bishops the first who was appointed to minister to those there was Marcus (4, 6, 3–4).[117]

The Bordeaux Pilgrim at the beginning of the fourth century knows of the custom of the Jews who were then permitted to come once a year (probably on the 9th of Ab) to the area of the old temple, not far from Hadrian's statue, to anoint the stones, to rend their garments and to weep in mourning over the fate of Jerusalem.[118] But it was no longer the same old city.

Hadrian built *colonia Aelia capitolina* on the site of the former Jerusalem. The *cardo maximus* of the new city led from north to south, roughly along the route of the present-day *Sûq* in the Old City, beginning at the Damascus Gate (or Bâb el-'Amûd, 'the gate of the Pillar', the name derived from the column which was erected at the north end of the *cardo maximus*, as can be seen on the Madaba Map)[119] and ending at the south wall. The *decumanus* coincided roughly with the *tarîq bâb Sitti Maryam* and led to the triple arch in the east wall of the city, which is called today the *Ecce Homo* Arch.[120] Thus it was that the old temple

[117] Cf. Justin Martyr, *Apol.* 1, 47, 6.—During all this period we hear very little about the Christians in Palestine and any part which they may have had in the revolt. Justin Martyr (*Apol.* 1, 31, 6) records: 'In the recent Jewish war, Bar Kocheba, the leader of the Jewish uprising, ordered that only the Christians should be subjected to dreadful torments, unless they renounced and blasphemed Jesus Christ' (tr. *Fathers of the Church* 6, 67; he is also quoted by Eusebius, *Eccl. Hist.* 4, 8, 4). P. Orosius (*Hist. adv. paganos* 7, 13; CSEL 5, 468): '. . . ultusque est [Hadrianus] Christianos, quos illi [Iudaei] Cocheba duce, cur sibi aduersum Romanos non adsentarentur, excruciabant; praecepitque, ne cui Iudaeo introeundi Hierosolymam esset licentia, Christianis tantum ciuitate permissa; quam ipse in optimum statum murorum exstructione reparauit et Aeliam uocari de praenomine suo praecepit.' Eusebius' *Chronicon* (in Jerome's translation, 283F; GCS 47, 201): 'Chochebas, dux Iudaicae factionis, nolentes sibi XPianos aduersum Romanum militem ferre subsidium omnimodis cruciatibus necat.'

[118] *Itinerarium Burdigalense* 591; CSEL 39, 22.

[119] M. Avi-Yonah, *The Madaba Mosaic Map with Introduction and Commentary* (Jerusalem: Israel Exploration Society, 1954) 52.

[120] See H. Vincent and F.-M. Abel, *Jérusalem: Recherches de topographie, d'archéologie et d'histoire. Tome second: Jérusalem nouvelle* (Paris: Gabalda, 1914) 29: The *Ecce Homo* Arch is judged by Vincent to be 'un débris de la porte orientale d'Aelia Capitolina'.

area was completely excluded from the new Roman colony.

The *Chronicon Paschale* for the year A.D. 119 (miscalculated; see above) records the following details in Hadrian's new city:

> He destroyed the temple of the Jews in Jerusalem and built there two public baths (*ta dyo dēmosia*), the theatre, the *capitolium* (*to trikamaron*), the four-porticoed nymphaeum (*tetranymphon*), and the circus (or amphitheatre, *dōdekapylon*), which was previously called the 'Steps' (*Anabathmoi*), and the Square (*tēn Kodran*). He divided the city into seven districts (*amphoda*), and set his own deputies up as district-rulers; to each of them he assigned a district. To this day each district goes by the name of its district-ruler. He gave his own name to the city, calling it Aelia.[121]

Not far from the intersection of the *cardo maximus* and the *decumanus maximus*, which was situated roughly at the Seventh Station of the *Via dolorosa*, the agora of Aelia was constructed. The remains of the gate of Ephraim were incorporated into its approach, and some remnants of its colonnade can still be seen today in the Russian hospice. At the edge of this forum the temple of Jupiter Capitolinus was erected, the *capitolium* or *Trikamaron* (so named because of its triple-vaulted cella).

On the old temple area was constructed the Square, the *Kodra*, a sanctuary sacred to Zeus and the area where the cult of Hadrian himself was carried out.

The Romans were once again in control of the city and the land. The garrison of the *Legio X Fretensis* took up its quarters anew on the upper hill of the city in the vicinity of the towers which remained from the old palace of Herod (near the Jaffa Gate). Over the gate leading to Bethlehem a dedication to the founder of the colony was inscribed together with the emblem of the Roman legion, a wild boar. Beginning with Eusebius, this figure has often been interpreted as a mockery intended to prevent the Jewish nation from attempting to enter the city which once belonged to it: 'in fronte eius portae, qua Bethleem

121 *PG* 92, 613. My interpretation of the expressions follows that of H. Vincent, *Jérusalem nouvelle*, 6–18.

egredimur, sus scalptus in marmore significans Romanae potestati subiacere Iudaeos'.[122]

But Roman contingents were scattered throughout the land as well. The new discoveries in the caves of the Wâdi Murabba'ât show that the Romans settled down there as well, perhaps to prevent survivors of the revolt, who had not been sold into slavery, from taking further refuge there. In the Murabba'ât caves were found two coins with the counter-minting of the *Legio X Fretensis*, a contract dated as late as A.D. 171 (?), and a Greek fragment mentioning the Emperor Commodus (180–192). It seems as though Roman soldiers stayed on in this area until the end of the second century.[123]

The defeat of the Jews in the Second Revolt sealed the fate which was to exclude them from the city and the temple area which for so many years had been the rallying point of the nation. After the destruction of Jerusalem in A.D. 70 the hope lived on that it would be rebuilt and restored to the nation. This hope began to see realization in the appearance of the messianic figure of Bar Cochba—but only to be disappointed. He was the last political leader whom the Jews had, until the foundation of the State of Israel in 1948.

That hope of a return to Jerusalem and of a restoration of the Temple is echoed in the fourteenth and seventeenth blessings of the *Šemônēh 'Eśrēh*:

> And to Jerusalem, your city, return in mercy and dwell in it, as you have said; rebuild it soon in our days as an everlasting building; and speedily set up therein the throne of David.
>
> Accept, O Lord our God, your people Israel, and receive in love and favour both the fire-offerings of Israel and their prayer; and may the service of your people Israel be ever acceptable to you. Let our eyes see your return to Zion in mercy.

[122] *Chronicon* 283 F (in Jerome's translation: GCS 47, 201).
[123] See DJD 2, 48.

15

THE OXYRHYNCHUS LOGOI OF JESUS AND THE COPTIC GOSPEL ACCORDING TO THOMAS*

In 1897 Bernard P. Grenfell and Arthur S. Hunt published a papyrus fragment, which had been found during the previous winter in an ancient dump of the hamlet of Behnesa on the edge of the Western Desert about 120 miles south of Cairo, where Oxyrhynchus, the capital of the Oxyrhynchite nome of ancient Egypt, stood in Roman times. This fragment, written on both sides in Greek uncials, contained a collection of eight 'Sayings of Our Lord', some being only partially preserved.[1] It is the remains of a literary work, not just a few notes or jottings, as is shown by the use of 'Jesus says' to introduce the sayings and the absence of any abbreviations except those normally found in biblical manuscripts. The verso of the fragment, written on the vertical fibres of the papyrus, appears to have preceded the recto, strangely enough; it bears the number 11 on its top margin, presumably a page number, which indicates that the fragment was part of a papyrus codex and not of a scroll.[2] Found together with other texts of the first three centuries A.D.,

* Originally published in *TS* 20 (1959) 505–60.

[1] *Logia Iēsou, Sayings of Our Lord from an Early Greek Papyrus* (London, 1897). [Hereafter GH, *Logia*.]

[2] We may ask what the preceding ten pages in the codex contained. The Coptic version preserved in the *Gospel according to Thomas* shows that the first Greek saying is equal to the twenty-seventh Coptic saying. The length of the twenty-six preceding sayings is not such as would take up ten pages of the

the fragment was dated by the first editors *c.* A.D. 150–300, 'probably written not much later than the year 200'.[3] This fragment is known today as Oxy P (=Oxyrhynchus Papyrus) 1.[4]

In 1904 the same editors, Grenfell and Hunt, published two other Oxyrhynchus fragments, one containing 'New Sayings of Jesus', the other a 'Fragment of a Lost Gospel'. The fragment of the New Sayings 'consists of forty-two incomplete lines on the back of a survey-list of various pieces of land', and has been dated 'to the middle or end of the third century; a later date than A.D. 300 is most unlikely'.[5] It must have been the beginning of a collection of sayings, for it contains a prologue and five sayings of Jesus, some again being only partially preserved. It is known today as Oxy P 654.[6]

The 'Fragment of a Lost Gospel' was made up actually of eight small scraps of a papyrus scroll, a well-written specimen dated not later than A.D. 250. In it we have four sayings of Jesus partially preserved. Though it was entitled by the first editors 'Fragment of a Lost Gospel', because it contained a question asked by disciples and thus gave some context to the saying, a feature that is absent in the other two fragments, it has long been obvious that it belongs in general to the same

---

codex, since we can now judge the length of the page—each page must have had about 38 lines. In all probability some other treatise preceded this Greek one, just as a number of treatises are found in the same codex in the Coptic version. There is, of course, no guarantee that the *Apocryphon of John* (*kata Iōhannēn apokryphon*), which precedes the *Gospel according to Thomas* in the Coptic codex, also preceded it in the Greek.

[3] GH, *Logia*, 6.

[4] Numbered thus in Bernard P. Grenfell and Arthur S. Hunt, *The Oxyrhynchus Papyri, Edited with Translations and Notes* (London, Part 1 [1891]) 1–3.

[5] *New Sayings of Jesus and Fragment of a Lost Gospel* (London, 1904) 9. [Hereafter GH, *New Sayings*.] Oxy P 657 (*Oxyrhynchus Papyri*, Part 4, 36 ff.) offers another example of a sacred text written on the back of a used papyrus; it contains fragments of the Epistle to the Hebrews, which had been copied on the back of a text of an *Epitome* of Livy (=Oxy P. 668).

[6] Numbered thus in *Oxyrhynchus Papyri*, Part 4 (1904) 1–22.

genre as the other two fragments. It contains the introductory phrase, 'Jesus says', and manifests the same sort of relation to the canonical Gospels that they do.[7] It is generally referred to today as Oxy P 655.[8]

After their discovery and first publication these fragments—or more precisely, the first two of them, Oxy P 1 and 654—were the subject of much discussion. The question of their identity, of their authenticity, and of the restoration of their partially preserved texts were the causes of many articles and small books. Only recently we have seen the publication of a work by J. Jeremias, *Unknown Sayings of Jesus*,[9] which treats these fragments in the larger context of the Agrapha (sayings attributed to Jesus, but not found in the canonical Gospels), no matter where preserved. Scholars like Batiffol, Deissmann, von Harnack, Klostermann, Lagrange, Preuschen, Reitzenstein, Sanday, C. Taylor, Wilamowitz-Moellendorff, and Zahn have worked over these texts and have tried to restore and interpret them. It seemed, indeed, that all that could be said about them had been said.[10]

But the whole subject has been reopened by the discovery in 1945 or 1946 of Coptic codices of ancient Chenoboskion near the modern village of Nag'- Ḥammâdi, some sixty miles north of Luxor in Upper Egypt. Chenoboskion (literally, 'a place for

[7] The relation of Oxy P 655 to the other two fragments has often been denied; see, e.g., the discussion in H. G. Evelyn White, *The Sayings of Jesus from Oxyrhynchus, Edited with Introduction, Critical Apparatus and Commentary* (Cambridge, 1920) xlix.–lii. [Hereafter: Evelyn White.]

[8] Numbered thus in *Oxyrhynchus Papyri*, Part 4 (1904) 22–8.

[9] Translated by R. H. Fuller (New York, 1957). [Hereafter: *Unknown Sayings*.]

[10] The bibliography of the Oxyrhynchus Sayings of Jesus is quite vast. While much of it is old and no longer pertinent, it contains at times observations which are still valuable in the light of the new Coptic material. I have decided, therefore, to offer as complete a listing of it as possible. It will be found at the end of this article. Unfortunately, it is not exhaustive, because I came across a number of titles with incomplete references and was not in a position to check them, as they were unavailable in the libraries to which I had access.

raising geese') is said to have been the place where Pachomius, the father of Christian Egyptian cenobitism, after release from involuntary service in the Roman army, was converted and baptized *c.* A.D. 320 and became the disciple of the hermit Palaemon, before founding his cenobitic monastery at Tabennisi on the right bank of the Nile. From a big jar found in the cemetery near Chenoboskion came thirteen codices, containing forty-four Coptic treatises, almost all of them Gnostic writings.[11]

One of these forty-four treatises is the *Gospel according to Thomas, peuaggelion pkata Thōmas.* It was published in 1956 as part of the first volume in the series, *Coptic Gnostic Papyri in the Coptic Museum at Old Cairo.*[12] It was written on ten leaves or twenty pages of a papyrus codex in the Sahidic dialect of Coptic, mixed with some Akhmimic or Sub-Akhmimic forms. Save for a few lacunae which are easily filled out the entire

[11] See J. Doresse, *Les livres secrets des Gnostiques d'Egypte* 1 : *Introduction aux écrits gnostiques coptes découverts à Khenoboskion* (Paris, 1958) 133–280. A convenient summary of the discovery, contents of the codices, and importance of the find can be found in E. Meyerovitch, 'The Gnostic Manuscripts of Upper Egypt', *Diogènes* [Engl. ed.] §25 (1959) 84–117. Pp. 115–17 contain a good bibliography of articles relating to the Coptic material. Cf. now J. M. Robinson, 'The Coptic Gnostic Library Today', *NTS* 14 (1967–68) 356–401. (This is an important article for sorting out the relation of the various Coptic tractates to the codices and for threading one's way through the maze of often confusing references to this literature. It also lists the main publications of the Coptic tractates. It has, however, little to do with the Oxyrhynchus papyri and their relation to the *Gospel according to Thomas.*) See also S. Giversen, 'Nag Hammadi Bibliography 1948–63', *ST* 17 (1963) 138–87; J. Simon, 'Bibliographie Copte', *Orientalia* 28 (1959) 93*–4*; 29 (1960) 48*–50*; 30 (1961) 64*–7*; 31 (1962) 53*–6*; 32 (1963) 116*–19*; 33 (1964) 126*–8*; 34 (1965) 219*–22*; 35 (1966) 142*–5*; 36 (1967) 162*–5*; M. Krause, 'Der Stand der Veröffentlichung der Nag Hammadi Texte', *The Origins of Gnosticism* (Studies in the History of Religions 12; Leiden: Brill, 1967) 61–89; R. Haardt, 'Zwanzig Jahre Erforschung der koptisch-gnostischen Schriften von Nag Hammadi', *Theologie und Philosophie* 42 (1967) 390–401; K. Rudolph, 'Gnosis und Gnostizismus, ein Forschungsbericht', *TRu* 34 (1969) 121–75, 181–231. These bibliographical articles deal with the whole area of the Nag' Hammâdi texts; a specific bibliography for the more important studies of the *Gospel according to Thomas* will be found at the end of this article (see pp. 426–33 below).

[12] Published by Pahor Labib (Cairo, 1956). The *Gospel according to Thomas*

text is well preserved. Palaeographically, the document has been variously dated by Coptic specialists: H.-Ch. Puech thinks that it comes 'du milieu ou de la première moitié du IIIe siècle';[13] G. Garitte says that it 'peut dater du IIIe ou du IVe siècle';[14] but J. Leipoldt dates it 'um 500',[15] while J. Doresse gives 'du milieu du IVe siècle'.[16] A date *c.* 400 is probably the safest for the copying of this text;[17] the date of composition is, of course, undoubtedly much earlier.

The *Gospel according to Thomas* is not a gospel in the sense of the canonical Matthew, Mark, Luke, or John, which contain a record of the words and deeds of Jesus, nor even in the sense of some of the apocryphal Gospels, which relate fantastic stories about the Holy Family in imitation of the canonical Gospels. The *Gospel according to Thomas* relates no episodes of the life of Christ and, in general, lacks all narrative and personal information about him. Even the instances in which the disciples or some others question Jesus cannot rightly be described as narrative, as they normally do no more than pose the question. After a prologue of four and a half lines, which itself contains a saying, this Gospel has preserved for us 114 sayings of Jesus, most of them simply introduced by the formula, 'Jesus said', *peǧe Iēsous.* The prologue, indeed, indicates the nature of the

---

is found on plates 80–99 with the title given at the end of the work as a sort of *explicit.* This edition contains only photographs of the papyrus pages; there is neither a modern Coptic transcription, a translation, nor a commentary. In addition to the *Gospel according to Thomas*, the volume contains part of the *Gospel of Truth* (pl. 1–46), the *Apocryphon of John* (pl. 47–80), the *Gospel according to Philip* (pl. 99–134), the *Hypostasis of the Archons* (pl. 134–45) and a Sethian Apocalypse (pl. 145–58).

13 'Un logion de Jésus sur bandelette funéraire', *RHR* 147 (1955) 127.

14 'Le premier volume de l'édition photographique des manuscrits gnostiques coptes et l'Evangile de Thomas', *Mus* 70 (1957) 61.

15 'Ein neues Evangelium? Das koptische Thomasevangelium übersetzt und besprochen', *TLZ* 83 (1958) 481.

16 *Les livres secrets des Gnostiques d'Egypte 2: L'Evangile selon Thomas ou les paroles secrètes de Jésus* (Paris, 1959) 23. [Hereafter: Doresse, *Thomas.*]

17 So W. C. Till, 'New Sayings of Jesus in the Recently Discovered Coptic "Gospel of Thomas"', *BJRL* 41 (1958–59) 451.

work as a collection of sayings. These sayings sometimes resemble maxims or proverbs, sometimes parables, but sometimes answer a question put by a disciple and thus form part of a conversation. They are strung together without any apparent logical order; once in a while catchword bonds (*Stichwortverbindungen*) can be the reason for joining two sayings. The collection of sayings is actually an artificial grouping of *dicta Iesu*, cast in a homogeneous format, which are most likely derived from various sources. Prof. Oscar Cullmann, in various lectures on the *Gospel according to Thomas*,[18] divided the sayings into four groups: (1) those which are word-for-word identical with certain sayings in the canonical Gospels; (2) those which are paraphrases or independent variants of canonical sayings; (3) those which reproduce sayings of Jesus which are not found in the NT, but are extant in patristic writings; (4) those which were previously unknown—a good half of the Gospel—and bear a very definite syncretistic, Gnostic stamp. As it stands, there is no doubt that the *Gospel according to Thomas* is an apocryphal work. I shall have more to say about this Gospel and the ancient witnesses to it toward the end of the article.

But now a word about the possible authenticity of these sayings, as this question will come up in the treatment of the individual texts. When one asks how authentic these Coptic sayings are, it should be clear that the answer will not be simple, given the complex nature of the sayings. As for the first group, they should be accorded the same authenticity as those of the NT. It is obviously quite possible that they have been merely lifted from the canonical Gospels; but we cannot exclude the possibility that the *Gospel according to Thomas* is tributary to an independent tradition, derived from one of the various oral or written forms that led to the formation of our canonical

[18] 'The Gospel of Thomas and the Problem of the Age of the Tradition Contained Therein', *Interpretation* 16 (1962) 418–38, especially 425; cf. *TLZ* 85 (1960) 321–34; *Protestantesimo* 15 (1960) 145–52.—I have some hesitation about the number of sayings that can really be classified in the first group; R. North (*CBQ* 24 [1962] 164) lists some twenty-five of them.

Gospels. In the case of the second and third groups we have to reckon seriously with the possibility of a different collection of sayings, i.e., different from those known to us in Mt, Mk, Lk, Jn, but that may have coexisted with them. The variants in the sayings that are found in the Synoptics themselves show us how the same saying has at times undergone modification in the refractory process of oral transmission or of editorial redaction. One must also reckon with the known creative additions and adaptations of sayings of Jesus that are recorded in the canonical Gospels. The same processes might well account for the variants that are found in the Coptic sayings, which we have called 'paraphrases'. Moreover, just as there are sayings of Jesus recorded in the NT outside of the Gospels (e.g. 1 Thes 4:15 ff.; Acts 20:35; 1 Cor 11:24; Ap 16:15), so those in the patristic writers cannot be rejected as unauthentic simply on the grounds that they do not occur in the Gospels. The fourth group of Coptic sayings, however, is so obviously Gnostic in character that we should be inclined to regard them rather as the product of the same type of imagination that produced many of the apocryphal Gospels. In fact, G. Quispel believes that they are derived from the apocryphal *Gospel of the Egyptians*.[19] Scholars will probably be divided as to the category in which some of the sayings are best classified; however, the classification used above is fairly objective, since in the first three groups the criterion is an outside control. In the second group one might dispute whether a given saying is a paraphrase or an entirely different saying. But in every case it will be necessary to judge each saying individually, a task of evaluation that will take a long time.[20]

It was, of course, a pleasant surprise to find that the Oxyrhynchus *logoi* of Jesus have turned up in the collection of the

[19] 'The Gospel of Thomas and the New Testament', *VC* 11 (1957) 189.

[20] See now the highly interesting and important discussion of H. Koester, '*Gnōmai diaphoroi:* The Origin and Nature of Diversification in the History of Early Christianity', *HTR* 58 (1965) 279–318.

Coptic sayings as part of the *Gospel according to Thomas*. When Oxy P 654 was first published, containing the name of Thomas, the editors discussed the possibility of a connection between the fragment and the *Gospel according to Thomas*, only to reject it.[21] In 1952 H.-Ch. Puech discovered the relation between the Oxyrhynchus papyri and the Coptic *Gospel according to Thomas*.[22] Thanks to the recovery of this Gospel, it is now certain that the three Oxyrhynchus fragments (1, 654, 655) are all parts of the same work;[23] they represent three different copies of the Greek text made at different times and give evidence of a fairly frequent copying of it in the third century A.D. On the basis of the Coptic version[24] we can now reconstruct many of the fragmentary lines of the Greek fragments with certainty—unfortunately, however, not all of them, for there are slight variants in the two recensions that still cause problems of interpretation. Oxy P 654=the prologue and the first six sayings of the Coptic Gospel; Oxy P 1=Coptic sayings 26, 27, 28, 29, 30, with the end of 77, 31, 32, 33; Oxy P 655=Coptic sayings 36, 37, 38, 39. (My numbering of the Coptic sayings is now following that which is commonly used [see note 27 below]; my numbering of the Greek sayings in Oxy P 654 has been made to conform to that numbering too.)

[21] GH, *New Sayings*, 30–2.

[22] 'Un logion de Jésus sur bandelette funéraire', *Bulletin de la société Ernest Renan*, n.s. 3 (1954) 126–9; see n. 13 above. Cf. Doresse, *Thomas*, 16, 21.

[23] Previously held by V. Bartlet, but generally rejected (see White, xlix.).

[24] The original form of this article regarded the Coptic version of the *Gospel according to Thomas* as an adapted translation of the Greek sayings in the Oxyrhynchus papyri. This view was challenged by no less an authority than G. Garitte, who thinks rather that the Oxyrhynchus *Logoi* are translated from a Coptic form of the Gospel (see 'Les "logoi" d'Oxyrhynque et l'apocryphe copte dit "Evangile de Thomas"', *Mus* 73 [1960] 151–72). Garitte's view was challenged by A. Guillaumont, 'Les *Logia* d'Oxyrhynchos sont-ils traduits du Copte?', *ibid.*, 325–33, to which Garitte replied, 'Les "logoi" d'Oxyrhynque sont traduits du Copte', *ibid.*, 335–49. Garitte was supported by H. Quecke, 'Het Evangelie volgens Thomas: Inleiding en commentaar', *Streven* 13 (1960) 452–3, and by P. Devos, *Analecta bollandiana* 78 (1960) 446–7. This question is far from resolved and many scholars still regard the Coptic text as an adapted translation from a Greek original. See

The first full translation of the *Gospel according to Thomas* to appear was that by J. Leipoldt in German.[25] The sayings in which we are interested in this paper were also translated into Latin by G. Garitte.[26] The translations of the Coptic sayings that we are using in this paper were worked out independently of these two translations and subsequently compared with them and others. A deluxe edition of the Gospel with better photographs of the papyrus pages, a Coptic transcription, a translation into French, English, and German, and commentary has been promised.[27]

It is my purpose in this essay to restudy the Greek fragments of Oxyrhynchus in the light of the Coptic translation. I have mentioned above the vast literature that was produced on the subject of these fragments. Many of the attempts to interpret and restore the fragments are now seen to have been in vain. However, many comments of former scholars are still valid and it is my aim to sift the existing publications for those which are still pertinent in the light of the new reconstruction that I propose for these texts. If my attempt to restore the Greek text seems bold or rash to anyone, let him recall the galaxy of names that attempted to do the same without any extrinsic guide or control. My restored text will be translated and commented

---

E. Haenchen, 'Literatur zum Thomasevangelium', *TRu* 27 (1961–62) 157–60 ('sein [Garitte's] Beweis hält nicht stand', p. 160); O. Cullmann, *Interpretation* 16 (1962) 421–2; J.-B. Bauer in *Geheime Worte Jesu: Das Thomasevangelium* (ed. R. M. Grant and D. N. Freedman; Frankfurt, 1960) 188–90. Cf. R. Kasser, *L'évangile selon Thomas: Présentation et commentaire théologique* (Neuchâtel: Delachaux et Niestlé, 1961) and H. Quecke, RechBib 6 (1962) 220–2. Whatever the answer to it is, the reconstruction of the Greek text of the Oxyrhynchus papyri must at present be made with the Coptic text in mind.

[25] See n. 15 above.

[26] See n. 14 above.

[27] An extract of this edition is available in A. Guillaumont, H.-Ch. Puech, G. Quispel, W. Till, and Y. 'Abd-al-Masiḥ, *The Gospel according to Thomas: Coptic Text Established and Translated* (Leiden: Brill; New York: Harper, 1959). I am following the numbering of sayings in this edition. See also J. Leipoldt, *Das Evangelium nach Thomas koptisch und deutsch* (TU 101; Berlin:

upon, and finally I shall conclude with some general remarks on the relation of the Greek fragments to the Coptic text.[28]

Oxy P 654

I begin the discussion of the Greek texts with Oxy P 654, for it contains the prologue which corresponds to that of the Coptic text. It is a long, narrow fragment ($9\frac{5}{8}'' \times 3\frac{1}{16}''$), containing 42 lines of which only the beginnings are preserved. In cases where the reconstruction of the line is certain due to the Coptic version, we are able to ascertain the normal number of letters on a line. For instance, line 4 contained 30 letters (16 restored); line 20 contained 28 (13 restored); line 25 contained 33 letters (15 restored); line 30 contained 29 letters (12 restored). This gives us a fairly certain norm to guide us in restoring other lines. I shall present first the unreconstructed text of Grenfell and Hunt,[29] then an English translation of the corresponding Coptic

---

Akademie-V., 1967); for other translations, see J. M. Robinson, *art. cit.* (n. 11 above) 388–9.

[28] The following are the articles that have appeared, dealing with the Oxyrhynchus *logoi* and the Coptic text: H.-Ch. Puech, 'Une collection de paroles de Jésus récemment retrouvée: l'évangile selon Thomas', *CRAIBL* 1957, 146–66. A. Guillaumont, 'Sémitismes dans les logia de Jésus retrouvés à Nag-Hamâdi', *JA* 246 (1958) 113–23. R. McL. Wilson, 'The Coptic "Gospel of Thomas"', *NTS* 5 (1958–59) 273–6. R. Kasser, 'Les manuscrits de Nag' Hammâdi: Faits, documents, problèmes', *RTP* 9 (1959) 357–70. O. Hofius, 'Das koptische Thomasevangelium und die Oxyrhynchus-Papyri Nr. 1, 654 und 655', *ET* 20 (1960) 21–42, 182–92. A. Rüstow, '*Entos hymōn estin:* Zur Deutung von Lukas 17, 20–21', *ZNW* 51 (1960) 197–224. J.-B. Bauer, 'Arbeitsaufgaben am koptischen Thomasevangelium', *VC* 15 (1961) 1–7. R. A. Kraft, Oxyrhynchus Papyrus 655 Reconsidered', *HTR* 54 (1961) 253–62. Guillaumont, A., '*Nēsteuein ton kosmon* (P. Oxy. 1, verso 1. 5–6)', *BIFAO* 61 (1962) 15–23. A. F. Walls, '"Stone" and "Wood" in Oxyrhynchus Papyrus I', *VC* 16 (1962) 71–6. W. Schrage, 'Evangelienzitate in den Oxyrhynchus-Logien und im koptischen Thomas-Evangelium', *Apophoreta* (Fest. E. Haenchen; BZNW 30; Berlin: Töpelmann, 1964) 251–68. A. Baker, '"Fasting to the World"', *JBL* 84 (1965) 291–4. T. F. Glasson, 'The Gospel of Thomas, Saying 3, and Deuteronomy xxx. 11–14', *ExpT* 78 (1966–67) 151–2. M. Marcovich, 'Textual Criticism on the *Gospel of Thomas*', *JTS* n.s. 20 (1969) 53–74. F. Altheim and R. Stiehl, *Die Araber in der alten Welt* (Berlin: De Gruyter) 5/2 (1969) 368–92. C. H. Roberts, 'The Gospel of Thomas: Logion 30A', *JTS* 21 (1970) 91–2.

[29] I give the text as it appeared in the preliminary editions (GH, *New*

saying, the full Greek text of the Oxyrhynchus saying (restored), a translation of the Greek, and finally comments on each saying.

In this revision of the essay I have changed the reconstruction of the Greek text only in a few instances. Part of the reason for the few changes is the use of my reconstruction in K. Aland, *Synopsis quattuor evangeliorum: Locis parallelis evangeliorum apocryphorum et patrum adhibitis* (Stuttgart: Württembergische Bibelanstalt, 1964) pp. 584–5 *et passim*. But the real reason is that I have not always been convinced that other attempts to reconstruct it are better than my own. Where changes have been made, I have acknowledged my dependence on others.

PROLOGUE AND FIRST SAYING

ΟΙ ΤΟΙΟΙ ΟΙ ΛΟΓΟΙ ΟΙ [
ΛΗΣΕΝ ΙΗΣ Ο ΖΩΝ Κ[
ΚΑΙ ΘΩΜΑ ΚΑΙ ΕΙΠΕΝ [
ΑΝ ΤΩΝ ΛΟΓΩΝ ΤΟΥΤ[
ΟΥ ΜΗ ΓΕΥΣΗΤΑΙ [

The prologue and first saying of the Coptic Gospel read as follows: 'These are the secret words which the living Jesus spoke, and Didymus Judas Thomas wrote them down. And he said, "Whoever discovers the interpretation (*hermēneia*)[30] of these words will not taste death!"' (Plate 80, lines 10–14).[31]

Sayings, 11 and 40; GH, *Logia*, 8) rather than that of the *editio princeps* (*Oxyrhynchus Papyri*, Part 1, p. 3; Part 4, pp. 3 and 23) because the preliminary editions present more objective readings of the fragments, not encumbered with the hypotheses that developed out of the preliminary publications. Any changes that the first editors subsequently made in the *editio princeps* will be noted.

30 The form of the Greek word found in parentheses in the English translation of the Coptic version is an exact transliteration of the form used by the Coptic. I add this form to the translation, for it will often shed light on the Greek text—as in this very case.

31 References to plates and lines are made according to the edition of P. Labib (see n. 12 above). I add these references, because they are the only sure way that now exists of referring to the Coptic Gospel. The various scholars who have so far discussed or translated the Gospel have divided the text up according to the sayings it contains. Some number 113, some 114, some 118.

On the basis of this Coptic version we may now restore the Greek text as follows:[32]

Οὗτοι οἱ {οι} λόγοι οἱ [ἀπόκρυφοι οὓς ἐλά]
λησεν Ἰη(σοῦ)ς ὁ ζῶν κ[αὶ ἔγραψεν Ἰούδας ὁ]
καὶ Θωμᾶ<ς> καὶ εἶπεν [ὅστις ἂν τὴν ἑρμηνεί]
αν τῶν λόγων τούτ[ων εὑρίσκῃ, θανάτου]
οὐ μὴ γεύσηται.

'These are the [secret] words [which] the living Jesus [sp]oke, an[d Judas who] (is) also (called) Thomas [wrote (them) down]. And he said, ["Whoever finds the interpre]tation of th[ese] words, will not taste [death!"]'

Comments

1. It is generally admitted that the first line contains 'obviously an uncorrected mistake' (Evelyn White, p. xxiii). The *editio princeps* reads {*hoi*} *toioi hoi logoi*; the editors insist that the second letter can only be an iota and try to explain *toios* as the equivalent of *toiosde* (*Oxyrhynchus Papyri*, Part 4, p. 4). However, many subsequent commentators such as Swete, Heinrici, Taylor, Wilamowitz-Moellendorff, and Evelyn White were not convinced by this questionable Greek construction and read the first line as I have given it, deleting the dittographical article before the noun. Cf. Bar 1:1, *houtoi hoi logoi tou bibliou hous egrapsen Barouch*; Lk 24:44.

logoi: The use of this word to designate the 'sayings' of Jesus in these fragments should be noted. Nowhere do we find *logia* used of these sayings; Grenfell and Hunt were, therefore, not accurate in entitling the preliminary publication of Oxy P 1 *Logia Iēsou*, which did not, of course, become apparent until the discovery of Oxy P 654. From the time of Herodotus on *logion* meant 'oracle', 'a saying derived from a deity'. In the LXX it denotes the 'word of God', having lost the Greek nuance of

[32] I am following the system of the Greek papyrologists in the use of square brackets [ ] to denote the restoration of lacunae, parentheses or round brackets ( ) to denote the resolution of abbreviations, angular brackets < > to denote my editorial additions, and braces {} to denote my editorial deletions.

'oracle' and acquired that of OT revelation. In this sense we find it in Acts 7:38; Rom 3:2; 1 Pt 4:11; Heb 5:12 (see G. Kittel, *TDNT* 4, 137–41). In A. Resch's collection of Agrapha (TU 30 [1906]) we find the word used only twice, and in each case it refers to the OT. See further J. Donovan, *The Logia in Ancient and Recent Literature* (Cambridge, 1927). The use of *logoi* here for the sayings of Jesus can be compared to Mt 15:12 and especially to Acts 20:35, *mnēmoneuein te tōn logōn tou Kyriou Iēsou hoti autos eipen.* See also Clement of Rome, *Ad Cor.* 13:1; 46:7 (ed. K. Bihlmeyer, pp. 42, 60) for the use of this word to designate the sayings of Jesus. Now that we know that the Greek fragments belong to a text of the *Gospel according to Thomas*, there is no longer room for the speculation that possibly they contain part of the *Logia* on which Papias wrote his commentary or of the *Logia* that Matthew collected (Eusebius, *Hist. Eccl.* 3, 39, 1 and 16). Consequently, it is better not to refer to the sayings either in the Oxyrhynchus fragments or in the Coptic *Gospel According to Thomas* (where the word used is *šaǧe*, 'word, saying') as *logia*, *pace* R. North (*CBQ* 24 [1962] 164, etc.). See further J. M. Robinson, '*Logoi sophōn:* Zur Gattung der Spruchquelle Q', *Zeit und Geschichte: Dankesgabe an Rudolf Bultmann zum 80. Geburtstag* (ed. E. Dinkler; Tübingen: Mohr, 1964) 77–96, esp. 79–84.

apokryphoi: Of all the adjectives previously suggested by the critics to modify 'sayings' only that of T. Zahn (*NKZ* 16 [1905] 178) has proved to be correct, as the Coptic *ᵉnšaǧe ethêp* shows, although it was not, ironically enough, acceptable to most scholars. The exact expression is to be found, moreover, in Hippolytus' *Elenchus* 7, 20 (GCS 26, 195): *basileidēs toinun kai Isidōros, . . . phēsin eirēkenai Matthian autois logous apokryphous, hous ēkouse para tou sōtēros kat' idian didachtheis.* Moreover, we find the same adjective used of both *logos* and *logia* in a text that is possibly related to this Gospel, viz., *Acta Thomae* 39 (ed. M. Bonnet, p. 156): *ho didymos tou Christou, ho apostolos tou hypsistou kai symmystēs tou logou tou Christou apokryphou, ho dechomenos autou ta apokrypha logia*. The same expression, *ᵉnšaǧe ethēp*, is found at the beginning of another Chenoboskion treatise ascribed to Thomas, the *Book of Thomas*. According to H.-Ch. Puech ('Les nouveaux écrits gnostiques découverts en Haute-Egypte: premier inventaire et essai d'identification', *Coptic Studies in Honor of Walter Ewing Crum* [=Second Bulletin of the Byzantine Institute; Boston, 1950] 105), this book begins, 'Paroles secrètes dites par le Sauveur à Jude et Thomas (*sic*) et consignées par Matthias'. Elsewhere Puech reveals the full title, *Book of Thomas the Athlete Written for the Perfect* (*CRAIBL* 1957, p. 149). We may ask in what sense the sayings of Jesus in this collection are to be regarded as 'secret' (for it is obvious that *apokryphos* does not have the later pejorative meaning of 'apocryphal' here), when many of the sayings contain words which Jesus pronounced openly and publicly. The 'hidden' character is rather to be found in the manner of interpretation which is found in this collection. The quotation from Hippolytus above tells us of 'hidden words' that Matthias had learned from the Saviour in private. This reveals a tradition which undoubtedly is to be traced to Mt 13:10–11, where Christ himself distinguished between the comprehension of the disciples and that of the crowd. The thirteenth Coptic saying illustrates this idea, moreover, when Jesus takes Thomas aside to tell him three words which he is not allowed to repeat to the other disciples. In this very saying we learn that eternal life is promised to him who succeeds in discovering the real meaning of the sayings in the collection. This probably refers to the different application or interpretation which is given to even the canonical sayings that are set in a different context. Such shifts in meaning were undoubtedly part of the esoteric interpretation which is intended by 'hidden' or 'secret'. J.-B. Bauer prefers to restore *kekrymmenoi* (*VC* 15 [1961] 5–7).

2. *ho zōn:* Former commentators often asked whether this adjective was to be referred to Christ's preresurrectional or postresurrectional existence. Leipoldt (col. 481) points out that

the Coptic *etonh* scarcely means, 'while he was living', and should probably be referred to the Risen Christ. But we need not deduce from this that the words recorded in this collection are postresurrectional sayings. There is nothing in the Coptic or Greek versions that supports this; on the contrary, a number of the sayings imply the preresurrectional phase.

[*Ioudas ho*] *kai Thōma*⟨*s*⟩ : The form *THŌMA* creates a problem. Most former commentators interpreted it as a dative in an expression like *kai ophtheis tois deka kai Thōma* (so, e.g., Evelyn White, p. 1). However, it is now clear from the Coptic that Thomas is the alleged compiler of the sayings and the subject of the sentence. At the end of line 2 we must certainly supply *k*[*ai egrapsen*. . . . This is confirmed by the title of the Gospel that is found at the end (Pl. 99): *peuaggelion pkata Thomas*. What, then, is the form of Thomas' name? In Jn 11:16; 20:24 we find Thomas referred to as *ho legomenos Didymos*, as generally in the Western tradition. Such a full form of the name is impossible here. In Jn 14:22 we read of a certain 'Judas, not the Iscariot', which the Curetonian Syriac version gives as 'Judas Thomas', a form which occurs elsewhere in Syriac writings. K. Lake (*HibbJ* 3 [1904–5] 339) suggested that this name be read here (in the dative). In fact, in the *Acta Thomae* we frequently find him referred to as *Ioudas ho kai Thōmas* (§11 [ed. M. Bonnet in R. A. Lipsius, *Acta apostolorum apocrypha* [Leipzig, 1903] p. 116]; also §20 [p. 130], §21 [p. 133] *et passim*). For the form of the name, cf. Acts 13:9, *Saulos ho kai Paulos*, and Blass-Debrunner, *Grammatik des neutestamentlichen Griechisch* (9th ed.; Göttingen, 1954) §268, 1. The real name of the Apostle was 'Judas the Twin'. *Didymos* is the Greek translation of the Hebrew *T*^{e}ʾ*ôm* or the Aramaic *T*^{e}ʾ*ômâ*. In Syriac "twin" is *tâʾmâ*, which shows that the Aramaic form of the proper name is actually influenced by the Hebrew in preserving the *ô*. The Greek form *Thōmas* is actually a genuine Greek name which has been substituted for a similarly sounding Semitic name, like *Simōn* for *Šim*^{e}ʿ*ôn*; cf. Blass-Debrunner §53, 2d. The author of *Acta Thomae* regards Thomas as the twin of our Lord and in the course of the writing they are mistaken for each other. In line 3 we must accordingly read *Thōma⟨s⟩*, since the nominative case is required.[33] M. Marcovich now points out (*JTS* 20 [1969] 53) that the omission of the final *s* on *Thōma* is common enough in the nominative; see E. Mayser, *Grammatik der griechischen Papyri aus der Ptolomäerzeit*, 1. 205.

3. *hermēnei*]*an:* The Coptic has preserved the Greek word for us, which makes the restoration certain.

4. *heuriskē:* Hofius' form *heurēsē* is surely wrong; one might possibly read *heurē*. Marcovich (*JTS* 20 [1969] 53) offers another possibility, *hostis . . . heurēsei*, but he wrongly judges that my *hostis an* is too long.

thanatou: The restoration of former commentators, suggested by Jn 8:52, is now certain. The compiler has modified the Johannine statement slightly in order to suit his prologue. The NT expression always lacks the article, whether used for physical or spiritual death; see Mt 16:28; Mk 9:1; Lk 9:27; Heb 2:9. Here, as in John, the idea of spiritual death is almost certainly intended. There is no apparent reason why this saying could not be authentic, if 'he said' refers to Jesus. E. Jacquier (*RB* 15 [1918] 114) regarded it as authentic. The only hesitation comes from the fact that the apodosis of our saying reflects a Jewish rephrasing of Jesus' statement, rather than the actual way it is recorded in John.

SECOND SAYING

ΜΗ ΠΑΥΣΑΣΘΩ Ο ΖΗ[
ΕΥΡΗ ΚΑΙ ΟΤΑΝ ΕΥΡΗ [
ΒΗΘΕΙΣ ΒΑΣΙΛΕΥΣΗ ΚΑ[
9 ΗΣΕΤΑΙ

The second Coptic saying: 'Jesus said, "Let him who seeks not give up seeking until he finds, and when (*hotan*) he finds, he

[33] I cannot agree with the translation of the Oxyrhynchus prologue as it is given by J. Doresse, *Thomas*, p. 89, which reads thus: 'Voici les paroles [cachées que] Jésus le Vivant a dites e[t qu'a transcrites Didyme Jude] et

will be bewildered; and if he is bewildered, he will marvel and he will become king over all"' (80:14–19).

In this case the Coptic version only helps in part, for it does not completely correspond to the Greek. The latter is shorter than the Coptic and contains a different ending. Since a form of the saying is preserved in Clement of Alexandria, former editors succeeded in restoring it quite well. We add nothing new to the restoration of this saying. The following form is derived from Evelyn White (p. 5):

[λέγει Ἰη(σοῦ)ς·]
μὴ παυσάσθω ὁ ζη[τῶν τοῦ ζητεῖν ἕως ἂν]
εὕρῃ, καὶ ὅταν εὕρῃ, [θαμβηθήσεται καὶ θαμ]
βηθεὶς βασιλεύσῃ κα[ὶ βασιλεύσας ἀναπα]
ήσεται.

'[Jesus says,] "Let him who see[ks] not cease [seeking until] he finds and when he finds, [he will be astounded, and] having been [astoun]ded, he will reign an[d having reigned], he will re[st]."'

Comments

5. After the last word of the first saying there is a *coronis*, a sign used to separate the sayings in this fragment. We may confidently restore in the lacuna at the end of the line *legei Iē(sou)s*, since this is the usual formula of introduction (see lines 9, 27, 36; Oxy P 1:4, 11, [23], 30, 36, 41). It should be noted that whereas the Coptic has the past tense in the introductory formula, *peǧe*, the Greek uses the present. The past would be more obvious, and the problem is to explain why the Greek version has the present tense. The use of the present tense is quite common in Mt, Mk, and Jn, less so in Lk; in the NT it has

---

Thomas'. From this it seems that Didyme Jude is not Thomas; moreover, there is no room to restore Didymus. The second relative pronoun which Doresse has introduced into his translation, obviously for the sake of smoothness, does not occur in the Coptic and I have not restored it in the Greek. My reconstruction was made independently of that proposed by H.-Ch. Puech (*Comptes rendus de l'Académie des Inscriptions et Belles-Lettres*, 1957, p. 153), with which it agrees substantially.

a historical sense normally. We find the exact expression in Jn 13:31. But this combination of the present *legei* and *Iēsous* without the article is otherwise unknown. Harnack (*Expositor*, ser. 5, vol. 6 [1897] 403, n. 2) took the use of the present with Jesus, instead of 'the Lord', as a sign of great antiquity, and he contrasted it with the use of *Kyrios* in the *Gospel according to the Egyptians*. Evelyn White (p. lxxv) believes that the anarthrous use of *Iēsous* is a mark of Johannine influence in the collection. Burney suggested (in W. Lock and W. Sanday, *Two Lectures on the 'Sayings of Jesus'* [Oxford, 1897] 47–8) that the formula is possibly a translation 'from a Neo-Hebrew or Aramaic original'. He cites as parallels *Pirqê 'Abôt* 1, 4, 5, 12. But it was often taken with Lock (*op. cit.*, 18) in a 'mystical' sense, meaning simply, 'This is a saying of Jesus'; 'this was said by Jesus in his lifetime and is still the utterance of him who is still a living Master' (see Evelyn White, pp. lxxiii–lxxvi). But since we also find the present used of the disciples (see Oxy P 654:32–33; 655:17), the 'mystical' sense must yield to the historical present, confirmed by the Coptic past.

6. *ho zētōn:* The saying is probably related to Mt 7:8, 'the one who searches finds'. But it is obviously a development of it.

tou zētein: This restoration (of Heinrici, *Theologische Studien und Kritiken* 78 [1905] 188–210) does not correspond exactly to the Coptic *efšine*, which is rather the 3 sg. m. pres. circumstantial, 'While he is seeking'. Something is needed to fill out the line, and since the circumstantial notion is already expressed in the participle, the infinitive is best retained.

7. [*thambēthēsetai*]*:* At this point the Greek text is shorter than the Coptic. But we are aided in the interpretation of the Greek by several passages from Clement of Alexandria. In *Stromata* 2, 9, 45 (GCS 15, 137) we find a text which is quite close to this fragment, but it is cited as derived from the *Gospel according to the Hebrews: kan tō kath' Hebraious euaggeliō ho thaumasas basileusei gegraptai kai ho basileusas anapaēsetai*. Again in *Stromata* 5, 14, 96 (GCS 15, 389) the saying is found in still fuller form: *ou pausetai*

ho zētōn heōs an heurē; heurōn de thambēthēsetai; thambētheis de basileusei; basileusas de epanapaēsetai. (Cf. M. R. James, *The Apocryphal New Testament, Being the Apocryphal Gospels, Acts, Epistles and Apocalypses* [Oxford, 1953] 2; Resch, *Agrapha*, 70–1; 215–16.) Is it possible that the *Gospel according to Thomas* has also quoted from the *Gospel according to the Hebrews*? In the present state of our knowledge it is impossible to answer this question. We may also ask in what sense the verb *thambēthēsetai* is to be understood. The context in which the saying is quoted in Clement of Alexandria is one in which he is trying to show that the beginning of philosophy is wonder. But this is hardly the meaning in the collection of sayings that we have here. Harnack interpreted it rather in the sense of joyful surprise, comparing the parable of the hidden treasure in Mt 13:24; cf. Evelyn White, p. 6; H. B. Swete, *ExpT* 15 (1903–4) 491.

8. *basileusē:* A misspelling for *basileusei*; at the period when the papyrus was written, *ē, ei, i, y* were all pronounced alike in Egyptian Greek. See further Oxy P 1:13 *sarkei* for *sarki* (in fact, '*sarkei* has been corrected by the original hand from *sarki*'; GH, *Logia*, p. 12); 1:16 *deipsōnta* for *dipsōnta*; 1:35 *geinōskontas* for *ginōskontas*; in 1:22 an epsilon has been inserted above the line in the word *ptōchian*; Oxy P 655:14 *heilikian* for *hēlikian*; 655:16 *hymein* for *hymein;* 655:19 *hēmein* for *hēmin*; Oxy P 654:10 reads *hēmas*, which should probably be *hymas;* 655:20 *esei* (a form acceptable even in earlier Greek for *esē*). Cf. E. Mayser, *Grammatik*, §11, 13, 15.

anapaēsetai: A vulgar form of *anapausetai*; cf. Ap 14:13; Clem. Alex., *Stromata* 2, 9, 45. The Coptic seems to have read here *ana panta*; or is this possibly a deliberate change of meaning that has been introduced?

Though J. H. Ropes (*Die Sprüche Jesu, die in den kanonischen Evangelien nicht überliefert sind* [TU 14/2; Leipzig, 1896] 128) believes that the saying is authentic, Resch (*Agrapha*, 215) called it apocryphal, and Jacquier (*art. cit.*, 101) labelled it doubtfully authentic.

THIRD SAYING

ΛΕΓΕΙ Ι[
ΟΙ ΕΛΚΟΝΤΕΣ ΗΜΑΣ [
Η ΒΑΣΙΛΕΙΑ ΕΝ ΟΥΡΑ[
ΤΑ ΠΕΤΕΙΝΑ ΤΟΥ ΟΥΡ[
ΤΙ ΥΠΟ ΤΗΝ ΓΗΝ ΕΣΤ[
ΟΙ ΙΧΘΥΕΣ ΤΗΣ ΘΑΛΑ[
ΤΕΣ ΥΜΑΣ ΚΑΙ Η ΒΑΣ[
ΕΝΤΟΣ ΥΜΩΝ [.]ΣΤΙ [
ΓΝΩ ΤΑΥΤΗΝ ΕΥΡΗ[
ΕΑΥΤΟΥΣ ΓΝΩΣΕΣΘΑΙ [
ΥΜΕΙΣ
ΕΣΤΕ ΤΟΥ ΠΑΤΡΟΣ ΤΟΥ Τ[
ΓΝΩΣΘΕ ΕΑΥΤΟΥΣ ΕΝ[
ΚΑΙ ΥΜΕΙΣ ΕΣΤΕ Η ΠΤΟ[

'Though no restoration of ll. 9–14 can hope to be very convincing, we think that a fairly good case can be made out in favour of our general interpretation' (GH, *New Sayings*, 16). As it turns out, neither the restoration of Grenfell and Hunt nor that of any of the subsequent commentators was correct. The difficulty lay in the fact that only the beginning of the lines of the Greek saying has been preserved and there was formerly no outside control or guide. Now, however, we have grounds for a fairly convincing restoration in the Coptic translation. The latter shows that we are dealing here with one long saying, not two, as was suggested by P. Parker (*ATR* 22 [1940] 196).[34] The third Coptic saying reads as follows: 'Jesus said, "If those who draw you on say to you, 'Behold, the kingdom is in the heaven', then the birds of the heaven shall be (there) before you. If they say to you, 'It is in the sea (*thalassa*)', then the fishes will be (there) before you. But (*alla*) the kingdom is within you and outside of you. When (*hotan*) you know yourselves, then (*tote*) they will know you (*or*: you will be known) and you will realize that you are the sons of the living Father. But if you do not know yourselves, then you are in poverty and you are poverty"' (80:19–27; 81:1–4).

[34] J. Doresse (*Thomas*, 89–90) likewise breaks up the second saying into two, without, however, giving any justifying reason.

Guided by this Coptic version, which is not in all respects identical, we may suggest the following restoration of the Greek text:

λέγει Ἰ*[η(σοῦ)ς· ἐὰν]*
οἱ ἕλκοντες ἡμᾶς [εἴπωσιν ὑμῖν· ἰδοὺ]
ἡ βασιλεία ἐν οὐρα[νῷ, ὑμᾶς φθήσεται]
τὰ πετεινὰ τοῦ οὐρ[ανοῦ· ἐὰν δ' εἴπωσιν ὅ]
τι ὑπὸ τὴν γῆν ἐστ[ιν, εἰσελεύσονται]
οἱ ἰχθύες τῆς θαλά[σσης φθάσαν]
τες ὑμᾶς καὶ ἡ βασ[ιλεία τοῦ θεοῦ]
ἐντὸς ὑμῶν [ἐ]στι [κἀκτός. ὃς ἂν ἑαυτὸν]
γνῷ, ταύτην εὑρή[σει καὶ ὅτε ὑμεῖς]
ἑαυτοὺς γνώσεσθαι, [εἰδήσετε ὅτι υἱοί]
ἐστε ὑμεῖς τοῦ πατρὸς τοῦ ζ[ῶντος· εἰ δὲ μὴ]
γνώσ<εσ>θε ἑαυτούς, ἐν [τῇ πτωχείᾳ ἐστὲ]
καὶ ὑμεῖς ἐστε ἡ πτω[χεία]

'Je[sus] says, ["If] those who draw you on [say to you, 'Behold,] the kingdom (is) in the heav[en',] the birds of the hea[ven will be (there) before you. But if they say th]at it is under the earth, the fishes of the se[a will enter before you]. And the king[dom of God] is within you [and outside (of you). Whoever] knows [himself,] will fin[d] it [and when you] know yourselves, [you will realize that] you are [sons] of the li[ving] Father. [But if you will not] know yourselves, [you are] in [poverty] and you are pov[erty.]"'

Comments

9. *I[ē(sou)s]:* Thanks to the Coptic version, we can now eliminate the often proposed restoration of J[udas], 'not the Iscariot'.

10. *hoi helkontes:* We have translated the Coptic above in function of the Greek participle; but it is just possible that the Coptic *netsōk hēttēut*^{e}*n* means 'those who go before you' (see W. E. Crum, *A Coptic Dictionary* [Oxford, 1939] 327a). But in neither case is the sense clear. Who are those who 'draw you on' or 'go before you'? It is now impossible to explain this word by appealing to Jn 6:44 or 12:32, as was done by the first editors

and many commentators since then. They appear to be opponents of Jesus, whose teachings he is refuting by reducing them to absurdity before he affirms that the kingdom is within and without.

hēmas: My translation corrects this word to *hymas*, which is demanded by the context, as many former editors saw, and also by the Coptic translation. On the interchange of eta and upsilon, see the note on line 8 above.

11. *hē basileia:* The absolute use of this word (without 'of God' or 'of heaven') can be paralleled by Mt 13:38; 24:14; 4:23; 8:12; Acts 20:25.

oura[nō: Restored in the singular because of the article with the word in the following line. Hofius' reconstruction of this line is a trifle too long.

13. *eiseleusontai . . . phthasan]tes hymas:* I am not happy about this reconstruction, because it does not exactly reflect the Coptic, but something similar is needed to fill up the space. For the use of the circumstantial participle of *phthanō* with a finite verb, cf. H. W. Smyth, *Greek Grammar* (Cambridge, 1956) §2062a; R. Kühner and B. Gerth, *Ausführliche Grammatik der griechischen Sprache*, Part 2, 4th ed. (Hanover, 1955) §482, Anm. 14.

15. *kai:* This conjunction is peculiar here, for we would expect an adversative, which is precisely what we have in the Coptic (*alla*, 'but').

hē bas[ileia tou theou]: It would also be possible to restore *tōn ouranōn.* Support for this restoration is had in a passage of Hippolytus, *Elenchus* 5, 7 (GCS 26, 83): *peri tēn . . . physin, hēnper phēsi* ⟨*tēn*⟩ *entos anthrōpou basileian ouranōn zētoumenēn, peri hēs diarrēdēn en tō kata Thōman epigraphomenō euangeliō paradidoasi. . . .* The Coptic version which we now have makes it all the more likely that the *Gospel according to Thomas* to which Hippolytus here refers is not the *Infancy Gospel of Thomas the Israelite*, but the one represented by the Oxyrhynchus fragments and the Coptic text. However, I have preferred to restore *tou theou*, because this saying is obviously a development of Lk 17:21, *idou gar hē basileia tou theou entos hymōn estin*. Moreover, in Oxy P 1:7–8 we find the expression *tēn basileian tou theou*, which is rendered in the Coptic (86:18–19) simply by *tm^e^ntero*, 'the kingdom' (absolutely), just as we find it here. For the possible use of Dt 30: 11–14 in this part of the saying, see T. F. Glasson, *ExpTim* 78 (1966–67) 151–2.

16. [*kaktos*]*:* This restoration is taken from the Coptic *s^e^mpet^e^n bal*, 'Outside'. The exact meaning of the kingdom being 'within you and without' is puzzling. L. Cerfaux and G. Garitte have devoted a study to the parables of the kingdom in this Coptic Gospel, but no attempt has been made by them to explain the sense of this phrase. See 'Les paraboles du royaume dans L'"Evangile de Thomas"', *Mus* 70 (1957) 307–27. See now A. Rüstow, '*Entos hymōn estin*', *ZNW* 51 (1960) 197–224; R. Sneed, '"The Kingdom of God is Within You" (Lk 17, 21)', *CBQ* 24 (1962) 363–82.

hos an heauton] *gnō:* There is a lack of correspondence here between the Greek and the Coptic, for the verb is 3 sg. 2 aor. subj., demanding a 3 sg. subject. We have simply adopted the restoration of this line given by former editors (see Evelyn White, pp. 8–9), which cannot be improved on.

17. *tautēn:* This pronoun must refer to the kingdom, as it is the only feminine in the preceding context. In Clement of Alexandria (*Paidagogos* 3, 1) we find the idea of the knowledge of oneself leading to a knowledge of God developed.

18. *heautous:* For the use of this pronoun as a reflexive with a verb in the 2 pl., see below l. 20 and Blass-Debrunner, §64, 1; Kühner-Gerth, §455, 7.

gnōsesthai: A misspelling for *gnōsesthe*; the diphthong *ai* was pronounced like epsilon, as in Modern Greek, at the time of the writing of this fragment. See further Oxy P 654:37 *-eitai* for *-eite*; Oxy P 1:5–6 *nēsteusētai* for *nēsteusēte*; 1:7 *heurētai* for *heurēte*. For the converse change see below line 23, *eperōtēse* for *eperōtēsai*. Cf. E. Mayser, *op. cit.*, §14.

eidēsete: Or possibly *eisesthe.*

19. *hymeis:* A correction written above the line.

z[ōntos]: GH, *New Sayings*, 11, read T[before the break in the papyrus, admitting that a pi is also possible (17). However, the traces of this letter are quite faint and can also be read as a zeta, which would agree with the Coptic *etonh*, 'who is living'. Cf. Jn 6:57 *ho zōn patēr*, and l. 2 of the prologue above. See also Rom 9:26 (=Hos 2:1).

20. *gnōsthe:* This form looks like a 2 pl. 2 aor. subj. midd. of *ginōskō*. But why should it be middle followed by a reflexive pronoun? Former commentators emended it to *gnōs⟨es⟩the*, a future middle form which would go well with the reflexive pronoun object, and which parallels *gnōsosthai* of 1:18.

en [tē ptōcheia este]: The association of poverty with a lack of knowledge reminds us of the explanations offered by some of the patristic writers why the Ebionites had a name apparently derived from *'ebyôn*, 'poor'. Cf. p. 438 below; 'Ebionites', *Dictionnaire de spiritualité* 4 (fasc. 25, 1958) 33.

21. *hē ptō[cheia:* GH, *New Sayings*, 11, read an omicron before the break in the papyrus. This must be read as an omega, as W. Schubart (*ZNW* 20 [1921] 222) previously suggested, but he restored the word *ptō[sis]*. The Coptic version makes our restoration certain. The word itself occurs in Oxy P 1:22.

To what extent this long saying is authentic is difficult to determine.

FOURTH SAYING

ΟΥΚ ΑΠΟΚΝΗΣΕΙ ΑΝΘ[
ΡΩΝ ΕΠΕΡΩΤΗΣΕ ΠΑ[
ΡΩΝ ΠΕΡΙ ΤΟΥ ΤΟΠΟΥ ΤΗ[
ΟΤΙ
ΣΕΤΕ ΠΟΛΛΟΙ ΕΣΟΝΤΑΙ Π[
ΟΙ ΕΣΧΑΤΟΙ ΠΡΩΤΟΙ ΚΑΙ [
ΣΙΝ

While former commentators succeeded in restoring the second part of this saying, their efforts were not so successful in the first part, as now appears from the Coptic version. The fourth Coptic saying: 'Jesus said, "The man old in his days will not hesitate[35] to ask a little child of seven days about the place (*topos*) of life, and he will live. For many (that are) first will be last and they will be(come) only one"' (81:4–10). The Greek text, which varies slightly, can be restored with great probability except for the last line.

[λέγει Ἰ(ησοῦ)ς·]
οὐκ ἀποκνήσει ἄνθ[ρωπος πλήρης ἡμε]
ρῶν ἐπερωτῆσε πα[ιδίον ἑπτὰ ἡμε]
ρῶν περὶ τοῦ τόπου τῆ[ς ζωῆς καὶ ζή]
σετε ὅτι πολλοὶ ἔσονται π[ρῶτοι ἔσχατοι καὶ]
οἱ ἔσχατοι πρῶτοι καὶ [ζωὴν αἰώνιον ἕξου]
σιν.

'[Jesus says,] "A ma[n full of d]ays will not hesitate to ask a ch[ild of seven da]ys about the place of [life and he will live.] For many (that are) fi[rst] will be [last and] the last will be first and they [will have eternal life]."'

Comments

22. *anthrōpos:* Of all the previous restorations of this line only C. Taylor's came close to the Coptic, *anthrōpos plērēs hēmerōn*. In fact, it is still acceptable. Also possible is *palaios hēmerōn*; so Hofius, appealing to Dn 7:9, 13, 22. This saying is to be compared with a similar one preserved in *A Manichaean Psalm-book*, published by C. R. C. Allberry (Manichaean Manuscripts in the Chester Beatty Collection, vol. 2 [Stuttgart, 1938] 192): 'The grey-haired old men, the little children instruct them. They that are six years old instruct them that are sixty years old.' Though there are differences of detail, the general idea is the same. Possibly the Psalm-book has borrowed from this passage.

23. *eperōtēse:* Misspelling for *eperōtēsai*; see note on line 18.

pa[idion hepta hēme]rōn: The passage quoted above (see note

[35] For some unknown reason J. Doresse (*Thomas*, 90) translates the future (*fnağnau*) as a jussive. Likewise, one wonders whence comes the expression 'il apparaîtra que' before 'many (that are) first will be last'.

on line 15) from Hippolytus (*Elenchus* 5, 7), quoting the *Gospel according to Thomas*, has a further expression that is interesting for this passage: *eme ho zētōn heurēsei en paidiois apo etōn hepta*. The idea of an old man being instructed by a small child was apparently a favourite with the Gnostics; see J. Doresse, *Thomas*, 126 ff.

24. *peri tou topou tē[s zōēs:* Cf. the Coptic saying §25 (Pl. 86, lines 4–5), in which the disciples ask, 'Show us the place (*topos*) in which you are, since (*epei*) there is need (*anankē*) for us to seek after it.' The answer given is not exactly *ad rem*, but the question shows that the idea of a 'place' of life or of the presence of Jesus concerned those who used this Gospel. According to J. Doresse (*Thomas*, 120), the same expression occurs in another Chenoboskion text, *The Dialogue of the Saviour* (MS. 1, p. 132?): 'Matthew says, "Lord, I wish [to question you] about the place of life."'

zēsete: This is Hofius' suggestion, which is surely better than my original one. It is a variant of *zēsetai* (see comment on line 18).

25. *hoti:* Inserted above the line.

polloi esontai . . . : Quoted *ad litteram* from Mk 10:31, whereas Mt 19:30 omits *hoi* before the second *eschatoi*. The form in Lk 13:30 is slightly different (Huck-Lietzmann, *Synopse*, p. 147). Cf. also Mt 20:16. Evelyn White (p. 16) has a remark that is worth quoting here. 'The Saying—however we restore it—is a remarkable instance of that salient characteristic of the Oxyrhynchus collection as a whole—the mixture of elements at once parallel to and divergent from the Synoptics. For while the first part of the Saying has nothing exactly similar in the Synoptics, it nevertheless seems related to a clearly marked group of episodes in the Gospels. On the other hand the second part of the Saying corresponds exactly with the Synoptic version. . . . The Synoptics and the Saying are indeed so close that it is incredible that the two are independent, and the evidence

. . . goes to show that it is the writer of the Sayings who is the borrower.'

26. *kai [zōēn aiōnion hexou]sin:* I am at a loss to restore the end of this saying properly according to the version in the Coptic. Is it possible that the Coptic has changed the text here or that it is based on a different Greek recension? Evelyn White (p. 15) restored [*zōēn klēronomēsou*]*sin*, but this yields thirty-four letters to the line. GH (*New Sayings*, 18) suggested, 'shall have eternal life'; cf. Jn 3:16, 36; 5:24. I prefer the latter, being one letter shorter. Lagrange's suggestion (*ibid.*) [*monoi zōēn hexou*]*sin* is also possible. See now M. Marcovich, *JTS* 20 (1969) 60–1.

FIFTH SAYING

ΛΕΓΕΙ ΙΗΣ   .[
ΘΕΝ ΤΗΣ ΟΨΕΩΣ ΣΟΥ ΚΑΙ [
ΑΠΟ ΣΟΥ ΑΠΟΚΑΛΥΦΗΣΕΤ[
ΤΙΝ ΚΡΥΠΤΟΝ Ο ΟΥ ΦΑΝΕ[
ΚΑΙ ΘΕΘΑΜΜΕΝΟΝ Ο Ο[

Except for the end of the first line, this saying was correctly restored by the first editors and subsequent commentators. The Coptic version now supplies the end of that line. The fifth Coptic saying: 'Jesus said, "Know what is before your face, and that which is hidden from you will be revealed to you. For (*gar*) there is nothing hidden which will not be revealed"' (81:10–14). The Greek text may now be restored as follows:

λέγει Ἰη(σοῦ)ς·   γ[νῶθι τὸ ὂν ἔμπροσ]
θεν τῆς ὄψεως σοῦ, καὶ [τὸ κεκαλυμμένον]
ἀπό σου ἀποκαλυφ<θ>ήσετ[αί σοι·   οὐ γάρ ἐσ]
τιν κρυπτὸν ὃ οὐ φανε[ρὸν γενήσεται]
καὶ θεθαμμένον ὃ ο[ὐκ ἐγερθήσεται].

'Jesus says, 'K[now what is be]fore your face, and [that which is hidden] from you will be reveal[ed to you. For there i]s nothing hidden which will not [be made] mani[fest] and (nothing) buried which will not [be raised up.]"'

Comments

27. *g[nōthi to on empros]then:* Thanks to the Coptic we can now eliminate the restoration of former commentators, 'Everything that is not before . . .', and restore an imperative. H.-Ch. Puech (*RHR* 147 [1955] 128) wonders whether we should not read a masculine *ton emprosthen*, in which case our Lord would be referring to himself. The Coptic *pet*^{e}*mp*^{e}*mto* ^{e}*mpekho ebol* can be translated either as 'what is' or 'who is'. If the neuter is read, we may compare Clement of Alexandria, *Stromata* 2, 9, 45: *thaumason ta paronta.*

28. [*to kekalymmenon*]*:* This part of the saying is variously preserved in the Synoptic tradition, with Luke giving us two versions of it. See Mk 4:22—Lk 8:17 and Mt 10:26—Lk 12:2 (Huck-Lietzmann, *Synopse*, p. 74). 'In the first of these groups, where Luke is clearly dependent upon Mark, the Saying occurs in a series of disconnected logia and is therefore without context; but in the second we find it in the Charge to the Twelve (*Matth.* x 5 ff.), or to the Seventy (*Luke* x 1 ff.), though the third evangelist defers some of the most characteristic matter—including the parallel to the present Saying—to chapter xii. Our authorities for the Saying in its two-fold form are, then, Mark (for Group I) and Q (for Group II). . . . Grenfell and Hunt consider it to agree with Matthew and Luke (Group II) in general arrangement, but with Mark in the language of the first clause of the second half. . . . Now the first clause of the second half of Saying IV coincides word for word with the Lucan parallel in Group I, and it therefore seems likely that Mark should be left out of the matter altogether. . . . It may, then, be claimed that the Saying is dependent partly upon the Q tradition, and partly upon the Lucan version of Mark's tradition' (Evelyn White, p. 18). Actually, the saying which is preserved in the Oxyrhynchus fragment and in the Coptic version is not exactly identical with any of the canonical forms of the saying; the greatest similarity is found in the third member of the saying with the beginning of Lk 8:17, while the second

member best resembles Mt 10:26, but the canonical version is in the negative, whereas the saying here is positive. The first and fourth members of the saying are not found in the canonical Gospels at all. H.-Ch. Puech (*art. cit.*, 128) has discovered this same saying also in the Manichaean *Kephalaia* 65 (Manichäische Handschriften der Staatlichen Museen Berlin, 1 [Stuttgart, 1940] 163): 'Know that which is before your face and what is hidden from you will be revealed to you.' He believes there is a deliberate suppression of reference to the resurrection here, evidence of a Gnostic theologoumenon.

29. *apokalyph⟨th⟩ēset[ai:* Corrected from the papyrus' *apokalyphēsetai.*

31. *thethammenon:* To be read as *tethammenon.* See next note. *ho ouk egerthēsetai:* Restoration of GH (*New Sayings*, 18). Cf. their note: 'Instead of "shall be raised" a more general expression such as "shall be made known" can be supplied; but this detracts from the picturesqueness of what is in any case a striking variation of a well-known saying.' The restoration has been confirmed by an inscription on a shroud found in the hamlet of Behnesa and bought in 1953. It is dated palaeographically to the fifth or sixth century A.D. and reads:

legei Iēsous: ouk estin tethamme
non ho ouk egerthēsetai.

'Jesus says, "There is nothing buried which will not be raised up."'

See H.-Ch. Puech, *art. cit.*, 127–8. We have then in the Greek a longer version than the Synoptic accounts or the Coptic traditions. Is it possible to say which was prior, the longer or the shorter? R. Bultmann (*Die Geschichte der synoptischen Tradition* [Göttingen, 1958] 95) and J. Jeremias (*Unknown Sayings*, 16) regard the saying as a secondary expansion of the canonical saying. I believe that this is the correct interpretation, certainly preferable to that suggested by Puech (*art. cit.*, 128–9), according to which the longer text would have been uttered by the Risen Christ and the whole saying would refer to his person (masculine *ton emprosthen*). He is inclined to regard the short version as 'propre au témoignages coptes . . . transmise par des documents émanant de gnostiques et de manichéens, c'est-à-dire de gens qui s'accordent à rejeter toute conception matérielle de la résurrection'. But the short version is also found in the canonical Gospels. The part of the saying that offers a paraphrase of the canonical saying should be regarded with the same authenticity; as for the last member, it is probably a literary embellishment of the canonical saying.

SIXTH SAYING

[..]ΕΤΑΖΟΥΣΙΝ ΑΥΤΟΝ Ο[
[..]ΓΟΥΣΙΝ ΠΩΣ ΝΗΣΤΕΥ[
[.....]ΜΕΘΑ ΚΑΙ ΠΩΣ [
[.....]ΑΙ ΤΙ ΠΑΡΑΤΗΡΗΣ[
[....]Ν ΛΕΓΕΙ ΙΗΣ[
[......]ΕΙΤΑΙ ΜΗ ΠΟΙΕΙΤ[
[....]ΗΣ ΑΛΗΘΕΙΑΣ ΑΝ[
[.........]Ν Α[.]ΟΚΕΚΡ[
[........]ΚΑΡΙ[..] ΕΣΤΙΝ [
[............]Ω ΕΣΤ[
[..............]ΙΝ[
. . . .

Though Grenfell and Hunt (*New Sayings*, 19) admitted that this saying was 'broken beyond hope of recovery', some commentators succeeded in correctly restoring some of the lines. Due to the Coptic version we can advance the restoration still farther; however, once again we are faced with two slightly different recensions. The sixth Coptic saying runs as follows: 'His disciples (*mathētēs*) asked him; they said to him, "Do you wish that we fast (*nēsteue*)? And in what way shall we pray, shall we give alms (*eleēmosynē*), and what shall we observe (*paratērei*) in eating?" Jesus said, "Do not lie, and what you hate do not do, for all will be revealed before heaven. For (*gar*) there is nothing hidden which will not be revealed, and nothing concealed that will remain without disclosure"' (81:13–14). From this Coptic version it is clear that the disciples were wondering to what extent they, as followers of Jesus, were to retain Jewish practices as the external observances of their religion. Jesus' answer insists rather on the internal aspects of religion. With this to guide us, we may now restore the Greek text thus:

[ἐξ]ετάζουσιν αὐτὸν ο[ἱ μαθηταὶ αὐτοῦ καὶ]
[λέ]γουσιν· πῶς νηστεύ[σομεν, καὶ πῶς προσ]
[ευξό]μεθα καὶ πῶς [ἐλεημοσύνην ποιή]
[σομεν, κ]αὶ τί παρατηρήσ[ομεν ὅταν δειπ]
[νῶμε]ν; λέγει Ἰη(σοῦ)ς· [μὴ ψεύδεσθε καὶ ὅ]
[τι μισ]εῖται μὴ ποιεῖ[τε· πάντα γὰρ ἔστ]
[αι πλήρ]ης ἀληθείας ἀν[τὶ τοῦ οὐρανοῦ· οὐ]
[δὲν γάρ ἐστι]ν ἀ[π]οκεκρ[υμμένον ὃ οὐ φανε]
[ρὸν ἔσται· μα]κάρι[ός] ἐστιν [ὃ ταῦτα μὴ ποιῶν].
[πάντα γὰρ ἐν φανερ]ῷ ἔστ[αι παρὰ τῷ πατρὶ ὃς]
[ἐν τῷ οὐρανῷ ἐστ]ιν. [

'[His disciples] ask him [and s]ay, "How [shall we] fast, [and how shall] we [pray] and how [shall we give alms, a]nd what shall [we] observe [when we sup?"] Jesus says, "[Do not lie and what] you [hate] do not do. [For all things will be full of (?)] truth bef[ore heaven. For there is nothing] hidden [which will not be (made) known. Ha]ppy is [he who does not do these things. For all] will be mani[fest before the Father who] is [in heaven.]"'

Comments

32. *exetazousin:* See Jn 21:12 for the use of this verb in disciples' questions. The question resembles in some ways that of the rich young man (Mt 19:16–22; Lk 18:18–22). It gives a bit of context to the saying, and in this respect resembles Oxy P 655:17 ff. Such an introduction we find in the following Coptic sayings: 12, 19, 21, 24, 37, 43, 51, 52, 53, 99, 113. In three cases the subject is simply 'they' (presumably 'the disciples'): 91, 100, 104. Elsewhere we find Mary speaking (21), Salome (61), a woman of the crowd (79), Simon Peter (13, 114), and Thomas (13).

33. *pōs:* It is clear that the Greek text has a slightly different

recension, for this occurrence of *pōs* does not correspond to the Coptic. We restore the future of the verb to make it similar to the construction of the rest of the Greek saying. The first three subjects about which the disciples inquire, viz., fasting, prayer, and almsgiving, are treated in Mt 6:2–4, 5–15, 16–18, but in reverse order.

34. *eleēmosynēn:* The singular of this noun occurs in Mt 6:2–4, and because the questions asked seem in some way related to this passage (see previous note), we have restored the singular. However, the plural is also possible, as can be seen from Acts 9:36; 10:2; 24:17.

35. *hotan deipnōmen:* This expression is not certain, but I am trying to render the Coptic *ena^{e}r paratêrei eou ^{e}nči* [for *^{e}nčin*?] *ouôm*, 'we shall observe what in eating?' The reconstruction is at best a conjecture. Hofius suggests rather [*peri tōn brōmatōn*, 'beim Essen'. Is this really better? Marcovich has accepted it.

36. *pseudesthe:* The aorist subjunctive would also be possible, but I have preferred the present imperative because another occurs in the following line. Cf. H. W. Smyth, *Greek Grammar*, §1800, 1840; Blass-Debrunner, §364, 3.

37. *mis*]*eitai:* A misspelling for *miseite*; see note on line 18. Despite the appeal to a misspelling, the reconstruction can be regarded as certain because of the Coptic version. It should be noted that Jesus does not answer the questions put by the disciples but insists on other things—a fact that former commentators were not able to ascertain.

How are we to restore the end of l. 37 and the beginning of l. 38? The last two letters before the break in l. 38 suggest the original of the Coptic *^{e}mp^{e}mto ebol ^{e}ntpe*, 'before heaven'. We have, accordingly, restored *an*[*ti tou ouranou*]. There is nothing in the Coptic that corresponds exactly to]*ēs alētheias*, which reminds us of Jn 1:14 but has an entirely different meaning, of course. The restoration here is highly questionable; Hofius' is no better. But cf. M. Marcovich, *JTS* 20 (1969) 65–6.

39. *apokekrymmenon:* See the preceding saying, ll. 28–30.

40. *makarios estin:* Is this part of the same saying? If so, then we have a different ending in the Greek that is not found in the Coptic. J. Doresse (*Thomas*, p. 91) treats this as part of a distinct saying. He has in his favour the fact that *makarios* is preserved in the Coptic of the following saying. But it would then seem that we must either shorten our restoration of l. 39 and the beginning of l. 40 or suppose that the usual introduction, 'Jesus says', has been omitted. Neither seems possible. Moreover, the letters that remain on the following lines do not seem to agree with any possible reconstruction of the Greek of the following Coptic saying. For an attempt to reconstruct it as a separate saying, see M. Marcovich, *JTS* 20 (1969) 66–7.

40. *tauta:* Refers to lying and doing what one abominates. However, the restoration of this and the next two lines is sheer conjecture on my part.

While certain elements of this saying are derived from the canonical Gospels and to that extent can be regarded as authentic sayings of Jesus, the saying as a whole is most likely the work of later compilers.

Oxy P 1

Fragment 1 measures $3\frac{3}{4}'' \times 5\frac{3}{4}''$ and represents the top part of a page from a papyrus codex. The top right-hand corner of the verso contains IA, the number 11, written in a later hand. 'As it was usual to foliate the right-hand pages of a book, the position of the numeral here is one good reason for supposing the leaf to have been so placed that the *verso* side came uppermost' (GH, *Logia*, 6). While most subsequent commentators accepted this decision of the first editors that the verso of the fragment preceded the recto, P. Batiffol questioned it.[36] That Grenfell and Hunt were correct is now shown by the order of the sayings preserved in the Coptic Gospel. Those on the verso precede those on the recto. Though the fragment has not been broken

[36] 'Les Logia du papyrus de Behnesa', *RB* 6 (1897) 502. A. Ehrhard (*Die altchristliche Literatur und ihre Erforschung von 1884–1900* [Freiburg i. B., 1900] 124) agreed with Batiffol. Also C. Bruston, *Les paroles de Jésus* (Paris, 1898).

vertically down the centre like Oxy P 654, the letters at the beginning of the lines have at times been so effaced that problems of restoration arise (especially at the beginning of the recto). However, since many of the lines are read with complete certainty, we can easily ascertain the number of letters on the normal line; line 1 has 17, line 6 has 16, line 20 has 19, line 29 has 17, line 36 has 18. A line-filler, shaped like a 7, is found at the end of three lines: 3 (with 13 letters), 17 (with 15 letters), 18 (with 14 letters). 21 lines are preserved on both the verso and the recto. As we shall see below, the verso must have contained at least 16 more lines. Consequently, we have only a little more than half of the papyrus page.

The eight sayings of Oxy P 1 correspond to the Coptic sayings 26, 27, 28, 29, 30 with the end of 77, 31, 32, 33. We shall number them here as sayings 7–14.

SEVENTH SAYING

ΚΑΙ ΤΟΤΕ ΔΙΑΒΛΕΨΕΙΣ
ΕΚΒΑΛΕΙΝ ΤΟ ΚΑΡΦΟΣ
ΤΟ ΕΝ ΤΩ ΟΦΘΑΛΜΩ
4 ΤΟΥ ΑΔΕΛΦΟΥ ΣΟΥ

We have unfortunately only the end of the Greek saying, but it is enough to show that it corresponds to the twenty-sixth Coptic saying of the *Gospel according to Thomas*, which reads as follows: 'Jesus said, "The splinter which is in your brother's eye you see, but (*de*) the beam which is in your own eye you do not see. When (*hotan*) you cast the beam out of your own eye,[37] then (*tote*) you will see clearly in order to cast the splinter out of your brother's eye"' (86:12–17).

Before we proceed to the restoration of this saying in its entirety, a preliminary problem must be discussed, which is raised by the first Greek word that is preserved in this fragment. The conjunction *kai* does not correspond to anything in the Coptic, where the adverb *tote* introduces the main clause. But

[37] Not 'la poutre qui est dans ton oeil' (J. Doresse, *Thomas*, 96).

it does correspond exactly to the canonical versions of Mt 7:5 and Lk 6:42, both of which do not have a subordinate temporal clause preceding but an imperative. Consequently, the clause immediately preceding the preserved part must be reconstructed according to the text of the canonical Gospels.

i [λέγει Ἰ(ησοῦ)ς·]
ii [βλέπεις τὸ κάρφος τὸ ἐν]
iii [τῷ ὀφθαλμῷ τοῦ ἀδελ]
iv [φοῦ σου, τὴν δὲ δόκον]
v [τὴν ἐν τῷ ἰδίῳ ὀφθαλμῷ]
vi [οὐ κατανοεῖς· ὑποκρι]
vii [τά, ἔκβαλε τὴν δόκον]
viii [ἐκ τοῦ ὀφθαλμοῦ σου]
1 καὶ τότε διαβλέψεις
2 ἐκβαλεῖν τὸ κάρφος
3 τὸ ἐν τῷ ὀφθαλμῷ
4 τοῦ ἀδελφοῦ σου.

['Jesus says, "You see the splinter in your brother's eye, but the beam in your own eye you do not see. Hypocrite, cast the beam out of your eye,] and then you will see in order to cast out the splinter which (is) in your brother's eye."'

Comments

Our restoration follows the wording of the Coptic version, except for the lines vi–vii, which we have discussed above. The vocabulary is Lucan, since the preserved part of the saying seems to be closer to Lk 6:42 than to Mt 7:5, as will be seen below.

2. *ekbalein:* GH (*Logia*, 10) noted that the preserved part of the saying 'agrees exactly with the wording of' Lk 6:42. However, a glance at a modern critical text of the NT reveals that the infinitive is found at the end of the verse. A. von Harnack (*Expositor*, ser. 5, vol. 6 [1897] 322) explained the discrepancy, noting that 'recent editors, following their preference for B [Vaticanus], have put *ekbalein* at the end, whereas all other Uncials, and also the Coptic version, show the word where we find it in the Papyrus'. This being so, the relation of the saying

to the Lucan version is clear. The close dependence of this saying on the canonical text assures it the same authenticity that the latter enjoys.

EIGHTH SAYING

ΛΕΓΕΙ
ΙΣ ΕΑΝ ΜΗ ΝΗΣΤΕΥΣΗ
ΤΑΙ ΤΟΝ ΚΟΣΜΟΝ ΟΥ ΜΗ
ΕΥΡΗΤΑΙ ΤΗΝ ΒΑΣΙΛΕΙ
ΑΝ ΤΟΥ ΘΥ ΚΑΙ ΕΑΝ ΜΗ
ΣΑΒΒΑΤΙΣΗΤΕ ΤΟ ΣΑΒ
ΒΑΤΟΝ ΟΥΚ ΟΨΕΣΘΕ ΤΟ
ΠΡΑ

While the Coptic is an almost exact reproduction of the Oxyrhynchus saying, it does not have the introductory *peğe IC* ('Jesus said') at the beginning. G. Garitte (*Mus* 70 [1957] 70) treats this saying as a continuation of the former, whereas J. Leipoldt (col. 486) and J. Doresse (*Thomas*, 96) separate them, following the Greek division. The twenty-seventh Coptic saying runs thus: '⟨Jesus said,⟩ "If you do not fast (*nēsteue*) to the world (*kosmos*), you will not find the kingdom; if you do not make the sabbath a (real) sabbath, you will not see the Father"' (86:17–20).

λέγει
Ἰ(ησοῦ)ς· ἐὰν μὴ νηστεύση
ται τὸν κόσμον, οὐ μὴ
εὕρηται τὴν βασιλεί
αν τοῦ θ(εο)ῦ· καὶ ἐὰν μὴ
σαββατίσητε τὸ σάβ
βατον, οὐκ ὄψεσθε τὸ(ν)
π(ατέ)ρα.

'Jesus says, "If you do not fast (to) the world, you will not find the kingdom of God; and if you do not make the sabbath a (real) sabbath, you will not see the Father."'

Comments

5. *nēsteusētai:* Misspelling for *nēsteusēte*; see note above on Oxy P 654:18.

ton kosmon: The accusative case here is strange, and former commentators made all sorts of suggestions regarding the interpretation of it. Comparing Clement of Alexandria's expression, *makarioi . . . hoi tou kosmou nēsteuontes* (*Stromata* 3, 15, 99), some regarded it 'as a clerical error for *tou kosmou*'! (e.g., C. Taylor, *The Oxyrhynchus Logia and the Apocryphal Gospels* [Oxford, 1899] 11–13). Others tried to make an accusative of time out of it.[38] However, the sense of the expression is now clear to us from the Coptic, which preserves for us the two Greek words, *nēsteue* and *kosmos* (possibly because the expression was strange to the Coptic translators too!), and adds the preposition *e*, 'to', before the latter word. Hence, the sense is 'to fast to the world'. Since we have no reason to consider the Greek defective, we must regard the accusative as one of respect. 'Fasting to the world' must mean a withdrawal from a worldly or secular outlook; it is an abstention from the world that involves becoming a 'solitary' (*monachos*). See now A. Guillaumont (*BIFAO* 61 [1962] 15–23); A. Baker, *JBL* 84 (1965) 291–4. Both writers have shown that in Syriac there are two forms of an expression which has the same basic meaning, 'abstaining from the world': *ṣūm min ʿālᵉmā* and *ṣūm lᵉʿālᵉmā*. The latter may underlie both the Greek *nēsteuein kosmon* (where the *l* would have been understood as the sign of the accusative) and the Coptic *nēsteue epkosmos* (where the *e* would have been written as the equivalent of the preposition *l*, in the dative).

[38] So Batiffol (*art. cit.*, 505), citing with approval the explanation of Herz (*Guardian*, 28 July 1897) that the Greek is an excessively literal (mis)translation of the Hebrew *'m l' tṣwmw lʿwlm*, which actually meant, 'si vous ne jeûnez toujours . . .'. The most far-fetched explanation was that of P. Cersoy (*RB* 7 [1898] 415–16), who suggested that the Greek translator of this originally Aramaic saying confused *ṣwm* ('a fast') with *ʿlm* ('world') and that we should therefore read here *tēn nēsteian*, a cognate accusative, parallel to the one we have in the second part.

7. *heurētai:* Misspelling for *heurēte*; see note above on Oxy P 654:18. Note that whereas the Greek has 'the kingdom of God', the Coptic simply has *tm*^{e}*ntero*, 'the kingdom'. See note on Oxy P 654:15.

8. *kai:* 'The use of this conjunction as a short formula of citation, meaning, "And *he saith*," is well established' (C. Taylor, *op. cit.*, 8). Cf. Heb 1:10; *Pirqê 'Abôt* 2, 5; Oxy P 1:15.

9. *sabbatisēte to sabbaton:* Being a construction with a cognate accusative (lit., 'to sabbatize the sabbath'), it explains the peculiar Coptic construction, where the repeated word is really superfluous, *etet*^{e}*nt*^{e}*meire* ^{e}*mpsambaton* ^{e}*ensabbaton*. (The dissimilation of *bb* to *mb* in the first occurrence of the word in Coptic, but not in the second, should be noted.) The Greek expression occurs in the LXX at Lv 23:32; 2 Chr 36:21. C. Taylor (*op. cit.*, pp. 14–15) showed that it does not simply mean 'to observe the (weekly) sabbath'. In Lv 23:32 it refers to the Day of Atonement, which is to be kept as a real sabbath. Hence, it is likely that we should understand the expression in this saying in a metaphorical sense or a spiritual sense. Cf. Heb 4:9 and Justin (*Dial. w. Trypho* 12, 3; *PG* 6, 500), who uses *sabbatizein* in the sense of a spiritual sabbath opposed to the formal Jewish observance; for him it consisted in abstention from sin. Cf. Resch, *Agrapha*, §74, p. 99.

10. *opsesthe ton patera:* Cf. Jn 6:46; 14:7–9 for the exact expression. Similar expressions: 'to see God' (Mt 5:8; Jn 1:18; 1 Jn 4:20; 3 Jn 11); 'to see the Lord' (Jn 21:18; 1 Cor 9:1; Heb 12:14). For the future indicative interchanging with the aorist subjunctive, see Blass-Debrunner, §365, 3.

I see no reason why this saying could not be an authentic one. E. Jacquier (*art. cit.*, p. 110) regarded it as 'probablement authentique'. But U. Holzmeister (*ZKT* 38 [1914] 118, n. 1) labelled it 'unecht'.

NINTH SAYING

ΛΕΓΕΙ $\overline{\text{ΙΣ}}$ Ε[Σ]ΤΗΝ
ΕΝ ΜΕΣΩ ΤΟΥ ΚΟΣΜΟΥ

ΚΑΙ ΕΝ ΣΑΡΚΕΙ ΩΦΘΗΝ
ΑΥΤΟΙΣ ΚΑΙ ΕΥΡΟΝ ΠΑΝ
ΤΑΣ ΜΕΘΥΟΝΤΑΣ ΚΑΙ
ΟΥΔΕΝΑ ΕΥΡΟΝ ΔΕΙΨΩ
ΤΑ ΕΝ ΑΥΤΟΙΣ ΚΑΙ ΠΟ
ΝΕΙ Η ΨΥΧΗ ΜΟΥ ΕΠΙ
ΤΟΙΣ ΥΙΟΙΣ ΤΩΝ ΑΝΩΝ
ΟΤΙ ΤΥΦΛΟΙ ΕΙΣΙΝ ΤΗ ΚΑΡ
ΔΙΑ ΑΥΤΩ[Ν] ΚΑΙ .. ΒΛΕΙΣ[39]
. . . .

Whereas the Coptic version of this saying has preserved it for us in its entirety, the Oxyrhynchus fragment has only the first half of it. The twenty-eighth Coptic saying reads thus: 'Jesus said, "I stood in the midst of the world (*kosmos*) and I revealed myself to them in flesh (*sarx*). I found them all drunken; I did not find any of them thirsty. My soul (*psychē*) was pained for the sons of men, for they are blind in their heart and do not see that they came into the world (*kosmos*) empty. They seek further to come out of the world (*kosmos*) empty. But (*plēn*) now they are drunk.[40] When (*hotan*) they set aside their wine, then (*tote*) they will do penance (*metanoei*)"' (86:20–31).

[39] But the *editio princeps* (*Oxyrhynchus Papyri*, Part 1, p. 3) reads:

ΚΑΙ ΟΥ ΒΛΕ
ΠΟΥΣΙΝ

[40] In my opinion neither J. Doresse nor G. Garitte has translated the end of this saying correctly. The Coptic reads: *plēn tenou setohe. hotan eušanneh pouērp tote sena^{e}rmetanoei*. J. Doresse (*Thomas*, 97) translates, 'Qu'il vienne cependant quelqu'un qui les redresse. Alors, quand ils auront cuvé leur vin, ils se repentiront'. G. Garitte (*Mus* 70 [1957] 71): 'ceterum (*plēn*) nunc . . .; quando impleverint cor suum, tum paenitentiam agent (*metanoein*).' The crucial form is *setohe* (3 pl. pres. ind. of *tihe*, 'to be drunk'; cf. Crum, *Coptic Dictionary*, 456b, *tohe* for *tahe*). My interpretation agrees with that of Leipoldt (col. 486). A little higher up, my interpretation differs from that of Doresse and Garitte again, in taking *ğe ^{e}ntauei* . . . (l. 27) as the object clause of *senau* and not as a subordinate clause parallel to *ğe h^{e}nb^{e}lle* . . . (again in agreement with Leipoldt). Doresse (*Thomas*, 97) has omitted the Oxyrhynchus parallel to this 28th Coptic saying.

It should be noted how closely the Coptic translates the Greek in this saying, where we have the Greek text. For instance, in 86:22 the Coptic reads *h*^{e}*nsarx*, where we might have expected the definite article; but it is the exact equivalent of the Greek. Likewise 86:23–24 reads *laau* ^{e}*nhêtou*, 'none among them', a literal rendering of *oudena . . . en autois*. Though we cannot generalize from this instance, it should nevertheless be borne in mind when a decision is to be made about the relation of the Coptic version to the Greek text in the Oxyrhynchus papyri.

λέγει Ἰ(ησοῦ)ς·　ἔ[σ]την
ἐν μέσῳ τοῦ κόσμου
καὶ ἐν σαρκεὶ ὤφθην
αὐτοῖς καὶ εὗρον πάν
τας μεθύοντας καὶ
οὐδένα εὗρον δειψῶ(ν)
τα ἐν αὐτοῖς καὶ πο
νεῖ ἡ ψυχή μου ἐπὶ
τοῖς υἱοῖς τῶν ἀν(θρώπ)ων
ὅτι τυφλοί εἰσιν τῇ καρ
δίᾳ αὐτῶ[ν] καὶ [οὐ] βλέπ
[ουσιν ὅτι ἤκουσιν εἰς]
[τὸν κόσμον κενοί·　ζη]
[τοῦσι δὲ πάλιν ἐξελ]
[θεῖν ἐκ τοῦ κόσμου κε]
[νοί.　πλὴν νῦν μεθύου]
[σιν·　ὅταν ἀποθῶνται]
[τὸν οἶνον αὐτῶν, τότε]
[μετανοήσουσιν.

'Jesus says, "I s[t]ood in the midst of the world and I appeared to them in flesh and I found them all drunken and I did not find one among them thirsting, and my soul is pained for the sons of men, for they are blind in their heart and do [not] se[e that they have come into the world empty. They seek further to go out of the world empty. But now they are drunk. When they put away their wine, then they will do penance]."'

Comments

As Garitte has already pointed out (*Mus* 70 [1959] 70, n. 5), the Coptic version makes impossible the attempt of some former commentators to join the end of the preserved part of the verso with the first line of the recto. Grenfell and Hunt (*Oxyrhynchus Papyri*, Part 1, p. 1) themselves protested against the 'current view that there is *a priori* probability in favour of only one line being lost at the bottom of the *verso*. The lacuna may have extended to five or even ten lines.' Garitte's conclusion: 'Si le texte grec était aussi long que le copte, la lacune doit être environ 17 lignes.' My own restoration of this and the following Greek saying yields sixteen lines (numbered with Roman numerals). The Coptic version, moreover, shows the unity of this saying, which was contested by P. Batiffol, who wanted to make two sayings out of it, mainly on the basis of the change of tense in the verbs (*RB* 6 [1897] 306–7).

The reader is referred to the treatment of this saying by J. Jeremias (*Unknown Sayings of Jesus*, 69–74), many of whose remarks are still valid.

11. *estēn . . . en sarkei ōphthēn:* Jesus here speaks as a 'Divine Being'; '. . . in these words we must recognize a backward glance upon His work on the part of the still living not the risen Christ' (A. von Harnack, *Expositor*, ser. 5, vol. 6 [1897] 330). The reason for this is the shift in tense from the past (in lines 11, 13, 14, 16) to the present (in lines 17, 20, 21). Evelyn White (p. xxxvi) thought that the whole saying betrays 'incipient rather than fully developed Johannism'. See the references below for verbal parallels to Johannine writing. The whole tone of the first part of the saying should, moreover, be compared with Mt 23:37, 'O Jerusalem, Jerusalem! . . . How often I have longed to gather your children around me, as a hen gathers her brood under her wings, but you refused!' Cf. Lk 13:34.

12. *en mesō tou kosmou:* Cf. Jn 1:9, 10; 3:17; 6:14; 11:27;

12:46; 16:28; 18:37. This use of *kosmos* is distinctively Johannine.

13. *en sarkei ōphthēn:* Cf. 1 Tm 3:16; Jn 1:14; 1 Jn 4:2–3.

15. *methyontas:* This notion has Pauline affinities, cf. 1 Thes 5:7–8. The figurative use of 'sobriety' recurs in 2 Tm 4:5; 1 Pt 1:13; 4:7; 5:8 (J. Jeremias, *Unknown Sayings*, 71).

16. *deipsōnta:* Some former commentators thought that Encratite influence was to be seen in the use of this word. However, it can more easily be explained as Johannine; cf. Jn 4:13–14; 6:35; 7:37, but also Mt 5:6. For the form see note above on Oxy P 654:8.

17. *ponei:* This phrase is certainly dependent on Is 53:11, *bouletai kyrios aphelein apo tou ponou tēs psychēs autou*, as has been generally recognized. Harnack also quoted Mt 26:38; Mk 14:34; Jn 12:27 for canonical statements about Jesus' troubled soul. The tone of the second part of this saying is closely related to that of the Synoptics. See J. Jeremias (*Unknown Sayings*, 71) for the Semitisms in this part of the saying. The Coptic version shows that we are dealing with one long saying here; it is not to be divided into two sayings at this point, as A. de Santos Otero has done (*Los Evangelios apócrifos*, 95–6).

20. *typhloi eisin tē kardia:* Evelyn White (p. 34) cites a parallel expression from the Greek *Gospel according to Thomas* (A viii; ed. Tischendorf): *nyn karpophoreitōsan ta sa, kai blepetōsan hoi typhloi tē kardia*. For the idea of spiritual blindness see Ps 68/69:24; Jn 9:39; Ap 3:17; Mt 15:14.

iv. *kenoi:* Cf. 1 Cor 15:58.

Though there is no direct parallel to this saying in the canonical Gospels there is nothing in it that prevents it from being regarded at least as substantially authentic. Cf. E. Jacquier, *RB* 15 (1918) 111.

TENTH SAYING

E

Recto 22 [....]..[.T]HN ΠΤΩΧΙΑ̅

The twenty-ninth Coptic saying reads as follows: 'Jesus said, "If the flesh (*sarx*) has come to be because of the spirit (*pneuma*), it is a marvel. But (*de*) if the spirit (*pneuma*) (has come to be) because of the body (*sōma*), it is a marvel of marvel(s).[41] But (*alla*) I marvel [. . . *sein?*][42] at this: how this (?) great wealth dwells in this poverty"' (86:31–5; 87:1–2).

Though we have no guarantee that the Coptic version is an exact reproduction of the Greek, one may suggest a tentative restoration somewhat as follows:

viii [λέγει]
ix [Ἰ(ησοῦ)ς· εἰ ἐγένετο ἡ σὰρξ]
x [ἕνεκεν τοῦ πνεύμα]
xi [τος, θαῦμά ἐστιν· εἰ δὲ]
xii [τὸ πνεῦμα ἕνεκεν τοῦ]
xiii [σώματος, θαῦμά ἐστι]
xiv [τῶν θαυμάτων· ἀλλὰ θαυ]
xv [μάζω ἐπὶ τούτῳ ὅτι ὁ]
xvi [τοσοῦτος πλοῦτος ἐνοι]
22 [κεῖ ταύ]τη[ν τ]ὴν πτωχεία(ν).

Comments

xv. *epi toutō:* Cf. Acts 3:12.

xvi. *ho tosoutos ploutos:* See Ap 18:17.

22. *ptōcheia(n):* The epsilon is inserted above the line; see note on Oxy P 654:8. The accusative can be used with the verb *enoikeō*; see Liddell-Scott-Jones, *s.v.*; E. Mayser, *Grammatik* 1/3 (1936) 219. There is no canonical saying that contains *ptōcheia*, nor any that resembles the full saying preserved in the Coptic.

ELEVENTH SAYING

[ΛΕΓ]ΕΙ [Ι̅Σ̅ ΟΠ]ΟΥ ΕΑΝ ΩΣΙΝ

[41] Reading *oušpēre* ^{e}*nšpēre pe* on Pl. 86, lines 33–4.

[42] On line 35 a word has been added that does not begin at the beginning of the line and does not otherwise seem to fit into the sentence, unless it is an adjective or adverb. Unfortunately, the first two or three letters of it have been lost; what remains of the end of it seems to be *sein*. My restoration disregards it.

[....]Ε[...]..ΘΕΟΙ ΚΑΙ[43]
[..]ΣΟ.Ε[..] ΕΣΤΙΝ ΜΟΝΟΣ
[..]ΤΩ ΕΓΩ ΕΙΜΙ ΜΕΤ ΑΥ
Τ[ΟΥ] ΕΓΕΙ[Ρ]ΟΝ ΤΟΝ ΛΙΘΟ̅
ΚΑΚΕΙ ΕΥΡΗΣΕΙΣ ΜΕ
ΣΧΙΣΟΝ ΤΟ ΞΥΛΟΝ ΚΑΓΩ
ΕΚΕΙ ΕΙΜΙ

It is this saying more than all the others that shows that the Coptic version is not a direct translation of the Greek, for we have here a bipartite saying, whereas the Coptic has preserved the two parts separately—the first part here in its proper place and order, but the second part as the conclusion of a longer, later saying. The text of the thirtieth Coptic saying: 'Jesus said, "In the place where there are three gods, they are gods. In the place where there are two or one, I am with him"' (87:2–5). And the text of the seventy-seventh Coptic saying: 'Jesus said, "I am the light which is over all of them. I am the All; the All has gone forth from me and the All has attained to me. Split wood, I am there; take up the stone, and you will find me there"' (94:22–28).

The first part of the Greek saying does not correspond exactly to the thirtieth Coptic saying, and so our restoration cannot be certain in this case. But taking a lead from the Coptic we may restore it thus:

[λέγ]ει ['Ι(ησοῦ)ς· ὅ]που ἐὰν ὦσιν
[γ' θε]ο[ί,] ε[ἰσὶ]ν θεοί· καὶ
[ὅ]π[ου] ε[ἷς] ἐστιν μόνος
[αὐ]τῷ, ἐγώ εἰμι μετ' αὐ
τ[οῦ]. ἔγει[ρ]ον τὸν λίθο(ν)
κἀκεῖ εὑρήσεις με,
σχίσον τὸ ξύλον, κἀγὼ
ἐκεῖ εἰμι.

[43] The *editio princeps* (*Oxyrhynchus Papyri*, Part 1, p. 3) gives the following reading, obviously dependent on restorations suggested by scholars:

[Β ΟΥΚ] Ε[ΙΣΙ]Ν ΑΘΕΟΙ ΚΑΙ
[Ο]ΠΟΥ Ε[ΙΣ] ΕΣΤΙΝ ΜΟΝΟΣ
[ΛΕ]ΓΩ ΕΓΩ....

'[Jesus sa]ys, "[Wh]ere there are [three g]o[ds, they ar]e gods. And where one is all alone to himself, I am with him. Take up the stone and there you will find me; split the wood and I am there."'

Comments

23. *hopou:* 'Immediately before *ou* there is part of a stroke which may very well be the end of the crossbar of *p*' (GH, *Logia*, 13). This reading is now confirmed by the Coptic.

24. [*g' the*]*o*[*i,*] *e*[*isi*]*n theoi:* Blass' brilliant restoration, followed by most commentators (see Evelyn White, p. 35), [*b',* *ouk*] *e*[*isi*]*n atheoi*, was certainly a step in the right direction. Objection cannot be made to the use of a cipher in a literary text, even side by side with a number written out, for several cases of this have been found, especially in the papyri; see Evelyn White, p. 36. The Coptic would suggest that we must read *three* instead of *two*. This, of course, yields a sentence in Greek that is as mysterious as the Coptic version. A. Guillaumont (*JA* 246 [1958] 114–16) suggests that a Semitic meaning underlies the use of *theoi* here, in that it reflects the use of Hebrew *ʾelōhîm*, such as one finds in Ps 82:1 and in the rabbinical interpretation of these (angelic) 'judges' in *Pirqê 'Abot* 3:7. On the other hand, M. Marcovich (*JTS* 20 [1969] 68) cites the suggestion that in the Coptic text the first mention of 'gods' may be dittographical, so that one should understand the text, 'Where they are three, they are gods'. In such case, one would restore *treis* at the beginning of line 24. This is an intriguing possibility; but it is hard to accept the idea of a dittography of this sort (with words intervening). Nor is it a case of horizontal or vertical dittography.

25. *heis estin monos:* The Greek does not correspond to the Coptic here, so we cannot force it. Who is intended here? A god or a man? The first sentence would suggest that a god is meant, but then we have an obvious problem on our hands: how is the speaker to be with him? In this second sentence we find the word 'god' neither in the Greek nor in the Coptic, and there is,

moreover, an obvious reference to Mt 18:20. For these reasons I prefer to think that the sentence refers to a man. A parallel to this saying is found in Ephraem's *Evangelii concordantis expositio* 14, 24 (*CSCO* 145, 144): 'Ubi unus erit, ibi sum et ego.' But see the full context and the discussion in A. Resch, *Agrapha*, §175, p. 201. See further *Pirqê 'Abôt* 3, 2; Str-B 1, 794.

26. *autō:* I prefer this reading, since Grenfell and Hunt (*Logia*, p. 9) first read a 't' after the lacuna. The verb *legō*, which is read by most commentators, disturbs the sense. C. Clemen (*Die christliche Welt*, 29 July 1897, p. 704, n. 4) compared *autō* to the Hebrew *l^{e}baddô*. C. H. Roberts ('The Gospel of Thomas: Logion 30^{A}', *JTS* 21 [1970] 91–2), having re-examined the papyrus itself, admits that the first letter after the lacuna can only be *g*, *t*, or (less probably) *p*. Rejecting my au]*tō* as 'linguistically weak', he prefers to remain with GH's *legō*.

27. *egeiron:* R. Reitzenstein (*ZNW* 6 [1905] 203) pointed out the occurrence of a part of this saying in a gloss of the *Etymologicum Gudianum*. Note that the order of the two members of this second part of the saying is reversed in the Coptic. See further A. F. Walls, *VC* 16 (1962) 71–6.

29. *kagō ekei eimi:* In what sense is this second part of the saying to be understood? It has often been interpreted in a pantheistic sense, or more precisely in a 'panchristic' sense, asserting the ubiquity of Jesus in the world. Cf. Eph 4:6. J. Jeremias (*Unknown Sayings*, 96, n. 2) gives a convenient list of those who so explained it. He rejects this interpretation and prefers that first suggested by H. Lisco and adopted by A. von Harnack, H. B. Swete, and Evelyn White. According to this interpretation, two pictorial illustrations are given to explain *how* Jesus is present to the individual—two kinds of strenuous work, lifting stones and splitting wood. The combination of these two types of work was probably suggested by Eccl 10:9, 'He who quarries stones may be hurt by them, while he who splits logs is endangered by them.' In contrast to the pessimism

of the Preacher, Jesus promises his abiding presence even in the most strenuous type of work.

Now the Coptic version definitely supports the 'panchristic' interpretation, if we take into consideration the full context of the Coptic saying. However, this may be a clear case in which the Coptic offers us a different redaction, for the second part of the Greek saying is separated from the first in the Coptic version, as we have already noted. Consequently, the interpretation offered by J. Jeremias may still be valid for the earlier (or at least different) Greek recension. He is, moreover, inclined to regard the second part of the Greek saying as authentic. E. Jacquier (*RB* 15 [1918] 112) called it 'douteuse'.

TWELFTH SAYING

ΛΕΓΕΙ ΙΣ ΟΥ
Κ ΕΣΤΙΝ ΔΕΚΤΟΣ ΠΡΟ
ΦΗΤΗΣ ΕΝ ΤΗ ΠΡΙΔΙ ΑΥ
Τ[Ο]Υ ΟΥΔΕ ΙΑΤΡΟΣ ΠΟΙΕΙ
ΘΕΡΑΠΕΙΑΣ ΕΙΣ ΤΟΥΣ
ΓΕΙΝΩΣΚΟΝΤΑΣ ΑΥΤΟ

This saying is exactly preserved in the Coptic version of the thirty-first saying. 'Jesus said, "No prophet (*prophētēs*) is accepted in his town; a physician does not heal (*therapeue*) those who know him"'(87:5–7). There is no need to repeat the Greek text in this case. It is translated as follows: 'Jesus says, "A prophet is not acceptable in his own homeland, nor does a physician work cures on those who know him."'

Comments

Parallels to the first part of this saying are to be found in Mt 13:57; Mk 6:4; Lk 4:24; Jn 4:44 (Huck-Lietzmann, *Synopse*, p. 18). But in no case is the wording identical. The closest parallel is offered by Lk, *oudeis prophētēs dektos estin en tē patridi autou*; but the longer forms of Mt and Mk begin in a way that is more similar to this fragment, *ouk estin prophētēs atimos ei mē en tē patridi autou kai en syggeneusin autou kai en tē oikia autou* (Mk 6:4).

Jn 4:44 echoes the Mt-Mk tradition. Luke's editorial handling of this saying in connection with one about a physician (4:23) makes us think that this saying is closer to his tradition than to the other Synoptics. See Evelyn White's comment on p. 42.

33. *poiei therapeias:* This phrase was considered to be an Aramaism by P. Cersoy (*RB* 7 [1898] 417–18); C. Taylor (*The Oxyrhynchus Logia and the Apocryphal Gospels*, 57) has pointed out that the same expression occurs in the *Protevangelium Jacobi* 20:2. Actually it reads *tas therapeias mou epeteloun* (ed. E. Amann, p. 256).

35. *geinōskontas:* For *ginōskontas*; see note on Oxy P 654:8.

The first part of this saying should be considered as authentic as the canonical parallels. The second may be authentic, or may be merely a saying constructed as an answer to the retort, 'Physician, heal thyself'.

THIRTEENTH SAYING

ΛΕΓΕΙ Ι̅Σ̅ ΠΟΛΙΣ ΟΙΚΟΔΟ
ΜΗΜΕΝΗ ΕΠ ΑΚΡΟΝ
[Ο]ΡΟΥΣ ΥΨΗΛΟΥΣ ΚΑΙ ΕΣ
ΤΗΡΙΓΜΕΝΗ ΟΥΤΕ ΠΕ
[Σ]ΕΙΝ ΔΥΝΑΤΑΙ ΟΥΤΕ ΚΡΥ
[Β]ΗΝΑΙ

Once again we have an almost exact correspondnece between the Greek and Coptic saying; the latter (the thirty-second) reads: 'Jesus said, "A city (*polis*) which is built upon a high mountain (and) is fortified cannot fall nor (*oude*) can it hide"' (87:7–10). Since the Greek text is almost perfectly preserved, there is no need to repeat it; it is translated as follows: 'Jesus says, "A city built upon the top of a high mountain and made fast can neither fall nor be hidden."'

Comments

The slight differences in the two versions may simply be translation peculiarities; the Coptic lacks the copula corresponding to *kai*, and repeats the verb 'to be able'. The whole saying is related to Mt 5:14, *ou dynatai polis krybēnai epanō orous keimenē.*

36. *oikodomēmenē:* To be corrected to *ōkodomēmenē.* GH (*Logia,* 15) pointed out that this participle is supported by a variant for Matthew's *keimenē* in the Syriac versions and in Tatian's *Diatessaron* 8, 41. W. Lock (*Two Lectures,* 13 and 26) found support for it also in a Latin version used by Hilary; A. Harnack in the Pseudo-Clementine *Hom.* 3, 67, 1 (GCS 42, 81).

37. *ep' akron orous hypsēlou:* Evelyn White (p. 44) thinks that this variant for Matthew's *epanō* is due to the influence of Is 2:2, *ep' akrou tōn oreōn,* or even of Is 28:4.

38. *hypsēlous:* An error by homoeoteleuton for *hypsēlou;* 'the scribe certainly wrote *hypsēlous,* but he appears to have partially rubbed out the *s*' (GH, *Logia,* 15).

There is no reason why the saying could not be regarded as authentic; but it is more likely a secondary expansion of Mt 5:14. I find it hard to see any connection between this saying and Mt 7:24–25, which has been suggested by various commentators.

FOURTEENTH SAYING

41 ΛΕΓΕΙ $\overline{\text{ΙΣ}}$ ΑΚΟΥΕΙΣ
[.]ΙΣΤΟΕ..ΤΙΟΝ ΣΟΥ ΤΟ[44]

This saying has been fully preserved for us in the thirty-third Coptic saying: 'Jesus said, "What you will hear in your ear (and) in[45] the other ear, preach upon your roof-tops. For (*gar*) no one lights a lamp and places it under a measuring-basket, nor (*oude*) does he put it in a hidden place; but (*alla*) he is wont to place it on a lampstand (*lychnia*) so that everyone who comes in and goes out may see its light"' (87:10–18). Only the beginning of the Greek text is preserved, and it corresponds more

[44] The *editio princeps* (*ibid.,* p. 3) gives the following reading and restoration:

42 [Ε]ΙΣ ΤΟ ΕΝ ΩΤΙΟΝ ΣΟΥ ΤΟ
[ΔΕ ΕΤΕΡΟΝ ΣΥΝΕΚΛΕΙΣΑΣ]

[45] I am indebted to G. W. MacRae, S.J., for the interpretation of this line.

or less to the Coptic; the initial pronoun is missing. We may restore it as follows:

41 λέγει Ἰ(ησοῦ)ς· ‹ὃ› ἀκούεις
[ε]ἰς τὸ ἓν ὠτίον σου, το[ῦ]
[το κήρυξον ἐπὶ τῶν]
[δωμάτων

'Jesus says, "What you hear in your one ear, preach that upon your roof-tops. . . ."'

Comments

41. *akoueis:* The present tense, whereas the Coptic has the future. Following the latter, we have also supplied a relative pronoun object to this verb. The Coptic version also supports the reading of line 42, which was generally adopted by the former commentators and the *editio princeps*.

The first part of the saying is an expanded version of Mt 10: 27 (cf. Lk 12:13).

The second part of the saying, which is preserved only in the Coptic version, is related to Mt 5:15; Lk 11:33; and to Mk 4: 21; Lk 8:16. See further M. Marcovich, *JTS* 20 (1969) 54–5.

Oxy P 655

The last group of Oxyrhynchus sayings of Jesus is found in the so-called Fragment of a Lost Gospel, Papyrus 655, the largest piece of which measures $3\frac{1}{4}'' \times 3\frac{1}{4}''$ and comprises the middle part of two narrow columns. It contains parts of at least four sayings[46] which correspond to the thirty-sixth to thirty-ninth Coptic sayings of the *Gospel according to Thomas*. We shall refer

[46] Fragment d of this text is very small and contains part of several words on five lines:

]TIN
]ΩTEINΩ
]OΣMΩ
]H
]ΣTIN
].

Fragment e may be part of d, although this is unlikely (see below); it has only two letters on it:]*KO*[. I made no attempt to deal with these fragments

to them as sayings 15–18. Some of the lines of col. I are completely preserved so that it is possible to determine the normal number of letters on a line: it varies between 12 letters in line 23 and 16 letters in lines 13, 18, 22.

FIFTEENTH SAYING

[...]ΠΟ ΠΡΩΙ Ε[.....
[....]Ε ΑΦ ΕΣΠ[.....
[....]ΡΩΙ ΜΗΤΕ [...
[......]ΜΩΝ ΤΙ ΦΑ[
[........] ΤΗ ΣΤ[.
[.......] ΤΙ ΕΝΔΥ[.
[..]ΣΘΕ [...]ΛΩ ΚΡΕΙ[.
[...]ΕΣ .[...] ΤΩΝ [..
ΝΩΝ ΑΤΙ[...]ΥΞΑ[.
ΝΕΙ ΟΥΔΕ Ν[..]ΕΙ .[.

---

in the original article. Subsequently, R. Kasser ('Les manuscrits de Nag' Hammâdi: Faits, documents, problèmes', *RTP* 9 [1959] 357–70) established the connection of frag. d with Coptic saying 24. R. A. Kraft (*HTR* 54 [1961] 261–2) sought to relate frag. e to the bottom of frag d. This attempt is, however, questionable, because though both fragments d and e come from the bottom of a column, as the lower straight margin indicates; the letters *KO* on frag. e are more or less on a line with *TIN* of the first line of frag. d. Consequently, frag. e scarcely represents the beginning of lines of the same column as frag. d. Moreover, the Greek text reconstructed by Kraft is scarcely better than Kasser's, which I follow below. Kraft's third line, though closer to the Coptic version, is too cryptic in Greek: the force of the parataxis comes through in the Coptic, but it is unfortunately lost in his form of the Greek text. The Coptic version of saying 24b runs: 'He said to them, "Whoever has ears let him hear. Within a man of light there is light and he lights the whole world (*kosmos*). When he does not shine, there is darkness."' The Greek saying can be reconstructed as follows:

[εἰ φῶς ἐσ]τιν
[ἐν ἀνθρώπῳ φ]ωτεινῷ,
[ἐν ὅλῳ τῷ κ]όσμῳ
[φωτίζει, εἰ δὲ μ]ή,
[σκοτεινός ἐ]στιν.

Its translation: 'If light is in a man of light, it shines in all the world; but if it is not, (then) it (the world) is in darkness.'—It is clear that this fragment d belonged to an earlier column in Oxy P 655.

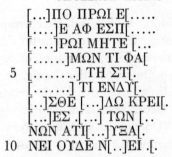

ΕΝ ΕΧΟΝΤ[...]ΝΔ[.
ΜΑ ΤΙ ΕΝ[....] ΚΑΙ
ϒΜΕΙΣ ΤΙΣ ΑΝ ΠΡΟΣΘΗ
ΕΠΙ ΤΗΝ ΕΙΛΙΚΙΑΝ
ϒΜΩΝ ΑϒΤΟ[..]ΩΣΕΙ
ϒΜΕΙΝ ΤΟ ΕΝΔϒΜΑ ϒ
ΜΩΝ

The thirty-sixth Coptic saying, which corresponds to this Oxyrhynchus fragmentary text, is much shorter than the Greek. It may represent a different Greek recension of the Gospel or a deliberate shortening of the text in the Coptic. At any rate, we can only use the Coptic as a control for the restoration of the first few lines of the Greek text. The Coptic version runs as follows: 'Jesus said, "Do not be solicitous from morning till evening and from evening till morning about what you are going to put on"' (87:24–7). Even this part of this saying does not correspond exactly to the beginning of the Greek text. We may restore it as follows:

[λέγει Ἰ(ησοῦ)ς· μὴ μεριμνᾶ]
[τε ἀ]πὸ πρωὶ ἕ[ως ὀψὲ]
[μήτ]ε ἀφ᾽ ἑσπ[έρας]
[ἕως π]ρωὶ μήτε [τῇ]
[τροφῇ ὑ]μῶν τί φά
[γητε μήτε] τῇ στ[ο]
[λῇ ὑμῶν] τί ἐνδύ
[ση]σθε. [πολ]λῷ κρεί[σ]
[σον]ές ἐ[στε] τῶν [κρί]
νων ἅτι[να α]ὐξά
νει οὐδὲ ν[ήθ]ει μ[ηδ]
ἐν ἔχοντ[α ἔ]νδ[υ]
μα. τί ἐν[δεῖτε] καὶ
ὑμεῖς; τίς ἂν προσθ<εί>η
ἐπὶ τὴν εἱλικίαν
ὑμῶν; αὐτὸ[ς δ]ώσει
ὑμεῖν τὸ ἔνδυμα ὑ
μῶν.

'[Jesus says, "Be not solicitous f]rom morning un[til evening, nor] from eve[ning until mo]rning either [for y]our [sustenance], what [you will] eat, [or] for [your] clo[thing], what you [will] put on. [You] are worth [far] more than [the lili]es whi[ch g]row but do not s[pi]n, a[nd] have n[o] clo[th]ing. And you, what do [you lack?] Who of you can add to his stature? *He* will [g]ive you your clothing."'

Comments

This saying is related to the canonical words recorded by Mt 6:25–32 and Lk 12:22–30, but we have either a different tradition preserved in this fragment or else a deliberate condensation. Lines 7–13 of the fragment can be compared with Mt 6:28 (=Lk 12:27); lines 13–16 with Mt 6:27 (=Lk 12:25). Cf. also *Acta Thomae* 36 (ed. Bonnet, p. 153). There is no reason why this form of the saying should not be given the same degree of authenticity that is accorded the canonical versions. E. Jacquier (*RB* 15 [1918] 116) regarded it as authentic, but J. Jeremias (*Unknown Sayings*, 86) would consider only the last three lines as authentic. He rejects the rest because he makes of this and the following saying but one unit. Since the following saying is marked with Gnostic ideas on sexual asceticism, it is not to be regarded as authentic (*ibid.*, 17). However, I do not believe that these two sayings should be treated as one. The change of subject in line 17 is the beginning of a new saying, as is now evident from several similar cases in the Coptic version. See note on Oxy P 654:32. This saying deals only with excessive solicitude for food and clothing and the correct dependence that the Christian should have on the Father.

1. This first line can now be restored confidently, thanks to the canonical version (Mt 6:28) and the Coptic, which supplies the negative form of the saying.

4. *trophē:* Suggested by Mt 6:25.

5. *stolē:* The first editors admitted that this word was not the happiest of restorations but nothing else seems to fit and no one else, as far as I can ascertain, has come up with a better solution. R. A. Kraft (*HTR* 54 [1961] 254) would rather read *tei st*[*o*]*lei*, maintaining that 'the difference between EI and H is

very difficult to detect in P. Ox. 655, since the vertical stroke of the E has very little curvature' (p. 258, n. 6). If this is a correct observation, it would involve a simple orthographic variant.

9. *hati[na a]uxanei:* For a different attempt to interpret these words, see R. A. Kraft, *HTR* 54 (1961) 258–9. Though his appeal to a form of the verb *xainein* (instead of *auxanein*) is attractive, it is based on dubious evidence (variants in the New Testament text tradition). Until more light is shed on this textual problem, I prefer to remain with my original reconstruction.

10. GH (*New Sayings*, p. 41) did not attempt to restore the end of this line nor the lacuna in line 12. In the *editio princeps* (*Oxyrhynchus Papyri*, Part 4, p. 25) they discuss the lacunae without bringing anything new to the problem, except the possibility of reading *en[deite]* in line 12. T. Zahn (*NKZ* 16 [1905] 97, n. 1) suggested the reading *[mēd]en echont[a e]nd[y]ma. ti en[dysesth]e kai hymeis*. But the verb *endysesthe* is too long for the lacuna, as is evident from a glance at Plate 2. Hence I suggest a combination of the first part suggested by Zahn with the verb *endeite* in line 12.

13. The corrected optative form was suggested by the first editors.

14. *heilikian:* A misspelling for *hēlikian*; see note on Oxy P 654:8. I have translated the word as 'stature', but it is also quite likely that the meaning 'age, length of life'—which is the more normal meaning of the word—should be used both here and in Mt 6:27 and Lk 12:25. See AG 345.

15. *autos:* This can only refer to the Father, as in Mt 6:26. Zahn refers also to 1 Cor 15:37–38.

16. *hymein:* For *hymin*; see note on Oxy P 654:8.

SIXTEENTH SAYING

ΛΕΓΟΥΣΙΝ ΑΥ
ΤΩ ΟΙ ΜΑΘΗΤΑΙ ΑΥΤΟΥ
ΠΟΤΕ ΗΜΕΙΝ ΕΜΦΑ
ΝΗΣ ΕΣΕΙ ΚΑΙ ΠΟΤΕ

ΣΕ ΟΨΟΜΕΘΑ ΛΕΓΕΙ
ΟΤΑΝ ΕΚΔΥΣΗΣΘΕ ΚΑΙ
ΜΗ ΑΙΣΧΥΝΘΗΤΕ
....
29 Θ[

The thirty-seventh Coptic saying is an almost exact reproduction of the Greek text, in so far as the latter is preserved. 'His disciples said, "On what day will you reveal yourself to us and on what day shall we see you?" Jesus said, "When (*hotan*) you take off your clothes (and) are not ashamed,[47] and take your tunics and lay them under your feet like little children and tread upon them, then (*tote*) [you will become] sons of the Living One and you will not fear"' (87:27–34; 88:1–2). Whereas the Coptic has omitted the translation of *autō* (line 17) and *autou* (line 18), it has added *Iēsous*, which is absent in the Greek. The first part of the saying is perfectly preserved in the Greek and needs no restoration; my attempt to complete it is, of course, based on the supposition that the Coptic and Greek corresponded substantially in the second part.

λέγουσιν αὐ
τῷ οἱ μαθηταὶ αὐτοῦ·
πότε ἡμεῖν ἐμφα
νὴς ἔσει καὶ πότε
σε ὀψόμεθα; λέγει·
ὅταν ἐκδύσησθε καὶ
μὴ αἰσχύνθητε
i [*καὶ λάβητε τοὺς χι*]
ii [*τῶνας ὑμῶν καὶ θῆτε*]
iii [*αὐτοὺς ὑπὸ τοὺς πό*]
iv [*δας ὑμῶν ὡς τὰ παι*]
v [*δία καὶ πατήσητε*]
vi [*αὐτούς, τότε τὸν υἱ*]
vii [*ὸν τοῦ ζῶντος ὄψεσ*]
viii *θ*[*ε οὐδὲ φοβηθήσεσθε*]

[47] The Coptic *etet*^{e}*nšakektēut*^{e}*n eheū* ^{e}*mpet*^{e}*nšipe*, 'when you take off your clothes (and) are not ashamed', has been mistranslated both by Leipoldt (col. 486: 'Wenn (*hotan*) ihr eure Scham auszieht') and by Garitte (*art. cit.*, 71: 'Quando (*hotan*) despoliabitis vos a pudore vestro et (au)feretis vesti-

'His disciples say to him, "When will you be revealed to us and when shall we see you?" He says, "When you take off your clothes and are not ashamed, and take your tunics and put them under your feet like little children and tread upon them, then you will see the Son of the Living One and you will not fear."'

Comments

19. *pote* . . .: This question recalls that put in the mouth of 'Judas, not the Iscariot' (most likely Judas Thomas, the alleged compiler of this Gospel), by the writer of the fourth canonical Gospel, 'Master, how does it happen that you are going to show yourself to us and not to the world?' (Jn 14:22).

hēmein: For *hēmin*; see note on Oxy P 654:0.

v. *patēsēte:* Clement of Alexandria (*Stromata* 3, 13, 92; GCS 15, 238) has preserved a quotation from the *Gospel according to the Egyptians*, which has a very similar statement ascribed to Jesus, 'To Salome's question, when the things about which he was speaking will be known, the Lord said, "When you tread upon the garment of shame, and when the two become one and the male (will be) with the female, neither male nor female."' See the discussion in Resch, *Agrapha*, pp. 252–4. Cf. H. C. Kee, '"Becoming a Child" in the Gospel of Thomas', *JBL* 82 (1963) 307–14, esp. 309–11; J. Z. Smith, 'The Garments of Shame', *History of Religions* 5 (1965–66) 217–38.

In this saying, at least as it is preserved for us in the Coptic version, we find the characteristic Gnostic ideas about sexual asceticism that were current in the second and third centuries A.D. These ideas force us to classify this saying in the category of J. Jeremias' 'tendentious inventions'.

SEVENTEENTH SAYING

30 ΛΕ[

Ο[

menta vestra et ponetis . . .'). On *kōk ahēu* see W. Till, *Koptische Grammatik* (Leipzig, 1955) §277.

TA[
ΓΥ[
KA[
N · [
KA[
HM[
ΣI[
[
[

Because of the fragmentary nature of this part of the fragment, no attempt was made in the past by commentators to restore these lines.[48] The lines that follow (41–6) correspond to the thirty-ninth Coptic saying; hence these lines (beginning at least with line 30) must correspond to the thirty-eighth. Is it possible to restore the Greek text on the basis of this Coptic saying? I have tried various possibilities, but none of them was so obvious as to be convincing, given the present reading of the fragment. Several points, however, should be noted. First of all, at least two blank lines are needed for the restoration of the following saying; these should normally be lines 39–40. But line 37 seems to contain the beginning of the word *hēmerai*, which corresponds to the Coptic. But then there is not room enough to complete the end of this saying in Greek with the present disposition of lines. However, if the fragment (c) is correctly spaced on the plate (and there is no reason to question the spacing of the editors), then at least *three* blank lines must be left between fragment (c) and (b). Secondly, in line 33 the second letter is far from certainly an upsilon; in fact, we may have there no more than one letter, gamma. The same is true of the second letter in line 38; in this case, there is a trace of a letter, but it could be almost anything.

The thirty-eighth Coptic saying: 'Jesus said, "Often have you desired (*epithymei*) to hear these words which I am saying to you, and you have no other from whom to hear them. There will be

[48] T. Zahn (*NKZ* 16 [1905] 99, n. 2) suggested the following possibilities: line 30 *le*[*gousin autō*]; 31 *ho*[*i mathētai autou*]; 33 *gy*[*nē* or *gy*[*mnos*; 35 *hēm*[*eis*.

days, when you will seek me (and) you will not find me"' (88: 2–7).

This saying is related to one that is preserved for us in Irenaeus, *Adv. haer.* 1, 20, 2, *pollakis epethymēsa⟨n⟩ akousai hena tōn logōn toutōn kai ouk eschon ton erounta.* See also Epiphanius, *Pan.* 34, 18, 13 (GCS 31, 34). Resch (*Agrapha*, §139, p. 179) thinks that it is an extracanonical parallel to Lk 10:24 and Mt 13:17. If we use these various leads, we arrive at a Greek form of the saying that is possible, but which is not altogether satisfying when an attempt is made to fit it to the letters that remain on the fragment.

30 λέ[γει Ἰ(ησοῦ)ς· π]
ο[λλάκις ἐπεθυμήσα]
τα[ι ἀκοῦσαι τοὺς λό]
γ[ους οὓς ὑμῖν λέγω]
κα[ὶ οὐκ ἔχετε τὸ]
35 ν [ἐροῦντα ὑμῖν]
κα[ὶ ἐλεύσονται]
ἡμ[έραι ὅτε ζητή]
38 σε[τέ με καὶ οὐχ εὑ]
i [ρήσετέ με.

Comments

I admit that my restoration is quite questionable in many places, but I propose it in the hope that someone will be fortunate enough to see more clearly and make the proper adjustments.

30. The breaking up of *pollakis*, as I have restored the text, is most improbable.

31. The ending *ai* on *epethymēsatai* instead of *epethymēsate* can be paralleled in these papyrus fragments; see note on Oxy P 654:18.

34. The breaking up of *ton* is proposed as a parallel to that of *ouk* in Oxy P 1:30–31 and 655:45–46.

36. *eleusontai hēmerai:* Cf. Mt 9:15. Cyprian, *Testimoniorum libri tres ad Quirinum* 3, 29 (CSEL 3, 143).

37. *zētēsete me:* Cf. Jn 7:34, 36.

EIGHTEENTH SAYING

[
[
ΕΛ[
ΤΗΣ [
ΚΡΥΨ[
ΕΙΣΗΛ[
ΕΙΣΕΡ[
ΚΑΝ[
ΔΕ ΓΕΙ[
ΜΟΙΩ[
ΚΕΡΑΙ[
ΡΑ[
....

As can be seen, lines 41–50 contain but a few letters (a maximum of five) at the beginning of the lines. V. Bartlet succeeded in identifying lines 41–6 as a variant of Lk 11:52, *ouai hymin tois nomikois, hoti ērate tēn kleida tēs gnōseōs; autoi ouk eisēlthate kai tous eiserchomenous ekōlysate* (GH, *New Sayings*, 44). C. Taylor (*op. cit.*, 23) subsequently identified lines 47–50 as related to Mt 10:16, *ginesthe oun phronimoi hōs hoi opheis kai akeraioi hōs hai peristerai*. They were both on the right track, as the Coptic version now shows, but we can still improve on their restoration. The thirty-ninth Coptic saying reads thus: 'Jesus said, "The Pharisees and the scribes have received the keys of knowledge (*gnōsis*); they have hidden them and have not (*oute*) entered, and those who wished to enter they have not permitted. But (*de*) you, become wise (*phronimos*) as the serpents and guileless (*akeraios*) as the doves"' (88:7–13). We may now restore the Greek text as follows:

i [λέγει]
['Ι(ησοῦ)ς· οἱ Φαρισαῖοι καὶ]
[οἱ γραμματεῖς ἀπ]
ἔλ[αβον τὰς κλεῖδας]
τῆς [γνώσεως καὶ ἀπέ]
κρυψ[αν αὐτάς· οὔτε]
εἰσῆλ[θον οὔτε τοὺς]

εἰσεϱ[χομένους ἀφῆ]
καν [εἰσελθεῖν. ὑμεῖς]
δὲ γεί[νεσθε φϱόνι]
μοι ὠ[ς οἱ ὄφεις καί ἀ]
κέϱαι[οι ὠς αἱ πεϱιστε]
ϱα[ί.

'Jesus says, "The Pharisees and the scribes have received the keys of knowledge and have hidden them; neither have they entered nor permitted those who would enter. But you become wise as the serpents and guileless as the doves."'

Comments

The Coptic now agrees with the Greek in every instance except in lines 44–5, where we had to restore the participle as in Lk 11:52, instead of the clause, 'those who wished to enter'.

40. *apelabon:* Having thus restored the text on the basis of the Coptic version, I read in G. Quispel's article (*VC* 11 [1957] 202, n. 17) that I had been anticipated by J. H. A. Michelsen, who suggested long ago reading *el*[*abon*], referring to Pseudo-Clementine *Hom.* 18, 15.

42. *gnōseōs:* Cf. Pseudo-Clementine *Hom.* 18, 16, 2 (GCS 42, 248): *apekrypton tēn gnōsin tēs basileias kai oute autoi eisēlthan oute tois boulomenois eiselthein pareschon.* This form is actually quite close to the Coptic.

apekrypsan: The Codex Bezae on Lk 11:52 reads a form of this verb instead of *ērate*. For a previous reconstruction that is close to my own, see A. de Santos Otero, *Los Evangelios apócrifos*, 83.

44. *eisēlthon:* Or *eisēlthan.*

45. *eiser*[*chomenous*]*:* I now prefer to follow Michelsen, Hofius, and Kraft in the reconstruction of this line.

47. *geinesthe:* For *ginesthe*; see note on Oxy P 654:8.

While E. Jacquier (*RB* 15 [1918] 117) was inclined to regard this saying as authentic, it is much more likely that in its present form it is a conflation of two canonical sayings.

Concluding Remarks

From the foregoing detailed comparison of the Greek sayings of Jesus preserved in the three Oxyrhynchus fragments with the Coptic Gospel it should be evident that we are dealing with two different copies of the *Gospel according to Thomas*. There can no longer be any doubt about the fact that the Oxyrhynchus fragments 1, 654, 655 are part of the *Gospel according to Thomas*. This conclusion is imposed on us by the prologue which introduces the fragments and, even more so, by the almost identical order of sayings within the fragments and the Coptic version. The identification of these fragments with the *Gospel according to Thomas* eliminates all the previous speculation about their relationship to the *logia* that Matthew collected, or to the *logia* on which Papias commented; nor are they part of the *Gospel according to the Egyptians* (so Harnack), nor of the *Gospel according to the Hebrews* (so Batiffol, Grenfell and Hunt, and the majority of critics after them), nor of the *Gospel of the Ebionites* (so Zahn)—not to mention the fantastic opinion of H. A. Redpath, that they are 'a fragment of perhaps some apocryphal gospel claiming to give a sort of *procès verbal* of the indictment or evidence used at the trial of Christ'.[49] The fact that in one or two instances this collection preserves a saying that is also found in one or other of these Gospels does not weaken in the least the identification which is now established. All that can be said on this score is that these other Gospels have preserved the same saying. In fact, given the peculiar character of the *Gospel according to Thomas* as a collection of Jesus' sayings, we would naturally expect some of the Agrapha preserved in other writings to turn up here.[50] Moreover, there are many more Coptic sayings which can be paralleled elsewhere than the few

[49] *Expositor*, ser. 5, vol. 6 (1897) 228.

[50] Apparently those entrusted with the official edition of the *Gospel according to Thomas* are convinced that the principal sources of the sayings are, beside the canonical Gospels, the *Gospels according to the Egyptians* and *according to the Hebrews*. So W. C. Till (*BJRL* 41 [1958–59] 451); H.-Ch. Puech (*CRAIBL*, 1957, p. 160); G. Quispel (*VC* 11 [1957] 194). Should

from the Oxyrhynchus papyri which we happen to have studied in this article.

While in most cases we found an almost word-for-word identity between the Greek and the Coptic versions, there are some differences which force us to conclude that we are not dealing with the same recension of the *Gospel according to Thomas* in the two languages. Allowance must be made, of course, for translation differences, which do not really prove a difference of recension. But there are variants, e.g., shorter and longer versions, or a change in order, which clearly point to a difference in recension. Though it is possible that another Greek recension existed, of which the Coptic is a faithful rendering, it is much more likely that the Coptic version is an adapted translation—most likely with adaptations made to suit some of the theologoumena of the Gnostics who used or translated the Gospel.

This difference of recension, however, is not such as to hinder us from using the Coptic as a guide for the restoration of the lacunae in the Greek text.[51] In some instances we had to depart from the Coptic version since the extant Greek words would not permit a literal translation back into Greek. Nevertheless, the Coptic recension supplies the tenor of the saying and enables us to correct many of the former restorations which were quite acceptable previously because of the lack of an extrinsic guide such as we now have in the Coptic.

---

not the similar positions taken by scholars in the past about the relation of the Oxyrhynchus fragments to these Gospels teach us to be more cautious? After all, what we know of these two Gospels is nothing more than a series of quotations preserved in various patristic writers. To postulate such a collection as the source of the complete Gospel which we now have is to go beyond the evidence. It may be that the *Gospel according to Thomas* is the source of the quotations found in those Gospels, or again maybe all three depend on a common source.

[51] The closeness of the relationship of the Greek and Coptic recensions can be seen from the following list, which attempts to sum up the degree of correspondence which exists between the various sayings. Sayings 10, 14, and 17 are so fragmentary that no judgment can be based on them. But Sayings 8, 12, and 13 are not fragmentary, and of these 12 is identical with

The Gospel to which these Oxyrhynchus fragments belong is not the *Infancy Gospel according to Thomas the Israelite Philosopher*.[52] It is rather another *Gospel according to Thomas*, which was well known in antiquity. I have cited above a passage from Hippolytus, who *c.* A.D. 230 tells us that the Naassenes, a Gnostic sect of the third century, used *to kata Thōman epigraphomenon euangelion*.[53] Likewise Origen mentioned a short time later a heterodox Gospel, *to kata Thōman euangelion*, which existed in his day together with a *Gospel according to Matthias*.[54] Eusebius probably echoed his information, when he spoke of *Thōma euaggelion* as one of those 'revered by the heretics under the name of the Apostles'. Jerome too derived from Origen his

---

the Coptic and the other two are almost identical, having slight variants which we may ascribe to translation and not to a different recension. In the case of the fragmentary sayings we must distinguish between (*a*) those which are split vertically down the centre (Prologue, Sayings 1–6 on Oxy P 654, 11 on Oxy P 1, 18 on Oxy P 655) and (*b*) those which lack a beginning or end, but have the remaining lines well preserved (Sayings 7, 9, and 16). In group *b* we have once again an almost identical correspondence in which the slight variants are most probably due to the translation and not to a difference in recension. In group *a* Saying 2 is shorter than the Coptic, Sayings 5, 6, 11 (=Coptic Sayings 30 and part of 77), 15 contain a longer and different ending, thus giving evidence of a different recension; possibly Saying 4 also belongs here. But the other sayings in this group (Prologue, 3, 18) manifest in their preserved parts an almost identical correspondence with the Coptic again. Hence the number of cases in which we find an exact or almost exact correspondence with the Coptic justifies our using the Coptic as a guide to the restoration of the Greek text, even though we do admit recensional differences, which we have carefully noted at the proper places.

[52] See M. R. James, *The Apocryphal New Testament*, 49–70. Anyone who compares the text of the Coptic *Gospel according to Thomas* with this Infancy Gospel will see that it is of an entirely different genre and a completely independent composition. At the time of Cullmann's lectures in the United States on the *Gospel according to Thomas* some Catholic newspapers quoted 'a leading Vatican Biblical expert', Mgr Garofalo, to this effect: the document on which Cullmann had lectured was 'only a new edition of a well-known apocryphal "Gospel of St Thomas" dating from the second century and recounting miracles performed by the Christ Child' (Baltimore *Catholic Review*, 3 April 1959, p. 4). This is not correct.

[53] *Elenchus* 5, 7, 20; GCS 26, 83.

[54] *Hom in Luc.* 1; GCS 49, 5.

knowledge of the existence of the Gospel (*evangelium, quod appellatur secundum Thomam*, transl. of Origen's *Hom. in Luc.* 1; *PL* 26, 233; GCS 49, 5; *evangelium iuxta Thomam, Comment. in Mt.*, Prol.; *PL* 26, 17).[55] But the testimony of Cyril of Jerusalem causes a problem, for he attributes the Gospel not to the Naassenes, as did Hippolytus, but to the Manicheans: *egrapsan kai Manichaioi kata Thōman euangelion.*[56] And in another place he says, 'Let no one read the *Gospel according to Thomas*, for it is not by one of the twelve apostles, but by one of the three wicked disciples of Manes.'[57] Patristic scholars have debated whether this *Gospel according to Thomas*, attributed by Hippolytus to the Naassenes and by Cyril to the Manicheans, is one and the same. J. Quasten suggested that the Manichean Gospel was 'merely a redaction, a working over of the Gnostic *Evangelium Thomae*'.[58] The heavily Gnostic character of many of the sayings in the Coptic Gospel has already led to the conclusion that the latter is most likely the Manichean version of which Cyril speaks. The deliberate change of ending in the fourth saying, which is paralleled in the Manichean *Kephalaia*, is certainly evidence in this direction, as H.-Ch. Puech has already pointed out.[59] Unfortunately, though it is clear that the Greek text in the Oxyrhynchus papyri represents a different recension, we are not in possession of any evidence to say that this represents the *Gospel according to Thomas* which Hippolytus ascribed to the Naassenes.

Though I have remarked above that this Coptic Gospel is

[55] See further Eusebius (*Hist. eccl.*, TU 5/2 [Leipzig 1889] 169); Ambrose (*Expos. ev. Luc.* 1, 2; CSEL 32, 11); Bede (*In Lucae ev. expositio* 1, prol.; *PL* 92, 307C); Peter of Sicily (*Hist. Manich.* 16; *PG* 104, 1265C); Ps.-Photius (C. *Manich.* 1, 14; *PG* 102, 41B); Ps.-Leontius of Byzantium (*De sectis* 3, 2; *PG* 86/1, 1213C); Timothy of Constantinople (*De recept. haeret.*; *PG* 86/1, 21C); Second Council of Nicaea (787), act. 6, 5 (Mansi 13, 293B); Gelasian Decree (TU 38/4 [Leipzig, 1912] 11, 295–6).

[56] *Catecheses* 4, 36; *PG* 33, 500B.

[57] *Catecheses* 6, 31; *PG* 33, 593A.

[58] *Patrology* 1 (Westminster, 1950) 123.

[59] '... il est aujourd'hui évident que l'*Evangile de Thomas* dont les anciens témoignages signalent la présence parmi les Ecritures manichéennes ne fait qu'un avec notre nouvel inédit' (*CRAIBL*, 1957, p. 153).

in no way a 'Gospel' in the sense of the canonical Matthew, Mark, Luke, and John, it is nevertheless significant that it is entitled *peuangelion*. Modern New Testament scholars are wont to define a gospel-form in function of the canonical writings, a composition including the words and deeds of Jesus. Yet the ancient compiler of this collection of sayings apparently had no qualms about calling it a 'Gospel'. May it not be possible that in a collection of sayings such as we have in the *Gospel according to Thomas*, an original idea of a Gospel as the 'good news' is preserved? We recall here Papias' statement about Matthew's collection of the *logia* and the postulated source of the Synoptics, Q. I suggest, therefore, that this fact be kept in mind when discussions are engaged in concerning the nature of this gospel-form, for the ancients obviously could also call a collection of sayings a 'Gospel', even if it did lack a Passion Narrative.[60]

I do not intend to enter into a discussion here of the relation of the sayings of the Coptic Gospel to the Synoptics or to John. This relation exists, but it can only be studied in the light of all of the sayings preserved, and we have been dealing in this paper only with the parallels to the Oxyrhynchus sayings. Moreover, such a study will require a long time yet, for each of the 114 sayings must be studied individually.

Undoubtedly the *Gospel according to Thomas* is one of the most important of the Chenoboskion texts, because it will shed new light on the Gospel tradition of the early Church. While it can and will be studied for the interest it might have as a Manichean Gnostic document, bringing new information to the history of that sect, it has a value which transcends this aspect, which it shares with the other Gnostic texts, in that it also has relevance for the New Testament. It is an apocryphal Gospel, and in no way can it enter the canon as 'the Fifth Gospel'.[61]

[60] *Pace* A. M. Farrer, 'On Dispensing with Q', *Studies in the Gospels: Essays in Memory of R. H. Lightfoot* (ed. D. E. Nineham; Oxford: Blackwell, 1957) 60.

[61] News about this Coptic Gospel stirred up the usual journalistic sensa-

Bibliography of the Oxyrhynchus Sayings

Anonymous, 'Extra-canonical Scriptures', *Academy* 52 (1897) 83; 'Further Research on the Logia', *The Independent*, 2 Sept. 1897, p. 13; Notice of GH, *Logia*, in *Critical Review of Theological and Philosophical Literature* 7 (1897) 485–6; Notice of GH, *New Sayings*, *ibid.*, 14 (1904) 467–8; Notice of GH, *Logia*, in *ChQR* 45 (1897) 215–20; 'The New Sayings of Jesus', *ibid.*, 58 (1904) 422–32; 'The New Logia', *The Independent*, 22 July 1897, p. 12; 'The Sayings of Christ', *ibid.*, 19 Aug 1897, pp. 8–9; 'The "Sayings of Jesus"', *Spectator* 79 (1897) 75–6; 'The Danger of False "Sayings of Christ"', *ibid.*, 107–8; 'What are the New Logia?', *Speaker*, 17 July 1897, pp. 64–5; Abbott, E. A., 'The Logia of Behnesa or the New "Sayings of Jesus"', *AJT* 2 (1898) 1–27; Andrews, H. T., 'Logia', *Encyclopaedia Britannica*, 11th ed., 16 (1911) 878–9; Bacon, B. W., 'The New Sayings of Jesus', *The Independent*, 22 July 1897, pp. 14–15; Badham, F. P., 'The New Logia', *Athenaeum* 3641 (7 Aug. 1897) 192–3; Bardenhewer, O., *Geschichte der altkirchlichen Litteratur* (Freiburg i. B.; vol. 1 [2nd ed.; 1913]) 511–12, 539–42; Bartlet, V., 'The New Logia', *Athenaeum* 3639 (23 July 1897) 129; 'The Oxyrhynchus "Sayings of Jesus"', *Contemporary Review* 87 (Jan.–June 1905) 116–25; 'The Oxyrhynchus "Sayings of Jesus" in a New Light', *Expositor*, ser. 8, vol. 23 (1922) 136–59; Review of C. Taylor, *The Oxyrhynchus Sayings of Jesus Found in 1903 . . .*, *Review of Theology and Philosophy* 1 (1905) 11–18; Review of Evelyn White, *JTS* 23 (1921–22) 293–300; Batiffol, P., 'Les logia du papyrus de Behnesa', *RB* 6 (1897) 501–15; 'Nouveaux fragments évangéliques de Behnesa', *ibid.*, n.s. 1 (1904) 481–93; Bauer, W., *Das Leben Jesu im Zeitalter der neutestamentlichen Apokryphen* (Tübingen, 1909); Berlin, M., 'The Logia', *JQR* 10 (1897–98)

tionalism. Unfortunately, it is not the first time that journalists announced to the world the discovery of a 'Fifth Gospel'. See F.-M. Braun, 'A propos d'un "Cinquième Evangile"', *VieInt* 34 (1935) 220–4. At that time it was a question of some *Fragments of an Unknown Gospel*, published by H. I. Bell and T. C. Skeat (London, 1935).

190; Besson, E., *Les logia agrapha: Paroles du Christ qui ne se trouvent pas dans les évangiles canoniques* (Bihorel-lez-Rouen, 1923); Blass, F., 'Das neue Logia-Fragment von Oxyrhynchus', *Evangelische Kirchenzeitung* 1897, pp. 498–500; Bonaccorsi, G., *I vangeli apocrifi, testo greco-latino e traduzione italiana* (Florence, 1948); **Buonaiuti, E.,** *Detti extracanonici di Gesù* (Scrittori cristiani antichi 11; Rome, 1925); Bruston, C., *Fragments d'un ancien recueil de paroles de Jésus* (Paris, 1905); *Les paroles de Jésus récemment découvertes en Egypte, et remarques sur le texte du fragment de L'Evangile de Pierre* (Paris, 1898); **C**abrol, F., 'Agrapha', *DACL* 1 (1907) 979–84; Causse, A., *Les nouveaux logia de Jésus* (Paris, 1898); Cersoy, P., 'Quelques remarques sur les logia de Benhesa [*sic*]', *RB* 7 (1898) 415–20; 'Un mot sur la deuxième sentence du papyrus découvert en 1897 à Behnesa', *L'Université Catholique*, n.s. 28 (1898) 150–3; Chiappelli, A., 'Le nuove Parole di Gesù scoperte in un papiro egizio', *Nuova Antologia*, ser. 4, vol. 71 (1897) 524–34; Christie, F. A., Review of GH, *Logia*, in *The New World* 6 (1897) 576–9; Clemen, C., 'Neugefundene Jesusworte?', *Die christliche Welt*, 29 July 1897, 702–5; Cobern, C. M., 'The Oldest Leaf of the New Testament', *Biblia* 10 (1897–98) 255–7; 'The Recently Discovered "Sayings of Christ" and the Oldest Leaf of the New Testament', *Homiletic Review*, 34 (1897) 505–10; Cotton, J. S., 'Greek Papyri from Egypt', *Biblia* 10 (1897–98) 153–9; 'Latest Views of the Logia', *ibid.*, 315–18; 'The Logia Not Pantheistic', *ibid.*, 213–14; Couard, L., *Altchristliche Sagen über das Leben Jesu und der Apostel* (Gütersloh, 1908); Cross, J. A., 'The Sayings of Jesus', *Expositor*, ser. 5, vol. 6 (1897) 257–67; **D**avidson, T., Review of GH, *Logia*, in *International Journal of Ethics* 8 (1897–98) 106–10; Deissmann, A., 'On the Text of the Second Logia Fragment from Oxyrhynchus', *Light from the Ancient East* (tr. by L. R. N. Strachan; London, 1910) App. 2, pp. 436–40 [first published in *Beilage zur Allgemeinen Zeitung* (Munich) no. 162, 18 July 1904, pp. 116 ff.]; Dietrich, E. L., *Ausserbiblische Worte Jesu: Grundtext und Übertragung* (Wiesbaden, 1950); Donovan, J., *The Logia in Ancient and Recent Literature*

(Cambridge, 1924); Dräseke, J., Review of GH, *Logia*, in *Wochenschrift für klassische Philologie* 14 (1897) 1171–4; D. R. J., 'Sentences de Jésus', *RevBén* 15 (1897) 433–9; Dunkerley, R., 'The Oxyrhynchus Gospel Fragments', *HTR* 23 (1930) 19–37; *The Unwritten Gospel, Ana and Agrapha of Jesus* (London, 1925); Durand, A., 'Bulletin d'archéologie biblique (part VI)', *Etudes* 72 (1897) 416–20; **E**. D. V., 'Recent Articles on the Logia', *Biblical World* 10 (1897) 304–8; Ehrhard, A., *Die altchristliche Literatur und ihre Erforschung von 1884–1900* I (Strassburger theologische Studien, erster Supplementband; Freiburg i. B., 1900) 124 ff.; Eisler, R., *Iēsous basileus ou basileusas* 2 (Heidelberg, 1930) 218–25; Esser, G., 'Die neu aufgefundenen Sprüche Jesu', *Katholik* 78 (1898) 137–51; **F**isher, F. H., 'The New Logia of Jesus', *ExpT* 9 (1897–98) 140–3; Fonseca, L. G. da, 'Agrapha', *VD* 2 (1922) 300–9; **G**ebhardt, O. von, Review of GH, *Logia*, in *Deutsche Literaturzeitung* 18 (1897) 1281–3; Gomez, J. J., *Loguia o dichos del Señor extraevangélicos: Estudio bíblico-histórico* (Murcia, 1935); Griffinhoofe, C. G., *The Unwritten Sayings of Christ: Words of Our Lord Not Recorded in the Four Gospels, Including Those Recently Discovered* (Cambridge, 1903); **H**arnack, A., *Über die jüngst entdeckten Sprüche Jesu* (Leipzig and Tübingen, 1897)[translated in *Expositor*, ser. 5, vol. 6 (1897) 321–40; 401–16]; 'Über einige Worte Jesu, die nicht in den kanonischen Evangelien stehen, nebst einem Anhang über die ursprüngliche Gestalt des Vater-Unsers', *Sitzungsberichte der königlichen preussischen Akademie der Wissenschaften* (1904) pp. 170–208; Harris, J. R., 'The "Logia" and the Gospels', *Contemporary Review* 72 (July–Dec., 1897) 341–8; Heinrici, G., 'Die neuen Herrensprüche', *Theologische Studien und Kritiken* 78 (1905) 188–210; Review of GH, *Logia*, in *TLZ* 22 (1897) 449–55; Review of Harnack, *Über die . . .*, in *ibid.*, 455–7; Review of GH, *New Sayings*, *ibid.*, 29 (1904) 428–31; Hennecke, E., 'Agrapha', *Realencyklopädie für protestantische Theologie und Kirche* 23 (3rd ed.; 1913) 16–25; *Neutestamentliche Apokryphen* (2nd ed.; Tübingen, 1924) pp. 35–7,

49–54, 56–8; Hilgenfeld, A., 'Neue Logia Jesu', *Zeitschrift für wissenschaftliche Theologie* 47 (n.s. 12, 1903–04) 414–18; 'Neue gnostische Logia Jesu', *ibid.*, 567–73; 'Die neuesten Logia-Funde von Oxyrhynchus', *ibid.*, 48 (n.s. 13, 1904–5) 343–53; Holtzmann, H., 'Literatur zum Neuen Testament: IV. Evangelienfrage', *Theologischer Jahresbericht* 17 (1897) 115–18; 18 (1898) 148–50; 'Neue Sprüche Jesu', *Protestantisches Monatsheft* 1 (1897) 385–92; Holtzmeister, U., 'Unbeachtete patristische Agrapha', *ZKT* 38 (1914) 113–43; 39 (1915) 98–118; Horder, W. G., *Newly Found Words of Jesus* (London, 1904); **J**acobs, J., 'The New "Logia"', *JQR* 10 (1897–98) 185–90; Jacobus, M. W., 'The Newly Discovered "Sayings of Jesus"', *Hartford Seminary Record* 8 (1897) 5–17; Jacquier, E., 'Les sentences de Jésus récemment découvertes', *L'université catholique* n.s. 27 (1897) 542–72; 'Les sentences du Seigneur extracanoniques (les Agrapha)', *RB* 15 (1918) 93–135; James, M. R., *The Apocryphal New Testament, Being the Apocryphal Gospels, Acts, Epistles and Apocalypses* (Oxford, 1953); 'The New Sayings of Christ', *Contemporary Review* 72 (July–Dec., 1897) 153–60; Jenkinson, J. H., *The Unwritten Sayings of the Lord* (London, 1925); Jeremias, J., *Unknown Sayings of Jesus* (tr. by R. H. Fuller; New York, 1957); Johnson, S. E., 'Stray Pieces of Early Christian Writing', *JNES* 5 (1946) 40–54; Jülicher, A., Review of GH, *Logia*, and Harnack, *Über die*, . . ., in *Göttingsche gelehrte Anzeigen* 159 (1897) 921–9; **K**lostermann, E., *Apocrypha II: Evangelien* (Kleine Texte 8; 3rd ed.; Berlin, 1929); *Apocrypha III: Agrapha, Slavische Josephusstücke, Oxyrhynchus-Fragment 1911* (Kleine Texte 11; 2nd ed.; Bonn, 1911); 'Zu den Agrapha', *ZNW* 6 (1905) 104–6; Krüger, G., Review of GH, *Logia*, and Harnack, *Über die* . . ., in *Literarisches Centralblatt*, 14 Aug. 1897, 1025–8; **L**agrange, M.-J., 'Une des paroles attribuées à Jésus', *RB* 30 (1921) 233–7; 'La seconde parole d'Oxyrhynque', *ibid.*, 31 (1922) 427–33; Lake, K., 'The New Sayings of Jesus and the Synoptic Problem', *HibbJ* 3 (1904–05) 332–41; Lataix, J., 'Une nouvelle série d'*Agrapha*', *Revue d'histoire et de littérature religieuses*

2 (1897) 433–8; Lock, W., 'The New Sayings of Jesus', *ChQR* 58 (1904) 422–32; Lock, W., and W. Sanday, *Two Lectures on the 'Sayings of Jesus' Recently Discovered at Oxyrhynchus* (Oxford, 1897); **M**cGiffert, A. C., 'The New-found Collection of Logia', *The Independent*, 26 Aug. 1897, pp. 8–9; Maas, A. J., 'Agrapha', *Catholic Encyclopedia* 1 (1907) 202–3; 'The Newly discovered "Sayings of Jesus"', *American Catholic Quarterly Review* 30 (1905) 253–67; Mangenot, E., 'Agrapha', *DTC* 1 (1903) 625–7; Michelsen, J. H. A., 'Nieuwontdekte fragmenten', *Teyler's Theologisch Tijdschrift* 3 (1905) 153 ff.; 'Uittreksels uit het Evangelie volgens Thomas', *ibid.* 7 (1909) 214–33; **N**icolassen, G. F., 'The Logia of Jesus', *Presbyterian Quarterly* (1898) 93–7; Nightingale, R. C., 'Sayings of Our Lord', *Sunday Magazine* (1897) 649–50; Noguer, N., 'Los dichos de Jesús llamados "Logia" y "Agrapha"', *Razón y fe* 51 (1918) 19–29; 204–26; **O**sborn, G., 'Note on P. Oxy 655', *JTS* 32 (1930–31) 179; **P**arker, P., 'The "Second" Saying from Oxyrhynchus', *ATR* 22 (1940) 195–8; Petrie, W. M. Flinders, 'The Harvest from Egypt', *Leisure Hour* (1897) 698–701; Pick, B., *Paralipomena: Remains of Gospels and Sayings of Christ* (Chicago, 1908); *The Extra-canonical Life of Christ* (New York, 1903); Preuschen, E., *Antilegomena: Die Rest der ausserkanonischen Evangelien und urchristlichen Überlieferungen* (2nd ed.; Giessen, 1905); *Zur Vorgeschichte des Evangelienkanons Programm* (Darmstadt, 1905); Purves, G. T., Review of GH, *Logia*, in *Presbyterian and Reformed Review* 9 (1897) 801–2; **R**auschen, G., *Monumenta minora saeculi secundi* (Florilegium patristicum 3; 2nd ed.; Bonn, 1914); Rawsley, H. D., *Sayings of Jesus: Six Village Sermons on the Papyrus Fragment* (London, 1897); Redpath, H. A., 'The So-called Logia and Their Relation to the Canonical Scriptures', *Expositor*, ser. 5, vol. 6 (1897) 224–30; Reitzenstein, R., 'Ein Zitat aus den *Logia Iēsou*', *ZNW* 6 (1905) 203; *Poimandres* (Leipzig, 1904) 239–42; Review of Evelyn White, in *Göttingsche gelehrte Anzeigen* 183 (1921) 165–74; Resch, A., *Agrapha: aussercanonische Evangelienfragmente gesammelt und untersucht* (TU 5/4;

Leipzig, 1889; 2nd ed.: 1906 [TU 15]); Réville, J., Review of GH, *Logia*, and Harnack, *Über die* . . ., in *Revue de l'histoire des religions* 36 (1897) 420–6; Rhyn, C. H. van, 'Nieuwe "worden van Jezus"', *Theologisch Studiën* 15 (1897) 403–13; Robertson, A. T., *The Christ of the Logia* (New York, 1924); Robertson, J. A., *Sayings of Jesus of Nazareth* (London, 1920); Robinson, J. A., 'Note by Professor Robinson', *Expositor* ser. 6, vol. 6 (1897) 417–21; Romeo, A., 'Agraphon', *Enciclopedia Cattolica* 1 (1948) 568–70; Ropes, J. H., 'Agrapha', *Hastings' Dictionary of the Bible* (New York, 1904) extra vol., 343–52; *Die Sprüche Jesu, die in den kanonischen Evangelien nicht überliefert sind: Eine kritische Bearbeitung des von D. Alfred Resch gesammelten Materials* (TU 14/2; Leipzig, 1896); 'What May We Expect from Christian Discoveries?', *Congregationalist*, 19 Aug. 1897, pp. 253–4; **S**antos Otero, A. de, *Los evangelios apócrifos* (Biblioteca de autores cristianos 148; Madrid, 1956) pp. 92–101; 81–3; Scholz, A. von, 'Zu den Logia Jesu', *TQ* 82 (1900) 1–22; Schubart, W., 'Das zweite Logion Oxyrhynchus Pap. IV 654', *ZNW* 20 (1921) 215–23; Selbie, J. A., '"The Logia"', *ExpT* 9 (1897–98) 548–9; 'The Oxyrhynchus Fragment', *ibid.*, 221; 'The Recently Discovered Logia', *ibid.*, 68–9; Semeria, G., *Le parole di Gesù recentemente scoperte e l'ultima fase della critica evangelica* (Genoa, 1898); Shahan, T. J., 'The Agrapha or "Unwritten Sayings" of our Lord', *AER* 25 (1901) 458–73; S. M., Review of GH, *Logia*, in *Biblical World* 10 (1897) 151–5; Swete, H. B., 'The New Oxyrhynchus Sayings, a Tentative Interpretation', *ExpT* 15 (1903–04) 488–95; 'The Oxyrhynchus Fragment', *ibid.*, 8 (1896–97) 544–50; *Zwei neue Evangelienfragmente* (Kleine Texte 31; 2nd ed.; Berlin, 1924); **T**aylor, C., *The Oxyrhynchus Logia and the Apocryphal Gospels* (Oxford, 1899); 'The Oxyrhynchus and Other Agrapha', *JTS* 7 (1905–06) 546–62; *The Oxyrhynchus Sayings of Jesus Found in* 1903 *with the Sayings called 'Logia' Found in* 1897 (Oxford, 1905); Thayer, J. H., 'The New "Sayings of Christ"', *The Independent*, 12 Aug. 1897, p. 16; Trabaud, H., 'Les nouvelles paroles de Jésus', *RTP* 31 (1898)

79–84; **U**ckeley, A., *Worte Jesu, die nicht in der Bibel stehen* (Biblische Zeit- und Streitfragen 7/3; Berlin, 1911); **V**aganay, L., 'Agrapha', *VDBS* 1 (1928) 159–98; Votaw, C. W., 'The Newly Discovered "Sayings of Jesus"', *Biblical World* 24 (1904) 261–77; 'The Oxyrhynchus Sayings of Jesus in Relation to the Gospel-making Movement of the First and Second Centuries', *JBL* 24 (1905) 79–90; **W**arschauer, J., *Jesus Saith: Studies in Some 'New Sayings' of Christ* (London, 1905); Weiss, J., 'Neue Logia', *TRu* 1 (1898) 227–36; Wessely, C., 'Les plus anciens monuments du christianisme écrits sur papyrus', *Patrologia orientalis* 4 (1908) 95 [1] 210 [116]; Wendland, P., *Die urchristlichen Literaturformen* (HNT herausg. von H. Lietzmann 1/3; Tübingen, 1912) 231 ff.; Evelyn White, H. G., 'The Fourth Oxyrhynchus Saying', *JTS* 14 (1912–13) 400–3; 'The Introduction to the Oxyrhynchus Sayings', *ibid.*, 13 (1911–12) 74–6; 'The Second Oxyrhynchus Saying', *ibid.*, 16 (1914–15) 246–50; *The Sayings of Jesus from Oxyrhynchus Edited with Introduction, Critical Apparatus and Commentary* (Cambridge, 1920); Wilamowitz-Moellendorff, U. von, 'Oxyrhynchus Papyri IV', *Göttingsche gelehrte Anzeigen* 166 (1904) 663–4; Wilkinson, J. H., *Four Lectures on the Early History of the Gospels* (London, 1898); Workman, W. P., 'Sayings of Jesus: A New Suggestion', *ExpT* 17 (1905–06) 191; Wright, G. F., 'The New "Sayings of Jesus"', *Bibliotheca sacra* 54 (1897) 759–70; **Z**ahn, T., 'Die jüngst gefundenen "Aussprüche Jesu"', *Theologisches Litteraturblatt* 18 (1897) 417–20; 425–31 [translated in *Lutheran Church Review* 17 (1898) 168–83]; 'Neue Funde aus der alten Kirche', *NKZ* 16 (1905) 94–105, 165–78.

ADDITIONAL BIBLIOGRAPHY 1969

Garitte, G., 'Le premier volume de l'édition photographique des manuscrits gnostiques coptes et "l'Evangile de Thomas"', *Mus* 70 (1957) 59–73. Quispel, G., 'The Gospel of Thomas and the New Testament', *VC* 11 (1957) 189–207. Cerfaux, L., and G. Garitte, 'Les paraboles du royaume dans l'"Evangile de

Thomas"', *Mus* 70, 307–27. Gershenson, D., and G. Quispel, 'Meristae', *VC* 12 (1958) 19–26. Quispel, G., 'L'Evangile selon Thomas et les Clémentines', *VC* 12 (1958) 181–96; 'Het Luikse "Leven van Jezus" en het jodenchristelijke "Evangelie der Hebreën"', *De nieuwe Taalgids* 51 (1958) 241–9; 'Neugefundene Worte Jesu', *Universitas* 13 (1958) 359–66. Leipoldt, J., 'Ein neues Evangelium? Das koptische Thomas-evangelium, übersetzt und besprochen', *TLZ* 83 (1958) 481–96. Prigent, P., 'Ce que l'oeil n'a pas vu, I Cor 2, 9: Histoire et préhistoire d'une citation', *TZ* 14 (1958) 416–29. Doresse, J., *Les livres secrets des gnostiques d'Egypte* (Paris: Plon, 1958). Quispel, G., 'Some Remarks on the Gospel of Thomas', *NTS* 5 (1958–59) 276–90. Wilson, R. McL., 'The Gospel of Thomas', *ExpT* 70 (1958–59) 324–5. Till, W. C., 'New Sayings of Jesus in the Recently Discovered Coptic "Gospel of Thomas"', *BJRL* 41 (1958–59) 446–58. Säve-Söderbergh, T., 'Thomasevangeliet', *SBU* 16 (1959) 28–49. Prigent, P., 'L'évangile selon Thomas: Etat de la question', *RHPR* 39 (1959) 39–45. Daniélou, J., 'Un recueil inédit de paroles de Jésus?', *Etudes* 302 (1959) 38–49. Quispel, G., 'L'évangile selon Thomas et le Diatessaron', *VC* 13 (1959) 87–117. Grant, R. M., 'Notes on the Gospel of Thomas', *VC* 13 (1959) 170–80. Collins, J. J., 'A Fifth Gospel?', *America* 101 (1959) 365–7. Bauer, J.-B., 'De agraphis genuinis evangelii secundum Thomam coptici', *VD* 37 (1959) 129–46. Puech, H.-Ch., 'Das Thomas-Evangelium', *Neutestamentliche Apokryphen in deutscher Übersetzung* (3rd ed.; ed. E. Hennecke and W. Schneemelcher; Tübingen: Mohr) 1 (1959) 199–223. Guillaumont, A., *et al.*, *The Gospel according to Thomas: Coptic Text Established and Translated* (New York: Harper; Leiden: Brill, 1959). Giversen, S., *Thomas Evangeliet: Indledning, oversaettelse og kommentarer* (Copenhagen: Gad, 1959). Doresse, J., *L'évangile selon Thomas ou les paroles secrètes de Jésus* (Les livres secrets des Gnostiques d'Egypte 2; Paris: Plon, 1959). Bauer, J.-B., 'Das Jesuswort "Wer mir nahe ist"', *TZ* 15 (1959) 446–50. Piper, O. A., 'The Gospel of Thomas', *PSB* 53 (1959–60)

18–24. Bartsch, H.-W., 'Das Thomas-Evangelium und die synoptischen Evangelien: Zu G. Quispels Bermerkungen zum Thomas-Evangelium', *NTS* 6 (1959–60) 249–61. McArthur, H. K., 'The Dependence of the Gospel of Thomas on the Synoptics', *ExpT* 7 (1959–60) 286–7. Quecke, H., 'Het Evangelie volgens Thomas: Inleiding en commentaar', *Streven* 13 (1959–60) 402–24. Unnik, W. C. van, *Evangelien aus dem Nilsand* (Frankfurt: Scheffler, 1960); *Newly Discovered Gnostic Writings: A Preliminary Survey of the Nag-Hammadi Find* (SBT 30; London: SCM, 1960). Wilson, R. McL., *Studies in the Gospel of Thomas* (London: Mowbray, 1960). Grant, R. M., 'Two Gnostic Gospels', *JBL* 79 (1960) 1–11. Nagel, W., 'Neuer Wein in alten Schläuchen (Mt 9, 17)', *VC* 14 (1960) 1–8. Roques, R., 'Gnosticisme et christianisme: L'évangile selon Thomas', *Irénikon* 33 (1960) 29–40. Smyth, K., 'Gnosticism in the *Gospel according to Thomas*', *HJ* 1 (1960) 189–98. Schäfer, K. T., 'Das neuentdeckte Thomasevangelium', *Bibel und Leben*, 1 (1960) 62–74; MacRae, G. W., 'The Gospel of Thomas—Logia Jesou', *CBQ* 22 (1960) 56–71. Piper, O. A., 'A New Gospel?', *Christian Century* 77 (1960) 96–9. Beare, F. W., 'The Gospel according to Thomas: A Gnostic Manual', *CJT* 9 (1960) 102–12. Cullmann, O., 'L'evangelo di Tommaso', *Protestantesimo* 15 (1960) 145–52. Roques, R., 'L'"évangile selon Thomas": Son édition critique et son identification', *RHR* 157 (1960) 187–218. Rüstow, A., '*Entos hymōn estin:* Zur Deutung von Lukas 17, 20–1', *ZNW* 51 (1960) 197–224. Wilson, R. McL., '"Thomas" and the Growth of the Gospels', *HTR* 53 (1960) 231–50. Schoedel, W. R., 'Naassene Themes in the Coptic Gospel of Thomas', *VC* 14 (1960) 225–34. Schippers, R., and T. Baarda, *Het Evangelie van Thomas: Apocriefe woorden van Jezus* (Boeketreeks 14; Kampen, 1960). McArthur, H. K., 'The Gospel according to Thomas', *New Testament Sidelights: Essays in Honor of A. C. Purdy* (ed. H. K. McArthur; Hartford: Seminary Foundation Press, 1960) 43–77. Munck, J., 'Bemerkungen zum koptischen Thomasevangelium', *ST* 14 (1960) 130–47. Regemorter, B. van, 'La reliure des manuscrits gnostiques découverts à Nag Hamadi', *Scriptorium* 14 (1960) 225–34. Quispel, G., 'L'évangile selon Thomas et le "texte occidental" du Nouveau Testament', *VC* 14 (1960) 204–15. Higgins, A. J. B., 'Non-Gnostic Sayings in the Gospel of Thomas', *NT* 4 (1960) 292–306. Cullmann, O., 'Das Thomasevangelium und die Frage nach dem Alter der in ihm enthaltenen Tradition', *TLZ* 85 (1960) 321–34. Giversen, S., 'Questions and Answers in the Gospel according to Thomas of pl. 81, 14–18 and pl. 83, 14–27', *AcOr* 25 (1960) 332–8. Schäfer, K. T., 'Der Primat Petri und das Thomas-Evangelium', *Die Kirche und ihre Ämter und Stände* (Festgabe J. Kard. Frings; ed. W. Corsten, *et al.*; Cologne: J. P. Bachem, 1960) 353–63. Harl, M., 'A propos de Logia de Jésus: Le sens du mot *monachos*', *REG* 73 (1960) 464–74. Rosa, G. de, 'Un quinto vangelo? Il "Vangelo secondo Tommaso"', *CC* 111/1 (1960) 496–512. Michaelis, W., *Das Thomas-Evangelium* (Calwer Hefte, 34; Stuttgart: Calwer, 1960). Leipoldt, J., and H.-M. Schenke, *Koptisch-gnostische Schriften aus den Papyrus-Codices von Nag-Hamadi* (Theologische Forschung 20; Hamburg-Bersgtedt: H. Reich, 1960) 7–30. Hunzinger, C.-H., 'Unbekannte Gleichnisse Jesu aus dem Thomas-Evangelium', *Judentum, Urchristentum, Kirche* (Fest. J. Jeremias; BZNW 26; Berlin: Töpelmann, 1960) 209–20; 'Aussersynoptisches Traditionsgut im Thomas-Evangelium', *TLZ* 85 (1960) 843–6. Krogmann, W., 'Helian, Tatian und Thomasevangelium', *ZNW* 51 (1960) 255–68. Kuhn, K. H., 'Some Observations on the Coptic Gospel according to Thomas', *Mus* 73 (1960) 317–23. Leipoldt, J., 'Bemerkungen zur Übersetzung des Thomasevangeliums', *TLZ* 85 (1960) 795–8. Grant, R. M., and D. N. Freedman, *The Secret Sayings of Jesus* (London: Collins; Garden City: Doubleday, 1960). Gärtner, B., *Ett nytt evangelium? Thomasevangeliets hemliga Jesusord* (Stockholm, 1960). Doresse, J., *Il vangelo secondo Tommaso: Versione dal copto e commento* (Milan, 1960); 'Le problème des "Paroles secrètes de Jésus" (L'Evangile de Thomas)', *La table ronde* 154 (Oct. 1960) 120–8.

Zandee, J., *Een geheim evangelie* (AO-reeks 807; Amsterdam, 1960). Cullmann, O., 'Das Thomasevangelium und seine Bedeutung für die Erforschung der kanonischen Evangelium', *Universitas* 15 (1960) 865–74. Montefiore, H. W., 'A Comparison of the Parables of the Gospel according to Thomas and of the Synoptic Gospels', *NTS* 7 (1960–61) 220–48. Walls, A. F., 'The References to Apostles in the Gospel of Thomas', *NTS* 7 (1960–61) 266–70. Wilson, R. McL., 'Thomas and the Synoptic Gospels', *ExpT* 72 (1960–61) 36–9. Masing, U., and K. Rätsep, 'Barlaam and Joasaphat and the Acts of Thomas, the Psalms of Thomas and the Gospel of Thomas', *Communio viatorum* 4/1 (1961) 29–36. Schierse, F. J., 'Nag-Hamadi und das Neue Testament', *SZ* 168 (1961) 47–62. Schippers, R., 'Het evangelie van Thomas een onafhankelijke traditie? Antwoord aan professor Quispel', *Gereformeerd theologisch tijdschrift* 61 (1961) 46–54. Cornelis, E. M. J. M., 'Quelques éléments pour une comparaison entre l'Evangile de Thomas et la notice d'Hippolyte sur les Naassènes', *VC* 15 (1961) 83–104. Bauer, J. B., 'Das milde Joch und die Ruhe, Matth. 11, 28–30', *TZ* 17 (1961) 99–106. Klijn, A. F. J., 'Das Thomasevangelium und das alt-syrische Christentum', *VC* 15 (1961) 146–59. Quecke, H., 'Das Evangelium nach Thomas', *Theologisches Jahrbuch* (ed. A. Dänhart; Leipzig, 1961) 226–36. Kasser, R., *'L'évangile selon Thomas: Présentation et commentaire théologique* (Neuchâtel: Delachaux et Niestlé, 1961). Haenchen, E., *Die Botschaft des Thomas-Evangeliums* (Theologische Bibliothek Töpelmann 6; Berlin: Töpelmann, 1961); 'Literatur zum Thomasevangelium', *TRu* 27 (1961) 147–78, 306–38. Gärtner, B., *The Theology of the Gospel according to Thomas* (tr. E. J. Sharpe; New York: Harper, 1961). Grobel, K., 'How Gnostic is the Gospel of Thomas?', *NTS* 8 (1961–62) 367–73. Reichelt, J., 'Das "Evangelium" nach Thomas', *Im Lande der Bibel* 8 (1962) 9–14. North, R., 'Chenoboskion and Q', *CBQ* 24 (1962) 154–70. Klijn, A. F. J., 'The "Single One" in the Gospel of Thomas', *JBL* 81 (1962) 271–8. Cullmann, O., 'The Gospel of Thomas and the Problem of the

Age of the Tradition Contained Therein: A Survey', *Int* 16 (1962) 418–38. Turner, H. E. W., and H. Montefiore, *Thomas and the Evangelists* (SBT 35; London: SCM, 1962). Quispel, G., 'Das Thomasevangelium und das Alte Testament', *Neotestamentica et patristica* (Fest. O. Cullmann; NovTSup 6; Leiden: Brill, 1962) 243–8. Quecke, H., 'L'Evangile de Thomas: Etat des recherches', *La venue du Messie* (RechBib 6; Bruges: Desclée de Brouwer, 1962) 217–41. R. E. Brown, 'The Gospel of Thomas and St John's Gospel', *NTS* 9 (1962–63) 155–77. Saunders, E. W., 'A Trio of Thomas Logia', *BibRes* 8 (1963) 43–59. Houghton, H. P., 'The Coptic Gospel of Thomas', *Aegyptus* 43 (1963) 107–40. Schneemelcher, W., and J. Jeremias, 'Sayings-Collections on Papyrus', *New Testament Apocrypha* (ed. R. Hennecke and W. Schneemelcher; tr. R. McL. Wilson; London: Lutterworth) 1 (1963) 97–113. Strobel, A., 'Textgeschichtliches zum Thomas-Logion 86 (Mt 8, 20; Luk 9, 58)', *VC* 17 (1963) 211–24. Schürmann, H., 'Das Thomasevangelium und das lukanische Sondergut', *BZ* 7 (1963) 236–60. Kee, H. C., '"Becoming a Child" in the Gospel of Thomas', *JBL* 82 (1963) 307–14. Garitte, G., 'Le nouvel évangile copte de Thomas', *L'Académie royale de Belgique*, Classe des lettres, Bulletin, ser. 5, tome 50/1–2 (Bruxelles: Palais des Académies, 1964) 33–54. Krogmann, W., 'Heiland und Thomasevangelium', *VC* 18 (1964) 65–73. Baker, A., 'Pseudo-Macarius and the Gospel of Thomas', *ibid.*, 215–25. Quispel, G., 'The Syrian Thomas and the Syrian Macarius', *ibid.*, 226–35. Haelst, J. van, 'A propos du catalogue raisonné des papyrus littéraires chrétiens d'Egypte, grecs et latins', *Actes du Xe congrès international des papyrologues . . . 1961* (ed. J. Wolski; Wroclaw: Polish Academy of Sciences, 1964) 215–25. Bauer, J.-B., 'The Synoptic Tradition in the Gospel of Thomas', *SE* 3 (TU 88; Berlin: Akademie-V., 1964) 314–17. Stead, G. C., 'Some Reflections on the Gospel of Thomas', *ibid.*, 390–402. Wilson, R. McL., 'The Gospel of Thomas', *ibid.*, 447–59. Vielhauer, P., '*Anapausis:* Zum gnostischen Hintergrund des Thomasevangeliums', *Apophoreta*

(Fest. E. Haenchen; BZNW 30; Berlin: Töpelmann, 1964) 281–99. Schrage, W., *Das Verhältnis des Thomas-Evangeliums zur synoptischen Tradition und zu den koptischen Evangeliensübersetzungen: Zugleich ein Beitrag zur gnostischen Synoptikerdeutung* (BZNW 29; Berlin: Töpelmann, 1964). Durso, M. H., 'The Gospel according to Thomas', *BT* 16 (Feb. 1965) 1067–74. Quispel, G., 'L'évangile selon Thomas et les origines de l'ascèse chrétienne', *Aspects du Judéo-Christianisme: Colloque de Strasbourg, 23–25 avril* 1964 (Paris: Presses universitaires de France, 1965) 35–52. Mees, M., 'Einige Überlegungen zum Thomasevangelium', *Vetera christianorum* 2 (1965) 151–65. Kosnetter, J., 'Das Thomasevangelium und die Synoptiker', *Wissenschaft im Dienste des Glaubens* (Fest. H. Peichl; ed. J. Kisser; Wien: Selbstverlag der Wiener katholischen Akademie, 1965) 29–49. Koester, H., '*Gnōmai diaphoroi:* The Origin and Nature of Diversification in the History of Early Christianity', *HTR* 58 (1965) 279–318. Janssens, Y., 'Deux "évangiles" gnostiques', *Byzantion* 35 (1965) 449–54. Baker, A., 'The *Gospel of Thomas* and the Diatessaron', *JTS* 16 (1965) 449–54. Smith, J. Z., 'The Garments of Shame', *History of Religions* 5 (1965–66) 217–38. Baker, A., 'The "Gospel of Thomas" and the Syriac "Liber graduum"', *NTS* 12 (1965–66) 49–55. Quispel, G., '"The Gospel of Thomas" and the "Gospel of the Hebrews"', *ibid.*, 371–82; 'Das Lied von der Perle', *Eranos-Jahrbuch 1965* 34 (Zurich, 1966) 9–32. Ménard, J.-E., 'L'Evangile selon Thomas et le Nouveau Testament', *Studia montis regii* 9 (1966) 147–53. Schmidt, K. O., *Die geheimen Herren-Worte des Thomas-Evangeliums: Weisweisungen Christi zur Selbstvollendung* (Pfullingen: Baum-V., 1966). Frend, W. H. C., 'The Gospel of Thomas: Is Rehabilitation Possible?', *JTS* 18 (1967) 13–26. Miller, B. F., 'A Study of the Theme of "Kingdom": The Gospel according to Thomas, Logion 18', *NT* 9 (1967) 52–60. Helmbold, A. K., *The Nag Hammadi Gnostic Texts and the Bible* (Baker Studies in Bibl. Archaeology; Grand Rapids: Baker, 1967) 55–63. Schoedel, W., 'The Gospel in the New Gospels', *Dialog* 6 (1957) 115–22. Karavidopoulos, I. D.,

To gnōstikon kata Thōman euangelion (Saloniki, 1967). Leipoldt, J., *Das Evangelium nach Thomas koptisch und deutsch* (TU 101; Berlin: Akademie-V., 1967). Quispel, G., *Makarius, das Thomasevangelium und das Lied von der Perle* (NT Sup 15; Leiden: Brill, 1967). Rengstorf, K. H., 'Urchristliches Kerygma und "gnostische" Interpretation in einigen Sprüchen des Thomasevangeliums', *The Origins of Gnosticism* (Studies in the History of Religions 12; Leiden: Brill, 1967) 563–74. Säve-Söderbergh, T., 'Gnostic and Canonical Gospel Traditions (With Special Reference to the Gospel of Thomas)', *ibid.*, 552–62. Ménard, J.-E., 'Le milieu syriaque de l'*Evangile selon Thomas* et de l'*Evangile selon Philippe*', *RevScRel* 42 (1968) 261–6. Summers, R., *The Secret Sayings of the Living Jesus: Studies in the Coptic Gospel According to Thomas* (Waco, Tex.: Word Books, 1968). Kim, Y. O., 'The Gospel of Thomas and the Historical Jesus', *Northeast Asia Journal of Theology* 2 (1969) 17–30.

16

THE QUMRAN SCROLLS, THE EBIONITES AND THEIR LITERATURE*

The importance of the Dead Sea Scrolls for both Old and New Testament study has been increasingly recognized, as these texts are published and studied. Though it will be many years before their exact value can be fully assessed, constant efforts are being made by scholars to interpret these documents. It is not surprising that some interpretations find almost immediate acceptance in scholarly circles, while others are rejected or subjected to long debate. For it is only by a gradual sifting process that the value and importance of these texts can be ascertained.

Shortly after the publication of three of the Qumran scrolls by the American Schools of Oriental Research, J. L. Teicher of Cambridge wrote an article in the *Journal of Jewish Studies*, in which he maintained that the Qumran sect, in whose midst these scrolls originated, was Ebionite.[1] This interpretation has not been accepted by most scholars, who prefer to regard the group who lived at Qumran as Essenes (or at least as a branch of the Essenes). Nevertheless, the fact was recognized that Teicher had indicated a source from which further information might be drawn.[2] Teicher continued to write a series of articles

* Originally published in *TS* 16 (1955) 335–72.

[1] 'The Dead Sea Scrolls—Documents of the Jewish Christian Sect of Ebionites', *JJS* 2 (1951) 67–99.

[2] A. Dupont-Sommer, *Nouveaux aperçus sur les manuscrits de la Mer Morte* (Paris: Maisonneuve, 1953) 205. W. F. Albright, 'Chronology of the Dead Sea Scrolls', Postscript to W. H. Brownlee's translation of the Dead Sea Manual of Discipline, *BASOR Suppl. Stud.* 10–12 (1951) 58, n. 3.

on the Ebionite sect of Qumran and the early Church.[3] Subsequently, however, Oscar Cullmann published an article in *Neutestamentliche Studien für Rudolf Bultmann*,[4] claiming that the remnants of the Essenes went over to the Ebionite group after the destruction of Jerusalem in A.D. 70. Another recent article, by Hans Joachim Schoeps, puts forth the theory that the Qumran sect, the Essenes of Philo and Josephus, the Ossaeans of Epiphanius, the disciples of John the Baptist, and the Ebionites (the latter as the descendants of the Jerusalem *Urgemeinde*) all became representatives of an apocalyptic-gnostic Judaism.[5] This brief survey of opinions suffices to show that the connection between the sect of Qumran and the Ebionites has been discussed in scholarly circles and that the question merits some attention. The present article intends to review the evidence for this connection and to sift the valid from the invalid claims that have been made. A *mise au point* is obviously needed, to see whether the parallels in tenets and practices of both groups are such as to warrant the assertion that the Qumran sect was Ebionite or passed over into Ebionism or even influenced the latter group.

The matter will be discussed under three main headings: the identification of the Ebionites; their literature; the comparison of Ebionites and the Qumran sect.

The sources of information regarding the Qumran sect are mainly the Dead Sea Scrolls, as published by the American Schools and the Hebrew University, as well as the Damascus

[3] Cf. *JJS* 2 (1950–51) 115–43; 3 (1952) 53–5; 111–18; 128–32; 139–50; 4 (1953) 1–13; 49–58; 93–103; 139–53; 5 (1954) 38; 93–9; *ZRGG* 3 (1951) 193–209; *VT* 5 (1955) 189–98.—Teicher has been followed by M.-A. Chevallier, *L'esprit et le messie dans le bas-judaïsme et le Nouveau Testament* (Etudes d'histoire et de philosophie religieuses 49; Paris: Presses universitaires de France, 1958) 115. See my review in *TS* 20 (1959) 451–5.

[4] 'Die neuentdeckten Qumrantexte und das Judenchristentum der Pseudoklementinen', BZNW 21 (1954) 35–51.

[5] 'Das gnostische Judentum in den Dead Sea Scrolls', *ZRGG* 6 (1954) 1–4 [hereafter referred to as Schoeps 2]; 'Ebionite Christianity', *JTS* 4 (1953) 219–24.

Document. The latter is generally recognized today as a work of this group, even though it was not found at Qumran originally. Any information that is drawn from other sources (e.g., Philo or Josephus) is valid only in so far as the identification of the Qumran sect as Essene is correct.

THE EBIONITES

Relatively little is known about the Ebionites. Most of the data concerning them has been preserved in patristic literature, and it is not easy to interpret. Scraps of information are found in Justin, Irenaeus, Tertullian, Origen, Hippolytus, Eusebius, and Jerome, while Epiphanius devotes a full chapter to them in his *Panarion*. Literary borrowing took place in some cases, so that it is not always easy to tell when the patristic writer is supplying data gathered from independent sources. In the preface of his *Theologie und Geschichte des Judenchristentums*, H. J. Schoeps claims to set a new landmark for scholarly research in the study of the Ebionites by being the first to take into account Rabbinic literature and the translation of the Old Testament by Symmachus, the Ebionite. The data from Symmachus are quite fragmentary and do not really concern us here.[6] The interpretation of the material in the Rabbinic sources is so intimately connected with the question of the identity of the *Mînîm*[7] that anything which might be gathered from such a discussion would remain quite problematical. Consequently, in

[6] The questions and problems connected with Symmachus and his translation of the Old Testament are so numerous that it is too hazardous to try to draw any definite conclusions from this source. Important as is the study made by Schoeps, one may still ask whether he has really proved his point; cf. the reviews of his books by R. Bultmann in *Gnomon* 26 (1954) 180, by G. Bornkamm in *ZKG* 64 (1952–53) 197, and by G. Mercati in *Biblica* 32 (1951) 329–35.

[7] Cf. H. J. Schoeps, *Theologie und Geschichte des Judenchristentums* (Tübingen: Mohr, 1949) 21–5 [hereafter referred to as Schoeps 1]. Also J. Thomas, *Le mouvement baptiste en Palestine et Syrie (150 v. J.-C.—300 apr. J.-C.)* (Gembloux: Duculot, 1935) 161–2. This author identifies the *Mînîm* with Ebionites and the *Nazōraioi*. But Ralph Marcus, 'Pharisees, Essenes and Gnostics', *JBL* 73

a discussion of the relationship between the sect of Qumran and the Ebionites, I prefer not to use these sources for information regarding the latter.

The English name, Ebionite, is derived from the Latin *Ebionitae*, found in Jerome (*Ep* 112, 13) and in the Latin translation of some of Origen's works of which the Greek originals are now lost (*Hom. in Luc.* 17; *Hom. in Gen.* 3, 5). Another Latin form is *Ebionaei*, found in Irenaeus (*Adv. haer* 1, 26, 2; 5, 1, 3), which is the transliteration of the Greek *Ebiōnaioi* (*Adv. haer.* 3, 21, 1; cf. Origen, *Contra Cels.* 2, 1; 5, 61, 65; *De Princ.* 4, 22; Eusebius, *Hist. Eccl.* 3, 27). This seems to be, in turn, a transliteration of the Aramaic *'ebyônāyê'*, derived from the Hebrew *'ebyônîm*, meaning 'the poor'. Another Greek form, *Ebiōnoi*, is found in Irenaeus (*Adv. haer.* 4, 33, 4), but this looks like a copyist's misspelling.

As the name of a sect, this word appears for the first time in Irenaeus (*Adv. haer.* 1, 26, 2 Latin: *Ebionaei*; 3, 21, 1 Greek: *Ebiōnaioi*). He offers no explanation of its meaning or origin, but several were given in antiquity. They were called Ebionites: (*a*) because of the poverty of their intelligence (Origen, *De princ.* 4, 22; *Hom. in Gen.* 3, 5; Eusebius, *Hist. Eccl.* 3, 27; Epiphanius, *Pan.* 30, 17); (*b*) because of the poverty of the law which they followed (Origen, *Contra Cels.* 2, 1); (*c*) because of the poverty of the opinions they had of Christ (Eusebius, *Hist. eccl.* 3, 27); (*d*) because they were 'poor in understanding, hope, and deeds' (Epiphanius, *Pan.* 30, 17). These are obviously

---

(1954) 159 remarks: '. . . it has become clearer in recent years that while the term *Minim* in the Rabbinic and patristic literature of the third century and afterwards may refer to Jewish Christians, in Tannaitic writings it chiefly designates Jewish Gnostics.' Prof. Marcus quotes L. Ginzberg: 'I may state with certainty that only in a very few places does Minim refer to Judeo-Christians, while in most cases it describes Jewish Gnostics' (*ibid.*, n. 4). Cf. also Bultmann, *op. cit.*, 179; and G. Bornkamm (*op. cit.*, 197) who speaks of the 'nur hypothetisch verwendbaren rabbinischen Zeugnisse über das Judenchristentum'.

pejorative afterthoughts, which scarcely give us a clue to the origin of the term.

Epiphanius (*Pan.* 30, 1; 30, 17; etc.) derived the name from a founder, named Ebion. Tertullian (*De praescrip.* 33; *De carne Christi* 14, 18) speaks of a man named Ebion. This notion, however, is associated with the ancient belief that the unorthodox teaching or opinion was named after those who started it (see Justin, *Dial. cum Tryph.* 35, 4). Despite this tradition, which also ascribes to Ebion certain fragments in the work *Doctrina patrum de incarnatione Verbi*, modern scholars are inclined to look on Ebion merely as an eponymous hero, a personification of the sect itself.[8] There is really no evidence that such a person ever existed, though some scholars in modern times have repeated the ancient allegation found in Tertullian, Jerome, and Epiphanius.[9]

We know from the New Testament that certain early Christians were referred to as 'the poor' (Rom 15:26; Gal 2:10). This undoubtedly refers to the poor members of the community at Jerusalem. But it is often thought that the name *Ebiōnaioi* grew out of a practice of referring to the early Jewish Christians in Jerusalem as the poor, especially after the destruction of the city in A.D. 70. At some time during the first two centuries (it is impossible to be more precise) this designation would have been restricted to Jewish Christians who lived in

[8] Cf. J. Thomas, *op. cit.*, 160; Schoeps 1, 9. The latter maintains that this idea of Ebion as a founder is due to Hippolytus, but he gives no references for this statement (cf. p. 9, n. 2). This is but one example of the carelessness that is found in this book amid an otherwise mammoth display of erudition, which makes it necessary to use Schoeps' work only with the greatest caution. Cf. Bornkamm's review, p. 196: 'leider in Zitaten und Literaturangaben fehlerreich'. Similarly Bultmann, *op. cit.*, 189. In the light of such criticism it is quite surprising to read the highly laudatory review of Schoeps' books written by P. Benoit, O.P., in *RB* 57 (1950) 604–9: 'un magistral exposé'; 'd'une richesse peu ordinaire'; '. . . par le soin scrupuleux qu'il met à prouver scientifiquement tout ce qu'il avance . . .'.

[9] See A. Hilgenfeld, *Die Ketzergeschichte des Urchristentums* (Leipzig, 1884) 423–36.

Palestine and Syria, and who continued to observe the Mosaic Law.

The Ebionites were, then, a Jewish-Christian group, first mentioned by Irenaeus *ca.* A.D. 175, which flourished during the second, third, and early fourth centuries (at least). In the New Testament there is mention of Jewish Christians, who believed in Christ but also observed the Mosaic Law (Acts 15:1 ff.; 21:21; Gal 2). This was the community at Jerusalem, headed by James, the 'brother of the Lord'. Remnants of this group after the destruction of Jerusalem may have developed into the Ebionite sect, acquiring heterodox notions in time from other sources, such as Cerinthus and the Elchesaites. Eusebius (*Hist. eccl.* 3, 5) tells us:

> The people of the church in Jerusalem were commanded by an oracle given by revelation before the war to those in the city who were worthy of it to depart and dwell in one of the cities of Perea which they called Pella. To it those who believed in Christ migrated from Jerusalem, that when holy men had altogether deserted the royal capital of the Jews and the whole land of Judaea, the judgement of God might at last overtake them for all their crimes against the Christ and his Apostles.[10]

It is important to note here that Eusebius does not call these emigrants by the name of Ebionites, nor have we any reason to assume that he was speaking of them specifically. They were merely some of the Christians of the original community of Jerusalem. Justin distinguished two sorts of Jewish Christians, those who observe the Mosaic Law but do not require its observance of all others, and those who maintain that this observance is necessary for salvation. Justin would communicate with the former, but not with the latter (*Dial. cum Tryph.* 47; 48). Schoeps equates the Ebionites with the more intransigent group.[11] By the time of Irenaeus there was definitely a sect named *Ebiōnaioi*, who were considered heretical by him and

[10] Kirsopp Lake's translation in the Loeb Classical Library, *Eusebius* 1, 201.

[11] Schoeps 1, 8.

were listed among the Gnostics (*Adv. haer.* 1, 26, 2). He mentions specifically that they rejected the virgin birth of Christ (5, 1, 3; 3, 21, 1) and denied the Incarnation (4, 33, 4).[12]

Tertullian adds no new details, except to speak of *Ebion*, not of the *Ebionaei*. One phrase of his, however, is interesting, for he mentions that Ebion was influenced by Cerinthus, 'non in omni parte consentiens' (*Adv. omn. haer.* 3.)[13] It is often admitted that the christological tenets of the Ebionites came from this Cerinthian influence. Hippolytus (*Philosoph.* 7, 34; 10, 22) adds a few details to our knowledge, but they are not important here (see Chart 1).

CHART 1

TENETS AND PRACTICES OF THE EBIONITES AND NAZORAIOI ACCORDING TO THE FATHERS

The Ebionites

a) they depend on Cerinthus and Carpocrates (Iren, Tertull, Hipp)
b) they believe in one God, the creator of the world (Iren, Tert, Hipp)
c) they use the gospel of Matthew only (Iren, Tert [?], Epiph)
d) they reject Paul as an apostate from the law (Iren, Orig, Epiph)
e) they interpret the prophets *curiosius* (Iren)
f) they practise circumcision (Iren, Orig, Epiph)
g) they observe the Sabbath (Euseb, Epiph)
h) they live according to the Jewish way of life, according to the Law (Iren, Tert, Hipp, Orig, Euseb, Epiph)

[12] It is important to remember that the type of patristic writing in which the Ebionites are usually mentioned is heresiography. They were classed as christological heretics; such a classification, though important to the theologian, leaves us, however, with a paucity of details for our comparison with the Qumran sect.

[13] Perhaps it would be better to describe this work as Pseudo-Tertullian; it is generally held today that cc. 46–53 of the *De praescriptione* are actually a digest of Hippolytus' lost *Syntagma*; cf. J. Quasten, *Patrology* 2 (Westminster, Md.: Newman, 1953) 169–70.

i) they face Jerusalem when they pray (Iren)
j) they hold the observance of the Mosaic Law as necessary for salvation (Hipp, Euseb)
k) they reject the virgin birth of Christ (Iren, Tert, Orig, Euseb, Epiph)
l) they hold Christ to be a mere man (Iren, Tert, Hipp, Euseb, Epiph)
m) they maintain Jesus had to merit his title, Christ, by fulfilling the Law (Hipp, Epiph)
n) they reject virginity and continence (Epiph)
o) they use purificatory baths (Epiph)
p) they use remedial baths (Epiph)
q) they admit baptism (Epiph)
r) they celebrate the mysteries with unleavened bread and mere water (Epiph)
s) they hold that Christ came to abrogate sacrifice in the temple (Epiph)
t) they believe that God set the devil and Christ to rule over this world and the world to come respectively (Epiph)
u) they give up all goods and possessions (Epiph)
v) they permit divorce (Epiph)
w) they admit Abraham, Isaac, Jacob, Moses, Aaron, Joshua, but none of the prophets (David, Solomon, Isaiah, Jeremiah, Daniel, Ezekiel, Elijah, Elisha) (Epiph)
x) they claim that Christ alone is the *prophētēs . . . tēs alētheias* (Epiph)
y) they use the book, *Periodoi Petrou dia Klēmentos* (Epiph)
z) they abstain from meat like Peter (Epiph)

The Nazōraioi

a) they believe in one God, Creator of the world (Epiph)
b) they use the Gospel of Matthew only (Euseb, Epiph)
c) they reject Paul as an apostate from the Law (Orig, Euseb)
d) they practise circumcision (Epiph)

e) they observe the Sabbath (Euseb, Epiph [Euseb says they observed Sunday too])

f) they follow the Jewish way of life according to the Law (Euseb, Epiph)

g) they do not reject the virgin birth of Christ (Orig, Euseb, Jerome; Epiph is not sure about this)

h) they deny Jesus' preexistence as God (Euseb)

i) they call Jesus the Son of God (Epiph, Jerome)

j) they believe in the resurrection of the dead (Epiph)

It is Origen who first distinguishes for us two kinds of Ebionites: those who admit the virgin birth of Christ, and those who reject it (*Contra Cels.* 5, 61). Both groups, however, reject the epistles of Paul (5, 65). Eusebius (*Hist. eccl.* 3, 27) has likewise recorded the fact of two groups of Ebionites:

But others the wicked demon, when he could not alienate them from God's plan in Christ, made his own, when he found them by a different snare. The first Christians gave these the suitable name of Ebionites because they had poor and mean opinions concerning Christ. They held him to be a plain and ordinary man who had achieved righteousness merely by the progress of his character and had been born naturally from Mary and her husband. They insisted on the complete observation of the Law, and did not think that they would be saved by faith in Christ alone and by a life in accordance with it. But there were others besides these who have the same name. These escaped the absurd folly of the first mentioned, and did not deny that the Lord was born of a Virgin and the Holy Spirit, but nevertheless agreed with them in not confessing his pre-existence as God, being the Logos and Wisdom. Thus they shared in the impiety of the former class, especially in that they were equally zealous to insist on the literal observance of the Law. They thought that the letters of the Apostle ought to be wholly rejected and called him an apostate from the Law. They used only the Gospel called according to the Hebrews and made little account of the rest. Like the former they used to observe the sabbath and the rest of the Jewish ceremonial, but on Sundays celebrated rites like ours in commemoration of the Saviour's resurrection. Wherefore from these practices they have obtained their name, for the name of Ebionites indicates the poverty of their intelligence, for this name means 'poor' in Hebrew.[14]

Epiphanius, who of all the patristic writers gives most space to the Ebionites, supplies names for the two groups. The more orthodox group, which probably admits the virgin birth of Christ (*Pan.* 29), is called *Nazōraioi*; the more heterodox group is labelled *Ebiōnaioi* (*Pan.* 30). The identification of the Nazoraioi as an orthodox group of Jewish Christians, related somehow to the Ebionites, is admitted by many scholars; but the identification has problems connected with it that we cannot discuss here.[15] It is complicated by the fact that Jerome equates *Ebionitae*, *Nazaraei*, and *Minaei*.[16] At any rate, we are sure that there was a definite group of christological heretics in the early centuries of the Church who were called Ebionites.

Among the details supplied by Epiphanius, mention is made of the influence of the Elchesaites on the Ebionites (*Pan.* 30, 17). He goes to the trouble of indicating that this influence affected the followers of Ebion, not Ebion himself. Elchesai was a heretical leader who preached (*ca.* A.D. 100) a doctrine of baptism unto the remission of sins which was heavily infected with Gnostic ideas (so, at least, it is usually judged). Schoeps,[17] following C. Schmidt and others, maintains that Epiphanius has confused the Ebionites with the Elchesaites, so that his

[14] Kirsopp Lake's translation, *op. cit.*, 261–3.

[15] Cf. J. Thomas, *op. cit.*, 156–70, for a detailed discussion and references to the literature on the subject. Schoeps (1, 8 ff.) likewise discusses the problem briefly.

[16] Cf. *Ep.* 112, 13 (*PL* 22, 924): 'Quid dicam de Ebionitis, qui Christianos esse se simulant? Usque hodie per totas Orientis synagogas inter Iudaeos haeresis est, quae dicitur Minaeorum, et a Pharisaeis nunc usque damnatur: quos vulgo Nazaraeos nuncupant, qui credunt in Christum Filium Dei, natum de virgine Maria, et eum dicunt esse, qui sub Pontio Pilato passus est, et resurrexit, in quem et nos credimus: sed dum volunt et Iudaei esse et Christiani, nec Iudaei sunt nec Christiani.'

[17] 1, 11; Schoeps is continually stressing throughout his book that the Ebionites were not Gnostics. He finds it convenient for his thesis to attribute all Gnostic elements that might be found in the Ebionite tenets to the Elchesaites. This may well be true, but it does not follow that Epiphanius

account of the Ebionites can be accepted only when there is outside control. It is true that Epiphanius adds details about the Ebionites not found elsewhere in patristic writings. If we glance at Chart 1, we will see that the items listed under *n–z* come from Epiphanius alone. Among these we find mention of dualism, various types of baths, peculiar ideas about the prophets, Christ—all of which have been associated with Jewish-Christian Gnosticism. Has Epiphanius confused the Ebionites with the Elchesaites? We just do not know. It is just as reasonable to admit the explanation given by J. Thomas,[18] that the Ebionites were influenced by three groups: the Essenes, the early Christians, the Elchesaites.

Before terminating this section on the identification of the Ebionites, I shall mention briefly the opinion of J. L. Teicher regarding the Qumran sect, which he maintains is Ebionite. One might be surprised that I am bringing up this point now. The reason is that, since Teicher does not depend upon a discussion of the Pseudo-Clementines for his 'proof' that the sect is Ebionite,[19] his view can be best set forth here.

From the description thus far given of the Ebionites, one might well wonder if there is any connection between them and the sect of Qumran. Certainly the climate of opinion in which the latter group lived was that of the Old Testament, as is evident to all who are acquainted with the Qumran literature.[20] The early Christian Church and certain New Testament writings,

---

has confused the Elchesaites and the Ebionites. Later Ebionites may well have been Gnostics, precisely because of the Elchesaite influence. Does not this seem to be indicated by the fact that Epiphanius notes a distinction between Ebion and later Ebionites?

[18] *Op. cit.*, 171–83; cf. Bultmann, *op. cit.*, 185.

[19] In his first article on the Ebionites and the Dead Sea Scrolls (cf. note 1 above) Teicher gives one reference to two places in the Pseudo-Clementines; cf. p. 98, n. 4. This is supposed to support his contention that Paul is the adversary referred to in the *pesher* on Habakkuk and in the Pseudo-Clementines.

[20] Cf. Karl Georg Kuhn, 'Die in Palästina gefundenen hebräischen Texte und das Neue Testament', *ZThK* 47 (1950) 207.

on the other hand, are definitely the framework and background of the Ebionite way of life, even though they have retained the observance of the Mosaic Law. This we know from patristic information and from the Pseudo-Clementine writings. Yet for Prof. Teicher the Qumran sect is Ebionite, Christ is the Teacher of Righteousness, and Paul is the 'Man of Lies'. The Ebionites, being Christians, were affected by Diocletian's edict of persecution, and so, rather than hand over their sacred books according to the royal decree, they hid them in the caves of Qumran. The Qumran sect is Ebionite because they are mentioned in the *pesher* on Habakkuk as *'ebyônîm* (12:3, 6); and Qumran is 'in the vicinity' of the spot in Transjordan where the Ebionites lived. Efforts were made to point out the weaknesses in the arguments of Prof. Teicher,[21] but he wrote on undaunted.[22]

The most serious difficulty, of course, with Teicher's opinion is that of chronology. The latest possible date for the deposit of the manuscripts is the destruction of Qumran in A.D. 68. Though the first explicit mention of the Ebionites dates from

[21] Cf., for instance, G. Vermès, 'Le "Commentaire d'Habacuc" et le Nouveau Testament', *Cahiers Sioniens* 5 (1951) 337–49; K. Elliger, *Studien zum Habakkuk-Kommentar* (Tübingen: Mohr) 244; H. J. Schoeps, 'Der Habakuk-Kommentar von 'Ain-Feshkha—ein Dokument der hasmonäischen Spätzeit', *ZAW* 63 (1951) 249–50. Also by Schoeps, 'Handelt es sich wirklich um ebionitische Dokumente?', *ZRGG* 3 (1951) 322. [Hereafter Schoeps 3.]

[22] Cf. n. 3 above for references to his articles. Just a few points will be mentioned here. For the identification of Jesus as the True Teacher and Paul as the 'Man of Lies' Teicher is relying on the article of G. Margoliouth, 'The Sadducean Christians of Damascus', *Athenaeum* 4335 (Nov. 26, 1910) 657–9, where the identification is merely asserted. Prof. Teicher does little more when he says, 'The "True Teacher" is, in fact, Jesus. He is addressed as such in Mark 12.14, "Master (Teacher) we know that thou art true."' This is the only evidence given that the *môreh haṣṣedeq* of the Qumran literature is Jesus. Another point is the problem of the Jewish Christians mentioned by Eusebius (*Hist. eccl.* 3, 5; quoted above). All we know is that they were early Christians from Jerusalem, most likely Jewish. Pella, the place to which they went according to Eusebius, is about 50–60 miles away from Qumran, as the crow flies, and on the other side of the Jordan—hardly 'in

Irenaeus (*ca.* A.D. 175), and though it is quite probable that they existed as a sect much earlier, there is simply no evidence for their existence in the first century A.D., either before or after the destruction of Jerusalem.[23] Consequently, the simple identification of the Qumran sect and the Ebionites is untenable.

EBIONITE LITERATURE

By Ebionite literature I mean here material embedded in the Pseudo-Clementine *Homilies* and *Recognitions*, often called merely the *Pseudoclementines* (PsC).[24] Various spurious works circulated in antiquity under the name of Clement of Rome, and among these was the romantic novel which exists today under the title

---

the vicinity of the 'Ain Feshkha cave' (*JJS* 2:93). Another gratuitous statement is the assertion that the Ebionites are mentioned by name in the *pesher* on Habakkuk (12:3, 6). K. Elliger (*op. cit.*, p. 244) has pointed out that the article would be necessary before *'ebyônîm* for this word to be capable of meaning 'the Ebionites'. The word has indeed turned up with the article in the *pesher* on the Psalms from Qumran Cave 4, where the words *'bywnym* and *'dt h'bywnym* are found. Cf. J. M. Allegro, 'A Newly Discovered Fragment of a Commentary on Psalm XXXVII from Qumrân', *PEQ* 86 (1954) 69–75; see now 4QPss[a] (=4Q*171*) 1–2 ii 9; 1, 3–4 iii 10 (DJD 5, 43–4). This still does not prove that *'ebyônîm* means 'Ebionites', for the word is obviously used in all places in the sense found so often in the Old Testament, God's poor. 1QpHab 12:10 can easily be translated 'who robbed the possessions of the poor'; meaning 'what little they had'. The parallelism between the 'poor' and the 'simple' in 1QpHab 12:3–4 cannot be disregarded. For other passages in the Qumran literature where *'bywnym* means the 'poor', cf. 1QM 11:9, 13; 13:12–14 ('a virtual self-designation of the [Qumran] group as "the poor"'—so L. E. Keck, *ZNW* 57 [1966] 71).

[23] Cf. A. Dupont-Sommer, *The Jewish Sect of Qumran and the Essenes* (London: Valentine Mitchell, 1954) 158: 'The excavations of Khirbet Qumrân, by establishing that the manuscripts were conveyed to their hiding-place about A.D. 66–70, show that Dr Teicher's dates are too late, and accordingly suffice to undermine the whole of his theory.' Cf. G. Vermès, *Les Manuscrits du Désert de Juda* (2nd ed.; Paris: Desclée, 1954) 36; Schoeps 2, 1. These authors' remarks are all based on the report of R. de Vaux, 'Fouille au Khirbet Qumrân', *RB* 60 (1953) 94; *CRAIBL*, 1953, p. 317; see now his *L'archéologie et les manuscrits de la Mer Morte* (Schweich Lectures, 1959; London: British Academy, 1961) and his answer to Teicher in 'Archaeology and the Dead Sea Scrolls', *Antiquity* 37 (1963) 126–7 (cf. pp. 25–30).

[24] For the purpose of this essay we do not have to consider the transla-

of *Homilies and Recognitions*. The PsC contain five documents: (*a*) the *Epistle of Peter to James*, instructing the latter that the accompanying writings are not to be entrusted to any but the initiated; (*b*) *Diamartyria* or *Contestatio*, the 'oath' to be taken by the initiated concerning these writings; (*c*) *Epistle of Clement to James*, telling of Peter's martyrdom, Clement's ordination, Peter's instruction to Clement his successor, and Peter's order to write down an epitome of his sermons in the various cities that it might be sent to James, the bishop of Jerusalem; this serves as an introduction to the *Homilies*, for Clement says that he is sending *Klēmentos tōn Petrou epidēmiōn kērygmatōn epitōme*; (*d*) *Homiliai*, 20 books of the 'Homilies'; (*e*) *Anagnorismoi*, 10 books of the 'Recognitions.'[25]

The *Homilies* (hereafter, *Hom*) and the *Recognitions* (hereafter, *Rec*) are two forms of a novel about the fate of the various members of the noble family of Clement of Rome. Clement himself is portrayed as a searcher for truth, going about to the various schools of philosophy for a solution of his doubts concerning the origin of the world, the immortality of the soul, etc. At length he hears that the Son of God has appeared in distant Judea. After a long journey, which takes him to Egypt and Palestine, he meets Peter in Caesarea, is instructed in the doctrine of the True Prophet, and becomes a Christian. He is invited by Peter to accompany him on his missionary journeys in pursuit of Simon Magus. Curious circumstances had brought about the break-up of Clement's family: his mother and two brothers leave Rome because of a warning his mother receives in a dream, and sail for Athens; but they are shipwrecked and separated. Finally, father, mother, and the three sons set out to

---

tion of the Old Testament by Symmachus, nor the *Gospel according to the Hebrews*, which are generally judged to be Ebionite compositions. The latter is 'some sort of reworking and extension of the Hebrew original of the canonical Gospel of Matthew' (J. Quasten, *op. cit.*, 1, 112). Cf. the remarks of Bornkamm, *op. cit.*, 197.

[25] The *Hom* are extant today in Greek; the text has recently been edited by Bernhard Rehm, *Die Pseudoklementinen: I, Homilien*, in the series, *Die*

find each other, and the successive recognitions of the members of the family, aided by the efforts of Peter, give the title of 'Recognitions' to one of the versions of this novel. The greater part of the novel is given over, however, to the sermons of Peter and his debates with Simon Magus. This is responsible for the title of the other extant version, 'Homilies'. Actually there is as much homiletic material in the *Recognitions* as there is recognition in the *Homilies*. Long passages parallel each other, sometimes with word-for-word identity.

Popular in the last century as the basis of the Tübingen-School theory of opposition between the Petrine and Pauline churches of early Christianity,[26] the PsC were first subjected to critical study by Adolf Hilgenfeld, a disciple of that same school, toward the end of the nineteenth century. Since the beginning of this century numerous scholars have worked over them; among these are especially Waitz, Heintze, Carl Schmidt, Cullmann, Thomas, Rehm, and Schoeps.[27] Waitz was the first

---

griechischen christlichen Schriftsteller der ersten Jahrhunderte 42 (Berlin: Akademie-Verlag, 1953). The *Rec* are extant only in a Latin translation (or, according to many scholars, a Latin adaptation) by Rufinus (*c.* A.D. 405). A new edition has been promised for the Berlin *Corpus*. For the time being we must use the text found in Migne, *PL* 1, 1158–1474. There is also a Syriac MS., dated A.D. 411, which contains the text of *Hom* 10–14 and *Rec* 1–4; cf. W. Frankenberg, *Die syrischen Clementinen mit griechischem Paralleltext* (Leipzig: Hinrichs, 1937; TU 48/3). A few other fragments also are extant; cf. J. Quasten, *op. cit.*, 1, 61. An English translation (which must now be checked against the new critical edition of the *Hom*) can be found in A. Roberts and Donaldson, *Ante-Nicene Christian Library* (Edinburgh: T. and T. Clark) 3 (Recognitions, 1875) 17 (Homilies, 1870).

[26] In the PsC Paul is alluded to, frequently under the designation of *inimicus homo* or *ho echthros anthrōpos*, being depicted as the adversary of James, the Bishop of Jerusalem. Though Peter is identified with the camp of James, we do not find Paul pictured as the enemy of Peter; the latter role is played by Simon Magus throughout. But the critics of the last century found no difficulty in asserting that the figure of Simon Magus was really a literary mask for the real opponent, Paul; cf. J. Chapman, 'On the Date of the Clementines', *ZNW* 9 (1908) 150–1.

[27] The chief works are: Hans Waitz, *Die Pseudoklementinen, Homilien und Rekognitionen, eine quellenkritische Untersuchung* (Leipzig: Hinrichs, 1904; TU

to subject the PsC to a searching literary analysis and to uncover the *Grundschrift* (hereafter, *G*). *G* was thought to have been a novel, composed of material that dates back to subapostolic times, in which Peter was the dominant figure. Though *G* is now lost, fragments of it are thought to be extant in the PsC, well reworked by different redactors.

G is considered to be a compilation, composed of fragments of five works: (*a*) the *Kērygmata Petrou*, sermons of Peter on his missionary journeys, digested by Clement; (*b*) the story of the wondrous deeds of Simon Magus and of his debates with Peter; (*c*) Appion-dialogues in *Hom* 4–6 and *Rec* 10: Clement argues with Appion against the latter's pagan ideas about fate, astrology, polytheism; cf. Eusebius, *Hist. eccl.*, 3, 38, 5; (*d*) the Graeco-Oriental Recognition-novel, about the members of the family of Clement of Rome; (*e*) Bardesanes' *Book of the Laws of the Lands*.[28]

The compilatory character of *G* is responsible for the impression of the reader that the *Hom* and *Rec* are quite a hodgepodge. Waitz maintained a date in the early third century for the composition of *G*; with slight variations this has been more or less generally admitted.[29] Practically all scholars admit today the existence of *G* and its compilatory character. The relationship of *G*, however, to the later reworkings, whether *Hom* and *Rec* represent independent versions of *G* or depend one on the other, is a question that has been hotly debated; it does not

---

25/4); Carl Schmidt, *Studien zu den Pseudoklementinen* (Leipzig: Hinrichs, 1929; TU 46/1); Oscar Cullmann, *Le problème littéraire et historique du roman pseudo-clémentin: Etude sur le rapport entre le Gnosticisme et le Judéo-Christianisme* (Paris: F. Alcan, 1930); J. Thomas, *op. cit.*, 174 ff.; Bernhard Rehm, 'Zur Entstehung der pseudoclementinischen Schriften', *ZNW* 37 (1938) 77–184; H. J. Schoeps 1, 37–61 *et passim*. An extensive bibliography is to be found in the last cited work; cf. also J. Quasten, *op. cit.*, 1, 62–3. See further H. J. Schoeps, 'Die Pseudoklementinen und das Urchristentum', *ZRGG* 10 (1958) 3–15.

[28] The inclusion of this last section is rather doubtful; cf. J. Quasten, *op. cit.*, 1, 263.

[29] C. Schoeps 1, 38.

concern us here. A Syriac version of *Hom* 10–14 and of *Rec* 1–4 is extant in a manuscript dated A.D. 411. Its text of *Hom* is slightly different at times from the Greek, and Schoeps is of the opinion that it represents an earlier form of the novel.[30]

It has been quite generally held that the PsC are Ebionite in origin; however, not all scholars agree. Evidence for the Ebionite origin comes from Epiphanius (*Pan.* 30, 15), who tells us that they used the *Periodoi Petrou dia Klēmentos*. This is the name by which *G* apparently went in antiquity.[31] Schoeps, following other scholars, maintains that the *Kērygmata Petrou* (hereafter, *KP*) were definitely the Ebionite writing among the sources of *G*, having been written by an Ebionite of the second century who led the defence of his co-religionists against the attacks of the Marcionite Gnosis.[32] The extent of the original *KP* was first determined by Waitz on the basis of the summary given in the third book of *Rec*, chap. 75. Clement mentions here that he has already sent to James a book of Peter's sermons, the contents of which he proceeds to summarize, dividing them into ten *tomoi*. Using this as a starting point, Waitz indicated the passages of the PsC that originally belonged to the *KP* section of *G*. This reconstruction of *KP* was checked by subsequent studies, accepted by many, expanded in slight details by still others, and enjoys a certain vogue today. However, as early as 1908 Dom John Chapman questioned the analysis.[33] In 1932 Ed. Schwartz and M. Goguel rejected it.[34] Schoeps is of the opinion that their arguments were answered by Waitz and others 'gebührend'.[35]

[30] *Ibid.*, 40.

[31] Cf. Origen, *Comm. in Gen.* according to *Philocalia* 23 (*PG* 12, 85); *Opus imperf. ad Matt.*, ser. 77; perhaps also Epiphanius, *Pan.* 30, 15; Jerome, *Comm. in Gal.* 1, 18; *Adv. Iovin.* 1, 14.

[32] Schoeps 1, 313; '. . . ein rein ebionitisches Werk aus der Zeit des antignostischen Kampfes . . .' (p. 58).

[33] *Op. cit.*, 147 ff.

[34] 'Unzeitgemässe Beobachtungen zu den Clementinen', *ZNW* 31 (1932) 151–99.

[35] Schoeps 1, 44.

However, Bernard Rehm, a student of Schwartz and editor of the latest critical edition of the *Hom*, has proposed an entirely different analysis of the redactions. While admitting an original G, he believes that the recognitive section was the nucleus (therefore not *KP*) about which the four other sections clustered. *G* was reworked in an early form of *Hom*, which was suspect in the Church at large, but found reception among the heretic Ebionites. An attempt to make the novel orthodox resulted in an early redaction of *Rec*. This analysis of Rehm cannot be lightly dismissed—and so the question arises whether there really were any *KP* at all. Bultmann, in his review of Schoeps' *Theologie*, states this question quite frankly and in the end admits his extreme scepticism, as do others, about the whole literary analysis of the sources of PsC.[36]

We have gone into details here merely to show how uncertain the reconstruction, extent, and original character of *KP* really are. Who is right, Schoeps and those he follows, or Rehm? Schoeps would have us believe that the *KP* were originally Ebionite, reworked later by Christians of different hues. Rehm proposes that the original *G* was Christian, later contaminated by Ebionite notions. It is obvious that the answer to this problem, if it can ever be found, will radically determine one's use of the *KP* in a comparison of Ebionite and Qumran tenets and practices. Cullmann has made such a comparison, utilizing the Qumran material that had been previously published, and the *KP*, apparently according to his own reconstruction of the document, as if this were a *chose acquise*. Nowhere in the article does he mention the analysis of Rehm, not even the summary given in the *Einleitung* of the latter's critical edition.

[36] *Op. cit.*, 181. Cf. Bornkamm, *op. cit.*, 197–8; J. Quasten, *op. cit.*, 1, 61–2. For Rehm's views see the introduction to his critical edition, *Die Pseudoklementinen*, cited above, pp. vii–ix; and especially his article, quoted in n. 27 above. Cf. E. Molland, 'La circoncision, le baptême et l'autorité du décret apostolique (Actes XV, 28 sq.) dans les milieux judéochrétiens des Pseudo-Clementines', *ST* 9 (1955) 1–8; G. Strecker, *Das Judenchristentum in den Pseudoklementinen* (TU 70; Berlin: Akademie-Verlag, 1958) 1–34.

In the following section of this paper I am going to compare the Ebionites and the sect of Qumran. For the sake of this comparison I shall accept the list of passages of the PsC which are judged by Schoeps as belonging to *KP*. His list represents the latest investigation and the widest range of passages that could pertain to the original *KP*.[37] The validity of such a list, of course, depends on how the previous questions are resolved. In all references to the PsC I shall indicate, in parentheses, whether or not the passage belongs to *KP*, according to this list (see Chart 2).

CHART 2

KĒRYGMATA PETROU

(found in the following passages of the PsC, according to the studies of Waitz, as modified by subsequent scholars, Bousset, Cullmann; the references in parentheses indicate the additions of Schoeps, *Theologie*, pp. 45-53)

Hom 1:18–20
2:6–12, 14–18, 33–4; 38–40, 43–52 (omit 6–12, 14–15, 34; add 41, 42)
3:17–28, 33–8, 43–56 (add 2–10; 39–42)
8:2–20 (add 21–3; omit 2–3)
9:1–23
11:16, 19–33 (add 35)
15:5–11
16:5–14, 16 (add 15, 21)
17:3, 6–19 (add 4–5)
18:6–10; 19–22
19:1–23
20:1–10

Rec 1:15–17, 22–4, 32–44, 46–71, 74 (omit 23; add 27–31, 45)
2:20–48, 55, 62–5 (omit 55, 62–5; add 66–7)
3:2–10, 12–30, 52–61 (add 33–8)
4:2–20 (add 1, 21, 25–6)
5:34–5
6:4–14

[37] Cf. Schoeps 1, 50–3. This list incorporates passages ascribed to *KP* by Waitz, Bousset, Cullmann, and Schoeps. Cf. Schoeps 1, 38 for a descrip-

COMPARISON OF THE EBIONITES AND THE SECT OF QUMRAN

I shall discuss in detail various points of similarity and dissimilarity that exist between the Ebionites and the Qumran sect, to see whether there is any basis for the assertion that the latter was or became Ebionite. It will be evident that I am not trying to trace the history of each idea or practice that I take up; nor am I trying to list all the possible sources from which either group may have derived its tenets and customs. I am concerned merely with the influence of Qumran on the Ebionites.

At the outset it should be noted that the PsC do not depict the Ebionites as living a communal existence, as does the Manual of Discipline with respect to the Qumran sect. There is nothing 'monastic'[38] about the group described in PsC. Hence the comparison will not be based on rules, ways of acting, punishments, etc., such as are found in 1QS.[39] But there are many other points that can well be compared.

Dualism

This term is used normally of those opposites which have been found in Gnostic literature, the Johannine and Pauline writings, Greek philosophy, and other writings. It should be obvious that the principle of contradiction, being a basic metaphysical principle, could be made the support for many sets of opposites which are not specifically 'dualistic'. Such notions as the levitical contrast of clean-unclean, God's creation of the heaven and the earth, the tree of the knowledge of good and evil, could be forced into a system of dualism. But we must be more specific; we must beware of trying to interpret every set of opposites as

tion of his 'orthodox' position in this matter. It is to be noted that Bornkamm (pp. 197–8) criticizes Schoeps for expanding the list of the other scholars 'ohne nähere Begründung'.

[38] Cf. Cullmann, 'Die neuentdeckten Qumrantexte und das Judenchristentum der Pseudoklementinen' [see n. 4] p. 42; unless otherwise noted, henceforth all references to Cullmann will be to this article.

[39] Millar Burrows, *The Dead Sea Scrolls of St Mark's Monastery* (New Haven: American Schools of Oriental Research) 1 (The Isaiah Manuscript and the Habakkuk Commentary, 1950); 2, fasc. 2 (The Manual of Discipline, 1951).

dualistic (in the sense usually intended by those who treat this question).

We can summarize the dualism of 1QS as follows: the members are to do good and avoid evil (1:4–5), to turn to the truth and away from perversity (6:15; cf. 1:5–6; 1:15–17; 5:1). This simple contrast of good-evil, truth-perversity soon appears more complex; for the members are to love the sons of light and hate the sons of darkness (1:10), to bless the men of God's lot and curse the men of Belial's lot (2:2, 5). These two groups of men are divided according to the divine appointment of two spirits (truth and perversity) which are to guide men until the period of visitation (3:17–19). These spirits are the 'prince of light' and the 'angel of darkness' (3:20–21). Truth is derived from the spring of light and perversity from the fountain of darkness (3:19–23). The angel of truth is on the side of the God of Israel (3:24), whose enemy is Belial (1:21–23; 7:1–3). For God loves the spirit of truth and hates the spirit of perversity (4:1). These two spirits are the source of all good and evil works of man in this world (3:26; 4:2 ff.). God has set them up to reign in equal parts with eternal, mutual enmity until the time of his visitation (4:17–19). Then God will destroy the spirit of perversity and the Truth will prevail (4:19). The spirits of truth and perversity both strive within the heart of man (4:23.)

Dualism is found as well in the War Scroll (1QM), but the system does not appear to be as developed as that in 1QS. This is slightly surprising, because 1QM is a manual for the conduct of God's war, in which the sons of light are to battle against the sons of darkness. The opposition of light and darkness is frequent enough; likewise that of God's lot and Belial's lot. But we find little mention of the opposition between truth and perversity. Columns 1 and 13 in particular contain dualistic concepts. A war is to be waged against the 'sons of darkness' (1:1, 7, 10, 16; 13:16; 14:17) by the 'sons of light' (1:1, 3, 9, 11, 13), against the 'lot of darkness' (1:1, 5, 11; 13:5) by the 'lot of light' (13:5, 9) or 'God's lot' (1:5; 13:6, 12; 15:1). We read of the 'army of Belial' (1:13; 11:8; 15:2–3; 18:3), the 'lot of Belial' (1:5; 4:2; 13:2, 4, 12; 14:10); the 'prince of light' (13:10), 'spirits of truth' (13:10); 'prince of the dominion of impiety' (17:5–6). It is God's war (11:1) that the sons of light are waging. The period of darkness reigns now, but in God's time the sons of light will prevail (1:8). For God has determined of old the day for the war to wipe out the sons of darkness (1:10).

In the Thanksgiving Psalms (1QH) we read that both the just man and the evil man proceed from God the Creator (4:38).

It is noteworthy that this dualism is lacking in 1QpHab and CD. As in the passage in 1QS 3:6, the contrast between clean and unclean might possibly be considered a manifestation of dualism (CD 6:17; 11:19–20; 12:20). But this is obviously an opposition known from the Levitical laws of the Bible.[40]

In the PsC there is also a dualism which can be compared with that of Qumran. God, the sole Creator of all, has differentiated all principles into pairs of opposites from the beginning—heaven, earth; day, night; light, fire; sun, moon; life, death (*Hom* 2:15 *KP*). This is the system that is known as the syzygies or combinations, according to which all things come in pairs (*Hom* 2:15, 33 *KP*). The smaller precedes the larger, the female the male, the inferior the superior, and evil precedes good (*Rec* 3:59 *KP*). Outside the passages thought to belong to the original *KP* we also find a dualism, the doctrine of the 'two paths', presided over by Belief and Unbelief (*Hom* 7:6–7).

Another way of expressing this dualism is the contrast of two kingdoms. 'The prophet of truth who appeared [on earth] taught us that the Maker and God of all gave two kingdoms to two, good and evil: granting to the evil the sovereignty over the present world along with the law, so that he [it] should have the right to punish those who act unjustly; but to the good He gave the eternal age to come. But He made each man free with

[40] Charles, *APOT* (Oxford: Clarendon Press, 1913) 2, 184, compares CD 6:17 with Ez 22:26.

the power to give himself up to whatsoever he prefers, either to the present evil or to the future good' (*Hom* 15:7 *KP*; 8:55 not *KP*). Elsewhere we learn that Christ is the ruler of the future ages as the King of righteousness, whereas the Tempter is the ruler of the present; that is why he tempted Christ saying, 'All the kingdoms of the present world are subject to me' (*Hom* 8:21 *KP* [according to Schoeps]). Truth and error are contrasted in *Rec* 6:4 *KP*. We will recall that Epiphanius recorded this opposition or dualism (*Pan.* 30, 16).

From the summaries given above it should be obvious that there is a definite similarity in the dualisms of Qumran and of the PsC. Cullmann has pointed out that in both cases there is a subordination of the dualistic system to Jewish monotheistic ideas. God set up the kings of the two domains in the PsC just as he set up the spirits of truth and perversity of 1QS.[41] Both Karl Georg Kuhn[42] and A. Dupont-Sommer[43] have related this Qumran dualism to Iranian sources. The latter maintains that precisely this subordination of the two spirits to the supreme God is found in the Iranian source.[44]

There seems, however, to be some difference of opinion among scholars about this Iranian influence. Quite recently H. Michaud has suggested an even more specific source of the Qumran dualism, i.e., Zervanism. Zervanism was a particular branch of Zoroastrianism, in which the protagonist, Ahura Mazda, and the antagonist in the dualistic system are both born of a superior deity, *Zurvan* or *chronos*, time. It dates from the time of the Achaemenian empire and was regarded as

[41] *Op. cit.*, 38–9.

[42] 'Die Sektenschrift und die iranische Religion', *ZThK* 49 (1952) 296–316.

[43] *Nouveaux aperçus sur les manuscrits de la Mer Morte* (Paris: Maisonneuve, 1953) 157–72.

[44] 'Ce qui frappe dans l'instruction du *Manuel*, c'est que les deux Esprits, comme dans les Gâthâ, restent subordonnés à Dieu: l'Esprit du bien n'est pas confondu avec Dieu, tandis qu'il est identifié avec Ahoura Mazda dans les speculations ultérieures du Mazdéisme' (p. 170). Cf. Engl. tr., p. 128.

heretical only in the time of the Sassanids. Michaud is of the opinion that the author of the Qumran theological system either knew the Zervanite myth of creation or was influenced by a system of thought that has been infected with it.[45] The possibility of such Iranian influence cannot be disregarded, but the full implication of this influence has not yet been explored. There is certainly no obstacle, theologically speaking, which would prevent such a dualism subordinated to a Supreme Being from being adopted either into the Jewish or Jewish-Christian way of thinking.

Cullmann has, however, pointed out a difference between the Qumran dualism and that of the PsC, i.e., that the opposition—light-darkness, truth-perversity—in 1QS is never brought into line with the opposition—male-female, light-fire—as it is in the PsC.[46] This is true, but it seems that the difference is much more fundamental. Kuhn has already described the Qumran dualism as ethical and eschatological, akin to the Iranian source.[47] This is true, for no pair of Qumran opposites can be found which is not to be understood in an ethical sense.[48] Light

[45] Kuhn (*op. cit.*, 311–12) asserts that the subordination to God in the Qumran literature is a feature not found in the Iranian source. That an Iranian source had influenced as well the PsC seems indicated by the interest shown in these writings in Nimrod-Zoroaster. Cullmann (*op. cit.*, 38, n. 14) pointed out the passages, *Hom* 9:4; *Rec* 1:30; to these we may add *Rec* 4:27–29 (all *KP*). For the ideas of Michaud, cf. 'Un mythe zervanite dans un des manuscrits de Qumrân', *VT* 5 (1955) 137–47. See further D. Winston, 'The Iranian Component in the Bible, Apocrypha, and Qumran: A Review of the Evidence', *History of Religions* 5 (1965–66) 183–216. H.-J. Schoeps, 'Iranisches in den Pseudoklementinen', *ZNW* 51 (1960) 1–10. R. G. Jones, 'The Manual of Discipline (1QS), Persian Religion and the Old Testament', *The Teacher's Yoke: Studies in Memory of Henry Trantham* (ed. E. J. Vardaman and J. L. Garrett, Jr.; Waco, Texas: Baylor University Press, 1964) 94–108. R. N. Frye, 'Zurvanism Again', *HTR* 52 (1959) 63–73.

[46] *Ibid.*, 39.

[47] *Op. cit.*, 305.

[48] This I maintain against W. Baumgartner, 'Die Bedeutung der Höhlenfunde aus Palästina für die Theologie', *Schweizerische theologische Umschau* 24 (1954) 62, who thinks that the opposition between the sons of light and the

and darkness are only symbols for the other pair, truth and perversity, good and evil, God and Belial. But in the PsC the dualism is definitely physical. *All* principles have been divided into opposites (*Hom* 2:15 *KP*); the *syzygies* dominate everything (*Hom* 2:15–16, 33; *Rec* 3:59 *KP*): heaven, earth; day, night; light, fire; sun, moon—as well as good, evil. The opposition in the ethical sphere is expressed in the PsC in terms of two kingdoms, two paths, two beings, whereas in 1QS it is a question of two spirits. This, of course, may be a mere manner of expression. But the dualism of Qumran, though similar in its general conception to that of the Ebionites, is of a simpler type. An ethical dualism, like that of Qumran, could have developed—especially under other influences—into a dualism that was both physical and ethical, like that of the PsC.

Before leaving this question of dualism, I must say a word about its possible Gnostic character. In the first article that Kuhn wrote on the ideas of the Qumran sect, he labelled its dualism as 'Gnostic'.[49] Later, in discussing its connection with Iranian religion, he showed how the ideas of 1QS confirmed the thesis once put forth by Bousset-Gressmann that the Jewish apocalyptic ideas of the last centuries B.C. had been affected by Persian thought. He emphasized the fact that the ethical character of the Qumran dualism definitely connected it with Old Iranian ideas and clearly separated it from Gnosticism.[50] Schoeps constantly rejected throughout his book the idea that the Ebionites were Gnostics.[51] He accused Epiphanius of confusing them with the Elchesaites, and of erroneously ascribing to them the Gnostic ideas of the latter. For him the PsC dualism

---

sons of darkness is physical. What the basis of this physical interpretation is, Baumgartner does not tell us.

[49] 'Die in Palästina gefundenen hebräischen Texte und das Neue Testament', *ZThK* 57 (1950) 210: 'eine palästinische-jüdische Sektenfrömmigkeit gnostischer Struktur'; p. 207: 'die dualistischgnostische Denkstruktur'.

[50] 'Die Sektenschrift und die iranische Religion', *op. cit.*, 315.

[51] Cf. Schoeps 1, 305–6: '*In Wirklichkeit sind die Ebioniten niemals Gnostiker gewesen, sondern im Gegenteil ihre allerschärfsten Gegner*' [emphasis supplied by Schoeps]. Cf. Bultmann's review, p. 188.

is nothing but a development of a trend, which has 'a legitimate Jewish root . . . for the *zûgôt*-principle is very ancient [*uralt*] in Judaism'.[52] Yet in an article written in 1954 Schoeps apparently abandoned this fundamental position; for he claims that he has finally realized that the Gnostic syzygy-system of Book 6 of *KP* is derived from the 1QS teaching of the two spirits.[53] This is a complete *volte-face*, the denial of a main contention in his book. Though the Qumran dualism could be the source of the Ebionite dualism of the PsC, we still have no real evidence for labelling either of them as Gnostic. It is to be hoped that the publication of the Gnostic Codices of Chenoboskion will shed light on the dualism of the PsC and give us a better understanding of early Gnositicism. But there is certainly no reason to call the Qumran dualism Gnostic.[54]

Teacher of Righteousness

The *môrēh haṣṣedeq* of 1QpHab (1:13; 2:2; 5:10; 7:4; 8:3; 9:9), of CD 1:11; 6:11; 20:1, 14, 28, 32), of 4QpPss[a] (1, 3–4 iii 15, 19; 3–10 iv 27), and of 4QpPss[b] (1:4; 2:2) has certain characteristics which resemble those of the *prophētēs alētheias* or *ho alēthēs prophētēs* of *KP* (*Hom* 1:18–19; 2:6 and *passim*). The latter is sometimes called merely 'the Prophet' (*Hom* 2:6) or 'the Teacher' (*Hom* 11:20, 28). This last description is also found for the Teacher of Righteousness in CD 20:28. But it should be

[52] *Ibid.*, 161. To be fair, we must indicate that he does admit in a footnote the possibility of the Persian source. The proof advanced for the *uralt* Jewish root is Rabbinic literature, whose antiquity is very hard to determine.

[53] 'Die Lehre [von den beiden Geistern] ist vielmehr Eigenbau, beste 'Ain-Feshkha Theologie. Jetzt weiss ich es endlich, *woher* die ebionitischen *Kerygmata Petrou* (K.P.), deren sechstes Buch die hochgnostische Syzygienlehre von den Gegensatzpaaren behandelt, ihre Lehre von den beiden Geistern bezogen haben' (Schoeps 2, 2).

[54] Cf. Heinrich Schlier, 'Das Denken der frühchristlichen Gnosis', *Neutestamentliche Studien für R. Bultmann*, *op. cit.*, 67–82, for an example of how different early Christian Gnosticism was from Qumran ideas. Bo Reicke has also recently pointed out another difference in that the God of Qumran is a *personal* God; see 'Traces cf Gnosticism in the Dead Sea Scrolls?', *NTS* 1 (1954) 140.

noted immediately that, whereas the identity of the Teacher of Righteousness in the Qumran documents is unknown, there can be no doubt that Jesus is the True Prophet of the PsC (cf. Epiphanius, *Pan.* 30, 18; *Hom* 3:52–56 *KP*).

The function of the Teacher of Righteousness is to lead men in the way of God's heart (CD 1:11); his words come from the mouth of God (1QpHab 2:2), for God has revealed to him all the mysteries of the words of his servants the prophets (7:4). The men of the community are to listen to him (CD 9:28, 32), and God will deliver from the house of condemnation all those who suffer for him and show their fidelity to him (1QpHab 2:7–8). He also seems to have been a priest (1QpHab 2:7),[55] 'persecuted' by the 'Man of the Lie', who rejected the Law (5:10; 11:5; CD 20:32). According to CD 6:11, someone is expected 'at the end of the days' and the phrase *ywrh hṣdq* plays on his name. Is it a reference to the Teacher of Righteousness? CD 19:35–20:1 seems to distinguish him from the Messiah expected 'from Aaron and from Israel'.[56]

[55] This is now confirmed by 4QpPss[a] 1,3–4 iii 15–16, where we read (2:15) *pšrw 'l hkwhn mwrh h*[*ṣdq*], 'its interpretation concerns the priest, the Teacher of [Righteousness whom] God has [or]dered to arise and [whom] he has established in order to build for him the congregation [of the Poor]' (see also 4QpPss[a] 1–2 ii 18; DJD 5, 44). J. L. Teicher denies, of course, that the Teacher of Righteousness was a priest; cf. *JJS* 3 (1952) 54; 5 (1954) 96: 'But he [the Teacher of Righteousness] was a teacher, not a sacrificing priest, and the term 'priest' applied to him in the Fragments is merely a metaphor.' 'The term *kohen* (priest) is thus equivalent to the term *doresh hatorah* (he who searches the scripture).' That the *dôreš hattôrāh*, 'the Interpreter of the Law', was a priestly figure in the Qumran literature is easily admitted. However, this does not mean that the Teacher of Righteousness was not a *kôhēn* ('priest') in the ordinary sense, i.e., a member of a priestly family closely related to the cultic service of the Jerusalem temple. He may have broken with the Jerusalem priests because of their laxity and corruption. But he is still regarded as *kôhēn*, and any attempt to water down the meaning of this term must offer some proof for the contention. On the other hand, CD 7:18 seems to think of an 'Interpreter of the Law' yet to come, a figure who seems to be distinct from the Teacher of Righteousness.

[56] See now R. E. Brown, 'The Teacher of Righteousness and the Messiah(s)', *The Scrolls and Christianity* (ed. M. Black; London: SPCK, 1969) 37–44, 109–12.

The function of the True Prophet in *KP* is similar to that of the Teacher of Righteousness at least in that he too is looked upon as the leader of the group, and the helper of mankind which is enshrouded in darkness and ignorance, communicating to it knowledge.[57] 'He alone is able to enlighten the souls of men, so that with our own eyes we may be able to see the way of eternal salvation' (*Hom* 1:19 *KP*; cf. *Rec* 1:15–16 *KP*). 'This is peculiar to the Prophet, to reveal the truth, even as it is peculiar to the sun to bring the day' (*Hom* 2:6 *KP*).

In this connection Cullmann speaks of an *Erlösergestalt* found in both sets of documents, whose specific role is to reveal the truth.[58] One may question whether the Teacher of Righteousness is aptly described as an *Erlösergestalt.* 1QpHab 8:2–3 is apparently the only passage (doubtful at that) that would lend itself to such an interpretation. For, though 'deliverance from the house of condemnation (*or* judgment)' might conceivably be understood in the sense of redemption, yet this may refer as well to some contemporary political situation, described by this vague expression, as do others in 1QpHab. As for the PsC, the True Prophet could be called an *Erlöser*; but Bultmann is undoubtedly right in stressing that the Pseudoclementine Christology is anything but soteriological in the Pauline sense, adopted by the early Church.[59]

As a revealer of truth, then, the Teacher of Righteousness and the True Prophet can be favourably compared, for their functions are definitely similar.[60] Nothing, however, warrants more than a possible connection between these two figures, when we are trying to trace the influence of Qumran on the Ebionites.

[57] K. Elliger, *op. cit.*, 285, and J. L. Teicher, *JJS* 2 (1951) 97, points out that the words *ṣdq* and *'mt* are really synonymous, so that we could well speak of the 'Teacher of Truth' or the 'True Teacher'. The other expression, however, has become customary already, so that it is retained here.

[58] *Op. cit.*, 39.

[59] *Op. cit.*, 183–6.

[60] Cullmann (*op. cit.*, 40) points out a dissimilarity in that the Teacher of

The Man of the Lie

The antagonist of the Teacher of Righteousness is described as the 'Man of the Lie' (cf. 1QpHab 2:1–2; 5:11; CD 20:15) or the 'Preacher of the Lie' (1QpHab 10:9; CD8:13): *'îš hakkāzāb*; *maṭṭîp hakkāzāb*. In the PsC, however, the antagonist of Christ, the True Prophet, is Satan, the prince of evil (*Hom* 8:21 *KP*). Peter, too, has an adversary throughout, Simon Magus. But there is an unnamed figure referred to as *inimicus homo*, *ho echthros anthrōpos*, *planos tis* (*Rec* 1:70, 71, 73; *Hom* 2:17; 11:35; *Ep. Petri* 2, 3), who is identified as the Apostle Paul on the basis of *Rec* 1:71, alluding to Acts 22:5. But it should be noted that he is definitely considered to be the adversary of James, the bishop of Jerusalem. It is, therefore, a gratuitous assertion to equate the *inimicus homo* of PsC with the *'îš hakkāzāb*, and to maintain on this basis that Paul is the antagonist referred to in the Qumran literature. Both the Qumran scrolls and the PsC speak of a figure who is an adversary, but the differing details prevent any further identification.[61]

Attitude toward the Old Testament

Under this heading we will discuss the attitude of both groups toward the prophets, the Pentateuch, the sacrifice of the Temple, and the priesthood.

a) *The prophets*. The Qumran sect not only held to the strict observance of the Torah, but also regarded the prophets of the Old Testament with great esteem. This is evident not only from statements of 1QS (1:3; 8:16), 4QpHos[a] (2:5), CD (7:17), 1QpHab (2:9), but also from the way they quote the prophets

---

Righteousness is a priest, whereas the True Prophet is not. See footnote 55 and compare 1QpHab 2:7 with 7:4. As for the PsC, the situation is not clear. From the general context we would not expect the True Prophet to be a priest, and *Rec* 1:46–48 (*KP*) are certainly difficult to understand if he were not one.

[61] Cullmann (*op. cit.*, 40) speaks of a *Lügenprophet* in 1QpHab 7:9. I can find no such character in 1QpHab, unless that is the translation he is using for *mṭyp hkzb* in 10:9.

(CD 7:10; 9:5) and from the writings they composed to interpret the biblical prophets (e.g., the *pesharim*, 1QpHab, 1QpMic, 1QpZeph, 3QpIs, 4QpIs^{a-e}, 4QpHos^{a-b}, 4QpNah, 4QpMic, 4QpZeph, 5QpMal.[62]

As for the Ebionites, Irenaeus tells us that they had developed their own way of expounding the prophets, 'quae autem sunt prophetica curiosius exponere nituntur' (*Adv. haer.* 1, 26, 2). What does *curiosius* mean? It has been explained (Schoeps 1, 159) in terms of the information supplied by the *Panarion* of Epiphanius (30, 17), where we learn that the Ebionites admitted Abraham, Isaac, Jacob, Moses, Aaron, and Joshua, but rejected all the prophets, David, Solomon, Isaiah, Jeremiah, Daniel, Ezekiel, Elijah, and Elisha together with their oracles.

This explanation, however, is not certain. *Curiosius* is the Latin translation of a lost Greek word. Since we have no reason to assume that it is not an accurate translation, we may legitimately ask what Irenaeus, writing *ca.* 175, could have meant by it. Epiphanius' statement about the rejection of the prophets remains, of course, a possible interpretation, but it represents more likely the attitude of a later stage of Ebionism. Between Irenaeus and Epiphanius (310–403), the Ebionites could have been subjected to other influences (Samaritan, for instance) with regard to the prophets. Certainly there is no foundation for the opinion of J. Thomas[63] that *curiosius* shows that some Ebionites were Gnostics. *Curiosus* means 'bestowing care or pains upon a thing, applying one's self assiduously', as well as 'curious, inquisitive'.[64] It is just as likely that the Ebionites of Irenaeus' time had something like *pesharim*, and that *curiosius* is his way of describing this detailed, careful exegesis of the prophets.

[62] See J. Milik, 'Fragments d'un Midrasch de Michée dans les manuscrits de Qumran', *RB* 59 (1952) 412–18; DJD 1, 77–80; 3, 95–6, 180; 5, 11–42.

[63] *Op. cit.*, 169.

[64] *Harper's Latin Dictionary* (N.Y.: American Book Co., 1907) 502; cf. also *Thesaurus linguae latinae* 4, 1493.

In the PsC Jesus is the only true prophet. Owing to their peculiar Christology, the Holy Spirit, who was believed to be in Christ, was also present in Adam, so that he too is called the 'only true prophet'. 'The only true prophet gave names to each animal' (*Hom* 3:21 *KP*). Moreover, 'the true prophet appeared to Moses' in Egypt (*Rec* 1:34 *KP*). This probably refers, not to Christ as such, but to the spirit which made him the True Prophet. 'Know then that Christ, who was from the beginning, and always, was ever present with the pious, though secretly, through all their generations; especially with those who waited for him to whom he frequently appeared' (*Rec* 1:52 *KP*). This attitude toward Christ is responsible for the Ebionite rejection of the prophets of the Old Testament.[65] But an even stranger reason is found in the view of the Old Testament prophets as representatives of female prophecy, having been born of women. The True Prophet, being the Son of *Man* represents male prophecy, and so is accepted on the principle of the syzygies (*Hom* 3:22–23).

There are a few references to the Old Testament prophets in the PsC.[66] But it is hard to deduce anything from these, because they may have passed into Ebionite literature via works that were more acceptable to them. One clear case is found in *Rec* 1:37, where Hos 6:6 is cited: 'For I delight in piety, not sacrifice.' This text of Hosea, however, is used by Matthew (9:13; 12:7).

The attitude of the Qumran sect toward the Old Testament prophets, then, is entirely different from that of the Ebionites, at least as they are known to us from Epiphanius and the PsC. Consequently, we cannot look to the tenets of Qumran as a source for the Ebionite attitude.

b) *The 'false pericopes'*. Epiphanius (*Pan*. 30, 18) tells us that the Ebionites did not accept the whole Pentateuch, but rejected certain passages of it (*oute gar dechontai tēn Pentateuchon Mōÿseōs*

[65] *Rec* 1:59; 68–69 *KP*.

[66] Cf. Schoeps 1, 160.

holēn, alla tina rēmata apoballousin). The PsC, too, know of falsehoods that have been added to the Law of Moses. 'The Scriptures have had joined to them many falsehoods against God' (*Hom* 2:38 *KP*). By labelling certain passages of the Pentateuch as false chapters, the Ebionites managed to eliminate those that seemed in conflict with their beliefs about God. Peter cites as examples the following: 'Neither was Adam a transgressor, who was fashioned by the hands of God; nor was Noah drunken, who was found righteous above all the world; nor did Abraham live with three wives at once, who, on account of his sobriety, was thought worthy of a numerous posterity; nor did Jacob associate with four—of whom two were sisters—who was the father of the twelve tribes, and who intimated the coming of the presence of our Master; nor was Moses a murderer, nor did he learn to judge from an idolatrous priest . . .' (*Hom* 2:52 *KP*).

There is not the slightest trace of such an attitude in the writings of the sect of Qumran.[67]

c) *Sacrifice*. Though there was formerly some hesitation about the attitude of the Qumran sect with regard to sacrifice, it seems clear from the War-Scroll that they did not reject it. In 1QM 2:5–6 we read: 'These shall be posted at the burnt-offerings and the sacrifices, to prepare an offering of incense, agreeable to the good pleasure of God, to make atonement on behalf of all his community, to burn flesh continually before him on the table of glory.' According to J. Baumgarten, 'We do not find in DSD [=1QS] any law concerning animal sacrifice. There are only figurative references to sacrificial offerings.'[68] But 'DSH and CDC [=1QS and CD] tell us of a sect which looked with disfavor upon the priests of the Temple of Jerusalem. They

[67] Cf. G. Vermès, *op. cit.*, 109–12. Bultmann (*op. cit.*, 187) maintains that this rejection of the false pericopes by the Ebionites presupposes a Gnostic rejection of the Old Testament, and is merely another example of the compromise made by the Ebionites between Gnosticism and Jewish-Christian tradition. The theory of the false pericopes represents a 'mysterion' transmitted by Peter to the Ebionite community. This is sheer speculation.

[68] 'Sacrifice and Worship among the Jewish Sectarians of the Dead Sea (Qumran) Scrolls', *HTR* 46 (1953) 149.

accused them of violating the sanctity of the Temple and the Holy City by failure to observe the laws of ritual purity and appropriating sacred property. The sectarians, who were themselves identified with the Zadokite priestly tradition, held that it was preferable, under such conditions, not to bring sacrifices to the altar. Consequently they entered a covenant to avoid the Sanctuary. In support of their position, they turned to Prophetic denunciations of sinful offerings. The Halakah of CDC, however, preserved several laws relating to the Temple and the sacrifices.'[69] This supports Josephus' testimony about the Essenes, who 'do not offer sacrifices, because they profess to have more pure lustrations' (*Ant.* 18, 1, 5).

But the Ebionites did reject sacrifice without a doubt. 'It is Jesus who has put out, by the grace of baptism, that fire which the priest kindled for sins' (*Rec* 1:48 *KP*; cf. also 1:36, 37, 39, 55, 62; *Hom* 3:45 all *KP*). Peter even preaches that the destruction of the Temple is due to the continuance of sacrifice at a time when it had been officially abolished (*Rec* 1:64 *KP*). This evidence from PsC agrees with the testimony of Epiphanius (*Pan* 30,16).

The radical difference of outlook here between the two sects prevents us from saying that the Ebionite attitude developed out of that of Qumran.[70]

d) *Priesthood.* The priesthood was a recognized group in the Qumran sect. Baumgarten has given a good summary of their attitude, as it is known from the scrolls published by the American Schools:

[69] *Ibid.*, 153–4. Cf. also p. 155 for a discussion of the following text of Josephus. See, however, J. Strugnell, *JBL* 77 (1958) 113–15.

[70] Bultmann (*op. cit.*, 187) would derive the Ebionite outlook from the attitude found in the primitive community of the Christian Church itself, not as dependent on passages in Mk 12:33, Mt 9:13; 12:7, but rather as coming from the attitude of the Jews among whom Christ lived. Jesus was not the opponent of the priests, as the prophets of the Old Law had been, but of the Scribes. As far as Jewish piety was concerned, the Synagogue had pressed the cult of the temple into the background, and so sacrifice had lost its meaning for early Christianity. In an article on 'L'opposition contre le

To the priests, DSD assigns an exalted position within the community. As in CDC, the sect is conceived as joining Aaron and Israel (DSD 5:6), but while the Israelite sectaries formed a 'holy house' (*bêt qōdeš*), the priests were to be established as a 'most holy institution' (*sôd qōdeš qodāšîm*) [1QS 8:5–6; cf. 8:8–9; 9:6]. Legal decisions were made 'according to the sons of Zadok, the priests who keep the Covenant, and according to the majority of the men of the community' [1QS 5:2–3; 5:9, 21–22; 6:19; 8:9]. DSD 9:7 provides that 'only the sons of Aaron shall have authority in matters of law and property'. In the council of the community there were twelve lay men and three priests (DSD 8:1). A priest was required to be present in every place where ten men formed a unit of the community. At the sessions of the sectarians, the priests were given preference in seating and procedure. A priest invoked the blessing over the bread and wine before communal meals (DSD 6:5–6). The priests also played a significant role in the annual covenant ceremony, which was one of the important institutions of the sect.[71]

In 1QM we learn that there are priests (7:10–15; 8:2–7, 13–14), but also 'leaders of the priests' (2:1), a 'chief priest' (2:1; 15:4; 16:13; 18:5),[72] and 'the priest appointed for the time of vengeance according to the vote of his brethren' (15, 6). The robes of the priests in battle are described (7:9–11), and the role the priests are to perform in the course of the battle is detailed (7:12–18). They are to blow the trumpets (7:15), encourage the soldiers (7:12), bless God and curse Belial (13:1–6).[73]

Temple de Jérusalem, motif commun de la théologie johannique et du monde ambiant', *NTS* 5 (1958–59) 157–73, O. Cullmann writes, '. . . nous constatons que les Pseudo-Clémentines qui adoptent en partie jusque dans leur moindres détails les idées et les usages de Qumran vont sur cette question du Temple et des sacrifices beaucoup plus loin que la secte de Qumran et se rapprochent, sur ce point, de l'attitude d'Etienne. Les Pseudo-Clémentines doivent être citées dans ce contexte du judaïsme ésoterique dont nous nous occupons . . . et encore leur radicalisme [i.e., des Pseudo-Clémentines] n'est-il qu'un développement naturel, pour ainsi dire, de l'attitude qumranienne à l'égard du Temple et de son culte' (p. 166).

[71] *Op. cit.*, 152; cf. G. Vermès, *op. cit.*, 78.

[72] Cf. H. L. Ginsberg, 'The Hebrew University Scrolls from the Sectarian Cache', *BASOR* 112 (1948) 20–1.

[73] This brief description shows that the function of the priest or *kôhēn* can

Such passages leave no doubt as to the status of the priests in the sect of Qumran. Levites, too, are often mentioned as a specific class. This is in sharp contrast to the attitude of the Ebionites as manifested by PsC. Their rejection of the priesthood logically follows the substitution of baptism for sacrifice. The priesthood had its function and meaning in history in the days when God *permitted* sacrifice, but that time has passed (*Rec* 1:48 KP). Cullmann looks upon this attitude as an extension of the attitude of the Qumran sect, adopted with reference to the official priesthood in the Temple.[74] 1 QpHab 8:8 ff. speaks of a 'wicked priest', who rebelled against the statutes of God, and 9:4 ff. of the 'priests of Jerusalem', who gather wealth and loot. Consequently, Cullmann may well be right in relating the Ebionite rejection of the priesthood to such a movement in Palestine as the Qumran disapproval of the official priesthood in Jerusalem.

The general conclusion to be drawn from the treatment of the attitudes of these two sects with regard to the Old Testament and its institutions is that they differ considerably. It is only in the last point that there is a possible kinship of ideas. For the rest the difference is radical.

Baths and Baptism

Several passages in the Qumran literature have been interpreted as referring to the bathing practices of the sect. Cullmann[75] cites 1QS 3:4, 9; 5:13–14. It will be profitable to examine these and other texts.

---

hardly be that as described by Teicher in his later article in *JJS* 5 (1954) 96; see footnote 55 above. According to 1QM 7:11 at the end of the description of the robes of the priests in battle it is prescribed that this battledress shall not be worn in the sanctuary. This same word, *miqdāš*, is used in 1QM 2:3 in a context where *'ôlôt* and *zebāḥîm* are also mentioned; so there is no reason to maintain that the priests of Qumran had nothing to do with sacrifice. One should also recall in this connection the possibility of sacrifice at Qumran itself; see R. de Vaux, *L'archéologie et les manuscrits de la Mer Morte* (London, 1961) 10–11.

[74] *Op. cit.*, 41.

[75] *Ibid.*, 44. Are we sure that 1QS 6:13 ff. refer to baths? M. H. Gottstein

He cannot be justified while he conceals his stubbornness of heart
And with darkened mind looks upon ways of light.
While in iniquity, he cannot be reckoned perfect.
He cannot purify himself by atonement,
Nor cleanse himself with water-for-impurity,
Nor sanctify himself with seas or rivers
Nor cleanse himself with any water for washing!
Unclean! Unclean! shall he be as long as he rejects God's laws
So as not to be instructed by the Community of his counsel
(1QS 3:3–6)

It is most probable that we have here a veiled reference to some bathing practice of the Qumran sect, to a purificatory bath perhaps. But it is remotely possible that this is a rhetorical way of stressing the uncleanness and guilt of the man who rejects God's laws. The same could be said of 1QS 3:9. But 1QS 4:20–21 is more explicit: 'Then God will purge with his truth all the deeds of man, and will refine for himself the frame of man by rooting out every spirit of falsehood from the bounds of his flesh, to cleanse him with a holy spirit from all wicked practices, sprinkling upon him a spirit of truth like water-for-impurity against all untrue abominations. . . .' However, the passage in 1QS 5:13 alludes to some bathing practice: 'He [the perverse one] may not enter into water to [be permitted to] touch the Purity of the holy men, for they will not be cleansed unless they have turned from their wickedness. . . .' Two passages in CD 10:11–12; 11:22) seem to be a mere repetition of the Levitical purity laws prescribed in Lv 11:40; 15:10. There is also one passage in 1QM 14:2–3 which may or may not refer to a purifactory bath. 'After they have gone up from among the slain to return to the camp, they will intone the hymn of Return. In

---

has gone to an opposite extreme in maintaining that the Qumran sect was not a baptist sect, whereas the Essenes are known to have been definitely such; cf. 'Anti-Essene traits in the DSS', *VT* 4 (1954) 141–7. Even Schoeps, who thinks that the identification of the 'Sadoqiten von 'Ain Feshkha' with the Essenes of Philo and Josephus is highly problematical, admits that Gottstein has gone too far (cf. Schoeps 2, 4); cf. R. North, S.J., 'The Qumrân "Sadducees"', *CBQ* 17 (1955) 44–68.

the morning they will wash their garments and cleanse themselves of the blood of the sinners' corpses.'

Perhaps no special meaning would be attached to references such as these, were it not for the fact that we know from other sources that the Essenes were a baptist sect (Josephus, *JW* 2, 129–32). Baumgarten has emphasized the adherence to stringent laws of purity and purification among the Essenes of Qumran.[76] Contact with a member of lower grade necessitates a purification (Josephus, *op. cit.* 2, 8; 2, 10). Excavations at Khirbet Qumran uncovered seven large cisterns, the nature of which was not at first definitely established. They have been considered as the bathing places of the Qumran sect; A. Dupont-Sommer called them 'swimming-pools' in the Postscript (dated 10 February 1954) to the English translation of his *Nouveaux aperçus sur les manuscrits de la Mer Morte*.[77] Partially roofed-over cisterns, fitted with steps by which one could descend to reach the water-level, are not unknown in Roman Palestine.[78] These cisterns were not baptisteries of any sort. However, there were also uncovered in the excavations at Khirbet Qumran at least two small baths, which undoubtedly did serve as places for ritual washings (see R. de Vaux, *L'archéologie*, pp. 98–9).

The conclusion, then, regarding the sect of Qumran is that it was baptist. Against the background of a general baptist movement, which is known to have existed in Palestine and

[76] *Op. cit.*, 155.

[77] The English title is *The Jewish Sect of Qumrân and the Essenes* (London: Valentine Mitchell, 1954) 167–8; Cullmann (*op. cit.*, 44) referred to these same excavated reservoirs or cisterns as proof that 'das Kloster von Qumrân ein wirkliches Taufzentrum war'.

[78] A stepped reservoir was found at Gezer; cf. R. A. S. Macalister, *Excavation of Gezer* (London: John Murray, 1912) 1, 274–6; 3, pl. LIV. Cf. also F. J. Bliss and R. A. S. Macalister, *Excavations in Palestine during the years 1898–1900* (London: Pal. Expl. Fund, 1902) 21. Mention is made here of a 'vaulted cistern' at Tell Zakarîyā. 'Similar stepped cisterns were excavated by me at Jerusalem' (p. 21). 'It is quite possible that we have here an ancient cistern vaulted over during the brief Roman occupation' (*ibid.*). See further, R. North, 'The Qumran Reservoirs', *BCCT* 100–32.

Syria between 150 B.C. and A.D. 300, the conclusion is even more plausible.[79]

There is a great deal of evidence for the bathing practices of the Ebionites both in Epiphanius (*Pan.* 30, 21) and the PsC. However, the one big difference in this regard is that they admitted Christian baptism as well. 'This is the service he [God] has appointed: to worship him only, and trust only in the Prophet of Truth, and to be baptized for the remission of sins, and thus by this pure baptism to be born again unto God by saving water . . .' (*Hom* 7:8 not *KP*; cf. *Rec* 1:39 *KP*). 'Unless a man be baptized in water, in the name of the threefold blessedness, as the true Prophet taught, he can neither receive the remission of sins nor enter into the Kingdom of heaven' (*Rec* 1:69 *KP*; cf. *Hom* 11:27 *KP*). This baptism is necessary before Peter and his followers will partake of food with a man (*Hom* 1:22 not *KP*; cf. 13:4–5 not *KP*).

But in addition to baptism, which is definitely considered an initiation-rite to be conferred only once in the PsC, there are other baths of a purificatory ritualistic character that remind one of the Essene practices mentioned above. These take place before meals and before prayer (*Hom* 8:2; 9:23 *KP*; 10:1 not *KP*; etc.). 'Peter rose early and went into the garden, where there was a great water-reservoir (*hydrochoeion*),[80] into which a full stream of water constantly flowed. There having bathed, and then having prayed, he sat down' (*Hom* 10:1 not *KP*; cf. 10:26 not *KP*: Peter bathes with others before a common meal; 11:1 not *KP*: Peter bathes before prayer; *Rec* 4:3 *KP*: Peter bathes in the sea before eating). Washing with water was prescribed after sexual intercourse (*Hom* 11:30, 33 *KP*). These baths are highly recommended by Peter in his preaching (*Hom*

[79] Cf. J. Thomas, *Le mouvement baptiste*, already referred to.

[80] The Syriac MS., containing parts of the *Hom* and *Rec*, unfortunately has a paraphrase for the Greek word, *hydrochoeion*, so that we are not given any clue to the Semitic word in question; e.g., *Hom* 10:1 reads *'tr dmy' sgy'' 'myn'yt rdyn hww*.

11:28 ff.; *Rec* 6:11 *KP*).[81] Such baths could well have been received into the Ebionite group from the Qumran sect; but, in view of the fact of a general baptist movement in Palestine and Syria at that time, we cannot restrict the source of this practice to Qumran alone.

As a matter of fact, there seems to be evidence of other influence. Epiphanius mentions the Elchesaites as the source of some of the baths in vogue among the Ebionites. 'Whenever any one of them is sick or bitten by a snake, he goes down into the water. There he makes use of all the invocations which Helxai composed, calling upon the heavens and the earth, salt and water, winds and the angels of justice (as they say), likewise bread and oil; then he says, 'Come to my aid, and free me from this pain"' (*Pan.* 30, 17). The similarity that exists between this practice and the 'oath' to be taken by the neophyte before he is entrusted with the sacred books and traditions of the Ebionites, described in *Diam.* 2, support this contention of other than Essene influence on the Ebionites. There is certainly nothing like this oath, taken by a stream of water with an invocation of elements, in the Qumran literature. J. Thomas maintains that they were influenced by the Christian Church, the Essenes, and the Elchesaites.[82]

Communal Meal

In 1QS 6:2 we learn about the Qumran sect that 'they shall eat communally'. 'When they arrange the table to eat or [arrange] the wine to drink, the priest shall first stretch out his hand to invoke a blessing with the first of the bread and/or

[81] The question of baths in the PsC is one that is involved in the discussion of sources. Most of the cases cited above of Peter's bath before meals and prayer are found in non-*KP* passages; the scene is Tripoli. Cullmann maintains that these passages represent later Ebionite practices (*op. cit.*, 45). It is precisely because of the bathing practices that J. Thomas decided to revise the usual theory of PsC sources and present his own (cf. *op. cit.*, 175). This cannot be discussed at length here. But it indicates once again the tenuous character of this entire comparison.

[82] *Ibid.*, 181.

wine' (6:4–6). 'He [the neophyte] shall not touch the drink of the Many until his completion of a second year among the men of the Community' (6:20; cf. 7:20). The room in which this communal meal was most likely taken has been found at Khirbet Qumran.[83] In the 'Two Column' Document (=1QSa) we hear of a Messiah of Israel sharing in the banquet of the sect, but he remains subordinate to the priest, whom Abbé Milik has identified as the Messiah of Aaron.[84]

As for the Ebionites of the PsC, I have already mentioned that they did not eat with the non-baptized (*Hom* 1:22; 3:4, 9; *Rec* 2:71 not *KP*). But they too had a communal meal. References to it are vague at times, but there seem to have been fixed places at table ('unusquisque ex more recognoscens proprii ordinis locum', *Rec* 4:37 not *KP*). Though the expression used to indicate the meal is often merely 'to partake of food' (*sitiōn metalabein, Hom* 8:2 *KP*; *trophēs metalabein*, 10:26 not *KP*; *cibum sumere, Rec* 4:37; 5:36 not *KP*), we meet on occasion a peculiar expression, *halōn metalabein*, 'to partake of salt' (*Hom* 4:6; 11:34; 19:25 not *KP*) or *meta tēn halōn koinōnian* (*Hom* 14:8 not *KP*; cf. *Ep. Clem.* 9, 1). Salt and bread are mentioned together in *Diam.* 4:3, and we even find the verb, *synalizesthai* (*Hom* 13:4 not *KP*).[85]

There is another set of expressions, which indicate that the Ebionites of the PsC celebrated the Eucharist. These are *klasas eucharistian* (*Hom* 11:36 not *KP*); *eucharistiam fragens cum eis* (*Rec* 6:15 not *KP*); *ton arton ep' eucharistia klasas kai epitheis halas* (*Hom* 14:1 not *KP*). Connection with the Christian Eucharist seems clear from the following passage: 'For I showed them that

[83] Cf. R. de Vaux, 'La seconde saison de fouilles à Khirbet Qumrân', *CRAIBL*, 1953, 310–11.

[84] 'Une lettre de Siméon bar Kokheba', *RB* 60 (1953) 291.

[85] This verb occurs in Acts 1:4, where it is variously interpreted; cf. W. Bauer, *Wörterbuch zum Neuen Testament* (4th ed.; Berlin, A. Töpelmann, 1952) col. 1425. Philo (*Vita Contemp.* 4, 9) mentions the use of salt at the meals of the Therapeutae, who have been generally considered as related to the Essenes.

in no way else could they be saved, unless through the grace of the Holy Spirit they hastened to be washed with the baptism of the threefold invocation, and received the eucharist of Christ the Lord . . .' (*Rec* 1:63 *KP*). Whether these were two separate types of communal meals is hard to say. The mention of bread and salt in *Hom* 14:1 recalls the passage in *Diam.* 4, 3, where there is no mention of the Eucharist. The question is further complicated by the fact that Epiphanius (*Pan.* 30, 16) mentions that the Ebionites celebrated the mysteries with unleavened bread and water.

The main fact, however, is certain, that a communal meal was found in both the Qumran sect and the Ebionites of the PsC. Whereas bread and wine figure in the former, bread, salt, and water (?) are found associated with the latter. In both cases the meal was only for the initiated. Neither similarities nor dissimilarities in this case should be overlooked in drawing conclusions.

Sacred Books

Mention of an enigmatic book of *H°gî* is found in CD 10:6; 13:2; 1QSa 1:7; and possibly in CD14:8, 'the book of Meditation', which is understood differently by various scholars. Dupont-Sommer thinks that this might refer to 1QS itself.[86] Others think that it refers to the Hebrew Scriptures. This is by no means certain, and we have no indication that the Qumran sect treated this book as secret. On the other hand, Josephus speaks of 'the books of the sect' which each member swears to preserve (*JW* 2, 8, 8 #142). The Manual of Discipline prescribes the concealment of 'the teaching of the Law' (1QS 9:17), but it is not easy to equate this with the preservation of secret books.

In the PsC the sermons of Peter were treated as secret writings, which were to be entrusted only to the initiated; cf. *Ep. Petr.* 1, 2; 3, 1; *Diam.* 1–3. It is in connection with these books that the period of probation is mentioned, which lasts for six

86 *Nouveaux aperçus*, 88–9; cf. Vermès, *op. cit.*, 176.

years (*Diam.* 1, 2; 2, 2). This is the only connection in which a probation is mentioned, whereas in the Qumran sect an elaborate process of initiation is found. It has nothing to do with the receiving of sacred books, but leads up to the acceptance as a full member of the Community.

Consequently, both on the score of sacred books and the probation or initiation connected with them, there is much more dissimilarity than similarity between the Qumran sect and the Ebionites of the PsC.

Community of Goods

Even though details may not be very clear, it is quite certain that the sect of Qumran practised some sort of communal poverty. 'All who dedicate themselves to his Truth shall bring all their mind and their strength and their property into the Community of God . . . to direct all their property according to his righteous counsels' (1QS 1:11–13; cf. 5:2). After a year's probation the novice's property will be handed over to the Custodian of Property of the Many (6:20), but it will not be pooled with the rest until the second year of probation is completed (6:22). 'If there be found among them a man who lies in the matter of wealth, and it become known, they shall exclude him from the Purity of the Many for one year, and he shall be fined one-fourth of his food-allowance' (6:25). No one may share in the property of those that transgress the laws of the community (7:25; 8:23; 9:22). The priests (sons of Aaron) will regulate the property (9:8) (see further, pp. 284–8 above).

Epiphanius (*Pan.* 30, 17) tells us that the Ebionites practised poverty, selling their goods as was the custom in the days of the Apostles. In the PsC poverty is praised and possessions are regarded as sinful (*Hom* 15:7 *KP*). 'To all of us possessions are sins' (*Hom* 15:9 *KP*). Yet, as Cullmann has pointed out,[87] the fact is that we find no practice of poverty in the PsC and do not see the members pooling their wealth as does the sect of Qum-

[87] *Op. cit.*, 47.

ran; it is thus an ideal rather than established practice. As previously mentioned, the Ebionites did not live a communal life (though they might have come together at times for communal meals). And though they might praise poverty, they could still judge as follows: 'One is not unquestionably righteous because he happens to be poor' (*Hom* 15:10 *KP*). This may be a bit surprising, in view of the fact that the group was known as Ebionite, a name which has often been explained in connection with the Hebrew word for 'the poor', as already discussed. Of course, Epiphanius' testimony stands as evidence to the contrary, but even here it is just possible that he or his sources have reasoned from the name to the practice, especially when the example of the Apostles could be cited in favour of early Church practices.[88]

At any rate, this is another significant difference between the sect of Qumran and the Ebionites, at least as they are known from the PsC.

CONCLUSION

To sum up, then, we can say that whereas there are many similarities between the sect of Qumran and the Ebionites, there are also striking dissimilarities. The Qumran dualism resembles the Ebionite in that it is subordinated to Jewish monotheism and both are ethical. But the Qumran dualism is ethical alone, whereas the Ebionite is also physical; the Qumran dualism is simpler (being a contrast merely of light-darkness, truth-perversity, good-evil, and two spirits), but the Ebionite is much more complex. In both groups we find two main figures: the Teacher of Righteousness and the Man of the Lie, the Prophet of Truth and the *inimicus homo*. In the Qumran literature they are protagonist and antagonist. The Ebionite Prophet of Truth has a role similar to that of the Teacher of Righteousness, whereas the *inimicus homo* can be compared with the Man of the Lie only in that he is an adversary. However,

[88] See further L. E. Keck, *ZNW* 57 (1966) 55–66.

we find a radical difference of outlook when we consider the attitude of the two groups toward the Old Testament and its institutions. Qumran esteems the Torah, the Prophets, the priests, and sacrifice (when their own rigid ideas of purity are observed by the priests during sacrifice). But the Ebionites reject the 'false pericopes' of the Pentateuch, reject the prophets of the Old Testament, reject priesthood, and claim that baptism has replaced sacrificial cult. Whereas the Ebionites admitted Christian baptism and had purificatory baths of different sorts, we find at Qumran only simple purificatory baths. Though both had some sort of a communal meal, bread and wine were used at Qumran, while the Ebionites used bread, salt, and water (?), and celebrated the Christian Eucharist. Some sort of sacred book (*H^ogî*) was used at Qumran, but we are not sure that it was a secret writing, so that it can scarcely be compared with the Sermons of Peter, which were to be entrusted only to the initiated among the Ebionites, who had passed a long probation. Whereas communal poverty was definitely practised at Qumran, there is no evidence of its practice in the PsC, where it is, however, praised. Epiphanius tells us, however, that the Ebionites did practise poverty.

From the preceding survey of the main points,[89] which have served as the basis of our comparison between the sect of Qumran and the Ebionites, several conclusions can be drawn. First, as already stated above, there is no real evidence for the identification of the sect of Qumran as Ebionite. This opinion is

[89] One main point has been purposely omitted; this is the question of 'knowledge' in the Qumran and Ebionite sects. To treat this point adequately would demand a separate paper in itself. From the standpoint of Qumran, we already have a good treatment of the question in the scrolls previously published, written by W. D. Davies, '"Knowledge" in the Dead Sea Scrolls and Matthew 11:25–30', *HTR* 46 (1953) 113–39. See esp. 129 ff., where he rejects the identification of Qumran 'knowledge' with any of three ways of understanding 'gnosticism' or 'gnosis'. Strangely enough, Cullmann has not considered this point. Cf. W. Baumgartner, *op. cit.*, 62, where the Qumran emphasis on wisdom and intelligence is labelled 'gnostic'. Cf. also Bo Reicke, *op. cit.*, 137–41.

contrary to that of J. L. Teicher of Cambridge, but finds itself in good company.[90] Secondly, it does not seem possible to admit that the Essenes of Qumran became the Ebionites. Cullmann's conclusion is: 'die Reste der Essener vom Toten Meer im Judenchristentum aufgingen.'[91] Such an opinion demands that the strict-living Qumran sect, adhering rigorously to the Torah, the teaching of the prophets, and their own ascetical rules of communal life, abandoned their main tenets and practices and became Christians. We have no evidence for this. As should be obvious to anyone reading this essay, I have utilized much of the material Cullmann has brought together in his enlightening article. Many of the similarities and dissimilarities here pointed out were indicated previously by him. Consequently, one is surprised to read at the end of his article that one group passed over into the other. It seems that the most we can say is that the sect of Qumran influenced the Ebionites in many ways; Essene tenets and practices were undoubtedly adopted or adapted into the Ebionite way of life. To try to state more than this is to overstep the limits set by the evidence we have at our disposal.[92]

In my discussion of dualism I rejected the idea that either the Qumran or the Pseudoclementine dualism was Gnostic. I

[90] Cullmann, *op. cit.*, 35; A. Dupont-Sommer, *Nouveaux aperçus*, 201–6; K. Elliger, *op. cit.*, 242–5; Schoeps 3, 322–8.

[91] *Op. cit.*, 50.

[92] It seems, too, that Cullmann has overemphasized the importance of the destruction of Jerusalem to the Ebionites of the PsC and to the sect of Qumran.—When this essay was reprinted in a slightly abridged form in K. Stendahl, *The Scrolls and the New Testament* (New York: Harper, 1957) 208–31, 291–8, it found itself in company with an article by O. Cullmann, 'The Significance of the Qumran Texts for Research into the Beginnings of Christianity', pp. 18–32, 251–2. Cullmann had the opportunity of including a note (on p. 252) in which he maintains that I have misunderstood his intention: 'I naturally do not mean that "the Essenes of Qumran became the Ebionites." What I say, however, is that after the dispersion of the community during the war of A.D. 70 the remnants of the sect were absorbed into the Jewish-Christian groups of the East Jordan district, which degenerated more and more into a Jewish sect, and were open to all kinds of

do not intend to claim that there is no Gnosticism at all in the PsC. It is, moreover, quite conceivable that many of the ideas of the Qumran writings would easily lend themselves to Gnostic adaptation. To admit this is not at all the same as to speak of a 'gnostisches Judentum' at Qumran, as Schoeps has done.

This discussion has tried to furnish a *mise au point* in the problem of the relationship between Qumran and the Ebionites. It is obvious that the last word has not yet been said.[93]

---

syncretistic influence.' I shall leave to others the judgment about whether I have misunderstood his intention. He has not always written so clearly as in the above-quoted note. For instance, in his article, 'Ebioniten' (*Die Religion in Geschichte und Gegenwart* [3rd ed.; Tübingen: Mohr], vol. 2 [1958], col. 298), he writes, 'Möglicherweise sind Reste der Qumransekte nach der Katastrophe von 70 nChr in den ebionitischen Gruppen des Ostjordanlandes aufgegangen.'

[93] See further my article, 'Ebionites', *Dictionnaire de Spiritualité* 4/25 (1958) cols. 32–40. F. Paschke, *Die beiden griechischen Klementinen-Epitomen und ihre Anhänge* (TU 90; Berlin: Akademie-V., 1966).

INDEX OF MODERN AUTHORS

INDEX OF SUBJECTS

INDEX OF SCRIPTURAL REFERENCES

APOCRYPHA (DEUTEROCANONICAL BOOKS)

INDEX OF PSEUDEPIGRAPHAL REFERENCES

TESTAMENT OF THE TWELVE PATRIARCHS

INDEX OF DEAD SEA SCROLLS REFERENCES